Welcome!

Set goals. Share your ideas. Collaborate with your peers. Reflect on your learning... myPerspectives is about YOU!

You will:

- *come up with your own perspectives on essential questions*
- *engage in thoughtful discussions with your peers*
- *make choices in what you read*
- *and maybe, even, re-examine your own thinking as a result!*

Contents

Lifelong Learning with *myPerspectives*

In the myPerspectives learning community, you explore essential questions, watch videos, read texts, listen to audio, collaborate with your peers, write about interesting topics - and more.

Above all, ***YOU*** *are at the center of your learning - sharing your perspectives, listening to others, and developing the skills and desire to learn that will last a lifetime!*

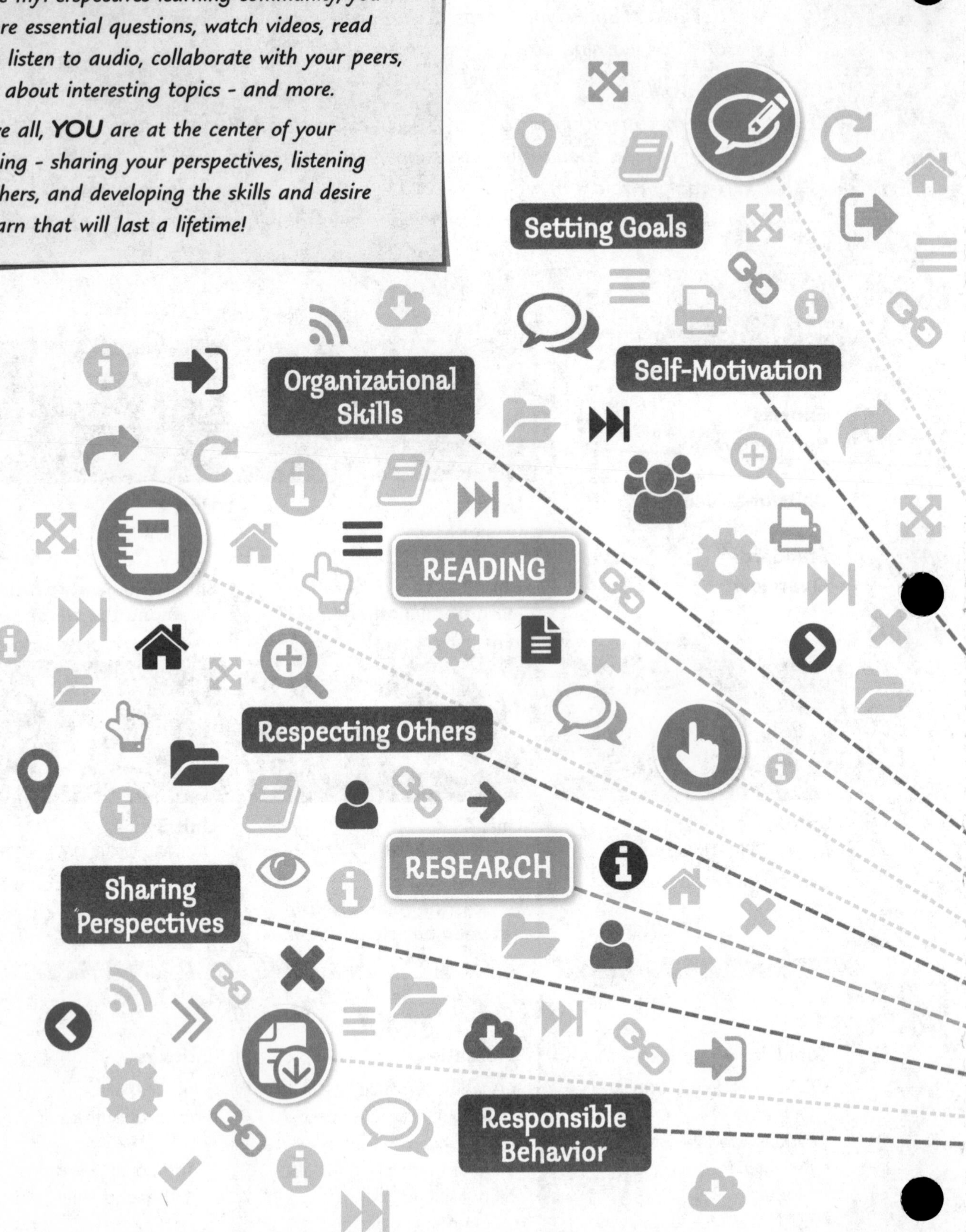

TEXAS Student Edition

myPerspectives

ENGLISH LANGUAGE ARTS

New York, New York Boston, Massachusetts
Chandler, Arizona Glenview, Illinois

ABOUT THE COVERS: *myPerspectives, Texas,* covers are designed to be fun, interesting, and inspiring. We want you to think differently about learning, make connections to the world around you, and bring in your own ideas, creativity, and perspectives. These illustrations highlight aspects of Texas that might be familiar to you and use art styles similar to those of famous painters such as Van Gogh, Matisse, and Seurat.

Pearson Education, Inc. 330 Hudson Street, New York, NY 10013

ISBN-13: 978-0-32-899134-1
ISBN-10: 0-32-899134-1
5 19

Making Decisions

Reflecting

Solving Problems

SPEAKING

LISTENING

Teamwork

Building Relationships

Social Engagement

WRITING

my Perspectives

ENGLISH LANGUAGE ARTS

myPerspectives is informed by a team of respected experts whose experiences working with students and study of instructional best practices have positively impacted education. From the evolving role of the teacher to how students learn in a digital age, our authors bring new ideas, innovations, and strategies that transform teaching and learning in today's competitive and interconnected world.

"The teaching of English needs to focus on engaging a new generation of learners. How do we get them excited about reading and writing? How do we help them to envision themselves as readers and writers? And, how can we make the teaching of English more culturally, socially, and technologically relevant? Throughout the curriculum, we've created spaces that enhance youth voice and participation and that connect the teaching of literature and writing to technological transformations of the digital age."

Ernest Morrell, Ph.D.

is the Coyle Professor of Literacy Education and the Inaugural Director of the Center for Literacy Education at the University of Notre Dame. He was formerly Macy Professor of English Education and Director of the Institute for Urban and Minority Education at Teachers College, Columbia University. Dr. Morrell is also past-president of the National Council of Teachers of English, a Fellow of the American Educational Research Association (AERA), and an appointed member of International Literacy Association's Literacy Research Panel.

Dr. Morrell works with schools, districts, and families across the country to infuse social and emotional learning, digital technologies, project based learning, and multicultural literature into literacy practices aimed at developing powerful readers and writers among all students. Dr. Morrell has influenced the development of *my*Perspectives in Assessment, Writing & Research, Student Engagement, and Collaborative Learning.

Elfrieda Hiebert, Ph.D.

is President and CEO of TextProject, a nonprofit that provides resources to support higher reading levels. She is also a research associate at the University of California, Santa Cruz. Dr. Hiebert has worked in the field of early reading acquisition for 45 years, first as a teacher's aide and teacher of primary-level students in California and, subsequently, as a teacher and researcher. Her research addresses how fluency, vocabulary, and knowledge can be fostered through appropriate texts. Dr. Hiebert has influenced the development of *my*Perspectives in Vocabulary, Text Complexity, and Assessment.

"The signature of complex text is challenging vocabulary. In the systems of vocabulary, it's important to provide ways to show how concepts can be made more transparent to students. We provide lessons and activities that develop a strong vocabulary and concept foundation—a foundation that permits students to comprehend increasingly more complex text."

Kelly Gallagher, M.Ed.

teaches at Magnolia High School in Anaheim, California, where he is in his thirty-third year. He is the former co-director of the South Basin Writing Project at California State University, Long Beach and the former president of the Secondary Reading Group for the International Literacy Association. Kelly is the author of several books on adolescent literacy, most notably *Readicide: How Schools Are Killing Reading and What You Can Do About It* and *Write Like This*. Kelly's latest book, co-written with Penny Kittle, is *180 Days: Two Teachers and the Quest to Engage and Empower Adolescents*. Mr. Gallagher has influenced the development of *my*Perspectives in Writing, Close Reading, and the Role of Teachers.

"The *my*Perspectives classroom is dynamic. The teacher inspires, models, instructs, facilitates, and advises students as they evolve and grow. When teachers guide students through meaningful learning tasks and then pass them ownership of their own learning, students become engaged and work harder. This is how we make a difference in student achievement—by putting students at the center of their learning and giving them the opportunities to choose, explore, collaborate, and work independently."

"It's critical to give students the opportunity to read a wide range of highly engaging texts and to immerse themselves in exploring powerful ideas and how these ideas are expressed. In *my*Perspectives, we focus on building up students' awareness of how academic language works, which is especially important for English language learners."

Jim Cummins, Ph.D.

is a Professor Emeritus in the Department of Curriculum, Teaching and Learning of the University of Toronto. His research focuses on literacy development in multilingual school contexts as well as on the potential roles of technology in promoting language and literacy development. In recent years, he has been working actively with teachers to identify ways of increasing the literacy engagement of learners in multilingual school contexts. Dr. Cummins has influenced the development of *my*Perspectives in English Language Learner and English Language Development support.

UNIT 1 Crossing Generations

Essential Question What can one generation learn from another?

INDEPENDENT LEARNING

These selections are available on Pearson Realize.

SHARE YOUR INDEPENDENT LEARNING

PERFORMANCE-BASED ASSESSMENT

UNIT REFLECTION

PEARSON realize

Go ONLINE for all lessons

 AUDIO

 VIDEO

 NOTEBOOK

 ANNOTATE

 INTERACTIVITY

 DOWNLOAD

 RESEARCH

BOOK CLUB

The novels below align to this unit.

REALISTIC FICTION

Esperanza Rising
Pam Muñoz Ryan

FANTASY ADVENTURE

The Fourteenth Goldfish
Jennifer L. Holm

These activities include items in TEKS Test format.

UNIT 2 Imagining the Future

UNIT INTRODUCTION

WHOLE-CLASS LEARNING

Comparing Across Genres

PERFORMANCE TASK

PEER-GROUP LEARNING

Comparing Within Genre

PERFORMANCE TASK

Essential Question Should humanity's future lie among the stars?

These selections are available on Pearson Realize.

SHARE YOUR INDEPENDENT LEARNING

UNIT REFLECTION

PEARSON realize™

Go ONLINE for all lessons

 AUDIO

 VIDEO

 NOTEBOOK

 ANNOTATE

 INTERACTIVITY

 DOWNLOAD

 RESEARCH

BOOK CLUB

The novels below align to this unit.

FANTASY ADVENTURE
James and the Giant Peach
Roald Dahl

SCIENCE-FICTION ADVENTURE
MiNRS
Kevin Sylvester

 These activities include items in TEKS Test format.

UNIT 3 Transformations

UNIT INTRODUCTION

WHOLE-CLASS LEARNING

PERFORMANCE TASK

PEER-GROUP LEARNING

PERFORMANCE TASK

Essential Question Can people really change?

INDEPENDENT LEARNING

REFLECTIVE ESSAY
Little Things Are Big
Jesús Colón

HISTORICAL NARRATIVE
The Story of Victor d'Aveyron, the Wild Child
Eloise Montalban

REALISTIC FICTION
A Retrieved Reformation
O. Henry

FABLE
The Grandfather and His Little Grandson
Leo Tolstoy

These selections are available on Pearson Realize.

SHARE YOUR INDEPENDENT LEARNING

PERFORMANCE-BASED ASSESSMENT

UNIT REFLECTION

PEARSON realize™

Go ONLINE for all lessons

 AUDIO
 VIDEO
 NOTEBOOK
 ANNOTATE
 INTERACTIVITY
 DOWNLOAD
 RESEARCH

BOOK CLUB

The novels below align to this unit.

REALISTIC FICTION
Stargirl
Jerry Spinelli

REALISTIC FICTION
Lost in the Sun
Lisa Graff

 These activities include items in TEKS Test format.

UNIT 4 Learning From Nature

UNIT INTRODUCTION

WHOLE-CLASS LEARNING

Comparing Within Genre

PERFORMANCE TASK

PEER-GROUP LEARNING

PERFORMANCE TASK

Essential Question What is the relationship between people and nature?

INDEPENDENT LEARNING

ADVENTURE STORY
from My Side of the Mountain
Jean Craighead George

REFLECTIVE ESSAY
from An American Childhood
Annie Dillard

FEATURE ARTICLE
A Young Tinkerer Builds a Windmill, Electrifying a Nation
Sarah Childress

NATURE WRITING
from Of Wolves and Men
Barry Lopez

These selections are available on Pearson Realize.

SHARE YOUR INDEPENDENT LEARNING

PERFORMANCE-BASED ASSESSMENT

UNIT REFLECTION

PEARSON realize™
Go ONLINE for all lessons

 AUDIO
 VIDEO
 NOTEBOOK
 ANNOTATE
 INTERACTIVITY
 DOWNLOAD
 RESEARCH

BOOK CLUB

The novels below align to this unit.

ADVENTURE
Hatchet
Gary Paulsen

REALISTIC FICTION
Hoot
Carl Hiaasen

These activities include items in TEKS Test format.

UNIT 5 Facing Adversity

UNIT INTRODUCTION

WHOLE-CLASS LEARNING

PEER-GROUP LEARNING

Essential Question How do we overcome obstacles?

INDEPENDENT LEARNING

These selections are available on Pearson Realize.

SHARE YOUR INDEPENDENT LEARNING

PERFORMANCE-BASED ASSESSMENT

UNIT REFLECTION

PEARSON realize™

Go ONLINE for all lessons

 AUDIO

 VIDEO

 NOTEBOOK

 ANNOTATE

 INTERACTIVITY

 DOWNLOAD

 RESEARCH

BOOK CLUB

The novels below align to this unit.

HISTORICAL FICTION ADVENTURE

The Cay
Theodore Taylor

REALISTIC FICTION

The Tequila Worm
Viola Canales

These activities include items in TEKS Test format.

Standards Overview

You will continue your journey toward college and career readiness as you read, write, discuss, and reflect on the texts in this program. The following listing provides you with an overview of the knowledge and skills you will gain over the course of the year.

Texas Essential Knowledge and Skills: Grade 7	
1	**Developing and sustaining foundational language skills: listening, speaking, discussion, and thinking—oral language.** The student develops oral language through listening, speaking, and discussion. The student is expected to:
A	listen actively to interpret a message and ask clarifying questions that build on others' ideas;
B	follow and give complex oral instructions to perform specific tasks, answer questions, or solve problems;
C	present a critique of a literary work, film, or dramatic production, employing eye contact, speaking rate, volume, enunciation, a variety of natural gestures, and conventions of language to communicate ideas effectively; and
D	engage in meaningful discourse and provide and accept constructive feedback from others.
2	**Developing and sustaining foundational language skills: listening, speaking, reading, writing, and thinking—vocabulary.** The student uses newly acquired vocabulary expressively. The student is expected to:
A	use print or digital resources to determine the meaning, syllabication, pronunciation, word origin, and part of speech;
B	use context such as contrast or cause and effect to clarify the meaning of words; and
C	determine the meaning and usage of grade-level academic English words derived from Greek and Latin roots such as *omni, log/logue, gen, vid/vis, phil, luc,* and *sens/sent.*
3	**Developing and sustaining foundational language skills: listening, speaking, reading, writing, and thinking—fluency.** The student reads grade-level text with fluency and comprehension. The student is expected to adjust fluency when reading grade-level text based on the reading purpose.
4	**Developing and sustaining foundational language skills: listening, speaking, reading, writing, and thinking—self-sustained reading.** The student reads grade-appropriate texts independently. The student is expected to self-select text and read independently for a sustained period of time.

5	**Comprehension skills: listening, speaking, reading, writing, and thinking using multiple texts.** The student uses metacognitive skills to both develop and deepen comprehension of increasingly complex texts. The student is expected to:
A	establish purpose for reading assigned and self-selected texts;
B	generate questions about text before, during, and after reading to deepen understanding and gain information;
C	make, correct, or confirm predictions using text features, characteristics of genre, and structures;
D	create mental images to deepen understanding;
E	make connections to personal experiences, ideas in other texts, and society;
F	make inferences and use evidence to support understanding;
G	evaluate details read to determine key ideas;
H	synthesize information to create new understanding; and
I	monitor comprehension and make adjustments such as re-reading, using background knowledge, asking questions, and annotating when understanding breaks down.
6	**Response skills: listening, speaking, reading, writing, and thinking using multiple texts.** The student responds to an increasingly challenging variety of sources that are read, heard, or viewed. The student is expected to:
A	describe personal connections to a variety of sources, including self-selected texts;
B	write responses that demonstrate understanding of texts, including comparing sources within and across genres;
C	use text evidence to support an appropriate response;
D	paraphrase and summarize texts in ways that maintain meaning and logical order;
E	interact with sources in meaningful ways such as notetaking, annotating, freewriting, or illustrating;
F	respond using newly acquired vocabulary as appropriate;
G	discuss and write about the explicit or implicit meanings of text;
H	respond orally or in writing with appropriate register, vocabulary, tone, and voice; and
I	reflect on and adjust responses as new evidence is presented.

7	**Multiple genres: listening, speaking, reading, writing, and thinking using multiple texts—literary elements.** The student recognizes and analyzes literary elements within and across increasingly complex traditional, contemporary, classical, and diverse literary texts. The student is expected to:
A	infer multiple themes within and across texts using text evidence;
B	analyze how characters' qualities influence events and resolution of the conflict;
C	analyze plot elements, including the use of foreshadowing and suspense, to advance the plot; and
D	analyze how the setting influences character and plot development.
8	**Multiple genres: listening, speaking, reading, writing, and thinking using multiple texts—genres.** The student recognizes and analyzes genre-specific characteristics, structures, and purposes within and across increasingly complex traditional, contemporary, classical, and diverse texts. The student is expected to:
A	demonstrate knowledge of literary genres such as realistic fiction, adventure stories, historical fiction, mysteries, humor, myths, fantasy, and science fiction;
B	analyze the effect of rhyme scheme, meter, and graphical elements such as punctuation and capitalization in poems across a variety of poetic forms;
C	analyze how playwrights develop characters through dialogue and staging;
D	analyze characteristics and structural elements of informational text, including:
	i. the controlling idea or thesis with supporting evidence;
	ii. features such as references or acknowledgements; and
	iii. organizational patterns that support multiple topics, categories, and subcategories;
E	analyze characteristics and structures of argumentative text by:
	i. identifying the claim;
	ii. explaining how the author uses various types of evidence and consideration of alternatives to support the argument; and
	iii. identifying the intended audience or reader; and
F	analyze characteristics of multimodal and digital texts.

9	**Author's purpose and craft: listening, speaking, reading, writing, and thinking using multiple texts.** The student uses critical inquiry to analyze the authors' choices and how they influence and communicate meaning within a variety of texts. The student analyzes and applies author's craft purposefully in order to develop his or her own products and performances. The student is expected to:
A	explain the author's purpose and message within a text;
B	analyze how the use of text structure contributes to the author's purpose;
C	analyze the author's use of print and graphic features to achieve specific purposes;
D	describe how the author's use of figurative language such as metaphor and personification achieves specific purposes;
E	identify the use of literary devices, including subjective and objective point of view;
F	analyze how the author's use of language contributes to mood, voice, and tone; and
G	explain the purpose of rhetorical devices such as direct address and rhetorical questions and logical fallacies such as loaded language and sweeping generalizations.

continued on next page

10	**Composition: listening, speaking, reading, writing, and thinking using multiple texts—writing process.** The student uses the writing process recursively to compose multiple texts that are legible and uses appropriate conventions. The student is expected to:
A	plan a first draft by selecting a genre appropriate for a particular topic, purpose, and audience using a range of strategies such as discussion, background reading, and personal interests;
B	develop drafts into a focused, structured, and coherent piece of writing by:
	i. organizing with purposeful structure, including an introduction, transitions, coherence within and across paragraphs, and a conclusion; and
	ii. developing an engaging idea reflecting depth of thought with specific facts, details, and examples;
C	revise drafts for clarity, development, organization, style, word choice, and sentence variety;
D	edit drafts using standard English conventions, including:
	i. complete complex sentences with subject-verb agreement and avoidance of splices, run-ons, and fragments;
	ii. consistent, appropriate use of verb tenses;
	iii. conjunctive adverbs;
	iv. prepositions and prepositional phrases and their influence on subject-verb agreement;
	v. pronoun-antecedent agreement;
	vi. subordinating conjunctions to form complex sentences and correlative conjunctions such as *either/or* and *neither/nor;*
	vii. correct capitalization;
	viii. punctuation, including commas to set off words, phrases, and clauses, and semicolons; and
	ix. correct spelling, including commonly confused terms such as *its/it's*, *affect/effect*, *there/their/they're*, and *to/two/too;* and
E	publish written work for appropriate audiences.

11	**Composition: listening, speaking, reading, writing, and thinking using multiple texts—genres.** The student uses genre characteristics and craft to compose multiple texts that are meaningful. The student is expected to:
A	compose literary texts such as personal narratives, fiction, and poetry using genre characteristics and craft;
B	compose informational texts, including multi-paragraph essays that convey information about a topic, using a clear controlling idea or thesis statement and genre characteristics and craft;
C	compose multi-paragraph argumentative texts using genre characteristics and craft; and
D	compose correspondence that reflects an opinion, registers a complaint, or requests information in a business or friendly structure.

12	**Inquiry and research: listening, speaking, reading, writing, and thinking using multiple texts.** The student engages in both short-term and sustained recursive inquiry processes for a variety of purposes. The student is expected to:
A	generate student-selected and teacher-guided questions for formal and informal inquiry;
B	develop and revise a plan;
C	refine the major research question, if necessary, guided by the answers to a secondary set of questions;
D	identify and gather relevant information from a variety of sources;
E	differentiate between primary and secondary sources;
F	synthesize information from a variety of sources;
G	differentiate between paraphrasing and plagiarism when using source materials;
H	examine sources for:
	i. reliability, credibility, and bias; and
	ii. faulty reasoning such as hyperbole, emotional appeals, and stereotype;
I	display academic citations and use source materials ethically; and
J	use an appropriate mode of delivery, whether written, oral, or multimodal, to present results.

Crossing Generations

PEARSON realize™

Go ONLINE for all lessons

AUDIO

VIDEO

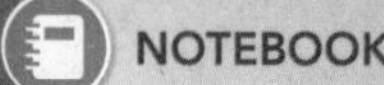
NOTEBOOK

ANNOTATE

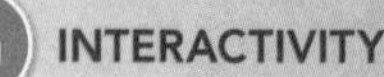
INTERACTIVITY

DOWNLOAD

RESEARCH

WATCH THE VIDEO

Grizzly Bear Teaches Her Cubs

DISCUSS IT What are some examples of things that one generation can learn from another?

Write your response before sharing your ideas.

UNIT 1

UNIT INTRODUCTION

Essential Question

What can one generation learn from another?

MENTOR TEXT:
PERSONAL NARRATIVE
Grounded

WHOLE-CLASS LEARNING

REALISTIC SHORT STORY

Two Kinds
from The Joy Luck Club
Amy Tan

FEATURE ARTICLE

The Case of the Disappearing Words
Alice Andre-Clark

PERFORMANCE TASK

WRITING PROCESS:
Write a Personal Narrative

PEER-GROUP LEARNING

HUMAN INTEREST STORY

Tutors Teach Seniors New High-Tech Tricks
Jennifer Ludden

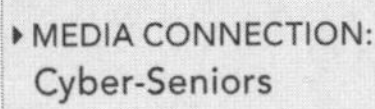

MEDIA CONNECTION: Cyber-Seniors

COMPARE ACROSS GENRES

MEMOIR

from **Mom & Me & Mom**
Maya Angelou

MEDIA: TELEVISION INTERVIEW

Learning to Love My Mother
Maya Angelou with Michael Maher

MEDIA: IMAGE GALLERY

Mother-Daughter Drawings
Mica and Myla Hendricks

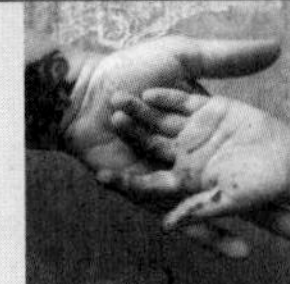

POETRY COLLECTION 1

Abuelita Magic
Pat Mora

Mother to Son
Langston Hughes

To James
Frank Horne

PERFORMANCE TASK

SPEAKING AND LISTENING:
Present a Personal Narrative

INDEPENDENT LEARNING

POETRY COLLECTION 2

Lineage
Margaret Walker

Family
Grace Paley

OPINION PIECE

"Gotcha Day" Isn't a Cause for Celebration
Sophie Johnson

MEDIA: DIGITAL STORYTELLING

Bridging the Generational Divide Between a Football Father and a Soccer Son
John McCormick

REALISTIC FICTION

Water Names
Lan Samantha Chang

REALISTIC FICTION

An Hour With Abuelo
Judith Ortiz Cofer

SHARE INDEPENDENT LEARNING

Share • Learn • Reflect

PERFORMANCE-BASED ASSESSMENT

Personal Narrative

You will write a personal narrative that explores the Essential Question for the unit.

UNIT REFLECTION

Goals • Texts • Essential Question

Unit Goals

VIDEO

Throughout this unit you will deepen your perspective about different generations by reading, writing, speaking, listening, and presenting. These goals will help you succeed on the Unit Performance-Based Assessment.

INTERACTIVITY

SET GOALS Rate how well you meet these goals right now. You will revisit your ratings later when you reflect on your growth during this unit.

SCALE	1	2	3	4	5
	NOT AT ALL WELL	NOT VERY WELL	SOMEWHAT WELL	VERY WELL	EXTREMELY WELL

ESSENTIAL QUESTION	Unit Introduction	Unit Reflection
I can read selections that express various points of view about different generations, and develop my own perspective.	1 2 3 4 5	1 2 3 4 5
READING	**Unit Introduction**	**Unit Reflection**
I can understand and use academic vocabulary words related to narrative nonfiction.	1 2 3 4 5	1 2 3 4 5
I can recognize elements of different genres, especially realistic fiction, informational texts, and poetry.	1 2 3 4 5	1 2 3 4 5
I can read a selection of my choice independently and make meaningful connections to other texts.	1 2 3 4 5	1 2 3 4 5
WRITING	**Unit Introduction**	**Unit Reflection**
I can write a focused, well-organized personal narrative.	1 2 3 4 5	1 2 3 4 5
I can complete Timed Writing tasks with confidence.	1 2 3 4 5	1 2 3 4 5
SPEAKING AND LISTENING	**Unit Introduction**	**Unit Reflection**
I can prepare and present a personal narrative.	1 2 3 4 5	1 2 3 4 5

TEKS
2.C. Determine the meaning and usage of grade-level academic English words derived from Greek and Latin roots such as *omni, log/logue, gen, vid/vis, phil, luc,* and *sens/sent.*

Academic Vocabulary: Nonfiction Narrative

Many English words have roots, or key parts, that come from ancient languages, such as Latin and Greek. Learn these roots and use the words as you respond to questions and activities in this unit.

PRACTICE Academic terms are used routinely in classrooms. Build your knowledge of these words by completing the chart.

1. **Review** each word, its root, and the mentor sentences.
2. **Determine** the meaning and usage of each word using the mentor sentences and a dictionary, if needed.
3. **List** at least two related words for each word.

WORD	MENTOR SENTENCES	PREDICT MEANING	RELATED WORDS
dialogue GREEK ROOT: ***-logue-*** "word"	1. The television show was known for its well-written *dialogue* between characters. 2. The confusion between Dina and Janet started a *dialogue* that cleared the air.		monologue; catalogue
consequence LATIN ROOT: ***-sequ-*** "follow"	1. A *consequence* of oversleeping is being late for school. 2. Earning an A on my math test was a positive *consequence* of studying all week.		
perspective LATIN ROOT: ***-spec-*** "look"	1. The examples from around the world gave the article a global *perspective*. 2. The personal essay was written from the author's *perspective*.		
notable LATIN ROOT: ***-not-*** "mark"	1. Every *notable* person in the city was invited to the mayor's fund-raising gala. 2. It had been a long, boring week, and nothing particularly *notable* had happened.		
contradict LATIN ROOT: ***-dict-*** "speak"	1. The facts of the case remain unclear because the witnesses' statements *contradict* each other. 2. The new test results *contradict* what we once thought to be true about the product.		

MENTOR TEXT | PERSONAL NARRATIVE

This selection is an example of a **personal narrative,** a type of nonfiction in which an author explores a personal experience. This is similar to the kind of writing you will develop in the Performance-Based Assessment at the end of the unit.

READ IT As you read, look at the way the writer vividly describes her grandmother and their relationship.

Grounded

1 Growing up I really didn't know my grandmother. She was a private person, and didn't talk about her past much, but I know she had one. She once told me that before she got married she was a backup singer in a band that I had actually heard of. But that's all she would say about it, no matter how often I prodded.

2 "El pasado es el pasado," she told me. *The past is the past.*

3 To me, she talked in Spanish. I talked back in English. We understood each other.

4 The thing I remember most about Grandma Sofia was how much she loved driving, especially since she came to live with us. She had a 1960s red Chevy Impala convertible that was all her own, a remnant of her band days. She loved driving with the top down, the radio blasting, singing at the top of her lungs when a good song came on. Driving was her independence, her freedom.

5 My parents, however, were concerned that she was getting too old to drive around by herself. One night, I overheard them:

6 "She's okay for now, but how long before she can't manage?"

7 "I'll speak to her tomorrow."

8 I felt sick at the thought of Grandma giving up her car. I knew what driving meant to her. I knew that without her wheels she'd feel ordinary—just another grandma, hovering and wise.

9 Sometimes it felt like Grandma and I were on the sidelines and my parents were in the middle, dragging us toward the center, where we did not want to be. I was often grounded for the smallest things. I didn't really mind, under normal circumstances.

10 One time—the time I'm writing about—circumstances were not normal. My parents had grounded me for the weekend of Luisa's

party, easily the social event of the season. No way was I going to miss it. But my parents weren't even going to be home! They were going to my Aunt Leticia's. It would just be me and Grandma. Me and Grandma and a 1966 red Chevy Impala convertible . . .

11 Saturday night arrived and I was itching to go to the party, so I did the unthinkable: I asked Grandma to drive me to Luisa's. I figured she didn't know about me being grounded. She looked at me quizzically and said she would. I got dressed and ran out to the car. She was waiting for me. I got in.

12 The sky was just beginning to darken, blue clouds against a darker blue sky. Soon it would be nighttime. Grandma looked a little uncomfortable. At first I thought it was because she knew about me being grounded. But then I wondered if maybe she didn't want to drive at night and didn't want to tell me.

13 At that moment, I wouldn't have minded getting out and going back home. I felt bad about Grandma. I felt bad about disobeying my parents. But how could I say any of this?

14 We took off. She drove slowly, maybe too slowly. But we didn't get very far. Suddenly she pulled over and stopped the car.

15 We must have been sitting in that car for five minutes, which is a long time if you're sitting in a car not talking. I couldn't ask her if she stopped because she was nervous about driving. And I couldn't ask if she stopped because she knew I was grounded.

16 Finally she turned to me. "Regresamos?" *Shall we turn back?*

17 "Sure," I replied. I was so relieved I could have cried.

18 "Bueno," she said, with a nod. She started the car and turned on the radio. It was a song we both knew by heart. But it was clear that Grandma and I could still learn a lot from each other. ❧

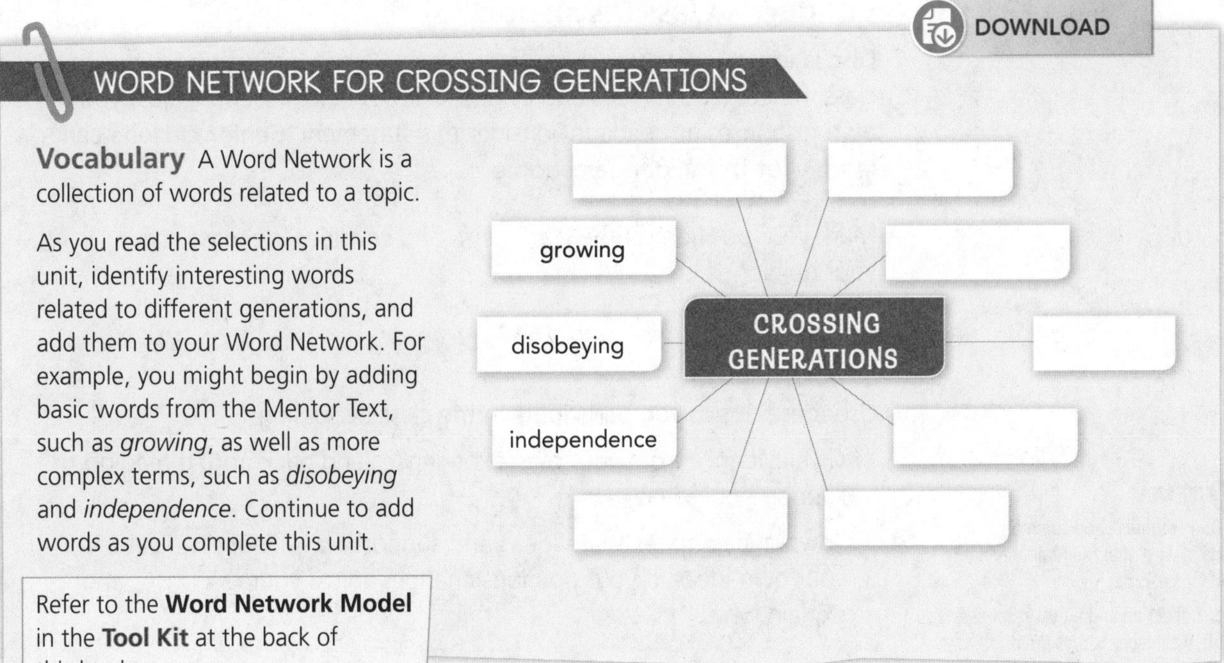

WORD NETWORK FOR CROSSING GENERATIONS

Vocabulary A Word Network is a collection of words related to a topic.

As you read the selections in this unit, identify interesting words related to different generations, and add them to your Word Network. For example, you might begin by adding basic words from the Mentor Text, such as *growing*, as well as more complex terms, such as *disobeying* and *independence*. Continue to add words as you complete this unit.

Refer to the **Word Network Model** in the **Tool Kit** at the back of this book.

Summary

A **summary** is a brief, complete overview of a text that maintains the meaning and logical order of the original work. It should not include your personal opinions.

NOTEBOOK

WRITE IT Write a summary of "Grounded."

Launch Activity

Conduct a Class Discussion

Discussions allow you to learn from others. When discussing an idea in class, reflect on the ideas and evidence your peers present. Adjust your own responses as needed. Consider this statement: **Senior citizens can learn a lot from younger people.**

Mark your position on the statement, and consider the reasons for your opinion.

○ Strongly Agree ○ Agree ○ Disagree ○ Strongly Disagree

Use these tips as you participate in the class discussion:

1. Give evidence from your own experiences and background reading to support your ideas.
2. As your classmates share ideas and supporting evidence, reflect on your own ideas. If your opinions change, adjust your responses and explain why.

TEKS

6.D. Paraphrase and summarize texts in ways that maintain meaning and logical order.

6.I. Reflect on and adjust responses as new evidence is presented.

QuickWrite

Consider class discussions, the video, and the Mentor Text as you think about the Essential Question.

Essential Question

What can one generation learn from another?

At the end of the unit, you will respond to the Essential Question again and see how your perspective has changed.

NOTEBOOK

WRITE IT Record your first thoughts here.

EQ Notes What can one generation learn from another?

As you read the selections in this unit, use a chart like the one shown to record your ideas and list details from the texts that support them. Taking notes as you go will help you clarify your thinking, gather relevant information, and be ready to respond to the Essential Question.

TITLE	MY IDEAS / OBSERVATIONS	TEXT EVIDENCE / INFORMATION

Refer to the **EQ Notes Model** in the **Tool Kit** at the back of this book.

Essential Question

What can one generation learn from another?

The famous Indian leader Mahatma Gandhi said, "Learn as if you were to live forever." You are always learning, from peers as well as from teachers, parents, and relatives. You will work with your whole class to explore ways in which generations can learn from each other.

INTERACTIVITY

Whole-Class Learning Strategies

Throughout your life, in school, in your community, and in your career, you will continue to learn and work in large-group environments.

Review these strategies and the actions you can take to practice them as you work with your whole class. Add ideas of your own to each category. Get ready to use these strategies during Whole-Class Learning.

STRATEGY	MY ACTION PLAN
Listen actively • Put away personal items to avoid becoming distracted. • Try to hear the speaker's full message before planning your own response.	
Demonstrate respect • Show up on time and make sure you are prepared for class. • Avoid side conversations while in class.	
Show interest • Be aware of your body language. For example, sit up in your chair. • Respond when the teacher asks for feedback.	
Interact and share ideas • If you're confused, other people probably are, too. Ask a question to help your whole class. • Build on the ideas of others by adding details or making a connection.	

CONTENTS

REALISTIC SHORT STORY

Two Kinds

from The Joy Luck Club

Amy Tan

A daughter feels stifled by her mother's high expectations.

FEATURE ARTICLE

The Case of the Disappearing Words

Alice Andre-Clark

Is the language we speak always something one generation can pass to the next?

PERFORMANCE TASK: WRITING PROCESS

Write a Personal Narrative

The Whole-Class readings illustrate the influence of one generation on another. After reading, you will write a personal narrative about an event in which you influenced someone from a different generation, or he or she influenced you.

TWO KINDS

The selection you are about to read is a realistic short story.

Reading Realistic Short Stories

A **short story** is a brief work of fiction. **Realistic short stories** are products of writers' imaginations, but seem true to real life.

REALISTIC SHORT STORY

Author's Purpose

- to entertain readers while providing an insight about life or human nature

Characteristics

- realistic settings that provide a backdrop for the action
- characters whose personal qualities influence a story's action and resolution
- conflicts that are resolved by the end of the story
- dialogue that sounds true to life
- themes that express general truths or observations about life or human nature

Structure

- a series of related events, or plot, that could happen in real life

Take a Minute!

NOTEBOOK

LIST IT Create four short story titles, two that are realistic, and two that are obviously not realistic. Write them here.

Share your story titles with a partner and decide which stories are probably realistic and which are not. Discuss your choices with your partner.

TEKS

7.B. Analyze how characters' qualities influence events and resolution of the conflict.

8.A. Demonstrate knowledge of literary genres such as realistic fiction, adventure stories, historical fiction, mysteries, humor, myths, fantasy, and science fiction.

Genre / Text Elements

Character, Conflict, and Resolution The people who take part in a story's action are the **characters.** Their **conflicts,** or problems, drive the story's events until they reach a **resolution,** or end.

Characters' qualities—their personality traits, likes, and dislikes—lead them to react to conflicts in distinct ways. These reactions propel a story forward and lead to its resolution.

TIP: An **external conflict** is a struggle between a character and an outside force. An **internal conflict** is a character's struggle with his or her own thoughts and feelings.

EXAMPLE: Characters' Qualities Influence Events and Resolutions

Conflict: A country is threatened by an evil overlord. Women are not allowed to be soldiers, but a teenaged girl wants to help in the fight.

	CHARACTER 1	CHARACTER 2
Qualities	brave but shy	brave and bold
Events	She stays in her village where she helps many people survive the war.	She becomes a skilled fighter, dresses as a boy, and joins the army.
Resolution	She becomes a local hero.	She becomes a national hero.

PRACTICE Read the chart and answer the question.

Conflict: A character's best friend goes missing on a hike.	
Story Events	*The main character...* • sets out alone to retrace his friend's steps • meets campers and borrows their drone to search the woods • finds his friend, who has broken his arm • makes a splint from twigs and a T-shirt
Resolution	helps his friend back home

Which character is most likely the one in this story? Explain your choice.
Character 1: moody loner; likes to take action before making a plan
Character 2: clever problem-solver; likes to consult with others

About the Author

If her mother had gotten her way, **Amy Tan** (b. 1952) would have two professions—doctor and concert pianist. Although Tan showed early promise in music, at 37 she became a successful fiction writer instead. Tan has written many books—most for adults, and some for children. Writing is sometimes tough, Tan admits, but she keeps this in mind: "A story should be a gift." That thought propels Tan to keep creating memorable characters and events.

TEKS

5.F. Make inferences and use evidence to support understanding.

Two Kinds

Concept Vocabulary

You will encounter the following words as you read "Two Kinds." Before reading, note how familiar you are with each word. Then, rank the words in order from most familiar (1) to least familiar (6).

INTERACTIVITY

WORD	YOUR RANKING
lamented	
indignity	
reproach	
discordant	
squabbling	
devastated	

Comprehension Strategy

ANNOTATE

Make Inferences

An **inference** is an educated guess you make about unstated information in a text. To make inferences, you connect details in a story with what you already know about life. Then, based on that combination of information, you develop an informed idea about the story's characters, setting, and events.

EXAMPLE

Here is an inference you might make as you read this story.

Story Passage: "My mother believed you could be anything you wanted to be in America. You could open a restaurant .... You could become rich."

Possible Inferences: The mother seems to be ambitious. She will probably be a strong character in the story.

PRACTICE As you read the story, write your inferences in the open space next to the text. Mark the evidence that led to each inference.

Two Kinds

from The Joy Luck Club

Amy Tan

BACKGROUND

In 1949, following years of civil war, the Communist Party seized control of China. A number of Chinese who feared Communists—like the mother in "Two Kinds"—fled to the United States. Many lost everything except their hopes for a better future. They placed these hopes on the shoulders of their children born in the new land.

AUDIO

ANNOTATE

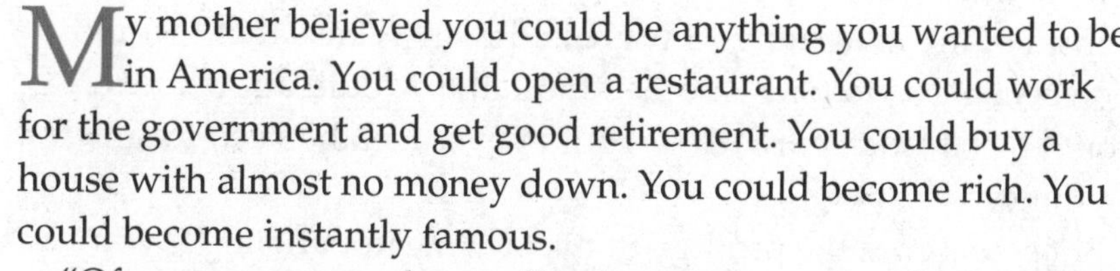

1 My mother believed you could be anything you wanted to be in America. You could open a restaurant. You could work for the government and get good retirement. You could buy a house with almost no money down. You could become rich. You could become instantly famous.

2 "Of course, you can be prodigy,[1] too," my mother told me when I was nine. "You can be best anything. What does Auntie Lindo know? Her daughter, she is only best tricky."

3 America was where all my mother's hopes lay. She had come here in 1949 after losing everything in China: her mother and father, her family home, her first husband, and two daughters, twin baby girls. But she never looked back with regret. There were so many ways for things to get better.

* * *

1. **prodigy** (PROD uh jee) *n.* child of unusually high talent.

CLOSE READ

ANNOTATE: Mark the italicized words in paragraphs 4 and 5.

QUESTION: What is different or unusual about these words?

CONCLUDE: What effect is created by the author's use of these words?

lamented (luh MEHNT ihd) *v.* expressed regret

indignity (ihn DIHG nuh tee) *n.* feeling that one has been disrespected

reproach (rih PROHCH) *n.* criticism or disapproval

4 We didn't immediately pick the right kind of prodigy. At first my mother thought I could be a Chinese Shirley Temple.[2] We'd watch Shirley's old movies on TV as though they were training films. My mother would poke my arm and say, "*Ni kan*"—You watch. And I would see Shirley tapping her feet, or singing a sailor song, or pursing her lips into a very round O while saying, "Oh my goodness."

5 "*Ni kan,*" said my mother as Shirley's eyes flooded with tears. "You already know how. Don't need talent for crying!"

6 Soon after my mother got this idea about Shirley Temple, she took me to a beauty training school in the Mission district and put me in the hands of a student who could barely hold the scissors without shaking. Instead of getting big fat curls, I emerged with an uneven mass of crinkly black fuzz. My mother dragged me off to the bathroom and tried to wet down my hair.

7 "You look like Negro Chinese," she **lamented**, as if I had done this on purpose.

8 The instructor of the beauty training school had to lop off these soggy clumps to make my hair even again. "Peter Pan is very popular these days," the instructor assured my mother. I now had hair the length of a boy's, with straight-across bangs that hung at a slant two inches above my eyebrows. I liked the haircut and it made me actually look forward to my future fame.

9 In fact, in the beginning, I was just as excited as my mother, maybe even more so. I pictured this prodigy part of me as many different images, trying each one on for size. I was a dainty ballerina girl standing by the curtains, waiting to hear the right music that would send me floating on my tiptoes. I was like the Christ child lifted out of the straw manger, crying with holy **indignity**. I was Cinderella stepping from her pumpkin carriage with sparkly cartoon music filling the air.

10 In all of my imaginings, I was filled with a sense that I would soon become *perfect*. My mother and father would adore me. I would be beyond **reproach**. I would never feel the need to sulk for anything.

11 But sometimes the prodigy in me became impatient. "If you don't hurry up and get me out of here, I'm disappearing for good," it warned. "And then you'll always be nothing."

* * *

12 Every night after dinner, my mother and I would sit at the Formica kitchen table. She would present new tests, taking her examples from stories of amazing children that she read in *Ripley's Believe It or Not*, or *Good Housekeeping*, *Reader's Digest*, and a dozen

2. **Shirley Temple** American child star of the 1930s. She starred in her first movie at age three and won an Academy Award at age six.

other magazines she kept in a pile in our bathroom. My mother got these magazines from people whose houses she cleaned. And since she cleaned many houses each week, we had a great assortment. She would look through them all, searching for stories about remarkable children.

13 The first night she brought out a story about a three-year-old boy who knew the capitals of all the states and even most of the European countries. A teacher was quoted as saying the little boy could also pronounce the names of the foreign cities correctly.

14 "What's the capital of Finland?" My mother asked me, looking at the magazine story.

15 All I knew was the capital of California, because Sacramento was the name of the street we lived on in Chinatown. "Nairobi!" I guessed, saying the most foreign word I could think of. She checked to see if that was possibly one way to pronounce "Helsinki" before showing me the answer.

16 The tests got harder—multiplying numbers in my head, finding the queen of hearts in a deck of cards, trying to stand on my head without using my hands, predicting the daily temperatures in Los Angeles, New York, and London.

17 One night I had to look at a page from the Bible for three minutes and then report everything I could remember. "Now Jehoshaphat had riches and honor in abundance and . . . that's all I remember, Ma," I said.

18 And after seeing my mother's disappointed face once again, something inside of me began to die. I hated the tests, the raised hopes and failed expectations. Before going to bed that night, I looked in the mirror above the bathroom sink and when I saw only my face staring back—and that it would always be this ordinary face—I began to cry. Such a sad, ugly girl! I made high-pitched noises like a crazed animal, trying to scratch out the face in the mirror.

19 And then I saw what seemed to be the prodigy side of me—because I had never seen that face before. I looked at my reflection, blinking so I could see more clearly. The girl staring back at me was angry, powerful. This girl and I were the same. I had new thoughts, willful thoughts, or rather thoughts filled with lots of won'ts. I won't let her change me, I promised myself. I won't be what I'm not.

20 So now on nights when my mother presented her tests, I performed listlessly, my head propped on one arm. I pretended to be bored. And I was. I got so bored I started counting the bellows of the foghorns out on the bay while my mother drilled me in other areas. The sound was comforting and reminded me of the cow jumping over the moon. And the next day, I played a game with myself, seeing if my mother would give up on me before eight

CLOSE READ

ANNOTATE: Mark words or phrases in paragraphs 18 and 19 that reveal the narrator's feelings.

QUESTION: Why might the author have chosen to reveal the contrasting emotions of the narrator?

CONCLUDE: What effect does this choice have on the reader?

bellows. After a while I usually counted only one, maybe two bellows at most. At last she was beginning to give up hope.

21 Two or three months had gone by without any mention of my being a prodigy again. And then one day my mother was watching *The Ed Sullivan Show*[3] on TV. The TV was old and the sound kept shorting out. Every time my mother got halfway up from the sofa to adjust the set, the sound would go back on and Ed would be talking. As soon as she sat down, Ed would go silent again. She got up, the TV broke into loud piano music. She sat down. Silence. Up and down, back and forth, quiet and loud. It was like a stiff embraceless dance between her and the TV set. Finally, she stood by the set with her hand on the sound dial.

22 She seemed entranced by the music, a little frenzied piano piece with this mesmerizing quality, sort of quick passages and then teasing lilting ones before it returned to the quick playful parts.

23 *"Ni kan,"* my mother said, calling me over with hurried hand gestures. "Look here."

24 I could see why my mother was fascinated by the music. It was being pounded out by a little Chinese girl, about nine years old, with a Peter Pan haircut. The girl had the sauciness of a Shirley Temple. She was proudly modest like a proper Chinese child. And

3. ***The Ed Sullivan Show*** popular television variety show that ran from 1948 to 1971.

she also did this fancy sweep of a curtsy, so that the fluffy skirt of her white dress cascaded slowly to the floor like the petals of a large carnation.

25 In spite of these warning signs, I wasn't worried. Our family had no piano and we couldn't afford to buy one, let alone reams of sheet music and piano lessons. So I could be generous in my comments when my mother bad-mouthed the little girl on TV.

26 "Play note right, but doesn't sound good! No singing sound," complained my mother.

27 "What are you picking on her for?" I said carelessly. "She's pretty good. Maybe she's not the best, but she's trying hard." I knew almost immediately that I would be sorry I said that.

28 "Just like you," she said. "Not the best. Because you not trying." She gave a little huff as she let go of the sound dial and sat down on the sofa.

29 The little Chinese girl sat down also to play an encore of "Anitra's Dance" by Grieg.[4] I remember the song, because later on I had to learn how to play it.

30 Three days after watching *The Ed Sullivan Show*, my mother told me what my schedule would be for piano lessons and piano practice. She had talked to Mr. Chong, who lived on the first floor of our apartment building. Mr. Chong was a retired piano teacher and my mother had traded housecleaning services for weekly lessons and a piano for me to practice on every day, two hours a day, from four until six.

31 When my mother told me this, I felt as though I had been sent to hell. I whined and then kicked my foot a little when I couldn't stand it anymore.

32 "Why don't you like me the way I am? I'm not a genius! I can't play the piano. And even if I could, I wouldn't go on TV if you paid me a million dollars!" I cried.

33 My mother slapped me. "Who ask you be genius?" she shouted. "Only ask you be your best. For you sake. You think I want you be genius? Hnnh! What for! Who ask you!"

34 "So ungrateful," I heard her mutter in Chinese, "If she had as much talent as she has temper, she would be famous now."

35 Mr. Chong, whom I secretly nicknamed Old Chong, was very strange, always tapping his fingers to the silent music of an invisible orchestra. He looked ancient in my eyes. He had lost most of the hair on top of his head and he wore thick glasses and had eyes that always looked tired and sleepy. But he must have been younger than I thought, since he lived with his mother and was not yet married.

36 I met Old Lady Chong once and that was enough. She had this peculiar smell like a baby that had done something in its pants.

4. **Grieg** (greeg) Edvard Grieg (1843–1907), Norwegian composer.

CLOSE READ

ANNOTATE: Mark the punctuation in paragraphs 32 and 33 that reveals how the mother and daughter communicate.

QUESTION: What does the punctuation suggest about the tone of the conversation?

CONCLUDE: How does the punctuation in these paragraphs help you to better understand the conflict between the mother and the daughter?

And her fingers felt like a dead person's, like an old peach I once found in the back of the refrigerator; the skin just slid off the meat when I picked it up.

37 I soon found out why Old Chong had retired from teaching piano. He was deaf. "Like Beethoven!"[5] he shouted to me. "We're both listening only in our head!" And he would start to conduct his frantic silent sonatas.

38 Our lessons went like this. He would open the book and point to different things, explaining their purpose: "Key! Treble! Bass! No sharps or flats! So this is C major! Listen now and play after me!"

39 And then he would play the C scale a few times, a simple chord, and then, as if inspired by an old, unreachable itch, he gradually added more notes and running trills and a pounding bass until the music was really something quite grand.

40 I would play after him, the simple scale, the simple chord, and then I just played some nonsense that sounded like a cat running up and down on top of garbage cans. Old Chong smiled and applauded and then said, "Very good! But now you must learn to keep time!"

41 So that's how I discovered that Old Chong's eyes were too slow to keep up with the wrong notes I was playing. He went through the motions in half-time. To help me keep rhythm, he stood behind me, pushing down on my right shoulder for every beat. He balanced pennies on top of my wrists so I would keep them still as I slowly played scales and arpeggios.[6] He had me curve my hand around an apple and keep that shape when playing chords. He marched stiffly to show me how to make each finger dance up and down, staccato[7] like an obedient little soldier.

42 He taught me all these things, and that was how I also learned I could be lazy and get away with mistakes, lots of mistakes. If I hit the wrong notes because I hadn't practiced enough, I never corrected myself. I just kept playing in rhythm. And Old Chong kept conducting his own private reverie.

43 So maybe I never really gave myself a fair chance. I did pick up the basics pretty quickly, and I might have become a good pianist at that young age. But I was so determined not to try, not to be anybody different that I learned to play only the most ear-splitting preludes, the most **discordant** hymns.

discordant (dihs KAWRD uhnt) *adj.* lacking harmony

44 Over the next year, I practiced like this, dutifully in my own way. And then one day I heard my mother and her friend Lindo Jong both talking in a loud bragging tone of voice so others could hear. It was after church, and I was leaning against the

5. **Beethoven** (BAY toh vuhn) Ludwig van Beethoven (1770–1827), German composer. Some of his greatest pieces were written when he was completely deaf.
6. **arpeggios** (ahr PEHJ ee ohz) *n.* notes in a chord played separately in quick succession.
7. **staccato** (stuh KAHT oh) *adv.* played crisply, with clear breaks between notes.

brick wall wearing a dress with stiff white petticoats. Auntie Lindo's daughter, Waverly, who was about my age, was standing farther down the wall about five feet away. We had grown up together and shared all the closeness of two sisters **squabbling** over crayons and dolls. In other words, for the most part, we hated each other. I thought she was snotty. Waverly Jong had gained a certain amount of fame as "Chinatown's Littlest Chinese Chess Champion."

squabbling (SKWAHB blihng) *v.* fighting noisily over small matters

45 "She bring home too many trophy," lamented Auntie Lindo that Sunday. "All day she play chess. All day I have no time do nothing but dust off her winnings." She threw a scolding look at Waverly, who pretended not to see her.

46 "You lucky you don't have this problem," said Auntie Lindo with a sigh to my mother.

47 And my mother squared her shoulders and bragged: "Our problem worser than yours. If we ask Jing-mei wash dish, she hear nothing but music. It's like you can't stop this natural talent."

48 And right then, I was determined to put a stop to her foolish pride.

* * *

49 A few weeks later, Old Chong and my mother conspired to have me play in a talent show which would be held in the church hall. By then, my parents had saved up enough to buy me a secondhand piano, a black Wurlitzer spinet with a scarred bench. It was the showpiece of our living room.

50 For the talent show, I was to play a piece called "Pleading Child" from Schumann's[8] *Scenes from Childhood*. It was a simple, moody piece that sounded more difficult than it was. I was supposed to memorize the whole thing, playing the repeat parts twice to make the piece sound longer. But I dawdled over it, playing a few bars and then cheating, looking up to see what notes followed. I never really listened to what I was playing. I daydreamed about being somewhere else, about being someone else.

51 The part I liked to practice best was the fancy curtsy: right foot out, touch the rose on the carpet with a pointed foot, sweep to the side, left leg bends, look up and smile.

52 My parents invited all the couples from the Joy Luck Club to witness my debut. Auntie Lindo and Uncle Tin were there. Waverly and her two older brothers had also come. The first two rows were filled with children both younger and older than I was. The littlest ones got to go first. They recited simple nursery rhymes, squawked out tunes on miniature violins, twirled Hula

8. **Schumann** (SHOO mahn) Robert Alexander Schumann (1810–1856), German composer.

Hoops, pranced in pink ballet tutus, and when they bowed or curtsied, the audience would sigh in unison, "Awww," and then clap enthusiastically.

53 When my turn came, I was very confident. I remember my childish excitement. It was as if I knew, without a doubt, that the prodigy side of me really did exist. I had no fear whatsoever, no nervousness. I remember thinking to myself, This is it! This is it! I looked out over the audience, at my mother's blank face, my father's yawn, Auntie Lindo's stiff-lipped smile, Waverly's sulky expression. I had on a white dress, layered with sheets of lace, and a pink bow in my Peter Pan haircut. As I sat down, I envisioned people jumping to their feet and Ed Sullivan rushing up to introduce me to everyone on TV.

CLOSE READ

ANNOTATE: In paragraph 54, mark descriptive words, and note what they describe.

QUESTION: Why does the author use positive and negative descriptions?

CONCLUDE: What effect do these descriptions have over the course of the paragraph?

54 And I started to play. It was so beautiful. I was so caught up in how lovely I looked that at first I didn't worry how I would sound. So it was a surprise to me when I hit the first wrong note and I realized something didn't sound quite right. And then I hit another and another followed that. A chill started at the top of my head and began to trickle down. Yet I couldn't stop playing, as though my hands were bewitched. I kept thinking my fingers would adjust themselves back, like a train switching to the right track. I played this strange jumble through two repeats, the sour notes staying with me all the way to the end.

55 When I stood up, I discovered my legs were shaking. Maybe I had just been nervous and the audience, like Old Chong, had seen me go through the right motions and had not heard anything wrong at all. I swept my right foot out, went down on my knee, looked up and smiled. The room was quiet, except for Old Chong, who was beaming and shouting "Bravo! Bravo! Well done!" But then I saw my mother's face, her stricken face. The audience clapped weakly, and as I walked back to my chair, with my whole face quivering as I tried not to cry, I heard a little boy whisper loudly to his mother, "That was awful," and the mother whispered back, "Well, she certainly tried."

56 And now I realized how many people were in the audience, the whole world it seemed. I was aware of eyes burning into my back. I felt the shame of my mother and father as they sat stiffly throughout the rest of the show.

57 We could have escaped during intermission. Pride and some strange sense of honor must have anchored my parents to their chairs. And so we watched it all: the eighteen-year-old boy with a fake moustache who did a magic show and juggled flaming hoops while riding a unicycle. The breasted girl with white makeup who sang from *Madama Butterfly* and got honorable mention. And the eleven-year-old boy who won first prize playing a tricky violin song that sounded like a busy bee.

58 After the show, the Hsus, the Jongs, and the St. Clairs from the Joy Luck Club came up to my mother and father.

59 "Lots of talented kids," Auntie Lindo said vaguely, smiling broadly.

60 "That was somethin' else," said my father, and I wondered if he was referring to me in a humorous way, or whether he even remembered what I had done.

61 Waverly looked at me and shrugged her shoulders. "You aren't a genius like me," she said matter-of-factly. And if I hadn't felt so bad, I would have pulled her braids and punched her stomach.

62 But my mother's expression was what **devastated** me: a quiet, blank look that said she had lost everything. I felt the same way, and it seemed as if everybody were now coming up, like gawkers at the scene of an accident, to see what parts were actually missing. When we got on the bus to go home, my father was humming the busy-bee tune and my mother was silent. I kept thinking she wanted to wait until we got home before shouting at me. But when my father unlocked the door to our apartment, my mother walked in and then went to the back, into the bedroom. No accusations. No blame. And in a way, I felt disappointed. I had been waiting for her to start shouting, so I could shout back and cry and blame her for all my misery.

devastated (DEH vuh stay tihd) *v.* destroyed; completely upset

* * *

63 I assumed my talent-show fiasco meant I never had to play the piano again. But two days later, after school, my mother came out of the kitchen and saw me watching TV.

64 "Four clock," she reminded me as if it were any other day. I was stunned, as though she were asking me to go through the talent-show torture again. I wedged myself more tightly in front of the TV.

65 "Turn off TV," she called from the kitchen five minutes later.

66 I didn't budge. And then I decided. I didn't have to do what my mother said anymore. I wasn't her slave. This wasn't China. I had listened to her before and look what happened. She was the stupid one.

67 She came out from the kitchen and stood in the arched entryway of the living room. "Four clock," she said once again, louder.

68 "I'm not going to play anymore," I said nonchalantly. "Why should I? I'm not a genius."

69 She walked over and stood in front of the TV. I saw her chest was heaving up and down in an angry way.

70 "No!" I said, and I now felt stronger, as if my true self had finally emerged. So this was what had been inside me all along.

71 "No! I won't!" I screamed.

72 She yanked me by the arm, pulled me off the floor, snapped off the TV. She was frighteningly strong, half pulling, half carrying me toward the piano as I kicked the throw rugs under my feet. She lifted me up and onto the hard bench. I was sobbing by now, looking at her bitterly. Her chest was heaving even more and her mouth was open, smiling crazily as if she were pleased I was crying.

73 "You want me to be someone that I'm not!" I sobbed. "I'll never be the kind of daughter you want me to be!"

74 "Only two kinds of daughters," she shouted in Chinese. "Those who are obedient and those who follow their own mind! Only one kind of daughter can live in this house. Obedient daughter!"

75 "Then I wish I wasn't your daughter. I wish you weren't my mother," I shouted. As I said these things I got scared. It felt like worms and toads and slimy things crawling out of my chest, but it also felt good, as if this awful side of me had surfaced, at last.

76 "Too late change this," said my mother shrilly.

77 And I could sense her anger rising to its breaking point. I wanted to see it spill over. And that's when I remembered the babies she had lost in China, the ones we never talked about. "Then I wish I'd never been born!" I shouted. "I wish I were dead! Like them."

78 It was as if I had said the magic words. Alakazam!—and her face went blank, her mouth closed, her arms went slack, and she backed out of the room, stunned, as if she were blowing away like a small brown leaf, thin, brittle, lifeless.

79 It was not the only disappointment my mother felt in me. In the years that followed, I failed her so many times, each time asserting my own will, my right to fall short of expectations. I didn't get straight A's. I didn't become class president. I didn't get into Stanford. I dropped out of college.

80 For unlike my mother, I did not believe I could be anything I wanted to be. I could only be me.

81 And for all those years, we never talked about the disaster at the recital or my terrible accusations afterward at the piano bench. All that remained unchecked, like a betrayal that was now unspeakable. So I never found a way to ask her why she had hoped for something so large that failure was inevitable.

82 And even worse, I never asked her what frightened me the most: Why had she given up hope?

83 For after our struggle at the piano, she never mentioned my playing again. The lessons stopped. The lid to the piano was closed, shutting out the dust, my misery, and her dreams.

84 So she surprised me. A few years ago, she offered to give me the piano, for my thirtieth birthday. I had not played in all those years. I saw the offer as a sign of forgiveness, a tremendous burden removed.

85 "Are you sure?" I asked shyly. "I mean, won't you and Dad miss it?"

86 "No, this your piano," she said firmly. "Always your piano. You only one can play."

87 "Well, I probably can't play anymore," I said. "It's been years."

88 "You pick up fast," said my mother, as if she knew this was certain. "You have natural talent. You could been genius if you want to."

89 "No I couldn't."

90 "You just not trying," said my mother. And she was neither angry nor sad. She said it as if to announce a fact that could never be disproved. "Take it," she said.

91 But I didn't at first. It was enough that she had offered it to me. And after that, every time I saw it in my parents' living room, standing in front of the bay windows, it made me feel proud, as if it were a shiny trophy I had won back.

* * *

92 Last week I sent a tuner over to my parents' apartment and had the piano reconditioned, for purely sentimental reasons. My mother had died a few months before and I had been getting things in order for my father, a little bit at a time. I put the jewelry in special silk pouches. The sweaters she had knitted in yellow, pink, bright orange— all the colors I hated—I put those in moth-proof boxes. I found some old Chinese silk dresses, the kind with little slits up the sides. I rubbed the old silk against my skin, then wrapped them in tissue and decided to take them home with me.

93 After I had the piano tuned, I opened the lid and touched the keys. It sounded even richer than I remembered. Really, it was a very good piano. Inside the bench were the same exercise notes with handwritten scales, the same secondhand music books with their covers held together with yellow tape.

94 I opened up the Schumann book to the dark little piece I had played at the recital. It was on the left-hand side of the page, "Pleading Child." It looked more difficult than I remembered. I played a few bars, surprised at how easily the notes came back to me.

95 And for the first time, or so it seemed, I noticed the piece on the right-hand side. It was called "Perfectly Contented." I tried to play this one as well. It had a lighter melody but the same flowing rhythm and turned out to be quite easy. "Pleading Child" was shorter but slower; "Perfectly Contented" was longer, but faster. And after I played them both a few times, I realized they were two halves of the same song. ❧

NOTEBOOK

Answer the questions in your notebook. Use text evidence to support your responses.

Response

1. **Personal Connections** What aspects of the story did you find surprising or funny? Explain.

Comprehension

2. **Reading Check (a)** In what ways does the mother pressure the narrator to change? **(b)** How does the narrator prepare for the talent show? **(c)** What happens when the narrator performs at the talent show?

3. **Strategy: Make Inferences (a)** Cite one inference you made that helped you understand something about a character that wasn't stated in the text. **(b)** What evidence did you use to make that inference? Explain.

Analysis

4. **(a) Compare and Contrast** How are the mother and the narrator similar and different? **(b) Analyze Cause and Effect** How do differences in the mother's and narrator's attitudes cause problems?

5. **(a) Make Inferences** Why do you think the mother was so determined to make the narrator into a prodigy? Cite text evidence that supports your response. **(b) Evaluate** Do you think the mother truly knows and understands her daughter? Explain.

6. **Make a Judgment** The mother criticizes the narrator for not being obedient and for not trying hard enough to succeed. Do the story's events prove or disprove that criticism? Explain.

EQ Notes What can one generation learn from another?

What have you learned about how people of different generations interact from reading this story? Go to your Essential Question Notes, and record your observations and thoughts about "Two Kinds."

TEKS

5.F. Make inferences and use evidence to support understanding.

6.C. Use text evidence to support an appropriate response.

TWO KINDS

Close Read

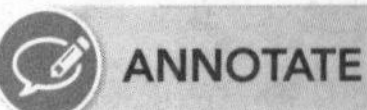

1. The model passage and annotation show how one reader analyzed paragraph 10 of the story. Find another detail in the passage to annotate. Then, write your own question and conclusion.

CLOSE-READ MODEL

In all of my imaginings, I was filled with a sense that I would soon become *perfect*. My mother and father would adore me. I would be beyond reproach. I would never feel the need to sulk for anything.

ANNOTATE: The author uses italics to emphasize a specific word.

QUESTION: Why is the word *perfect* emphasized?

CONCLUDE: The narrator believes that the only way her parents will be satisfied with her is if she is without fault.

MY **QUESTION:**

MY **CONCLUSION:**

2. For more practice, answer the Close-Read notes in the selection.
3. Choose a section of the story you found especially important. Mark important details. Then, jot down questions and write your conclusions in the open space next to the text.

 RESEARCH

Inquiry and Research

 NOTEBOOK

Research and Extend Often, you have to generate your own research questions. Sometimes, however, your teacher will give you research questions to explore. Practice responding to teacher-guided questions by conducting a brief, informal inquiry to find facts about the setting of this story:

The main setting of this story is San Francisco's Chinatown in the 1950s. How many people lived there at that time? In what part of the city was the neighborhood located?

Cite at least three facts you discover during your research.

 TEKS

7.B. Analyze how characters' qualities influence events and resolution of the conflict.

12.A. Generate student-selected and teacher-guided questions for formal and informal inquiry.

Genre / Text Elements

Character, Conflict, and Resolution A **character's qualities**—including his or her appearance, age, feelings, and thoughts—influence the nature of the conflict in a story. The conflict, in turn, moves the story forward until it ends in the **resolution**. This means that *who* a character is determines what happens in a story and how it resolves.

NOTEBOOK

INTERACTIVITY

PRACTICE Complete the activity and answer the questions.

1. **(a) Support** Find a passage from the story that reveals each of the narrator's qualities listed in the chart.
   (b) Connect In the blank row, add another quality the narrator possesses and a passage that reveals it.

NARRATOR'S QUALITIES	PASSAGE THAT REVEALS QUALITY
Self-Confident	
Stubborn	
Lazy	

2. **(a) Analyze** In paragraphs 18–19, the narrator observes a dramatic change in her sense of self. What is that change? **(b) Analyze Cause and Effect** Note two ways in which this change influences the narrator's actions and the story events that come later.

3. **(a) Summarize** Reread paragraphs 75–78. How does the narrator's conflict with her mother abruptly end? **(b) Evaluate** Is the resolution happy? Explain. **(c) Interpret** Reread paragraph 79 to the end of the story. How does the resolution change over time? Explain.

4. **Speculate** Explain how the story's events and resolution might have unfolded if the narrator were different in each of the following ways:
   (a) She works hard at piano practice.
   (b) She does whatever her mother wants.

TWO KINDS

Concept Vocabulary

NOTEBOOK

Why These Words? The vocabulary words relate to the idea of conflict. For example, the narrator fantasizes that she might one day be beyond *reproach*. The word *reproach* describes the heavy criticism that she feels as a result of her mother's actions.

lamented	reproach	squabbling
indignity	discordant	devastated

PRACTICE Answer the questions.

1. What other words in the selection connect to the concept of conflict, or struggle?
2. Why might a person who experiences *indignity* feel upset or angry?
3. Why might a famous chef feel that his or her cooking is beyond *reproach*?
4. Why might someone's neighbors complain about *discordant* music coming from a loudspeaker?
5. What advice can you give people to help them avoid *squabbling* with each other?
6. If a student *lamented* after taking a test, how did the student do?
7. What kind of weather might have *devastated* an apple orchard?

WORD NETWORK

Add words that are related to the idea of generations from the text to your Word Network.

Word Study

NOTEBOOK

Latin Prefix: *in-* The prefix *in-*, which appears in the vocabulary word *indignity,* means "not." When this prefix is added to a base word, the new word takes on the opposite meaning of the base word.

PRACTICE Complete the following items.

1. When people have *dignity*, they are worthy of honor and respect. Write a definition of the word *indignity* that uses your knowledge of the prefix *in-*.
2. Define these words that contain the prefix *in-: incorrect, inactive, incomplete*.

TEKS

10.D.vii. Edit drafts using standard English conventions, including correct capitalization.

Conventions

Nouns and Pronouns A **common noun** names a person, place, thing, or idea, and is not capitalized. A **proper noun** names a specific person, place, thing, or idea, and is capitalized. A **possessive noun** shows ownership.

COMMON NOUNS	PROPER NOUNS	POSSESSIVE NOUNS
mother, daughter, country, street, month	Mr. Chong, China, Main Street, April	the audience's reaction Lucas's piano the musicians' bows the children's concert

TIP: Note that, unlike possessive nouns, possessive pronouns do not use apostrophes to show possession.

A **personal pronoun** takes the place of a noun, or several nouns, or another pronoun referred to earlier in the text. A **possessive pronoun** shows possession or ownership.

PERSONAL PRONOUNS	I, me, we, us, you, he, him, she, her, it, they, them
POSSESSIVE PRONOUNS	my, mine, our, ours, your, yours, his, hers, its, their, theirs

NOTEBOOK

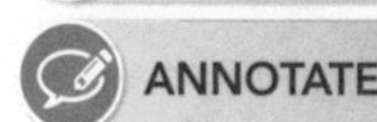
ANNOTATE

READ IT Reread paragraph 29 of "Two Kinds." Mark the nouns. Then, classify each noun as common or proper. Finally, identify the possessive noun in the paragraph.

WRITE IT

A. Edit the sentences. Replace the underlined nouns with appropriate pronouns.

1. When the daughter performed, the daughter's playing was sloppy.

2. My father listened patiently, although my father did not want to be there.

3. The youngest children played first. Most of the youngest children were prepared.

B. Write three sentences about an important scene between the mother and daughter in the selection. Include at least one of each type of noun and pronoun in your sentences. Edit your sentences to be sure you have capitalized all proper nouns.

TWO KINDS

Composition

A **retelling** is a new version of a story. In a retelling, at least one important story element from the original version is changed.

EDITING PRACTICE As you edit your draft, make sure you haven't confused the words *its* and *it's*. *Its* is the possessive form of the pronoun *it*. *It's* is a contraction that means "it is" or "it has."

ASSIGNMENT

Choose a scene from the story, and write a **retelling** of the scene from the mother's point of view.

- Review the story, and note important details that can help you identify the mother's character traits and motives. Use these details to ensure that you accurately portray the mother's character.
- Present a clear sequence of events, and establish the conflict for the scene that you chose.
- Use narrative techniques, such as dialogue and description, to convey the mother's thoughts and feelings.

Use New Words

Try to use one or more of the concept vocabulary words in your writing: *lamented, indignity, reproach, discordant, squabbling, devastated.*

NOTEBOOK

Reflect on Your Writing

PRACTICE Think about the choices you made as you wrote. Also, consider what you learned by writing. Share your experiences by responding to these questions.

1. How did writing from the mother's point of view help you to better understand her perspective?

2. What characteristics of short stories did you use in your writing? Which narrative technique do you think was most effective in portraying the mother's character?

3. **WHY THESE WORDS?** The words you choose make a difference in your writing. Which words did you specifically choose to bring the mother's point of view to life?

6.H. Respond orally or in writing with appropriate register, vocabulary, tone, and voice.

10.D.ix. Edit drafts using standard English conventions, including correct spelling, including commonly confused terms such as *its/it's, affect/ effect, there/their/they're,* and *to/two/too*.

11.A. Compose literary texts such as personal narratives, fiction, and poetry using genre characteristics and craft.

Speaking and Listening

A **monologue** is a speech presented by one character. The character expresses thoughts and feelings he or she may not have shared with other characters in the story.

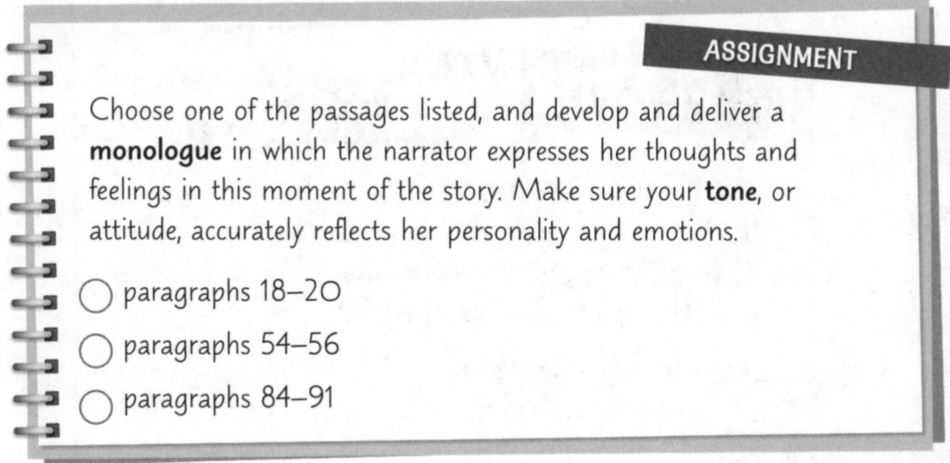

ASSIGNMENT

Choose one of the passages listed, and develop and deliver a **monologue** in which the narrator expresses her thoughts and feelings in this moment of the story. Make sure your **tone**, or attitude, accurately reflects her personality and emotions.

- ◯ paragraphs 18–20
- ◯ paragraphs 54–56
- ◯ paragraphs 84–91

Plan Your Monologue Use the following questions to gather ideas and prepare notes to guide your delivery.

- How can you begin in a way that grabs listeners' interest?
- How might events from earlier in the story affect the narrator now?
- How can you show changes in the narrator's feelings?
- What specific vocabulary can you use to vividly portray the narrator's personality?

TIP: Remember to stay in character. Include cues in your notes to keep you on track.

Practice Your Delivery Vary your **tone,** or the emotional qualities of your voice, to show what the narrator is feeling.

Present and Evaluate Use a guide like the one shown to evaluate your own monologue as well as those of your classmates.

PRESENTATION EVALUATION GUIDE

Rate each statement on a scale of 1 (not demonstrated) to 5 (demonstrated).

Statement	1	2	3	4	5
The speaker communicated events from the narrator's point of view.	◯	◯	◯	◯	◯
The speaker's tone communicated shifts in feeling.	◯	◯	◯	◯	◯
The monologue was clear and expressive.	◯	◯	◯	◯	◯

EQ Notes Before moving on to a new selection, go to your Essential Question Notes and record any additional thoughts or observations you may have about "Two Kinds."

THE CASE OF THE DISAPPEARING WORDS

The selection you are about to read is a feature article.

Reading Feature Articles

A **feature article** is a longer work of journalism that reports information in an in-depth way.

FEATURE ARTICLES

Author's Purpose

- to present information about newsworthy events, issues, or people and explain why they are important and relevant
- to bring readers' attention to a subject in a powerful way

Characteristics

- a title that engages readers' interest
- a clear controlling idea
- a variety of evidence, including quotations, facts, statistics, examples, and anecdotes
- diction, or word choice, that clarifies a complex subject

Structure

- often starts with a "lead," or an engaging first paragraph or section
- may use a variety of organizational patterns that show time order as well as causes or effects

Take a Minute!

NOTEBOOK

FIND IT Think of a subject you enjoy, such as sports or music. Do a quick Internet search to find a feature article related to that subject. Jot down the title and publication.

TEKS

8.D.i. Analyze characteristics and structural elements of informational text, including the controlling idea or thesis with supporting evidence.

Genre / Text Elements

Controlling Idea and Supporting Evidence A feature article expresses a **controlling idea**—a thesis or main point—in a way that entertains readers. The author weaves together different kinds of **supporting evidence** to bring the topic to life and develop the thesis. Consider this example.

TIP: A controlling idea is not a topic. A topic is what an article is about. A controlling idea is what it means.

EXAMPLE

Controlling Idea: Disc golf is one of the most exciting new games to come along in years.

TYPES OF EVIDENCE	EXAMPLES
facts: statements that can be proved true	In disc golf, players throw Frisbee-like discs into baskets.
statistics: numerical data (percentages, estimates, averages), gained from research	As of 2016, an estimated 12 million people have played disc golf in the United States.
examples: specific instances of a general idea	Disc golf courses will soon be everywhere. For example, Texas currently has 376 courses and more on the way.
anecdotes: brief stories that illustrate a point	I played disc golf on opening day in El Paso. I'm not a great athlete, so it was challenging, but still fun.

PRACTICE The following items are pieces of evidence that support the controlling idea from the example. State whether each item is a plain fact, a statistic, an example, or an anecdote. Then, explain how it supports the controlling idea.

1. About 34% of disc golf players are between the ages of 30–39. ______________

2. People of all ages can play disc golf. For example, there is now a league for seniors. ______________

3. Players try to get their discs into the baskets in as few throws as possible. ______________

4. These 7th grade girls said they "hated" sports until they played disc golf. They went on to petition their school to start a program. ______________

The Case of the Disappearing Words

About the Author

Born in Rochester, New York, **Alice Andre-Clark** now lives in New Jersey. She studied Social Welfare at Harvard Kennedy School and Public Policy at Harvard University Graduate School of Arts and Sciences.

Concept Vocabulary

You will encounter the following words as you read "The Case of the Disappearing Words." Before reading, note how familiar you are with each word. Using a scale of 1 (do not know it at all) to 5 (know it very well), indicate your knowledge of each word.

INTERACTIVITY

WORD	YOUR RATING
fluently	
linguists	
term	
lecture	
recording	
pronouncing	

Comprehension Strategy

ANNOTATE

Make Predictions

Predictions are a type of guess you make about the information and ideas a text will include. Informational texts often have features that add to or organize the content. Before you read, scan the text for these features. Use the information they provide to make predictions. Then, correct or confirm your predictions as you read on.

- **titles and subtitles:** indicate the topic and may suggest a controlling idea
- **subheads:** indicate the ideas that appear in a particular section
- **images:** illustrate important ideas or information
- **captions:** suggest how images connect to ideas

PRACTICE Before you read, scan the text features in the article, and use your observations to write three predictions. Then, read on to either confirm your predictions or to correct them.

TEKS
5.C. Make, correct, or confirm predictions using text features, characteristics of genre, and structures.

The Case of the Disappearing Words

Saving the World's Endangered Languages

Alice Andre-Clark

BACKGROUND

You already know about endangered animals and plants, living things that are at risk of disappearing from Earth. Alice Andre-Clark believes that many languages are also endangered. But are languages living things? Decide for yourself as you read.

AUDIO

ANNOTATE

1 During World War II, American Navajo speakers worked with the United States military to create a secret code in their language that the Germans couldn't crack. Now Navajo children are unlikely to grow up speaking the language **fluently**. The Taa language of southern Africa is one of the most complex in the world, combining five distinct clicks of the tongue with other sounds to produce between 80 and 120 different consonants. Today, this unique language has only a few thousand speakers

fluently (FLOO ehnt lee) *adv.* easily and smoothly

Breton is a Celtic language spoken in the Brittany region of France, where parents were once forbidden from giving children Breton names.

linguists (LIHN gwihsts) *n.* people who study how languages work

left. Earth is home to around 7,000 languages, but **linguists** are rushing to catalog them because around half are expected to disappear by 2100.

Why They Disappear

2 Languages tend to become endangered when a dominant culture swallows up a smaller culture. Sometimes younger generations stop learning a language because parents want children to fit in and get jobs in the majority culture. Sometimes societies force minorities to give up language and traditions. Many Native American children of the late nineteenth and early twentieth centuries were required to attend boarding schools where educators forbade them from speaking their native

languages. In China today, the government limits the time teachers may speak the language Uighur. Many Uighur language speakers feel their culture may be at risk.

Categories of Danger

3 The United Nations regularly releases lists of endangered languages, placing each in one of five categories. A "vulnerable" language is one that many children speak at home, but few speak outside of their homes. Zuni, spoken by 9,000 of New Mexico's Pueblo peoples, is vulnerable. A "definitely endangered" language is one that older generations speak, but children no longer learn in the home. Dakota, a language of the Great Plains with 675 speakers, is definitely endangered.

4 A "severely endangered" language is one that parents may understand but don't speak much. Grandparents are the primary speakers. Oklahoma's Chickasaw, with 600 speakers, mostly age 50 or older, is one example. A "critically endangered" language is one that few people younger than grandparents speak, and grandparents don't speak it often. New York's and Canada's Onondaga, with about 50 speakers, is critically endangered. An "extinct" language has no living native speakers—the last native speaker of Alaska's Eyak language died in 2008.

Why Save Them?

5 You could ask the same question of an endangered species of animal. Why should we save it? The answer is that having a variety of species benefits our environment. In the same way that different species create biodiversity, languages contribute to cultural diversity. Learning about and protecting endangered languages benefits our understanding of other cultures. A language's vocabulary paints a fascinating picture of a society's way of life. We know a little more about India's Gta' speakers when we learn that they have words like *nosor* (noh SAWR), meaning "to free someone from a tiger," *bno* (buh NOH), "a ladder made from a single bamboo tree," and *gotae* (goh TA), "to bring something from a hard-to-reach place with a long stick."

6 Languages can show how a society looks at the world and what it values. In Apache culture, a sense of place is so important that storytellers use descriptive names for land features, such as "White Rocks Lie Above in a Compact Cluster." Facing setbacks with laughter is important in the Jewish tradition, so it may not be surprising that the Jewish language Yiddish has words to describe two kinds of fools. A *schlemiel* is the kind who spills soup on other people, and the unlucky *schlimazel* is the one on whom soup always gets spilled.

CLOSE READ

ANNOTATE: In paragraph 5, mark words from another language and their definitions.

QUESTION: Why does the author call attention to these particular words and definitions?

CONCLUDE: What do these words show about this language?

term (turhm) *n.* word or expression that has a specific meaning

lecture (LEHK shuhr) *v.* talk in a critical way that seems unfair

7 A language may contain hidden knowledge that the rest of the world has not yet discovered. The **term** for eelgrass in Mexico's Seri language alerted scientists that eelgrass, unlike most sea grasses, is a nutritious food. The Seri word *moosni hant cooit* (mohs nee ahnt koh eet), meaning "green turtle that descends," revealed something no one else knew—that green turtles hibernate, or overwinter, on the sea floor.

8 A language may describe something in a way that is funny, sharp, or beautifully poetic. In Welsh, it rains not cats and dogs, but old wives and walking sticks. If a Basque speaker tells you, "Don't take the beans out of your lap," you're being asked not to get on your high horse and **lecture** (which would probably be hard to do with a lap full of beans). The elegant Seri term for a car muffler means "into which the breathing descends."

9 Sometimes a language provides the exact right way to describe something that always needed a great word. The Cherokee word *ukvhisdi* (oh kuh huhs dee) is what you say to a cute baby

Garifuna is the last living remnant of languages once spoken by native peoples in the Caribbean islands. Now it's spoken mainly in Belize, Honduras, and Guatemala.

or kitten. If your neighbor pops in every day, you might be dealing with what the Ojibway call *mawadishiweshkiwin,* the habit of making visits too often. The Cheyenne capture a hilariously embarrassing moment with *mémestátamao'ó,* to laugh so hard you fart.

Me'phaa is a language of Guerrero, Mexico, where Spanish dominates.

How to Save a Language

10 Linguists at projects like the Endangered Language Alliance are working to learn from speakers of disappearing languages, **recording** them singing songs, telling stories, **pronouncing** common words like the names of the colors, and explaining vocabulary that is important in their culture, such as the words that describe traditional arts or native plants.

11 Yet many speakers of endangered languages aren't content just to preserve scraps of their native languages in a digital museum. They hope that new generations will learn them, and that they will again become living languages. Different cultures have come up with different ways of bringing their languages back to life. Cherokee speakers can use an app that lets them text in their native alphabet. Yiddish speakers can enjoy weekly radio shows. In Wales, a community of writers is producing new science fiction (they had to come up with a Welsh word for "alien"), and young people in Chile are performing Huilliche-language hip-hop songs.

12 If an endangered language is going to make a real comeback, it'll probably get its start in schools. From 1896 to 1986, public schools in Hawaii did not teach the Hawaiian language. Then educators began opening "language nests," preschools where kids speak nothing but Hawaiian. Now there are elementary schools where kids not only take most classes in Hawaiian, but also learn about native traditions like gardening with Hawaiian plants and extending hospitality. Students can keep learning in Hawaiian into college and beyond—the University of Hawaii offers a Ph.D. in the Hawaiian language.

recording (ree KAWR dihng) *v.* storing sounds in a form, such as a digital file, so that they can be heard again in the future

pronouncing (proh NOWN sihng) *v.* speaking words correctly

The Language That Came Back to Life

13 Can a language with zero native speakers come back to life? At least one did. In 1881, a Jewish newspaper editor and linguist named Eliezer Ben-Yehuda immigrated to Jerusalem. Ben-Yehuda imagined the founding of a Jewish nation, and he thought that nation needed a language of its own. Back then, people learned Hebrew mostly just to read religious texts, but it was no one's native language. He and his wife decided to raise their family to speak nothing but Hebrew.

14 Ben-Yehuda realized that the 3,000-year-old language needed two kinds of help. First, it had to have young speakers. He persuaded teachers and rabbis to hold all their classes in Hebrew. Second, Hebrew needed lots of new words. He wrote a dictionary that added new words to this ancient language for modern things like dolls, omelets, ice cream, and bicycles. Hebrew grew from 8,000 words to 50,000. Today it is one of the official languages of Israel, with over 4 million speakers.

Gurung is a Tibeto-Burman language from the Himalayas in Nepal.

NOTEBOOK

Answer the questions in your notebook. Use text evidence to support your responses.

Response

1. **Personal Connections** What did you find most surprising about this article? Cite a specific passage or detail that led to your response.

Comprehension

2. **Reading Check (a)** According to the article, about how many languages currently exist in the world? **(b)** Identify the five categories the United Nations assigns to endangered languages. Briefly define what each category means for a language.

3. **Strategy: Make Predictions (a)** Note a text feature that helped you make a prediction prior to reading the article. Were you able to confirm this prediction or did you have to correct it? **(b)** How did this strategy affect your reading?

Analysis

4. **Analyze Cause and Effect** According to the author, what are the main reasons languages are disappearing?

5. **(a) Analyze** According to the author, how does a culture's language show what life is like for the people who speak it? Explain.
   (b) Support Identify two examples from the article that support your response.

6. **(a) Draw Conclusions** Based on the article, what can you conclude is an important part of any effort save an endangered language? Explain your answer, citing text evidence. **(b) Connect** Why do you think this element is so important?

EQ Notes What can one generation learn from another?

What have you learned about the ways different generations teach one another from reading this article? Go to your Essential Question Notes and record your observations and thoughts about "The Case of the Disappearing Words."

TEKS

5.C. Make, correct, or confirm predictions using text features, characteristics of genre, and structures.

6.C. Use text evidence to support an appropriate response.

THE CASE OF THE DISAPPEARING WORDS

Close Read

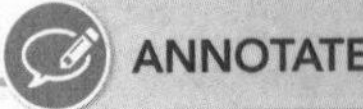

1. The model passage and annotation show how one reader analyzed paragraph 11. Find another detail in the passage to annotate. Then, write your own question and conclusion.

CLOSE-READ MODEL

Yet many speakers of endangered languages aren't content just to preserve scraps of their native languages in a digital museum. They hope that new generations will learn them, and that they will again become living languages. Different cultures have come up with different ways of bringing their languages back to life.

ANNOTATE: There is an interesting contrast between these phrases.

QUESTION: Why does the author emphasize this contrast?

CONCLUDE: The contrast highlights the difference between preserving bits of a dead language and keeping languages alive.

MY **QUESTION:**

MY **CONCLUSION:**

2. For more practice, answer the Close-Read note in the selection.
3. Choose a section of the feature article you found especially important. Mark important details. Then, jot down questions and write your conclusions in the open space next to the text.

Inquiry and Research

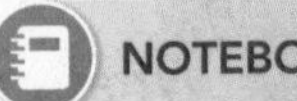

Research and Extend Extend your learning by generating 2 or 3 questions you could use to guide more research on a culture or organization named in the article. Then, perform a brief, informal inquiry to get answers to one of your questions. Use Internet and print resources.

TEKS

8.D.i. Analyze characteristics and structural elements of informational text, including the controlling idea or thesis with supporting evidence.

12.A. Generate student-selected and teacher-guided questions for formal and informal inquiry.

Genre / Text Elements

Controlling Idea and Supporting Evidence Feature articles weave together different kinds of **supporting evidence** in ways that keep readers interested and build a **controlling idea**—a main point or thesis. Supporting evidence may include facts, statistics, anecdotes, and examples.

TIP: Each section or paragraph of an article develops a key idea that contributes to the larger controlling idea.

A typical informational text follows a structure that presents, develops, and reinforces the controlling idea:

- an introduction that states the controlling idea
- body paragraphs that develop the controlling idea
- a conclusion that reinforces the controlling idea and presents an insight

INTERACTIVITY

PRACTICE Complete the activity and answer the questions.

1. **Analyze** Reread paragraph 1. Use the chart to identify the different types of evidence used to support the key idea of the paragraph.

KEY IDEA: The diversity of languages people currently speak is declining very quickly.		
TYPE OF EVIDENCE	EXAMPLE FROM THE PARAGRAPH	HOW IT SUPPORTS THE KEY IDEA
FACT		
STATISTIC		
EXAMPLE		
ANECDOTE		

2. **(a) Analyze** Reread paragraphs 13–14. What key idea is expressed in these paragraphs? **(b) Support** Identify examples of two types of evidence that support it.

3. **Interpret** In your own words, state the controlling idea of the article. Cite two different types of evidence that support your response. Explain each choice.

4. **Analyze** Explore how the article's structure develops the controlling idea: **(a)** Which paragraphs make up the introduction? **(b)** Where does the author state the controlling idea? **(c)** How do the subheads help to develop the controlling idea? **(d)** With what memorable point does the writer conclude?

THE CASE OF THE DISAPPEARING WORDS

Concept Vocabulary

NOTEBOOK

Why These Words? All of the vocabulary words relate to language as an idea. For example, *linguists* study language and may listen to a *recording* of native speakers.

fluently	linguists	term
lecture	recording	pronouncing

PRACTICE Answer the questions.

1. How might your knowledge of these vocabulary words help you discuss languages more precisely?

2. Use one vocabulary word to complete each sentence.

   (a) The reporter is ____________ his interview for a broadcast tomorrow.

   (b) It takes practice to speak a foreign language ____________ .

   (c) Before her trip to Spain, Amy practiced ____________ words in Spanish.

   (d) People are more likely to take your advice if you don't ____________ them.

   (e) *Scarlet* is a more specific ____________ for the color red.

   (f) Some ____________ study how children learn language.

WORD NETWORK

Add words that are related to the idea of generations from the text to your Word Network.

Word Study

NOTEBOOK

Latin Root Word: *lingua* The Latin root word *lingua* means "language" or "tongue." The vocabulary word *linguists* is built on this root word.

PRACTICE Complete the following items.

1. **(a)** Explain how the root word *lingua* contributes to the meaning of the word *linguist.* **(b)** The prefix *bi-* means "two." Given this information, explain what you think *bilingual* means. Use a dictionary to confirm your thinking.

2. Write a sentence that correctly uses the word *linguists.*

TEKS

2.C. Determine the meaning and usage of grade-level academic English words derived from Greek and Latin roots such as *omni, log/logue, gen, vid/vis, phil, luc,* and *sens/sent.*

Author's Craft

Author's Perspective An **author's perspective** is the way in which he or she views a topic. For example, an author with personal knowledge of a subject will write about it differently than someone who has only read about it. Sometimes, the author directly states his or her perspective. More often, perspective is suggested through word choice and details.

- **Word Choice:** Words with strong positive or negative meanings may suggest a distinct perspective.
- **Details:** An author's choices of facts and examples can also suggest a particular perspective.

TIP: Perspective is a lens, or way of looking at a topic. You see a topic differently depending on the lens you use.

INTERACTIVITY

PRACTICE **Answer the questions and complete the activity.**

1. **(a)** Identify at least four different languages the author discusses.
   (b) Interpret What does her choice to discuss multiple languages suggest about her perspective on her subject? Explain.
2. **Speculate** Imagine that the author had explained the problem using examples from only one language. How would that reflect a very different perspective?
3. **(a) Analyze** Use the chart to analyze the positive and negative meanings of the subheads in the article. The first row has been done for you.
   (b) Make Inferences What do the subheads tell you about the author's perspective on the topic of threatened languages? Explain.

SUBHEAD	POSITIVE OR NEGATIVE?	WHY?
Why They Disappear	negative	The word *disappear* sounds scary; it suggests a permanent loss.
Categories of Danger		
Why Save Them?		
How to Save a Language		
The Language That Came Back to Life		

THE CASE OF THE DISAPPEARING WORDS

Composition

A **travel guide** is a type of writing that provides visitors with information to better appreciate a place. It may offer suggestions for sites to visit as well as explanations of an area's culture and language.

TIP: When you **synthesize,** you include information from more than one source in order to arrive at your own insight. Make sure you haven't relied solely on a single source, but have truly synthesized information to express your own ideas.

ASSIGNMENT

Write a **travel guide entry** about a place in the world that is experiencing threats to its language. Identify and gather relevant information from at least two different types of sources, such as an encyclopedia and a web article. Synthesize the information by answering the following questions in your own words:

- Who speaks the language?
- Why is the language threatened?
- Are any efforts being made to save it? If so, what are they?

Finally, choose two words or phrases from the language that have particularly interesting meanings to include in your entry.

Use New Words

Refer to your Word Network to use new basic vocabulary you have learned. Also, try to include one or more of these vocabulary words in your writing: *fluently, linguists, term, lecture, recording, pronouncing.*

NOTEBOOK

Reflect on Your Writing

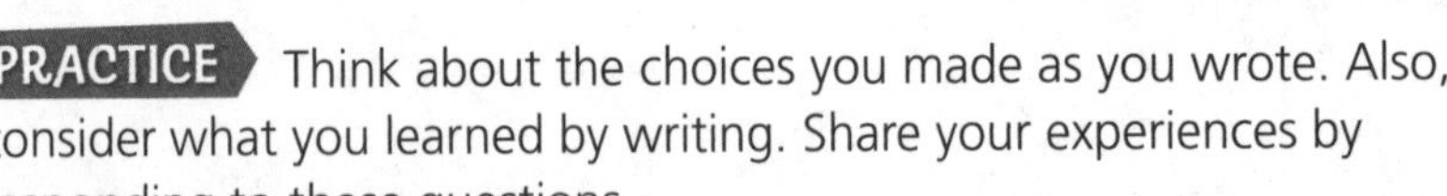

PRACTICE Think about the choices you made as you wrote. Also, consider what you learned by writing. Share your experiences by responding to these questions.

1. Was it easy or difficult to synthesize information from different sources? Explain.

2. What was the most interesting thing you learned from your research? Why?

3. **WHY THESE WORDS?** The words you choose make a difference in your writing. Which words did you specifically choose to strengthen your description of an endangered language?

TEKS

2.A. Use print or digital resources to determine the meaning, syllabication, pronunciation, word origin, and part of speech.

6.F. Respond using newly acquired vocabulary as appropriate.

6.H. Respond orally or in writing with appropriate register, vocabulary, tone, and voice.

12.D. Identify and gather relevant information from a variety of sources.

12.F. Synthesize information from a variety of sources.

Speaking and Listening

An **oral presentation** is a speech that provides an audience with useful information.

ASSIGNMENT

Choose an endangered language mentioned in the article. Research words and expressions from that language and choose three that you think are interesting. Then, deliver an **oral presentation** of your findings. Summarize the information about the endangered language you chose, and explain the words and phrases you included.

- Be sure you know how to properly pronounce the words or phrases from the language. Practice pronouncing them as you rehearse.
- You may have come across English words in your research that you want to say but aren't sure how to pronounce. Use a print or digital dictionary to confirm the correct pronunciations.
- Speak clearly and make eye contact with your audience periodically during your presentation.

Evaluate Presentations

Use a guide like the one shown to evaluate your own presentation as well as those of your classmates.

EQ Notes Before moving on to a new selection, go to your Essential Question Notes and record any additional thoughts or observations you may have about "The Case of the Disappearing Words."

PRESENTATION EVALUATION GUIDE

Rate each statement on a scale of 1 (not demonstrated) to 5 (demonstrated).

Statement	1	2	3	4	5
The speaker presented a summary that provided a basic overview of the language.	○	○	○	○	○
The speaker clearly pronounced and explained the example words and phrases.	○	○	○	○	○
The speaker spoke clearly, pronounced words correctly, and made appropriate eye contact with the audience.	○	○	○	○	○

Write a Personal Narrative

A **personal narrative** is a true story about a meaningful event in your life. Writers share personal narratives to communicate insights about their experiences.

ASSIGNMENT

Write a **personal narrative** that answers this question:

What experience helped you see how people of different generations can influence one another?

Include details about a conflict you faced and the reasons the experience was important. Use the elements of personal narratives in your writing.

ELEMENTS OF PERSONAL NARRATIVES

Purpose: to share a real-life story that is meaningful to you

Characteristics

- first-person point of view, with you as the narrator
- a clear focus on a specific experience
- a conflict, or problem, related to the experience
- vivid portrayals of characters who are real people and settings that are real places
- reflection on the deeper meaning of the experience
- narrative craft, such as the use of dialogue and description
- standard English conventions

Structure

- a well-organized structure that includes
  - an engaging beginning
  - a chronological organization of events
  - a strong, purposeful ending or conclusion that reflects on your experience and connects to the specific conflict, events, and characters in the narrative

TEKS

11.A. Compose literary texts such as personal narratives, fiction, and poetry using genre characteristics and craft.

Take a Closer Look at the Assignment

1. What is the assignment asking me to do (in my own words)? Use a dictionary or ask your teacher if any of the words in the assignment are unclear to you.

2. Is a specific **audience** mentioned in the assignment?

   ○ Yes If "yes," who is my main audience?

   ○ No If "no," who do I think my audience is or should be?

3. Is my **purpose** for writing specified in the assignment?

   ○ Yes If "yes," what is the purpose?

   ○ No If "no," why am I writing this narrative (not just because it's an assignment)?

4. Does the assignment ask me to include specific **narrative characteristics** and craft?

   ○ Yes If "yes," what are they?

   ○ No If "no," what types of elements do I think I need?

5. Does the assignment ask me to organize my ideas in a certain way?

   ○ Yes If "yes," what structure does it specify?

   ○ No If "no," how can I best order my ideas?

AUDIENCE

Your **audience** is your reader.

- Choose an experience that will engage readers' curiosity, but make sure it is one you feel comfortable sharing.
- Describe people or places with which your audience may not be familiar.

PURPOSE

A specific **purpose,** or reason, for writing, leads to a more focused narrative.

Vague Purpose: *I'll write about fishing.*

Specific Purpose: *I'll write about the day my aunt taught me to fish.*

NARRATIVE CHARACTERISTICS

Narrative characteristics are the building blocks of any story. In a personal narrative, these elements are real rather than imagined. Use details to bring them to life.

- **Characters:** people who take part in the action
- **Setting:** the place and time of the action
- **Conflict and Plot:** obstacle or problem that leads to a related sequence of events

Planning and Prewriting

Before you draft, discover the narrative you want to tell. Complete the activities to get started.

Discover Your Topic: Freewrite!

Topics for a personal narrative come mainly from your memories and experiences. Write freely for three minutes without stopping. Try one of these strategies to begin.

- Imagine a photo album of your life. Choose one image and write about it.
- List places you associate with strong feelings. Freewrite about one.
- Recall conversations that mattered to you. Freewrite about one.

After you're done with your freewrite, briefly discuss your ideas with a partner. Which ones get the most positive responses?

NOTEBOOK

WRITE IT What experience helped you see how people of different generations can influence one another?

 TEKS

10.A. Plan a first draft by selecting a genre appropriate for a particular topic, purpose, and audience using a range of strategies such as discussion, background reading, and personal interests.

Structure Your Narrative: Make a Plan

NOTEBOOK

A. Choose a Focus Review your freewriting and pull out the strongest idea. Describe it here in a few words.

B. Write Your Message Write one sentence that explains what you learned from this experience. Also, list strong details you want to make sure to include.

C. Plan a Structure Plan how you will describe the **sequence of events** so that readers understand who was involved, what happened, and where and when events occurred.

Who was involved?

What happened?

Where and when did events happen?

How did the experience end?

MESSAGE

Your **message,** or central idea, is the insight you want your narrative to convey. Hint at this message early in your narrative to help explain its personal value.

SEQUENCE OF EVENTS

The **sequence,** or order of events in a narrative, should flow in a logical way that readers can follow.

- Establish the setting and people who are involved in the story early on.
- Show how a conflict or problem arose and what people did as a result.
- Use chronological order, narrating events in the order in which they occurred.
- Show how the conflict ended.

CONCLUSION

A well-structured personal narrative has a **conclusion** in which you share reflections on your experience. To make that connection clear in your conclusion, refer to the specific conflict, key events, and important characters in your narrative.

Drafting

Apply the planning work you've done and write a first draft. Consider how you will develop your characters to bring them to life for readers.

Read Like a Writer

Reread the third paragraph of the Mentor Text. Mark details that give you a vivid sense of the grandmother's personality. One observation has been done for you.

MENTOR TEXT

from Grounded

The thing I remember most about Grandma Sofia was how much she loved driving, especially since she came to live with us. She had a 1960s red Chevy Impala convertible that was all her own, a remnant of her band days. She loved driving with the top down, the radio blasting, singing at the top of her lungs when a good song came on. Driving was her independence, her freedom.

These vivid, specific details about the car help show the grandmother's personality.

Mark other details that convey a strong sense of the grandmother's character.

NOTEBOOK

WRITE IT Follow the Mentor Text example by using vivid details to portray someone who plays an important role in your narrative.

DEPTH OF THOUGHT

As you draft the rest of your narrative, make your writing vivid and precise.

- **Conflict** Make sure you clearly show the conflict and why it was important.
- **Characters** Show how people look and act. Use dialogue that adds their unique voices.
- **Setting** Use specific details related to sight, sound, smell, and touch to help readers picture places in your narrative.
- **Development** Create a clear sequence of events. For each new moment or event, start a new paragraph.

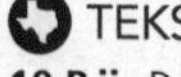

TEKS

10.B.ii. Develop drafts into a focused, structured, and coherent piece of writing by developing an engaging idea reflecting depth of thought with specific facts, details, and examples.

Create Coherence

A **coherent** piece of writing "holds together" and conveys a unified whole. Use these strategies to create coherence in your narrative.

- Write a beginning that gives a clear sense of what your narrative is about and who is involved.
- Use vivid details and precise verbs to show what people do and say.
- Use correct **pronoun-antecedent agreement** so that readers always know to whom you are referring in your narrative.

TIP: A coherent narrative does not confuse readers. Even if there are multiple characters, readers understand which person is speaking or taking an action.

Personal Pronouns

	Singular	Plural
First Person	*I, me, my, mine*	*we, us, our, ours*
Second Person	*you, your, yours*	*you, your, yours*
Third Person	**Feminine:** *she, her, hers* **Masculine:** *he, him, his* **Neutral:** *it, its*	*they, them, their, theirs*

PRONOUN-ANTECEDENT AGREEMENT

A **pronoun** is a word you can use in place of a noun or another pronoun. The **antecedent** is the word or words the pronoun replaces. A personal pronoun must agree with its antecedent in person, number, and gender.

In these examples, notice that each underlined pronoun agrees with its highlighted antecedent in person, number, and gender:

- *I reminded Grandma Sofia to bring the car keys with her.*
- *My parents were concerned. I heard them talking.*

NOTEBOOK

WRITE IT Write a scene from your narrative. Use correct pronoun-antecedent agreement.

AGREEMENT IN NUMBER

When a pronoun has a compound antecedent (two or more words joined by "and," "or," or "nor"), agreement can be tricky.

- two singular antecedents joined by "and" = plural pronoun

EXAMPLE:
Ann and Emma finished *their* work.

- two singular antecedents joined by "or" or "nor" = singular pronoun

EXAMPLE:
Neither *Ann nor Emma* finished *her* work.

Revising

ANNOTATE

Now that you have a first draft, revise it to be sure it describes events and conveys meaning as vividly as possible. When you revise, you "re-see" your writing, checking for the following elements:

Clarity: precision of your descriptions and sharpness of your ideas

Development: full portrayals with vivid and precise details

Organization: clear flow of events

Style and Tone: variety of sentences and accuracy of word choices; a level of formality that suits your audience and purpose

Read Like a Writer

Review the revisions made to the Mentor Text. Then, answer the questions in the white boxes.

MENTOR TEXT

from Grounded

My parents, however, were concerned that she was getting too old to drive around by herself. One night, I overheard them: ~~saying they'd have to do something soon.~~ *"She's okay for now, but how long before she can't manage?" "I'll speak to her tomorrow."*

The addition of dialogue makes the scene more vivid and meaningful.

I felt sick at the thought of Grandma giving up her car. I knew what driving meant to her. I knew that without her wheels she'd feel ordinary—just another grandma, ~~very overprotective~~ *hovering* and wise.

Why do you think the writer changed this word choice?

Sometimes it felt like Grandma and I were on the sidelines and my parents were in the middle, dragging us toward the center, where we did not want to be. I was often grounded for the smallest things. I didn't really mind, under normal circumstances.

One time—the time I'm writing about—circumstances were not normal. ~~Then, there was that time my~~ My parents had grounded me for the weekend of Luisa's party, easily the social event of the season. No way was I going to miss it. But my parents weren't even going to be home! They were going to my Aunt Leticia's. It would just be me and Grandma. Me and Grandma and a 1966 ~~car~~ *red Chevy Impala convertible* . . .

Why do you think the writer changed this sentence?

The addition of a precise detail clarifies the writer's excitement.

TEKS

10.C. Revise drafts for clarity, development, organization, style, word choice, and sentence variety.

Take a Closer Look at Your Draft

Now, revise your draft. Use the Revision Guide for Personal Narrative to evaluate and improve your narrative.

REVISION GUIDE FOR PERSONAL NARRATIVE

EVALUATE	TAKE ACTION
Clarity	
Is the message of my narrative clear?	If the point of your narrative isn't clear, **add** a conclusion that explains what the experience showed or taught you.
Will readers who do not know me understand my narrative?	Imagine that you do not know anything about your own story. **Add** information that is missing. For example, instead of writing *Leah attached the fishing line*, write *My cousin Leah attached the fishing line*.
Development	
Is my narrative complete?	**Add** another scene or **clarify** reactions so that your readers fully understand the story and your message.
Have I used a variety of techniques to show what happened?	If your narrative seems dull or repetitive, introduce variety. **Include** descriptive details, **replace** explanations with dialogue, and **add** important observations or thoughts.
Organization	
Does the order of events make sense?	**Picture** each event in your mind to make sure you have described the sequence accurately. If you haven't, **number** the events in your draft, **reorder** details, and then remove the numbering.
Does my narrative ramble or lose focus?	**Remove** unnecessary scenes or ideas that distract from your message.
Style and Tone	
Have I used precise words, sharp dialogue, and vivid descriptive details?	**Replace** weak words with precise choices and explanations with dialogue. **Add** sensory details to bring scenes to life.
Is my tone appropriate for a personal narrative?	**Replace** overly formal language with words and phrases that reflect your natural speech.
Are sentence types and lengths varied?	If your sentences are too similar (all short or all long) create variety: 1. **Break** a long, confusing sentence into two shorter sentences. 2. **Combine** two short sentences into one longer sentence. 3. **Rewrite** some sentences as questions or exclamations.

Editing

Don't let errors weaken the power of your narrative. Reread your draft and fix mistakes to create a finished work.

Read Like a Writer

Look at how the writer of the Mentor Text edited an early draft. Then, follow the directions in the white boxes.

MENTOR TEXT

from Grounded

At that moment, I wouldn't have minded getting out and going back Home. I felt bad about grandma. I felt bad about disobeying my Parents. But how could I say any of this?

We took off. She drove slowly, maybe too slowly. But we didn't get very far. Suddenly they pulled over and stopped the car.

We must have been sitting in that car for five minutes, which is a long time if you're sitting in a car not talking. I couldn't ask her if she stopped because she was nervous about driving. And I couldn't ask if she stopped because she knew I was grounded.

The writer added a transition to help clarify the sequence of events.

Fix three capitalization errors.

Fix the incorrect pronoun-antecedent agreement.

Focus on Sentences

Pronoun-Antecedent Agreement Using pronouns in place of some nouns makes your storytelling sound more natural and your sentences less repetitive. Keep in mind that a personal pronoun must agree with its antecedent in person, number, and gender. For example:

Incorrect Person: _Drivers_ know _you_ have to obey speed limits.

Correct Person: _Drivers_ know _they_ have to obey speed limits.

PRACTICE Fix errors in pronoun-antecedent agreement in these sentences. Then, check your own draft for correctness.

1. Grandma hesitated but agreed to drive me in their car.
2. Grandma chose songs to sing, based on whether it inspired her.
3. Grandma loved singing at the top of your lungs.

EDITING TIPS

- Mark the antecedent and consider its person, number, and gender.
- Mark any pronoun that goes with the antecedent and make sure the person, number, and gender match.
- Replace pronouns that do not agree with ones that do.

TEKS

10.D.v. Edit drafts using standard English conventions, including pronoun-antecedent agreement; **10.D.vii.** Edit drafts using standard English conventions, including correct capitalization.

Focus on Capitalization and Punctuation

Capitalization: Proper Nouns A common noun names a person, place, thing, or idea, and does not have to be capitalized. A proper noun names a specific person, place, thing, or idea, and must be capitalized.

EXAMPLES:

I knew that Grandmother was not just another grandmother. Her car was a Chevy Impala.

Drive east of the Rocky Mountains. Then, hike the rocky path.

Punctuation: Dialogue Follow these rules to punctuate dialogue correctly:

- Place every word spoken aloud inside quotation marks.
  EXAMPLE: *"Mac," I said, "you're not making sense."*
- Set a new paragraph for each new speaker.
  EXAMPLE: *"I know I'm right," she replied.*

  "No, you're not," Mike insisted. "This is crazy."
- If the dialogue requires punctuation, place it inside the quotation mark.
  EXAMPLE: *"This is exciting!" Elle exclaimed.*
- Use a comma to separate dialogue from narration.
  EXAMPLE: *I asked the group, "What do we do now?"*

EDITING TIPS

- Read your narrative aloud to catch errors and check that dialogue sounds natural.
- Use resources, such as a grammar handbook, to clarify grammar rules or to confirm that your corrections are accurate.

PRACTICE Correct capitalization and punctuation errors in the sentences. Then, review your own draft for correctness.

1. Dad, grandma's chevy is important to her I said

2. Will you teach me to drive I asked. You're too young sofia exclaimed.

3. We drove to austin, Texas, to see her old Recording Studio.

Publishing and Presenting

Make It Multimodal

Share your personal narrative with your class. Choose one of these options.

OPTION 1 Create a slideshow based on your narrative. You can use existing photos or make illustrations.

OPTION 2 Record your personal narrative to share as part of a podcast or community blog. Consider adding music and sound effects to enhance your recording.

PEER-GROUP LEARNING

Essential Question

What can one generation learn from another?

What people value can change from one generation to the next, but there are always some common threads despite these differences. You can gain new insight and knowledge when you understand the values and challenges facing other generations. You will work in a group to continue your exploration of the relationship between generations.

VIDEO

INTERACTIVITY

Peer-Group Learning Strategies

Throughout your life, in school, in your community, and in your career, you will continue to learn and work with others.

Look at these strategies and the actions you can take to practice them as you work in small groups. Add ideas of your own for each category. Use these strategies during Peer-Group Learning.

STRATEGY	MY PEER-GROUP ACTION PLAN
Prepare • Complete your assignments so that you are prepared for group work. • Take notes on your reading so that you can share ideas with others in your group.	
Participate fully • Make eye contact to signal that you are paying attention. • Use text evidence when making a point.	
Support others • Build off ideas from others in your group. • Ask others who have not yet spoken to do so.	
Clarify • Paraphrase the ideas of others to be sure your understanding is correct. • Ask follow-up questions.	

CONTENTS

HUMAN INTEREST STORY

Tutors Teach Seniors New High-Tech Tricks

Jennifer Ludden

It's never too late to learn something new.

▸ MEDIA CONNECTION: Cyber-Seniors

COMPARE ACROSS GENRES

MEMOIR

from Mom & Me & Mom

Maya Angelou

Can forgiveness and love overcome disappointment and sadness?

MEDIA: TELEVISION INTERVIEW

Learning to Love My Mother

Maya Angelou with Michael Maher

Maya Angelou talks about her complicated relationship with her mother.

MEDIA: IMAGE GALLERY

Mother-Daughter Drawings

Mica and Myla Hendricks

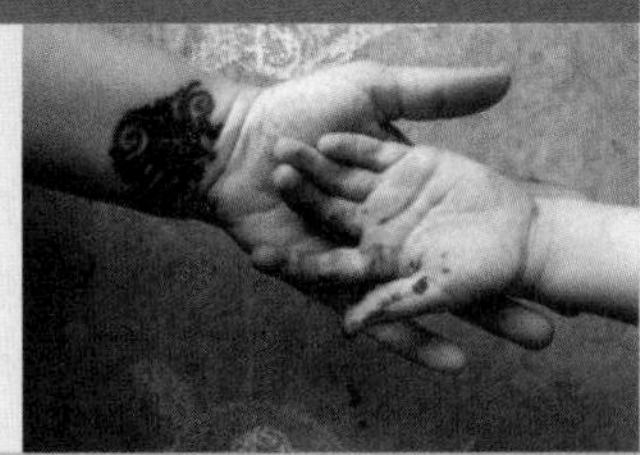

What happens when an artist collaborates with her four-year-old child?

POETRY COLLECTION 1

Abuelita Magic

Pat Mora

Mother to Son

Langston Hughes

To James

Frank Horne

The bonds between generations are stronger than the difficulties of life.

PERFORMANCE TASK

Present a Personal Narrative

The Peer-Group readings explore the insights that people of different generations share with each other. After reading, your group will present autobiographical anecdotes about learning from people of different generations.

Working as a Group

1. Discuss the Topic

With your group, discuss the following question:

> What kinds of ideas and experience can young people and adults share?

As you take turns speaking, work to create an open and meaningful exchange of ideas. Listen to one another carefully, and support creative thinking. Share thoughtful examples that illustrate your ideas. After all group members have shared, discuss the similarities and differences among your responses.

2. List Your Rules

As a group, decide on the rules that you will follow as you work together. Two samples are provided. Add two more of your own. You may add or revise rules as you work through the readings and activities together.

- Everyone should participate in group discussions.
- People should not interrupt.

___

___

3. Apply the Rules

Practice working as a group. Share what you've discovered about how people of different generations can learn from each other. Make sure each person in the group contributes. Take notes and be prepared to share with the class one thing that you heard from another group member.

4. Name Your Group

Choose a name that reflects the unit topic.

Our group's name: ___

5. Create a Communication Plan

Decide how you want to communicate with one another. For example, you might use online collaboration tools, email, or instant messaging.

Our group's plan:

___

___

1.D. Engage in meaningful discourse and provide and accept constructive feedback from others. **6.C.** Use text evidence to support an appropriate response.

 INTERACTIVITY

Making a Schedule

First, find out the due dates for the peer-group activities. Then, preview the texts and activities with your group and make a schedule for completing the tasks.

SELECTION	ACTIVITIES	DUE DATE
Tutors Teach Seniors New High-Tech Tricks		
from Mom & Me & Mom Learning to Love My Mother		
Mother-Daughter Drawings		
Abuelita Magic Mother to Son To James		

 NOTEBOOK

Using Text Evidence

When you respond to literature, you use text evidence to support your ideas. Apply these tips to choose the right text evidence for any purpose.

Understand the Question: Different kinds of questions call for different kinds of evidence. For example, if you are *analyzing,* you are looking for specific details. If you are *interpreting,* you are looking for specific details that connect to build a larger meaning.

Notice Key Details: Notice details that stand out and make you feel strongly about a character or an idea. These details are probably important and may become evidence for your position or interpretation.

Evaluate Your Choices: The evidence you use should clearly relate to the question you are answering. For example, if a question asks about a character's motivations, choose evidence that shows *why* he or she felt, thought, and acted a certain way. Other details may be interesting, but are not relevant.

Use strong and effective text evidence to support your responses as you read, discuss, and write about the selections.

TUTORS TEACH SENIORS NEW HIGH-TECH TRICKS

The selection you are about to read is a human interest story.

Reading Human Interest Stories

A **human interest story** is a form of journalism that focuses on the more personal side of current events.

HUMAN INTEREST STORIES

Author's Purpose

- to inform readers while entertaining them and engaging their emotions

Characteristics

- a controlling idea, or thesis
- a variety of evidence, such as facts, descriptions, and quotations
- a tone that reflects the writer's feelings
- details that engage readers' emotions

Structure

- a lead, or opening section, that pulls readers in
- information that answers basic questions: *who, what, where, when, why,* and *how*

Take a Minute!

NOTEBOOK

FIND IT Work with a partner to find a human interest story in a daily newspaper or magazine, in print or online. Jot down the title.

Why do you think this is a human interest story?

TEKS

8.D. Analyze characteristics and structural elements of informational text.

9.F. Analyze how the author's use of language contributes to mood, voice, and tone.

Genre / Text Elements

Language and Tone Unlike many other types of journalism, human interest stories allow reporters to express their opinions. Sometimes, a writer simply states what he or she thinks about the story or the people in it. More often, the writer's **tone**, or attitude toward the subject and reader, suggests those opinions. The writer's choices of details and his or her **diction,** or word choice, create the tone.

TIP: In passage 1, positive words (*success, smiling, hugs*) create a joyful tone. In passage 2, negative words (*doomed, cages, discard*) create a grim tone.

EXAMPLE: Notice how the two example passages report the same event but highlight different details and convey different tones.

PASSAGE 1	PASSAGE 2
Oak Town's Adopt-a-Dog Day was a major success. Smiling broadly, Director Mae Woods moved among the crowd, shaking hands, giving out hugs, and patting heads, both human and canine.	The joy of Adopt-a-Dog Day did not reach dozens of pets still doomed to live in cages. After the event, Director Mae Woods visited the animals no one took home. "I do my best," she reported, "but it's tough." She feels that too many people treat pets like objects they can discard.

PRACTICE Work on your own to read the passage. Mark details that contribute to the tone, and answer the questions that follow.

Dan and Su Linn's story begins with a wallet—just an ordinary wallet left behind in a taxi by an absent-minded dentist. "I was running late. I do it all the time," he reported. Dan was the next passenger in the taxi, and he's not the type of person to leave a lost wallet lying around. When he tried to call the absent-minded dentist, he dialed Su Linn by mistake. Dan is a singer with a wonderful voice. That voice stopped Su Linn in her tracks. "I didn't want to hang up," she says. "I fell in love with a voice." One year later, Dan sang for her at their wedding. And the dentist? He got his wallet back, along with a thank-you note, and—later—a wedding invitation.

1. How would you describe the author's tone? Which details create that tone?

2. What emotional effect might this passage have on readers? Explain.

About the Author

Jennifer Ludden (b. 1967) is a correspondent for National Public Radio (NPR). Ludden has won and shared in several awards for her work as a foreign reporter covering the Middle East, Europe, and West and Central Africa. She graduated from Syracuse University in 1988.

Tutors Teach Seniors New High-Tech Tricks

Concept Vocabulary

ANNOTATE

As you read "Tutors Teach Seniors New High-Tech Tricks," you will encounter these words.

struggling	impairments	frustrated

Context Clues The **context** of a word is the other words and phrases that appear close to it in the text. **Cause-and-effect clues** suggest how one thing leads to, or causes, another. By understanding cause-and-effect clues, you can figure out word meanings.

EXAMPLE My computer stopped working after it was infected with a nasty *worm*.

Analysis The word *nasty* means "unpleasant," and it describes a worm that has *infected* a computer and caused it to stop working. A *worm* must mean "a computer bug" or "problem."

PRACTICE As you read this article, study the context to determine the meanings of unfamiliar words. Mark your observations in the open space next to the text.

Comprehension Strategy

ANNOTATE

Make Connections

When you **make connections to personal experiences** while reading, you look for relationships between elements of a text and your prior knowledge, or what you already know from your own life. As you read, be aware of your reactions. Notice similarities and differences between your life experiences and the ones described in a text. Ask yourself the following types of questions:

- How does this description make me feel, and why?
- Does this example remind me of anything?
- Have I met anyone like the person described in this article, or experienced a similar situation?
- Does this text change how I view aspects of my own life?

PRACTICE As you read, write the connections you make to your personal experiences in the open space next to the text.

TEKS

2.B. Use context such as contrast or cause and effect to clarify the meaning of words.

5.E. Make connections to personal experiences, ideas in other texts, and society.

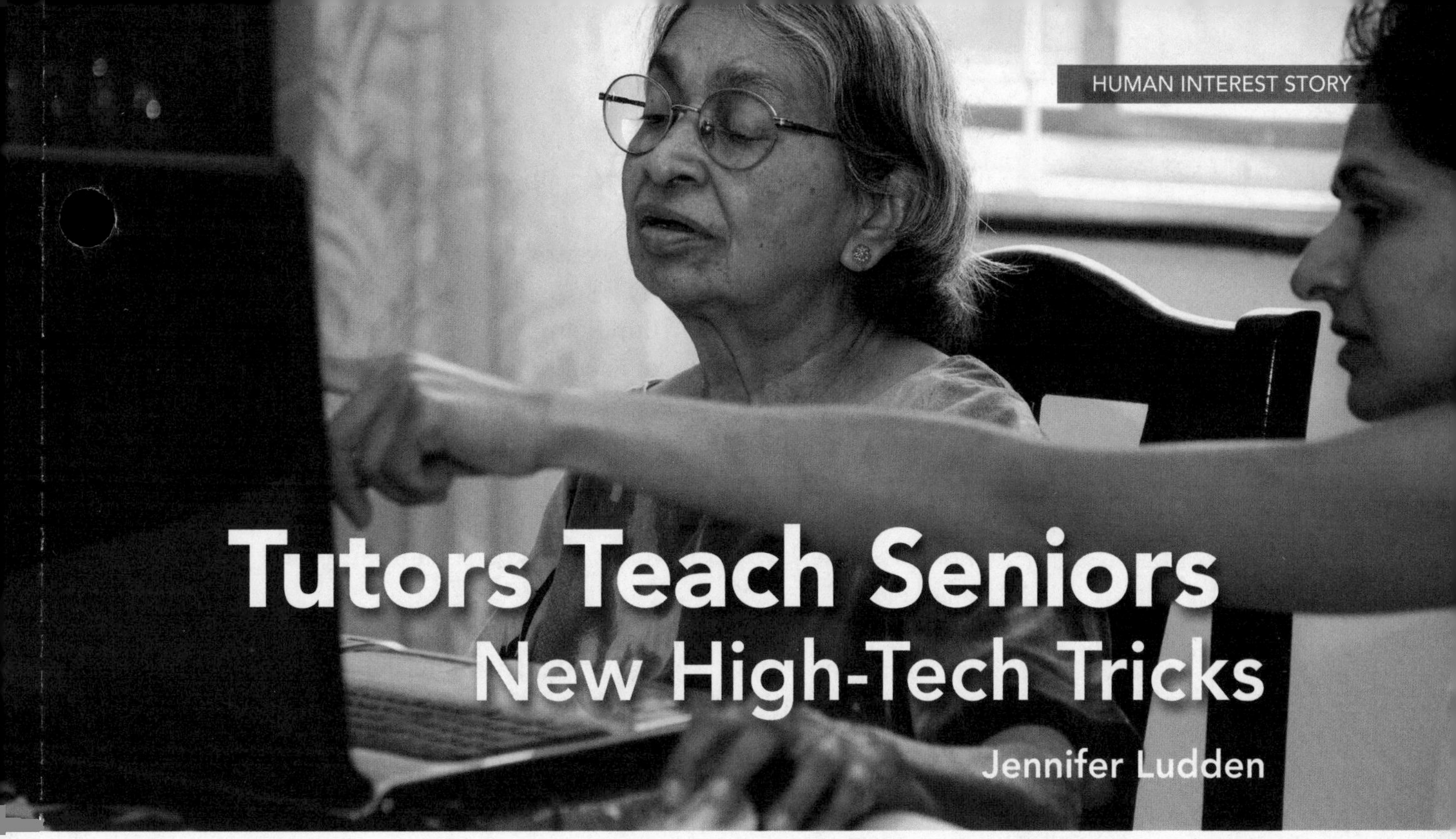

Tutors Teach Seniors New High-Tech Tricks

Jennifer Ludden

BACKGROUND

Modern technology allows us to easily connect with one another. People can instantaneously share photographs and have face-to-face conversations with friends and family both down the street and on the other side of the world. However, technology changes so quickly that senior citizens are often left behind.

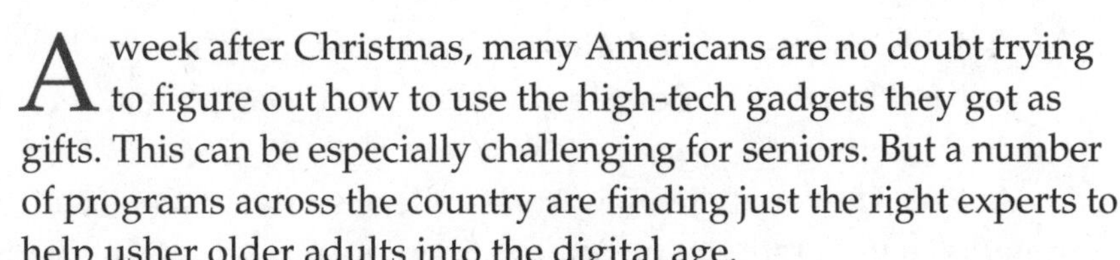

1 A week after Christmas, many Americans are no doubt trying to figure out how to use the high-tech gadgets they got as gifts. This can be especially challenging for seniors. But a number of programs across the country are finding just the right experts to help usher older adults into the digital age.

2 For Pamela Norr, of Bend, Ore., the light bulb went off as she, yet again, was trying to help her own elder parents with a tech problem. To whom did she turn?

3 "My teenage kids," she says.

4 Norr happens to head the Central Oregon Council on Aging, and thus was born TECH—Teenager Elder Computer Help.

5 "I thought if my parents need it, probably other seniors need it, too," she says.

6 High school students studying computer tech or involved with the National Honor Society sign up to teach local senior citizens about Facebook, Skype, smartphones, even something as seemingly simple as a camera. Norr discovered that many seniors had been given digital cameras by their children.

7 "They were going around town taking all these great pictures that they wanted to send to their family members," she says. But

Mark context clues or indicate another strategy you used that helped you determine meaning.

struggling (STRUHG lihng) *v.*

MEANING:

impairments (ihm PAIR muhnts) *n.*

MEANING:

frustrated (FRUHS trayt ehd) *adj.*

MEANING:

they "couldn't figure out how to connect to the USB port[1] or take out the SIM card.[2]"

8 Many elders have moved to central Oregon to retire. Sigrid Scully, 84, signed up for a TECH class because she was **struggling** to stay connected with far-flung family.

9 "My kids were not returning calls," she says. "They don't write letters. They are so knowledgeable about texting and email, and so I needed to get to know how to do that."

10 Scully worried she'd never catch on. She'd read a computer manual once, but didn't understand words like "icon" or "cookies." She says her teen tutor was personable and used plain language.

11 "So many teenagers think that seniors are just old people that don't know anything," she says. "And actually, the camaraderie and knowledge that we can transmit to one another is so wonderful and so helpful. I had that feeling with this class."

Sensitivity Training

12 "It has made me think about what life was like without Facebook and the Internet," says 15-year-old Tucker Rampton, who's helped train about a dozen Oregon seniors. He's been surprised to have to explain email, something he thought everyone had mastered. Then again, a lot of seniors ask him about Twitter, which Rampton admits he knows nothing about. He says teaching tech to seniors has changed his perspective.

13 "I think it's a very good idea to work on your patience," he says, "and be more understanding when it comes to what's going on in their minds."

14 At Pace University in New York, college students who tutor seniors in local retirement homes are prepped with sensitivity training.

15 "They get to feel what it's like to be 70, 80, 90 years old," says associate professor Jean Coppola, who directs the program. "They wear specially prepared glasses that give them different visual **impairments**."

16 Coppola also has students do things like tape two fingers together—to simulate the effects of arthritis or a stroke—then try to navigate a mouse. By the time they're at the computer with an elder, she says, they're not **frustrated** at all.

17 "They'll say something a hundred times because they've worn cotton balls or earplugs in their ear," she says. "They understand that they have to speak up, articulate their words."

MEDIA CONNECTION

Cyber-Seniors

DISCUSS IT **What benefits do young people get when they teach seniors about technology and the Internet?**

Write your response before sharing your ideas.

1. **USB port** *n.* computer hardware for connecting other devices to computers.
2. **SIM card** *n.* smart card used in cell phones to store identification information.

18 Coppola says the whole thing is a bonding experience for both generations. Applause often breaks out the first time a senior receives an email. Some have been able to see new grandchildren for the first time through emailed photos.

19 Pamela Norr, in Oregon, says young trainers also gain new confidence. They see that the seniors are "not criticizing me for the way I dress," she says, "or clucking their tongue. They're actually respecting me for the knowledge base that I have."

20 Perhaps most unexpected, some teen trainers and seniors have even become friends. They keep in touch long after class ends—through Facebook, of course. ❧

BUILD INSIGHT

NOTEBOOK

Work on your own to answer the questions in your notebook. Use text evidence to support your responses.

Response

1. **Personal Connections** Do you think having young people teach seniors about technology is a good idea? Why or why not?

Comprehension

2. **Strategy: Make Connections to Personal Experiences** **(a)** Cite one connection you made to your own experiences while reading this human interest story. **(b)** Was this strategy useful? Explain.

Analysis and Discussion

3. **Analyze Cause and Effect** Reread paragraphs 12–13. How do Tucker Rampton's experiences teaching seniors change his perspective? Explain.
4. **(a)** In the Pace University program, what sensitivity training do college students receive? **(b)** **Generalize** What do these details suggest about ways in which people in general might better understand or sympathize with one another? Explain.
5. **Get Ready for Close Reading** Choose a passage from the text that you find especially interesting or important. You'll discuss the passage with your group during Close-Read activities.

WORKING AS A GROUP

Discuss your responses to the Analysis and Discussion questions with your group.

- Note agreements and disagreements.
- Consider changes of opinion.

If necessary, revise your original answers to reflect what you learn from your discussion.

EQ Notes What can one generation learn from another?

What have you learned about how people of different generations can learn from each other by reading this human interest story? Go to your Essential Question Notes, and record your observations and thoughts about "Tutors Teach Seniors New High-Tech Tricks."

TEKS

5.E. Make connections to personal experiences, ideas in other texts, and society.

6.C. Use text evidence to support an appropriate response.

TUTORS TEACH SENIORS NEW HIGH-TECH TRICKS

Close Read

ANNOTATE

PRACTICE **Complete the following activities. Use text evidence to support your responses.**

1. **Present and Discuss** With your group, share the passages from the human interest story that you found especially interesting. Discuss what you notice, the questions you have, and the conclusions you reach. For example, you might focus on the following passages:
   - Paragraphs 1–3: Discuss how the lead, or opening section, introduces the subject. Does it grab your interest?
   - Paragraphs 8–11: Discuss why the author included Sigrid Scully's story.
2. **Reflect on Your Learning** What new ideas or insights did you uncover during your second reading of the text?

NOTEBOOK

LANGUAGE STUDY

Concept Vocabulary

Why These Words? The vocabulary words are related.

struggling	impairments	frustrated

1. With your group, determine what the words have in common. Write your ideas.
2. Add another word that fits the category: ____________________
3. Use each vocabulary word in a sentence. Include context clues that hint at each word's meaning.

Word Study

Suffix *-ment* The suffix *-ment* means "the result of an action." When added to a verb (the action), the suffix creates a noun. Use a dictionary to find the meaning of the following words that contain the suffix *-ment*: *advertisement, amusement, settlement*. Explain how the suffix *-ment* contributes to the meaning of each word.

WORD NETWORK

Add words that are related to the idea of generations from the text to your Word Network.

TEKS

2.A. Use print or digital resources to determine the meaning, syllabication, pronunciation, word origin, and part of speech.

9.F. Analyze how the author's use of language contributes to mood, voice, and tone.

Genre / Text Elements

Language and Tone In this human interest story, the author describes how a group of people noticed a problem and found a solution for it. The author's choices of details and her **diction**, or word choice, help to create her **tone,** or attitude toward the subject. Tone can be described using the same adjectives we use to describe emotions and behavior; for example, *cold, warm, funny, friendly, angry,* or *frustrated*.

TIP The author's choice of **quotations**, or other people's exact words, contributes to the overall tone of an article.

PRACTICE Work with your group to complete the activity and answer the questions.

NOTEBOOK

INTERACTIVITY

1. **Distinguish** Reread the article, and use the chart to note examples of two types of diction: **(a)** words and phrases that relate to the problems seniors face; **(b)** words and phrases that relate to the solution—the tutoring program and its effects.

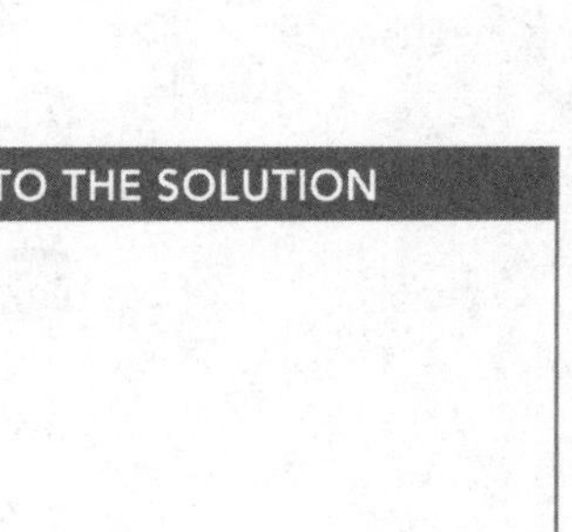

DICTION RELATED TO THE PROBLEM	DICTION RELATED TO THE SOLUTION

2. Review your word lists. **(a) Evaluate** Which list has more words? **(b) Interpret** What does the author's diction show about the aspects of the story she has chosen to emphasize? Explain.

3. **Describe** Cite two adjectives you think accurately describe the author's tone. Explain your choices, citing text evidence.

4. **(a) Analyze** What mood, or feeling, do you think most people would experience after reading this article? Explain your reasons, and cite specific details from the text that support them. **(b) Connect** What connections do you see between the author's tone and the article's effects on the reader?

5. **Speculate** Why do you think serious newscasts often feature human interest stories at the end? In your explanation, include a discussion of the importance of tone.

TUTORS TEACH SENIORS NEW HIGH-TECH TRICKS

Author's Craft

Controlling Idea and Supporting Evidence A **controlling idea** is an author's main point, the message he or she wants readers to understand. The author develops that idea with **supporting evidence**, or information. In this article, the author relies heavily on direct quotations gathered from her interviews with the people profiled.

TIP: In addition to direct quotations, journalists may paraphrase information. A **paraphrase** is a restatement of another person's ideas or insights in different words.

Direct Quotations: the exact words of another person	
Purposes	support ideas, introduce new ideas, answer questions
	provide specific examples of general ideas
	emphasize the personalities of real people
	show the perspectives of multiple people

PRACTICE Work on your own to complete the activity and answer the questions. Then, discuss your responses with your group.

1. **Analyze** Reread the text, and find a quotation from each person noted in the chart. Explain specific ways in which each quotation supports the controlling idea.

Controlling Idea: A program in which young people teach seniors to use technology benefits everyone.		
PERSON	QUOTATION	EXPLANATION
Pamela Norr (program director)		
Sigrid Scully (senior participant)		
Tucker Rampton (teen participant)		
Jean Coppola (associate professor)		

2. **Speculate** Imagine that the author had included quotations from only one person. Would this strengthen or weaken the development of her controlling idea? Explain.

3. **(a) Paraphrase** Choose one direct quotation from your chart, and rewrite it as a paraphrase. **(b) Evaluate** What is lost by this change? What, if anything, is gained? Explain.

TEKS

1.B. Follow and give complex oral instructions to perform specific tasks, answer questions, or solve problems.

8.D.i. Analyze characteristics and structural elements of informational text, including the controlling idea or thesis with supporting evidence.

Speaking and Listening

Oral instructions are step-by-step directions that are presented aloud to listeners.

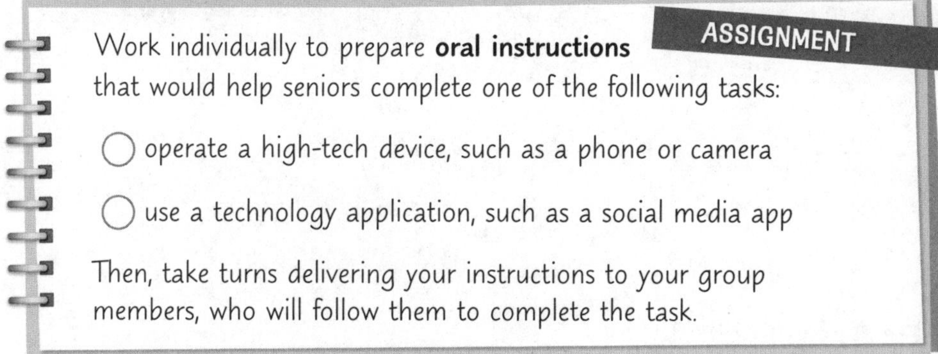

Choose a Specific Task Select a device or application on which to focus your instructions. First, complete the task yourself, noting the steps you take.

Prepare Your Instructions Review your notes and be sure you have not skipped any steps. For example, the first step in most instructions is to turn a device on—don't assume that people following your instructions will have done so already. Then, follow these steps to create an outline that will guide your delivery:

- Create a numbered list in which you describe the steps in the exact order they must be done.
- Use time-order words, such as *first, next, then,* and *finally*, to clarify the order of each step.

TIP: Include visuals, such as diagrams or screenshots, to help you explain complicated steps.

Present and Evaluate As you present your instructions, speak clearly and do not rush. When it is your turn to follow instructions, listen closely. Use a guide like the one shown to evaluate your own instructions as well as those of your classmates.

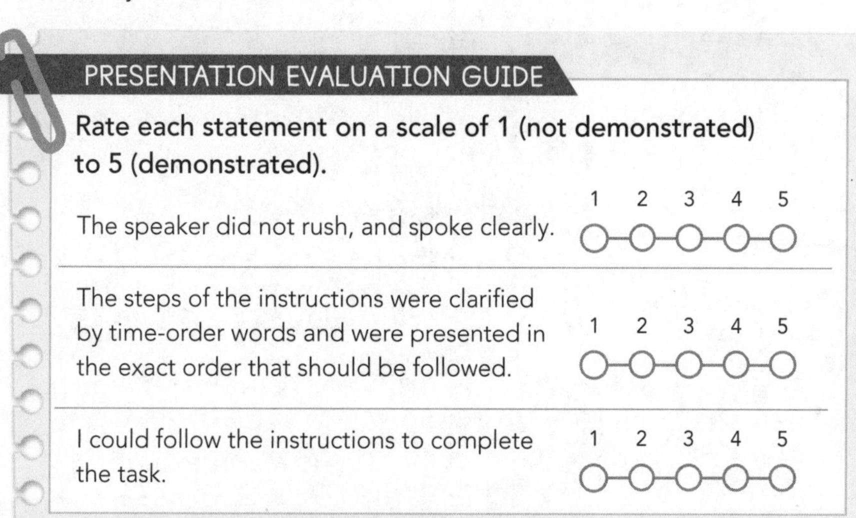
PRESENTATION EVALUATION GUIDE

Rate each statement on a scale of 1 (not demonstrated) to 5 (demonstrated).

Statement	1	2	3	4	5
The speaker did not rush, and spoke clearly.	○	○	○	○	○
The steps of the instructions were clarified by time-order words and were presented in the exact order that should be followed.	○	○	○	○	○
I could follow the instructions to complete the task.	○	○	○	○	○

EQ Notes Before moving on to a new selection, go to your Essential Question Notes and record any additional thoughts or observations you may have about "Tutors Teach Seniors New High-Tech Tricks."

from MOM & ME & MOM

Nonfiction and Media

A **memoir** is a type of narrative nonfiction in which an author shares memories of his or her life. A **television interview** is a structured conversation between two or more people that is aired on a television show.

LEARNING TO LOVE MY MOTHER

MEMOIR

Author's Purpose

- to relate true experiences and express insights about them

Characteristics

- based on memories and true events
- uses literary devices, such as dialogue and description
- uses first-person point of view
- presents characters—who are real people
- takes place in a certain setting, or time and place
- focuses on a specific time in or aspect of the writer's life

Structure

- often, relates events in chronological order
- may be organized in chapters or sections

TELEVISION INTERVIEW

Purpose

- to share a noteworthy person's experiences, knowledge, and insights

Characteristics

- one-on-one conversation, or dialogue, between an interviewer and interviewee, or subject
- sense of immediacy and authority because the interviewee has unique information or knowledge
- may include nonverbal media, such as images

Structure

- question-and-answer format
- often, includes an introduction or background segment

Genre / Text Elements

Literary Devices: Dialogue and Description Even though memoirs are a type of nonfiction, they often include storytelling devices, such as **dialogue** and **description**, that make them seem like fiction. Dialogue is usually set off from the rest of a text by quotation marks. Adjectives or verbs in nearby text may describe the person's emotions or behavior as he or she speaks.

LITERARY DEVICE	EXAMPLE	PURPOSES
Dialogue: words people or characters in a narrative speak aloud; their conversations	*"What do you want from me, Marty?" I asked.* *"Nothin'," Marty muttered. "But I always treated you like a son."*	• shows what characters are like and how they interact • moves the plot forward • makes a text more vivid
Description: words and phrases related to the senses (sight, hearing, taste, touch, smell) that show what people, places, and objects are like	*The forest pool is a near-perfect circle of still green water troubled now and then by the splash of a fish.*	• shows how the narrator or other people in a narrative perceive their environment • creates a specific mood, or emotional quality • gives necessary information

PRACTICE Work on your own to read the passage, and mark the description. Use a different mark to identify the dialogue. Then, answer the questions.

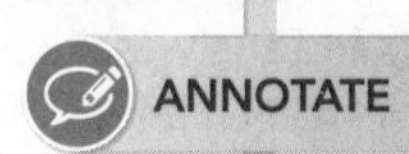

ANNOTATE

NOTEBOOK

Metal wheels screamed against iron rails as the train rounded the curve. I gasped and grabbed Alan's hand. *"Too fast, too fast!"* I cried, heart pounding.

Alan glanced at me. "Hey," he said, squeezing my hand. "Stop being nuts. We're fine."

None of the other passengers seemed nervous. I heard the gentle hum of voices and the occasional peal of laughter. No sobs of terror, no cries of anguish. "I just hate trains," I sighed.

1. What do descriptions in paragraphs 1 and 3 tell you about the situation? Explain.

2. What aspects of the characters' personalities do you learn from dialogue? Explain.

TEKS

8.D. Analyze characteristics and structural elements of informational text.

9.E. Identify the use of literary devices, including subjective and objective point of view.

from MOM & ME & MOM

Compare Nonfiction and Media

In this lesson, you will read an excerpt from Maya Angelou's memoir *Mom & Me & Mom* and watch an interview with the author. You will then compare the memoir and the interview.

LEARNING TO LOVE MY MOTHER

About the Author

Born Marguerite Johnson, **Maya Angelou** (1928–2014) struggled with racism, poverty, and ill treatment early in her life. Across her long career she was a dancer, an actress, a singer, a teacher, and a writer. Angelou became one of the best-known African American authors in the world, and she was an activist for women and for the African American community.

from Mom & Me & Mom

Concept Vocabulary

ANNOTATE

As you read the memoir, you will encounter these words.

supervision	charitable	philanthropist

Base Words Base, or "inside" words, along with context clues can help you figure out what some words mean.

EXAMPLE

Unfamiliar Word in Context: An <u>*artisan*</u> made the lovely bowl.

Base Word: *art*, or "something made with skill and imagination"

Conclusion: *Artisan* must mean some sort of artist.

PRACTICE As you read, notice base words that help you define unfamiliar words. Mark your observations in the open space next to the text.

Comprehension Strategy

ANNOTATE

Evaluate Details to Determine Key Ideas

Most memoir writers describe scenes and situations rather than simply stating their key ideas. As you read, mark details that seem important. Evaluate them by taking notes that capture your thinking. Then, determine how the details connect to larger, key ideas.

EXAMPLE

Marked Details: I had become too <u>frightened</u> to accept the idea that <u>I was going to meet my mother at last.</u>

Notes about Key Ideas: The author never met her mom before and she's scared. Maybe one key idea is about facing difficult feelings.

PRACTICE As you read, mark details and take notes in the open space next to the text. Then, evaluate the details to determine key ideas.

TEKS

5.G. Evaluate details read to determine key ideas.

6.E. Interact with sources in meaningful ways such as notetaking, annotating, freewriting, or illustrating.

from Mom & Me & Mom

Maya Angelou

BACKGROUND

When Maya Angelou was 3 years old and her brother Bailey was 5, her parents divorced and sent the children off to live with their grandmother in Stamps, Arkansas. When Maya was 13, she and Bailey were sent back to San Francisco to live with their mother, Vivian Baxter.

AUDIO

ANNOTATE

Chapter 3

1 My grandmother made arrangements with two Pullman car[1] porters and a dining car waiter for tickets for herself, my brother, and me. She said she and I would go to California first and Bailey would follow a month later. She said she didn't want to leave me without adult **supervision**, because I was a thirteen-year-old girl. Bailey would be safe with Uncle Willie. Bailey thought he was looking after Uncle Willie, but the truth was, Uncle Willie was looking after him.

Mark base words or indicate another strategy you used that helped you determine meaning.

supervision (soo pehr VIH zhun) *n.*

MEANING:

2 By the time the train reached California, I had become too frightened to accept the idea that I was going to meet my mother at last.

3 My grandmother took my hands. "Sister, there is nothing to be scared for. She is your mother, that's all. We are not surprising her.

1. **Pullman car** *n.* type of railroad sleeping car built by the Pullman Company.

When she received my letter explaining how Junior was growing up, she invited us to come to California."

4 Grandmother rocked me in her arms and hummed. I calmed down. When we descended the train steps, I looked for someone who could be my mother. When I heard my grandmother's voice call out, I followed the voice and I knew she had made a mistake, but the pretty little woman with red lips and high heels came running to my grandmother.

5 "Mother Annie! Mother Annie!"

6 Grandmother opened her arms and embraced the woman. When Momma's arms fell, the woman asked, "Where is my baby?"

7 She looked around and saw me. I wanted to sink into the ground. I wasn't pretty or even cute. That woman who looked like a movie star deserved a better-looking daughter than me. I knew it and was sure she would know it as soon as she saw me.

8 "Maya, Marguerite, my baby." Suddenly I was wrapped in her arms and in her perfume. She pushed away and looked at me. "Oh baby, you're beautiful and so tall. You look like your daddy and me. I'm so glad to see you."

9 She kissed me. I had not received one kiss in all the years in Arkansas. Often my grandmother would call me and show me off to her visitors. "This is my grandbaby." She would stroke me and smile. That was the closest I had come to being kissed. Now Vivian Baxter was kissing my cheeks and my lips and my hands. Since I didn't know what to do, I did nothing.

10 Her home, which was a boardinghouse,[2] was filled with heavy and very uncomfortable furniture. She showed me a room and said it was mine. I told her I wanted to sleep with Momma. Vivian said, "I suppose you slept with your grandmother in Stamps, but she will be going home soon and you need to get used to sleeping in your own room."

11 My grandmother stayed in California, watching me and everything that happened around me. And when she decided that everything was all right, she was happy. I was not. She began to talk about going home, and wondering aloud how her crippled son was getting along. I was afraid to let her leave me, but she said, "You are with your mother now and your brother will be coming soon. Trust me, but more than that trust the Lord. He will look after you."

12 Grandmother smiled when my mother played jazz and blues very loudly on her record player. Sometimes she would dance just because she felt like it, alone, by herself, in the middle of the floor. While Grandmother accepted behavior so different, I just couldn't get used to it.

2. **boardinghouse** *n.* house where people rent one or more rooms for either short or long periods of time.

13 My mother watched me without saying much for about two weeks. Then we had what was to become familiar as "a sit-down talk-to."

14 She said, "Maya, you disapprove of me because I am not like your grandmother. That's true. I am not. But I am your mother and I am working some part of my anatomy[3] off to pay for this roof over your head. When you go to school, the teacher will smile at you and you will smile back. Students you don't even know will smile and you will smile. But on the other hand, I am your mother. If you can force one smile on your face for strangers, do it for me. I promise you I will appreciate it."

15 She put her hand on my cheek and smiled. "Come on, baby, smile for Mother. Come on. Be **charitable**."

16 She made a funny face and against my will, I smiled. She kissed me on my lips and started to cry. "That's the first time I have seen you smile. It is a beautiful smile. Mother's beautiful daughter can smile."

17 I was not used to being called beautiful.

18 That day, I learned that I could be a giver simply by bringing a smile to another person. The ensuing[4] years have taught me that a kind word or a vote of support can be a charitable gift. I can move over and make another place for another to sit. I can turn my music up if it pleases, or down if it is annoying.

19 I may never be known as a **philanthropist**, but I certainly want to be known as charitable.

Mark base words or indicate another strategy you used that helped you determine meaning.

charitable (CHAIR ih tuh buhl) *adj.*

MEANING:

philanthropist (fih LAN thruh pihst) *n.*

MEANING:

* * *

20 I was beginning to appreciate her. I liked to hear her laugh because I noticed that she never laughed at anyone. After a few weeks it became clear that I was not using any title when I spoke to her. In fact, I rarely started conversations. Most often, I simply responded when I was spoken to.

21 She asked me into her room. She sat on her bed and didn't invite me to join her.

22 "Maya, I am your mother. Despite the fact that I left you for years, I am your mother. You know that, don't you?"

23 I said, "Yes, ma'am." I had been answering her briefly with a few words since my arrival in California.

24 "You don't have to say 'ma'am' to me. You're not in Arkansas."

25 "No, ma'am. I mean no."

26 "You don't want to call me 'Mother,' do you?"

27 I remained silent.

28 "You have to call me something. We can't go through life without you addressing me. What would you like to call me?"

3. **anatomy** (uh NAT uh mee) *n.* the structure of the body.
4. **ensuing** *adj.* following.

29 I had been thinking of that since I first saw her. I said, "Lady."

30 "What?"

31 "Lady."

32 "Why?"

33 "Because you are beautiful, and you don't look like a mother."

34 "Is Lady a person you like?"

35 I didn't answer.

36 "Is Lady a person you might learn to like?"

37 She waited as I thought about it.

38 I said, "Yes."

39 "Well, that's it. I am Lady, and still your mother."

40 "Yes, ma'am. I mean yes."

41 "At the right time I will introduce my new name."

42 She left me, turned up the player, and sang loudly with the music. The next day I realized she must have spoken to my grandmother.

43 Grandmother came into my bedroom. "Sister, she is your mother and she does care for you."

44 I said, "I'll wait until Bailey gets here. He will know what to do, and whether we should call her Lady."

Chapter 4

45 Mother, Grandmother, and I waited at the railway station. Bailey descended from the train and saw me first. The smile that took over his face made me forget all the discomfort I had felt since coming to California.

46 His eyes found Grandmother and his smile changed to a grin, and he waved to her. Then he saw Mother and his response broke my heart. Suddenly he was a lost little boy who had been found at last. He saw his mother, his home, and then all his lonely birthdays were gone. His nights when scary things made noise under the bed were forgotten. He went to her as if hypnotized. She opened her arms and she clasped him into her embrace. I felt as if I had stopped breathing. My brother was gone, and he would never come back.

47 He had forgotten everything, but I remembered how we felt on the few occasions when she sent us toys. I poked the eyes out of each doll, and Bailey took huge rocks and smashed to bits the trucks or trains that came wrapped up in fancy paper.

48 Grandmother put her arm around me and we walked ahead of the others back to the car. She opened the door and sat in the backseat. She looked at me and patted the seat beside her. We left the front seat for the new lovers.

49 The plan was that Grandmother would return to Arkansas two days after Bailey arrived. Before Lady and Bailey Jr. reached the car I said to Grandmother, "I want to go back home with you, Momma."

50 She asked, "Why?"

51 I said, "I don't want to think of you on that train all alone. You will need me."

52 "When did you make that decision?" I didn't want to answer.

53 She said, "When you saw the reunion of your brother and his mother?" That she should have such understanding, being an old woman and country, too: I thought it was amazing. It was just as well that I had no answer, because Bailey and his mother had already reached the car.

54 Vivian said to Grandmother, "Mother Annie, I didn't look for you two. I knew you would go to the car." Bailey didn't turn to look at me. His eyes were glued to his mother's face. "One thing about you that cannot be denied, you are a true sensible woman."

55 Grandmother said, "Thank you, Vivian. Junior?"

56 She had to call twice to get his attention, "Junior, how was the train? Did somebody make food for your trip? How did you leave Willie?"

57 Suddenly he remembered there was someone else in the world. He grinned for Grandmother. "Yes, ma'am, but none of them can cook like you."

58 He turned to me and asked, "What's happening, My? Has California got your tongue? You haven't said a word since I got in the car."

59 I made my voice as cold as possible. I said, "You haven't given me a chance."

60 In a second he said, "What's the matter, My?"

61 I had hurt him and I was glad. I said, "I may go back to Stamps with Momma." I wanted to break his heart.

62 "No, ma'am, you will not." My grandmother's voice was unusually hard.

63 My mother asked, "Why would you leave now? You said all you were waiting on was your brother. Well, here he is." She started the car and pulled out into traffic.

64 Bailey turned back to her. He added, "Yep, I'm in California."

65 Grandmother held my hand and patted it. I bit the inside of my mouth to keep from crying.

66 No one spoke until we reached our house. Bailey dropped his hand over the back of the front seat. When he wiggled his fingers, I grabbed them. He squeezed my fingers and let them go and drew his hand back to the front seat. The exchange did not escape Grandmother's notice, but she said nothing. ❧

* * *

BUILD INSIGHT

NOTEBOOK

Work on your own to answer the questions in your notebook. Use text evidence to support your responses.

Response

1. **Personal Connections** Do you sympathize with the author's feelings when Bailey arrives? Explain.

Comprehension

2. **Strategy: Evaluate Details to Determine Key Ideas (a)** Cite one example of a detail you evaluated that helped you determine a key idea. **(b)** Would you recommend this strategy to other readers? Why, or why not?

WORKING AS A GROUP

Discuss your responses to the Analysis and Discussion questions with your group.

If necessary, revise your original answers to reflect what you learn from your discussion.

Analysis and Discussion

3. **Interpret** What does Angelou learn when she smiles for her mother?
4. **Compare and Contrast** Why do you think Angelou's reaction to seeing her mother again differs so much from her brother's reaction? Cite details that support your answer.
5. **Analyze** In paragraph 46, the author says, "My brother was gone, and he would never come back." What do you think she means by this statement?
6. **Get Ready for Close Reading** Choose a passage from the text that you find especially interesting or important. You'll discuss the passage with your group during Close-Read activities.

EQ Notes

What can one generation learn from another?

What has this memoir taught you about people of different generations? Go to your Essential Question Notes and record your observations and thoughts about *Mom & Me & Mom*.

from MOM & ME & MOM

Close Read

ANNOTATE

PRACTICE **Complete the following activities. Use text evidence to support your responses.**

1. **Present and Discuss** With your group, share passages from the memoir that you found especially interesting. Discuss what you notice, the questions you have, and the conclusions you reach. For example, you might focus on the following passages:
   - Paragraphs 20–44: Discuss this scene and the reasons for the author's confusion about what to call her mother.
   - Paragraph 66: Discuss what Bailey does and the responses of both Angelou and her grandmother.
2. **Reflect on Your Learning** What new ideas or insights did you uncover during your second reading of the text?

NOTEBOOK

LANGUAGE STUDY

Concept Vocabulary

Why These Words? The vocabulary words are related.

supervision	charitable	philanthropist

1. With your group, determine what the words have in common. Write your ideas.
2. Add another word that fits the category: ____________________
3. Use each vocabulary word in a sentence. Include context clues that hint at each word's meaning.

Word Study

Greek Root: *-phil-* The word *philanthropist* is built on the Greek roots *-phil-* which means "love for," and *-anthrop-,* which means "human." Use a dictionary to find the meanings of the following words: *audiophile, philosophy,* and *bibliophile*. Explain how *-phil-* contributes to the meanings of all three words. Then, write sentences for each word, demonstrating its usage.

TEKS

2.C. Determine the meaning and usage of grade-level academic English words derived from Greek and Latin roots such as *omni, log/logue, gen, vid/vis, phil, luc,* and *sens/sent.*

5.G. Evaluate details read to determine key ideas.

from MOM & ME & MOM

Genre / Text Elements

Literary Devices: Dialogue and Description The use of **dialogue** and **description** helps a memoir writer portray his or her experiences so that they come alive for readers. Writers also employ **exposition**, or explanations. Maya Angelou uses all three devices to build a vivid picture and convey insights. Consider the examples.

EXAMPLES: Literary Devices in Mom & Me & Mom

DEVICE	PASSAGE	PURPOSE
Dialogue: characters' spoken words; conversations	*"Sister, there is nothing to be scared for. She is your mother, that's all...."*	• shows what characters are like and how they interact • moves the plot forward • makes a text more vivid
Description: sensory language that creates word pictures in readers' minds	*the pretty little woman with red lips and high heels came running...*	• shows how characters see people and places • adds to a specific mood
Exposition: explanations	*My grandmother made arrangements with two Pullman car porters and a dining car waiter for tickets ....*	• gives basic information about situations • provides background

INTERACTIVITY

PRACTICE Work with your group to complete the activity and answer the questions.

1. **Analyze** Use the chart to cite details in the memoir that relate to the author's mother. Identify the device or devices used in each passage and explain what they show about the author's feelings.

PASSAGE	DETAIL(S)	DEVICE(S)	EXPLANATION
Paragraph 8			
Paragraph 12			
Paragraphs 21–22			

2. **(a) Summarize** In paragraph 11, summarize the information given in exposition. **(b) Connect** Why is this information important?

3. **(a) Distinguish** Cite details in paragraph 46 that show what happens when Bailey sees his family. **(b) Interpret** How does this description support the author's feeling that her brother "was gone"?

TEKS

9.E. Identify the use of literary devices, including subjective and objective point of view.

10.D.vi. Edit drafts using standard English conventions, including subordinating conjunctions to form complex sentences and correlative conjunctions such as *either/or* and *neither/nor.*

Conventions

Subordinating Conjunctions and Complex Sentences A **conjunction** is a word that joins words or groups of words. It also creates a relationship between the elements that are joined. A **subordinating conjunction** joins a subordinate, or dependent, clause to an independent clause to create a complex sentence. It creates a relationship of time, cause and effect, manner, or comparison.

SUBORDINATING CONJUNCTIONS	TYPE OF RELATIONSHIP	EXAMPLES FROM THE TEXT
after, before, once, since, until, when, while	Time	*When we descended the train steps, I looked for someone who could be my mother.*
because, so that, that	Cause and Effect	*She said she didn't want to leave me without adult supervision, because I was a thirteen-year-old girl.*
as, as if, as though, like	Manner	*I felt as if I had stopped breathing.*
although, while, more than, less than, than	Comparison	*While Grandmother accepted behavior so different, I just couldn't get used to it.*

NOTEBOOK

READ IT Work on your own to complete the activities.

1. Identify the subordinating conjunction in each sentence. Then, tell what kind of relationship the conjunction creates.

   a. No one spoke until we reached our house.

   b. He went to her as if he were hypnotized.

2. Reread paragraph 20 of *Mom & Me & Mom*. Mark and then label two examples of a subordinate clause. Some sentences have more than one.

WRITE IT Edit the following pairs of sentences. Use the subordinating conjunction indicated to change one independent clause into a dependent clause. Then, connect it to the remaining clause to create a single complex sentence. Finally, write a complex sentence of your own.

1. Martina is a great person. She is not very punctual. *(although)*

2. I slammed the door. The glass fell off the table. (after)

from MOM & ME & MOM

Compare Nonfiction and Media

The interview features Maya Angelou describing some of the experiences she wrote about in her memoir. Pay attention to similarities and differences in the ways the memoir and the interview tell the author's story.

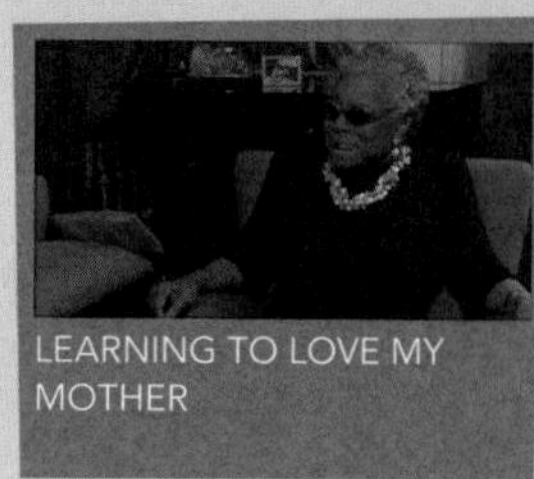

LEARNING TO LOVE MY MOTHER

About the Interviewer

Michael Maher has produced and filmed numerous videos, including many for *BBC News Magazine*. In most of his work—even when he is the interviewer—he is not very visible, and the focus of the video doesn't stray from the subject.

Learning to Love My Mother

Media Vocabulary

These words describe characteristics of TV interviews, a type of multimodal text. Use them as you analyze, discuss, and write about the selection.

interview subject: the person being interviewed	• The subject is someone with special knowledge, experience, or status. He or she has wisdom or insight to share with viewers.
set: where the interview takes place	• Uses color and other visual elements to create a mood that fits the personality of the subject. • The set may be a television studio or a more personal place, such as the subject's home.
tone: the emotional quality of the conversation between the interviewer and the subject	• The overall tone of an interview will reflect the topic and interviewer's purpose. • Word choice, vocal qualities, and facial expressions set the tone of an interview.

Comprehension Strategy

NOTEBOOK

Evaluate Details to Determine Key Ideas

As you watch and listen to any media, take notes about details that seem striking or important. Then, evaluate the details by deciding which ones help most to develop larger, key ideas. Be sure to note the time code of each detail, as this will make it easier for you to revisit those sections.

EXAMPLE

Details from "Learning to Love My Mother"

- Grandmother was patient, spoke slowly. (time code 00:25)
- Vivian Baxter spoke fast, danced. (time code 00:28)

Evaluate Details: These details are important. They contribute to a key idea about the mother-daughter relationship.

PRACTICE As you watch the interview, take notes about important details. Then, evaluate the details to determine key ideas.

TEKS

5.G. Evaluate details read to determine key ideas.

6.E. Interact with sources in meaningful ways such as notetaking, annotating, freewriting, or illustrating.

8.F. Analyze characteristics of multimodal and digital texts.

Learning to Love My Mother

Maya Angelou with Michael Maher

BACKGROUND

When Maya Angelou was three years old, she and her brother were sent to live with their grandmother. Their mother, Vivian Baxter, was not ready to be tied down with a family. Ten years later, the two children returned to live with their mother. More than 70 years later, Angelou wrote about this transition in her memoir *Mom & Me & Mom*. In this interview, she tells Michael Maher some of the lessons she learned from her experiences.

TAKE NOTES As you watch and listen, take notes to record key ideas.

NOTEBOOK

Work on your own to answer the questions in your notebook. Use text evidence to support your responses.

Response

1. **Personal Connections** Angelou mentions several lessons she learned from her relationship with her mother. Which one do you find most powerful? Explain.

Comprehension

2. **(a)** Why did Vivian Baxter, Angelou's mother, abandon her children? **(b)** How does Vivian Baxter later react to Angelou's calling her "Lady"?

3. **Strategy: Evaluate Details to Determine Key Ideas** Do the details about President Obama and Martin Luther King, Jr., contribute to a key idea in this interview? Explain your answer.

WORKING AS A GROUP

Discuss your responses to the Analysis and Discussion questions with your group.

- Note agreements and disagreements.
- Summarize insights.
- Consider changes of opinion.

If necessary, revise your original answers to reflect what you learn from your discussion.

Analysis and Discussion

4. **(a) Distinguish** What qualities did Angelou see in her mother after she had lived with her for awhile? **(b) Analyze** How did Angelou's recognition of these qualities affect her feelings for her mother? Explain.

5. **(a)** According to Angelou, what would Vivian Baxter have thought about the election of an African American president? **(b) Make Inferences** What does this detail suggest about Vivian Baxter's personality and the effect she had on her daughter?

6. **(a)** What one message does Angelou pray someone will hear in her book? **(b) Make Inferences** Why do you think this one message is so important to her?

EQ Notes What can one generation learn from another?

What have you learned about different generations from watching this interview? Go to your Essential Question Notes and record your observations and thoughts about "Learning to Love My Mother."

TEKS

5.G. Evaluate details read to determine key ideas.

Close Review

 NOTEBOOK

LEARNING TO LOVE MY MOTHER

Watch the interview again. As you watch, take notes about important details and jot down your observations. Note time codes so you can find important elements again later. Then, write a question and your conclusion.

MY **QUESTION:**

MY **CONCLUSION:**

Inquiry and Research

 RESEARCH

Research and Extend Briefly research Maya Angelou's life and her many accomplishments. Explain how this new knowledge adds to your appreciation of the interview.

Media Vocabulary

 NOTEBOOK

These words describe characteristics of multimodal texts. Practice using them as you write and discuss your responses.

interview subject	set	tone

1. If you were conducting this interview, what location would you choose? Explain.

2. Identify one question you wished the interviewer had asked Angelou. Explain your thinking.

3. How would you describe the emotional quality of this interview? Explain, citing details from the video.

 TEKS

6.F. Respond using newly acquired vocabulary as appropriate.

8.F. Analyze characteristics of multimodal and digital texts.

from MOM & ME & MOM

LEARNING TO LOVE MY MOTHER

Compare Nonfiction and Media

Multiple Choice

NOTEBOOK

These questions are based on the excerpt from the memoir *Mom & Me & Mom* and the interview "Learning to Love My Mother." Choose the best answer to each question.

1. When the author travels by train to California, how does she feel?

A She feels happy to be leaving Stamps, Arkansas.

B She feels sad to leave her brother behind.

C She feels excited to be meeting her mother at last.

D She feels frightened to be meeting her mother at last.

2. Read paragraph 20 from the memoir and the transcript of a similar section in the interview. What do you learn from the interview that Angelou does *not* share in her memoir?

Memoir

I was beginning to appreciate her. I liked to hear her laugh because I noticed she never laughed at anyone. After a few weeks it became clear that I was not using any title when I spoke to her. In fact, I rarely started conversations. Most often, I simply responded when I was spoken to.

Television Interview

00:45: INTERVIEWER: . . . What allowed you to somewhat establish a relationship?

00:56: ANGELOU: She loved me. And she told me. She said, "I really wasn't ready to be a parent." And I realized there are some people who are great parents to small people. My mother was just the opposite.

F Her mother was eager for children.

G Her mother had been unprepared for children.

H Her mother did not laugh at anyone.

J Her mother did not appreciate people.

3. In both the memoir and the interview, what important idea does Angelou share?

A She learned to be kinder from the experience.

B She wished that her childhood had been easier.

C She hopes to forgive her mother someday.

D She knew that her grandmother loved her mother.

TEKS

6.B. Write responses that demonstrate understanding of texts, including comparing sources within and across genres.

10.B.i. Develop drafts into a focused, structured, and coherent piece of writing by organizing with purposeful structure, including an introduction, transitions, coherence within and across paragraphs, and a conclusion.

Short Response

1. **(a) Describe** In the memoir, what overall impression does the author give of her mother's appearance and behavior? **(b) Synthesize** Cite at least one detail in the interview that adds to that portrayal. Explain.

2. **(a) Synthesize** What information do the photos and video included in the interview add to the viewers' understanding of Angelou's life? **(b) Speculate** The young Angelou had difficulty understanding her mother. Do you think she would have understood her own adult self? Explain.

3. **Connect** In the TV interview, Angelou says that her mother loved her. Which details in the memoir suggest that love? Cite at least one statement and one action and explain your choices.

Answer the questions in your notebook. Use text evidence to support your responses.

Timed Writing

A **comparison-and-contrast essay** is a piece of writing in which you discuss the similarities and differences between two or more topics.

ASSIGNMENT

Maya Angelou gave the interview "Learning to Love My Mother" to promote her memoir *Mom & Me & Mom*. Write a **comparison-and-contrast essay** in which you explain which text provides a more vivid sense of Angelou's experience.

- Which source allows you to better understand Angelou and her family?
- Which source offers more detail, and why?

5-MINUTE PLANNER

1. Read the assignment carefully and completely.
2. Decide what you want to say—your controlling idea or thesis. Make sure to state it in your introduction, develop it in your body paragraphs, and restate it in your conclusion.
3. Decide which examples you'll use from the two sources.
4. Organize your ideas, making sure to note details you learn from the memoir that you don't learn from the interview, and vice versa.

EQ Notes Before moving on to a new selection, go to your Essential Question Notes and record any additional thoughts and observations you may have about *Mom & Me & Mom* and "Learning to Love My Mother."

About the Author

Mica Angela Hendricks was born into a military family and traveled to many countries. As a child, she would carry a sketchbook everywhere she went. People who didn't know her well would simply call her "that girl who draws." Hendricks is now an illustrator and has collaborated with her four-year-old daughter, Myla, on the sketchbook "Share With Me."

Mother-Daughter Drawings

Media Vocabulary

These words describe characteristics of drawings. Here, the drawings are presented with captions to create a type of multimodal text. Use these words as you analyze, discuss, and write about the selection.

composition: arrangement of elements in a work of visual art	• Artists consider color, line, shape, space, form, and texture when composing an image. • Composition may emphasize one part of an image over others.
light and shadow: elements that define and enhance parts of an image	• An artist's use of light and shadow can make a two-dimensional shape look three-dimensional—a circle becomes a sphere. • Varying degrees of light and shadow may create different moods.
proportion: sizes of objects in relation to each other or the background	• Realistic proportions make objects seem true to life. • Exaggerated proportions make objects seem odd, imaginary, or dreamlike.

Comprehension Strategy

NOTEBOOK

Synthesize Information

When you **synthesize information**, you pull together ideas from different sources in order to develop your own perspective. You allow your thinking about a topic to grow and change. To synthesize as you read, follow these steps:

- Identify important points in a text.
- Consider connections, similarities, and differences among those points.
- Use these sentence starters to organize your thinking and express your new understanding:
  At first I thought ______________________.
  Then, I learned ______________________.
  Now I think ______________________.

PRACTICE As you study this gallery of visual art, synthesize your observations of the drawings and the caption text to create a new understanding. Jot your ideas in the Notes sections.

TEKS

5.H. Synthesize information to create new understanding.

8.F. Analyze characteristics of multimodal and digital texts.

Mother-Daughter Drawings

Mica and Myla Hendricks

BACKGROUND

Artist Mica Angela Hendricks had always tried to teach her four-year-old daughter Myla the importance of sharing. But it's easier to talk about sharing than to do it. Mica found that out when Myla noticed her mother drawing in a sketchbook and asked if she could draw in it too. Mica was afraid Myla would ruin her drawings, but decided she had to set a good example by practicing what she preached, especially after Myla quoted her words back to her: "If you can't share, we might have to take it away."

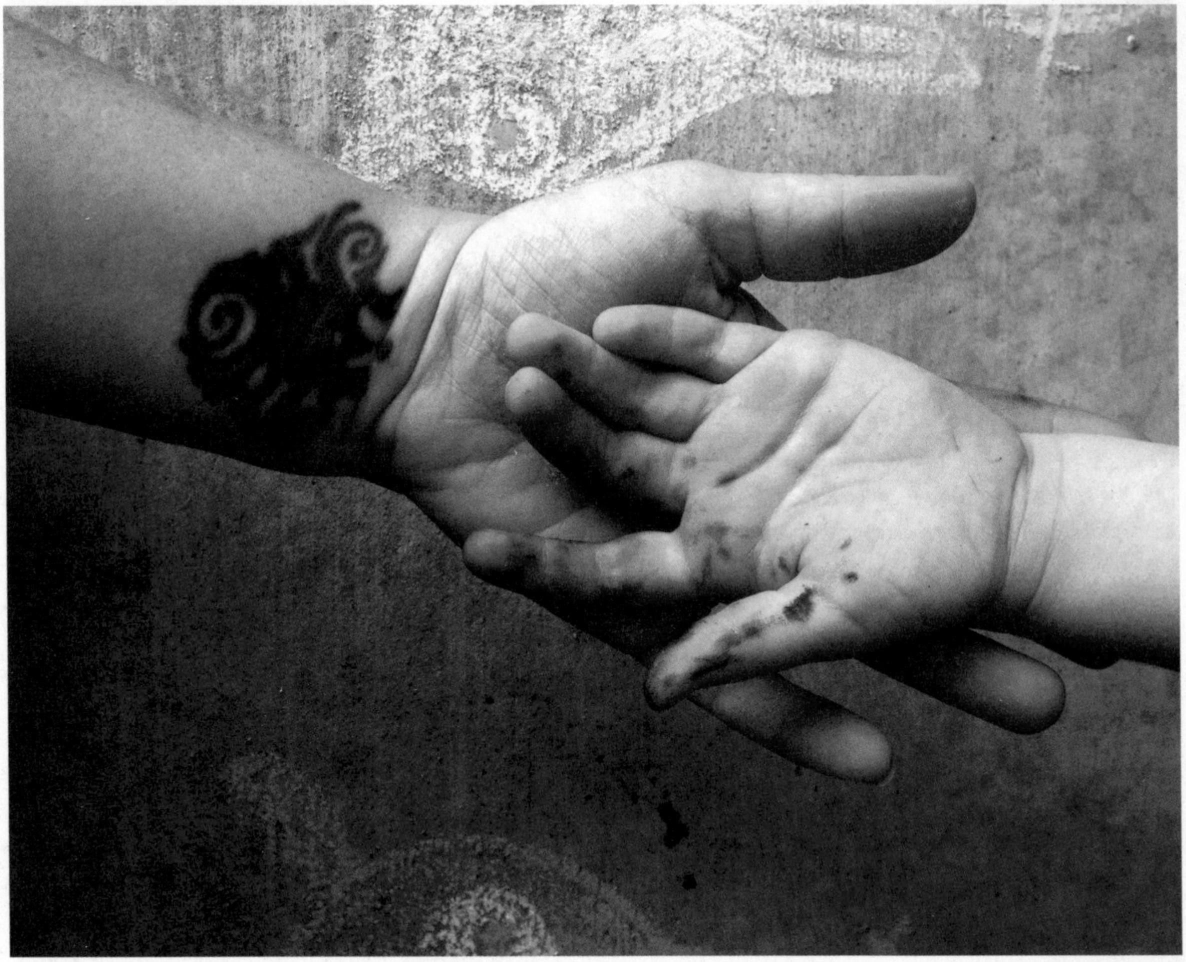

IMAGE 1: Mica had just drawn a woman's face from an old photograph. She let Myla draw the woman's body and then used acrylic paint to add color, highlights, and texture to the entire piece.

TAKE NOTES

IMAGE 2: Mica was impressed that her collaboration with her daughter turned out so well and wanted to try it again.

TAKE NOTES

IMAGE 3: Mica began filling her sketchbook with drawings of heads and letting Myla draw the bodies.

TAKE NOTES

IMAGE 4: At first, Mica tried telling Myla what kind of bodies to draw. She soon realized the drawings turned out better when Myla did what she wanted. "In most instances, kids' imaginations *way* outweigh a grown-up's," Mica says.

TAKE NOTES

IMAGE 5: Working with her daughter taught Mica that giving up control is not just fun, but necessary. "Those things you hold so dear cannot change and grow and expand unless you loosen your grip on them a little," she says.

TAKE NOTES

NOTEBOOK

Response

1. **Personal Connections** Which drawing did you like the best? Why?

Work on your own to answer the questions in your notebook. Use text evidence to support your responses.

Comprehension

2. **Reading Check** **(a)** Why did Mica let Myla draw in the sketchbook? **(b)** What did she think would happen? **(c)** What actually happened?

3. **Strategy: Synthesize Information** **(a)** Explain at least one way in which your understanding of the art changed when you synthesized your observations of the drawings with information from the captions. **(b)** How might the strategy of synthesizing help you in other school tasks, such as writing a research paper? Explain.

Analysis and Discussion

4. **(a) Contrast** What are some of the most striking differences between the parts of the drawings Mica drew and the parts that Myla drew? **(b) Modify** How might the drawings be different if Mica had not collaborated with her daughter? Explain.

5. In the text accompanying Image 5, Mica says, "Those things you hold so dear cannot change and grow and expand unless you loosen your grip on them a little." **(a) Interpret** What does she mean by that statement? **(b) Connect** In what ways do you think this idea comes through in the drawings? Explain.

6. **Take a Position** In the creation of art, which matters more, imagination or skill? Explain your thinking, using these drawings as evidence.

WORKING AS A GROUP

Discuss your responses to the Analysis and Discussion questions with your group.

Make sure you comprehend routine language, including the words *contrast* and *interpret*, used in the questions. Your responses should show your understanding of those words.

EQ Notes What can one generation learn from another?

What have you learned about the ways different generations teach one another from reading and viewing this image gallery? Go to your Essential Question Notes and record your observations and thoughts about "Mother-Daughter Drawings."

TEKS

5.H. Synthesize information to create new understanding.

6.A. Describe the personal connections to a variety of sources, including self-selected text.

6.C. Use text evidence to support an appropriate response.

MOTHER-DAUGHTER DRAWINGS

Close Review

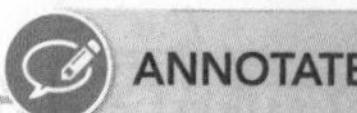

Review the text and images in "Mother-Daughter Drawings." As you review, take notes about important details and jot down your observations. Then, write a question and your conclusion. Share your notes with your group.

MY **QUESTION:**

MY **CONCLUSION:**

Media Vocabulary

NOTEBOOK

These words describe characteristics of multimodal texts. Practice using them as you analyze the drawings and discuss the questions.

composition	light and shadow	proportion

1. Why do you think Image 1 is made up of four separate photographs? What is the effect of this choice?

2. What mood is suggested by Image 2? Which details or elements of the drawing create that mood?

3. **(a)** In Image 5, how does the size of the head relate to other parts of the body? **(b)** What is the effect? Explain.

TEKS

6.F. Respond using newly acquired vocabulary as appropriate.

8.F. Analyze characteristics of multimodal and digital texts.

Speaking and Listening

A **presentation** is a way of providing information to an audience using a combination of words, images, video, and audio.

ASSIGNMENT

Mica Hendricks learned a valuable lesson when she shared her sketchbook with her daughter. With your group, write or retell a story that taught someone an unexpected but positive lesson. Choose one of the following options:

- ◯ Write a new narrative.
- ◯ Choose a story to retell.

Then, deliver your story as a **multimedia presentation**. Make sure everyone in the group has a speaking role.

Choose Images Consider how you can use images to enhance the story.

- Do you want images that show specific events, people, or places?
- Do you want images that are less specific but create a certain mood?

Choose Other Media Choose music or audio to enhance your images and text.

Organize Your Presentation Create a logical sequence for the text you'll speak. Then, identify images and other media that will go with each section. Write the name of the person who will speak during each segment. Use the graphic organizer to capture your notes.

EQ Notes Before moving on to a new selection, go to your Essential Question Notes and record any additional thoughts or observations you may have about "Mother-Daughter Drawings."

Rehearse and Present Practice your presentation with your group. Make sure you transition smoothly between speakers.

Reflect and Discuss Reflect on your experience working as a group:

- Was your process effective? Did everyone participate equally?
- Mica Hendricks was surprised by the experience of working with her daughter. Did you learn anything from this process that surprised you?

POETRY COLLECTION 1

Each selection you are about to read is an example of lyric poetry.

Reading Lyric Poetry

A **lyric poem** is a type of poem that sounds musical and expresses the thoughts and feelings of a single speaker.

LYRIC POETRY

Author's Purpose

- to use highly focused, imaginative language and form to capture the emotions or realization of a moment

Characteristics

- focuses on a moment in time
- expresses an insight, or new understanding
- has a speaker, or voice that "tells" the poem
- uses words for both sound and meaning; uses imagery and figurative language
- may break some of the rules of standard English

Structure

- expresses ideas in lines, or horizontal sets of words, that are often grouped into stanzas
- may use graphical, or visual, elements to reinforce or add meaning

Take a Minute!

NOTEBOOK

FIND IT Work with a partner to find a lyric poem online or in this program. Read aloud one stanza. What do you notice about the feeling or sound of the poem?

TEKS

8.B. Analyze the effect of rhyme scheme, meter, and graphical elements such as punctuation and capitalization in poems across a variety of poetic forms.

Genre / Text Elements

Graphical Elements in Poetry The arrangement of words, **lines**, and **stanzas** in a poem creates *graphical*, or visual, effects. Poets may use other graphical elements, as well. These elements make a poem look a certain way, and that affects how it is read and what it means:

- line lengths, which may be long or short
- stanza lengths, which may be just one line or many lines
- spacing, including use of "white" (empty) space
- punctuation and capitalization, which may be unconventional
- italic, bold, and other text treatments

EXAMPLE

The chair where you sat
Is   empty.
Your place at the table
Is   bare.
Your sweet clear rich voice
Is   silent.

But my heart my *heart* my *heart* my *heart*
sees … hears … remembers

TIP:

- Lines 2, 4, 6: White space emphasizes a sense of absence.
- Line 7: Italics emphasize a heartbeat-like rhythm.
- Line 8: Punctuation shows a struggle to find words.

ANNOTATE

NOTEBOOK

PRACTICE Work on your own to complete the activity. Then, discuss your responses with your group.

1. Read the poem, and mark the following: **(a)** short lines; **(b)** unconventional punctuation and capitalization; **(c)** use of white space.

Ana can
NOT "Sit still!"
Ana   r-u-n-s & hops(!)
up
      steps
               r-u-n-s & hops(!)
      down
steps!
Ana, STOP! No never no ever for Ana
is 3 & free & whe-e!-e-e! e-e!

2. Explain how one element you marked adds to the poem's meaning.

POETRY COLLECTION 1

Abuelita Magic • Mother to Son • To James

Concept Vocabulary

As you read Poetry Collection 1, you will encounter these words.

flung	catapulted	lurched

Context Clues The context of a word is the other words and phrases that appear close to it in the text. Clues in the context can help you figure out word meanings. **Contrast clues** show differences that can help you define an unfamiliar word.

EXAMPLE The winner *glides* across the finish line, while the rest of the runners stumble behind.

Analysis: *Stumble* is a verb that means "move in an awkward, uneven way." The sentence presents a contrast, so *glide* must mean "move in a smooth, continuous way."

PRACTICE As you read these poems, study the context to determine the meaning of unfamiliar words. Mark your observations in the open space next to the text.

Comprehension Strategy

Create Mental Images

By **creating mental images** as you read lyric poetry, you can more easily understand difficult passages and deepen your understanding of the poem.

- As you read, notice language that refers to color, shape, space, and texture.
- Focus on a word or phrase, and consider the image that comes to mind.

EXAMPLE

Notice the words related to shape and texture in these lines from "Mother to Son." Use them to see this scene in your mind.

It's had tacks in it, / And splinters, / And boards torn up, / And places with no carpet on the floor—/ Bare.

PRACTICE As you read this collection of lyric poetry, deepen your understanding by marking vivid details and pausing to create mental images.

TEKS

2.B. Use context such as contrast or cause and effect to clarify the meaning of words.

5.D. Create mental images to deepen understanding.

About the Poets

Abuelita Magic

BACKGROUND

Pat Mora's grandparents moved to the United States during the Mexican Revolution in 1910. Growing up in Texas, Mora spoke Spanish at home, English at school, and appreciated family members who could tell stories and "make words flow or fly" in both languages. Despite Mora's love for language, in this poem she celebrates a grandmother—an *abuelita*—who communicates in a language without words.

Pat Mora (b. 1942) has been a teacher, university administrator, museum director, and consultant. She is now a writer of award-winning poetry, nonfiction, and bilingual books for children. In 1997, she founded Children's Day/Book Day, or *El día de los niños/El día de los libros*, which has been celebrated on April 30 ever since. Born in El Paso, Texas, she lives in Santa Fe, New Mexico.

Mother to Son

BACKGROUND

Even after the abolition of slavery, life was very hard for most African Americans. Poetry, music, and the other arts were creative outlets that allowed them to express the hardships of their lives and to find inspiration.

Langston Hughes (1902–1967) was an African American writer known for jazz-inspired poems that portrayed African American life in America. His work was controversial. Some critics worried that it played into racial stereotypes. Others praised Hughes for reaching everyday people by using language and themes "familiar to anyone who had the ability simply to read."

To James

BACKGROUND

From 1914 through 1937, Harlem, a neighborhood in New York City, was the setting for an awakening of African American culture that came to be known as the Harlem Renaissance. During this period, African American writers such as Langston Hughes and Frank Horne searched for the truest way to express their experiences. Each developed a unique style that ultimately helped shape not just African American culture but also world culture.

Frank Horne (1899–1974) was an African American writer and activist. As a director at the U.S. Housing Authority, he fought to end segregated housing. As a poet, he fought discrimination with poems that conveyed dignity and pride.

Abuelita Magic

Pat Mora

The new mother cries with her baby
in the still desert night,
sits on the dirt floor of the two-room house,
rocks the angry bundle
tears sliding down her face.

The *abuelita* wakes, shakes her head,
finds a dried red chile,
slowly shakes the wrinkled pod
so the seeds rattle
                    ts . ss, ts . ss
The *abuelita*
                    ts . ss, ts . ss
gray-haired shaman[1]
                    ts . ss, ts . ss
cures her two children
                    ts . ss
with sleep

1. **shaman** *n.* figure who uses traditional healing methods and spirituality, sometimes seen as magical, to cure the sick.

Mother to Son

Langston Hughes

AUDIO

ANNOTATE

Well, son, I'll tell you:
Life for me ain't been no crystal stair.
It's had tacks in it,
And splinters,
And boards torn up,
And places with no carpet on the floor—
Bare.
But all the time
I'se been a-climbin' on,
And reachin' landin's,
And turnin' corners,
And sometimes goin' in the dark
Where there ain't been no light.
So boy, don't you turn back.
Don't you set down on the steps
'Cause you finds it's kinder hard.
Don't you fall now—
For I'se still goin', honey,
I'se still climbin',
And life for me ain't been no crystal stair.

To James

Frank Horne

Do you remember
How you won
That last race . . . ?
How you **flung** your body
At the start . . .
How your spikes
Ripped the cinders[1]
In the stretch . . .
How you **catapulted**
Through the tape . . .
Do you remember . . . ?
Don't you think
I **lurched** with you
Out of those starting holes . . . ?
Don't you think
My sinews[2] tightened
At those first
Few strides . . .
And when you flew into the stretch

Mark context clues or indicate another strategy you used that helped you determine meaning.

flung (FLUHNG) *v.*

MEANING:

catapulted
(KA tuh puhl tihd) *v.*

MEANING:

lurched (LURCHT) *v.*

MEANING:

1. **cinders** *n.* ashes.
2. **sinews** *n.* strong tissue that connects muscle to bone.

Was not all my thrill
Of a thousand races
In your blood . . . ?
At your final drive
Through the finish line
Did not my shout
Tell of the
Triumphant ecstasy
Of victory . . . ?
Live
As I have taught you
To run, Boy—
It's a short dash
Dig your starting holes
Deep and firm
Lurch out of them
Into the straightaway
With all the power
That is in you
Look straight ahead
To the finish line
Think only of the goal
Run straight
Run high
Run hard
Save nothing
And finish
With an ecstatic burst
That carries you
Hurtling
Through the tape
To victory. . . .

NOTEBOOK

Work on your own to answer the questions in your notebook. Use text evidence to support your responses.

Response

1. **Personal Connections** Which of the three poems most vividly reminds you of something you have experienced? Describe your response.

Comprehension

2. **Reading Check (a)** In "Abuelita Magic," who does the grandmother help? **(b)** In "Mother to Son," what lesson does the mother want her son to learn? **(c)** In "To James," what event does the speaker refer to at the beginning of the poem?

3. **Strategy: Create Mental Images (a)** Which moment or detail in each poem were you able to picture most clearly? Why? **(b)** In what ways did this strategy add to your reading experience?

Analysis and Discussion

WORKING AS A GROUP

Discuss your responses to the Analysis and Discussion questions with your group.

- Note agreements and disagreements.
- Summarize insights.
- Consider changes of opinion.

If necessary, revise your original answers to reflect what you learn from your discussion.

4. **Make Inferences** In "Abuelita Magic," what can you infer about the grandmother when the speaker refers to her as a "shaman"?

5. **(a) Analyze** In lines 8–13 and 18–20 of "Mother to Son," what personal qualities does the mother demonstrate? **(b) Draw Conclusions** Why do you think she uses herself as an example in her message to her son?

6. **(a) Analyze** Reread lines 12–18 in "To James." How does the speaker react to James's physical efforts? **(b) Connect** What do these reactions show about the speaker's emotional connection to James? Explain.

7. **Get Ready for Close Reading** Choose a passage from the text that you find especially interesting or important. You'll discuss the passage with your group during Close-Read activities.

EQ Notes **What can one generation learn from another?**

What have these poems taught you about people of different generations? Go to your Essential Question Notes and record your observations and thoughts about Poetry Collection I.

TEKS

5.D. Create mental images to deepen understanding.

6.A. Describe personal connections to a variety of sources, including self-selected texts.

6.C. Use text evidence to support an appropriate response.

6.I. Reflect on and adjust responses as new evidence is presented.

POETRY COLLECTION I

Close Read

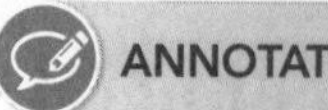

ANNOTATE

PRACTICE **Complete the following activities. Use text evidence to support your responses.**

1. **Present and Discuss** With your group, share the passages from the poems that you found especially interesting. Discuss what you notice, the questions you have, and the conclusions you reach. For example, you might discuss the following passages:
   - "Abuelita Magic," lines 1–5: Discuss the details that show what the setting of the poem is like.
   - "Mother to Son," lines 2–13: Discuss the nature of the life the speaker has lived.
   - "To James," lines 29–51: Discuss the attitude toward life the speaker hopes to have inspired in James.
2. **Reflect on Your Learning** What new ideas or insights did you uncover during your second reading of the text?

WORD NETWORK

Add words that are related to the idea of generations from the text to your Word Network.

NOTEBOOK

LANGUAGE STUDY

Concept Vocabulary

Why These Words? The vocabulary words are related.

flung	catapulted	lurched

1. With your group, determine what the words have in common. Write your ideas.
2. Add another word that fits the category: ____________________
3. Use each vocabulary word in a sentence that describes a person or an object in motion.

Word Study

Synonyms and Antonyms Reread lines 12–14 from "To James." With your group, use a print or digital thesaurus to choose two synonyms and two antonyms for *lurched*. Then, rewrite lines 12–14 twice. In the first version, replace *lurched* with one of the synonyms. In the second version, replaced *lurched* with one of the antonyms. Discuss how replacing a word changes the poem.

TEKS

2.A. Use print or digital resources to determine the meaning, syllabication, pronunciation, word origin, and part of speech.

6.F. Respond using newly acquired vocabulary as appropriate.

8.B. Analyze the effect of rhyme scheme, meter, and graphical elements such as punctuation and capitalization in poems across a variety of poetic forms.

Genre / Text Elements

Graphical Elements in Poetry Graphical, or visual, elements affect how a poem looks, how readers follow the flow of words, and what the poem means.

GRAPHICAL ELEMENTS IN POETRY	
Line Length	• Even line lengths make a poem look orderly. • Varied line lengths make a poem look expressive.
White Space	Empty space suggests pauses or adds meaning.
Punctuation	• Conventional punctuation may guide readers. • Unconventional or no punctuation may leave the reading of a poem more open.
Capitalization	• Each line may start with a capital letter, which adds a sense of order. • Capitalization may stress certain words.

TIP Punctuation marks suggest meaning.
- An ellipsis (...) shows a pause, an ongoing thought, or a struggle to speak.
- A dash (—) shows an urgent interruption.

NOTEBOOK

PRACTICE Work on your own to answer the questions. Then, discuss your responses with your group. In your responses, use new vocabulary you have learned, such as *graphical* and *line length*.

1. **Interpret** In lines 10 to 18 of "Abuelita Magic," how does the use of white space and punctuation add to the poem's effect?

2. **(a) Distinguish** In "Mother to Son," how does line 7 differ from the other lines? **(b) Interpret** What is the effect? Explain.

3. **Analyze** In "Mother to Son," how does punctuation affect the way you read line 17? Explain.

4. **(a) Distinguish** In "To James," how does line 29 differ from the other lines? **(b) Interpret** What is the effect? Explain.

5. **(a) Interpret** In "To James," what do the ellipses suggest about the questions the speaker is asking? **(b) Analyze** Why do you think the poem ends with an ellipsis? Explain.

6. **(a) Compare and Contrast** How is the use of capitalization in the three poems similar and different? **(b) Interpret** What is the effect of the use of capitalization in each poem?

POETRY COLLECTION I

Author's Craft

Figurative Language: Metaphor **Figurative language** creates imaginative comparisons that help to convey meaning in poetry in surprising and powerful ways. They show how a speaker feels and how he or she perceives the world. **Metaphors** are one type of figurative language.

METAPHOR	EXAMPLE
Basic Metaphor: shows similarities between two seemingly unlike things; it presents one thing as though it *is* another.	*Hope is a flame.*
Extended Metaphor: builds a comparison over several lines, a section, or an entire poem	*Hope is a flame* *A spark in the darkness* *Pale at first but then* *Brighter, growing* *Becoming bonfires of belief*

Two of the poems in this collection, "Mother to Son" and "To James," center around extended metaphors.

NOTEBOOK

PRACTICE Work on your own to analyze extended metaphors in "Mother to Son" and "To James." Then, discuss your responses with your group.

1. **Analyze** In "Mother to Son," to what object does the speaker compare her life? What is the metaphor she uses?

2. **Analyze** Trace how the poet develops the extended metaphor in "Mother to Son":
   (a) Lines 1–7: What do descriptive details tell you about the type of life the mother has lived? Explain.

   (b) Lines 8–13: What do details about the mother's actions tell you about the ways in which she responded to challenges? Cite specific details that support your thinking.

   (c) Lines 14–20: In line 14, how does the poem change? In what ways does the poet continue and deepen the metaphor? Explain.

3. **(a)** In "To James," what events does the speaker describe in lines 1–28? **(b) Analyze** What metaphor begins in line 29? **(c) Connect** How does the rest of the poem develop that metaphor?

4. **(a) Generalize** How does the speaker want James to live his life? **(b) Interpret** In what ways does the metaphor help to convey that message?

TEKS

9.D. Describe how the author's use of figurative language such as metaphor and personification achieves specific purposes.

10.B.ii. Develop drafts into a focused, structured, and coherent piece of writing by developing an engaging idea reflecting depth of thought with specific facts, details, and examples.

10.E. Publish written work for appropriate audiences.

11.A. Compose literary texts such as personal narratives, fiction, and poetry using genre characteristics and craft.

Composition

A **lyric poem** uses language in highly focused, imaginative ways to express the thoughts and feelings of a single speaker.

ASSIGNMENT

Work on your own to write a **lyric poem** that captures a moment in time. Focus your poem on a single event or observation. Choose details that work together, or cohere, to create a powerful image. Experiment with structures, such as line lengths and punctuation, to emphasize the meaning of your poem.

TIP Before you start to write, reread the poems in this collection, noting how each poet uses descriptive details and graphical elements to create vivid messages.

Plan Your Poem Come up with an engaging idea, one that truly interests you. Gather vivid descriptive details that bring that idea to life. Consider using metaphors that present ideas in unexpected ways.

Develop Your Draft As you write your poem, explore your ideas from different angles, showing the depth of your thinking. Pay attention to these elements as you write:

- **Focus:** Unlike most prose, a poem is condensed. Convey meaning with metaphors and descriptive details rather than a lot of explanation.
- **Structure:** Line lengths, line breaks, capitalization, and punctuation can reinforce meaning. Use these graphical elements to make your most important ideas stand out.
- **Coherence:** Choose details that create a single strong impression.

Publish Your Work A **chapbook** is a small collection of poetry. Work with your group to publish a chapbook of the poems you wrote independently. Follow these steps:

- Gather the poems everyone has written. If possible, use word processing software to type them using the same fonts. Make sure each poet's name appears with the poem he or she wrote.
- Create a table of contents that includes each poem's title, its author, and the number of the page on which it appears.
- Give your collection a title and choose an image to use on the cover.
- Once you are happy with the design, print multiple copies, and bind the pages as books.
- Share your chapbooks with your class or another appropriate audience. You may also find out about adding them to the collections of your school or local libraries.

EQ Notes Before moving on to a new selection, go to your Essential Question Notes and record any additional thoughts or observations you may have about Poetry Collection 1.

SOURCES

- Tutors Teach Seniors New High-Tech Tricks
- *from* Mom & Me & Mom
- Learning to Love My Mother
- Abuelita Magic
- Mother to Son
- To James

Present a Personal Narrative

ASSIGNMENT

You have read selections about conflicts and connections between generations. With your group, present an **autobiographical anecdote**, a brief true story, about an event in your life. Use your anecdote to respond to the following question:

What new knowledge or skills have you learned from someone of a different generation?

Prepare and Plan

Analyze the Texts Each of the texts in this section presents insights into the lessons different generations can teach one another. With your group, identify the lessons each text conveys. Use this chart to summarize your ideas.

TITLE	LESSON TAUGHT / SUPPORTING DETAILS
Tutors Teach Seniors New High-Tech Tricks	
from Mom & Me & Mom	
Learning to Love My Mother	
Abuelita Magic	
Mother to Son	
To James	

Determine a Topic Use your summaries to inspire your own anecdote. Jot down two or three ideas and discuss them with your group. Which is the most interesting or powerful? Which most clearly answers the assignment question?

Apply Narrative Techniques Work on your own to write your anecdote. Describe what happened in time order. Use details to show what the situation was like and use dialogue to show what people said and how they interacted.

Rehearse and Present

Organize Your Presentation Work as a group to revise your anecdotes and to plan an effective sequence in which to present them.

- Have each group member read his or her anecdote aloud.
- Provide and accept constructive feedback, working together to make sure each anecdote is strong and vivid. When you are providing feedback, begin by saying what worked well. Then, offer specific suggestions for elements that could be strengthened. When you accept feedback, be receptive and listen closely to your peers' suggestions.
- Consider the mood, or emotional quality, of each anecdote. Then, decide the effect you want your presentation to have. Choose an order that creates the effect you want. For example, you might want to start with a funny anecdote and end with an inspirational one.

TIP: Constructive feedback is information someone can actually use and apply. Be specific and provide suggestions rather than criticism.

Share Your Presentations Once you are satisfied with your presentation, deliver it to the class. Then, invite discussion and questions from your audience. Respond to the questions thoughtfully.

Listen and Ask Questions

Listen to the Presentations As your peers deliver their presentations, listen actively to interpret the messages of their anecdotes. Use these tips:

- Take notes, but keep your attention on the speakers.
- Don't write whole sentences. Instead, jot down key words that will jog your memory later.
- Notice details that affect you in a strong way.
- Listen for details the speakers emphasize, comparisons they make, and differences they point out. Notice how they end the anecdote. With what impression does it leave you?

Discuss Interpretations As a class, engage in a meaningful conversation about the anecdotes related in each presentation. Share your interpretations, and ask clarifying questions of the presenters to make sure you understand their ideas. Consider their answers thoughtfully, and build on one another's ideas. Use these sentence frames as examples to guide your questions and comments during the discussion:

SENTENCE FRAMES

I agree with that point and find it interesting. I also think ____________.

My viewpoint is a little different. What would you say about ____________________?

Yes, that's true! But I wonder about ______________________.

 TEKS

1.A. Listen actively to interpret a message and ask clarifying questions that build on others' ideas.

1.D. Engage in meaningful discourse and provide and accept constructive feedback from others.

Essential Question

What can one generation learn from another?

People of different generations may have unique ways of looking at the world. How can learning about different perspectives broaden your own views? In this section, you will choose a text about different generations to read independently. Get the most from this section by establishing a purpose for reading. Ask yourself, "What do I hope to gain from my independent reading?" Here are just a few purposes you might consider:

Read to Learn Think about the selections you have already read. What questions do you still have about the unit topic?

Read to Enjoy Read the descriptions of the texts. Which one seems most interesting and appealing to you?

Read to Form a Position Consider your thoughts and feelings about the Essential Question. Are you still undecided about some aspect of the topic?

Reading Digital Texts

Digital texts like the ones you will read in this section are electronic versions of print texts. They have a variety of characteristics:

- can be read on various devices
- text can be re-sized
- may include highlighting or other annotation tools
- may have bookmarks, audio links, and other helpful features

Independent Learning Strategies

Throughout your life, in school, in your community, and in your career, you will need to rely on yourself to learn and work on your own. Use these strategies to keep your focus as you read independently for sustained periods of time. Add ideas of your own for each category.

STRATEGY	MY ACTION PLAN
Create a schedule • Be aware of your deadlines. • Make a plan for each day's activities.	
Read with purpose • Use a variety of comprehension strategies to deepen your understanding. • Think about the text and how it adds to your knowledge.	
Take notes • Record key ideas and information. • Review your notes before sharing what you've learned.	

TEKS
4. Self-select text and read independently for a sustained period of time; **5.A.** Establish purpose for reading assigned and self-selected text; **8.F.** Analyze characteristics of multimodal and digital texts.

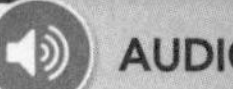
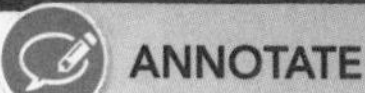

CONTENTS

Choose one selection. Selections are available online only.

POETRY COLLECTION 2: LYRIC POETRY

Lineage

Margaret Walker

Family

Grace Paley

What do you inherit from your ancestors?

OPINION PIECE

"Gotcha Day" Isn't a Cause for Celebration

Sophie Johnson

Can you yearn for a past that you barely remember?

MEDIA: DIGITAL STORYTELLING

Bridging the Generational Divide Between a Football Father and a Soccer Son

John McCormick

How do a father and son find common ground in a disagreement?

REALISTIC FICTION

Water Names

Lan Samantha Chang

An eerie tale that has been passed down for generations.

REALISTIC FICTION

An Hour With Abuelo

Judith Ortiz Cofer

A grandfather still has the ability to surprise his grandson.

SHARE YOUR INDEPENDENT LEARNING

Reflect on and evaluate the information you gained from your Independent Reading selection. Then, share what you learned with others.

Close-Read Guide

Tool Kit
Close-Read Guide and **Model Annotation**

Establish your purpose for reading. Then, read the selection through at least once. Use this page to record your close-read ideas.

Selection Title: ____________ Purpose for Reading: ____________

Minutes Read: ____________

INTERACTIVITY

Close Read the Text

Zoom in on sections you found interesting. **Annotate** what you notice. Ask yourself **questions** about the text. What can you **conclude**?

Analyze the Text

1. Think about the author's choices of literary elements, techniques, and structures. Select one and record your thoughts.

2. What characteristics of digital texts did you use as you read this selection, and in what ways? How do the characteristics of a digital text affect your reading experience? Explain.

QuickWrite

Choose a paragraph from the text that grabbed your interest. Explain the power of this passage.

Share Your Independent Learning

Essential Question

What can one generation learn from another?

When you read something independently, your understanding continues to grow as you share what you have learned with others.

NOTEBOOK

Prepare to Share

CONNECT IT One of the most important ways to respond to a text is to notice and describe your personal reactions. Think about the text you explored independently and the ways in which it connects to your own experiences.

- What similarities and differences do you see between the text and your own life? Describe your observations.
- How do you think this text connects to the Essential Question? Describe your ideas.

Learn From Your Classmates

DISCUSS IT Share your ideas about the text you explored on your own. As you talk with others in your class, take notes about new ideas that seem important.

Reflect

EXPLAIN IT Review your notes, and mark the most important insight you gained from these writing and discussion activities. Explain how this idea adds to your understanding of generations.

TEKS

6.A. Describe personal connections to a variety of sources, including self-selected texts.
6.E. Interact with sources in meaningful ways such as notetaking, annotating, freewriting, or illustrating.

Personal Narrative

ASSIGNMENT

In this unit, you read different perspectives about the ways in which people of different generations can learn from one another. You also practiced writing personal, nonfiction narratives. Now, apply what you have learned.

Write a **personal narrative** that reflects your new understanding of the Essential Question.

Essential Question

What can one generation learn from another?

Review and Evaluate Your EQ Notes

INTERACTIVITY

Review your Essential Question Notes and your QuickWrite from the beginning of the unit. Have your ideas changed?

○ Yes	○ No
Identify at least three pieces of evidence that changed your ideas about people of different generations.	Identify at least three pieces of evidence that reinforced your initial ideas.
1.	**1.**
2.	**2.**
3.	**3.**

State your ideas now:

How might you express your thinking about the ways in which we learn from people across generations in a personal narrative?

Share Your Perspective

The **Personal Narrative Checklist** will help you stay on track.

PLAN Before you write, read the Checklist and make sure you understand all the items.

DRAFT As you write, pause occasionally to make sure you're meeting the Checklist requirements.

Use New Words Refer to your Word Network to vary your word choice. Also, consider using one or more of the Academic Vocabulary terms you learned at the beginning of the unit: ***dialogue, consequence, perspective, notable, contradict.***

REVIEW AND EDIT After you have written a first draft, evaluate it against the Checklist. Make any changes needed to strengthen the structure, message, and language of your writing. Then, reread your narrative and fix any errors you find.

EQ Notes Make sure you have pulled in details from your Essential Question Notes to support your ideas.

INTERACTIVITY

PERSONAL NARRATIVE CHECKLIST

My personal narrative clearly contains...

- ○ an introduction that establishes the characters, or real people, setting, and situation.
- ○ events that show conflicts begin and develop.
- ○ a conclusion that shows how conflicts resolve, or come to an end.
- ○ a clear point of view with you as the narrator.
- ○ descriptive details and language that paints a picture for readers.
- ○ correct use of standard English conventions, including pronoun-antecedent agreement.
- ○ no punctuation or spelling errors.

TEKS

11.A. Compose literary texts such as personal narratives, fiction, and poetry, using genre characteristics and craft.

Revising and Editing

Read this draft and think about corrections the writer might make. Then, answer the questions that follow.

[1] At the oaktown park, I met Ranger Jim, a bald man with a scratchy voice. [2] He was clearly popular with visitors, but I didn't get it. [3] He was one of the older rangers—and probably forgetful—so why were they still working? [4] It seemed old-fashioned to meet for a guided hike. [5] The park's app covered everything.

[6] Well, the app gave facts, but Jim had lived adventures, and as I listened, I lived them, too. [7] I could picture Jim as a teenager like me. [8] I could feel the heat of wildfires and hear thundering waterfalls.

[9] "I see you like apps," Jim said, glancing at the phone in my hand. [10] I reddened, as I'd forgotten it in my enjoyment of his stories.

[11] "I, uh, want to develop apps of my own someday," I mumbled.

[12] "I'd be happy to share tips said Jim. [13] "After all, you were kind enough to download the app I developed."

[14] That day I learned something.

1. How should the capitalization in sentence 1 be corrected?

A Replace *oaktown park* with *Oaktown park*.

B Replace *Ranger Jim* with *Ranger jim*.

C Replace *oaktown park* with *Oaktown Park*.

D Replace *Ranger Jim* with *ranger jim*.

2. What change should be made to sentence 3 to correct the pronoun-antecedent error?

F Replace *older* with *oldest*.

G Replace *He* with *Jim*.

H Change *were they* to *was they*

J Change *were they* to *was he*.

3. What is the BEST way to combine sentences 4 and 5?

A Because it seemed old-fashioned to meet for a guided hike if the park's app covered everything.

B It seemed old-fashioned to meet for a guided hike because the park's app covered everything.

C Given the park's app, why meet for a guided hike?

D A guided hike, due to the park's app, seemed old-fashioned.

4. Which answer choice accurately corrects the punctuation of dialogue in sentence 12?

F "I'd be happy to share tips", said Jim.

G "I'd be happy to share tips" said Jim.

H "I'd be happy to share tips," said Jim.

J Make no change.

Reflect on the Unit

 NOTEBOOK

 INTERACTIVITY

RESEARCH

Reflect On the Unit Goals

Review your Unit Goals chart from the beginning of the unit. Then, complete the activity and answer the question.

1. In the Unit Goals chart, rate how well you meet each goal now.
2. In which goals were you most and least successful?

Reflect On the Texts

VOTE! Use this Selection Ballot to vote for the texts you liked the most and the least. Then, discuss the reasons for your choices.

SELECTION BALLOT

Title	Liked Most [choose one]	Liked Least [choose one]
Two Kinds *from* The Joy Luck Club		
The Case of the Disappearing Words		
Tutors Teach Seniors New High-Tech Tricks		
from Mom & Me & Mom		
Learning to Love My Mother		
Mother-Daughter Drawings		
Abuelita Magic / Mother to Son / To James		
Your Independent Reading Selection:		

Reflect On the Essential Question

Life-Lessons Guide Create an inspirational guide, using quotations from characters, authors, and people you encountered as you explored the Essential Question: **What can one generation learn from another?**

- Review the texts in the unit to locate quotations that made an impression on you. Include at least five quotations.
- For each quotation, cite the name of the character or person quoted as well as the selection title and author. Then, briefly explain how this quotation affected your ideas about the Essential Question.

Tip: As you collect quotations, make sure that your guide book represents a wide range of generations and perspectives.

 TEKS

10.D.v. Edit drafts using standard English conventions, including pronoun-antecedent agreement; **10.D.vi.** Edit drafts using standard English conventions, including subordinating conjunctions to form complex sentences and correlative conjunctions such as *either/or* and *neither/nor;* **10.D.vii.** Edit drafts using standard English conventions, including correct capitalization.

UNIT 2

Imagining the Future

PEARSON realize

Go ONLINE for all lessons

 AUDIO

 VIDEO

 NOTEBOOK

 ANNOTATE

 INTERACTIVITY

 DOWNLOAD

 RESEARCH

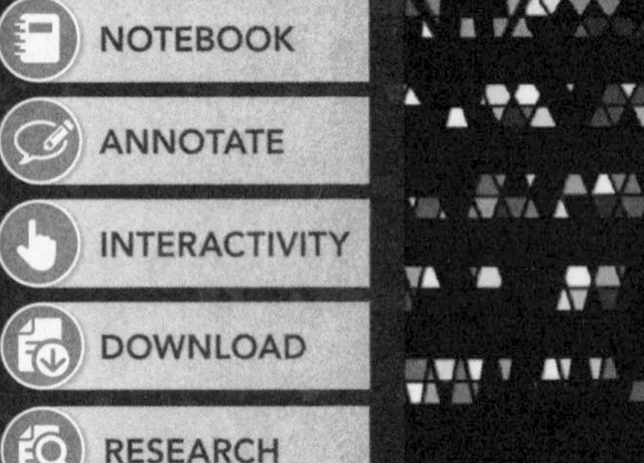

Earth Views

DISCUSS IT Why are people curious about our galaxy and what lies beyond?

Write your response here before sharing your ideas.

UNIT 2

UNIT INTRODUCTION

Essential Question

Should humanity's future lie among the stars?

MENTOR TEXT:
ARGUMENT
Leaving Main Street

 WHOLE-CLASS LEARNING

COMPARE ACROSS GENRES

SCIENCE-FICTION FANTASY

Dark They Were, and Golden-Eyed
Ray Bradbury

MEDIA: RADIO PLAY

Dark They Were, and Golden-Eyed
Ray Bradbury and Michael McDonough

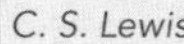

PERFORMANCE TASK

WRITING PROCESS
Write an Argument

 PEER-GROUP LEARNING

POETRY COLLECTION

Science-Fiction Cradlesong
C. S. Lewis

First Men on the Moon
J. Patrick Lewis

SCIENCE-FICTION ADVENTURE

The Last Dog
Katherine Paterson

COMPARE WITHIN GENRE

PERSUASIVE ESSAY

Mars Can Wait. Oceans Can't.
Amitai Etzioni

PERSUASIVE ESSAY

***from* Packing for Mars**
Mary Roach

PERFORMANCE TASK

SPEAKING AND LISTENING
Present an Argument

INDEPENDENT LEARNING

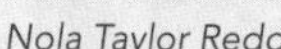

NEWS ARTICLE

Future of Space Exploration Could See Humans on Mars, Alien Planets
Nola Taylor Redd

▸ MEDIA CONNECTION
Video: 100-Year Starship

MAGAZINE ARTICLE

Danger! This Mission to Mars Could Bore You to Death!
Maggie Koerth-Baker

INTERVIEW

Neil deGrasse Tyson on the Future of U.S. Space Exploration After *Curiosity*
Neil deGrasse Tyson and Keith Wagstaff

MEDIA: VIDEO BIOGRAPHY

Ellen Ochoa: Director, Johnson Space Center
Ellen Ochoa

SHARE INDEPENDENT LEARNING

Share • Learn • Reflect

PERFORMANCE-BASED ASSESSMENT

Argumentative Essay

You will write an argumentative essay in response to the Essential Question for the unit.

UNIT REFLECTION

Goals • Texts • Essential Question

Unit Goals

Throughout this unit you will deepen your perspective about imagination and the future by reading, writing, speaking, listening, and presenting. These goals will help you succeed on the Unit Performance-Based Assessment.

SET GOALS Rate how well you meet these goals right now. You will revisit your ratings later, when you reflect on your growth during this unit.

SCALE	1	2	3	4	5
	NOT AT ALL WELL	NOT VERY WELL	SOMEWHAT WELL	VERY WELL	EXTREMELY WELL

ESSENTIAL QUESTION	Unit Introduction	Unit Reflection
I can read selections that express different points of view about imagination and the future and develop my own perspective.	1 2 3 4 5	1 2 3 4 5
READING	**Unit Introduction**	**Unit Reflection**
I can understand and use academic vocabulary words related to argument.	1 2 3 4 5	1 2 3 4 5
I can recognize elements of different genres, especially persuasive essays, informational texts, and science fiction.	1 2 3 4 5	1 2 3 4 5
I can read a selection of my choice independently and make meaningful connections to other texts.	1 2 3 4 5	1 2 3 4 5
WRITING	**Unit Introduction**	**Unit Reflection**
I can write a focused, well-organized argumentative essay.	1 2 3 4 5	1 2 3 4 5
I can complete Timed Writing tasks with confidence.	1 2 3 4 5	1 2 3 4 5
SPEAKING AND LISTENING	**Unit Introduction**	**Unit Reflection**
I can prepare and deliver a critique of a literary work or dramatic production.	1 2 3 4 5	1 2 3 4 5

TEKS

2.C. Determine the meaning and usage of grade-level academic English words derived from Greek and Latin roots such as *omni, log/logue, gen, vid/vis, phil, luc,* and *sens/sent.*

Academic Vocabulary: Argument

Many English words have roots, or key parts, that come from ancient languages, such as Latin and Greek. Learn these roots and use the words as you respond to questions and activities in this unit.

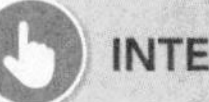

PRACTICE Academic terms are used routinely in classrooms. Build your knowledge of these words by completing the chart.

1. With a partner, **read aloud** each word, its root, and the mentor sentences.
2. **Determine** the meaning and usage of each word using the mentor sentences and a dictionary, if needed.
3. **List** at least two related words for each word.

WORD	MENTOR SENTENCES	PREDICT MEANING	RELATED WORDS
justify LATIN ROOT: ***-jus-*** "law"; "right"	1. Raymond had to *justify* his position on a controversial subject during the debate. 2. Lucy decided to *justify* her lateness by saying she was stuck in traffic.		justice; justification
dissent LATIN ROOT: ***-sent-*** "feel"	1. Robin expressed her *dissent* from the opinion of the majority of the people in the class. 2. The king used all of his power to quash political *dissent* within his country.		
certainty LATIN ROOT: ***-cert-*** "sure"	1. It was a *certainty* that everyone would want to play the popular new game. 2. The astronomers knew with *certainty* that the comet would return again.		
discredit LATIN ROOT: ***-cred-*** "believe"	1. The scientist had to *discredit* his partner's work because the correct procedure was not followed. 2. The lawyer used facts to *discredit* the testimony of the star witness.		
assumption LATIN ROOT: ***-sum-*** "take up"	1. The scientist made an *assumption* about life on Mars based on his experiments. 2. It is not wise to make an *assumption* if you do not have all the facts.		

MENTOR TEXT | ARGUMENT

This selection is an example of an **argument,** a type of nonfiction in which an author states and defends a position on a topic. This is similar to the type of writing you will develop in the Performance-Based Assessment at the end of the unit.

READ IT As you read, look at the way the writer advances the argument that people are born to explore the unknown.

Leaving Main Street

AUDIO

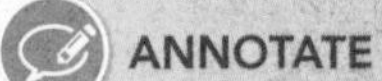
ANNOTATE

1 In July, 2015, the world watched in awe as close-up photographs of Pluto streamed back to Earth from three billion miles away. The spacecraft *New Horizons* had traveled nine years to study the dwarf planet at the edge of our solar system.

2 As a result of the mission, scientists discovered that Pluto is not just a giant ball of ice. It has a molten core, tectonic plates, and volcanic activity, just as Earth does. It may even support some form of life. The *New Horizons* mission has been hailed as a triumph of human ingenuity, and a huge leap forward for the future of space exploration.

3 Yet it almost didn't happen. The mission had to overcome some serious challenges before it could get underway—such as repeated threats to defund it.

4 There have always been naysayers who've questioned the need for space exploration. The argument goes that the United States has more important things to spend its money on, such as ending hunger and poverty.

5 Others argue that a successful space program adds to our national prestige, helps the economy, creates jobs, and improves national security. It inspires students to pursue innovative projects and careers in science and technology. At a cost of six-tenths of a percent of the federal budget, it's well worth the price: The cost of exploration is vastly outweighed by the idea of extending humankind's sphere of influence to outer space.

6 But these are not the real reasons for continuing the space program, says Michael Griffin in *Air & Space Magazine*. Griffin makes the point that people go to space for reasons that are not necessarily logical. In other words, money doesn't have much to

do with it. "When we contemplate committing large sums of money to a project, we tend to dismiss reasons that are emotional or value-driven," Griffin says. He goes on to say that Americans need the prospect of exploring space.

7 Humans explore space because it's in our genes. We're hardwired with certain built-in features that compel us in that direction. Here's how it breaks down:

8 First, there is something about the human condition that strives to be the best, or the first, at something. Our ancestors survived by outperforming others.

9 In addition, humans are by nature curious about exploring new places. Everyone remembers being a kid and wanting to see what's "over there." Humans will not tolerate boundaries; their dream is to explore what's beyond.

10 Likewise, humans have always created monuments to commemorate their great achievements so that the next generation will remember who they are and how they spent their time here. What we want to be remembered for is finding life on other worlds, maybe even for landing on Mars.

11 Finally, NASA's space program inspires competition and innovation. The Hubble Space Telescope and the robotic missions to the planets have been shining examples of what can be achieved when a project is based on goals set by scientists rather than by politicians.

12 If we stop exploring space, soon society will have forgotten what it's like to be human. It's human to wonder about things we can't see, to look for what's over the horizon. And how can we be so narrow-minded as to think we're the only ones out there? ❧

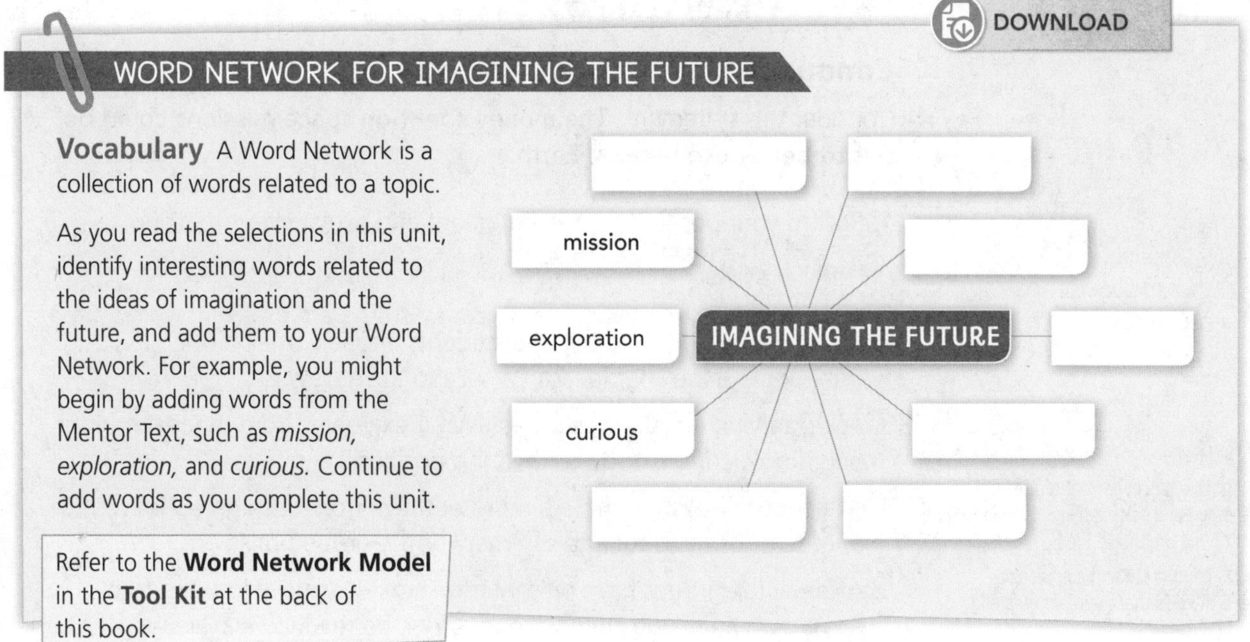

WORD NETWORK FOR IMAGINING THE FUTURE

Vocabulary A Word Network is a collection of words related to a topic.

As you read the selections in this unit, identify interesting words related to the ideas of imagination and the future, and add them to your Word Network. For example, you might begin by adding words from the Mentor Text, such as *mission, exploration,* and *curious.* Continue to add words as you complete this unit.

Refer to the **Word Network Model** in the **Tool Kit** at the back of this book.

Summary

A **summary** is a brief, complete overview of a text that maintains the meaning and logical order of ideas in the original. It should not include your personal opinions.

NOTEBOOK

WRITE IT Write a summary of "Leaving Main Street."

Launch Activity

Conduct a Four-Corner Debate

Consider this statement: **The money spent on space missions could be put to better use here on Earth.**

1. Record your position on the statement and explain your thinking.

   ◯ Strongly Agree ◯ Agree ◯ Disagree ◯ Strongly Disagree

2. Form a group with like-minded students in one corner of the classroom. Share your ideas in a collaborative way.
3. Ask clarifying questions, such as "What examples from the text or your prior knowledge led you to take this position?"
4. After your discussion, have a representative from each group present a brief two- or three-minute summary of the group's position.
5. After all the groups have presented their views, move into the four corners again. If you change your corner, be ready to explain why.

TEKS

1.A. Listen actively to interpret a message and ask clarifying questions that build on others' ideas.

6.D. Paraphrase and summarize texts in ways that maintain meaning and logical order.

QuickWrite

Consider class discussions, presentations, the video, and the Mentor Text as you think about the Essential Question.

Essential Question

Should humanity's future lie among the stars?

At the end of the unit, you will respond to the Essential Question again and see how your perspective has changed.

NOTEBOOK

WRITE IT Record your first thoughts here.

DOWNLOAD

EQ Notes Should humanity's future lie among the stars?

As you read the selections in this unit, use a chart like the one shown to record your ideas and list details from the texts that support them. Taking notes as you go will help you clarify your thinking, gather relevant information, and be ready to respond to the Essential Question.

TITLE	MY IDEAS / OBSERVATIONS	TEXT EVIDENCE / INFORMATION

Refer to the **EQ Notes Model** in the **Tool Kit** at the back of this book.

Essential Question

Should humanity's future lie among the stars?

Some people gaze up at a starry sky and wonder at its beauty. Some people look up at the same sky and imagine who or what is up there. You will work with your whole class to explore different perspectives on imagining the future.

VIDEO

INTERACTIVITY

Whole-Class Learning Strategies

Throughout your life, in school, in your community, and in your career, you will continue to learn and work in large-group environments.

Review these strategies and the actions you can take to practice them as you work with your whole class. Add ideas of your own for each category. Get ready to use these strategies during Whole-Class Learning.

STRATEGY	MY ACTION PLAN
Listen actively • Put away personal items to avoid becoming distracted. • Try to hear the speaker's full message before planning your own response.	
Demonstrate respect • Show up on time and make sure you are prepared for class. • Avoid side conversations while in class.	
Make personal connections • Recognize that literature explores human experience—the details may differ from your own life, but the emotions it expresses are universal. • Actively look for ways in which your personal experiences help you find meaning in a text. • Consider how your own experiences help you understand characters' actions and reactions.	

CONTENTS

COMPARE ACROSS GENRES

DARK THEY WERE, AND GOLDEN-EYED (short story)

Fiction and Drama

A **science-fiction fantasy** is a work of fiction that combines futuristic or science-based elements with magical ones. A **radio-play adaptation** is an audio drama that is based on an existing story.

DARK THEY WERE, AND GOLDEN-EYED (radio play)

SCIENCE-FICTION FANTASY

Author's Purpose

- to tell an imaginative story

Characteristics

- settings that feature imaginary elements (other worlds, advanced technology, magic that is real)
- characters that may be human or non-human
- a narrator, or voice that tells the story
- conflicts, or problems, that are often caused by the setting
- a theme, or insight about life

Structure

- Exposition, or explanation, as well as dialogue and description convey the story's setting and plot.

RADIO PLAY ADAPTATION

Author's Purpose

- to retell an original work of fiction as an audio drama

Characteristics

- often part of a radio show or podcast
- settings, characters, conflicts, events, language, theme, and plot based on those of an original story
- announcer or narrator
- background music
- sound effects

Structure

- Dialogue, or characters' spoken words, convey the story's setting and plot.

Genre / Text Elements

Setting The **setting** of a story is the time and place in which it occurs. Science-fiction usually features imaginary settings, such as the future. To achieve their purpose of making alien settings clear and vivid, science-fiction writers often use **figurative language,** such as personification, metaphors, and similes. This is language that works imaginatively rather than literally.

- **Personification** presents nonhuman things as though they have human qualities: *The forest is lonely without the owls.*
- **Metaphors** imply a similarity between two unlike things: *The suns of yellow flowers blaze in the vase.*
- **Similes** use the words "like" or "as" to state a similarity between two unlike things: *The flowers are like blazing suns.*

TIP: In the examples, personification gives human feelings to the forest. The metaphor suggests and the simile states a similarity between suns and flowers.

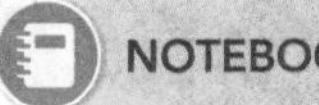

PRACTICE Identify items 1–4 as either personification, metaphor, or simile. Explain how you made your determination. Then, answer question 5.

1. The mirror of the lake reflects the moons.

2. The storm won its argument with the Martian colony.

3. Gravity held on, unwilling to let the spaceship go.

4. The sea is like a sheet of silver covering the planet.

5. Given these examples, describe the purpose you think figurative language might serve in a science-fiction story.

TEKS

8.A. Demonstrate knowledge of literary genres such as realistic fiction, adventure stories, historical fiction, mysteries, humor, myths, fantasy, and science fiction.

9.D. Describe how the author's use of figurative language such as metaphor and personification achieves specific purposes.

DARK THEY WERE, AND GOLDEN-EYED
(short story)

Compare Fiction and Drama

In this lesson, you will read the short story "Dark They Were, and Golden-Eyed" and listen to a radio play performance of it. You will then compare the short story to the radio play.

DARK THEY WERE, AND GOLDEN-EYED
(radio play)

About the Author

As a boy, **Ray Bradbury** (1920–2012) loved magicians, circuses, and science-fiction stories. He began writing at the age of 12 and went on to become one of the most celebrated writers of science fiction and fantasy. *The Martian Chronicles*, a collection of Bradbury's stories about Earth's colonization of Mars, was published in 1950 and is considered a classic today.

Dark They Were, and Golden-Eyed

Concept Vocabulary

INTERACTIVITY

You will encounter the following words as you read the short story. Before reading, note how familiar you are with each word. Then, rank the words in order from most familiar (1) to least familiar (6).

WORD	YOUR RANKING
submerged	
forlorn	
canals	
immense	
atmosphere	
mosaic	

Comprehension Strategy

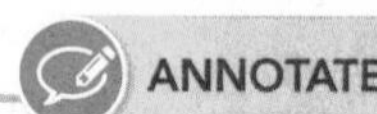
ANNOTATE

Make Inferences

Inferences are educated guesses you make based on evidence in a story. Making inferences as you read will add to your understanding and enjoyment. To make inferences, notice clues in a text, and think about what they suggest about characters or events.

EXAMPLE

This is an inference you might make as you read this story:

In paragraph 82, Mr. Bittering thinks, "Aren't you frightened? Aren't you afraid?"
Inference: No one else is upset. Mr. Bittering may be the only one who senses something is wrong.

PRACTICE As you read the story, note inferences in the open space next to the text. Mark evidence that supports each one.

TEKS
5.F. Make inferences and use evidence to support understanding.

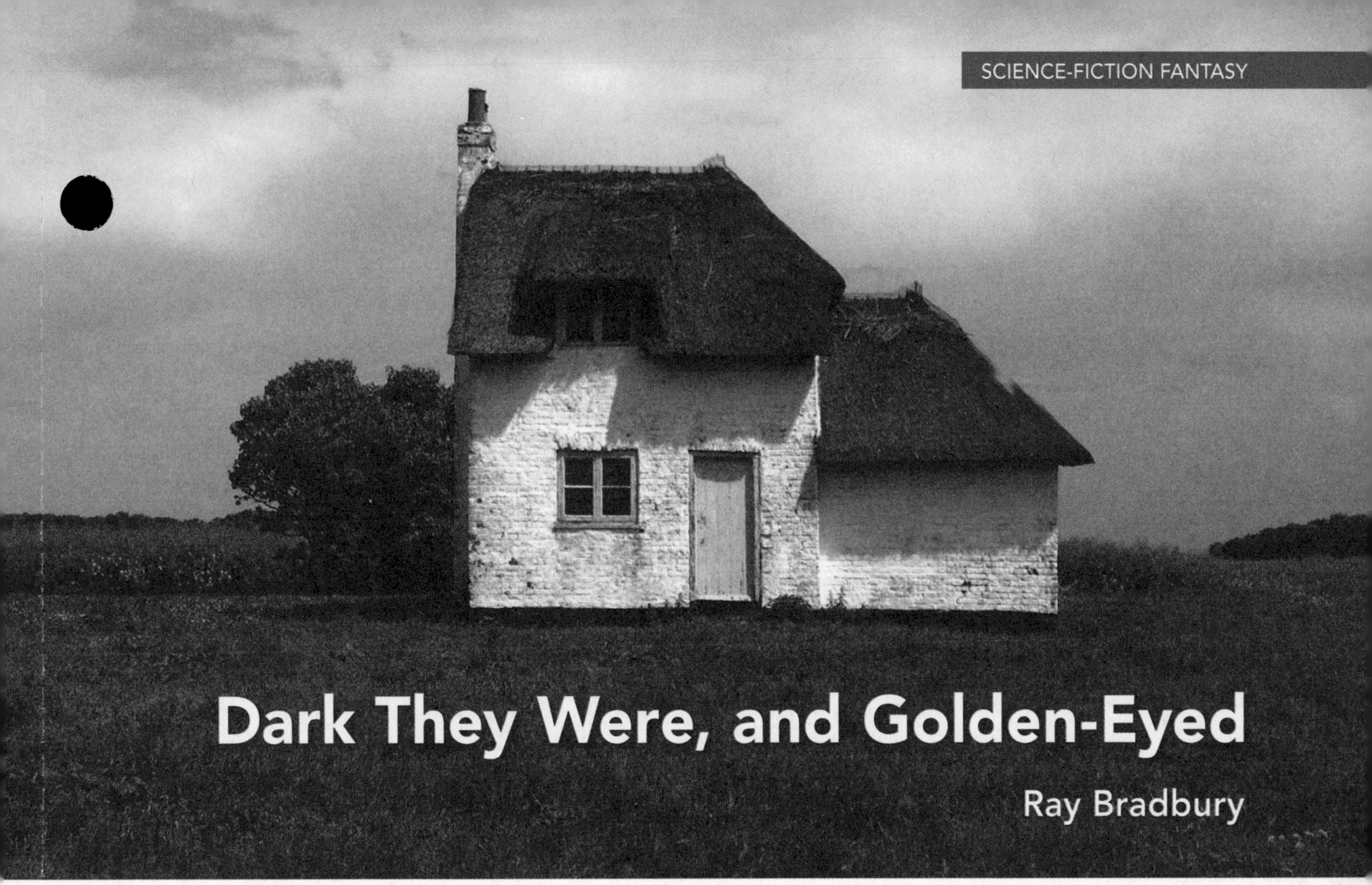

Dark They Were, and Golden-Eyed

Ray Bradbury

BACKGROUND

The astronomer Carl Sagan once wrote, "Mars has become a kind of mythic arena onto which we have projected our earthly hopes and fears." People have always been fascinated by the possibility of alien life on Mars. In this story, author Ray Bradbury does away with hard science, choosing instead to explore the aura of mystery that has always surrounded the Red Planet.

AUDIO

ANNOTATE

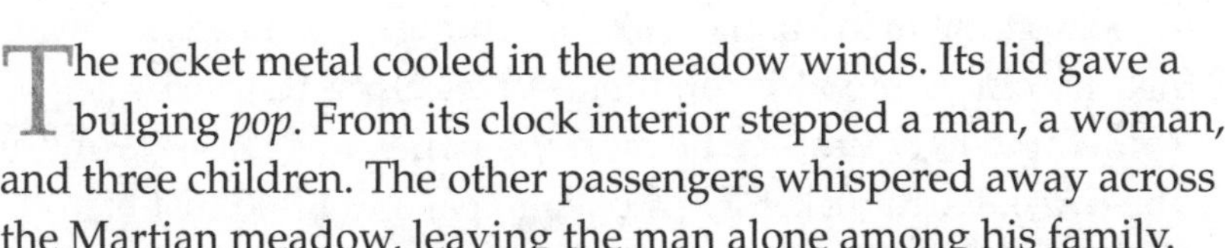

1 The rocket metal cooled in the meadow winds. Its lid gave a bulging *pop*. From its clock interior stepped a man, a woman, and three children. The other passengers whispered away across the Martian meadow, leaving the man alone among his family.

2 The man felt his hair flutter and the tissues of his body draw tight as if he were standing at the center of a vacuum. His wife, before him, seemed almost to whirl away in smoke. The children, small seeds, might at any instant be sown to all the Martian climes.

3 The children looked up at him, as people look to the sun to tell what time of their life it is. His face was cold.

4 "What's wrong?" asked his wife.

5 "Let's get back on the rocket."

6 "Go back to Earth?"

7 "Yes! Listen!"

8 The wind blew as if to flake away their identities. At any moment the Martian air might draw his soul from him, as marrow

CLOSE READ

ANNOTATE: In paragraph 2, mark the things that are being compared.

QUESTION: What is unusual about these comparisons?

CONCLUDE: What mood or overall impression has Bradbury created with these comparisons?

submerged (suhb MURJD) *adj.* completely covered with a liquid

comes from a white bone. He felt **submerged** in a chemical that could dissolve his intellect and burn away his past.

9 They looked at Martian hills that time had worn with a crushing pressure of years. They saw the old cities, lost in their meadows, lying like children's delicate bones among the blowing lakes of grass.

10 "Chin up, Harry," said his wife. "It's too late. We've come over sixty million miles."

11 The children with their yellow hair hollered at the deep dome of Martian sky. There was no answer but the racing hiss of wind through the stiff grass.

12 He picked up the luggage in his cold hands. "Here we go," he said—a man standing on the edge of a sea, ready to wade in and be drowned.

13 They walked into town.

14 Their name was Bittering. Harry and his wife Cora; Dan, Laura, and David. They built a small white cottage and ate good breakfasts there, but the fear was never gone. It lay with Mr. Bittering and Mrs. Bittering, a third unbidden partner at every midnight talk, at every dawn awakening.

15 "I feel like a salt crystal," he said, "in a mountain stream, being washed away. We don't belong here. We're Earth people. This is Mars. It was meant for Martians. For heaven's sake, Cora, let's buy tickets for home!"

16 But she only shook her head. "One day the atom bomb will fix Earth. Then we'll be safe here."

17 "Safe and insane!"

18 *Tick-tock, seven o'clock* sang the voice-clock; *time to get up*. And they did.

19 Something made him check everything each morning—warm hearth, potted blood-geraniums—precisely as if he expected something to be amiss. The morning paper was toast-warm from the 6 A.M. Earth rocket. He broke its seal and tilted it at his breakfast place. He forced himself to be convivial.[1]

20 "Colonial days all over again," he declared. "Why, in ten years there'll be a million Earthmen on Mars. Big cities, everything! They said we'd fail. Said the Martians would resent our invasion. But did we find any Martians? Not a living soul! Oh, we found their empty cities, but no one in them. Right?"

21 A river of wind submerged the house. When the windows ceased rattling Mr. Bittering swallowed and looked at the children.

22 "I don't know," said David. "Maybe there're Martians around we don't see. Sometimes nights I think I hear 'em. I hear the wind. The sand hits my window. I get scared. And I see those towns way

1. **convivial** (kuhn VIHV ee uhl) *adj.* social and friendly.

up in the mountains where the Martians lived a long time ago. And I think I see things moving around those towns, Papa. And I wonder if those Martians *mind* us living here. I wonder if they won't do something to us for coming here."

23 "Nonsense!" Mr. Bittering looked out the windows. "We're clean, decent people." He looked at his children. "All dead cities have some kind of ghosts in them. Memories, I mean." He stared at the hills. "You see a staircase and you wonder what Martians looked like climbing it. You see Martian paintings and you wonder what the painter was like. You make a little ghost in your mind, a memory. It's quite natural. Imagination." He stopped. "You haven't been prowling up in those ruins, have you?"

24 "No, Papa." David looked at his shoes.

25 "See that you stay away from them. Pass the jam."

26 "Just the same," said little David, "I bet something happens. "

27 Something happened that afternoon.

28 Laura stumbled through the settlement, crying. She dashed blindly onto the porch.

29 "Mother, Father—the war, Earth!" she sobbed. "A radio flash just came. Atom bombs hit New York! All the space rockets blown up. No more rockets to Mars, ever!"

30 "Oh, Harry!" The mother held onto her husband and daughter.

31 "Are you sure, Laura?" asked the father quietly.

32 Laura wept. "We're stranded on Mars, forever and ever!"

33 For a long time there was only the sound of the wind in the late afternoon.

34 Alone, thought Bittering. Only a thousand of us here. No way back. No way. No way. Sweat poured from his face and his hands and his body; he was drenched in the hotness of his fear. He wanted to strike Laura, cry, "No, you're lying! The rockets will come back!" Instead, he stroked Laura's head against him and said, "The rockets will get through someday."

35 "Father, what will we do?"

36 "Go about our business, of course. Raise crops and children. Wait. Keep things going until the war ends and the rockets come again."

37 The two boys stepped out onto the porch.

38 "Children," he said, sitting there, looking beyond them, "I've something to tell you."

39 "We know," they said.

40 In the following days, Bittering wandered often through the garden to stand alone in his fear. As long as the rockets had spun a silver web across space, he had been able to accept Mars. For he had always told himself: Tomorrow, if I want, I can buy a ticket and go back to Earth.

CLOSE READ

ANNOTATE: Mark details in the beginning of paragraph 34 that describe Bittering's inner thoughts.

QUESTION: Why are these thoughts expressed in incomplete sentences, with a lot of repetition?

CONCLUDE: What does this use of language help reveal about Bittering's emotional state?

CLOSE READ

ANNOTATE: Mark examples of descriptive language in paragraph 41.

QUESTION: What idea about Mars does this use of language suggest?

CONCLUDE: How does this passage build suspense?

41 But now: The web gone, the rockets lying in jigsaw heaps of molten girder and unsnaked wire. Earth people left to the strangeness of Mars, the cinnamon dusts and wine airs, to be baked like gingerbread shapes in Martian summers, put into harvested storage by Martian winters. What would happen to him, the others? This was the moment Mars had waited for. Now it would eat them.

42 He got down on his knees in the flower bed, a spade in his nervous hands. Work, he thought, work and forget.

43 He glanced up from the garden to the Martian mountains. He thought of the proud old Martian names that had once been on those peaks. Earthmen, dropping from the sky, had gazed upon hills, rivers, Martian seats left nameless in spite of names. Once Martians had built cities, named cities; climbed mountains, named mountains; sailed seas, named seas. Mountains melted, seas drained, cities tumbled. In spite of this, the Earthmen had felt a silent guilt at putting new names to these ancient hills and valleys.

44 Nevertheless, man lives by symbol and label. The names were given.

45 Mr. Bittering felt very alone in his garden under the Martian sun, anachronism[2] bent here, planting Earth flowers in a wild soil.

46 Think. Keep thinking. Different things. Keep your mind free of Earth, the atom war, the lost rockets.

47 He perspired. He glanced about. No one watching. He removed his tie. Pretty bold, he thought. First your coat off, now your tie. He hung it neatly on a peach tree he had imported as a sapling from Massachusetts.

48 He returned to his philosophy of names and mountains. The Earthmen had changed names. Now there were Hormel Valleys, Roosevelt Seas, Ford Hills, Vanderbilt Plateaus, Rockefeller Rivers,[3] on Mars. It wasn't right. The American settlers had shown wisdom, using old Indian prairie names: Wisconsin, Minnesota, Idaho, Ohio, Utah, Milwaukee, Waukegan, Osseo. The old names, the old meanings.

49 Staring at the mountains wildly, he thought: Are you up there? All the dead ones, you Martians? Well, here we are, alone, cut off! Come down, move us out! We're helpless!

50 The wind blew a shower of peach blossoms.

51 He put out his sun-browned hand and gave a small cry. He touched the blossoms and picked them up. He turned them, he touched them again and again. Then he shouted for his wife.

52 "Cora!"

53 She appeared at a window. He ran to her.

2. **anachronism** (uh NA kruh nih zuhm) *n.* something that seems to belong to the past instead of the present.

3. **Hormel Valleys . . . Rockefeller Rivers** the colonists have named places on Mars after well-known families from mid-twentieth-century America.

54 "Cora, these blossoms!"

55 She handled them.

56 "Do you see? They're different. They've changed! They're not peach blossoms any more!"

57 "Look all right to me," she said.

58 "They're not. They're wrong! I can't tell how. An extra petal, a leaf, something, the color, the smell!"

59 The children ran out in time to see their father hurrying about the garden, pulling up radishes, onions, and carrots from their beds.

60 "Cora, come look!"

61 They handled the onions, the radishes, the carrots among them.

62 "Do they look like carrots?"

63 "Yes . . . no." She hesitated. "I don't know."

64 "They're changed."

65 "Perhaps."

66 "You know they have! Onions but not onions, carrots but not carrots. Taste: the same but different. Smell: not like it used to be." He felt his heart pounding, and he was afraid. He dug his fingers into the earth. "Cora, what's happening? What is it? We've got to get away from this." He ran across the garden. Each tree felt his touch. "The roses. The roses. They're turning green!"

67 And they stood looking at the green roses.

68 And two days later Dan came running. "Come see the cow. I was milking her and I saw it. Come on!"

69 They stood in the shed and looked at their one cow.

70 It was growing a third horn.

71 And the lawn in front of their house very quietly and slowly was coloring itself like spring violets. Seed from Earth but growing up a soft purple.

72 "We must get away," said Bittering. "We'll eat this stuff and then we'll change—who knows to what? I can't let it happen. There's only one thing to do. Burn this food!"

73 "It's not poisoned."

74 "But it is. Subtly, very subtly. A little bit. A very little bit. We mustn't touch it."

75 He looked with dismay at their house. "Even the house. The wind's done something to it. The air's burned it. The fog at night. The boards, all warped out of shape. It's not an Earthman's house any more."

76 "Oh, your imagination!"

77 He put on his coat and tie. "I'm going into town. We've got to do something now. I'll be back."

78 "Wait, Harry!" his wife cried.

79 But he was gone.

80 In town, on the shadowy step of the grocery store, the men sat with their hands on their knees, conversing with great leisure and ease.

81 Mr. Bittering wanted to fire a pistol in the air.

82 What are you doing, you fools! he thought. Sitting here! You've heard the news—we're stranded on this planet. Well, move! Aren't you frightened? Aren't you afraid? What are you going to do?

83 "Hello, Harry," said everyone.

84 "Look," he said to them. "You did hear the news, the other day, didn't you?"

85 They nodded and laughed. "Sure. Sure, Harry."

86 "What are you going to do about it?"

87 "Do, Harry, do? What *can* we do?"

88 "Build a rocket, that's what!"

89 "A rocket, Harry? To go back to all that trouble? Oh, Harry!"

90 "But you *must* want to go back. Have you noticed the peach blossoms, the onions, the grass?"

91 "Why, yes, Harry, seems we did," said one of the men.

92 "Doesn't it scare you?"

93 "Can't recall that it did much, Harry."

94 "Idiots!"

95 "Now, Harry."

96 Bittering wanted to cry. "You've got to work with me. If we stay here, we'll all change. The air. Don't you smell it? Something in the air. A Martian virus, maybe; some seed, or a pollen. Listen to me!"

97 They stared at him.

CLOSE READ

ANNOTATE: Mark details in paragraphs 83–95 that indicate disagreement between Bittering and the other men.

QUESTION: Why might Bradbury have chosen to build conflict through the use of dialogue?

CONCLUDE: Would this passage be as effective if it had been written as description rather than dialogue? Explain.

98 "Sam," he said to one of them.

99 "Yes, Harry?"

100 "Will you help me build a rocket?"

101 "Harry, I got a whole load of metal and some blueprints. You want to work in my metal shop on a rocket, you're welcome. I'll sell you that metal for five hundred dollars. You should be able to construct a right pretty rocket, if you work alone, in about thirty years."

102 Everyone laughed.

103 "Don't laugh."

104 Sam looked at him with quiet good humor.

105 "Sam," Bittering said. "Your eyes—"

106 "What about them, Harry?"

107 "Didn't they used to be gray?"

108 "Well now, I don't remember."

109 "They were, weren't they?"

110 "Why do you ask, Harry?"

111 "Because now they're kind of yellow-colored."

112 "Is that so, Harry?" Sam said, casually.

113 "And you're taller and thinner—"

114 "You might be right, Harry."

115 "Sam, you shouldn't have yellow eyes."

116 "Harry, what color eyes have *you* got?" Sam said.

117 "My eyes? They're blue, of course."

118 "Here you are, Harry." Sam handed him a pocket mirror. "Take a look at yourself."

119 Mr. Bittering hesitated, and then raised the mirror to his face.

120 There were little, very dim flecks of new gold captured in the blue of his eyes.

121 "Now look what you've done," said Sam a moment later. "You've broken my mirror."

122 Harry Bittering moved into the metal shop and began to build the rocket. Men stood in the open door and talked and joked without raising their voices. Once in a while they gave him a hand on lifting something. But mostly they just idled and watched him with their yellowing eyes.

123 "It's suppertime, Harry," they said.

124 His wife appeared with his supper in a wicker basket.

125 "I won't touch it," he said. "I'll eat only food from our Deepfreeze. Food that came from Earth. Nothing from our garden."

126 His wife stood watching him. "You can't build a rocket."

127 "I worked in a shop once, when I was twenty. I know metal. Once I get it started, the others will help," he said, not looking at her, laying out the blueprints.

128 "Harry, Harry," she said, helplessly.

129 "We've got to get away, Cora. We've *got* to!"

130 The nights were full of wind that blew down the empty moonlit sea meadows past the little white chess cities lying for their twelve-thousandth year in the shallows. In the Earthmen's settlement, the Bittering house shook with a feeling of change.

131 Lying abed, Mr. Bittering felt his bones shifted, shaped, melted like gold. His wife, lying beside him, was dark from many sunny afternoons. Dark she was, and golden-eyed, burnt almost black by the sun, sleeping, and the children metallic in their beds, and the wind roaring **forlorn** and changing through the old peach trees, the violet grass, shaking out green rose petals.

forlorn (fawr LAWRN) *adj.* abandoned or deserted

132 The fear would not be stopped. It had his throat and heart. It dripped in a wetness of the arm and the temple and the trembling palm.

133 A green star rose in the east.

134 A strange word emerged from Mr. Bittering's lips.

135 "*Iorrt. Iorrt.*" He repeated it.

136 It was a Martian word. He knew no Martian.

137 In the middle of the night he arose and dialed a call through to Simpson, the archaeologist.

138 "Simpson, what does the word *Iorrt* mean?"

139 "Why that's the old Martian word for our planet Earth. Why?"

140 "No special reason."

141 The telephone slipped from his hand.

142 "Hello, hello, hello, hello," it kept saying while he sat gazing out at the green star. "Bittering? Harry, are you there?"

143 The days were full of metal sound. He laid the frame of the rocket with the reluctant help of three indifferent men. He grew very tired in an hour or so and had to sit down.

144 "The altitude," laughed a man.

145 "Are you *eating*, Harry?" asked another.

146 "I'm eating," he said, angrily.

147 "From your Deepfreeze?"

148 "Yes!"

149 "You're getting thinner, Harry."

150 "I'm not."

151 "And taller."

152 "Liar!"

153 His wife took him aside a few days later. "Harry, I've used up all the food in the Deepfreeze. There's nothing left. I'll have to make sandwiches using food grown on Mars."

154 He sat down heavily.

155 "You must eat," she said. "You're weak."

156 "Yes," he said.

CLOSE READ

ANNOTATE: Mark the Martian word Mr. Bittering says in paragraph 135.

QUESTION: Why does the author have Bittering speak Martian at this point in the story?

CONCLUDE: In what way is this event significant?

157 He took a sandwich, opened it, looked at it, and began to nibble at it.

158 "And take the rest of the day off," she said. "It's hot. The children want to swim in the **canals** and hike. Please come along."

159 "I can't waste time. This is a crisis!"

160 "Just for an hour," she urged. "A swim'll do you good."

161 He rose, sweating. "All right, all right. Leave me alone. I'll come."

162 "Good for you, Harry."

163 The sun was hot, the day quiet. There was only an **immense** staring burn upon the land. They moved along the canal, the father, the mother, the racing children in their swimsuits. They stopped and ate meat sandwiches. He saw their skin baking brown. And he saw the yellow eyes of his wife and his children, their eyes that were never yellow before. A few tremblings shook him, but were carried off in waves of pleasant heat as he lay in the sun. He was too tired to be afraid.

164 "Cora, how long have your eyes been yellow?"

165 She was bewildered. "Always, I guess."

166 "They didn't change from brown in the last three months?"

167 She bit her lips. "No. Why do you ask?"

canals (kuh NALZ) *n.* artificial waterways for transportation or irrigation

immense (ih MEHNS) *adj.* very large

168 "Never mind."

169 They sat there.

170 "The children's eyes," he said. "They're yellow, too."

171 "Sometimes growing children's eyes change color."

172 "Maybe *we're* children, too. At least to Mars. That's a thought." He laughed. "Think I'll swim."

173 They leaped into the canal water, and he let himself sink down and down to the bottom like a golden statue and lie there in green silence. All was water-quiet and deep, all was peace. He felt the steady, slow current drift him easily.

174 If I lie here long enough, he thought, the water will work and eat away my flesh until the bones show like coral. Just my skeleton left. And then the water can build on that skeleton—green things, deep water things, red things, yellow things. Change. Change. Slow, deep, silent change. And isn't that what it is up *there*?

175 He saw the sky submerged above him, the sun made Martian by **atmosphere** and time and space.

atmosphere (AT muhs fihr) *n.* the gas surrounding the earth; the air

176 Up there, a big river, he thought, a Martian river; all of us lying deep in it, in our pebble houses, in our sunken boulder houses, like crayfish hidden, and the water washing away our old bodies and lengthening the bones and—

177 He let himself drift up through the soft light.

178 Dan sat on the edge of the canal, regarding his father seriously.

179 "*Utha*," he said.

180 "What?" asked his father.

181 The boy smiled. "You know. *Utha's* the Martian word for 'father.'"

182 "Where did you learn it?"

183 "I don't know. Around. *Utha!*"

184 "What do you want?"

185 The boy hesitated. "I—I want to change my name."

186 "Change it?"

187 "Yes."

188 His mother swam over. "What's wrong with Dan for a name?"

189 Dan fidgeted. "The other day you called Dan, Dan, Dan. I didn't even hear. I said to myself, That's not my name. I've a new name I want to use."

190 Mr. Bittering held to the side of the canal, his body cold and his heart pounding slowly. "What is this new name?"

191 "Linnl. Isn't that a good name? Can I use it? Can't I, please?"

192 Mr. Bittering put his hand to his head. He thought of the silly rocket, himself working alone, himself alone even among his family, so alone.

193 He heard his wife say, "Why not?"

194 He heard himself say, "Yes, you can use it."

195 "Yaaa!" screamed the boy. "I'm Linnl, Linnl!"

196 Racing down the meadowlands, he danced and shouted.

197 Mr. Bittering looked at his wife. "Why did we do that?"

198 "I don't know," she said. "It just seemed like a good idea."

199 They walked into the hills. They strolled on old **mosaic** paths, beside still pumping fountains. The paths were covered with a thin film of cool water all summer long. You kept your bare feet cool all the day, splashing as in a creek, wading.

200 They came to a small deserted Martian villa with a good view of the valley. It was on top of a hill. Blue marble halls, large murals, a swimming pool. It was refreshing in this hot summertime. The Martians hadn't believed in large cities.

201 "How nice," said Mrs. Bittering, "if we could move up here to this villa for the summer."

202 "Come on," he said. "We're going back to town. There's work to be done on the rocket."

203 But as he worked that night, the thought of the cool blue marble villa entered his mind. As the hours passed, the rocket seemed less important.

204 In the flow of days and weeks, the rocket receded and dwindled. The old fever was gone. It frightened him to think he had let it slip this way. But somehow the heat, the air, the working conditions—

205 He heard the men murmuring on the porch of his metal shop.

206 "Everyone's going. You heard?"

207 "All going. That's right."

208 Bittering came out. "Going where?" He saw a couple of trucks, loaded with children and furniture, drive down the dusty street.

209 "Up to the villas," said the man.

210 "Yeah, Harry. I'm going. So is Sam. Aren't you Sam?"

211 "That's right, Harry. What about you?"

212 "I've got work to do here. "

213 "Work! You can finish that rocket in the autumn, when it's cooler."

214 He took a breath. "I got the frame all set up."

215 "In the autumn is better." Their voices were lazy in the heat.

216 "Got to work," he said.

217 "Autumn," they reasoned. And they sounded so sensible, so right.

218 "Autumn would be best," he thought. "Plenty of time, then."

219 No! cried part of himself, deep down, put away, locked tight, suffocating. No! No!

220 "In the autumn," he said.

221 "Come on, Harry," they all said.

222 "Yes," he said, feeling his flesh melt in the hot liquid air. "Yes, in the autumn. I'll begin work again then."

mosaic (moh ZAY ihk) *adj.* made of many small pieces of colored glass or stone

CLOSE READ

ANNOTATE: Mark the words or ideas that are repeated in paragraphs 212–222.

QUESTION: Why are these words or ideas repeated so often? What is happening to Bittering as the discussion progresses?

CONCLUDE: What important change has occurred as Bittering echoes the words of others?

223 "I got a villa near the Tirra Canal," said someone.

224 "You mean the Roosevelt Canal, don't you?"

225 "Tirra. The old Martian name."

226 "But on the map—"

227 "Forget the map. It's Tirra now. Now I found a place in the Pillan Mountains—"

228 "You mean the Rockefeller Range," said Bittering.

229 "I mean the Pillan Mountains," said Sam.

230 "Yes," said Bittering, buried in the hot, swarming air. "The Pillan Mountains."

231 Everyone worked at loading the truck in the hot, still afternoon of the next day.

232 Laura, Dan, and David carried packages. Or, as they preferred to be known, Ttil, Linnl, and Werr carried packages.

233 The furniture was abandoned in the little white cottage.

234 "It looked just fine in Boston," said the mother. "And here in the cottage. But up at the villa? No. We'll get it when we come back in the autumn."

235 Bittering himself was quiet.

236 "I've some ideas on furniture for the villa," he said after a time. "Big, lazy furniture."

237 "What about your encyclopedia? You're taking it along, surely?"

238 Mr. Bittering glanced away. "I'll come and get it next week."

239 They turned to their daughter. "What about your New York dresses?"

240 The bewildered girl stared. "Why, I don't want them any more."

241 They shut off the gas, the water, they locked the doors and walked away. Father peered into the truck.

242 "Gosh, we're not taking much," he said. "Considering all we brought to Mars, this is only a handful!"

243 He started the truck.

244 Looking at the small white cottage for a long moment, he was filled with a desire to rush to it, touch it, say good-bye to it, for he felt as if he were going away on a long journey, leaving something to which he could never quite return, never understand again.

245 Just then Sam and his family drove by in another truck.

246 "Hi, Bittering! Here we go!"

247 The truck swung down the ancient highway out of town. There were sixty others traveling in the same direction. The town filled with a silent, heavy dust from their passage. The canal waters lay blue in the sun, and a quiet wind moved in the strange trees.

248 "Good-bye, town!" said Mr. Bittering.

249 "Good-bye, good-bye," said the family, waving to it.

250 They did not look back again.

251 Summer burned the canals dry. Summer moved like flame upon the meadows. In the empty Earth settlement, the painted houses flaked and peeled. Rubber tires upon which children had swung in back yards hung suspended like stopped clock pendulums in the blazing air.

252 At the metal shop, the rocket frame began to rust.

253 In the quiet autumn Mr. Bittering stood, very dark now, very golden-eyed, upon the slope above his villa, looking at the valley.

254 "It's time to go back," said Cora.

255 "Yes, but we're not going," he said quietly. "There's nothing there any more."

256 "Your books," she said. "Your fine clothes.

257 "Your *Illes* and your fine *ior uele rre*," she said.

258 "The town's empty. No one's going back," he said. "There's no reason to, none at all."

259 The daughter wove tapestries and the sons played songs on ancient flutes and pipes, their laughter echoing in the marble villa.

260 Mr. Bittering gazed at the Earth settlement far away in the low valley. "Such odd, such ridiculous houses the Earth people built."

261 "They didn't know any better," his wife mused. "Such ugly people. I'm glad they've gone."

262 They both looked at each other, startled by all they had just finished saying. They laughed.

263 "Where did they go?" he wondered. He glanced at his wife. She was golden and slender as his daughter. She looked at him, and he seemed almost as young as their eldest son.

264 "I don't know," she said.

265 "We'll go back to town maybe next year, or the year after, or the year after that," he said, calmly. "Now—I'm warm. How about taking a swim?"

266 They turned their backs to the valley. Arm in arm they walked silently down a path of clear-running spring water.

* * *

267 Five years later a rocket fell out of the sky. It lay steaming in the valley. Men leaped out of it, shouting.

268 "We won the war on Earth! We're here to rescue you! Hey!"

269 But the American-built town of cottages, peach trees, and theaters was silent. They found a flimsy rocket frame rusting in an empty shop.

270 The rocket men searched the hills. The captain established headquarters in an abandoned bar. His lieutenant came back to report.

271 "The town's empty, but we found native life in the hills, sir. Dark people. Yellow eyes. Martians. Very friendly. We talked a bit,

CLOSE READ

ANNOTATE: Mark details in paragraphs 269–278 that reveal the findings of the rescue mission from Earth.

QUESTION: Why has Bradbury chosen to include this scene? What clues to the colonists' fate are hinted at?

CONCLUDE: Does this lingering mystery improve or weaken the story? Explain.

not much. They learn English fast. I'm sure our relations will be most friendly with them, sir."

272 "Dark, eh?" mused the captain. "How many?"

273 "Six, eight hundred, I'd say, living in those marble ruins in the hills, sir. Tall, healthy. Beautiful women."

274 "Did they tell you what became of the men and women who built this Earth settlement, Lieutenant?"

275 "They hadn't the foggiest notion of what happened to this town or its people."

276 "Strange. You think those Martians killed them?"

277 "They look surprisingly peaceful. Chances are a plague did this town in, sir."

278 "Perhaps. I suppose this is one of those mysteries we'll never solve. One of those mysteries you read about."

279 The captain looked at the room, the dusty windows, the blue mountains rising beyond, the canals moving in the light, and he heard the soft wind in the air. He shivered. Then, recovering, he tapped a large fresh map he had thumbtacked to the top of an empty table.

280 "Lots to be done, Lieutenant." His voice droned on and quietly on as the sun sank behind the blue hills. "New settlements. Mining sites, minerals to be looked for. Bacteriological specimens taken. The work, all the work. And the old records were lost. We'll have a job of remapping to do, renaming the mountains and rivers and such. Calls for a little imagination.

281 "What do you think of naming those mountains the Lincoln Mountains, this canal the Washington Canal, those hills—we can name those hills for you, Lieutenant. Diplomacy. And you, for a favor, might name a town for me. Polishing the apple. And why not make this the Einstein Valley, and farther over . . . are you *listening*, Lieutenant?"

282 The lieutenant snapped his gaze from the blue color and the quiet mist of the hills far beyond the town.

283 "What? Oh, *yes*, sir!" ❧

NOTEBOOK

Response

1. **Personal Connections** Describe your initial reaction to this story. For example, did anything surprise you? Did any part of it disturb you? Explain your responses.

Answer the questions in your notebook. Use text evidence to support your responses.

Comprehension

2. **Reading Check** **(a)** What causes the people from Earth to become stranded on Mars? **(b)** What change does Harry first notice in the world around him? **(c)** What does the rescue crew find when they arrive on Mars after five years?

3. **Strategy: Make Inferences** **(a)** Note two inferences you made as you read the story. What text evidence supports each inference? **(b)** Did this strategy help you better understand the characters and events? Explain.

Analysis

4. **(a)** After the Bitterings arrive on Mars, what disaster happens on Earth? **(b) Analyze Cause and Effect** How does this disaster affect the Bitterings?

5. **Interpret** When Mr. Bittering says his first Martian word, he does not know what it means. What does this detail suggest is happening to Mr. Bittering?

6. **(a) Contrast** How do the houses built by the Earth people differ from the ones built by the Martians? **(b) Draw Conclusions** What can you conclude about Martians and Earth people from this contrast in their homes? Use text evidence to support your response.

7. **(a) Analyze** How does the wind affect the characters in the beginning, middle, and end of the story? **(b) Synthesize** What might the wind mean in this story? Use text evidence to support your responses.

Should humanity's future lie among the stars?

What have you learned about imagination and the future from reading this story? Go to your Essential Question Notes and record your observations and thoughts about "Dark They Were, and Golden-Eyed."

TEKS

5.F. Make inferences and use evidence to support understanding.

6.A. Describe personal connections to a variety of sources, including self-selected texts.

6.C. Use text evidence to support an appropriate response.

DARK THEY WERE, AND GOLDEN-EYED

Close Read

ANNOTATE

1. The model passage and annotation show how one reader analyzed paragraph 251 of the story. Find another detail in the passage to annotate. Then, write your own question and conclusion.

CLOSE-READ MODEL

Summer burned the canals dry. Summer moved like flame upon the meadows. In the empty Earth settlement, the painted houses flaked and peeled. Rubber tires upon which children had swung in back yards hung suspended like stopped clock pendulums in the blazing air.

ANNOTATE: I notice that many words contain the letter *m*.

QUESTION: What effect does this repetition create?

CONCLUDE: The repeated sound creates a drowsy mood.

MY **QUESTION:**

MY **CONCLUSION:**

2. For more practice, answer the Close-Read notes in the selection.
3. Choose a section of the story that you found especially important. Mark important details. Then, jot down questions and write your conclusions in the open space next to the text.

RESEARCH

NOTEBOOK

Inquiry and Research

Research and Extend Ray Bradbury's fictional Mars is based on some facts and a lot of imagination. Write down three details about the physical setting of Mars in this story. Using these details, generate two to three of your own questions about what Mars is really like. Then, conduct a brief informal inquiry to answer your questions. Use a variety of sources, including government web sites.

TEKS

9.D. Describe how the author's use of figurative language such as metaphor and personification achieves specific purposes.

9.F. Analyze how the author's use of language contributes to mood, voice, and tone.

12.A. Generate student-selected and teacher-guided questions for formal and informal inquiry.

12.D. Identify and gather relevant information from a variety of sources.

Genre / Text Elements

Setting and Figurative Language In this story, the **setting** is important because it creates the characters' problems. To help readers understand what this alien setting is like, Ray Bradbury uses **figurative language,** including **similes, metaphors,** and **personification.**

EXAMPLES FROM THE STORY

Simile: *Rubber tires...hung suspended like stopped clock pendulums*

Metaphor: *the rockets had spun a silver web across space*

Personification: *the wind roaring forlorn and changing*

Bradbury's use of figurative language serves a variety of purposes. It helps show how the setting looks, and it also gives the story a specific **mood**, or feeling.

 NOTEBOOK

 INTERACTIVITY

PRACTICE Complete the activity and answer the questions.

1. **Analyze** Passages from the story appear in the chart. Identify each as either a simile, a metaphor, or personification. In the final column, explain the purpose of each example—what it shows about the setting and the mood it helps create.

PASSAGE	TYPE OF FIGURATIVE LANGUAGE	WHAT IT SHOWS
The children, small seeds, might at any instant be sown to all the Martian climes. (paragraph 2)		
They saw the old cities, . . . lying like children's delicate bones ... (paragraph 9)		
This was the moment Mars had waited for. Now it would eat them. (paragraph 41)		

2. **(a) Distinguish** Find and write down another example of each type of figurative language in the story.

Simile

Metaphor

Personification

(b) Interpret Choose the example that best helps you understand the setting and its impact on the characters. Explain your choice.

DARK THEY WERE, AND GOLDEN-EYED

Concept Vocabulary

NOTEBOOK

Why These Words? The vocabulary words describe Bradbury's vision of Mars. For example, the Bitterings' house is *submerged* by a river of wind, which also roars "*forlorn* and changing through the old peach tree."

submerged	canals	atmosphere
forlorn	immense	mosaic

PRACTICE

1. How do the vocabulary words sharpen the reader's understanding of what life is like for the Bitterings on Mars?

2. What other words in the selection help describe an alien world?

3. Use each concept word in a sentence that demonstrates your understanding of the word's meaning.

4. Challenge yourself to replace the concept word in each sentence with a synonym. How does the word change affect the meaning of your sentence? For example, which sentence is stronger? Which has a more positive meaning?

WORD NETWORK

Add words that are related to the ideas of imagination and the future from the text to your Word Network.

Word Study

NOTEBOOK

Synonyms and Nuance Words that have the same basic meaning are called **synonyms.** Often, however, there are subtle shades of meaning, or **nuances,** between synonyms. For example, the basic meaning of *forlorn* is "sad," but its nuances indicate that it is a type of sadness caused by abandonment or loneliness.

1. Identify the basic meaning of these synonyms, and then describe their differences in nuance: *yellow / golden.*

2. Using a thesaurus, find two other words related to *forlorn*. Record a definition for each synonym, and then use each synonym in a sentence that reflects its nuances, or shades of meaning.

TEKS

6.F. Respond using newly acquired vocabulary as appropriate.

10.C. Revise drafts for clarity, development, organization, style, word choice, and sentence variety.

Conventions

Sentence Structures A sentence is made up of one or more clauses. There are two types of clauses:

- **independent clause:** a group of words that has a subject and a verb and can stand by itself as a complete thought
- **dependent clause:** a group of words that has a subject and a verb but is not a complete thought

The structure of a sentence is determined by the number and types of clauses it contains.

SENTENCE STRUCTURE	EXAMPLE FROM THE STORY
simple sentence: one independent clause	Atom bombs hit New York!
compound sentence: two or more independent clauses linked by a connecting word (conjunction), such as *or, and,* or *but*	He felt his heart pounding, and he was afraid.
complex sentence: one independent clause and one or more dependent clauses	If we stay here, we'll all change.
compound-complex sentence: two or more independent clauses and one or more dependent clauses	We'll eat this stuff and then we'll change—who knows to what?

TIP: In the examples, the independent clauses are underlined once, and the dependent clauses are underlined twice.

ANNOTATE

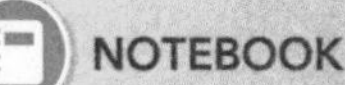
NOTEBOOK

READ IT Reread the story, and find another example of each type of sentence. Then, mark the independent clauses. Use another mark to identify the dependent clauses.

WRITE IT Write a brief paragraph about the story. Then, revise it to add greater sentence variety, including at least one of each type of sentence—simple, compound, complex, and compound-complex.

DARK THEY WERE, AND GOLDEN-EYED
(short story)

Compare Fiction and Drama

The text and audio versions of "Dark They Were, and Golden-Eyed" tell the same story. Pay attention to how experiencing the story is different when you read it and when you listen to it.

DARK THEY WERE, AND GOLDEN-EYED
(radio play)

About the Producer

Michael McDonough is a professional sound designer and the producer of the *Bradbury 13* series. For *Bradbury 13*, McDonough wrote all the scripts and created spectacular original sound effects. McDonough first learned sound design as a student at Brigham Young University and went on to work on dozens of films and television shows.

Dark They Were, and Golden-Eyed

Media Vocabulary

These words describe characteristics of radio plays, a type of multimodal text. Use them as you analyze, discuss, and write about the selection.

sound effects: sounds produced artificially for a radio production	• Sound effects indicate settings and actions (city noises; the dropping of a book). • Certain sound effects help create mood (the squeak of a rusty door; the screech of an owl).
actors' delivery: the ways in which actors speak their lines	• Voices in a radio play need to be distinct so listeners know which character is speaking. • A speaker's pitch, volume, and pacing take on even more importance in a radio play.
background music: music that is not the focus of the performance	• Background music can signal changes in scene or mood. • Specific melodies might be used with particular characters or settings.

Comprehension Strategy

NOTEBOOK

Create Mental Images

When you listen to an audio play, deepen your understanding by **creating mental images.** "See" the setting, characters, and actions in your mind.

- **Listen for emotion in characters' voices.**
  EXAMPLE: Breathless, fast speech helps you "see" a character who is anxious or excited.
- **Listen for sound effects** that tell you what characters are doing, or what is happening around them.
  EXAMPLE: Sounds of spaceships lifting off and landing help you "see" a busy spaceport.
- **Listen to the music.** Notice the mood of the music. Imagine how characters in such a mood might look and act.

PRACTICE As you listen to the play, use the Notes section to briefly describe the mental images you create.

TEKS

5.D. Create mental images to deepen understanding.

8.F. Analyze characteristics of multimodal and digital texts.

Dark They Were, and Golden-Eyed

Michael McDonough, Producer

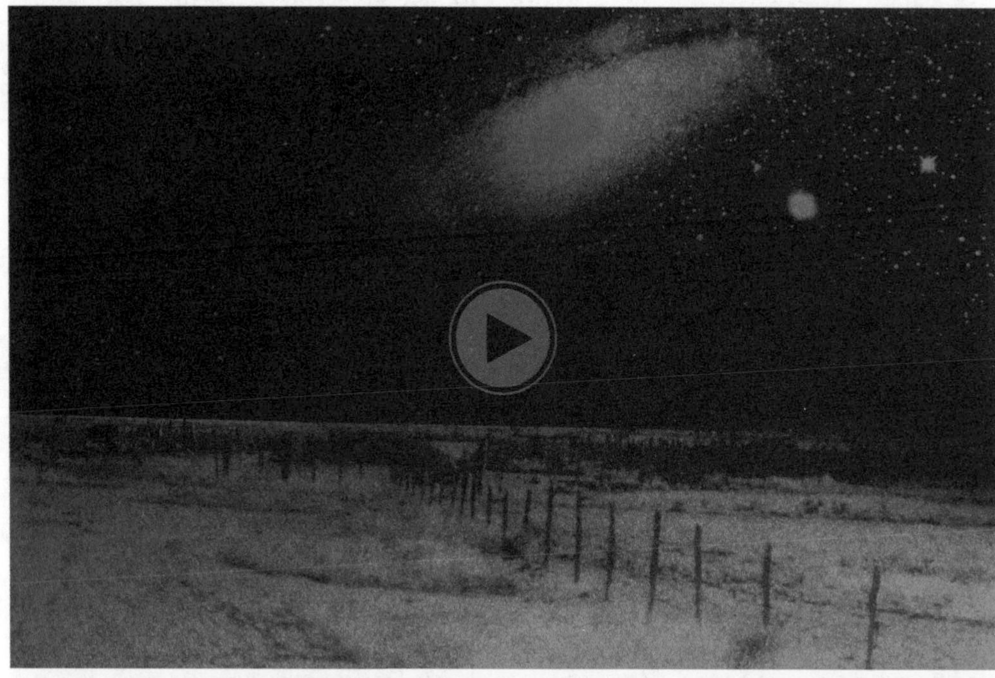

BACKGROUND

During the 1930s and 1940s, radio plays were a highly popular form of entertainment. However, with the rise of television, radio plays all but disappeared. In 1984, National Public Radio aired *Bradbury 13*, a series of radio adaptations of Ray Bradbury's works that re-create the feel of classic radio drama.

AUDIO

NOTEBOOK

TAKE NOTES Deepen and confirm your understanding of the radio play by taking notes as you listen.

NOTEBOOK

Answer the questions in your notebook. Use text evidence to support your responses.

Response

1. How do you think most listeners would react to this radio play, especially if they have not read the original story? Explain.

Comprehension

2. What does the spaceship pilot announce at the beginning of the play?

3. **(a)** In the story, how does the author let readers know that bombs have blown up all Earth rockets? **(b)** What elements does the radio play add to that scene?

4. **(a)** What physical changes do the Bitterings first notice in themselves? **(b)** In what other ways do the Earth people physically change?

5. **Strategy: Create Mental Images** Which elements of the radio play helped you the most to "see" the characters and action in your mind? Explain, citing at least one specific example.

Analysis

6. **Compare and Contrast** **(a)** In what way is the opening scene of the radio play similar to that of the story? **(b)** In what way does the opening scene differ from the story?

7. **(a)** Note at least two items the Bitterings leave behind when they move to the villa in the hills. **(b) Interpret** Why are these items no longer important to them?

8. **Evaluate** Some critics believe that science-fiction fantasy stories like this one are *not* about the future. These critics think the stories are actually about concerns people have in the present. If that is true, what aspects of present-day life do you think this story might be addressing? Explain your thinking.

Should humanity's future lie among the stars?

What have you learned about imagination and the future from listening to this radio play? Go to your Essential Question Notes and record your observations and thoughts about the radio play adaptation of "Dark They Were, and Golden-Eyed."

TEKS

5.D. Create mental images to deepen understanding.

6.F. Respond using newly acquired vocabulary as appropriate.

12.D. Identify and gather relevant information from a variety of sources.

Close Review

Listen to the radio play again. As you listen, take notes about important details and jot down your observations. Note time codes so you can find important elements again later. Then, write a question and your conclusion.

DARK THEY WERE, AND GOLDEN-EYED (radio play)

MY **QUESTION:**

MY **CONCLUSION:**

Inquiry and Research

Research and Extend Choose one of the following topics to research: the story's author, the series called *Bradbury 13*, or the history of radio plays in general. Gather relevant information from a variety of sources. Explain how this new knowledge helps deepen your understanding of the radio play.

Media Vocabulary

These words describe characteristics of multimodal texts. Practice using them in your responses.

sound effects	actors' delivery	background music

1. In what ways has the Martian environment been brought to life in the radio play?

2. How would you evaluate the actors' performances?

3. How are changes of scene indicated in the radio play?

DARK THEY WERE, AND GOLDEN-EYED (short story)

DARK THEY WERE, AND GOLDEN-EYED (radio play)

Compare Fiction and Drama

Multiple Choice

NOTEBOOK

These questions are based on the short story and radio play versions of "Dark They Were, and Golden-Eyed." Choose the best answer to each question.

1. In both the story and the play, when the family first arrives on Mars, what does Mr. Bittering want to do right away?

   A He wants to visit the ancient Martian cities.

   B He wants to get back on the rocket and return to Earth.

   C He wants to get to work building a rocket.

   D He wants to start building a villa in the mountains.

2. Read paragraphs 118 to 121 from the story and the transcript of a similar section in the radio play. What happens in the story that does *not* happen in the play?

Short Story

"Here you are, Harry." Sam handed him a pocket mirror. "Take a look at yourself."

Mr. Bittering hesitated, and then raised the mirror to his face.

There were little, very dim flecks of new gold captured in the blue of his eyes.

"Now look what you've done," said Sam a moment later. "You've broken my mirror."

Radio Play

SAM: Is that so? Harry, what color are your eyes?

HARRY: My eyes? They're blue.

SAM: Take a look in this mirror. See for yourself.

HARRY: [gasps] No! They're turning yellow.

SAM: Welcome to the club, Harry.

   F Harry gasps when he sees himself.

   G Harry looks at himself in a mirror.

   H Harry sees that his eyes are turning yellow.

   J Harry breaks the mirror.

3. At the end of both the story and the play, what do members of the rescue team start to do?

   A They start to repair the houses the townspeople left behind.

   B They develop a plan to drive the Martians out of their villas.

   C They start to give Earth names to the mountains, hills, and canals.

   D They prepare to leave Mars because they failed in their mission.

TEKS

6.B. Write responses that demonstrate understanding of texts, including comparing sources within and across genres.

11.B. Compose informational texts, including multi-paragraph essays that convey information about a topic, using a clear controlling idea or thesis statement and genre characteristics and craft.

NOTEBOOK

Answer the questions in your notebook. Use text evidence to support your responses.

Short Response

1. **(a) Analyze** In the story, how does the author show the importance of the Martian wind? **(b) Analyze** How does the radio play show the importance of the wind?

2. **Interpret** In the radio play, after the Bitterings move to the villa, sound effects include bird song. Birds are not mentioned in the story. Why do you think the radio play includes bird sounds at this point?

3. **(a) Describe** What is life like in the Martian villas? **(b) Contrast** How is that lifestyle different from that of the Earth people? **(c) Evaluate** Which version of the story—the original text or the radio play—presents a stronger contrast between Martian and Earth ways of living? Explain.

Timed Writing

A **comparison-and-contrast essay** is a piece of writing in which you discuss similarities and differences among two or more topics.

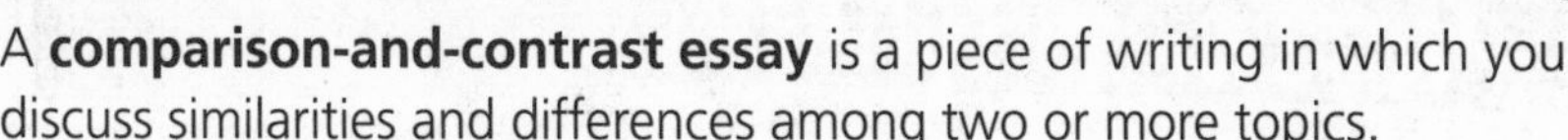

ASSIGNMENT

Write a **comparison-and-contrast essay** in which you explain how each version of "Dark They Were, and Golden-Eyed" brings the setting and characters to life. Include an evaluation that tells which version is more effective.

5-MINUTE PLANNER

1. Read the assignment carefully and completely.
2. Decide what you want to say—your controlling idea, or thesis.
3. Decide which examples you'll use from the story and play.
4. Organize your ideas, making sure to address these points:
   - Explain how the story and radio play are similar.
   - Explain important differences between the two.
   - Explain which version of the story you think is more effective and why.

EQ Notes Before moving on to a new selection, go to your Essential Question Notes and record any additional thoughts and observations you may have about the text and radio play versions of "Dark They Were, and Golden-Eyed."

Write an Argument: Editorial

Editorials are short persuasive essays that appear in newspapers and on news sites. People write them to express their opinions about current events or problems.

ASSIGNMENT

Write an **editorial** in which you take a position on the following question:

Is space exploration important?

Support your position with evidence from your reading, your background knowledge, and your own observations. Use the elements of an editorial in your writing.

ELEMENTS OF AN EDITORIAL

Purpose: to explain and defend your position

Characteristics

- a clear claim that relates to an engaging idea and shows depth of thought
- different types of evidence, including specific facts, details, and examples
- precise word choices and an appropriately formal tone
- well-chosen transitions and other elements of craft
- standard English conventions, including correct use of subordinating conjunctions and punctuation

Structure

- a well-organized structure that includes:
  - an interesting introduction
  - a logical flow of ideas from paragraph to paragraph
  - a strong conclusion

TEKS

11.C. Compose multi-paragraph argumentative texts using genre characteristic and craft.

Take a Closer Look at the Assignment

NOTEBOOK

1. What routine classroom words do I notice in the assignment? What is it asking me to do (in my own words)?

2. Is a specific **audience** mentioned in the assignment?

   ◯ Yes If "yes," who is my main audience?

   ◯ No If "no," who do I think my audience is or should be?

3. Is my **purpose** for writing specified in the assignment?

   ◯ Yes If "yes," what is the purpose?

   ◯ No If "no," why am I writing this editorial (not just because it's an assignment)?

4. **(a)** Does the assignment ask me to use specific **types of evidence**?

   ◯ Yes If "yes," what are they?

   ◯ No If "no," what types of evidence do I think I need?

   (b) Where will I get the evidence? What details can I pull from my EQ Notes?

5. Does the assignment ask me to organize my ideas in a certain way?

   ◯ Yes If "yes," what structure does it require?

   ◯ No If "no," how can I best order my ideas?

AUDIENCE

Always keep your **audience**, or reader, in mind when you write.

- Choose words your audience will understand.
- Explain elements that may be unfamiliar to your audience.

PURPOSE

A specific **purpose**, or reason for writing, will lead to a stronger editorial.

General Purpose: *In this editorial, I'll argue that sports are great.*

Specific Purpose: *In this editorial, I'll convince readers that we need a skate park.*

EVIDENCE

Varied **evidence**, or supporting details, will make your editorial stronger.

- **Facts:** information that can be proved true
- **Expert Opinion:** words of people who have special knowledge
- **Personal Observation:** explanations of your own knowledge or experience
- **Anecdote:** brief story that illustrates a situation
- **Examples:** specific instances of a general idea

Planning and Prewriting

Before you draft, decide what you want to say and how you want to say it. Consider the texts you have read and listened to in this unit as well as any background reading you have done on your own. If you need more information to determine your position, briefly research other perspectives on the topic. Then, complete the activities to get started.

Discover Your Thinking: Freewrite!

Keep your topic in mind as you write quickly and freely for at least three minutes without stopping.

- Don't worry about your spelling and grammar (you'll fix mistakes later).
- When time is up, pause and look at what you wrote.
- Mark ideas or points that seem strong or interesting. Repeat the process as many times as necessary to get all your ideas out. For each round, start with the strong ideas you marked. Focus on those as you again write quickly and freely.

NOTEBOOK

WRITE IT Is space exploration important?

TEKS

10.A. Plan a first draft by selecting a genre appropriate for a particular topic, purpose, and audience using a range of strategies such as discussion, background reading, and personal interests. **10.B.i.** Develop drafts into a focused, structured, and coherent piece of writing by organizing with purposeful structure, including an introduction, transitions, coherence within and across paragraphs, and a conclusion.

Structure Ideas: Make a Plan

NOTEBOOK

A. Choose a Focus Review your freewriting and pull out the main points you want to make. Don't worry about the order.

B. Write a Claim

C. Plan a Structure Figure out the content for each section of your editorial.

I. **Introduction:** Plan how you'll engage your reader and show that your topic is important. Consider telling a story or describing a scene.

II. **Body:** List your points and evidence in a logical order.

III. **Conclusion:** Plan how you can leave your reader with a strong impression. Consider including an unusual statement or a memorable image.

CLAIM

A **claim** is your main idea, position, or point. Begin by writing a "working" claim—just one sentence. As you draft and revise, you may change or refine your claim.

STRUCTURE

A clear **structure**, or organization of ideas and evidence, helps readers follow your thinking. These two types of structures work well with arguments:

- **Order of Importance:** Start with your strongest point, follow with your next strongest point, and so on.
- **Nestorian Order:** Start with your second strongest point. Add other points and end with your strongest point.

Drafting

ANNOTATE

Apply the planning work you've done, and write a first draft. Start with your introduction, which should interest readers in your topic. Then, explore ways to create a coherent piece of writing.

Read Like a Writer

Reread the first few paragraphs of the Mentor Text. Mark details that you think engage readers' interest. One observation has been done for you.

MENTOR TEXT

from Leaving Main Street

In July, 2015, the world watched in awe as close-up photographs of Pluto streamed back to Earth from three billion miles away. The spacecraft *New Horizons* had traveled nine years to study the dwarf planet at the edge of our solar system.

As a result of the mission, scientists discovered that Pluto is not just a giant ball of ice. It has a molten core, tectonic plates, and volcanic activity, just as Earth does. It may even support some form of life. The *New Horizons* mission has been hailed as a triumph of human ingenuity, and a huge leap forward for the future of space exploration

Yet it almost didn't happen.

Which details in the text grab your attention? Mark them.

After a series of long sentences, this short sentence is like a STOP sign. It tells readers to pay attention.

NOTEBOOK

WRITE IT Write your introduction. Follow the Mentor Text structure, and use a series of longer sentences. Then, add a short sentence for contrast.

DEPTH OF THOUGHT

As you draft, make your writing thoughtful and persuasive.

- **Tone** Your attitude, or tone, should reinforce your thinking. Strive for a formal tone, but don't try to sound like someone you are not.
- **Development** Support your points with varied evidence, including facts, details, and examples. For example, if you use an anecdote, add a fact or statistic to drive the point home.

TEKS

10.B.i. Develop drafts into a focused, structured, and coherent piece of writing by organizing with purposeful structure, including an introduction, transitions, coherence within and across paragraphs, and a conclusion; **10.B.ii.** Develop drafts into a focused, structured, and coherent piece of writing by developing an engaging idea reflecting depth of thought with specific facts, details, and examples; **10.D.vi.** Edit drafts using standard English conventions, including subordinating conjunctions to form complex sentences and correlative conjunctions such as *either/or* and *neither/nor*.

Create Coherence

As you draft your editorial, make sure that the transitions from sentence to sentence and paragraph to paragraph are **coherent**. This means that all the parts of your editorial clearly connect and create a unified whole.

One strategy for creating coherence is using **subordinating conjunctions** to create **complex sentences.** The particular subordinating conjunction you choose tells the reader the exact logical relationship between your ideas.

COMPLEX SENTENCES

A **complex sentence** has one independent clause and one dependent clause.

- An **independent clause** has a subject and a verb and expresses a complete thought.
- A **dependent clause** has a subject and a verb, but it does not express a complete thought. It often begins with a **subordinating conjunction.**

Sample Subordinating Conjunctions

Relationship Between Ideas	Subordinating Conjunctions
show contrast	*although, even though, whereas*
show cause	*because, since*
show effect	*in order that, so that*
show place	*where, wherever*
show time	*after, before, once, until, while*

WRITE IT Write a paragraph of your editorial here. Make sure your draft is coherent by including only specific facts and examples that convey your position and reflect the depth of thought of your idea. Then, edit your paragraph, making sure you use accurate transition words and subordinating conjunctions that mean exactly what you want to say.

SENTENCE VARIETY

Too many short, choppy sentences can make your writing repetitive. Maintain readers' interest and create variety in your writing by using subordinating conjunctions to create some complex sentences.

EXAMPLE:

- We need to be more curious. Curiosity can sometimes be dangerous.
- We need to be more curious **even though** curiosity can sometimes be dangerous.

Revising

ANNOTATE

Now that you have a first draft, revise it to be sure it is as persuasive as possible. When you revise, you "re-see" your writing, checking for the following elements:

Clarity: sharpness of your ideas

Development: full explanations with strong supporting details

Organization: logical flow of ideas

Style and Tone: well-written, varied sentences and precise word choices; a level of formality that suits your audience and purpose

Read Like a Writer

Review the revisions made to the Mentor Text. Then, answer the questions in the white boxes.

MENTOR TEXT

from Leaving Main Street

Humans explore space~~. It's~~ *because it's* in our genes. We're hardwired with certain built-in features that compel us in that direction. Here's how it breaks down:

First, there is something about the human condition that strives to be the best, or the first, at something. Our ancestors survived by outperforming others. ~~Many of us also like to be right, but that may not be as important.~~

In addition, humans are by nature curious about exploring new places. *Everyone remembers being a kid and wanting to see what's "over there."* Humans will not tolerate boundaries; their dream is to explore what's beyond.

Finally, NASA's space program inspires competition and innovation. The Hubble Space Telescope and the robotic missions to the planets have been shining examples of what can be achieved when a project is based on goals set by scientists rather than by politicians.

Likewise, humans ~~Humans~~ have always created monuments to commemorate their great achievements *so that the* ~~. The~~ next generation will remember who they are and how they spent their time here. What we want to be remembered for is finding life on other worlds, maybe even for landing on Mars.

Why do you think the writer changed the wording?

Why do you think the writer chose to delete this sentence?

This detail provides an example readers will relate to.

Why has the writer reordered these paragraphs?

The writer has created a complex sentence using the subordinating conjunction *so that* in order to show a cause-and-effect relationship between two ideas.

TEKS

10.C. Revise drafts for clarity, development, organization, style, word choice, and sentence variety.

Take a Closer Look at Your Draft

Now, revise your draft. Use the Revision Guide for Argument to evaluate and strengthen your editorial.

REVISION GUIDE FOR ARGUMENT

EVALUATE	TAKE ACTION
Clarity	
Is my claim strong and clear?	If your claim isn't clear, **replace** it with a question. Then, **answer** the question by stating your position in a direct, forceful way.
Development	
Have I given enough supporting evidence for every idea?	• **Mark** each supporting detail and the idea it supports. • **Move** any detail that is not in the same paragraph as the idea it supports. • **Add** or **delete** details if necessary.
Have I used varied evidence?	• **Add** facts or expert statements to strengthen your opinions. • **Add** anecdotes or examples to illustrate your facts.
Organization	
Have I organized my ideas in a logical way?	If the structure doesn't work, **reorganize** ideas and details. Print your paper, and then cut out the paragraphs. Physically **rearrange** them until you find a better order. Then, **add** transitions to make the flow of ideas clear.
Does my introduction engage readers?	**Add** a question, anecdote, quotation, or strong detail to interest your audience.
Have I ended my editorial in a memorable way?	**Add** a quotation, a call to action, an insight, or a strong statement to conclude.
Style and Tone	
Are my word choices precise and vivid?	Review your draft and **mark** any vague words, such as *nice, good, bad,* or *important*. **Replace** those words with vivid words that will make your ideas more interesting and persuasive, such as *valuable, destructive,* or *influential.*
Is my tone suitable for an editorial, in which I attempt to persuade my audience?	**Replace** any slang or overly casual language with more formal options. For example, instead of saying, "Space exploration is *cool,*" say "Space exploration is *both necessary and interesting.*"
Have I used a variety of sentence types?	If most of your sentences are all very short or all very long, create sentence variety: **Break up** long sentences, and **combine** closely related shorter sentences.

Editing

Don't let errors distract readers from your ideas. Reread your draft, and fix mistakes to create a finished persuasive work.

Read Like a Writer

Look at how the writer of the Mentor Text edited her draft. Then, follow the directions in the white boxes.

MENTOR TEXT

from Leaving Main Street

But these are not the real reasons for continuing the space program, says Michael Griffin in *Air & Space Magazine*. Griffin makes the point that people go to space for reasons that are not *necessarily* ~~necesarily~~ logical. In other words, money doesn't have much to do with it. "When we contemplate committing large sums of money to a project we tend to dismis reasons that are emotional or *value-driven* ~~valuedriven~~," Griffin says. He goes on to say that Americans need the prospect of exploring space.

The writer fixed two spelling errors.

Find and fix an error in which a comma is missing after a dependent clause at the beginning of a complex sentence.

Find and fix another spelling error.

Focus on Sentences

Complex Sentences In a complex sentence, make sure the subordinating conjunction you have chosen shows the correct logical relationship between ideas. The wrong subordinating conjunction will misrepresent your ideas and confuse your readers.

PRACTICE Find and fix the incorrect subordinating conjunctions in these complex sentences. Then, check your own draft for correctness.

1. Trees don't yet grow on Mars when they eventually will.
2. Although I applied to NASA, I waited patiently to hear from them.
3. Before you support my application, I'll surely be admitted.
4. Progress is slow unless space exploration is so expensive.
5. We've been very determined where we made our decision.

EDITING TIPS

1. Mark the subordinating conjunction in each sentence.
2. Replace the incorrect subordinating conjunction with one that shows an accurate relationship between ideas.

TEKS

10.D.vi. Edit drafts using standard English conventions, including subordinating conjunctions to form complex sentences and correlative conjunctions such as *either/or* and *neither/nor;* **10.D.viii.** Edit drafts using standard English conventions, including punctuation, including commas to set off words, phrases, and clauses, and semicolons.

Focus on Spelling and Punctuation

Spelling: *-ful* or *-full?* The word *full* has two *l*'s. However, the suffix *-ful* has only one *l*. Words with two or more syllables, like *cheerful* and *successful*, end with the single-*l* suffix. Check your editorial for any words ending with this suffix, and make sure you have spelled them correctly.

Punctuation: Dependent Clauses There are two common patterns of complex sentences. To determine whether you need to use a comma to set off the dependent clause, follow these general rules:

- Dependent Clause + Independent Clause = Comma
  EXAMPLE: *If we don't find another solar system, all that time will have been wasted.*
- Independent Clause + Dependent Clause = No Comma
  EXAMPLE: *All that time will have been wasted if we don't find another solar system.*

EDITING TIPS

- If you are writing on a computer, print out your draft.
- Read your draft aloud, word by word, to catch omissions, typos, and other problems.

PRACTICE Add commas to these sentences if necessary. Then, review your own draft for correctness.

1. Before we head to outer space we should improve the earth.

2. I've wanted to be an astronaut since I was a child.

3. Although they had a rough landing they were happy to be out of the skies.

Publishing and Presenting

Broaden Your Audience

Share your editorial with your class or school community. Choose one of these options:

OPTION 1 Post your editorial to a class or school blog or website. Respectfully comment on the editorials of others, and respond politely to the comments your editorial receives.

OPTION 2 Pair up with a classmate whose editorial expresses a different point of view than yours. Take turns presenting your ideas to the class. After your presentation, answer questions from listeners.

Essential Question

Should humanity's future lie among the stars?

Some people think that space exploration is the way we will transform our dreams of the future into reality. Others think it is a big waste of time and money. You will read selections that examine different aspects of this subject. Work in a small group to continue your investigation into different perspectives on imagination and the future.

VIDEO

INTERACTIVITY

Peer-Group Learning Strategies

Throughout your life, in school, in your community, and in your career, you will continue to learn and work with others.

Look at these strategies and the actions you can take to practice them as you work in small groups. Add ideas of your own for each category. Use these strategies during Peer-Group Learning.

STRATEGY	MY PEER-GROUP ACTION PLAN
Prepare • Complete your assignments so that you are prepared for group work. • Take notes on your reading so that you can share ideas with others in your group.	
Participate fully • Make eye contact to signal that you are paying attention. • Use text evidence when making a point.	
Support others • Build off ideas from others in your group. • Ask others who have not yet spoken to do so.	
Clarify • Paraphrase the ideas of others to be sure that your understanding is correct. • Ask follow-up questions.	

CONTENTS

PERFORMANCE TASK

Present an Argument

The Peer-Group readings present different perspectives on exploring outer space. After reading, you will present a critique of one of the fiction selections from this unit.

Working as a Group

NOTEBOOK

1. Take a Position

Discuss the following question with your group:

> Would you rather stay here on Earth or experience life on another planet?

As you take turns sharing your positions, be sure to provide reasons to support your ideas. Make sure you understand one another, and ask questions when you need clarification of a word or an idea. After all group members have shared, discuss the challenges you might encounter if you were living on another planet.

2. List Your Rules

As a group, decide on the rules that you will follow as you work together. Two samples are provided. Add two more of your own. You may add or revise rules as you work through the readings and activities together.

- Everyone should participate in group discussions.
- People should not interrupt.

____

____

3. Apply the Rules

Practice working as a group. Share what you have learned about the possibility of living in space. Make sure each person in the group contributes. Take notes and be prepared to share with the class one thing that you heard from another member of your group.

4. Name Your Group

Choose a name that reflects the unit topic.

Our group's name: ____

5. Create a Communication Plan

Decide how you want to communicate with one another. For example, you might use online collaboration tools, email, or instant messaging.

Our group's plan:

____

____

TEKS

1.A. Listen actively to interpret a message and ask clarifying questions that build on others' ideas.

6.G. Discuss and write about the explicit or implicit meanings of text.

Making a Schedule

First, find out the due dates for the peer-group activities. Then, preview the texts and activities with your group and make a schedule for completing the tasks.

SELECTION	ACTIVITIES	DUE DATE
Science-Fiction Cradlesong First Men on the Moon		
The Last Dog		
Mars Can Wait. Oceans Can't. *from* Packing for Mars		

Analyzing Explicit and Implicit Meanings

Literature is rich in meanings that are both explicit and implicit. You will be asked to discuss and write about both types of meaning as you work with your group.

- **Explicit meanings** don't require interpretation. They are directly stated. Many informational texts and arguments convey explicit meanings more often than implicit ones.
- **Implicit meanings** are suggested by details. Readers make inferences and draw connections to figure them out. Literary genres may include some explicit meanings, but the key meanings are usually implicit.

Apply these strategies to identify and interpret both kinds of meaning:

- *To identify explicit meanings,* mark passages that directly state or explain ideas. Paraphrase these ideas, restating them in your own words, to make sure you understand them.
- *To interpret implicit meanings,* mark details that stand out. Then, consider how the details relate to one another, and whether other details have similar or different qualities. Make inferences about the deeper ideas the details suggest.

POETRY COLLECTION

The selections you are about to read are lyric poems.

Reading Lyric Poetry

Lyric poetry expresses the thoughts and feelings of a single speaker, is usually brief, and often has a musical quality.

LYRIC POETRY

Author's Purpose

- to use focused, imaginative language and form to capture emotion and thought

Characteristics

- describes a moment in time
- expresses an insight or new understanding
- has a speaker or voice that "tells" the poem
- uses language with multiple layers of meaning
- uses words for both sound and meaning
- may break some grammatical rules

Structure

- divided into lines that are often organized into groups, or stanzas
- may use rhyme, rhyme scheme, and meter, or set rhythmic patterns

Take a Minute!

DISCUSS IT With a partner, discuss different poems you have read and liked. Which ones might be considered lyric?

TEKS

8.B. Analyze the effect of rhyme scheme, meter, and graphical elements such as punctuation and capitalization in poems across a variety of poetic forms.

Genre / Text Elements

Meter and Rhyme Scheme The stressed and unstressed syllables of words give language natural rhythms. Poets use these rhythms to craft meter. Likewise, similar sounds in words create rhyme that poets use to craft rhyme schemes.

- **Meter** is a pattern of stressed and unstressed syllables. A **foot** is a unit of meter. For example, this line has three feet, each with one stressed syllable followed by an unstressed syllable: **Ed**mund | **ate** his | **oat**meal.
- A **rhyme scheme** is a pattern made by rhyming words at the ends of poetic lines. The words that form the patterns may be *exact rhymes (sun / run)*, or *slant rhymes* that have similar but not exact ending sounds (*prove / love*). Rhyme schemes create multiple effects: They help make poems memorable and easy to recite. They also create different moods, such as bright and lively or dark and eerie.

TIP: A **foot** can begin or end in the middle of a word. Poetic lines can have any number of feet.

EXAMPLE: *from* "A Lazy Day," Paul Laurence Dunbar

- Stressed syllables are set in bold. The vertical bars separate metrical feet. The meter makes this rhythm: tee TUM tee TUM.
- The rhyme scheme (*abab*) is noted by a letter for each rhyming sound.

*The **trees** | bend **down** | a**long** | the **stream,*** (a)
*Where **anch** | ored **swings** | my **ti** | ny **boat.*** (b)
*The **day** | is **one** | to **drowse** | and **dream*** (a)
*And **list** | the **thrush** | 's **throt** | tling **note.*** (b)

ANNOTATE

NOTEBOOK

PRACTICE Read the first stanza of a poem by John Greenleaf Whittier entitled "What the Birds Said." Then, work on your own to answer the questions.

The birds against the April wind
Flew northward, singing as they flew;
They sang, "The land we leave behind
Has swords for corn-blades, blood for dew."

1. **(a)** Mark the stressed and unstressed syllables in each line. **(b)** How many feet does each line contain?
2. **(a)** Use the letter system (*abc*) to identify the rhyme scheme. **(b)** Which rhyme is exact and which is slant? Explain.
3. Read the stanza aloud. Describe the effect of the meter and rhyme.

POETRY COLLECTION

Science-Fiction Cradlesong

First Men on the Moon

Concept Vocabulary

As you read the poems, you will encounter these words.

vast	wanderlust	awe

Print Resources A **print dictionary** is a reference book that provides a great deal of information about words. You can use it to find a word's meaning, pronunciation, syllabication, part of speech, and origin.

SAMPLE DICTIONARY ENTRY

terrestrial *adj.* (tuh RES tree uhl) [1400–50; late ME < L *terrestri(s)* pertaining to earth (der. of *terrra* earth) + AL] **1.** of or relating to Earth or its inhabitants **2.** living on or relating to land rather than water

This entry tells you that *terrestrial* is an adjective that has four syllables and two meanings. Its origin is the Latin word *terrestri*, which was derived from the Latin word *terra*, which means "earth."

PRACTICE As you read the poems, use a print dictionary to find the meanings and pronunciations of unfamiliar words. Use the open space next to the text to note definitions and other useful information.

Comprehension Strategy

Adjust Fluency

Poetry presents reading challenges that are different from those of prose. When your purpose is to read and understand poetry, **adjust your fluency** to better appreciate its compact and imaginative language. For example, pay attention to the punctuation, which clarifies meaning and indicates where you should pause, slow down, or stop. Follow these guidelines.

- comma (,) or semicolon (;) = brief pause
- period (.) = full stop
- question mark (?) = full stop with a slight lift in the tone of voice
- ellipses (...) = extended pause
- dash (—) = abrupt interruption

PRACTICE As you read and analyze these poems, adjust your fluency to fit your reading purpose.

2.A. Use print or digital resources to determine the meaning, syllabication, pronunciation, word origin, and part of speech.

3. Adjust fluency when reading grade-level text based on the reading purpose.

About the Poems

Science-Fiction Cradlesong

BACKGROUND

During the second half of C. S. Lewis's writing career, science fiction became more popular as the idea of space flight started to become a reality. The space age began in 1957, when the Soviet Union launched the first satellite into Earth's orbit. In 1961, Yuri Gagarin became the first man to travel into space.

C. S. Lewis (1898–1963) was an Irish author best known for his classic *Chronicles of Narnia*, a fantasy series about four young siblings and their adventures in the magical land of Narnia. He wrote more than thirty books, and most of his writings teach moral lessons. Lewis taught medieval literature at Oxford University and Cambridge University in England.

First Men on the Moon

BACKGROUND

On July 20, 1969, *Apollo 11* astronauts Neil Armstrong and Edwin "Buzz" Aldrin became the first human beings to set foot on the moon. Upon exiting the lunar module, *Eagle*, Armstrong famously said, "That's one small step for a man, one giant leap for mankind." Armstrong and Aldrin explored the moon's surface for about two hours, conducting experiments, collecting samples, and taking photographs. They also planted an American flag.

J. Patrick Lewis was born in Gary, Indiana, in 1942. He served as the United States Children's Poet Laureate from 2011 to 2013. Lewis taught economics for 25 years before he became a full-time writer. He has written more than fifty books of poetry for children and several books of poetry for adults, including *Gulls Hold Up the Sky*.

Reading Poetry

The language of poetry uses a wide variety of language structures, some of which break conventional rules. For example, as you read poetry, you may notice the following kinds of structures:

- sentence fragments
- inversion, where the usual subject-verb order is switched
- alternative capitalization or punctuation
- compressed language that may not have obvious surface meanings

Try to accept that you may not understand the full meaning of a poem when you read it for the first time. Often, poetry reveals its meaning over multiple readings.

Science-Fiction Cradlesong

C. S. Lewis

By and by Man will try
To get out into the sky,
Sailing far beyond the air
From Down and Here to Up and There.
Stars and sky, sky and stars
Make us feel the prison bars.

Suppose it done. Now we ride
Closed in steel, up there, outside;
Through our port-holes see the **vast**
Heaven-scape go rushing past.
Shall we? All that meets the eye
Is sky and stars, stars and sky.

Points of light with black between
Hang like a painted scene
Motionless, no nearer there
Than on Earth, everywhere
Equidistant[1] from our ship.
Heaven has given us the slip.

Hush, be still. Outer space
Is a concept, not a place.
Try no more. Where we are
Never can be sky or star.
From prison, in a prison, we fly;
There's no way into the sky.

1. **Equidistant** (ee kwuh DIHS tuhnt) *adj.* equally distant.

AUDIO

ANNOTATE

Use a dictionary or indicate another strategy you used that helped you determine meaning.

vast (vast) *adj.*

MEANING:

First Men on the Moon

J. Patrick Lewis

"The *Eagle* has landed!"

— Apollo 11 Commander Neil A. Armstrong

"A magnificent desolation!"

— Air Force Colonel Edwin E. "Buzz" Aldrin, Jr.

July 20, 1969

AUDIO

ANNOTATE

That afternoon in mid-July,
Two pilgrims watched from distant space
The moon ballooning in the sky.
They rose to meet it face-to-face.

Their spidery spaceship, *Eagle*, dropped
Down gently on the lunar sand.
And when the module's engines stopped,
Rapt silence fell across the land.

The first man down the ladder, Neil,
Spoke words that we remember now—
"One small step…" It made us feel
As if we were there too, somehow.

When Neil planted the flag and Buzz
Collected lunar rocks and dust,
They hopped like kangaroos because
Of gravity. Or **wanderlust**?

A quarter million miles away,
One small blue planet watched in **awe**.
And no one who was there that day
Will soon forget the sight they saw.

Use a dictionary or indicate another strategy you used that helped you determine meaning.

wanderlust
(WAHN der luhst) *n.*
MEANING:

awe (AW) *n.*
MEANING:

Response

1. **Personal Connections** Which poem did you find more interesting or appealing? Why?

Work on your own to answer the questions in your notebook. Use text evidence to support your responses.

Comprehension

2. **Reading Check (a)** In the first stanza of "Science-Fiction Cradlesong," what does the speaker say "Man" will try to do? **(b)** What does the speaker ask readers to imagine in the second stanza of "Science-Fiction Cradlesong"? **(c)** What is the *Eagle* in "First Men on the Moon"?

3. **Strategy: Adjust Fluency (a)** How did you adjust your fluency to suit your purpose for reading these poems? **(b)** Cite one example of a line that became clearer to you when you read it according to punctuation. Explain.

Analysis and Discussion

4. **Make Inferences** In "Science-Fiction Cradlesong," what motivates the human desire to explore space? Use evidence from the poem to support your inference.

5. **Analyze** In line 19 of "Science-Fiction Cradlesong," the speaker addresses the reader with the words "Hush, be still." Why are these words appropriate, given the poem's title? Explain.

6. **Interpret** In "First Men on the Moon," why do you think the poet refers to the astronauts by their first names? What effect does this choice have?

7. **Get Ready for Close Reading** Choose a passage from the texts that you find especially interesting or important. You'll discuss the passage with your group during Close-Read activities.

WORKING AS A GROUP

Discuss your responses to the Analysis and Discussion questions with your group.

- Note agreements and disagreements.
- Summarize insights.
- Consider changes of opinion.

If necessary, revise your original answers to reflect what you learn from your discussion.

EQ Notes Should humanity's future lie among the stars?

What have you learned about imagination and the future from reading these poems? Go to your Essential Question Notes and record your observations and thoughts about "Science-Fiction Cradlesong" and "First Men on the Moon."

TEKS

3. Adjust fluency when reading grade-level text based on the reading purpose.

5.F. Make inferences and use evidence to support understanding.

6.C. Use text evidence to support an appropriate response.

6.I. Reflect on and adjust responses as new evidence is presented.

POETRY COLLECTION

Close Read

PRACTICE **Complete the following activities. Use text evidence to support your responses.**

1. **Present and Discuss** With your group, share the passages from the poems that you found especially interesting. Discuss what you notice, the questions you have, and the conclusions you reach. For example, you might focus on the following passages:
   - First and last stanzas of "Science-Fiction Cradlesong": Discuss the references to prison. Why does the speaker believe Earth is a prison?
   - Line 2 of "First Men on the Moon": Discuss the use of the word "pilgrims" to describe the astronauts.
2. **Reflect on Your Learning** What new ideas or insights did you uncover during your second reading of the text?

LANGUAGE STUDY

Concept Vocabulary

Why These Words? The vocabulary words are related.

vast	wanderlust	awe

1. With your group, determine what the words have in common. Write your ideas.

2. Add another word that fits the category. ____________________

Word Study

Connotation and Denotation The **denotation** of a word is its dictionary definition. The **connotation** is the shade of meaning or emotional qualities the word expresses. For example, the denotation of *vast* is similar to that of *gigantic*. The words are synonyms. However, they have very different connotations.

1. Work on your own to find another synonym for *vast* in a thesaurus. Then, rewrite lines 7–10 of "Science-Fiction Cradlesong," replacing *vast* with the synonym.
2. With your group, read your revised lines. Discuss how the synonyms change the meaning and whether the new lines are stronger or weaker than the original.

WORD NETWORK

Add words that are related to imagination and the future from the text to your Word Network.

TEKS

6.F. Respond using newly acquired vocabulary as appropriate.

8.B. Analyze the effect of rhyme scheme, meter, and graphical elements such as punctuation and capitalization in poems across a variety of poetic forms.

Genre / Text Elements

Meter and Rhyme Scheme **Meter** is the rhythm created by the pattern of stressed and unstressed syllables in each line of a poem. To identify meter, say the lines out loud and listen for a pattern of beats. Mark the pattern and then count how many times it occurs within each line. Here are some common types of metrical feet.

TIP: Metrical names identify the type and number of feet in each line. For example, iambic pentameter has five (*penta* = five) feet of iambs.

TYPE OF FOOT	EXAMPLE	METRICAL NAME
Iamb: one unstressed and one stressed syllable	That **time** | of **year** | thou **mayst** | in **me** | be**hold** (5 feet)	iambic pentameter
Trochee: one stressed and one unstressed syllable	**Ty**ger!| **Ty**ger! | **Burn**ing | **bright**. (4 feet)	trochaic tetrameter

Rhyme scheme is the pattern of end rhymes in a poem. Poets use rhyme schemes to create musical effects or to create mood. Follow these steps to identify rhyme scheme:

1. Mark the word at the end of the first line with an *a*. Then, mark all other end words that rhyme with that word *a*.
2. Mark the next end word that has a different final sound with a *b*. Then, mark all other end words that rhyme with that word *b*.
3. Continue on, using a new letter to indicate each new set of rhymes.
4. Record the pattern stanza by stanza. Leave a space to indicate stanza breaks. For example: *abab cc efef*.

 NOTEBOOK

PRACTICE Work with your group to discuss and answer the questions. As you speak and write, use the terms you have learned, such as *trochee* and *iamb*.

1. **Analyze** Does "First Men on the Moon" use iambs or trochees? Explain.
2. **(a) Analyze** Which poem has a more consistent meter? Explain.
   (b) Make a Judgment Which poem uses meter to better effect? Discuss with your group, and support your opinion with details.
3. **Analyze** Identify the rhyme scheme of each poem using the *abc* system.
4. **(a) Compare and Contrast** In each poem, what effect does the rhyme create? **(b) Evaluate** Would the poems be as effective without rhyme schemes? Explain.

POETRY COLLECTION

Author's Craft

Author's Purpose and Message Poetry is an art form, which means the author's **purpose,** or reason for writing, is complex. Likewise, the **message**, or theme, of a poem is multi-layered. However, some poems convey messages that are similar to those of an essay.

- Like a paragraph in prose, the structures of poetry—the lines and stanzas—help the poet achieve a purpose. Each poetic stanza introduces a new idea that relates to or develops a message.
- To determine the message of the poem, **paraphrase**, or restate the idea of each stanza in your own words.
- Consider how the logic of the poem builds line by line and stanza by stanza to express a central message.

INTERACTIVITY

NOTEBOOK

PRACTICE Work with your group to answer the questions and complete the activity. Seek help from other groups or your teacher as needed.

1. **Paraphrase** Use the chart to paraphrase each stanza of "Science-Fiction Cradlesong." Make sure to maintain the meaning and logical order of the original. What main point does the speaker express in each stanza?

STANZA	PARAPHRASE
1	
2	
3	
4	

2. **(a) Analyze** In "Science-Fiction Cradlesong," what point does the speaker make in line 18? **(b) Connect** How does this point relate to lines 21 and 24? **(c) Summarize** What is the speaker's overall message?

3. **(a) Analyze** In "First Men on the Moon," who is the "we" the speaker mentions in stanza three? **(b) Connect** How does that reference connect to the last stanza? **(c) Summarize** What message does the poem convey about the importance of the moon landing?

4. **Draw Conclusions** What do you think the poet's purpose was for writing "First Men on the Moon"? In what ways does the structure of the poem help him achieve that purpose?

TEKS

6.D. Paraphrase and summarize texts in ways that maintain meaning and logical order.

9.A. Explain the author's purpose and message within a text.

9.B. Analyze how the use of text structure contributes to the author's purpose.

Speaking and Listening

An **illustrated version** of a literary work includes the original text as well as pictures that show how an artist imagines and interprets the work.

ASSIGNMENT

Work with your group to create an **illustrated version** of either "Science-Fiction Cradlesong" or "First Men on the Moon" to present to a class of young children. Choose one of the following options:

◯ picture book, either digital or print

◯ graphic novel

The illustrations should capture the major ideas and insights of the poem and convey them in a visual way to a young audience.

Discuss and Plan As a group, discuss the poem you will illustrate and make some decisions about the effect you want to achieve. Make sure the images you plan are appropriate for an audience of young children.

- Will you illustrate each stanza or only parts of stanzas?
- Will you use the text of the poem as captions or as part of the images?
- What qualities of the poem do you want to emphasize?

Use the chart to capture your decisions.

INTERACTIVITY

TEXT TO ILLUSTRATE	CONTENT OF ILLUSTRATION

Create the Illustrations You may draw, paint, collage, use art software, or use and modify photographs. You may also create images on paper and then photograph or scan them to create a digital text.

Provide and Accept Feedback Share your illustrated version with the class and ask for feedback. In particular, make sure your work is appropriate for the intended audience of young children. Listen and accept feedback from your classmates and then make any necessary changes.

Publish and Present If possible, print your work as a picture book and share it in a story session for an elementary school class.

EQ Notes Before moving on to a new selection, go to your Essential Question Notes and record any additional thoughts or observations you may have about this Poetry Collection.

 TEKS

1.D. Engage in meaningful discourse and provide and accept constructive feedback from others.

6.E. Interact with sources in meaningful ways such as notetaking, annotating, freewriting, or illustrating.

10.E. Publish written work for appropriate audiences.

THE LAST DOG

The selection you are about to read is a science-fiction adventure story.

Reading Science-Fiction Adventure Stories

A **science-fiction adventure story** is a brief work of fiction in which danger and futuristic science or technology play important roles.

SCIENCE-FICTION ADVENTURE

Author's Purpose

- to tell an exciting and imaginative story

Characteristics

- The setting is imaginary (the future, another planet, etc.) and dangerous.
- Characters may be human or non-human (aliens, robots, etc.).
- Conflicts are often caused by the setting, harsh social rules, or technology.
- Science and technology play a key role in the story.
- Conveys a theme, or message about life.

Structure

- The plot features elements of danger and builds suspense in readers.

Take a Minute!

NOTEBOOK

LIST IT Work with a partner to list at least two examples of science-fiction adventures you have read or seen. Consider novels, stories, TV shows, and movies.

What do you like and dislike about these types of stories?

TEKS

7.C. Analyze plot elements, including the use of foreshadowing and suspense, to advance the plot.

8.A. Demonstrate knowledge of literary genres such as realistic fiction, adventure stories, historical fiction, mysteries, humor, myths, fantasy, and science fiction.

Genre / Text Elements

Foreshadowing, Suspense, and Plot The plot of any adventure story is driven by conflicts that involve danger and put characters at risk. Uncertainty about a character's fate builds **suspense**, or tension, in readers. The writer adds to the suspense through **foreshadowing**, or the use of clues that hint at what *could* happen. The reader learns enough to understand the threat, but not enough to be certain of the outcome.

TIP: Foreshadowing also helps to advance the plot because it connects details from early in a story with events that happen later.

EXAMPLE: FORESHADOWING CLUE	WHAT IT SUGGESTS
Lucia's compass was smoothed by use. It had helped her find her way home so many times. "Can't lose this," she thought, clutching it to her heart as she felt the jungle close in around her.	Details about the compass and the jungle foreshadow, or hint at, problems that may arise later in the plot. These details suggest Lucia's danger and build suspense.

PRACTICE Read the passage. Then, answer the questions that follow.

"The light is fading," Aden thought. She had only wanted to see the first colony for herself, but her hovercar had broken down and now she was lost. In the wilds...at night...alone. She hadn't seen any of *them.* But what were those sparks in the glassy grass? And the clicking sounds. Crickets? "But there are no insects on this planet," she thought.

1. **(a)** Mark clues in the passage that foreshadow later events.
   (b) What kinds of events seem possible? Explain.

2. Which details in the passage create suspense?

About the Author

The daughter of two American missionaries, **Katherine Paterson** (b. 1932) was born in China and lived there during her early childhood years. Paterson became a renowned writer of children's novels. She has twice won the Newbery Medal and National Book Award.

The Last Dog

Concept Vocabulary

ANNOTATE

As you read "The Last Dog," you will encounter these words.

threatening	extinct	mutation

Context Clues The context of a word is the other words and phrases that appear close to it in the text. Clues in the context can help you figure out a word's meaning.

Antonym, or Contrast, is a type of context clue that shows differences.

EXAMPLE The **insolent** robot had to be replaced with a polite robot.

Analysis: Since an insolent robot was replaced with a polite one, *insolent* probably means the opposite of *polite*, or "rude; disrespectful."

EXAMPLE One robot was **diminutive,** but the other was gigantic.

Analysis: Since a "gigantic" robot is contrasted with a "diminutive" robot, *diminutive* must mean the opposite of *gigantic*, or "very small."

PRACTICE As you read "The Last Dog," study the context to determine the meanings of unfamiliar words. Mark your observations in the open space next to the text.

Comprehension Strategy

ANNOTATE

Make Predictions

Predictions are a type of guess you make about events that will happen later in a story. Good readers make predictions and then correct or confirm them as they read on. You can use the characteristics of the genre you are reading to make predictions.

- Notice details in the text and consider what they tell you about the characters and setting.
- Use your knowledge of science-fiction adventure stories to predict the conflicts characters might face and ways they might react.
- As you keep reading, correct the predictions that were wrong and confirm the ones that were right.

PRACTICE Read the first two paragraphs of this story. Then, write two predictions about Brock in the open space next to the text. Return to these predictions later and correct or confirm them.

TEKS

2.B. Use context such as contrast or cause and effect to clarify the meaning of words.

5.C. Make, correct, or confirm predictions using text features, characteristics of genre, and structures.

SCIENCE-FICTION ADVENTURE

The Last Dog

Katherine Paterson

AUDIO

ANNOTATE

BACKGROUND

In this science-fiction story, the author imagines a future in which people live in a sealed dome and believe that the outside world is unsafe and in ruins. The story's main character discovers something that everyone thinks can't exist—and it changes everything.

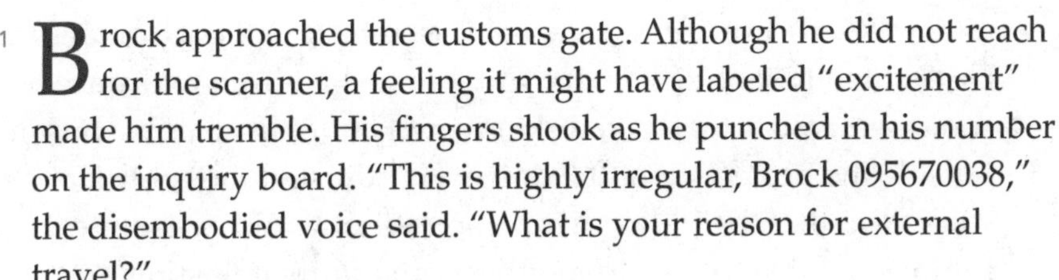

1 Brock approached the customs gate. Although he did not reach for the scanner, a feeling it might have labeled "excitement" made him tremble. His fingers shook as he punched in his number on the inquiry board. "This is highly irregular, Brock 095670038," the disembodied voice said. "What is your reason for external travel?"

2 Brock took a deep breath. "Scientific research," he replied. He didn't need to be told that his behavior was "irregular." He'd never heard of anyone doing research outside the dome—actual rather than virtual research. "I—I've been cleared by my podmaster and the Research Team. . . ."

3 "Estimated time of return?" So, he wasn't to be questioned further.

4 "Uh, 1800 hours."

5 "Are you wearing the prescribed dry suit with helmet and gloves?"

6 "Affirmative."

7 "You should be equipped with seven hundred fifty milliliters of liquid and food tablets for one day travel."

8 "Affirmative." Brock patted the sides of the dry suit to be sure.

9 "Remember to drink sparingly. Water supply is limited." Brock nodded. He tried to lick his parched lips, but his whole mouth felt dry. "Is that understood?"

10 "Affirmative." Was he hoping customs would stop him? If he was, they didn't seem to be helping him. Well, this was what he wanted, wasn't it? To go outside the dome.

11 "Turn on the universal locator, Brock 095670038, and proceed to gate."

12 Why weren't they questioning him further? Were they eager for him to go? Ever since he'd said out loud in group speak that he wanted to go outside the dome, people had treated him strangely—that session with the podmaster and then the interview with the representative from Research. Did they think he was a deviant?[1] Deviants sometimes disappeared. The word was passed around that they had "gone outside," but no one really knew. No deviant had ever returned.

13 The gate slid open. Before he was quite ready for it, Brock found himself outside the protection of the dome. He blinked. The sun—at least it was what was called "the sun" in virtual lessons—was too bright for his eyes even inside the tinted helmet. He took a deep breath, one last backward look at the dome, which, with the alien sun gleaming on it, was even harder to look at than the distant star, and started across an expanse of brown soil [was it?] to what he recognized from holograms as a line of purplish mountains in the distance.

14 It was, he pulled the scanner from his outside pouch and checked it, "hot." Oh, that was what he was feeling. Hot. He remembered "hot" from a virtual lesson he'd had once on deserts. He wanted to take off the dry suit, but he had been told since he could remember that naked skin would suffer irreparable burning outside the protection of the dome. He adjusted the control as he walked so that the unfamiliar perspiration would evaporate. He fumbled a bit before he found the temperature adjustment function. He put it on twenty degrees centigrade and immediately felt more comfortable. No one he really knew had ever left the dome (stories of deviants exiting the dome being hard to verify), but there was all this equipment in case someone decided to venture out. He tried to ask the clerk who outfitted him, but the woman was evasive. The equipment was old, she said. People used to go out, but the outside environment was **threatening**, so hardly anyone (she looked at him carefully now), hardly anyone ever used it now.

Mark context clues or indicate another strategy you used that helped you determine meaning.

threatening (THREHT uhn ihng) *adj.*

MEANING:

15 Was Brock, then, the only normal person still curious about the outside? Or had all those who had dared to venture out perished, discouraging further forays? Perhaps he *was* a deviant for wanting to see the mountains for himself. When he'd mentioned it to others, they had laughed, but there was a hollow sound to the laughter.

1. **deviant** (DEE vee uhnt) *n.* strange, irregular person.

16 If he never returned, he'd have no one to blame but himself. He knew that. While his podfellows played virtual games, he'd wandered into a subsection of the historical virtuals called "ancient fictions." Things happened in these fictions more—well, more densely than they did in the virtuals. The people he met there—it was hard to describe—but somehow they were more *actual* than dome dwellers. They had strange names like Huck Finn and M. C. Higgins the Great. They were even a little scary. It was their insides. Their insides were very loud. But even though the people in the ancient fictions frightened him a bit, he couldn't get enough of them. When no one was paying attention, he went back again and again to visit them. They had made him wonder about that other world—that world outside the dome.

17 Perhaps, once he had realized the danger the ancient fictions posed, he should have left them alone, but he couldn't help himself. They had made him feel hollow, hungry for something no food pellet or even virtual experience could satisfy. And now he was in that world they spoke of and the mountains of it were in plain view.

18 He headed for the purple curves. Within a short distance from the dome, the land was clear and barren, but after he had been walking for an hour or so he began to pass rusting hulks and occasional ruins of what might have been the dwellings of ancient peoples that no one in later years had cleared away for recycling or vaporization.

19 He checked the emotional scanner for an unfamiliar sensation. "Loneliness," it registered. He rather liked having names for these new sensations. It made him feel a bit "proud," was it? The scanner was rather interesting. He wondered when people had stopped using them. He hadn't known they existed until, in that pod meeting, he had voiced his desire to go outside.

20 The podmaster had looked at him with a raised eyebrow and a sniff. "Next thing you'll be asking for a scanner," he said.

21 "What's a scanner?" Brock asked.

22 The podmaster requisitioned one from storage, but at the same time, he must have alerted Research, because it was the representative from Research who had brought him the scanner and questioned him about his expressed desired for an Actual Adventure—a journey outside the dome.

23 "What has prompted this, uh—unusual ambition?" the representative had asked, his eyes not on Brock but on the scanner in his hand. Brock had hesitated, distracted by the man's fidgeting with the strange instrument. "I—I'm interested in scientific research," Brock said at last.

24 So here he was out of the pod, alone for the first time in his life. Perhaps, though, he should have asked one of his podfellows to

come along. Or even the pod robopet. But the other fellows all laughed when he spoke of going outside, their eyes darting back and forth. Nothing on the outside, they said, could equal the newest Virtual Adventure. He suddenly realized that ever since he started interfacing with the ancient fictions, his fellows had given him that look. They did think he was odd—not quite the same as a regular podfellow. Brock didn't really vibe with the pod robopet. It was one of the more modern ones, and when they'd programmed its artificial intelligence they'd somehow made it too smart. The robopet in the children's pod last year was older, stupider, and more "fun" to have around.

25 He'd badly underestimated the distance to the mountains. The time was well past noon, and he had at least three kilometers to go. Should he signal late return or turn about now? He didn't have much more than one day's scant supply of water and food tablets. But he was closer to the hills than to the dome. He felt a thrill ["excitement"] and pressed on.

Mark context clues or indicate another strategy you used that helped you determine meaning.

extinct (ehk STIHNGKT) *adj.*

MEANING:

26 There were actual trees growing on the first hill. Not the great giants of virtual history lessons, more scrubby and bent. But they were trees, he was sure of it. The podmaster had said that trees had been **extinct** for hundreds of years. Brock reached up and pulled off a leaf. It was green and had veins. In some ways it looked like his own hand. He put the leaf in his pack to study later. He didn't want anyone accusing him of losing his scientific objectivity.[2] Only deviants did that. Farther up the hill he heard an unfamiliar burbling sound. No, he knew that sound. It was water running. He'd heard it once when the liquid dispenser had malfunctioned. There'd been a near panic in the dome over it. He checked the scanner. There was no caution signal, so he hurried toward the sound.

27 It was a—a "brook"—he was sure of it! Virtual lessons had taught that there were such things outside in the past but that they had long ago grown poisonous, then in the warming climate had dried up. But here was a running brook, not even a four-hour journey from his dome. His first impulse was to take off his protective glove and dip a finger in it, but he drew back. He had been well conditioned to avoid danger. He sat down clumsily on the bank. Yes, this must be grass. There were even some tiny flowers mixed in the grass. Would the atmosphere poison him if he unscrewed his helmet to take a sniff? He punched the scanner to read conditions, but the characters on the scanner panel danced about uncertainly until, at length, the disembodied voice said "conditions unreadable." He'd better not risk it.

28 He pushed the buttons now for liquid and pellets. A tube appeared in his mouth. It dropped a pellet on his tongue. From

2. **objectivity** (ob jehk TIHV uh tee) *n.* perspective based on facts, not feelings or opinions.

the tube he sucked liquid enough to swallow his meal. What was it they called outside nourishment in the history virtuals? Pecnec? Something like that. He was having a *pecnec* in the woods by a brook. A hasty consulting of the scanner revealed that what he was feeling was "pleasure." He was very glad he hadn't come with an anxious podfellow or, worse, an advanced robopet that would, no doubt, be yanking at his suit already, urging him back toward the dome.

29 It was then, in the middle of the post-*pecnec* satisfaction, that he heard the new sound. Like that programmed into a robopet, yet different. He struggled to his feet. The dry suit from storage was certainly awkward when you wanted to stand up or sit down. Nothing on the scanner indicated danger, so he went into the scrubby woods toward the sound. And stopped abruptly.

30 Something was lying under the shadow of a tree. Something about a meter long. It was furred and quite still. The sound was not coming from it. And then he saw the small dog—the puppy. He was sure it was a puppy, nosing the stiff body of what must once have been its mother, making the little crying sounds that he'd heard from the brook. Later, much later, he realized that he should have been wary. If the older dog had died of some extradomal[3] disease, the puppy might have been a carrier. But at the time, all he could think of was the puppy, a small creature who had lost its mother.

31 He'd found out about mothers from the Virtuals. Mothers were extinct in the dome. Children were conceived and born in the lab and raised in units of twelve in the pods, presided over by a bank of computers and the podmaster. Nuclear families,[4] as everyone knew, had been wasteful of time, energy, and space. There was an old proverb: The key to survival is efficiency. So though Brock could guess the puppy was "sad" (like that fictions person, Jo, whose podmate expired), he didn't know what missing a mother would feel like. And who would whimper for a test tube?

32 Brock had never seen a dog, of course, but he'd seen plenty of dog breed descriptions on the science/history virtuals. Dogs had been abundant once. They filled the ancient fictions. They even had names there—Lassie, Toto, Sounder. But now dogs were extinct, gone during the dark ages when the atmosphere had become warm and poisonous. The savages who had not had the intelligence or wealth to join the foresighted dome crafters had killed all animals wild or domesticated for food before they had eventually died out themselves. It was all in one of the very first virtual lessons. He had seen that one many times. He never confessed to anyone how, well, sad it made him feel.

3. **extradomal** *adj.* from outside the dome.
4. **nuclear families** groups consisting of parents and their children.

33 But obviously, dogs were not quite extinct. Cautiously, he moved toward the small one.

34 "Alert. Alert. Scanning unknown object."

35 Brock pushed the off button. "Are you sure you want to turn off scanner?"

36 "Affirmative." He stuck the scanner into his pouch.

37 The puppy had lifted its head at the sound of his voice. It looked at him, head cocked, as though deciding whether to run or stay.

38 "It's all right, dog," Brock said soothingly. "I won't hurt you." He stayed still. He didn't want to frighten the little beast. If it ran, he wasn't sure he'd be able to catch it in his clumsy dry suit.

39 Slowly he extended his gloved hand. The dog backed away anxiously, but when Brock kept the hand extended, the puppy slowly crept toward him and sniffed, making whimpering sounds. It wasn't old enough to be truly afraid, it seemed. The pup licked his glove tentatively, then backed away again. It was looking for food, and plasticine gloves weren't going to satisfy.

40 Brock looked first at the dead mother, whose source of nourishment must have long dried up, then around the landscape. What would a dog eat? A puppy on its own? He took off his glove and reached through his pouch into the inside pocket that held his pellet supply. Making every move slow and deliberate so as not to startle the dog, he held out a pellet. The dog came to his hand, licked it, then the pellet. It wrinkled its nose. Brock laughed. He didn't need the scanner now to tell him that what he felt was "pleasure." He loved the feel of the rough tongue on his palm and the little furred face, questioning him.

41 "It's all right, fellow. You can eat it."

42 As though understanding, the pup gulped down the pellet. Then looked around for more, not realizing that it had just bolted

down a whole meal. When the dog saw there was no more coming, it ran over to the brook. Brock watched in horror as it put its head right down into the poisonous stream and lapped noisily.

43 "Don't!" Brock cried.

44 The puppy turned momentarily at the sound, then went back to drinking, as though it was the most normal thing in the world. Well, it was, for the dog. Where else would a creature in the wild get liquid? If the streams were not all dried up, they must have learned to tolerate the water. But then, it was breathing the poisoned atmosphere, wasn't it? Why hadn't it hit Brock before? This was a fully organic creature on the outside *without any life support system*. What could that mean? Some amazing **mutation** must have occurred, making it possible for at least some creatures to breathe the outside atmosphere and drink its poisoned water. Those who couldn't died, those who could survived and got stronger. Even the ancient scientist Darwin[5] knew that. And Brock had come upon one of these magnificent mutants!

Mark context clues or indicate another strategy you used that helped you determine meaning.

mutation (myoo TAY shuhn) *n.*

MEANING:

45 The puppy whimpered and looked up at Brock with large, trusting eyes. How could he think of it as a mutant specimen? It was a puppy. One who had lost its mother. What would it eat? There was no sign of food for a carnivore. Perhaps way back in the mountains some small mammals had also survived, keeping the food chain going, but the puppy would not live long enough to find its way there, much less know how to hunt with its mother gone. For the first time in his life something deep inside Brock reached out toward another creature. The thought of the puppy languishing here by the side of its dead parent until it, too . . .

46 "Your name is Brog, all right?" The ancient astronomers had named stars after themselves. He had discovered something just as wonderful. Didn't he have the right to name it sort of after himself while preserving the puppy's uniqueness? "Don't worry, Brog. I won't let you starve."

47 Which is why Brock appeared at the customs portal after dark, the front of his dry suit stained, carrying a wriggling *Canis familiaris*[6] of uncertain breed.

48 If there had been any way to smuggle the dog in, Brock would have. But he couldn't for the life of him figure out how. As it was, every alarm in the area went off when he stepped into the transitional cubicle. The disembodied voice of the monitor queried him.

49 "Welcome back, Brock 095670038. You're late."

50 "Affirmative."

51 "And you are carrying contraband."

52 "I pulled a leaf."

5. **Darwin** Charles Darwin (1809–1882); scientist who first formulated the theory of evolution.
6. ***Canis familiaris*** (KAY nihs fuh mihl ee AR ihs) scientific name for a dog.

53 "Deposit same in quarantine bins."

54 "Affirmative."

55 "Sensors denote warm-blooded presence not on official roster."

56 "I found a dog," Brock mumbled.

57 "Repeat."

58 "A dog."

59 "*Canis familiaris* is extinct."

60 "Well, maybe it's just a robopet that got out somehow."

61 "Correction. Robopets are bloodless. Leave dry suit for sterilization and proceed to quarantine inspection."

62 The officials in quarantine inspection, who rarely had anything to inspect, were at first nervous and then, as they watched the puppy happily licking Brock's face, interested despite themselves. An actual dog! None of them had ever seen one, of course, and Brock's dog was so much, well, more vital than a robopet. And although, on later reflection, they knew they should have terminated or expelled it, they couldn't quite bring themselves to do so that night.

63 "It will have to go to Research," the chief inspector finally declared.

64 "Permission requested to hand carry the dog known as Brog to Research," Brock said. There was a bit of an argument about that. Several inspectors sought the honor, but the chief declared that Brock, having shed his dry suit and being already contaminated, should be placed with the dog in a hermetically sealed air car and transported to Research.

65 The scientists in Research were predictably amazed to see a live *Canis familiaris*. But being scientists and more objective than the lower-grade quarantine inspectors, they kept a safe distance both physically and psychically from the creature. Only the oldest scientist, dressed in proper protective clothing, came into the laboratory with Brock and the dog. He scanned and poked and prodded the poor little fellow until it began to whimper in protest.

66 "Brog needs to rest," said Brock, interrupting the scientist in the midst of his inspection. "She's (for by this time gender had been indisputably established) had a hard day. And if there's some actual food available—she's not used to pellets."

67 "Of course, of course," said one of the researchers through the speaker in the observation booth. "How thoughtless. Send someone out for a McLike burger without sauce. She may regard it as meat. Anyhow, it will seem more like food to her than a pellet, affirmative, Brock?"

68 The scientists, Brock soon realized, were looking to him for advice. He was, after all, the discoverer of the last dog. It gave him sudden scientific status. Brock had sense enough to take advantage of this. After Brog had swallowed the McLike burger in three quick gulps, Brock insisted that he be allowed to stay

with Brog, so that he might interact and sleep with her. "She's not like us," he explained. "She's used to tumbling about and curling up with other warm bodies. In the old myths," he added, "puppies separated from their litters cried all night long. She will need constant interaction with another warm-blooded creature or she might well die of," he loved using his new vocabulary, "loneliness."

69 The scientists agreed. After all, research was rather like quarantine, and since Brock had touched the dog ungloved and unprotected, he might well have picked up some germ from her. It was better to keep them both isolated in the research lab where proper precautions would be taken.

70 For nearly a week, Brock lived with Brog in the research center, eating McLike burgers, playing "fetch," teaching Brog to "sit," "heel," "come"—all the commands he could cull from the ancient texts. The dog quickly learned to obey Brock's commands, but it wasn't the automatic response of a robopet. Brog delighted in obedience. She wanted to please Brock, and those few times when she was too busy nosing about the lab and failed to obey instantly, those times when Brock's voice took on a sharp tone of reproof, the poor little thing put her tail between her legs, looked up at him with sorrowful eyes, begging to be forgiven. Brock was tempted to speak sharply to her even when there was no need, for the sight of her drooping ears and tail, her mournful eyes, was so dear to him that he did what Travis Coates had done to Old Yeller. He hugged her. There was no other way to explain it. He simply put his arms around her and held her to his chest while she beat at him with her tail and licked his face raw. Out of the corner of his eye he was aware that one of the scientists was watching. Well, let him watch. Nothing was as wonderful as feeling this warmth toward another creature.

71 For the first week, the researchers seemed quite content to observe dog and boy from their glass-paneled observation booth and speak copious notes into their computers. Only the oldest of them would come into the lab and actually touch the alien creature, and he always wore a sterile protective suit with gloves. The others claimed it would interfere with objectivity if they got close to the dog, but they all seemed to behave positively toward Brog. No mention was made to Brock of his own less than-objective behavior. So Brock was astounded to awake in the middle of the night to the sounds of an argument. Someone had forgotten to turn off the communication system.

72 "Cloning—it's the only thing to do. If she's the last, we owe it to posterity to keep the line going."

73 "And how are we going to raise a pack of dogs in a dome? One is nearly eating and drinking us out of test tube and petri dish. We can't go on this way. As drastic as it may seem, we have

to be realistic. Besides, no one has had the chance to do actual experiments since the dark ages. Haven't you ever, just once, yearned to compare virtual research with actual?"

74 "What about the boy? He won't agree. Interfacing daily with the dog, he's become crippled by primal urges."

75 "Can you think what chaos might ensue if a flood of primordial[7] emotions were to surface in a controlled environment such as ours?" another asked. "Apparently, emotions are easily triggered by interactions with primitive beasts, like dogs."

76 "Shh. Not now. The speaker is—" The system clicked off.

77 But Brock had already heard. He knew he had lost anything resembling scientific objectivity. He was no longer sure objectivity was a desirable trait. He rather enjoyed being flooded by "primordial emotions." But he was more worried for Brog than for himself. It wasn't hard to figure out what the scientists meant by "actual experiments." Cloning would be bad enough. Ten dogs who looked just like Brog so no one would know how special, how truly unique Brog was. But experiments! They'd cut her open and examine her internal organs, the way scientists had in the dark ages. They'd prod her with electric impulses and put chips in her brain. They'd try to change her personality or modify her behavior. They'd certainly try to make her eat and drink less!

78 In the dark, he put his arm around Brog and drew her close. He loved the terrible smell of her breath and the way she snored when she slept. They'd probably fix that, too.

79 The next day he played sick. Brog, faithful dog that she was, hung around him whimpering, licking his face. The scientists showed no particular concern. They were too busy plotting what they might do with Brog.

80 Brock crept to the nearest terminal[8] in the lab. It was already logged in. The scientists had been doing nothing but research on *Canis familiaris*. COMMON CANINE DISEASES. Brock scrolled down the list with descriptions. No, *distemper* wouldn't do. The first symptom was loss of appetite. He couldn't make Brog fake that. On and on it went—no, *heartworms* wouldn't do. What he needed was a disease that might affect *Homo sapiens* as well as *Canis familiaris*. Here it was! "Rabies: A viral disease occurring in animals and humans, especially in dogs and wolves. Transmitted by bite or scratch. The early stages of the disease are most dangerous, for an otherwise healthy and friendly appearing animal will suddenly bite without provocation."

81 Rabies was it! Somehow he would have to make Brog bite him. There was no antirabies serum in the dome, he felt sure. There were no animals in the dome. Why would they use precious space

7. **primordial** (pry MAWR dee uhl) *adj.* very ancient and basic.
8. **terminal** *n.* computer.

to store an unneeded medication? So they'd have to expel him as well as Brog for fear of spreading the disease. He shivered, then shook himself. No matter what lay on the outside, he could not stand to go back to the life he had lived in the dome before he met Brog.

82 He crept back to bed, pulling the covers over Brog. When one of the scientists came into the observation booth, Brock pinched Brog's neck as hard as he could. Nothing. He pinched again, harder. Brog just snuggled closer, slobbering on his arm.

83 Disgusted, Brock got out of bed. Brog hopped down as well, rubbing against his leg. Pinching obviously was not going to do it. While the scientist on duty in the booth was bending over a computer terminal, Brock brought his foot down on Brog's paw. A tiny *yip* was all he got from that cruel effort—not enough sound even to make the man look up.

84 "Feeling better, Brock 095670038?" The oldest researcher had come into the lab.

85 "Affirmative," Brock answered.

86 "And how are you, puppy-wuppy?" The old man tickled Brog under her chin with his gloved hand. *If I were a dog, I'd bite someone like that*, thought Brock, but Brog, of course, simply licked the researcher's glove and wagged her tail.

87 That was when he got his great idea. He waited to execute it until the proper moment. For the first time, all the scientists had gathered in the lab, all of them in protective garb, some of them twitching nervously in their chairs. They were sitting in a circle around Brock and Brog, explaining what must be done.

88 "It has to be done for the sake of science," they began. Then they went on to, "For the sake of the dome community, which is always, as you well know, short on food, and particularly short on water." Brock listened to their arguments, nodding solemnly, pretending to agree. "It won't be as if she'll really be gone, you know. We've made virtuals of her—a special series just for you to keep. You can virtually play with her whenever you like."

89 That was the cue. Brock turned and bit Brog on the tail so hard that the blood started. Brog, surprised and enraged, spun around and bit Brock on the nose.

90 There was a shocked silence. Every scientist leaned backward, body pressed hard against his or her chair back. Every eye was on the two of them.

91 "I—I don't know what got into me," Brock said. "I've been feeling very weird." The scientists continued to stare. "I was checking the historical records. . . ."

92 All of the scientists fled the room. Someone ran to a computer terminal. When Brock offered to take Brog out of the dome and let her loose in the mountains, no one argued. Neither did they

say, "Hurry back," or even, "Take care." No one came close as he loaded his pouch with water and food pellets. The customs gate monitor asked no questions.

93 Out of sight of the dome, Brog was delirious with joy, jumping and running about in circles around Brock's boots. Why wasn't the atmosphere choking Brog if it was as poisonous as the dome dwellers claimed? His heart beating rapidly, Brock unscrewed his helmet just enough to let in a little of the outside atmosphere. Nothing happened. In fact, he seemed to be breathing perfectly normally. He took off the helmet entirely. He was still breathing freely. But his heart was beating so hard, he couldn't be sure. He waited for the choking sensation he had been warned of. It didn't occur. Could they be wrong? Could the outside world have healed itself? Perhaps—perhaps the reason the scanner had so much trouble reading the outside atmosphere was because it wasn't within the range of computerized expectations.

94 Could it be? Could it be that fear had kept the dome dwellers prisoner many years longer than a poisoned environment would have?

95 He unfastened the dry suit and slowly stepped out of it into the sunlight.

96 It was wonderful how much faster he could walk without the clumsy suit. "Who knows?" Brock said to a frisking Brog. "Who knows, maybe out here you aren't the last dog. Your mother had to come from somewhere."

97 Brog barked happily in reply.

98 "And maybe, just maybe, where there are dogs, there are humans as well."

99 They stopped at the brook where they'd met, and both of them had a long drink. Brock no longer carried a scanner, but he knew what he felt was excitement. The water was delicious. ❧

NOTEBOOK

Response

1. **Personal Connections** At what points in the story did you feel worried or concerned? At what points did you feel hopeful? Explain your responses.

Work on your own to answer the questions in your notebook. Use text evidence to support your responses.

Comprehension

2. **Reading Check (a)** Where does Brock live? **(b)** What do people in Brock's community believe about the world outside the dome? **(c)** What does Brock discover about the world beyond the dome?

3. **Strategy: Make Predictions (a)** Which characteristics of science-fiction adventures did you use to make predictions about the story? **(b)** Were you able to confirm your predictions, or did you have to correct them? Explain.

Analysis and Discussion

4. **Draw Conclusions** Brock often checks his scanner to identify sensations, such as being hot, and emotions, such as loneliness. What does Brock's need to check his scanner so often suggest about life in the dome?

5. **Analyze** How does Brock's decision to go outside the dome change him? Explain, citing evidence from the text.

6. **(a) Connect** One possible theme of the story is: Advanced technology leaves an emptiness in people. Which story details support this theme? Explain your choices. **(b) Synthesize** State another theme you think this story expresses. Cite specific story details that support your idea.

7. **Get Ready for Close Reading** Choose a passage from the text that you find especially interesting or important. You'll discuss the passage with your group during Close-Read activities.

WORKING AS A GROUP

Discuss your responses to the Analysis and Discussion questions with your group.

- Note agreements and disagreements.
- Summarize insights.
- Consider changes of opinion.

If necessary, revise your original answers to reflect what you learn from your discussion.

EQ Notes Should humanity's future lie among the stars?

What have you learned about imagination and the future from reading this story? Go to your Essential Question Notes and record your observations and thoughts about "The Last Dog."

TEKS

5.C. Make, correct, or confirm predictions using text features, characteristics of genre, and structures.

6.A. Describe personal connections to a variety of sources, including self-selected texts.

6.C. Use text evidence to support an appropriate response.

6.I. Reflect on and adjust responses as new evidence is presented.

THE LAST DOG

Close Read

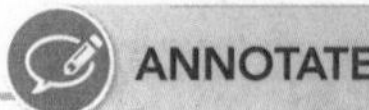

ANNOTATE

PRACTICE Complete the following activities.
Use text evidence to support an appropriate response.

1. **Present and Discuss** With your group, share the passages from the story that you found especially interesting. Discuss what you notice, the questions you have, and the conclusions you reach. For example, you might focus on the following passages:
   - Paragraphs 12 and 26: Discuss what it means to be "deviant" in Brock's society.
   - Paragraph 16: Discuss the author's use of **allusions**, or references to well-known people, events, or literary works from outside the story.
   - Paragraphs 1–11 and 92–93: Discuss the portrayal of the customs gate monitor at the beginning and end of the story.
2. **Reflect on Your Learning** What new ideas or insights did you uncover during your second reading of the text?

WORD NETWORK

Add words that are related to the ideas of imagination and the future from the text to your Word Network.

NOTEBOOK

LANGUAGE STUDY

Concept Vocabulary

Why These Words? The vocabulary words are related.

threatening	extinct	mutation

1. With your group, determine what the words have in common. Write your ideas.
2. Add another word that fits the category: ____________________
3. Use each vocabulary word in a sentence. Include context clues that hint at each word's meaning.

Word Study

Latin Suffix: *-tion* In the story, Brock thinks that the puppy is the product of a *mutation* that enables her to survive in the outside world. The word *mutation* is built from the verb *mutate*, meaning "to change," and the Latin suffix *-tion,* which turns a verb into a noun. Based on that information, identify the meaning of *mutation*.

TEKS

6.F. Respond using newly acquired vocabulary as appropriate.

7.C. Analyze plot elements, including the use of foreshadowing and suspense, to advance the plot.

Genre / Text Elements

Foreshadowing, Suspense, and Plot Foreshadowing is the use of clues that hint at events that could happen later in the plot of a story. Foreshadowing has important effects in adventure stories:

- It creates **suspense**, or a feeling of tense curiosity, that makes a reader want to keep reading.
- It creates a sense that the story holds together even if the ending is a surprise.

Foreshadowing is the technique and suspense is the effect. Together, they help to create continuity and advance the plot of a story, linking details logically and engaging readers' emotions to pull them through the narrative.

INTERACTIVITY

NOTEBOOK

PRACTICE Work on your own to respond to the questions, using vocabulary you have learned, such as *foreshadowing*. Then, discuss your answers with your group.

1. **(a) Analyze** Complete the chart by analyzing each foreshadowing clue and determining what it makes readers think or ask about Brock's world. **(b) Explain** How does each clue create suspense? Explain.

FORESHADOWING CLUE	THOUGHTS OR QUESTIONS	CREATION OF SUSPENSE
"Remember to drink...supply is limited." (paragraph 9)		
He was having...toward the dome. (paragraph 28)		
For the first...positively toward Brog. (paragraph 71)		

2. **(a) Analyze** Identify one other instance of foreshadowing in the story and explain the questions it raises in your mind. **(b) Connect** How are these questions answered by the story's events?

3. **Analyze** In what ways does foreshadowing help to connect the story's events and advance the plot? Cite examples from your answers to items 1 and 2 to support your response.

4. **(a) Analyze** Describe a moment in the story in which you felt suspense and were concerned about a character's fate. Which details caused your reaction, and why? **(b) Connect** Explain why suspense is an important element in fiction and how it helps to advance a plot.

Conventions

Verb Tenses A **verb** expresses an action or a state of being. Verbs have different **tenses**, or forms, that tell when something happens or exists. The chart shows the three simple tenses of verbs.

VERB TENSE	EXAMPLE FROM "THE LAST DOG"
Present tense indicates a current state of being, an action that occurs regularly, or states a general truth.	Water supply **is** limited. Brog **needs** to rest.
Past tense indicates an action that has already happened.	There **were** actual trees growing on the first hill.
Future tense indicates an action that will happen.	Anyhow, it **will seem** more like food to her than a pellet, affirmative, Brock?

To ensure that you are using consistent verb tenses, identify the time in which an action or events occur. Then, use the verb tense that is appropriate for that time frame. In situations where related events happen in different time frames, you may need to shift verb tenses. Unintentional shifts in tense, however, cause confusion. If events happen, situations occur, or people experience thoughts or feelings in the same time frame, stick with the same verb tense.

EXAMPLE

Incorrect: *Brock* ***exits*** *the dome and* ***explored*** *the land.*

Correct: *Brock* ***exits*** *the dome and* ***explores*** *the land.*

ANNOTATE

READ IT Reread the story, and mark examples of three different verb tenses—present, past, and future. Work on your own, then share your examples with your group.

WRITE IT The following paragraph contains unnecessary shifts in verb tenses. Work on your own to edit the paragraph, choosing an appropriate verb tense and making it consistent.

Our school celebrated space exploration this coming Friday. Students displayed cool projects, including space ice cream. Plus, famous astronauts spoke, and I can't wait to hear them.

TIP: Reading your work aloud may help you to identify unintentional shifts in verb tense.

10.D.ii. Edit drafts using standard English conventions, including consistent, appropriate use of verb tenses.

11.A. Compose literary texts such as personal narratives, fiction, and poetry using genre characteristics and craft.

Composition

A **revised ending** shows how a story could have concluded if the author had made different choices. The new ending should still make sense and provide a believable conclusion to the story's conflicts.

EDITING TIP
Review your draft to ensure that any shifts in verb tenses are deliberate and to correct any that are confusing.

ASSIGNMENT

Write your own version of the last seven paragraphs of this story. Begin your **revised ending** with the words "Out of sight of the dome." For your revision, choose one of the following options:

- ◯ Change the narrator, and write from the perspective of the puppy, Brog.
- ◯ Add a new character who influences the story's final events.

Work on your own to do this assignment. Then, share and discuss your revised ending with your group.

Plan Your Story Think carefully about how your revised ending will change the way readers see Brock and his conflicts. For example, will a different understanding of the puppy or the addition of a new character affect the choices Brock makes? Take notes in a chart like the one shown. Then, write your revised ending.

INTERACTIVITY

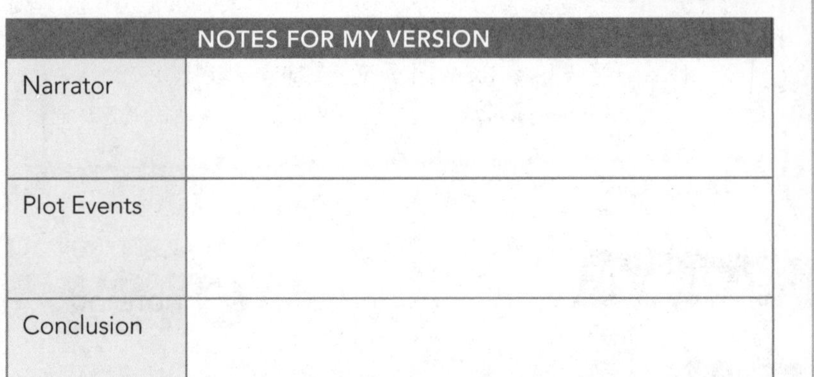

NOTES FOR MY VERSION	
Narrator	
Plot Events	
Conclusion	

EQ Notes Before moving on to a new selection, go to your Essential Question Notes and record any additional thoughts or observations you may have about "The Last Dog."

Draft Your Story As you write, choose descriptive details that create vivid pictures in your reader's mind. Help readers to "see" and "hear" the characters and events.

Reflect on Your Writing Share your revised endings as a group and discuss the similarities and differences in your choices.

MARS CAN WAIT. OCEANS CAN'T.

A **persuasive essay** is a brief work of nonfiction in which the writer tries to convince readers to do something specific or to think a certain way about a situation or an idea.

from PACKING FOR MARS

PERSUASIVE ESSAY

Author's Purpose

- to convince or persuade readers; to argue for or against an idea

Characteristics

- a statement of the writer's claim
- various types of supporting evidence, such as facts, examples, data, or anecdotes
- a counterclaim, or opposing position, that the author disproves by offering a counterargument
- language that shows the writer's awareness of his or her reader, or audience

Structure

- an introduction, a body, and a conclusion that flow in a logical way and make the author's ideas clear

Take a Minute!

NOTEBOOK

MARK IT Read the list of phrases. Then, mark ones that you would most likely see in a persuasive essay. Discuss your choices with a partner.

I question whether	Great party!	On the other hand
I cannot agree	Equally important	Wait here
First, choose your paint	There is no doubt	Dinner will be served

TEKS

8.E.i. Analyze characteristics and structures of argumentative text by identifying the claim.

8.E.ii. Analyze characteristics and structures of argumentative text by explaining how the author uses various types of evidence and consideration of alternatives to support the argument.

Genre / Text Elements

Claim and Supporting Evidence A **claim** is the writer's position, the idea he or she wants readers to accept. In effective persuasion, the writer tailors the argument to the **audience**, or readers, he or she is trying to convince. The writer chooses reasons and varied **evidence** that will appeal to the audience's sense of logic, to their emotions, or to both.

TYPE OF EVIDENCE	EXAMPLE
facts: information, including dates and numerical data, that can be proved true	In 1969, American astronauts landed on the moon. Approximately, 600 million people watched on TV.
expert opinions: information from those who have special knowledge of a subject	According to Carl Sagan, "The nitrogen in our DNA, the calcium in our teeth, the iron in our blood … were made in the interiors of collapsing stars."
examples: specific instances of a general idea	For instance, blankets used by marathon runners were invented for the space program.
personal observations: explanations from the writer's experience or knowledge	Watching the meteor shower, I realized how much we can learn from exploring the cosmos.
anecdotes: brief stories that illustrate a situation	As *Opportunity* completed 26 miles on Mars, NASA scientists celebrated with their own marathon.

NOTEBOOK

PRACTICE Work with a partner to label the type of evidence represented by each item. Then, choose the one that best supports this claim: *Earth still has many unknown wonders deserving of exploration.*

1. While studying the Marianas Trench, I saw how much we still don't know about Earth.

2. Martian rover *Spirit* launched on June 10, 2003.

3. When he was still a teen, José Hernández was inspired to become an astronaut after hearing a radio story about Franklin Chang-Diaz.

4. New species, such as a walking catfish, are still being found on Earth.

MARS CAN WAIT. OCEANS CAN'T.

Compare Nonfiction

In this lesson, you will read two persuasive essays that offer different perspectives on the importance of space exploration. You will then compare the authors' arguments.

from PACKING FOR MARS

About the Author

Amitai Etzioni (b. 1929) is a University Professor at George Washington University. He was previously a professor at Harvard Business School and Columbia University. Etzioni was also Senior Advisor to the White House under President Jimmy Carter. His work appears frequently in newspapers, such as the *New York Times, Washington Post*, and *Wall Street Journal*.

Mars Can Wait. Oceans Can't.

Concept Vocabulary

As you read the persuasive essay, you will encounter these words.

dire	looming	severe

Context Clues Clues in the context can help you determine word meanings.

Antonym, or contrast, is a type of context clue that shows differences.

EXAMPLE The professor was *taciturn*; however, her assistant was friendly and outgoing.

PRACTICE As you read, study the context to determine the meanings of unfamiliar words. Mark your observations in the open space next to the text.

Comprehension Strategy

Generate Questions

Generating questions can help you deepen your understanding of a text and gain more information.

1. **Before you read,** preview the text, including the title and any images. Write questions you hope the text will answer.
2. **As you read,** notice details that raise questions in your mind. Jot your questions down, and read on.
3. **After you read,** pause to reflect on the questions you asked before and during reading. Then, write down any additional questions that you have.

PRACTICE Before, during, and after you read the essay, write questions in the open space next to the text.

TEKS

2.B. Use context such as contrast or cause and effect to clarify the meaning of words.

5.B. Generate questions about text before, during, and after reading to deepen understanding and gain information.

PERSUASIVE ESSAY

Mars Can Wait. Oceans Can't.

Amitai Etzioni

BACKGROUND

In March 2012, Canadian deep-sea explorer James Cameron reached the bottom of Challenger Deep at the southern end of the Mariana Trench in the Pacific Ocean. Alone in a specially designed submarine, he collected samples and took videos—a skill for which he was already known, having directed two of the world's highest-grossing movies: *Titanic* and *Avatar.*

 AUDIO

 ANNOTATE

1 While space travel still gets a lot of attention, not enough attention has been accorded to a major new expedition to the deepest point in the ocean, some seven miles deep—the recent journey by James Cameron, on behalf of *National Geographic*.

2 The cover story of the prestigious journal *Foreign Affairs* lays out the "Case for Space." *60 Minutes* recently ran a story about the **dire** effects on Florida's space industry of scaling back our extraterrestrial endeavors. Newt Gingrich gained attention earlier this year by calling for building a permanent base on the moon. And President Obama has talked of preparing to eventually send Americans into orbit around Mars.

3 Actually, there are very good reasons to stop spending billions of dollars on manned space missions, to explore space in ways that are safer and much less costly, and to grant much higher priority to other scientific and engineering mega-projects, the oceans in particular.

4 The main costs of space exploration arise from the fact that we are set on sending humans, rather than robots. The reasons such efforts drive up the costs include: A human needs a return ticket, while a robot can go one way. Space vehicles for humans must be

Mark context clues or indicate another strategy you used that helped you determine meaning.

dire (DY ur) *adj.*

MEANING:

made safe, while we can risk a bunch of robots without losing sleep. Robots are much easier to feed, experience little trouble when subject to prolonged weightlessness, and are much easier to shield from radiation. And they can do most tasks humans can.

5 British astronomer royal Martin Rees writes, "I think that the practical case (for manned flights) gets weaker and weaker with every advance in robotics and miniaturization. It's hard to see any particular reason or purpose in going back to the moon or indeed sending people into space at all." Nobel Laureate Steven Weinberg calls manned missions "an incredible waste of money" and argues that "for the cost of putting a few people on a very limited set of locations on Mars we could have dozens of unmanned, robotic missions roving all over Mars."

6 The main argument for using humans is a public relations one. As Neil deGrasse Tyson puts it in *Foreign Affairs*, "China's latest space proclamations could conceivably produce another 'Sputnik moment' [1] for the United States, spurring the country into action after a relatively fallow period in its space efforts." Also, astronauts are said to inspire our youth to become scientists and explorers. However, it is far from established that we cannot achieve the same effects by making other R&D[2] projects our main priority.

7 Take the oceans, about which we know much less than the dark side of the moon. Ninety percent of the ocean floor has not even been charted, and while we have been to the moon, the technology to explore the ocean's floors is still being developed. For example, a permanent partially submerged sea exploration station, called the *SeaOrbiter*, is currently in development.

8 The oceans play a major role in controlling our climate. But we have not learned yet how to use them to cool us off rather than contribute to our overheating. Ocean organisms are said to hold the promise of cures for an array of diseases. An examination of the unique eyes of skate (ray fish) led to advances in combating blindness, the horseshoe crab was crucial in developing a test for bacterial contamination, and sea urchins helped in the development of test-tube fertilization.

9 The toadfish's ability to regenerate its central nervous system is of much interest to neuroscientists. A recent Japanese study concluded that the drug eribulin, which was derived from sea sponges, is effective in combating breast, colon, and urinary cancer.

10 Given the **looming** crisis of water scarcity, we badly need more efficient and less costly methods to desalinate ocean water. By 2025, 1.8 billion people are expected to suffer from **severe** water

Mark context clues or indicate another strategy you used that helped you determine meaning.

looming (LOO mihng) *adj.*

MEANING:

severe (suh VEER) *adj.*

MEANING:

1. **'Sputnik moment'** the moment in October 1957 when the Soviet Union launched Sputnik, the first artificial satellite, thus starting a "space race" with the United States.
2. **R&D** research and development.

scarcity, with that number jumping to 3.9 billion by 2050—well over a third of the entire global population.

11 If the oceans do not make your heart go pitter-patter, how about engineering a bacteria that eats carbon dioxide—and thus helps protect the world from overheating—AND excretes fuel which will allow us to drive our cars and machines, without oil? I cannot find any evidence that people young or old, Americans or citizens of other nations, would be less impressed or less inspired with such a breakthrough than with one more set of photos of a far away galaxy or a whole Milky Way full of stars.

12 Space enthusiasts claim that space exploration has generated major spinoffs for our life right here on Earth. Tyson quotes President Obama suggesting that the Apollo mission[3] "produced technologies that have improved kidney dialysis and water purification systems; sensors to test for hazardous gases; energy-saving building materials; and fire-resistant fabrics used by firefighters and soldiers," and adds a few more innovations to the list: "digital imaging, implantable pacemakers, collision-avoidance systems on aircraft, precision LASIK eye surgery, and global positioning satellites."

13 Of course, the space environment is radically different from the one on Earth. Materials and technologies that are suited for a vacuum, zero gravity, and extreme cold and heat are not the ones we typically can use on Earth.

14 Elias Carayannis, professor of Science, Technology, Innovation and Entrepreneurship at The George Washington University, notes "government agencies—particularly those such as the National Space and Aeronautics Administration that are continually pressured to justify their activities—tout the spin-off value of their investments in sometimes quite extravagant claims." Products such as Velcro, Tang, and Teflon that are often cited as spinoffs of space technology did not actually result from the space program.

15 Space promoters tell us, once every few months, that there are signs that there might be or has been water on one of the planets that might make "life" possible. I wonder if some of those who hear these reports interpret them to mean that we expect to find a civilization out there, one that we could ally with, say against the Chinese. What scientists are really talking about is organic material, the kind found in any compost —not a reason to spend billions of dollars of public funds.

16 In short, do not cry for Mars. It is not going away. We can send R2D2 to explore it and still keep a whole pile of dough for important and inspiring exploration missions right here on Earth, starting at the beach nearest you. ❧

3. **Apollo mission** first manned mission to the moon.

NOTEBOOK

Work on your own to answer the questions in your notebook. Use text evidence to support your responses.

Response

1. **Personal Connections** After reading the text, would you rather explore the oceans or the skies? Why?

Comprehension

2. **Reading Check (a)** According to the author, what is the main reason space exploration is so costly? **(b)** Identify two reasons the author gives for making ocean exploration a priority.

3. **Strategy: Generate Questions (a)** Cite one question you generated about the essay before reading and one you generated during your reading. **(b)** What additional question can you generate now that you have read the full text? **(c)** In what ways does asking questions deepen your understanding and help you gain more information from a text?

WORKING AS A GROUP

Discuss your responses to the Analysis and Discussion questions with your group.

- Note agreements and disagreements.
- Summarize insights.
- Consider changes of opinion.

If necessary, revise your original answers to reflect what you learn from your discussion.

Analysis and Discussion

4. **(a) Analyze** Why does the author suggest that ocean exploration could benefit human health? **(b) Support** Identify two details that the author uses to support this idea.

5. **(a) Analyze** Why does the author think that the possibility of water on other planets is *not* significant? **(b) Evaluate** Does this information affect your views about space exploration? Why or why not?

6. **Get Ready for Close Reading** Choose a passage from the text that you find especially interesting or important. You'll discuss the passage with your group during Close-Read activities.

EQ Notes **Should humanity's future lie among the stars?**

What have you learned about imagination and the future from reading this essay? Go to your Essential Question Notes and record your observations and thoughts about "Mars Can Wait. Oceans Can't."

TEKS

5.B. Generate questions about text before, during, and after reading to deepen understanding and gain information.

6.A. Describe personal connections to a variety of sources, including self-selected texts.

6.C. Use text evidence to support an appropriate response.

6.I. Reflect on and adjust responses as new evidence is presented.

MARS CAN WAIT. OCEANS CAN'T.

Close Read

ANNOTATE

PRACTICE Complete the following activities. Use text evidence to support your responses.

1. **Present and Discuss** With your group, share the passages from the essay that you found especially interesting. Discuss what you notice and why you chose the passage. If you have difficulty expressing yourself, use gestures or make a drawing to get your ideas across. You may choose to focus on one of these passages:
   - Paragraphs 1–2: Discuss why the author refers to famous people and well-known news sources.
   - Paragraph 6: Discuss the author's assertion that the argument for sending humans to space involves "public relations."
2. **Reflect on Your Learning** What new ideas or insights did you uncover during your second reading of the text?

NOTEBOOK

LANGUAGE STUDY

Concept Vocabulary

Why These Words? The vocabulary words are related.

dire	looming	severe

1. With your group, determine what the words have in common. Write your ideas.
2. Add another word that fits the category: ______________________
3. Use each vocabulary word in a sentence. Include context clues that hint at each word's meaning.

Word Study

Synonyms Words that have the same basic meanings are **synonyms**. Often, synonyms have different **connotations**, or emotional associations, even though their definitions are similar. Use a thesaurus to find three synonyms for the vocabulary word *looming*. Then, go back into the text, and replace the word *looming* with each of the synonyms. How does each synonym affect the meaning of the sentence?

WORD NETWORK

Add words that are related to the ideas of imagination and the future from the text to your Word Network.

TEKS

2.A. Use print or digital resources to determine the meaning, syllabication, pronunciation, word origin, and part of speech.

6.F. Respond using newly acquired vocabulary as appropriate.

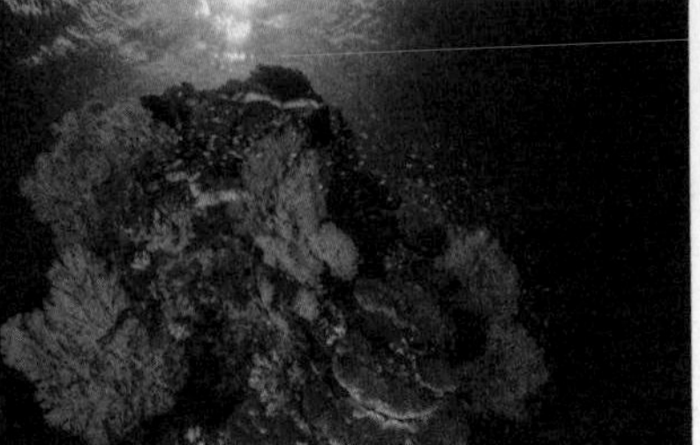

MARS CAN WAIT. OCEANS CAN'T.

TIP: Evidence comes in different forms, including facts, expert opinions, examples, personal observations, and anecdotes.

Genre / Text Elements

Claim and Supporting Evidence In effective persuasive writing, an author states and defends a **claim**. He or she gives logical reasons to support the claim and chooses **evidence** that shows the reasons are valid. Strong persuasive writers also demonstrate awareness of their **audience**, or reader:

- They anticipate **counterclaims**, or opposing views readers might hold.
- They address the counterclaims head on, and disprove them with additional, alternative reasons and evidence that support the main claim.

 NOTEBOOK

 INTERACTIVITY

PRACTICE Work with your group to analyze the characteristics and structures of the essay. Seek help from your teacher or other groups if necessary.

1. **(a) Analyze** What is the author's claim? **(b) Connect** Complete the chart by finding one example of each type of evidence in the essay and explaining how it supports the claim.

TYPE OF EVIDENCE	EXAMPLE	HOW IT SUPPORTS THE CLAIM
fact		
expert opinion		
example		
personal observation		
anecdote		

2. **(a) Analyze** Cite two counterclaims that the author addresses in the essay. **(b) Connect** Explain the reasons and evidence he uses to disprove those opposing views.

3. **(a) Analyze** What audience do you think the author is trying to reach in this essay? Do they mainly agree or disagree with him? Explain. **(b) Evaluate** Do you think the intended audience would find his argument convincing? Why, or why not?

 TEKS

8.E.i. Analyze characteristics and structures of argumentative text by identifying the claim.

8.E.ii. Analyze characteristics and structures of argumentative text by explaining how the author uses various types of evidence and consideration of alternatives to support the argument.

9.F. Analyze how the author's use of language contributes to mood, voice, and tone.

Author's Craft

Diction and Tone Diction is the type of language—the words and expressions—a writer chooses. **Tone** is the writer's attitude toward the subject.

A writer's diction may be informal, formal, technical, sophisticated, and so on. A writer's tone can reflect any emotion or attitude a person can feel. Tone might be described, for example, as soothing, hostile, friendly, or stern. Diction is always a key part of tone.

EXAMPLES

Notice how the two example sentences have the same meaning but very different diction and tones.

Sentence 1:
Potential space explorers are not thinking sensibly.

Sentence 2:
I think anyone who wants to explore space is crazy!

TIP: Formal diction (*potential, sensibly*) gives sentence 1 a serious tone. **Informal diction** (*crazy*) and the use of first person (*I think*) give sentence 2 a lighter tone.

 ANNOTATE

 INTERACTIVITY

 NOTEBOOK

PRACTICE Work on your own to complete the activities. Then, discuss your responses with your group.

1. Read the passage from the essay, and mark words and phrases that suggest the author's tone, or attitude toward the subject. Also, note word choices that seem casual, technical, or just interesting.

   If the oceans do not make your heart go pitter-patter, how about engineering a bacteria that eats carbon dioxide—and thus helps protect the world from overheating—AND excretes fuel which will allow us to drive our cars and machines, without oil? I cannot find any evidence that people young or old, Americans or citizens of other nations, would be less impressed or less inspired with such a breakthrough than with one more set of photos of a far away galaxy or a whole Milky Way full of stars.

2. **(a) Interpret** Mark the answer choice that best describe's Etzioni's overall tone.

   ◯ engaging and instructive

   ◯ formal and unfeeling

   ◯ sarcastic and funny

   (b) Support Explain the reasons for your answer. Cite specific words and phrases from the essay that support your thinking.

MARS CAN WAIT. OCEANS CAN'T.

Compare Nonfiction

The persuasive essay you are about to read offers a different perspective on the importance of space exploration. Pay attention to the similarities and differences in how the authors advance their arguments.

from PACKING FOR MARS

About the Author

Mary Roach (b. 1959) grew up in New Hampshire. After graduating from Wesleyan University, she pursued a career in writing. She has written for *Wired, National Geographic*, and the *New York Times Magazine*, and is known for her popular science books.

from Packing for Mars

Concept Vocabulary

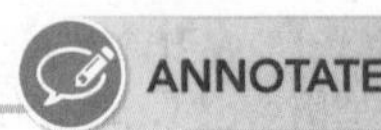
ANNOTATE

As you read the essay, you will encounter these words.

frivolity	impractical	squandered

Print Resources A typical thesaurus entry provides a word's part of speech as well as lists of synonyms and antonyms.

SAMPLE THESAURUS ENTRY

promulgate *v. synonyms:* announce, declare, notify, promote, publicize *antonyms*: hide, conceal, repress, withhold

In this example, synonyms *(declare, promote)* and antonyms *(hide, withhold)* can help you determine the meaning of the more challenging word *promulgate*.

PRACTICE As you read the essay, use a thesaurus to determine the meanings of unfamiliar words. Mark your observations in the open space next to the text.

Comprehension Strategy

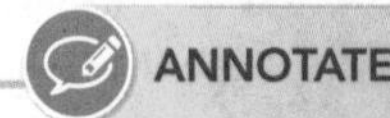
ANNOTATE

Make Connections

You can gain more insight into a text by **making connections** to other texts you have read. Ask yourself questions, such as *How is this text similar to and different from other texts on the subject?* Doing so will deepen your understanding of the text you are reading and the topic as a whole. To make connections to other texts, consider the following elements:

- controlling ideas, claims, and insights
- supporting evidence and details
- word choice and style

PRACTICE As you read the essay, use the open space next to the text to jot down connections you make to other texts you have read.

TEKS

2.A. Use print or digital resources to determine the meaning, syllabication, pronunciation, word origin, and part of speech.

5.E. Make connections to personal experiences, ideas in other texts, and society.

PERSUASIVE ESSAY

from Packing for Mars

Mary Roach

BACKGROUND

It was in 1783 that people first took to the sky on a hot-air balloon designed by the Montgolfier brothers. In 1903, the Wright brothers took flight in the first powered airplane. And in 2000, the first crew arrived to take up residence on the International Space Station. Today, people are contemplating the first manned mission to Mars.

AUDIO

ANNOTATE

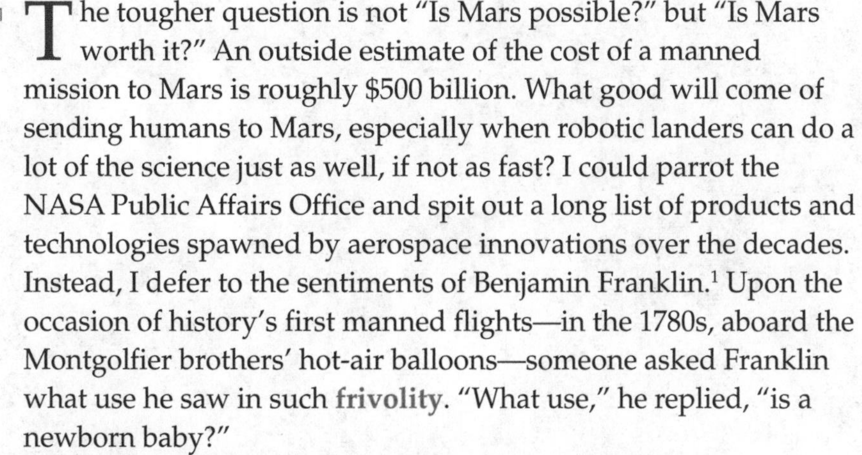

1 The tougher question is not "Is Mars possible?" but "Is Mars worth it?" An outside estimate of the cost of a manned mission to Mars is roughly $500 billion. What good will come of sending humans to Mars, especially when robotic landers can do a lot of the science just as well, if not as fast? I could parrot the NASA Public Affairs Office and spit out a long list of products and technologies spawned by aerospace innovations over the decades. Instead, I defer to the sentiments of Benjamin Franklin.[1] Upon the occasion of history's first manned flights—in the 1780s, aboard the Montgolfier brothers' hot-air balloons—someone asked Franklin what use he saw in such **frivolity**. "What use," he replied, "is a newborn baby?"

2 It might not be that hard to raise the funds. If the nations involved were to approach their respective entertainment conglomerates, an impressive hunk of funding could be raised.

Use a thesaurus or indicate another strategy you used that helped you determine meaning.

frivolity (frih VAHL ih tee) *n.*

MEANING:

1. **Benjamin Franklin** (1706–1790) American author, scientist, and statesman who was famous for his inventions.

The more you read about Mars missions, the more you realize it's the ultimate reality TV.

3 I was at a party the day the Phoenix robotic lander touched down on Mars. I asked the party's host, Chris, if he had a computer I could use to watch the NASA TV coverage. At first it was just Chris and I watching. By the time *Phoenix* had plowed intact through the Martian atmosphere and was about to release its parachute for the descent, half the party was upstairs crowded around Chris's computer. We weren't even watching *Phoenix*. The images hadn't yet arrived. (It takes about twenty minutes for signals to travel between Mars and Earth.) The camera was trained on Mission Control at the Jet Propulsion Laboratory. It was standing room with engineers and managers, people who'd spent years working on heat shields and parachute systems and thrusters, all of which, in this final hour, could fail in a hundred different ways, each of those failures having been planned for with backup hardware and contingency software. One man stared at his computer with the fingers of both hands crossed. The touchdown signal arrived, and everyone was up on their feet making noise. Engineers bear-hugged each other so enthusiastically that they knocked their glasses crooked. Someone began passing out cigars. We all yelled too and some of us got a little choked up. It was inspiring, what these men and women had done. They flew a delicate scientific instrument more than 400

As they watch from the control room, engineers celebrate the successful completion of a space mission.

million miles to Mars and set it down as gently as a baby, exactly where they wanted it.

4 We live in a culture in which, more and more, people live through simulations. We travel via satellite technology, we socialize on computers. You can tour the Sea of Tranquility on Google Moon and visit the Taj Mahal via Street View.[2] Anime fans in Japan have been petitioning the government for the right to legally marry a two-dimensional character. Fundraising has begun on a $1.6 billion resort in the rim of a simulated Martian crater in the desert outside Las Vegas. (They can't simulate Martian gravity, but the boots of the spacesuits will be "a little more bouncy.") No one goes out to play anymore. Simulation is becoming reality.

5 But it isn't anything like reality. Ask an M.D.[3] who spent a year dissecting a human form tendon by gland by nerve, whether learning anatomy on a computer simulation would be comparable. Ask an astronaut whether taking part in a space simulation is anything like being in space. What's different? Sweat, risk, uncertainty, inconvenience. But also, awe. Pride. Something ineffably splendid and stirring. One day at Johnson Space Center, I visited Mike Zolensky, the curator of cosmic dust and one of the caretakers of NASA's meteorite collection. Every now and then, a piece of asteroid slams into Mars hard enough that the impact hurls small chunks of the Martian surface way out into space, where they continue to travel until they are snagged by some other planet's gravitational pull. Occasionally that planet is Earth. Zolensky opened a case and lifted out a Martian meteorite as heavy as a bowling ball and handed it to me. I stood there taking in its hardness and heft, its *realness*, making an expression that I'm sure I'd never before had call to make. The meteorite wasn't beautiful or exotic-looking. Give me a chunk of asphalt and some shoe polish and I can make you a simulated Mars meteorite. What I can't possibly simulate for you is the feeling of holding a 20-pound divot of Mars in your hands.

6 The nobility of the human spirit grows harder for me to believe in. War, zealotry, greed, malls, narcissism. I see a backhanded nobility in excessive, **impractical** outlays of cash prompted by nothing loftier than a species joining hands and saying "I bet we can do this." Yes, the money could be better spent on Earth. But would it? Since when has money saved by government redlining[4] been spent on education and cancer research? It is always **squandered**. Let's squander some on Mars. Let's go out and play. ❧

Use a thesaurus or indicate another strategy you used that helped you determine meaning.

impractical (ihm PRAC tih cuhl) *adj.*

MEANING:

squandered (SKWAHN duhrd) *v.*

MEANING:

2. **Google Moon . . . Street View** technology that displays photographic views of the moon and streets around the world respectively.
3. **M.D.** *abbrev.* medical doctor.
4. **government redlining** practice of denying services, such as banking or insurance, to people in areas that are unfairly regarded as high risk.

NOTEBOOK

Work on your own to answer the questions in your notebook. Use text evidence to support your responses.

Response

1. **Personal Connections** Did this essay make you excited about the future? Why or why not? Cite a specific passage or detail that led to your response.

Comprehension

2. **Reading Check (a)** According to the author, what is the main question concerning Mars? **(b)** What position does the author take on the idea of simulated experiences? **(c)** At the end of the essay, what does the author want people to think or do?

3. **Strategy: Make Connections (a)** Cite one connection you made to ideas in another text while reading this essay. What did you learn? **(b)** Was this strategy useful? Why or why not?

WORKING AS A GROUP
Discuss your responses to the Analysis and Discussion questions with your group.
- Note agreements and disagreements.
- Summarize insights.
- Consider changes of opinion.

If necessary, revise your original answers to reflect what you learn from your discussion.

Analysis and Discussion

4. **Interpret** Reread the first paragraph. What point is the author making when she quotes Benjamin Franklin?

5. **Analyze** In paragraph 2, the author describes the Mars mission as the "ultimate reality TV." Which details support her observation?

6. **(a) Generalize** What point does the writer make about simulations versus real exploration? **(b) Evaluate** Do you agree with the author's position on this point? Why or why not?

7. **Get Ready for Close Reading** Choose a passage from the text that you find especially interesting or important. You'll discuss the passage with your group during Close-Read activities.

TEKS

5.E. Make connections to personal experiences, ideas in other texts, and society.

6.A. Describe personal connections to a variety of sources, including self-selected texts.

6.C. Use text evidence to support an appropriate response.

EQ Notes

Should humanity's future lie among the stars?

What have you learned about imagination and the future from reading this persuasive essay? Go to your Essential Question Notes and record your observations and thoughts about *Packing for Mars*.

Close Read

from PACKING FOR MARS

PRACTICE Complete the following activities. Use text evidence to support your responses.

1. **Present and Discuss** With your group, share the passages from the essay that you found especially interesting. Discuss what you notice, the questions you have, and the conclusions you reach. For example, you might focus on the following passages:
   - Paragraph 1: Discuss how the author uses questions to make a point.
   - Paragraph 4: Discuss the author's statement that "Simulation is becoming reality."
   - Paragraph 6: Discuss whether the author truly thinks resources would be *squandered* by Mars exploration.
2. **Reflect on Your Learning** What new ideas or insights did you uncover during your second reading of the text?

NOTEBOOK

LANGUAGE STUDY

Concept Vocabulary

Why These Words? The vocabulary words are related.

frivolity	impractical	squandered

1. With your group, determine what the words have in common. Write your ideas in your notebook.

2. Add another word that fits the category. ____________________

3. Use each vocabulary word in a sentence. Include context clues that hint at each word's meaning.

Word Study

Antonyms All three vocabulary words often have negative shades of meaning. In this essay, the author turns those meanings into positives. Find at least one **antonym,** or word that has an opposite meaning, for each word. Then, use each word in a paragraph about Mars exploration.

WORD NETWORK

Add words that are related to the ideas of imagination and the future from the text to your Word Network.

from PACKING FOR MARS

TIP: Remember that there are different forms of evidence, including facts (which include numerical data), expert opinions, personal observations, examples, and anecdotes.

Genre / Text Elements

Claim, Evidence, and Audience In persuasive writing, an author attempts to convince an **audience**, or group of readers, to accept a **claim**, or position. The author takes the audience's knowledge, beliefs, and interest level into account, framing issues and presenting **evidence** in ways readers will understand and find compelling. The chart shows some of the ways in which a writer molds a text to suit the intended audience.

PERSUADING A GENERAL AUDIENCE, THE AUTHOR...	PERSUADING AN EXPERT AUDIENCE, THE AUTHOR...
defines specialized terms.	assumes readers know specialized terms.
gives general background.	provides little general background.
engages readers' interest with humor, stories, or pop culture references.	assumes readers' interest.
uses casual, friendly language.	uses formal, technical language.

NOTEBOOK

PRACTICE Work on your own to answer the questions. Then, discuss your responses with your group.

1. **Analyze** What is the author's claim in this essay—what does she want readers to do or believe?

2. In paragraph 1, the author says she won't list products that resulted from the space program as evidence of its value. Consider the alternative: **(a) Draw Conclusions** How would such a list support her argument? **(b) Interpret** Why do you think she chose not to include it? Explain.

3. **Analyze** What audience is the author trying to reach? Explain, citing details that reflect her understanding of this audience.

4. **(a) Connect** In paragraph 1, what idea does the quote by Ben Franklin support? **(b) Make Inferences** What opinion does this suggest the author's audience may hold about Mars exploration?

5. **Connect** Explain how each type of evidence reflects the author's attempts to engage her audience: **(a)** anecdote about the Martian meteorite; **(b)** examples of technology that affects our lives.

TEKS

8.E.i. Analyze characteristics and structures of argumentative text by identifying the claim.

8.E.ii. Analyze characteristics and structures of argumentative text by explaining how the author uses various types of evidence and consideration of alternatives to support the argument.

8.E.iii. Analyze characteristics and structures of argumentative text by identifying the intended audience or reader.

9.F. Analyze how the author's use of language contributes to mood, voice, and tone.

Author's Craft

Language: Diction and Voice A writer's **voice** is his or her personality on the page—the sense of a real person who sees the world in a unique way. While every element of a text contributes to a writer's voice, his or her **diction**, or word choice, is the main ingredient. Diction can have many different qualities. For example, it may be serious, playful, idiomatic, sophisticated, formal, or informal.

EXAMPLES

Here are examples of the many kinds of diction Mary Roach uses in this essay.

FORMAL	INFORMAL	PLAYFUL	IDIOMATIC
I defer to the sentiments of Benjamin Franklin	*an impressive hunk of funding*	*Give me a chunk of asphalt and some shoe polish*	*spit out a long list of products*

TIP: An **idiom** is an expression that has a meaning you can't get from the literal meanings of the words. For example, if you *let the cat out of the bag,* you revealed a secret. You didn't free a cat.

Note that Roach combines different types of diction throughout her writing. Even single sentences may have different kinds of words. This varied diction adds to her distinct voice.

INTERACTIVITY

NOTEBOOK

PRACTICE Work together with your group to complete the activity, and answer the questions.

1. **Categorize** Use the chart to label each example of diction from the essay as formal, informal, playful, or idiomatic.

EXAMPLE	TYPE OF DICTION
Engineers bear-hugged each other (paragraph 3)	
Something ineffably splendid and stirring (paragraph 5)	
where they continue to travel until they are snagged (paragraph 5)	
Let's go out and play (paragraph 6)	

2. **(a) Synthesize** When you read a text, you "meet" a writer on the page. Choose two passages that you think best introduce you to this writer, revealing her unique voice. **(b) Describe** Using the examples you chose, describe the writer's voice in this essay.

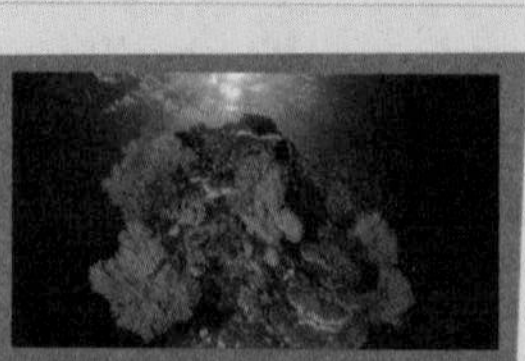

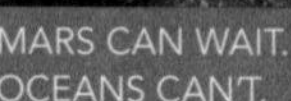

MARS CAN WAIT. OCEANS CAN'T.

from PACKING FOR MARS

Compare Within Genre: Argument

Multiple Choice

NOTEBOOK

These questions are based on "Mars Can Wait. Oceans Can't." and the essay from *Packing for Mars*. Choose the best answer to each question.

1. Which answer choice BEST states the *main* disagreement between these two authors?

A Etzioni does not think human space exploration is worth the cost and effort, but Roach thinks it is.

B Roach sees no value in ocean exploration, but Etzioni does.

C Etzioni does not trust scientists to spend money wisely, but Roach does.

D Roach wants to collect more Martian rocks, but Etzioni does not find rocks interesting.

2. Read the passage from each essay. Then, choose the answer that BEST summarizes the difference between the two authors' points of view.

from "Mars Can Wait. Oceans Can't."

Actually, there are very good reasons to stop spending billions of dollars on manned space missions, to explore space in ways that are safer and much less costly…

from *Packing for Mars*

It might not be that hard to raise the funds. If the nations involved were to approach their respective entertainment conglomerates, an impressive hunk of funding could be raised.

F Etzioni wants entertainment companies to pay for robotic missions in space, but Roach wants them to pay for manned missions.

G Etzioni thinks human space exploration is dangerous, but Roach isn't worried about safety.

H Roach thinks entertainment companies would fund manned missions to Mars, but Etzioni thinks they won't be interested.

J Roach thinks that entertainment companies would fund manned space missions. Etzioni thinks there are cheaper ways to explore space.

3. Which question do the two authors answer in opposite ways?

A Are manned missions to Mars possible?

B Are manned missions to Mars worth the expense and effort?

C Is ocean exploration more important than space exploration?

D Is space exploration dangerous to human beings?

TEKS

5.F. Make inferences and use evidence to support understanding.

6.B. Write responses that demonstrate understanding of texts, including comparing sources within and across genres.

NOTEBOOK

Short Response

1. **(a) Analyze** What practical benefits does Etzioni think we might gain through ocean exploration? Explain. **(b) Analyze** Does Roach care whether human space exploration has practical benefits? Explain. **(c) Make Inferences** How might Etzioni react to Roach's ideas about the value of "frivolity" or "play"? Explain.

2. **(a) Analyze** What main benefits does Etzioni see in having robots explore space? **(b) Contrast** Why does Roach feel robotic exploration is not enough?

3. **(a) Interpret** Etzioni dismisses the argument for manned space missions as a matter of "public relations." What does he mean by that? **(b) Speculate** How might Roach respond to that argument? Explain.

Answer the questions in your notebook. Use text evidence to support your responses.

Timed Writing

A **persuasive essay** is a brief work of nonfiction in which the writer tries to convince readers to do something specific or to think a certain way about a situation or an idea.

ASSIGNMENT

Write a **persuasive essay** in which you compare the two essays and explain which argument you find more inspiring. Which essay presents a view of exploration that you prefer? State a clear claim and support your position with evidence from both essays.

EQ Notes Before moving on to a new selection, go to your Essential Question Notes and record any additional thoughts and observations you may have about "Mars Can Wait. Oceans Can't" and the essay from *Packing for Mars*.

5-MINUTE PLANNER

1. Read the assignment carefully and completely.
2. Decide what you want to say—your claim, or position.
3. Choose supporting evidence from both essays.
4. Organize your ideas, keeping these points in mind:
   - Summarize each author's view of exploration and the future.
   - Clearly connect the evidence you cite from each essay to your own ideas.

SOURCES

- Dark They Were, and Golden-Eyed (short story)
- Dark They Were, and Golden-Eyed (radio play)
- Science-Fiction Cradlesong
- First Men on the Moon
- The Last Dog

Present an Argument

A **critique** is a detailed analysis and assessment of a literary work. In a critique, you may point out weaknesses in a text, explain the strengths of a text, or do both.

ASSIGNMENT

Choose a selection—whether text or audio—from this unit and write a **critique** that has the following characteristics:

- an analysis of a character, conflict, setting, theme, or other element of the text
- a well-supported claim about the work's effectiveness
- accurate use of content-area vocabulary, especially literary terms

Deliver a **presentation** of your critique to your group.

Plan and Write

Choose a Text To choose a work, review the questions you've answered and the activities you've completed for each one. Remind yourself of characters, conflicts, events, or language that truly interested you. Choose a selection that you like and find engaging.

Find a Focus Narrow your topic by asking a question about the text you chose. Here are some sample questions; you may also develop your own.

- What makes this character's motivations believable or unbelievable for me?
- Which details make the setting come to life?
- How does the language create a vivid experience for me as a reader?
- In what ways is the theme important for people to understand?

Develop Your Claim Reread the text you chose to note details that relate to your question. As you work to answer the question, the points you want to make will become clear. Sharpen your answer to develop your claim.

Write Your Critique Draft your critique as a brief essay, leaving extra space in the margins for notes that will help you deliver your presentation orally. Use strong, memorable language and accurate content-area vocabulary to express your ideas clearly and defend your point of view.

TEKS
11.C. Compose multi-paragraph argumentative texts using genre characteristics and craft.

Rehearse and Present

Now, rehearse the delivery of your critique. Use the Speaking Guide to guide your rehearsal and strengthen your presentation.

SPEAKING GUIDE

SKILL	TIPS	What worked well? Why?	What didn't? Why?
Eye Contact Use eye contact to connect with listeners.	• Don't stare. Let your gaze sweep across listeners' faces. • Make eye contact after sharing a key point, such as your main idea.		
Speaking Rate Adjust the speed at which you talk to make your presentation more interesting.	• Slow down to add drama. • Speed up to add excitement.		
Volume Vary the volume of your voice.	• Use volume to draw your listeners' attention to a word, phrase, or idea. • Don't yell or whisper.		
Enunciation Say each word clearly so that listeners can understand you.	• Use and pronounce content-area vocabulary correctly. • Don't over-enunciate or exaggerate.		
Gestures Use body language and hand movements that feel natural.	• Don't stand stiffly. • Don't overuse gestures. Make the ones you use count.		
Conventions Follow the rules of standard English.	• Avoid slang, unless you're using it to make a point. • Recognize that this is not an informal conversation. Use correct grammar.		

Listen and Evaluate

As each member of your group delivers his or her critique, listen respectfully. You may take notes, but keep your attention on the speaker. Consider each speaker's ideas as well as the strengths and weaknesses of his or her delivery. Once everyone is done, discuss the presentations. Share constructive feedback thoughtfully and accept it from your classmates.

TEKS

1.C. Present a critique of a literary work, film, or dramatic production, employing eye contact, speaking rate, volume, enunciation, a variety of natural gestures, and conventions of language to communicate ideas effectively.

1.D. Engage in meaningful discourse and provide and accept constructive feedback from others.

Essential Question

Should humanity's future lie among the stars?

Some people imagine a future in which people spread out among the stars, while others see one in which humanity improves life on Earth. In this section, you will choose a selection about our imagination and the future to read independently. Get the most from this section by establishing a purpose for reading. Ask yourself, "What do I hope to gain from my independent reading?" Here are just a few purposes you might consider:

Read to Learn Think about the selections you have already read. What questions do you still have about the unit topic?

Read to Enjoy Read the descriptions of the texts. Which one seems most interesting and appealing to you?

Read to Form a Position Consider your thoughts and feelings about the Essential Question. Are you still undecided about some aspect of the topic?

Reading Digital Texts

Digital texts, like the ones you will read in this section, are electronic versions of print texts. They have a variety of characteristics:

- can be read on various devices
- text can be resized
- may include annotation tools
- may have bookmarks, audio features, links, and other helpful elements

Independent Learning Strategies

Throughout your life, in school, in your community, and in your career, you will need to rely on yourself to learn and work on your own. Use these strategies to keep your focus as you read independently for sustained periods of time. Add ideas of your own for each category.

STRATEGY	MY ACTION PLAN
Create a schedule • Be aware of your deadlines. • Make a plan for each day's activities.	
Read with purpose • Use a variety of comprehension strategies to deepen your understanding. • Think about the text and how it adds to your knowledge.	
Take notes • Record key ideas and information. • Review your notes before sharing what you've learned.	

TEKS

4. Self-select text and read independently for a sustained period of time; **5.A.** Establish purpose for reading assigned and self-selected texts; **8.F.** Analyze characteristics of multimodal and digital texts.

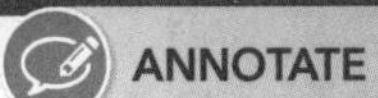

CONTENTS

Choose one selection. Selections are available online only.

SHARE YOUR INDEPENDENT LEARNING

Reflect on and evaluate the information you gained from your Independent Reading selection. Then, share what you learned with others.

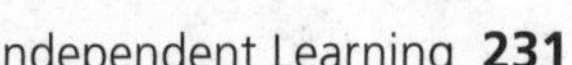

Close-Read Guide

Tool Kit
Close-Read Guide and **Model Annotation**

Establish your purpose for reading. Then, read the selection through at least once. Use this page to record your close-read ideas.

Selection Title: ____________ Purpose for Reading: ____________

Minutes Read: ____________

INTERACTIVITY

Close Read the Text

Zoom in on sections you found interesting. **Annotate** what you notice. Ask yourself **questions** about the text. What can you **conclude**?

Analyze the Text

1. Think about the author's choices of literary elements, techniques, and structures. Select one and record your thoughts.

2. What characteristics of digital texts did you use as you read this selection, and in what ways? How do the characteristics of a digital text affect your reading experience? Explain.

QuickWrite

Choose a paragraph from the text that grabbed your interest. Explain the power of this passage.

Share Your Independent Learning

Essential Question

Should humanity's future lie among the stars?

When you read something independently, your understanding continues to grow as you share what you have learned with others.

NOTEBOOK

Prepare to Share

CONNECT IT One of the most important ways to respond to a text is to notice and describe your personal reactions. Think about the text you explored independently and the ways in which it connects to your own experiences.

- What similarities and differences do you see between the text and your own life? Describe your observations.
- How do you think this text connects to the Essential Question? Describe your ideas.

Learn From Your Classmates

DISCUSS IT Share your ideas about the text you explored on your own. As you talk with others in your class, take notes about new ideas that seem important.

Reflect

EXPLAIN IT Review your notes, and mark the most important insight you gained from these writing and discussion activities. Explain how this idea adds to your understanding of imagination and the future.

TEKS

6.A. Describe personal connections to a variety of sources, including self-selected texts.

6.E. Interact with sources in meaningful ways such as notetaking, annotating, freewriting, or illustrating.

Argumentative Essay

ASSIGNMENT

In this unit, you read different perspectives about the ways in which we imagine humanity's future. You also practiced writing editorials and other arguments. Now, apply what you have learned.

Write an **argumentative essay** in which you state and defend a claim in response to the Essential Question.

Essential Question

Should humanity's future lie among the stars?

Review and Evaluate Evidence

INTERACTIVITY

Review your Essential Question Notes and your QuickWrite from the beginning of the unit. Has your position changed?

○ Yes	○ No
Identify at least three pieces of evidence that convinced you to change your mind. **1.** **2.** **3.**	Identify at least three pieces of evidence that reinforced your initial position. **1.** **2.** **3.**

State your position now:

What other evidence might you need to support your position?

Share Your Perspective

The **Argumentative Essay Checklist** will help you stay on track.

PLAN Before you write, read the Checklist and make sure you understand all the items.

DRAFT As you write, pause occasionally to make sure you're meeting the Checklist requirements.

Use New Words Refer to your Word Network to vary your word choice. Also, consider using one or more of the Academic Vocabulary terms you learned at the beginning of the unit: ***justify, dissent, certainty, discredit, assumption.***

REVIEW AND EDIT After you have written a first draft, evaluate it against the Checklist. Make any changes needed to strengthen your claim, structure, transitions, and language. Then, reread your essay and fix any errors you find.

EQ Notes Make sure you have pulled in details from your Essential Question Notes to support your claim.

INTERACTIVITY

ARGUMENTATIVE ESSAY CHECKLIST

My essay clearly contains . . .

- ○ a claim that shows depth of thought.
- ○ varied types of supporting evidence, including facts, details, and examples.
- ○ a purposeful structure that includes an introduction, logical connections among body paragraphs, and a strong conclusion.
- ○ use of transitional words and phrases that accurately show how ideas are related.
- ○ correct use of standard English conventions, including consistent verb tenses and correct subject-verb agreement in all sentence types.
- ○ no punctuation or spelling errors.

TEKS

11.C. Compose multi-paragraph argumentative texts using genre characteristics and craft.

Revising and Editing

Read this draft and think about corrections the writer might make. Then, answer the questions that follow.

[1] Many students may dream of becoming astronauts. [2] They should learn how to fly first. [3] If they do not know what it is like to spread their own wings, to catch a wave of wind, how can they have maneuvered around in space? [4] Esteemed philosopher M. C. Interstellar notes, "Astronauts should be the smartest birds in the sky."

[5] Would-be astronauts should also learn to dance since they can move gracefully through space. [6] To prepare for the stretches of solitude and loneliness, they should retreat to the woods alone for a week. [7] Although they will have plenty of work to do to convince others they will come out ready to travel to space. [8] Indeed, retired astronaut Clay Anderson has commented that he applied 15 times, over many years, before NASA accepted him. [9] His experience happens a ton, as many applicants can attest.

1. Which answer choice BEST combines sentences 1 and 2 into a single complex sentence that retains the original meaning?

A Many students dream of becoming astronauts so they can learn how to fly first.

B Before they dream of becoming astronauts, many students want to learn how to fly first.

C Although many students may dream of becoming astronauts, they should learn how to fly first.

D After they learn how to fly, many students may dream of becoming astronauts.

2. What change should be made to correct a verb tense error in sentence 3?

F Change *do not know* to *will not know*

G Change *to spread* to *to have spread*

H Delete *to catch a wave of wind*

J Change *have maneuvered* to *maneuver*

3. Where should a comma be inserted in sentence 7 to set off a dependent clause?

A After *although*

B After *do*

C After *others*

D After *out*

4. Which answer choice BEST revises sentence 9 to match the formal tone of the rest of the passage?

F Many applicants can attest, that his experience is super typical.

G As many applicants can or would like to attest his experience is common.

H As many applicants would say if they were asked his experience happens a lot.

J His experience is common, as many applicants can attest.

Reflect on the Unit

NOTEBOOK

INTERACTIVITY

RESEARCH

Reflect On the Unit Goals

Review your Unit Goals chart from the beginning of the unit. Then, complete the activity and answer the question.

1. In the Unit Goals chart, rate how well you meet each goal now.
2. In which goals were you most and least successful?

Reflect On the Texts

VOTE! Which selections in this unit inspire you and which don't? Use the ballot to vote for the texts you find most and least inspiring.

SELECTION BALLOT

Title	Most Inspiring [choose one]	Least Inspiring [choose one]
Dark They Were, and Golden-Eyed (SCIENCE-FICTION FANTASY)		
Dark They Were, and Golden-Eyed (RADIO PLAY ADAPTATION)		
Science-Fiction Cradlesong / First Men on the Moon		
The Last Dog		
Mars Can Wait. Oceans Can't.		
from Packing for Mars		
Your Independent Reading Selection:		

Reflect On the Essential Question

Reading/Viewing List Make a list of texts and media that you would recommend to someone who wants to explore the Essential Question: **Should humanity's future lie among the stars?**

- List selections from this unit. Conduct research to find two more. In addition to print texts, consider movies, newscasts, and websites.
- For each selection you add, briefly explain how it will help students explore the Essential Question.

TIP: As you conduct research, keep records of the websites you visit; the dates you access them; and the titles and authors of texts you find.

TEKS

10.C. Revise drafts for clarity, development, organization, style, word choice, and sentence variety; **10.D.ii.** Edit drafts using standard English conventions, including consistent, appropriate use of verb tenses; **10.D.vi.** Edit drafts using standard English conventions, including subordinating conjunctions to form complex sentences and correlative conjunctions such as *either/or* and *neither/nor*; **10.D.viii.** Edit drafts using standard English conventions, including punctuation, including commas to set off words, phrases, and clauses, and semicolons.

UNIT 3

Transformations

PEARSON realize™

Go ONLINE for all lessons

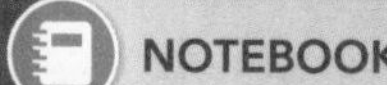
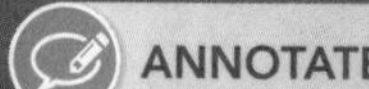

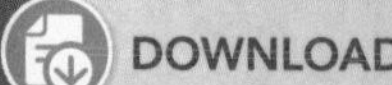

WATCH THE VIDEO

A Transformation

DISCUSS IT What sorts of transformations occur in nature and in the human experience?

Write your response before sharing your ideas.

UNIT 3

UNIT INTRODUCTION

Essential Question

Can people really change?

MENTOR TEXT: SHORT STORY
The Golden Windows

WHOLE-CLASS LEARNING

COMPARE ACROSS GENRES

DRAMA

A Christmas Carol: Scrooge and Marley, Acts I and II
based on the novel by Charles Dickens

NOVEL EXCERPT

from **A Christmas Carol**
Charles Dickens

▸ MEDIA CONNECTION
from Scrooge

PERFORMANCE TASK

WRITING PROCESS
Write a Short Story

PEER-GROUP LEARNING

REALISTIC SHORT STORY

Thank You, M'am
Langston Hughes

SCIENCE JOURNALISM

Learning Rewires the Brain
Alison Pearce Stevens

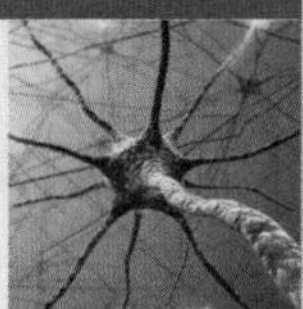

COMPARE WITHIN GENRE

LYRIC POETRY

Trying to Name What Doesn't Change
Naomi Shihab Nye

NARRATIVE POETRY

I Myself
Ángel González

PERFORMANCE TASK

SPEAKING AND LISTENING
Deliver a Dramatic Adaptation

INDEPENDENT LEARNING

REFLECTIVE ESSAY

Little Things Are Big
Jesús Colón

HISTORICAL NARRATIVE

The Story of Victor d'Aveyron, the Wild Child
Eloise Montalban

REALISTIC FICTION

A Retrieved Reformation
O. Henry

FABLE

The Grandfather and His Little Grandson
Leo Tolstoy

SHARE INDEPENDENT LEARNING

Share • Learn • Reflect

PERFORMANCE-BASED ASSESSMENT

Short Story

You will write a short story that explores the Essential Question for the unit.

UNIT REFLECTION

Goals • Texts • Essential Question

Unit Goals

VIDEO

Throughout this unit you will deepen your perspective about transformations by reading, writing, speaking, listening, and presenting. These goals will help you succeed on the Unit Performance-Based Assessment.

INTERACTIVITY

SET GOALS Rate how well you meet these goals right now. You will revisit your ratings later, when you reflect on your growth during this unit.

SCALE

1	2	3	4	5
NOT AT ALL WELL	NOT VERY WELL	SOMEWHAT WELL	VERY WELL	EXTREMELY WELL

ESSENTIAL QUESTION	Unit Introduction	Unit Reflection
I can read selections that express different points of view about transformations and develop my own perspective.	1 2 3 4 5	1 2 3 4 5
READING	**Unit Introduction**	**Unit Reflection**
I can understand and use academic vocabulary words related to fiction.	1 2 3 4 5	1 2 3 4 5
I can recognize elements of different genres, especially drama, fiction, and poetry.	1 2 3 4 5	1 2 3 4 5
I can read a selection of my choice independently and make meaningful connections to other texts.	1 2 3 4 5	1 2 3 4 5
WRITING	**Unit Introduction**	**Unit Reflection**
I can write an engaging and meaningful short story.	1 2 3 4 5	1 2 3 4 5
I can complete Timed Writing tasks with confidence.	1 2 3 4 5	1 2 3 4 5
SPEAKING AND LISTENING	**Unit Introduction**	**Unit Reflection**
I can prepare and deliver a dramatic adaptation.	1 2 3 4 5	1 2 3 4 5

TEKS

2.C. Determine the meaning and usage of grade-level academic English words derived from Greek and Latin roots such as *-omni, log/logue, gen, vid/vis, phil, luc,* and *sens/sent.*

Academic Vocabulary: Fiction

Many English words have roots, or key parts, that come from ancient languages, such as Latin and Greek. Learn these roots and use the words as you respond to questions and activities in this unit.

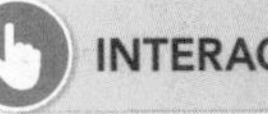

PRACTICE Academic terms are used routinely in classrooms. Build your knowledge of these words by completing the chart.

1. **Review** each word, its origin, and mentor sentences.
2. With a partner, read the words and mentor sentences aloud. Then, **determine** the meaning and usage of each word. Use a dictionary, if needed.
3. **List** at least two related words for each word.

WORD	MENTOR SENTENCES	PREDICT MEANING	RELATED WORDS
ingenious LATIN ROOT: ***-gen-*** "birth"; "produce"	1. No one else could have imagined the new, *ingenious* invention. 2. Julia came up with an *ingenious* solution to the problem.		generation; genuine genius
omniscient LATIN ROOT: ***-omni-*** "all"; "every"	1. An *omniscient* narrator can tell the reader what all the characters in a story are thinking. 2. Anyone who claims to be *omniscient* must be lying because no one knows everything.		
envision LATIN ROOT: ***-vis-*** "see"	1. I *envision* a future in which everyone lives in harmony. 2. The writer's description helped me *envision* the beautiful scenery.		
lucid LATIN ROOT: ***-luc-*** "light"	1. Elena's *lucid* explanation made the complex process seem simple. 2. Octavio wasn't *lucid* until his fever finally died down.		
sensation LATIN ROOT: ***-sens-*** "feel"; "think"	1. The new action-adventure movie is an instant *sensation*. 2. As she boarded the plane, Eve had a nagging *sensation* that she had forgotten something important.		

MENTOR TEXT | SHORT STORY

This selection is an example of a short story, a brief fictional narrative.

This story models the type of writing you will develop in the Performance-Based Assessment at the end of the unit.

READ IT As you read, notice how the author chooses words that paint a vivid picture of the setting.

AUDIO

ANNOTATE

The Golden Windows

Laura E. Richards

1 All day long the little boy had worked hard, in field and barn and shed, for his people were poor farmers, and could not pay a workman; but at sunset there came an hour that was all his own, for his father had given it to him. Then the boy would go up to the top of a hill and look across at another hill that rose some miles away. On this far hill stood a house with windows of clear gold and diamonds. They shone and blazed so that it made the boy wink to look at them: but after a while the people in the house put up shutters, as it seemed, and then it looked like any common farmhouse. The boy supposed they did this because it was supper-time; and then he would go into the house and have his supper of bread and milk, and so to bed.

2 One day the boy's father called him and said: "You have been a good boy, and have earned a holiday. Take this day for your own; but remember that God gave it, and try to learn some good thing."

3 The boy thanked his father and kissed his mother; then he put a piece of bread in his pocket, and started off to find the house with the golden windows.

4 It was pleasant walking. His bare feet made marks in the white dust, and when he looked back, the footprints seemed to be following him, and making company for him. His shadow, too, kept beside him, and would dance or run with him as he pleased; so it was very cheerful.

5 By and by he felt hungry; and he sat down by a brown brook that ran through the alder hedge by the roadside, and ate his bread, and drank the clear water. An apple tree, which nestled beside wildflowers, was heavy with fruit. Then he scattered the crumbs for the birds, as his mother had taught him to do, and went on his way.

6 After a long time he came to a high green hill; and when he had climbed the hill, there was the house on the top; but it seemed that the shutters were up, for he could not see the golden windows. He came up to the house, and then he could well have wept, for the windows were of clear glass, like any others, and there was no gold anywhere about them.

7 A woman came to the door, and looked kindly at the boy, and asked him what he wanted.

8 "I saw the golden windows from our hilltop," he said, "and I came to see them, but now they are only glass."

9 The woman shook her head and laughed.

10 "We are poor farming people," she said, "and are not likely to have gold about our windows; but glass is better to see through."

11 She bade the boy sit down on the broad stone step at the door, and brought him a cup of milk and a cake, and bade him rest; then

she called her daughter, a child of his own age, and nodded kindly at the two, and went back to her work.

12 The little girl was barefooted like himself, and wore a brown cotton gown, but her hair was golden like the windows he had seen, and her eyes were blue like the sky at noon. She led the boy about the farm, and showed him her black calf with the white star on its forehead, and he told her about his own at home, which was red like a chestnut, with four white feet. Then when they had eaten an apple together, and so had become friends, the boy asked her about the golden windows. The little girl nodded, and said she knew all about them, only he had mistaken the house.

13 "You have come quite the wrong way!" she said. "Come with me, and I will show you the house with the golden windows, and then you will see for yourself."

14 They went to a knoll that rose behind the farmhouse, and as they went the little girl told him that the golden windows could only be seen at a certain hour, about sunset.

15 "Yes, I know that!" said the boy.

16 When they reached the top of the knoll, the girl turned and pointed; and there on a hill far away stood a house with windows of clear gold and diamond, just as he had seen them. And when they looked again, the boy saw that it was his own home.

17 Then he told the little girl that he must go; and he gave her his best pebble, the white one with the red band, that he had carried for a year in his pocket; and she gave him three horse-chestnuts, one red like satin, one spotted, and one white like milk. He kissed her, and promised to come again, but he did not tell her what he had learned; and so he went back down the hill, and the little girl stood in the sunset light and watched him.

18 The way home was long, and it was dark before the boy reached his father's house; but the lamplight and firelight shone through the windows, making them almost as bright as he had seen them from the hilltop; and when he opened the door, his mother came to kiss him, and his little sister ran to throw her arms about his neck, and his father looked up and smiled from his seat by the fire.

19 "Have you had a good day?" asked his mother.

20 Yes, the boy had had a very good day.

21 "And have you learned anything?" asked his father.

22 "Yes!" said the boy. "I have learned that our house has windows of gold and diamond." ❧

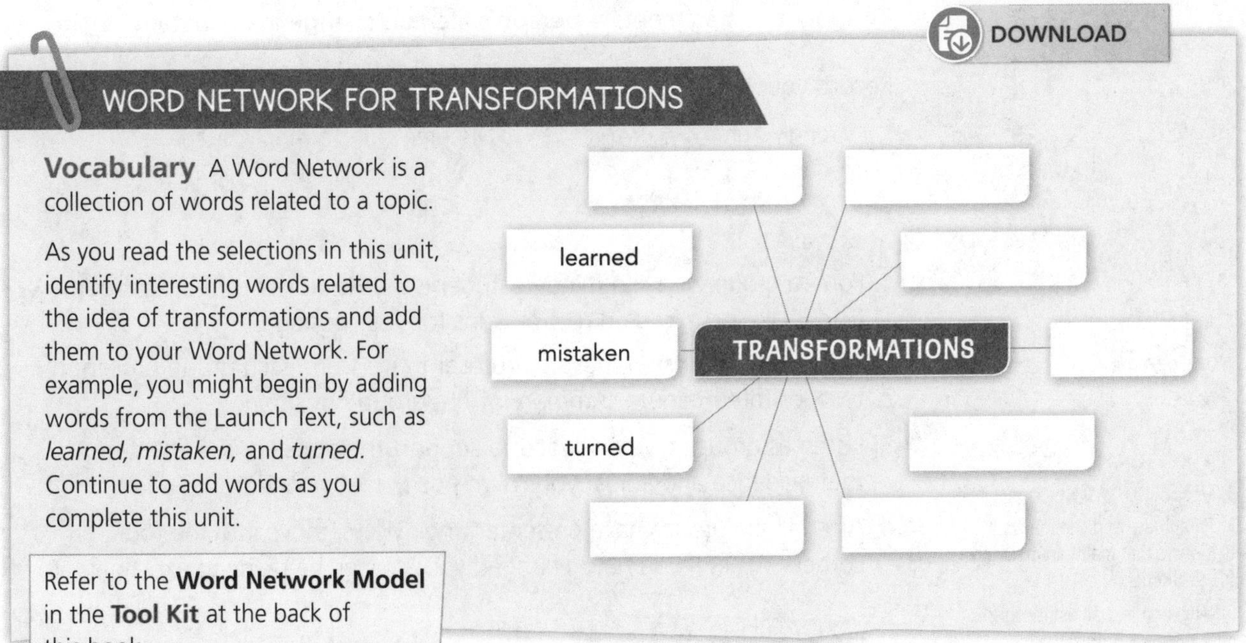

WORD NETWORK FOR TRANSFORMATIONS

Vocabulary A Word Network is a collection of words related to a topic.

As you read the selections in this unit, identify interesting words related to the idea of transformations and add them to your Word Network. For example, you might begin by adding words from the Launch Text, such as *learned, mistaken,* and *turned.* Continue to add words as you complete this unit.

Refer to the **Word Network Model** in the **Tool Kit** at the back of this book.

Summary

A **summary** is a brief, complete overview of a text that maintains the meaning and logical order of ideas of the original. It should not include your personal opinions.

NOTEBOOK

WRITE IT Write a summary of "The Golden Windows." In your summary, use basic words you learned as you read the story.

Launch Activity

Conduct a Four-Corner Debate

Consider this statement: **A person's life can change in an instant.**

Record your position on the statement and explain your thinking.

○ Strongly Agree ○ Agree ○ Disagree ○ Strongly Disagree

1. Form a group with like-minded students in one corner of the classroom. Discuss your choice and give reasons for your position.
2. After your discussion, have a representative from each group present a two- or three-minute summary of the group's position.
3. Listen as groups give evidence to support their positions. Reflect on that evidence and adjust your own position as needed.
4. After all the groups have presented their views, move into the four corners again. If you have changed your corner, be ready to explain why.

TEKS

6.D. Paraphrase and summarize texts in ways that maintain meaning and logical order.

6.I. Reflect on and adjust responses as new evidence is presented.

QuickWrite

Consider class discussions, presentations, the video, and the Mentor Text as you think about the Essential Question.

Essential Question

Can people really change?

At the end of the unit, you will respond to the Essential Question again and see how your perspective has changed.

NOTEBOOK

WRITE IT Record your first thoughts here.

DOWNLOAD

EQ Notes Can people really change?

As you read the selections in this unit, use a chart like the one shown to record your ideas and list details from the texts that support them. Taking notes as you go will help you clarify your thinking, gather relevant information, and be ready to respond to the Essential Question.

TITLE	MY IDEAS / OBSERVATIONS	TEXT EVIDENCE / INFORMATION

Refer to the **EQ Notes Model** in the **Tool Kit** at the back of this book.

Essential Question

Can people really change?

It's a common expression that "people change"—but do they? If so, how? You will work with your whole class to explore the concept of transformation and what it means to truly change.

VIDEO

INTERACTIVITY

Whole-Class Learning Strategies

Throughout your life, in school, in your community, and in your career, you will continue to learn and work in large-group environments.

Review these strategies and the actions you can take to practice them as you work with your whole class. Add ideas of your own for each category. Get ready to use these strategies during Whole-Class Learning.

STRATEGY	MY ACTION PLAN
Listen actively • Put away personal items to avoid becoming distracted. • Try to hear the speaker's full message before planning your own response.	
Demonstrate respect • Show up on time and make sure you are prepared for class. • Avoid side conversations while in class.	
Show interest • Be aware of your body language. For example, sit up in your chair. • Respond when the teacher asks for feedback.	
Interact and share ideas • If you're confused, other people probably are, too. Ask a question to help your whole class. • Build on the ideas of others by adding details or making a connection.	

CONTENTS

COMPARE ACROSS GENRES

DRAMA

A Christmas Carol: Scrooge and Marley, Acts I and II

based on the novel by Charles Dickens

How will Ebenezer Scrooge survive the ghosts of Christmas?

NOVEL EXCERPT

from A Christmas Carol

Charles Dickens

Can a humble family's Christmas celebration inspire Ebenezer Scrooge to change?

▸ MEDIA CONNECTION: *from* Scrooge

PERFORMANCE TASK: WRITING PROCESS

Write a Short Story

The Whole-Class readings dramatize moments of truth for Ebenezer Scrooge. After reading, you will write a short story about a character that has a significant, possibly transforming, life experience.

A CHRISTMAS CAROL: SCROOGE AND MARLEY, ACTS I AND II

The selection you are about to read is a drama.

Compare Across Genres

This play is a dramatic adaptation of the novel *A Christmas Carol*, a classic book by Charles Dickens. After reading the play, you will read an excerpt from the novel and compare it to the dramatic adaptation.

Reading Drama

A **drama,** or play, is a narrative written to be performed by actors.

DRAMA

Author's Purpose

- to tell a story to be performed by actors in front of an audience

Characteristics

- characters who take part in the story's action
- setting, or the time and place in which the story's action occurs; may have multiple settings
- various types of dramatic speech, including dialogue and monologue
- stage directions that describe how characters speak and behave
- stage directions may indicate other performance elements, such as sets, lighting, and costumes

Structure

- written in script form and organized in sections called acts and scenes
- plot, or related sequence of events, driven by one or more conflicts

Take a Minute!

DISCUSS IT With a partner, discuss plays you've seen in school or elsewhere that you enjoyed. Which were your favorites, and why? What qualities in the script or the performance made them fun to watch, moving, or exciting?

8.A. Demonstrate knowledge of literary genres such as realistic fiction, adventure stories, historical fiction, mysteries, humor, myths, fantasy, and science fiction.

8.C. Analyze how playwrights develop characters through dialogue and staging.

Genre/Text Elements

Dialogue, Stage Directions, and Character Development Plays are stories that are brought to life by a script, director, and actors. Scripts are like a recipe for the final product—the play. They contain information about the characters, their conversations, their actions, and their development. Here are two basic elements of a script:

- **Dialogue:** conversation among characters
  Most plays convey characters' personalities, thoughts, and reactions through dialogue—the words they say. Dialogue can reveal how characters change or develop over the course of a play.
- **Stage Directions:** playwright's directions or notes in a script
  Stage directions often include notes about how characters should speak. Sometimes, they include information about the setting, sound effects, and costumes.

EXAMPLE Consider how two different stage directions affect the development of the character.

[*A backstage dressing room.* Kate, *sits in front of a mirror.* Peg *is pinning up Kate's hair.*]

Version 1
Kate. *[barely able to contain her excitement]* Oh, I feel grand! I can just see my reviews tomorrow—"Kate West! Huge Star!"

Version 2
Kate. *[slumped; with sarcasm]* Oh, I feel grand! I can just see my reviews tomorrow—"Kate West! Huge Star!"

NOTEBOOK

PRACTICE **Read the passage and analyze what you learn about characters from the dialogue and stage directions. Then, answer the questions.**

[Kate's *dressing room, later that night.* Kate *sits before a mirror while* Peg *brushes her hair.*]

Kate. [*suddenly angry*] What are you doing? My hair looks awful!

Peg. [*wearily*] It's fine, Miss West. You always look fine.

Kate. [*narrowing her eyes*] Well, I don't care–you've ruined me! I'm going to look terrible tonight!

Peg. [*unconsciously, then catching herself*] Yes, Miss West. I mean, of course not, Miss West.

1. What do you learn about the characters from dialogue?
2. What do you learn about the characters from stage directions? Explain, citing details from the passage.

About Adaptations

During his lifetime, British novelist **Charles Dickens** (1812–1870) was one of the best-selling writers in England. Readers loved his vivid stories, which are full of unforgettable characters, realistic settings, dark humor, and social commentary. Since Dickens's death, his popularity has only grown. His many novels have served as the basis for countless other works, including movies, plays, operas, and ballets. This dramatic adaptation of his novel *A Christmas Carol* retells the famous tale of the miser Ebenezer Scrooge in two powerful acts.

A Christmas Carol: Scrooge and Marley, Act I

Concept Vocabulary

You will encounter the following words as you read *A Christmas Carol: Scrooge and Marley,* Act I. Before reading, note how familiar you are with each word. Then, rank the words in order from most familiar (1) to least familiar (6).

WORD	YOUR RANKING
covetous	
morose	
resolute	
impossible	
malcontent	
miser	

Comprehension Strategy

Paraphrase

When you **paraphrase** a text, you restate it in your own words while maintaining the meaning and logical order of the original. Doing so can help you better understand what you read. When you encounter a complex passage, paraphrase to clarify its meaning.

EXAMPLE

Consider this passage from Scene 2, paragraph 15:

> ***Nephew.*** *There are many things from which I have derived good, by which I have not profited, I daresay.*

Paraphrase: Many things that helped me did not earn me any money.

PRACTICE As you read, use the open space next to the text to write paraphrases of challenging passages. Make sure your paraphrases maintain the meaning and order of the original text.

TEKS
6.D. Paraphrase and summarize texts in ways that maintain meaning and logical order.

A Christmas Carol: Scrooge and Marley

Act I

a drama based on the novel
by Charles Dickens

BACKGROUND

Charles Dickens's novel, *A Christmas Carol,* from which this play was adapted, shows sympathy for the struggles of the poor. The story is set in England during the nineteenth century, a time of rapid industrial growth. In this booming economy, the wealthy lived in luxury, but the poor and the working class suffered.

AUDIO

ANNOTATE

CHARACTERS

Jacob Marley, a specter
Ebenezer Scrooge, not yet dead, which is to say still alive
Bob Cratchit, Scrooge's clerk
Fred, Scrooge's nephew
Thin Do-Gooder
Portly Do-Gooder
Specters (Various), carrying money-boxes
The Ghost of Christmas Past
Four Jocund Travelers
A Band of Singers
A Band of Dancers
Little Boy Scrooge
Young Man Scrooge
Fan, Scrooge's little sister
The Schoolmaster
Schoolmates
Fezziwig, a fine and fair employer
Dick, young Scrooge's co-worker
Young Scrooge
A Fiddler
More Dancers
Scrooge's Lost Love
Scrooge's Lost Love's Daughter
Scrooge's Lost Love's Husband
The Ghost of Christmas Present
Some Bakers
Mrs. Cratchit, Bob Cratchit's wife
Belinda Cratchit, a daughter
Martha Cratchit, another daughter
Peter Cratchit, a son
Tiny Tim Cratchit, another son
Scrooge's Niece, Fred's wife
The Ghost of Christmas Future, a mute Phantom
Three Men of Business
Drunks, Scoundrels, Women of the Streets
A Charwoman
Mrs. Dilber
Joe, an old second-hand goods dealer
A Corpse, very like Scrooge
An Indebted Family
Adam, a young boy
A Poulterer
A Gentlewoman
Some More Men of Business

READING DRAMA

The language of plays reflects the ways in which people routinely speak and uses a wide variety of language structures. As you read this play, look for language structures, such as declarative, interrogative, exclamatory, and imperative sentences.

Declarative: a statement
It's not my business.

Interrogative: a question
What are you doing, Cratchit?

Exclamatory: an urgent statement
It is the very thing he likes!

Imperative: a command
Don't say it, Cratchit.

THE PLACE OF THE PLAY Various locations in and around the City of London, including Scrooge's Chambers and Offices; the Cratchit Home; Fred's Home; Scrooge's School; Fezziwig's Offices; Old Joe's Hide-a-Way.

THE TIME OF THE PLAY The entire action of the play takes place on Christmas Eve, Christmas Day, and the morning after Christmas, 1843.

Scene 1

1 [*Ghostly music in auditorium. A single spotlight on* Jacob Marley, D.C. *He is ancient; awful, dead-eyed. He speaks straight out to auditorium.*]

2 **Marley.** [*Cackle-voiced*] My name is Jacob Marley and I am dead. [*He laughs.*] Oh, no, there's no doubt that I am dead. The register of my burial was signed by the clergyman, the clerk, the undertaker . . . and by my chief mourner . . . Ebenezer Scrooge . . . [*Pause; remembers*] I am dead as a doornail.

3 [*A spotlight fades up, Stage Right, on* Scrooge, *in his counting-house*[1] *counting. Lettering on the window behind* Scrooge *reads: "Scrooge and Marley, Ltd." The spotlight is tight on* Scrooge's *head and shoulders. We shall not yet see into the offices and setting. Ghostly music continues, under.* Marley *looks across at* Scrooge; *pitifully. After a moment's pause*]

1. **counting-house** *n.* office for keeping financial records and writing business letters.

4 I present him to you: Ebenezer Scrooge . . . England's most tightfisted hand at the grindstone, Scrooge! a squeezing, wrenching, grasping, scraping, clutching, **covetous**, old sinner! secret, and self-contained, and solitary as an oyster. The cold within him freezes his old features, nips his pointed nose, shrivels his cheek, stiffens his gait; makes his eyes red, his thin lips blue; and speaks out shrewdly in his grating voice. Look at him. Look at him . . .

covetous (KUHV uh tuhs) *adj.* greedy and jealous

CLOSE READ

ANNOTATE: Mark the use of descriptive words in paragraph 4.

QUESTION: Why might the playwright have chosen these words?

CONCLUDE: How does the playwright's word choice affect the reader's understanding of Scrooge's character?

5 [Scrooge *counts and mumbles.*]

6 **Scrooge.** They owe me money and I will collect. I will have them jailed, if I have to. They owe me money and I will collect what is due me.

7 [Marley *moves towards* Scrooge; *two steps. The spotlight stays with him.*]

8 **Marley.** [*Disgusted*] He and I were partners for I don't know how many years. Scrooge was my sole executor, my sole administrator, my sole assign, my sole residuary legatee,[2] my sole friend and my sole mourner. But Scrooge was not so cut up by the sad event of my death, but that he was an excellent man of business on the very day of my funeral, and solemnized[3] it with an undoubted bargain. [*Pauses again in disgust*] He never painted out my name from the window. There it stands, on the window and above the warehouse door: Scrooge and Marley. Sometimes people new to our business call him Scrooge and sometimes they call him Marley. He answers to both names. It's all the same to him. And it's cheaper than painting in a new sign, isn't it? [*Pauses; moves closer to* Scrooge] Nobody has ever stopped him in the street to say, with gladsome looks, "My dear Scrooge, how are you? When will you come to see me?" No beggars implored him to bestow a trifle, no children ever ask him what it is o'clock, no man or woman now, or ever in his life, not once, inquire the way to such and such a place. [Marley *stands next to* Scrooge *now. They share, so it seems, a spotlight.*] But what does Scrooge care of any of this? It is the very thing he likes! To edge his way along the crowded paths of life, warning all human sympathy to keep its distance.

9 [*A ghostly bell rings in the distance.* Marley *moves away from* Scrooge, *now, heading* D. *again. As he does, he "takes" the light:* Scrooge *has disappeared into the black void beyond.* Marley *walks* D.C., *talking directly to the audience. Pauses*]

10 The bell tolls and I must take my leave. You must stay a while with Scrooge and watch him play out his scroogey life. It is now the story: the once-upon-a-time. Scrooge is busy in his counting-house. Where else? Christmas eve and Scrooge is busy in his counting-house. It is cold, bleak, biting weather outside: foggy withal: and, if you listen closely, you can hear the people in the court go wheezing up and down, beating their hands upon their breasts, and stamping their feet upon the pavement stones to warm them . . .

11 [*The clocks outside strike three.*]

12 Only three! and quite dark outside already: it has not been light all day this day.

13 [*This ghostly bell rings in the distance again.* Marley *looks about him. Music in.* Marley *flies away.*]

14 [*N.B.* Marley's *comings and goings should, from time to time, induce the explosion of the odd flash-pot, I.H.*]

2. **sole residuary legatee** *n.* legal term for a person who inherits someone's home after he or she dies.

3. **solemnized** *v.* honored or remembered. Marley is being sarcastic.

Scene 2

1 *[Christmas music in, sung by a live chorus, full. At conclusion of song, sound fades under and into the distance. Lights up in set: offices of Scrooge and Marley, Ltd.* Scrooge *sits at his desk, at work. Near him is a tiny fire. His door is open and in his line of vision, we see* Scrooge's clerk, Bob Cratchit, *who sits in a dismal tank of a cubicle, copying letters. Near* Cratchit *is a fire so tiny as to barely cast a light: perhaps it is one pitifully glowing coal?* Cratchit *rubs his hands together, puts on a white comforter*[4] *and tries to heat his hands around his candle.* Scrooge's Nephew *enters, unseen.]*

4. **comforter** *n.* long, woolen scarf.

2 **Scrooge.** What are you doing, Cratchit? Acting cold, are you? Next, you'll be asking to replenish your coal from my coal-box, won't you? Well, save your breath, Cratchit! Unless you're prepared to find employ elsewhere!

3 **Nephew.** [*Cheerfully; surprising* Scrooge] A merry Christmas to you, Uncle! God save you!

4 **Scrooge.** Bah! Humbug![5]

5. **Humbug** *interj.* nonsense.

5 **Nephew.** Christmas a "humbug," Uncle? I'm sure you don't mean that.

6 **Scrooge.** I do! Merry Christmas? What right do you have to be merry? What reason have you to be merry? You're poor enough!

7 **Nephew.** Come, then. What right have you to be dismal? What reason have you to be **morose**? You're rich enough.

morose (muh ROHS) *adj.* gloomy; ill-tempered

8 **Scrooge.** Bah! Humbug!

9 **Nephew.** Don't be cross, Uncle.

10 **Scrooge.** What else can I be? Eh? When I live in a world of fools such as this? Merry Christmas? What's Christmastime to you but a time of paying bills without any money; a time for finding yourself a year older, but not an hour richer. If I could work my will, every idiot who goes about with "Merry Christmas" on his lips, should be boiled with his own pudding, and buried with a stake of holly through his heart. He should!

CLOSE READ

ANNOTATE: Mark words in paragraph 10 that show Scrooge's attitude toward Christmas.

QUESTION: What does Scrooge think of people, such as his nephew, that celebrate Christmas?

CONCLUDE: What does this attitude reveal about Scrooge's character?

11 **Nephew.** Uncle!

12 **Scrooge.** Nephew! You keep Christmas in your own way and let me keep it in mine.

13 **Nephew.** Keep it! But you don't keep it, Uncle.

14 **Scrooge.** Let me leave it alone, then. Much good it has ever done you!

15 **Nephew.** There are many things from which I have derived good, by which I have not profited, I daresay. Christmas among the rest. But I am sure that I always thought of Christmas time, when it has come round—as a good time: the only time I know of, when men and women seem to open their shut-up hearts freely, and to think of people below them as if they really were fellow-passengers to the grave, and not another race of creatures bound on other journeys. And therefore, Uncle, though it has never put a scrap of gold or silver in my pocket, I believe that it has done me good, and that it *will* do me good; and I say, God bless it!

16 [*The Clerk in the tank applauds, looks at the furious* Scrooge *and pokes out his tiny fire, as if in exchange for the moment of impropriety.* Scrooge *yells at him.*]

17 **Scrooge.** [*To the clerk*] Let me hear another sound from *you* and you'll keep your Christmas by losing your situation. [*To the nephew*] You're quite a powerful speaker, sir. I wonder you don't go into Parliament.[6]

6. **Parliament** national legislative body of Great Britain, in some ways like the U.S. Congress.

18 **Nephew.** Don't be angry, Uncle. Come! Dine with us tomorrow.

19 **Scrooge.** I'd rather see myself dead than see myself with your family!

20 **Nephew.** But, why? Why?

21 **Scrooge.** Why did you get married?

22 **Nephew.** Because I fell in love.

23 **Scrooge.** That, sir, is the only thing that you have said to me in your entire lifetime which is even more ridiculous than "Merry Christmas!" [*Turns from* Nephew] Good afternoon.

24 **Nephew.** Nay, Uncle, you never came to see me before I married either. Why give it as a reason for not coming now?

25 **Scrooge.** Good afternoon, Nephew!

26 **Nephew.** I want nothing from you; I ask nothing of you; why cannot we be friends?

27 **Scrooge.** Good afternoon!

28 **Nephew.** I am sorry with all my heart, to find you so **resolute**. But I have made the trial in homage to Christmas, and I'll keep my Christmas humor to the last. So A Merry Christmas, Uncle!

resolute (REHZ uh loot) *adj.* determined

29 **Scrooge.** Good afternoon!

30 **Nephew.** And a Happy New Year!

31 **Scrooge.** Good afternoon!

32 **Nephew.** [*He stands facing* Scrooge.] Uncle, you are the most . . . [*Pauses*] No, I shan't. My Christmas humor is intact . . . [*Pause*] God bless you, Uncle . . . [Nephew *turns and starts for the door; he stops at* Cratchit's *cage.*] Merry Christmas, Bob Cratchit . . .

33 **Cratchit.** Merry Christmas to you sir, and a very, very happy New Year . . .

34 **Scrooge.** [*Calling across to them*] Oh, fine, a perfection, just fine . . . to see the perfect pair of you; husbands, with wives and children to support . . . my clerk there earning fifteen shillings a week . . . and the perfect pair of you, talking about a Merry Christmas! [*Pauses*] I'll retire to Bedlam![7]

7. **Bedlam** *n.* hospital in London for the mentally ill.

35 **Nephew.** [*To* Cratchit] He's **impossible**!

impossible (ihm POS uh buhl) *adj.* disagreeable; unreasonable

36 **Cratchit.** Oh, mind him not, sir. He's getting on in years, and he's alone. He's noticed your visit. I'll wager your visit has warmed him.

37 **Nephew.** Him? Uncle Ebenezer Scrooge? *Warmed?* You are a better Christian than I am, sir.

38 **Cratchit.** [*Opening the door for* Nephew; *two* Do-Gooders *will enter, as* Nephew *exits*] Good day to you, sir, and God bless.

39 **Nephew.** God bless . . . [*One man who enters is portly, the other is thin. Both are pleasant.*]

40 **Cratchit.** Can I help you, gentlemen?

41 **Thin Man.** [*Carrying papers and books; looks around* Cratchit *to* Scrooge] Scrooge and Marley's, I believe. Have I the pleasure of addressing Mr. Scrooge, or Mr. Marley?

42 **Scrooge.** Mr. Marley has been dead these seven years. He died seven years ago this very night.

43 **Portly Man.** We have no doubt his liberality[8] is well represented by his surviving partner . . . [*Offers his calling card*]

8. **liberality** *n.* generosity.

44 **Scrooge.** [*Handing back the card; unlooked at*] . . . Good afternoon.

45 **Thin Man.** This will take but a moment, sir . . .

46 **Portly Man.** At this festive season of the year, Mr. Scrooge, it is more than usually desirable that we should make some slight provision for the poor and destitute, who suffer greatly at the present time. Many thousands are in want of common necessities; hundreds of thousands are in want of common comforts, sir.

47 **Scrooge.** Are there no prisons?

48 **Portly Man.** Plenty of prisons.

49 **Scrooge.** And aren't the Union workhouses still in operation?

50 **Thin Man.** They are. Still, I wish that I could say that they are not.

51 **Scrooge.** The Treadmill[9] and the Poor Law[10] are in full vigor, then?

52 **Thin Man.** Both very busy, sir.

53 **Scrooge.** Ohhh, I see. I was afraid, from what you said at first, that something had occurred to stop them from their useful course. [*Pauses*] I'm glad to hear it.

54 **Portly Man.** Under the impression that they scarcely furnish Christian cheer of mind or body to the multitude, a few of us are endeavoring to raise a fund to buy the Poor some meat and drink, and means of warmth. We choose this time, because it is a time, of all others, when Want is keenly felt, and Abundance rejoices. [*Pen in hand; as well as notepad*] What shall I put you down for, sir?

55 **Scrooge.** Nothing!

56 **Portly Man.** You wish to be left anonymous?

57 **Scrooge.** I wish to be left alone! [*Pauses; turns away; turns back to them*] Since you ask me what I wish, gentlemen, that is my answer. I help to support the establishments that I have mentioned: they cost enough: and those who are badly off must go there.

58 **Thin Man.** Many can't go there; and many would rather die.

59 **Scrooge.** If they would rather die, they had better do it, and decrease the surplus population. Besides—excuse me—I don't know that.

60 **Thin Man.** But you might know it!

61 **Scrooge.** It's not my business. It's enough for a man to understand his own business, and not to interfere with other people's. Mine occupies me constantly. Good afternoon, gentlemen!

62 [Scrooge *turns his back on the gentlemen and returns to his desk.*]

63 **Portly Man.** But, sir, Mr. Scrooge . . . think of the poor.

64 **Scrooge.** [*Turns suddenly to them. Pauses*] Take your leave of my offices, sirs, while I am still smiling.

65 [*The* Thin Man *looks at the* Portly Man. *They are undone. They shrug. They move to the door.* Cratchit *hops up to open it for them.*]

66 **Thin Man.** Good day, sir . . . [*To* Cratchit] A merry Christmas to you, sir . . .

9. **the Treadmill** kind of mill wheel turned by the weight of people treading steps arranged around it; this device is used to punish prisoners.

10. **Poor Law** the original 16th-century Poor Laws called for overseers of the poor in each neighborhood to provide relief for the needy. The New Poor Law of 1834 made the workhouses in which the poor sometimes lived and worked extremely harsh and unattractive places.

CLOSE READ

ANNOTATE: Mark the words in paragraph 54 that describe the Portly Man's reasons for asking for help.

QUESTION: What do these details reveal about the setting?

CONCLUDE: How does this information affect your understanding of the drama?

67 **Cratchit.** Yes. A Merry Christmas to both of you . . .

68 **Portly Man.** Merry Christmas . . .

69 [Cratchit *silently squeezes something into the hand of the* Thin Man.]

70 **Thin Man.** What's this?

71 **Cratchit.** Shhhh . . .

72 [Cratchit *opens the door; wind and snow whistle into the room.*]

73 **Thin Man.** Thank you, sir, thank you.

74 [Cratchit *closes the door and returns to his workplace.* Scrooge *is at his own counting table. He talks to* Cratchit *without looking up.*]

75 **Scrooge.** It's less of a time of year for being merry, and more a time of year for being loony . . . if you ask me.

76 **Cratchit.** Well, I don't know, sir . . . [*The clock's bell strikes six o'clock.*] Well, there it is, eh, six?

77 **Scrooge.** Saved by six bells, are you?

78 **Cratchit.** I must be going home . . . [*He snuffs out his candle and puts on his hat.*] I hope you have a . . . very very lovely day tomorrow, sir . . .

79 **Scrooge.** Hmmm. Oh, you'll be wanting the whole day tomorrow, I suppose?

80 **Cratchit.** If quite convenient, sir.

81 **Scrooge.** It's not convenient, and it's not fair. If I was to stop half-a-crown for it, you'd think yourself ill-used, I'll be bound?

82 [Cratchit *smiles faintly.*]

83 **Cratchit.** I don't know, sir . . .

84 **Scrooge.** And yet, you don't think me ill-used when I pay a day's wages for no work . . .

85 **Cratchit.** It's only but once a year . . .

86 **Scrooge.** A poor excuse for picking a man's pocket every 25th of December! But I suppose you must have the whole day. Be here all the earlier the next morning!

87 **Cratchit.** Oh, I will, sir. I will. I promise you. And, sir . . .

88 **Scrooge.** Don't say it, Cratchit.

89 **Cratchit.** But let me wish you a . . .

CLOSE READ

ANNOTATE: Mark details in paragraphs 78–95 that show Cratchit's attitude toward Scrooge.

QUESTION: Why might the playwright have included this exchange between Cratchit and Scrooge?

CONCLUDE: What does this conversation reveal about Cratchit's character?

90 **Scrooge.** Don't say it, Cratchit. I warn you . . .

91 **Cratchit.** Sir!

92 **Scrooge.** Cratchit!

93 [Cratchit *opens the door.*]

94 **Cratchit.** All right, then, sir . . . well . . . [*Suddenly*] Merry Christmas, Mr. Scrooge!

95 [*And he runs out the door, shutting same behind him.* Scrooge *moves to his desk; gathering his coat, hat, etc. A* Boy *appears at his window . . . .*]

96 **Boy.** [*Singing*] "Away in a manger . . ."

97 [Scrooge *seizes his ruler and whacks at the image of the* Boy *outside. The* Boy *leaves.*]

98 **Scrooge.** Bah! Humbug! Christmas! Bah! Humbug! [*He shuts out the light.*]

99 *A note on the crossover, following Scene 2:*

100 [Scrooge *will walk alone to his rooms from his offices. As he makes a long slow cross of the stage, the scenery should change. Christmas music will be heard, various people will cross by* Scrooge, *often smiling happily.*]

101 *There will be occasional pleasant greetings tossed at him.*

102 Scrooge, *in contrast to all, will grump and mumble. He will snap at passing boys, as might a horrid old hound.*

103 *In short,* Scrooge's *sounds and movements will define him in contrast from all other people who cross the stage: he is the misanthrope,*[11] *the* **malcontent**, *the* **miser**. *He is* Scrooge.

11. **misanthrope** (MIHS uhn throhp) *n.* a person who hates or distrusts everyone.

malcontent (MAL kuhn tehnt) *n.* a person who is always unhappy

miser (MY zuhr) *n.* greedy person who keeps and refuses to spend money, even at the expense of his or her own comfort

104 *This statement of* Scrooge's *character, by contrast to all other characters, should seem comical to the audience.*

105 *During* Scrooge's *crossover to his rooms, snow should begin to fall. All passers-by will hold their faces to the sky, smiling, allowing snow to shower them lightly.* Scrooge, *by contrast, will bat at the flakes with his walking-stick, as might an insomniac swat at a sleep-stopping, middle-of-the-night swarm of mosquitoes. He will comment on the blackness of the night, and, finally, reach his rooms and his encounter with the magical specter:*[12] Marley, *his eternal mate.*]

12. **specter** *n.* ghost.

Scene 3

1 **Scrooge.** No light at all . . . no moon . . . *that* is what is at the center of Christmas Eve: dead black: void . . .

2 [Scrooge *puts his key in the door's keyhole. He has reached his rooms now. The door knocker changes and is now* Marley's *face. A musical sound: quickly: ghostly.* Marley's *image is not at all angry, but looks at* Scrooge *as did the old* Marley *look at* Scrooge. *The hair is curiously stirred; eyes wide open, dead: absent of focus.* Scrooge *stares wordlessly here. The face, before his very eyes, does deliquesce.*[13] *It is a knocker again.* Scrooge *opens the door and checks the back of same, probably for* Marley's *pigtail. Seeing nothing but screws and nuts,* Scrooge *refuses the memory.*]

13. **deliquesce** (dehl ih KWEHS) *v.* melt away.

3 Pooh, pooh!

4 [*The sound of the door closing resounds throughout the house as thunder. Every room echoes the sound.* Scrooge *fastens the door and walks across the hall to the stairs, trimming his candle as he goes; and then he goes slowly up the staircase. He checks each room: sitting room, bedrooms, lumber-room. He looks under the sofa, under the table: nobody there. He fixes his evening gruel on the hob,*[14] *changes his jacket.* Scrooge *sits near the tiny low-flamed fire, sipping his gruel. There are various pictures on the walls: all of them now show likenesses of* Marley. Scrooge *blinks his eyes.*]

14. **gruel on the hob** thin broth warming on a ledge at the back or side of the fireplace.

5 Bah! Humbug!

6 [Scrooge *walks in a circle about the room. The pictures change back into their natural images. He sits down at the table in front of the fire. A bell hangs overhead. It begins to ring, of its own accord. Slowly, surely, begins the ringing of every bell in the house. They continue ringing for nearly half a minute.* Scrooge *is stunned by the phenomenon. The bells cease their ringing all at once. Deep below* Scrooge, *in the basement of the house, there is the sound of clanking, of some enormous chain being dragged across the floors; and now up the stairs. We hear doors flying open.*]

7 Bah still! Humbug still! This is not happening! I won't believe it!

8 [Marley's Ghost *enters the room. He is horrible to look at: pigtail, vest, suit as usual, but he drags an enormous chain now, to which is fastened cash-boxes, keys, padlocks, ledgers, deeds, and heavy purses fashioned of steel. He is transparent.* Marley *stands opposite the stricken* Scrooge.]

9 How now! What do you want of me?

10 **Marley.** Much!

11 **Scrooge.** Who are you?

12 **Marley.** Ask me who I was.

13 **Scrooge.** Who were you then?

14 **Marley.** In life, I was your business partner: Jacob Marley.

15 **Scrooge.** I see . . . can you sit down?

16 **Marley.** I can.

17 **Scrooge.** Do it then.

18 **Marley.** I shall. [Marley *sits opposite* Scrooge, *in the chair across the table, at the front of the fireplace.*] You don't believe in me.

19 **Scrooge.** I don't.

20 **Marley.** Why do you doubt your senses?

21 **Scrooge.** Because every little thing affects them. A slight disorder of the stomach makes them cheat. You may be an undigested bit of beef, a blot of mustard, a crumb of cheese, a fragment of an underdone potato. There's more of gravy than of grave about you, whatever you are!

22 [*There is a silence between them.* Scrooge *is made nervous by it. He picks up a toothpick.*]

23 Humbug! I tell you: humbug!

24 [Marley *opens his mouth and screams a ghostly, fearful scream. The scream echoes about each room of the house. Bats fly, cats screech, lightning flashes.* Scrooge *stands and walks backwards against the wall.* Marley *stands and screams again. This time, he takes his head and lifts it from his shoulders. His head continues to scream.* Marley's *face again appears on every picture in the room: all screaming.* Scrooge, *on his knees before* Marley.]

25 Mercy! Dreadful apparition,[15] mercy! Why, O! why do you trouble me so?

26 **Marley.** Man of the worldly mind, do you believe in me, or not?

27 **Scrooge.** I do. I must. But why do spirits such as you walk the earth? And why do they come to me?

28 **Marley.** It is required of every man that the spirit within him should walk abroad among his fellow-men, and travel far and wide; and if that spirit goes not forth in life, it is condemned to do so after death. [Marley *screams again; a tragic scream; from his ghostly bones.*] I wear the chain I forged in life. I made it link by link, and yard by yard. Is its pattern strange to you? Or would you know,

15. **apparition** *n.* ghost.

you, Scrooge, the weight and length of the strong coil you bear yourself? It was full as heavy and long as this, seven Christmas Eves ago. You have labored on it, since. It is a ponderous chain.

29 [*Terrified that a chain will appear about his body,* Scrooge *spins and waves the unwanted chain away. None, of course, appears. Sees* Marley *watching him dance about the room.* Marley *watches* Scrooge; *silently.*]

30 **Scrooge.** Jacob. Old Jacob Marley, tell me more. Speak comfort to me, Jacob . . .

31 **Marley.** I have none to give. Comfort comes from other regions, Ebenezer Scrooge, and is conveyed by other ministers, to other kinds of men. A very little more, is all that is permitted to me. I cannot rest, I cannot stay, I cannot linger anywhere . . . [*He moans again.*] My spirit never walked beyond our counting-house—mark me!—in life my spirit never roved beyond the narrow limits of our moneychanging hole; and weary journeys lie before me!

32 **Scrooge.** But you were always a good man of business, Jacob.

33 **Marley.** [*Screams word "business"; a flash-pot explodes with him.*] *BUSINESS!!!* Mankind was my business. The common welfare was my business; charity, mercy, forbearance, benevolence, were, all, my business. [Scrooge is *quaking.*] Hear me, Ebenezer Scrooge! My time is nearly gone.

34 **Scrooge.** I will, but don't be hard upon me. And don't be flowery, Jacob! Pray!

35 **Marley.** How is it that I appear before you in a shape that you can see, I may not tell. I have sat invisible beside you many and many a day. That is no light part of my penance. I am here tonight to warn you that you have yet a chance and hope of escaping my fate. A chance and hope of my procuring, Ebenezer.

36 **Scrooge.** You were always a good friend to me. Thank'ee!

37 **Marley.** You will be haunted by Three Spirits.

38 **Scrooge.** Would that be the chance and hope you mentioned, Jacob?

39 **Marley.** It is.

40 **Scrooge.** I think I'd rather not.

41 **Marley.** Without their visits, you cannot hope to shun the path I tread. Expect the first one tomorrow, when the bell tolls one.

42 **Scrooge.** Couldn't I take 'em all at once, and get it over, Jacob?

CLOSE READ

ANNOTATE: Mark the words in paragraphs 30–34 that show Scrooge's reaction to Marley.

QUESTION: What do these words reveal about Scrooge at this point in the play?

CONCLUDE: What does Scrooge's reaction in these paragraphs suggest about his character?

43 **Marley.** Expect the second on the next night at the same hour. The third upon the next night when the last stroke of twelve has ceased to vibrate. Look to see me no more. Others may, but you may not. And look that, for your own sake, you remember what has passed between us!

44 [Marley *places his head back upon his shoulders. He approaches the window and beckons to* Scrooge *to watch. Outside the window, specters fly by, carrying money-boxes and chains. They make a confused sound of lamentation.* Marley, *after listening a moment, joins into their mournful dirge. He leans to the window and floats out into the bleak, dark night. He is gone.*]

45 **Scrooge.** [*Rushing to the window*] Jacob! No, Jacob! Don't leave me! I'm frightened! [*He sees that* Marley *has gone. He looks outside. He pulls the shutter closed, so that the scene is blocked from his view. All sound stops. After a pause, he re-opens the shutter and all is quiet, as it should be on Christmas Eve. Carolers carol out of doors, in the distance.* Scrooge *closes the shutter and walks down the stairs. He examines the door by which* Marley *first entered.*] No one here at all! Did I imagine all that? Humbug! [*He looks about the room.*] I did imagine it. It only happened in my foulest dream-mind, didn't it? An undigested bit of . . . [*Thunder and lightning in the room; suddenly*] Sorry! Sorry!

46 [*There is silence again. The lights fade out.*]

Scene 4

1 [*Christmas music, choral, "Hark the Herald Angels Sing," sung by an onstage choir of children, spotlighted, D.C. Above,* Scrooge *in his bed, dead to the world, asleep, in his darkened room. It should appear that the choir is singing somewhere outside of the house, of course, and a use of scrim*[16] *is thus suggested. When the singing is ended, the choir should fade out of view and* Marley *should fade into view, in their place.*]

2 **Marley.** [*Directly to audience*] From this point forth . . . I shall be quite visible to you, but invisible to him. [*Smiles*] He will feel my presence, nevertheless, for, unless my senses fail me completely, we are—you and I—witness to the changing of a miser: that one, my partner in life, in business, and in eternity: that one: Scrooge. [*Moves to staircase, below* Scrooge] See him now. He endeavors to pierce the darkness with his ferret eyes.[17] [*To audience*] See him, now. He listens for the hour.

3 [*The bells toll.* Scrooge *is awakened and quakes as the hour approaches one o'clock, but the bells stop their sound at the hour of twelve.*]

16. **scrim** *n.* see-through fabric backdrop used to create special effects in the theater.

17. **ferret eyes** A ferret is a small, weasel-like animal used for hunting rabbits. This expression means to stare continuously, the way a ferret hunts.

4 **Scroge.** [*Astonished*] Midnight! Why this isn't possible. It was past two when I went to bed. An icicle must have gotten into the clock's works! I couldn't have slept through the whole day and far into another night. It isn't possible that anything has happened to the sun, and this is twelve at noon! [*He runs to window; unshutters same; it is night.*] Night, still. Quiet, normal for the season, cold. It is certainly not noon. I cannot in any way afford to lose my days. Securities come due, promissory notes,[18] interest on investments: these are things that happen in the daylight! [*He returns to his bed.*] Was this a dream?

5 [Marley *appears in his room. He speaks to the audience.*]

6 **Marley.** You see? He does not, with faith, believe in me fully, even still! Whatever will it take to turn the faith of a miser from money to men?

7 **Scrooge.** Another quarter and it'll be one and Marley's ghostly friends will come. [*Pauses; listens*] Where's the chime for one? [*Ding, dong*] A quarter past [*Repeats*] Half-past! [Repeats] A quarter to it! But where's the heavy bell of the hour one? This is a game in which I lose my senses! Perhaps, if I allowed myself another short doze . . .

8 **Marley.** . . . Doze, Ebenezer, doze.

9 [*A heavy bell thuds its one ring; dull and definitely one o'clock. There is a flash of light.* Scrooge *sits up, in a sudden. A hand draws back the curtains by his bed. He sees it.*]

10 **Scrooge.** A hand! Who owns it! Hello!

11 [*Ghostly music again, but of a new nature to the play. A strange figure stands before* Scrooge*—like a child, yet at the same time like an old man: white hair, but unwrinkled skin, long, muscular arms, but delicate legs and feet. Wears white tunic; lustrous belt cinches waist. Branch of fresh green holly in its hand, but has its dress trimmed with fresh summer flowers. Clear jets of light spring from the crown of its head. Holds cap in hand. The Spirit is called* Past.]

12 Are you the Spirit, sir, whose coming was foretold to me?

13 **Past.** I am.

14 **Marley.** Does he take this to be a vision of his green grocer?

15 **Scrooge.** Who, and what are you?

16 **Past.** I am the Ghost of Christmas Past.

17 **Scrooge.** Long past?

18 **Past.** Your past.

18. **promissory notes** *n.* written promises to pay someone a certain sum of money.

CLOSE READ

ANNOTATE: Mark details in paragraph 4 that describe the setting.

QUESTION: Why might the playwright have included these details?

CONCLUDE: How do these details work together to increase the tension?

19 **Scrooge.** May I ask, please, sir, what business you have here with me?

20 **Past.** Your welfare.

21 **Scrooge.** Not to sound ungrateful, sir, and really, please do understand that I am plenty obliged for your concern, but, really, kind spirit, it would have done all the better for my welfare to have been left alone altogether, to have slept peacefully through this night.

22 **Past.** Your reclamation, then. Take heed!

23 **Scrooge.** My what?

24 **Past.** [*Motioning to* Scrooge *and taking his arm*] Rise! Fly with me! [*He leads* Scrooge *to the window.*]

25 **Scrooge.** [*Panicked*] Fly, but I am a mortal and cannot fly!

26 **Past.** [*Pointing to his heart*] Bear but a touch of my hand here and you shall be upheld in more than this!

27 [Scrooge *touches the spirit's heart and the lights dissolve into sparkly flickers. Lovely crystals of music are heard. The scene dissolves into another. Christmas music again*]

Scene 5

1 [Scrooge *and the* Ghost of Christmas Past *walk together across an open stage. In the background, we see a field that is open; covered by a soft, downy snow: a country road.*]

2 **Scrooge.** Good Heaven! I was bred in this place. I was a boy here!

3 [Scrooge *freezes, staring at the field beyond.* Marley's *ghost appears beside him; takes* Scrooge's *face in his hands, and turns his face to the audience.*]

4 **Marley.** You see this Scrooge: stricken by feeling. Conscious of a thousand odors floating in the air, each one connected with a thousand thoughts, and hopes, and joys, and care long, long forgotten. [*Pause*] This one—this Scrooge—before your very eyes, returns to life, among the living. [*To audience, sternly*] You'd best pay your most careful attention. I would suggest rapt.[19]

5 [*There is a small flash and puff of smoke and* Marley *is gone again.*]

6 **Past.** Your lip is trembling, Mr. Scrooge. And what is that upon your cheek?

19. **rapt** *adj.* giving complete attention; totally carried away by something.

7 **Scrooge.** Upon my cheek? Nothing . . . a blemish on the skin from the eating of overmuch grease . . . nothing . . . [*Suddenly*] Kind Spirit of Christmas Past, lead me where you will, but quickly! To be stagnant in this place is, for me, unbearable!

8 **Past.** You recollect the way?

9 **Scrooge.** Remember it! I would know it blindfolded! My bridge, my church, my winding river! [*Staggers about, trying to see it all at once. He weeps again.*]

10 **Past.** These are but shadows of things that have been. They have no consciousness of us.

11 [*Four jocund travelers enter, singing a Christmas song in four-part harmony—"God Rest Ye Merry Gentlemen."*]

12 **Scrooge.** Listen! I know these men! I remember the beauty of their song!

13 **Past.** But, why do you remember it so happily? It is Merry Christmas that they say to one another! What is Merry Christmas to you, Mr. Scrooge? Out upon Merry Christmas, right? What good has Merry Christmas ever done you, Mr. Scrooge? . . .

14 **Scrooge.** [*After a long pause*] None. No good. None . . . [*He bows his head.*]

15 **Past.** Look, you, sir, a school ahead. The schoolroom is not quite deserted. A solitary child, neglected by his friends, is left there still.

16 [Scrooge *falls to the ground; sobbing as he sees, and we see, a small boy, the young* Scrooge, *sitting and weeping, bravely, alone at his desk: alone in a vast space, a void.*]

17 **Scrooge.** I cannot look on him!

18 **Past.** You must, Mr. Scrooge, you must.

19 **Scrooge.** It's me. [*Pauses; weeps*] Poor boy. He lived inside his head . . . alone . . . [*Pauses; weeps*] poor boy. [*Pauses; stops his weeping*] I wish . . . [*Dries his eyes on his cuff*] ah! it's too late!

20 **Past.** What is the matter?

21 **Scrooge.** There was a boy singing a Christmas Carol outside my door last night. I should like to have given him something: that's all.

22 **Past.** [*Smiles; waves his hand to* Scrooge] Come. Let us see another Christmas.

CLOSE READ

ANNOTATE: Mark words in paragraphs 15–19 that describe Scrooge's emotions and behavior.

QUESTION: What does the playwright reveal through these words?

CONCLUDE: What can you conclude about the Ghost of Christmas Past's effect on Scrooge based on this description?

23 [*Lights out on a little boy. A flash of light. A puff of smoke. Lights up on older boy*]

24 **Scrooge.** Look! Me, again! Older now! [*Realizes*] Oh, yes . . . still alone.

25 [*The boy—a slightly older* Scrooge—*sits alone in a chair, reading. The door to the room opens and a young girl enters. She is much, much younger than this slightly older* Scrooge. *She is, say, six, and he is, say, twelve. Elder* Scrooge *and the* Ghost of Christmas Past *stand watching the scene, unseen.*]

26 **Fan.** Dear, dear brother, I have come to bring you home.

27 **Boy.** Home, little Fan?

28 **Fan.** Yes! Home, for good and all! Father is so much kinder than he ever used to be, and home's like heaven! He spoke so gently to me one dear night when I was going to bed that I was not afraid to ask him once more if you might come home; and he said "yes" . . . you should; and sent me in a coach to bring you. And you're to be a man and are never to come back here, but first, we're to be together all the Christmas long, and have the merriest time in the world.

29 **Boy.** You are quite a woman, little Fan!

30 [*Laughing; she drags at boy, causing him to stumble to the door with her. Suddenly we hear a mean and terrible voice in the hallway. Off. It is the* Schoolmaster.]

31 **Schoolmaster.** Bring down Master Scrooge's travel box at once! He is to travel!

32 **Fan.** Who is that, Ebenezer?

33 **Boy.** O! Quiet, Fan. It is the Schoolmaster, himself!

34 [*The door bursts open and into the room bursts with it the* Schoolmaster.]

35 **Schoolmaster.** Master Scrooge?

36 **Boy.** Oh, Schoolmaster, I'd like you to meet my little sister, Fan, sir . . .

37 [*Two boys struggle on with* Scrooge's *trunk.*]

38 **Fan.** Pleased, sir . . . [*She curtsies.*]

39 **Schoolmaster.** You are to travel, Master Scrooge.

40 **Scrooge.** Yes, sir, I know sir . . .

41 [*All start to exit, but* Fan *grabs the coattail of the mean old* Schoolmaster.]

42 **Boy.** Fan!

43 **Schoolmaster.** What's this?

44 **Fan.** Pardon, sir, but I believe that you've forgotten to say your goodbye to my brother, Ebenezer, who stands still now awaiting it . . . [*She smiles, curtsies, lowers her eyes.*] pardon, sir.

45 **Schoolmaster.** [*Amazed*] I . . . uh . . . harumph . . . uhh . . . well, then . . . [*Outstretches hand*] Goodbye, Scrooge.

46 **Boy.** Uh, well, goodbye, Schoolmaster . . .

47 [*Lights fade out on all but* Boy *looking at* Fan; *and* Scrooge *and* Past *looking at them.*]

48 **Scrooge.** Oh, my dear, dear little sister, Fan . . . how I loved her.

49 **Past.** Always a delicate creature, whom a breath might have withered, but she had a large heart . . .

50 **Scrooge.** So she had.

51 **Past.** She died a woman, and had, as I think, children.

52 **Scrooge.** One child.

53 **Past.** True. Your nephew.

54 **Scrooge.** Yes.

55 **Past.** Fine, then. We move on, Mr. Scrooge. That warehouse, there? Do you know it?

56 **Scrooge.** Know it? Wasn't I apprenticed[20] there?

57 **Past.** We'll have a look.

58 [*They enter the warehouse. The lights crossfade with them, coming up on an old man in Welsh wig:* Fezziwig.]

59 **Scrooge.** Why, it's old Fezziwig! Bless his heart; it's Fezziwig, alive again!

60 [Fezziwig *sits behind a large, high desk, counting. He lays down his pen; looks at the clock: seven bells sound.*]

61 Quittin' time . . .

62 **Fezziwig.** Quittin' time . . . [*He takes off his waistcoat and laughs: calls off*] Yo ho, Ebenezer! Dick!

63 [Dick Wilkins *and* Ebenezer Scrooge—*a young man version—enter the room.* Dick *and* Ebenezer *are* Fezziwig's *apprentices.*]

64 **Scrooge.** Dick Wilkins, to be sure! My fellow-'prentice! Bless my soul, yes. There he is. He was very much attached to me, was Dick. Poor Dick! Dear, dear!

65 **Fezziwig.** Yo ho, my boys. No more work tonight. Christmas Eve, Dick. Christmas, Ebenezer!

66 [*They stand at attention in front of* Fezziwig; *laughing*]

67 Hilli-ho! Clear away, and let's have lots of room here! Hilliho, Dick! Chirrup, Ebenezer!

68 [*The young men clear the room, sweep the floor, straighten the pictures, trim the lamps, etc. The space is clear now. A fiddler enters, fiddling.*]

69 Hi-ho, Matthew! Fiddle away . . . where are my daughters?

70 [*The fiddler plays. Three young daughters of* Fezziwig *enter followed by six young adult male suitors. They are dancing to the music. All employees come in: workers, clerks, housemaids, cousins, the baker, etc. All dance. Full number wanted here. Throughout the dance, food is brought into the feast. It is "eaten" in dance, by the dancers.* Ebenezer

20. **apprenticed** (uh PREHN tihst) *v.* received instruction in a trade as well as food and housing or wages in return for work.

dances with all three of the daughters, as does Dick. *They compete for the daughters, happily, in the dance.* Fezziwig *dances with his daughters.* Fezziwig *dances with* Dick *and* Ebenezer. *The music changes:* Mrs. Fezziwig *enters. She lovingly scolds her husband. They dance. She dances with* Ebenezer, *lifting him and throwing him about. She is enormously fat. When the dance is ended, they all dance off, floating away, as does the music.* Scrooge *and the* Ghost of Christmas Past *stand alone now. The music is gone.*]

71 **Past.** It was a small matter, that Fezziwig made those silly folks so full of gratitude.

72 **Scrooge.** Small!

73 **Past.** Shhh!

74 [*Lights up on* Dick *and* Ebenezer]

75 **Dick.** We are blessed, Ebenezer, truly, to have such a master as Mr. Fezziwig!

76 **Young Scrooge.** He is the best, best, the very and absolute best! If ever I own a firm of my own, I shall treat my apprentices with the same dignity and the same grace. We have learned a wonderful lesson from the master, Dick!

77 **Dick.** Ah, that's a fact, Ebenezer. That's a fact!

78 **Past.** Was it not a small matter, really? He spent but a few pounds[21] of his mortal money on your small party. Three or four pounds, perhaps. Is that so much that he deserves such praise as you and Dick so lavish now?

79 **Scrooge.** It isn't that! It isn't that, Spirit. Fezziwig had the power to make us happy or unhappy; to make our service light or burdensome; a pleasure or a toil. The happiness he gave is quite as great as if it cost him a fortune.

80 **Past.** What is the matter?

81 **Scrooge.** Nothing particular.

82 **Past.** Something, I think.

83 **Scrooge.** No, no. I should like to be able to say a word or two to my clerk just now! That's all!

84 [Ebenezer *enters the room and shuts down all the lamps. He stretches and yawns.* The Ghost of Christmas Past *turns to* Scrooge *all of a sudden.*]

85 **Past.** My time grows short! Quick!

CLOSE READ

ANNOTATE: Mark details in paragraphs 70–76 that describe young Scrooge's behavior and personality.

QUESTION: Why might the playwright have included these descriptions?

CONCLUDE: How do these details deepen your understanding of Scrooge?

21. **pounds** *n.* common type of money used in Great Britain.

86 [*In a flash of light,* Ebenezer *is gone, and in his place stands an* Older Scrooge, *this one a man in the prime of his life. Beside him stands a young woman in a mourning dress. She is crying. She speaks to the man, with hostility.*]

87 **Woman.** It matters little . . . to you, very little. Another idol has displaced me.

88 **Man.** What idol has displaced you?

89 **Woman.** A golden one.

90 **Man.** This is an even-handed dealing of the world. There is nothing on which it is so hard as poverty; and there is nothing it professes to condemn with such severity as the pursuit of wealth!

91 **Woman.** You fear the world too much. Have I not seen your nobler aspirations fall off one by one, until the masterpassion, Gain, engrosses you? Have I not?

92 **Scrooge.** No!

93 **Man.** What then? Even if I have grown so much wiser, what then? Have I changed towards you?

94 **Woman.** No . . .

95 **Man.** Am I?

96 **Woman.** Our contract is an old one. It was made when we were both poor and content to be so. You are changed. When it was made, you were another man.

97 **Man.** I was not another man: I was a boy.

98 **Woman.** Your own feeling tells you that you were not what you are. I am. That which promised happiness when we were one in heart is fraught with misery now that we are two . . .

99 **Scrooge.** No!

100 **Woman.** How often and how keenly I have thought of this, I will not say. It is enough that I have thought of it, and can release you . . .

101 **Scrooge.** [*Quietly*] Don't release me, madame . . .

102 **Man.** Have I ever sought release?

103 **Woman.** In words. No. Never.

104 **Man.** In what then?

105 **Woman.** In a changed nature: in an altered spirit. In everything that made my love of any worth or value in your sight. If this has never been between us, tell me, would you seek me out and try to win me now? Ah, no!

106 **Scrooge.** Ah, yes!

107 **Man.** You think not?

108 **Woman.** I would gladly think otherwise if I could, heaven knows! But if you were free today, tomorrow, yesterday, can even I believe that you would choose a dowerless girl[22]—you who in your very confidence with her weigh everything by Gain; or, choosing her, do I not know that your repentance and regret would surely follow? I do; and I release you. With a full heart, for the love of him you once were.

109 **Scrooge.** Please, I . . . I . . .

110 **Man.** Please, I . . . I . . .

111 **Woman.** Please. You may—the memory of what is past half makes me hope you will—have pain in this. A very, very brief time, and you will dismiss the memory of it, as an unprofitable dream, from which it happened well that you awoke. May you be happy in the life that you have chosen for yourself . . .

112 **Scrooge.** No!

113 **Woman.** Yourself . . . alone . . .

114 **Scrooge.** No!

115 **Woman.** Goodbye, Ebenezer . . .

116 **Scrooge.** Don't let her go!

117 **Man.** Goodbye.

118 **Scrooge.** No!

119 [*She exits.* Scrooge *goes to younger man: himself.*]

120 You fool! Mindless loon! You fool!

121 **Man.** [*To exited woman*] Fool. Mindless loon. Fool . . .

122 **Scrooge.** Don't say that! Spirit, remove me from this place.

123 **Past.** I have told you these were shadows of the things that have been. They are what they are. Do not blame me, Mr. Scrooge.

124 **Scrooge.** Remove me! I cannot bear it!

22. **a dowerless girl** girl without a dowry, the property or wealth a woman brings to her husband in marriage.

CLOSE READ

ANNOTATE: In paragraphs 111–122, mark Scrooge's words to his younger self.

QUESTION: What do these words reveal about the ways in which Scrooge's feelings have changed?

CONCLUDE: How does this change deepen the reader's understanding of Scrooge's personality?

125 [*The faces of all who appeared in this scene are now projected for a moment around the stage: enormous, flimsy, silent.*]

126 Leave me! Take me back! Haunt me no longer!

127 [*There is a sudden flash of light: a flare.* The Ghost of Christmas Past *is gone.* Scrooge *is, for the moment, alone onstage. His bed is turned down, across the stage. A small candle burns now in* Scrooge's *hand. There is a child's cap in his other hand. He slowly crosses the stage to his bed, to sleep.* Marley *appears behind* Scrooge, *who continues his long, elderly cross to bed.* Marley *speaks directly to the audience.*]

128 **Marley.** Scrooge must sleep now. He must surrender to the irresistible drowsiness caused by the recognition of what was. [*Pauses*] The cap he carries is from ten lives past: his boyhood cap . . . donned atop a hopeful hairy head . . . askew, perhaps, or at a rakish angle. Doffed now in honor of regret.[23] Perhaps even too heavy to carry in his present state of weak remorse . . .

129 [Scrooge *drops the cap. He lies atop his bed. He sleeps. To audience*]

130 He sleeps. For him, there's even more trouble ahead. [Smiles] For you? The play house tells me there's hot cider, as should be your anticipation for the specter Christmas Present and Future, for I promise you both. [*Smiles again*] So, I pray you hurry back to your seats refreshed and ready for a miser—to turn his coat of gray into a blazen Christmas holly-red. [*A flash of lightning. A clap of thunder. Bats fly. Ghostly music.* Marley *is gone.*] ❧

23. **donned . . . regret** To *don* and *doff* a hat means to put it on and take it off, *askew* means "crooked," and *at a rakish angle* means "having a dashing or jaunty look."

NOTEBOOK

Answer the questions in your notebook. Use text evidence to support your responses.

Response

1. **Personal Connections** In your opinion, what is the meanest thing Scrooge does in Act I? Explain.

Comprehension

2. **Reading Check (a)** In what year and city is Act I set? **(b)** When Marley was alive, what relationship did he have with Scrooge? **(c)** What does Scrooge say to people who wish him a "Merry Christmas"?

3. **Strategy: Paraphrase (a)** Provide an example of a challenging passage in Act I that you paraphrased. **(b)** In what ways did this strategy help you better understand the text? Explain.

Analysis

4. **(a) Connect** In Scene 3, why is Marley dragging a chain of cash-boxes and other metal objects? **(b) Make Inferences** What does the chain suggest about the life Marley lived? Explain.

5. **(a)** What scenes from his past does Scrooge visit? **(b) Draw Conclusions** How did each event in his life contribute to his current attitude and personality? Explain.

6. **Interpret** Why is the past so painful to Scrooge? Cite details from the text to support your interpretation.

EQ Notes Can people really change?

What have you learned about transformations from reading Act I of this drama? Go to your Essential Question Notes and record your observations and thoughts about A *Christmas Carol: Scrooge and Marley,* Act I.

TEKS

6.A. Describe personal connections to a variety of sources, including self-selected texts.

6.C. Use text evidence to support an appropriate response.

6.D. Paraphrase and summarize texts in ways that maintain meaning and logical order.

A CHRISTMAS CAROL: SCROOGE AND MARLEY, ACT I

Close Read

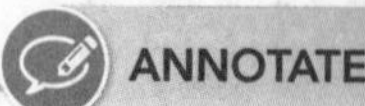

1. The model passage shows how one reader analyzed part of Scene 5, paragraph 4. Find another detail in the passage to annotate. Then, write your own question and conclusion.

CLOSE-READ MODEL

Marley. You see this Scrooge: stricken by feeling. Conscious of a thousand odors floating in the air, each one connected with a thousand thoughts, and hopes, and joys, and care long, long forgotten. [*Pause*] This one—this Scrooge—before your very eyes, returns to life, among the living.

ANNOTATE: I notice that the playwright has used lots of *s*'s in this monologue.

QUESTION: Why might the playwright have made this choice?

CONCLUDE: The repeated *s* sound makes it seem as if Marley were hissing or whispering, creating an eerie mood.

MY **QUESTION:**

MY **CONCLUSION:**

2. For more practice, answer the questions in the Close-Read notes in the selection.

3. Choose a section of the drama that you found especially important. Mark important details. Then, jot down questions and write your conclusions in the open space next to the text.

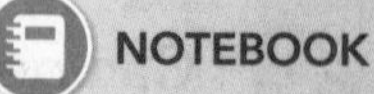

Inquiry and Research

Research and Extend In Act I, Scene 2, Scrooge refers to workhouses and the Poor Law. Briefly research the Poor Law and workhouses in Victorian England. Identify at least two relevant sources, and gather information. How does your research increase your understanding of the play's setting?

TEKS

8.C. Analyze how playwrights develop characters through dialogue and staging.

12.D. Identify and gather relevant information from a variety of sources.

Genre / Text Elements

Dialogue and Character Development In a play, some information about characters is provided in stage directions. However, most of the details that develop each character's personality come through **dialogue**. What characters say and how they say it shows readers or viewers what they are like. Consider how the example reveals the nephew's friendly, forgiving nature. Even though Scrooge is cold and unkind to him, he continues to speak gently.

EXAMPLE

Scrooge. Why did you get married?
Nephew. Because I fell in love.
Scrooge. That, sir, is the only thing that you have said to me in your entire lifetime which is even more ridiculous than "Merry Christmas!" *[Turns from Nephew]* Good afternoon.
Nephew. Nay, Uncle, you never came to see me before I married either. Why give it as a reason for not coming now?
Scrooge. Good afternoon, Nephew!
Nephew. I want nothing from you; I ask nothing of you; why cannot we be friends?

PRACTICE Complete the activity and answer the questions.

1. **Analyze** Use the chart to analyze how each example of dialogue helps develop the characters' personalities.

EXAMPLE OF DIALOGUE	WHAT DIALOGUE SHOWS
Cratchit. *I must be going...Merry Christmas, Mr. Scrooge!* (Scene 2, paragraphs 78–94)	
Scrooge. *Oh, my dear, dear...Fezziwig, alive again!* (Scene 5, paragraphs 48–59)	

2. **(a) Distinguish** Choose a passage of dialogue from Act I that you think is especially effective in developing Scrooge's character. **(b) Analyze** Explain your choice, noting specific character traits the passage reveals.

A CHRISTMAS CAROL: SCROOGE AND MARLEY, ACT I

Concept Vocabulary

 NOTEBOOK

Why These Words? The vocabulary words relate to Scrooge's character and personality in Act I of the play. For example, Scrooge shows he is a *miser* by refusing to share his coal with Bob Cratchit.

covetous	resolute	malcontent
morose	impossible	miser

PRACTICE Answer the questions.

1. What other words in Act I help you better understand Scrooge and his personality?
2. What might someone do if he or she were *covetous*?
3. How might a person behave if he or she were *morose*?
4. Describe a situation in which someone might be *resolute*.
5. What character traits might cause a person to be viewed as *impossible*?
6. How would a *malcontent* behave at a party?
7. What actions and behaviors might be expected of a *miser*?

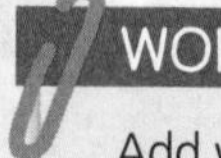

WORD NETWORK

Add words that are related to transformations from the text to your Word Network.

Word Study

 NOTEBOOK

Latin Prefix: *mal-* The Latin prefix *mal-* means "bad." As an adjective, the word *malcontent* means "dissatisfied with current conditions or circumstances." As a noun, *malcontent* means "a discontented, or unhappy, person."

PRACTICE Complete the activities.

1. Write your own sentence that correctly uses the word *malcontent*, either as a noun or an adjective.
2. Using a dictionary or thesaurus, find three other words that have the prefix *mal-*. For each word, note the definition, and write a sentence that correctly uses the word.

 TEKS

2.A. Use print or digital resources to determine the meaning, syllabication, pronunciation, word origin, and part of speech.

6.F. Respond using newly acquired vocabulary as appropriate.

9.E. Identify the use of literary devices, including subjective and objective point of view.

Author's Craft

Subjective and Objective Points of View In this play, Marley is both a character in the story and a guide to the action. He is the figure that starts the conflict and moves the plot forward, but he also steps away from the story in order to give background information and explain situations. This dual role represents two different types of point of view—subjective and objective.

- As a character, Marley has a **subjective point of view**. This means he expresses only his own ideas, thoughts, and experiences.
- As a guide to the story, he has an **objective point of view**. He expresses attitudes that many characters share and gives information that is widely known within the setting of the play.

Consider how the example from scene 4 provides objective information.

EXAMPLE

Marley. *[Directly to audience]* From this point forth ... I shall be quite visible to you, but invisible to him. *[Smiles]* He will feel my presence, nevertheless, for, unless my senses fail me completely, we are—you and I—witness to the changing of a miser: that one, my partner in life, in business, and in eternity: that one: Scrooge. *[Moves to staircase, below Scrooge]* See him now. He endeavors to pierce the darkness with his ferret eyes. *[To audience]* See him, now. He listens for the hour.

Marley delivers a number of long speeches in the play. Sometimes, they clearly show just one of these points of view. In some cases, they show both.

NOTEBOOK

PRACTICE Complete the activity and answer the questions.

1. **(a) Analyze** Which point of view, subjective or objective, is used in each of the passages listed in the chart? **(b) Connect** Explain what each passage tells you about characters or situations in the story.

PASSAGE	POINT OF VIEW	EXPLANATION
I present him to you: ... Look at him . . . (Scene 1, paragraph 4)		
I have none to give... weary journeys lie before me! (Scene 3, paragraph 31)		

2. **Evaluate** What do you think about the role Marley plays in this drama? Do you find his dual role as both a participant in the action and a guide effective? Why or why not?

A Christmas Carol: Scrooge and Marley, Act II

Concept Vocabulary

You will encounter the following words as you read Act II of the play. Before reading, note how familiar you are with each word. Then, rank the words in order from most familiar (1) to least familiar (6).

WORD	YOUR RANKING
parallel	
altered	
strive	
dispelled	
earnest	
infinitely	

Comprehension Strategy

Monitor Comprehension

When you **monitor your comprehension,** you check in with yourself as you read. If you find you are not fully understanding a text, make adjustments. For example, you might pause to **annotate** the text or take notes about details that seem important. Doing so may help you understand challenging language or complex ideas. Here are some ways you might annotate a text:

- highlight, underline, or circle key words, phrases, and ideas
- signal important passages with symbols (arrows, stars)
- take notes about your observations or reactions in the margins

PRACTICE As you read, monitor your comprehension and make adjustments as needed. For example, you might annotate and take notes about important details.

TEKS

5.I. Monitor comprehension and make adjustments such as re-reading, using background knowledge, asking questions, and annotating when understanding breaks down.

6.E. Interact with sources in meaningful ways such as notetaking, annotating, freewriting, or illustrating.

DRAMA

A Christmas Carol: Scrooge and Marley

Act II

a drama based on the novel by Charles Dickens

BACKGROUND

In mid-nineteenth century England, millions of peasants moved to the cities. There, they lived in overcrowded slums. Adults and many children worked up to 12 hours a day, 6 days a week. In contrast, factory owners and professionals lived in grand houses with at least one—and often many—servants. These differences in social conditions play a part in *A Christmas Carol.*

AUDIO

ANNOTATE

Scene 1

1 [*Lights. Choral music is sung. Curtain.* Scrooge, *in bed, sleeping, in spotlight. We cannot yet see the interior of his room.* Marley, *opposite, in spotlight equal to* Scrooge's. Marley *laughs. He tosses his hand in the air and a flame shoots from it, magically, into the air. There is a thunder clap, and then another; a lightning flash, and then another. Ghostly music plays under. Colors change.* Marley's *spotlight has gone out and now reappears, with* Marley *in it, standing next to the bed and the sleeping* Scrooge. Marley *addresses the audience directly.*]

2 **Marley.** Hear this snoring Scrooge! Sleeping to escape the nightmare that is his waking day. What shall I bring to him now? I'm afraid nothing would astonish old Scrooge now. Not after what he's seen. Not a baby boy, not a rhinoceros, nor anything in between would astonish Ebenezer Scrooge just now. I can think of nothing . . . [*Suddenly*] that's it! Nothing! [*He speaks confidentially.*] I'll have the

clock strike one and, when he awakes expecting my second messenger, there will be no one . . . nothing. Then I'll have the bell strike twelve. And then one again . . . and then nothing. Nothing . . . [*Laughs*] nothing will . . . astonish him. I think it will work.

3 [*The bell tolls one.* Scrooge *leaps awake.*]

4 **Scrooge.** One! One! This is it; time! [*Looks about the room*] Nothing!

5 [*The bell tolls midnight.*]

6 Midnight! How can this be? I'm sleeping backwards.

7 [*One again*]

8 Good heavens! One again! I'm sleeping back and forth! [*A pause.* Scrooge *looks about.*] Nothing! Absolutely nothing!

9 [*Suddenly, thunder and lightning.* Marley *laughs and disappears. The room shakes and glows. There is suddenly springlike music.* Scrooge *makes a run for the door.*]

10 **Marley.** Scrooge!

11 **Scrooge.** What?

12 **Marley.** Stay you put!

13 **Scrooge.** Just checking to see if anyone is in here.

14 [*Lights and thunder again: more music.* Marley *is of a sudden gone. In his place sits the* Ghost of Christmas Present*—to be called in the stage directions of the play,* Present*—center of room. Heaped up on the floor, to form a kind of throne, are turkeys, geese, game, poultry, brawn, great joints of meat, suckling pigs, long wreaths of sausages, mince-pies, plum puddings, barrels of oysters, red hot chestnuts, cherry-cheeked apples, juicy oranges, luscious pears, immense twelfth cakes, and seething bowls of punch, that make the chamber dim with their delicious steam. Upon this throne sits* Present, *glorious to see. He bears a torch, shaped as a Horn of Plenty.*[1] Scrooge *hops out of the door, and then peeks back again into his bedroom.* Present *calls to* Scrooge.]

1. **Horn of Plenty** horn overflowing with fruits, flowers, and grain, representing wealth and abundance.

15 **Present.** Ebenezer Scrooge. Come in, come in! Come in and know me better!

16 **Scrooge.** Hello. How should I call you?

17 **Present.** I am the Ghost of Christmas Present. Look upon me.

18 [Present *is wearing a simple green robe. The walls around the room are now covered in greenery, as well. The room seems to be a perfect grove now: leaves of holly, mistletoe and ivy reflect the stage lights. Suddenly, there is a mighty roar of flame in the fireplace and now the hearth burns*

with a lavish, warming fire. There is an ancient scabbard girdling the Ghost's *middle, but without sword. The sheath is gone to rust.*]

19 You have never seen the like of me before?

20 **Scrooge.** Never.

21 **Present.** You have never walked forth with younger members of my family: my elder brothers born on Christmases past.

22 **Scrooge.** I don't think I have. I'm afraid I've not. Have you had many brothers, Spirit?

23 **Present.** More than eighteen hundred.

24 **Scrooge.** A tremendous family to provide for! [Present *stands*] Spirit, conduct me where you will. I went forth last night on compulsion, and learnt a lesson which is working now. Tonight, if you have aught to teach me, let me profit by it.

25 **Present.** Touch my robe.

26 [Scrooge *walks cautiously to* Present *and touches his robe. When he does, lightning flashes, thunder claps, music plays. Blackout*]

Scene 2

1 [*PROLOGUE*: Marley *stands spotlit,* L. *He speaks directly to the audience.*]

2 **Marley.** My ghostly friend now leads my living partner through the city's streets.

3 [*Lights up on* Scrooge *and* Present]

4 See them there and hear the music people make when the weather is severe, as it is now.

5 [*Winter music. Choral group behind scrim, sings. When the song is done and the stage is re-set, the lights will fade up on a row of shops, behind the singers. The choral group will hum the song they have just completed now and mill about the streets,*[2] *carrying their dinners to the bakers' shops and restaurants. They will, perhaps, sing about being poor at Christmastime, whatever.*]

6 **Present.** These revelers, Mr. Scrooge, carry their own dinners to their jobs, where they will work to bake the meals the rich men and women of this city will eat as their Christmas dinners. Generous people these . . . to care for the others, so . . .

CLOSE READ

ANNOTATE: Mark the details in paragraphs 5–6 that describe the setting.

QUESTION: Why might the playwright have chosen to begin the scene with these details?

CONCLUDE: How does this information help you better understand the play?

2. **mill about the streets** walk around aimlessly.

3. **incense** (IHN sehns) *n.* any of various substances that produce a pleasant odor when burned.

7 [Present *walks among the choral group and a sparkling incense*[3] *falls from his torch on to their baskets, as he pulls the covers off of the baskets. Some of the choral group become angry with each other.*]

8 **Man #1.** Hey, you, watch where you're going.

9 **Man #2.** Watch it yourself, mate!

10 **[Present** *sprinkles them directly, they change.*]

11 **Man #1.** I pray go in ahead of me. It's Christmas. You be first!

12 **Man #2.** No, no. I must insist that YOU be first!

13 **Man #1.** All right, I shall be, and gratefully so.

14 **Man #2.** The pleasure is equally mine, for being able to watch you pass, smiling.

15 **Man #1.** I would find it a shame to quarrel on Christmas Day . . .

16 **Man #2.** As would I.

17 **Man #1.** Merry Christmas then, friend!

18 **Man #2.** And a Merry Christmas straight back to you!

19 [*Church bells toll. The choral group enter the buildings: the shops and restaurants; they exit the stage, shutting their doors closed behind them. All sound stops.* Scrooge *and* Present *are alone again.*]

20 **Scrooge.** What is it you sprinkle from your torch?

21 **Present.** Kindness.

22 **Scrooge.** Do you sprinkle your kindness on any particular people or on all people?

23 **Present.** To any person kindly given. And to the very poor most of all.

24 **Scrooge.** Why to the very poor most?

25 **Present.** Because the very poor need it most. Touch my heart . . . here, Mr. Scrooge. We have another journey.

26 [Scrooge *touches the* Ghost's *heart and music plays, lights change color, lightning flashes, thunder claps. A choral group appears on the street, singing Christmas carols.*]

Scene 3

1 [Marley *stands spotlit in front of a scrim on which is painted the exterior of* Cratchit's *four-roomed house. There is a flash and a clap and* Marley *is gone. The lights shift color again, the scrim flies away, and we*

are in the interior of the Cratchit *family home.* Scrooge *is there, with the spirit* (Present), *watching* Mrs. Cratchit *set the table, with the help of* Belinda Cratchit *and* Peter Cratchit, *a baby, pokes a fork into the mashed potatoes on his highchair's tray. He also chews on his shirt collar.*]

2 **Scrooge.** What is this place, Spirit?

3 **Present.** This is the home of your employee, Mr. Scrooge. Don't you know it?

4 **Scrooge.** Do you mean Cratchit, Spirit? Do you mean this is Cratchit's home?

5 **Present.** None other.

6 **Scrooge.** These children are his?

7 **Present.** There are more to come presently.

8 **Scrooge.** On his meager earnings! What foolishness!

9 **Present.** Foolishness, is it?

10 **Scrooge.** Wouldn't you say so? Fifteen shillings[4] a week's what he gets!

4. **fifteen shillings** small amount of money for a week's work.

11 **Present.** I would say that he gets the pleasure of his family, fifteen times a week times the number of hours a day! Wait, Mr. Scrooge. Wait, listen and watch. You might actually learn something . . .

12 **Mrs. Cratchit.** What has ever got your precious father then? And your brother, Tiny Tim? And Martha warn't as late last Christmas by half an hour!

13 [Martha *opens the door, speaking to her mother as she does.*]

14 **Martha.** Here's Martha, now, Mother! [*She laughs. The* Cratchit Children *squeal with delight.*]

15 **Belinda.** It's Martha, Mother! Here's Martha!

16 **Peter.** Marthmama, Marthmama! Hullo!

17 **Belinda.** Hurrah! Martha! Martha! There's such an enormous goose for us, Martha!

18 **Mrs. Cratchit.** Why, bless your heart alive, my dear, how late you are!

19 **Martha.** We'd a great deal of work to finish up last night, and had to clear away this morning, Mother.

20 **Mrs. Cratchit.** Well, never mind so long as you are come. Sit ye down before the fire, my dear, and have a warm, Lord bless ye!

21 **Belinda.** No, no! There's Father coming. Hide, Martha, hide!

22 [Martha *giggles and hides herself.*]

23 **Martha.** Where? Here?

24 **Peter.** Hide, hide!

25 **Belinda.** Not there! *THERE!*

26 [Martha *is hidden.* Bob Cratchit *enters, carrying* Tiny Tim *atop his shoulder. He wears a threadbare and fringeless comforter hanging down in front of him.* Tiny Tim *carries small crutches and his small legs are bound in an iron frame brace.*]

27 **Bob and Tiny Tim.** Merry Christmas.

28 **Bob.** Merry Christmas my love, Merry Christmas Peter, Merry Christmas Belinda. Why, where is Martha?

29 **Mrs. Cratchit.** Not coming.

30 **Bob.** Not coming: Not coming upon Christmas Day?

31 **Martha.** [*Pokes head out*] Ohhh, poor Father. Don't be disappointed.

32 **Bob.** What's this?

33 **Martha.** 'Tis I!

34 **Bob.** Martha! [*They embrace.*]

35 **Tiny Tim.** Martha! Martha!

36 **Martha.** Tiny Tim!

37 [Tiny Tim *is placed in* Martha's *arms.* Belinda *and* Peter *rush him offstage.*]

38 **Belinda.** Come, brother! You must come hear the pudding singing in the copper.

39 **Tiny Tim.** The pudding? What flavor have we?

40 **Peter.** Plum! Plum!

41 **Tiny Tim.** Oh, Mother! I love plum!

42 [*The children exit the stage giggling.*]

43 **Mrs. Cratchit.** And how did little Tim behave?

44 **Bob.** As good as gold, and even better. Somehow he gets thoughtful sitting by himself so much, and thinks the strangest things you ever heard. He told me, coming home, that he hoped people saw him in the church, because he was a cripple, and it might be pleasant to them to remember upon Christmas Day, who made lame beggars walk and blind men see. [*Pauses*] He has the oddest ideas sometimes,

CLOSE READ

ANNOTATE: Mark the pauses and the sound effect in paragraph 44.

QUESTION: Why might the playwright have included the pauses and sound effect in the dialogue?

CONCLUDE: What can you conclude about Bob Cratchit's state of mind as a result of these details?

but he seems all the while to be growing stronger and more hearty . . . one would never know. [*Hears* Tim's *crutch on floor outside door*]

45 **Peter.** The goose has arrived to be eaten!

46 **Belinda.** Oh, mama, mama, it's beautiful.

47 **Martha.** It's a perfect goose, Mother!

48 **Tiny Tim.** To this Christmas goose, Mother and Father I say . . . [*Yells*] Hurrah! Hurrah!

49 **Other Children.** [*Copying* Tim] Hurrah! Hurrah!

50 [*The family sits round the table.* Bob and Mrs. Cratchit *serve the trimmings, quickly. All sit; all bow heads; all pray.*]

51 **Bob.** Thank you, dear Lord, for your many gifts . . . our dear children; our wonderful meal; our love for one another; and the warmth of our small fire—[*Looks up at all*] A merry Christmas to us, my dear. God bless us!

52 **All.** [*Except* Tim] Merry Christmas! God bless us!

53 **Tiny Tim.** [*In a short silence*] God bless us every one.

54 [*All freeze. Spotlight on* Present *and* Scrooge]

55 **Scrooge.** Spirit, tell me if Tiny Tim will live.

56 **Present.** I see a vacant seat . . . in the poor chimney corner, and a crutch without an owner, carefully preserved. If these shadows remain unaltered by the future, the child will die.

57 **Scrooge.** No, no, kind Spirit! Say he will be spared!

58 **Present.** If these shadows remain unaltered by the future, none other of my race will find him here. What then? If he be like to die, he had better do it, and decrease the surplus population.

59 [Scrooge *bows his head. We hear* Bob's *voice speak* Scrooge's *name.*]

60 **Bob.** Mr. Scrooge . . .

61 **Scrooge.** Huh? What's that? Who calls?

62 **Bob.** [*His glass raised in a toast*] I'll give you Mr. Scrooge, the Founder of the Feast!

63 **Scrooge.** Me, Bob? You toast *me*?

64 **Present.** Save your breath, Mr. Scrooge. You can't be seen or heard.

65 **Mrs. Cratchit.** The Founder of the Feast, indeed! I wish I had him here, that miser Scrooge. I'd give him a piece of my mind to feast upon, and I hope he'd have a good appetite for it!

66 **Bob.** My dear! Christmas Day!

67 **Mrs. Cratchit.** It should be Christmas Day, I am sure, on which one drinks the health of such an odious, stingy, unfeeling man as Mr. Scrooge . . .

68 **Scrooge.** Oh. Spirit, must I? . . .

69 **Mrs. Cratchit.** You know he is, Robert! Nobody knows it better than you do, poor fellow!

70 **Bob.** This is Christmas Day, and I should like to drink to the health of the man who employs me and allows me to earn my living and our support and that man is Ebenezer Scrooge . . .

71 **Mrs. Cratchit.** I'll drink to his health for your sake and the day's, but not for his sake . . . a Merry Christmas and a Happy New Year to you, Mr. Scrooge, wherever you may be this day!

72 **Scrooge.** Just here, kind madam . . . out of sight, out of sight . . .

73 **Bob.** Thank you, my dear. Thank you.

74 **Scrooge.** Thank you, Bob . . . and Mrs. Cratchit, too. No one else is toasting me, . . . not now . . . not ever. Of that I am sure . . .

CLOSE READ

ANNOTATE: In paragraphs 62–71, mark words and phrases that highlight the differences between Mrs. Cratchit's and Bob Cratchit's attitudes toward Scrooge.

QUESTION: Why might the playwright have chosen to show this contrast in their attitudes through their dialogue?

CONCLUDE: What does the contrast reveal about the personality of each character?

75 **Bob.** Children . . .

76 **All.** Merry Christmas to Mr. Scrooge.

77 **Bob.** I'll pay you sixpence, Tim, for my favorite song.

78 **Tiny Tim.** Oh, Father, I'd so love to sing it, but not for pay. This Christmas goose—this feast—you and Mother, my brother and sisters close with me: that's my pay—

79 **Bob.** Martha, will you play the notes on the lute, for Tiny Tim's song.

80 **Belinda.** May I sing, too, Father?

81 **Bob.** We'll all sing.

82 [*They sing a song about a tiny child lost in the snow—probably from Wordsworth's poem.* Tim *sings the lead vocal; all chime in for the chorus. Their song fades under, as the* Ghost of Christmas Present *speaks.*]

83 **Present.** Mark my words, Ebenezer Scrooge. I do not present the Cratchits to you because they are a handsome, or brilliant family. They are not handsome. They are not brilliant. They are not well-dressed, or tasteful to the times. Their shoes are not even waterproofed by virtue of money or cleverness spent. So when the pavement is wet, so are the insides of their shoes and the tops of their toes. These are the Cratchits, Mr. Scrooge. They are not highly special. They are happy, grateful, pleased with one another, contented with the time and how it passes. They don't sing very well, do they? But, nonetheless, they do sing . . . [*Pauses*] think of that, Scrooge. Fifteen shillings a week and they do sing . . . hear their song until its end.

84 **Scrooge.** I am listening. [*The chorus sings full volume now, until . . . the song ends here.*] Spirit, it must be time for us to take our leave. I feel in my heart that it is . . . that I must think on that which I have seen here . . .

85 **Present.** Touch my robe again . . .

86 [Scrooge *touches* Present's *robe. The lights fade out on the* Cratchits, *who sit, frozen, at the table.* Scrooge *and* Present *in a spotlight now. Thunder, lightning, smoke. They are gone.*]

Scene 4

1 [Marley *appears* D.L. *in single spotlight. A storm brews. Thunder and lightning.* Scrooge *and* Present *"fly" past,* U. *The storm continues, furiously, and, now and again,* Scrooge *and* Present *will zip past in their travels.* Marley *will speak straight out to the audience.*]

2 **Marley.** The Ghost of Christmas Present, my co-worker in this attempt to turn a miser, flies about now with that very miser, Scrooge, from street to street, and he points out partygoers on their way to Christmas parties. If one were to judge from the numbers of people on their way to friendly gatherings, one might think that no one was left at home to give anyone welcome . . . but that's not the case, is it? Every home is expecting company and . . . [*He laughs.*] Scrooge is amazed.

3 [Scrooge *and* Present *zip past again. The lights fade up around them. We are in the* Nephew's *home, in the living room.* Present *and* Scrooge *stand watching the* Nephew: Fred *and his wife, fixing the fire.*]

4 **Scrooge.** What is this place? We've moved from the mines!

5 **Present.** You do not recognize them?

6 **Scrooge.** It is my nephew! . . . and the one he married . . .

7 [Marley *waves his hand and there is a lightning flash. He disappears.*]

8 **Fred.** It strikes me as sooooo funny, to think of what he said . . . that Christmas was a humbug, as I live! He believed it!

9 **Wife.** More shame for him, Fred!

10 **Fred.** Well, he's a comical old fellow, that's the truth.

11 **Wife.** I have no patience with him.

12 **Fred.** Oh, I have! I am sorry for him; I couldn't be angry with him if I tried. Who suffers by his ill whims? Himself, always . . .

13 **Scrooge.** It's me they talk of, isn't it, Spirit?

14 **Fred.** Here, wife, consider this. Uncle Scrooge takes it into his head to dislike us, and he won't come and dine with us. What's the consequence?

15 **Wife.** Oh . . . you're sweet to say what I think you're about to say, too, Fred . . .

16 **Fred.** What's the consequence? He don't lose much of a dinner by it, I can tell you that!

17 **Wife.** Ooooooo, Fred! Indeed, I think he loses a very good dinner . . . ask my sisters, or your bachelor friend, Topper . . . ask any of them. They'll tell you what old Scrooge, your uncle, missed: a dandy meal!

18 **Fred.** Well, that's something of a relief, wife. Glad to hear it! [*He hugs his wife. They laugh. They kiss.*] The truth is, he misses much yet. I mean to give him the same chance every year, whether he likes it or not, for I pity him. Nay, he is my only uncle and I feel for the old

miser . . . but, I tell you, wife: I see my dear and perfect mother's face on his own wizened cheeks and brow: brother and sister they were, and I cannot erase that from each view of him I take . . .

19 **Wife.** I understand what you say, Fred, and I am with you in your yearly asking. But he never will accept, you know. He never will.

20 **Fred.** Well, true, wife. Uncle may rail at Christmas till he dies. I think I shook him some with my visit yesterday . . . [*Laughing*] I refused to grow angry . . . no matter how nasty he became . . . [*Whoops*] It was HE who grew angry, wife! [*They both laugh now.*]

21 **Scrooge.** What he says is true, Spirit . . .

22 **Fred and Wife.** Bah, humbug!

23 **Fred.** [*Embracing his wife*] There is much laughter in our marriage, wife. It pleases me. You please me . . .

24 **Wife.** And you please me, Fred. You are a good man . . . [*They embrace.*] Come now. We must have a look at the meal . . . our guests will soon arrive . . . my sisters, Topper . . .

25 **Fred.** A toast first . . . [*He hands her a glass*] A toast to Uncle Scrooge . . . [*Fills their glasses*]

26 **Wife.** A toast to him?

27 **Fred.** Uncle Scrooge has given us plenty of merriment, I am sure, and it would be ungrateful not to drink to his health. And I say . . . *Uncle Scrooge!*

28 **Wife.** [*Laughing*] You're a proper loon,[5] Fred . . . and I'm a proper wife to you . . . [*She raises her glass.*] Uncle Scrooge! [*They drink. They embrace. They kiss.*]

29 **Scrooge.** Spirit, please, make me visible! Make me audible! I want to talk with my nephew and my niece!

30 [*Calls out to them. The lights that light the room and* Fred *and wife fade out.* Scrooge *and* Present *are alone, spotlit.*]

31 **Present.** These shadows are gone to you now, Mr. Scrooge. You may return to them later tonight in your dreams. [*Pauses*] My time grows short, Ebenezer Scrooge. Look you on me! Do you see how I've aged?

32 **Scrooge.** Your hair has gone gray! Your skin, wrinkled! Are spirits' lives so short?

33 **Present.** My stay upon this globe is very brief. It ends tonight.

34 **Scrooge.** Tonight?

5. **a proper loon** silly person.

35 **Present.** At midnight. The time is drawing near!

36 [*Clock strikes 11:45.*]

37 Hear those chimes? In a quarter hour, my life will have been spent! Look, Scrooge, man. Look you here.

38 [*Two gnarled baby dolls are taken from* Present's *skirts.*]

39 **Scrooge.** Who are they?

40 **Present.** They are Man's children, and they cling to me, appealing from their fathers. The boy is Ignorance; the girl is Want. Beware them both, and all of their degree, but most of all beware this boy, for I see that written on his brow which is doom, unless the writing be erased.

41 [*He stretches out his arm. His voice is now amplified: loudly and oddly.*]

42 **Scrooge.** Have they no refuge or resource?

43 **Present.** Are there no prisons? Are there no workhouses? [*Twelve chimes*] Are there no prisons? Are there no workhouses?

44 [*A* Phantom, *hooded, appears in dim light,* D., *opposite.*]

45 Are there no prisons? Are there no workhouses?

46 [Present *begins to deliquesce.* Scrooge *calls after him.*]

47 **Scrooge.** Spirit, I'm frightened! Don't leave me! Spirit!

48 **Present.** Prisons? Workhouses? Prisons? Workhouses . . .

49 [*He is gone.* Scrooge *is alone now with the* Phantom, *who is, of course, the* Ghost of Christmas Future. *The* Phantom *is shrouded in black. Only its outstretched hand is visible from under his ghostly garment.*]

50 **Scrooge.** Who are you, Phantom? Oh, yes. I think I know you! You are, are you not, the Spirit of Christmas Yet to Come? [*No reply*] And you are about to show me the shadows of the things that have not yet happened, but will happen in time before us. Is that not so, Spirit? [*The* Phantom *allows* Scrooge *a look at his face. No other reply wanted here. A nervous giggle here.*] Oh, Ghost of the Future, I fear you more than any Specter I have seen! But, as I know that your purpose is to do me good and as I hope to live to be another man from what I was, I am prepared to bear you company. [Future *does not reply, but for a stiff arm, hand and finger set, pointing forward.*] Lead on, then, lead on. The night is waning fast, and it is precious time to me. Lead on, Spirit!

51 [Future *moves away from* Scrooge *in the same rhythm and motion employed at its arrival.* Scrooge *falls into the same pattern, a considerable space apart from the* Spirit. *In the space between them,* Marley *appears. He looks to* Future *and then to* Scrooge. *He claps his hands. Thunder and lightning. Three* Businessmen *appear, spotlighted singularly: One is* D.L.; *one is* D.R.; *one is* U.C. *Thus, six points of the stage should now be spotted in light.* Marley *will watch this scene from his position,* C. Scrooge *and* Future *are* R. *and* L. *of* C.]

52 **First Businessman.** Oh, no, I don't know much about it either way, I only know he's dead.

53 **Second Businessman.** When did he die?

54 **First Businessman.** Last night, I believe.

55 **Second Businessman.** Why, what was the matter with him? I thought he'd never die, really . . .

56 **First Businessman.** [*Yawning*] Goodness knows, goodness knows . . .

57 **Third Businessman.** What has he done with his money?

58 **Second Businessman.** I haven't heard. Have you?

59 **First Businessman.** Left it to his Company, perhaps. Money to money; you know the expression . . .

CLOSE READ

ANNOTATE: Mark the words and phrases that the Ghost of Christmas Present repeats in paragraphs 43–48.

QUESTION: Why might the playwright have chosen to have the Ghost of Christmas Present repeat these words and phrases upon departing?

CONCLUDE: What effect does this repetition have on the reader?

60 **Third Businessman.** He hasn't left it to *me*. That's all I know . . .

61 **First Businessman.** [*Laughing*] Nor to me . . . [*Looks at* Second Businessman] You, then? You got his money???

62 **First Businessman.** [*Laughing*] Me, me, his money? Nooooo!

63 [*They all laugh.*]

64 **Third Businessman.** It's likely to be a cheap funeral, for upon my life, I don't know of a living soul who'd care to venture to it. Suppose we make up a party and volunteer?

65 **Second Businessman.** I don't mind going if a lunch is provided, but I must be fed, if I make one.

66 **First Businessman.** Well, I am the most disinterested among you, for I never wear black gloves, and I never eat lunch. But I'll offer to go, if anybody else will. When I come to think of it, I'm not all sure that I wasn't his most particular friend: for we used to stop and speak whenever we met. Well, then . . . bye, bye!

67 **Second Businessman.** Bye, bye . . .

68 **Third Businessman.** Bye, bye . . .

69 [*They glide offstage in three separate directions. Their lights follow them.*]

70 **Scrooge.** Spirit, why did you show me this? Why do you show me businessmen from my streets as they take the death of Jacob Marley? That is a thing past. You are *future!*

71 [Jacob Marley *laughs a long, deep laugh. There is a thunder clap and lightning flash, and he is gone.* Scrooge *faces* Future, *alone on stage now.* Future *wordlessly stretches out his arm-hand-and-finger-set, pointing into the distance,* U. *There, above them, scoundrels "fly" by, half-dressed and slovenly. When this scene has passed, a woman enters the playing area. She is almost at once followed by a second woman; and then a man in faded black; and then, suddenly, an old man, who smokes a pipe. The old man scares the other three. They laugh, anxious.*]

72 **First Woman.** Look here, old Joe, here's a chance! If we haven't all three met here without meaning it!

73 **Old Joe.** You couldn't have met in a better place. Come into the parlor. You were made free of it long ago, you know; and the other two ain't strangers [*He stands; shuts a door. Shrieking*] We're all suitable to our calling. We're well matched. Come into the parlor. Come into the parlor . . . [*They follow him* D. Scrooge *and* Future *are now in their midst, watching; silent. A truck comes in on which is set a small wall with fireplace and a screen of rags, etc. All props for the scene.*] Let me just rake this fire over a bit . . .

74 [*He does. He trims his lamp with the stem of his pipe. The First* Woman *throws a large bundle on to the floor. She sits beside it, crosslegged, defiantly.*]

75 **First Woman.** What odds then? What odds, Mrs. Dilber? Every person has a right to take care of themselves. HE always did!

76 **Mrs. Dilber.** That's true indeed! No man more so!

77 **First Woman.** Why, then, don't stand staring as if you was afraid, woman! Who's the wiser? We're not going to pick holes in each other's coats, I suppose?

78 **Mrs. Dilber.** No, indeed! We should hope not!

79 **First Woman.** Very well, then! That's enough. Who's the worse for the loss of a few things like these? Not a dead man, I suppose?

80 **Mrs. Dilber.** [*Laughing*] No, indeed!

81 **First Woman.** If he wanted to keep 'em after he was dead, the wicked old screw, why wasn't he natural in his lifetime? If he had been, he'd have had somebody to look after him when he was struck with Death, instead of lying gasping out his last there, alone by himself.

82 **Mrs. Dilber.** It's the truest word that was ever spoke. It's a judgment on him.

83 **First Woman.** I wish it were a heavier one, and it should have been, you may depend on it, if I could have laid my hands on anything else. Open that bundle, old Joe, and let me know the value of it. Speak out plain. I'm not afraid to be the first, nor afraid for them to see it. We knew pretty well that we were helping ourselves, before we met here, I believe. It's no sin. Open the bundle, Joe.

84 **First Man.** No, no, my dear! I won't think of letting you being the first to show what you've . . . earned . . . earned from this. I throw in mine.

85 [*He takes a bundle from his shoulder, turns it upside down, and empties its contents out on to the floor.*]

86 It's not very extensive, see . . . seals . . . a pencil case . . . sleeve buttons . . .

87 **First Woman.** Nice sleeve buttons, though . . .

88 **First Man.** Not bad, not bad . . . a brooch there . . .

89 **Old Joe.** Not really valuable, I'm afraid . . .

90 **First Man.** How much, old Joe?

91 **Old Joe.** [*Writing on the wall with chalk*] A pitiful lot, really. Ten and six and not a sixpence more!

CLOSE READ

ANNOTATE: In paragraph 75, mark the word that is emphasized.

QUESTION: Why did the playwright choose to emphasize this word?

CONCLUDE: How does emphasizing this word reveal the First Woman's attitude toward the man of whom she speaks?

92 **First Man.** You're not serious!

93 **Old Joe.** That's your account and I wouldn't give another sixpence if I was to be boiled for not doing it. Who's next?

94 **Mrs. Dilber.** Me! [*Dumps out contents of her bundle*] Sheets, towels, silver spoons, silver sugar-tongs . . . some boots . . .

95 **Old Joe.** [*Writing on wall*] I always give too much to the ladies. It's a weakness of mine and that's the way I ruin myself. Here's your total comin' up . . . two pounds-ten . . . if you asked me for another penny, and made it an open question, I'd repent of being so liberal and knock off half-a-crown.

96 **First Woman.** And now do MY bundle, Joe.

97 **Old Joe.** [*Kneeling to open knots on her bundle*] So many knots, madam . . . [*He drags out large curtains; dark*] What do you call this? Bed curtains!

98 **First Woman.** [*Laughing*] Ah, yes, bed curtains!

99 **Old Joe.** You don't mean to say you took 'em down, rings and all, with him lying there?

100 **First Woman.** Yes, I did, why not?

101 **Old Joe.** You were born to make your fortune and you'll certainly do it.

102 **First Woman.** I certainly shan't hold my hand, when I can get anything in it by reaching it out, for the sake of such a man as he was. I promise you, Joe. Don't drop that lamp oil on those blankets, now!

103 **Old Joe.** His blankets?

104 **First Woman.** Whose else's do you think? He isn't likely to catch cold without 'em, I daresay.

105 **Old Joe.** I hope that he didn't die of anything catching? Eh?

106 **First Woman.** Don't you be afraid of that. I ain't so fond of his company that I'd loiter about him for such things if he did. Ah! You may look through that shirt till your eyes ache, but you won't find a hole in it, nor a threadbare place. It's the best he had, and a fine one, too. They'd have wasted it, if it hadn't been for me.

107 **Old Joe.** What do you mean "They'd have wasted it"?

108 **First Woman.** Putting it on him to be buried in, to be sure. Somebody was fool enough to do it, but I took it off again . . .

109 [*She laughs, as do they all, nervously.*]

110 If calico[6] ain't good enough for such a purpose, it isn't good enough then for anything. It's quite as becoming to the body. He can't look uglier than he did in that one!

111 **Scrooge.** [*A low-pitched moan emits from his mouth; from the bones.*] *OOOOOOooooooOOOOOooooooOOOOOOOO ooooooOOOOOOoooooOO!*

112 **Old Joe.** One pound six for the lot. [*He produces a small flannel bag filled with money. He divvies it out. He continues to pass around the money as he speaks. All are laughing.*] That's the end of it, you see! He frightened every one away from him when he was alive, to profit us when he was dead! Hah ha ha!

113 **All.** HAHAHAHAhahahahahahah!

114 **Scrooge.** *OOoooOOoooOOOoooOOOoooOOoooOOoooOOOooo!* [*He screams at them.*] Obscene demons! Why not market the corpse itself, as sell its trimming??? [*Suddenly*] Oh, Spirit, I see it, I see it! This unhappy man—this stripped-bare corpse . . . could very well be my own. My life holds **parallel**! My life ends that way now!

115 [Scrooge *backs into something in the dark behind his spotlight.* Scrooge *looks at* Future, *who points to the corpse.* Scrooge *pulls back the blanket. The corpse is, of course,* Scrooge, *who screams. He falls aside the bed; weeping.*]

116 Spirit, this is a fearful place. In leaving it, I shall not leave its lesson, trust me. Let us go!

117 [Future *points to the corpse.*]

118 Spirit, let me see some tenderness connected with a death, or that dark chamber, which we just left now, Spirit, will be forever present to me.

119 [Future *spreads his robes again. Thunder and lightning. Lights up, U., in the* Cratchit *home setting.* Mrs. Cratchit *and her daughters, sewing*]

120 **Tiny Tim's Voice.** [*Off*] And He took a child and set him in the midst of them.

121 **Scrooge.** [*Looking about the room; to* Future] Huh? Who spoke? Who said that?

122 **Mrs. Cratchit.** [*Puts down her sewing*] The color hurts my eyes. [Rubs her eyes] That's better. My eyes grow weak sewing by candlelight. I shouldn't want to show your father weak eyes when he comes home . . . not for the world! It must be near his time . . .

6. **calico** (KAL ih koh) *n.* coarse and inexpensive cotton cloth.

CLOSE READ

ANNOTATE: Mark the sounds and sound effects in paragraphs 111–114.

QUESTION: Why do you think the playwright chose to include these details?

CONCLUDE: What effect does this choice have on the reader?

parallel (PAR uh lehl) *adj.* having the same direction or nature; similar

123 **Peter.** [*In corner, reading. Looks up from book*] Past it, rather. But I think he's been walking a bit slower than usual these last few evenings, Mother.

124 **Mrs. Cratchit.** I have known him walk with . . . [*Pauses*] I have known him walk with Tiny Tim upon his shoulder and very fast indeed.

125 **Peter.** So have I, Mother! Often!

126 **Daughter.** So have I.

127 **Mrs. Cratchit.** But he was very light to carry and his father loved him so, that it was not trouble—no trouble. [Bob, *at door*]

128 And there is your father at the door.

129 [Bob Cratchit *enters. He wears a comforter. He is cold, forlorn.*]

130 **Peter.** Father!

131 **Bob.** Hello, wife, children . . .

132 [*The daughter weeps; turns away from* Cratchit.]

133 Children! How good to see you all! And you, wife. And look at this sewing! I've no doubt, with all your industry, we'll have a quilt to set down upon our knees in church on Sunday!

134 **Mrs. Cratchit.** You made the arrangements today, then, Robert, for the . . . service . . . to be on Sunday.

135 **Bob.** The funeral. Oh, well, yes, yes, I did. I wish you could have gone. It would have done you good to see how green a place it is. But you'll see it often. I promised him that I would walk there on Sunday, after the service. [*Suddenly*] My little, little child! My little child!

136 **All Children.** [*Hugging him*] Oh, Father . . .

137 **Bob.** [*He stands*] Forgive me. I saw Mr. Scrooge's nephew, who you know I'd just met once before, and he was so wonderful to me, wife . . . he is the most pleasant-spoken gentleman I've ever met . . . he said "I am heartily sorry for it and heartily sorry for your good wife. If I can be of service to you in any way, here's where I live." And he gave me this card.

138 **Peter.** Let me see it!

139 **Bob.** And he looked me straight in the eye, wife, and said, meaningfully, "I pray you'll come to me, Mr. Cratchit, if you need some help. I pray you do." Now it wasn't for the sake of anything that he might be able to do for us, so much as for his kind way. It seemed as if he had known our Tiny Tim and felt with us.

140 **Mrs. Cratchit.** I'm sure that he's a good soul.

141 **Bob.** You would be surer of it, my dear, if you saw and spoke to him. I shouldn't be at all surprised, if he got Peter a situation.

142 **Mrs. Cratchit.** Only hear that, Peter!

143 **Martha.** And then, Peter will be keeping company with someone and setting up for himself!

144 **Peter.** Get along with you!

145 **Bob.** It's just as likely as not, one of these days, though there's plenty of time for that, my dear. But however and whenever we part from one another, I am sure we shall none of us forget poor Tiny Tim—shall we?—or this first parting that was among us?

146 **All Children.** Never, Father, never!

147 **Bob.** And when we recollect how patient and mild he was, we shall not quarrel easily among ourselves, and forget poor Tiny Tim in doing it.

148 **All Children.** No, Father, never!

149 **Little Bob.** I am very happy, I am. I am. I am very happy.

150 [Bob *kisses his little son, as does* Mrs. Cratchit, *as do the other children. The family is set now in one sculptural embrace. The lighting fades to a gentle pool of light, tight on them.*]

151 **Scrooge.** Specter, something informs me that our parting moment is at hand. I know it, but I know not how I know it.

152 [Future *points to the other side of the stage. Lights out on* Cratchits. Future *moves slowing, gliding.* Scrooge *follows.* Future *points opposite.* Future *leads* Scrooge *to a wall and a tombstone. He points to the stone.*]

153 Am I that man those ghoulish parasites[7] so gloated over? [*Pauses*] Before I draw nearer to that stone to which you point, answer me one question. Are these the shadows of things that will be, or the shadows of things that MAY be, only?

154 [Future *points to the gravestone.* Marley *appears in light well* U. *He points to grave as well. Gravestone turns front and grows to ten feet high. Words upon it:* Ebenezer Scrooge: *Much smoke billows now from the grave. Choral music here.* Scrooge *stands looking up at gravestone.* Future *does not at all reply in mortals' words, but points once more to the gravestone. The stone undulates and glows. Music plays, beckoning* Scrooge. Scrooge *reeling in terror*]

155 Oh, no. Spirit! Oh, no, no!

156 [Future's *finger still pointing*]

7. **ghoulish parasites** (GOOL ish PAR uh syts) referring to the men and women who stole and divided Scrooge's goods after he died.

157 Spirit! Hear me! I am not the man I was. I will not be the man I would have been but for this intercourse. Why show me this, if I am past all hope?

158 [Future *considers* Scrooge's logic. *His hand wavers.*]

altered (AWL tuhrd) *adj.* changed

159 Oh. Good Spirit, I see by your wavering hand that your good nature intercedes for me and pities me. Assure me that I yet may change these shadows that you have shown me by an **altered** life!

160 [Future's *hand trembles; pointing has stopped.*]

strive (STRYV) *v.* make a great effort; try very hard

161 I will honor Christmas in my heart and try to keep it all the year. I will live in the Past, the Present, and the Future. The Spirits of all Three shall **strive** within me. I will not shut out the lessons that they teach. Oh, tell me that I may sponge away the writing that is upon this stone!

162 [Scrooge *makes a desperate stab at grabbing* Future's *hand. He holds firm for a moment, but* Future, *stronger than* Scrooge, *pulls away.* Scrooge *is on his knees, praying.*]

163 Spirit, dear Spirit, I am praying before you. Give me a sign that all is possible. Give me a sign that all hope for me is not lost. Oh, Spirit, kind Spirit, I beseech thee: give me a sign . . .

164 [Future *deliquesces, slowly, gently.* The Phantom's *hood and robe drop gracefully to the ground in a small heap. Music in. There is nothing in them. They are mortal cloth. The* Spirit *is elsewhere.* Scrooge *has his sign.* Scrooge *is alone. Tableau. The light fades to black.*]

Scene 5

1 [*The end of it.* Marley, *spotlighted, opposite* Scrooge, *in his bed, spotlighted.* Marley *speaks to audience, directly.*]

2 **Marley.** [*He smiles at* Scrooge.] The firm of Scrooge and Marley is doubly blessed; two misers turned; one, alas, in Death, too late; but the other miser turned in Time's penultimate nick.[8] Look you on my friend, Ebenezer Scrooge . . .

8. **in Time's penultimate nick** just at the last moment.

3 **Scrooge.** [*Scrambling out of bed; reeling in delight*] I will live in the Past, in the Present, and in the Future! The Spirits of all Three shall strive within me!

4 **Marley.** [*He points and moves closer to Scrooge's bed.*] Yes, Ebenezer, the bedpost is your own. Believe it! Yes, Ebenezer, the room is your own. Believe it!

5 **Scrooge.** Oh, Jacob Marley! Wherever you are, Jacob, know ye that I praise you for this! I praise you . . . and heaven . . . and Christmastime! [*Kneels facing away from* Marley] I say it to you on my knees, old Jacob, on my knees! [*He touches his bed curtains.*] Not torn down. My bed curtains are not at all torn down! Rings and all, here they are! They are here: I am here: the shadows of things that would have been, may now be **dispelled**. They will be, Jacob! I know they will be!

dispelled (dihs PEHLD) *v.* driven away; scattered

6 [*He chooses clothing for the day. He tries different pieces of clothing and settles, perhaps, on a dress suit, plus a cape of the bed clothing: something of color.*]

7 I am light as a feather, I am happy as an angel. I am as merry as a schoolboy. [*Yells out window and then out to audience*] Merry Christmas to everybody! Merry Christmas to everybody! A Happy New Year to all the world! Hallo here! Whoop! Whoop! Hallo! Hallo! I don't know what day of the month it is! I don't care! I don't know anything! I'm quite a baby! I don't care! I don't care a fig! I'd much rather be a baby than be an old wreck like me or Marley! (Sorry, Jacob. wherever ye be!) Hallo! Hallo there!

8 [*Church bells chime in Christmas Day. A small boy, named* Adam, *is seen now* D.R., *as a light fades up on him.*] Hey, you boy! What's today? What day of the year is it?

9 **Adam.** Today, sir? Why, it's Christmas Day!

10 **Scrooge.** It's Christmas Day, is it? Whoop! Well, I haven't missed it after all, have I? The Spirits did all they did in one night. They can do anything they like, right? Of course they can! Of course they can!

11 **Adam.** Excuse me, sir?

12 **Scrooge.** Huh? Oh, yes, of course. What's your name, lad?

13 [Scrooge *and* Adam *will play their scene from their own spotlights.*]

14 **Adam.** Adam, sir.

15 **Scrooge.** Adam! What a fine, strong name! Do you know the poulterer's[9] in the next street but one, at the corner?

16 **Adam.** I certainly should hope I know him, sir!

17 **Scrooge.** A remarkable boy! An intelligent boy! Do you know whether the poulterer's have sold the prize turkey that was hanging up there? I don't mean the little prize turkey, Adam. I mean the big one!

18 **Adam.** What, do you mean the one they've got that's as big as me?

19 **Scrooge.** I mean, the turkey the size of Adam: that's the bird!

20 **Adam.** It's hanging there now, sir.

21 **Scrooge.** It is? Go and buy it! No, no. I am absolutely in **earnest.** Go and buy it and tell 'em to bring it here, so that I may give them the directions to where I want it delivered, as a gift. Come back here with the man, Adam, and I'll give you a shilling. Come back here with him in less than five minutes, and I'll give you half-a-crown!

22 **Adam.** Oh, my sir! Don't let my brother in on this.

23 [Adam *runs offstage.* Marley *smiles.*]

24 **Marley.** An act of kindness is like the first green grape of summer: one leads to another and another and another. It would take a queer man indeed to not follow an act of kindness with an act of kindness. One simply whets the tongue for more . . . the taste of kindness is too too sweet. Gifts—goods—are lifeless. But the gift of goodness one feels in the giving is full of life. It . . . is . . . a . . . wonder.

CLOSE READ

ANNOTATE: In paragraphs 12–22, mark words that show Scrooge's attitude and behavior toward Adam.

QUESTION: What do these word choices reveal about Scrooge?

CONCLUDE: How does Scrooge's attitude and behavior toward Adam reveal a transformation in his character?

9. **poulterer's** (POHL tuhr uhrz) *n.* British term for a person or a store that sells poultry.

earnest (UR nihst) *n.* serious mental state; not joking

25 [*Pauses; moves closer to* Scrooge, *who is totally occupied with his dressing and arranging of his room and his day. He is making lists,* etc. Marley *reaches out to* Scrooge.]

26 **Adam.** [Calling, off] I'm here! I'm here!

27 [Adam *runs on with a man, who carries an enormous turkey.*]

28 Here I am, sir. Three minutes flat! A world record! I've got the poultryman and he's got the poultry! [*He pants, out of breath.*] I have earned my prize, sir, if I live . . .

29 [*He holds his heart, playacting.* Scrooge *goes to him and embraces him.*]

30 **Scrooge.** You are truly a champion, Adam . . .

31 **Man.** Here's the bird you ordered, sir . . .

32 **Scrooge.** *Oh, my, MY!!!* Look at the size of that turkey, will you! He never could have stood upon his legs, that bird! He would have snapped them off in a minute, like sticks of sealingwax! Why you'll never be able to carry that bird to Camden-Town, I'll give you money for a cab . . .

33 **Man.** Camden-Town's where it's goin', sir?

34 **Scrooge.** Oh, I didn't tell you? Yes, I've written the precise address down just here on this . . . [*Hands paper to him*] Bob Cratchit's house. Now he's not to know who sends him this. Do you understand me? Not a word . . . [*Handing out money and chuckling*]

35 **Man.** I understand, sir, not a word.

36 **Scrooge.** Good. There you go then . . . this is for the turkey . . . [*Chuckle*] . . . and this is for the taxi. [*Chuckle*] . . . and this is for your world-record run, Adam . . .

37 **Adam.** But I don't have change for that, sir.

38 **Scrooge.** Then keep it, my lad. It's Christmas!

39 **Adam.** [*He kisses* Scrooge's *cheek, quickly.*] Thank you, sir. Merry, Merry Christmas! [*He runs off.*]

40 **Man.** And you've given me a bit overmuch here, too, sir . . .

41 **Scrooge.** Of course I have, sir. It's Christmas!

42 **Man.** Oh, well, thanking you, sir. I'll have this bird to Mr. Cratchit and his family in no time, sir. Don't you worry none about that. Merry Christmas to you, sir, and a very happy New Year, too . . .

43 [*The man exits.* Scrooge *walks in a large circle about the stage, which is now gently lit. A chorus sings Christmas music far in the distance. Bells chime as well, far in the distance. A gentlewoman enters and passes.* Scrooge *is on the streets now.*]

44 **Scrooge.** Merry Christmas, madam . . .

45 **Woman.** Merry Christmas, sir . . .

46 [*The portly businessman from the first act enters.*]

47 **Scrooge.** Merry Christmas, sir.

48 **Portly Man.** Merry Christmas, sir.

49 **Scrooge.** Oh, you! My dear sir! How do you do? I do hope that you succeeded yesterday! It was very kind of you. A Merry Christmas.

50 **Portly Man.** Mr. Scrooge?

51 **Scrooge.** Yes, Scrooge is my name though I'm afraid you may not find it very pleasant. Allow me to ask your pardon. And will you have the goodness to—[*He whispers into the man's ear.*]

CLOSE READ

ANNOTATE: In paragraphs 49–56, mark words and phrases that indicate the Portly Man's reaction to Scrooge.

QUESTION: Why might the playwright have included these details?

CONCLUDE: What does the Portly Man's reaction show about Scrooge's character at this point in the play?

52 **Portly Man.** Lord bless me! My dear Mr. Scrooge, are you *serious!?!*

53 **Scrooge.** If you please. Not a farthing[10] less. A great many back payments are included in it, I assure you. Will you do me that favor?

54 **Portly Man.** My dear sir, I don't know what to say to such munifi—

55 **Scrooge.** [*Cutting him off*] Don't say anything, please. Come and see me. Will you?

56 **Portly Man.** I will! I will! Oh I will, Mr. Scrooge! It will be my pleasure!

57 **Scrooge.** Thank'ee, I am much obliged to you. I thank you fifty times. Bless you!

58 [Portly Man *passes offstage, perhaps by moving backwards.* Scrooge *now comes to the room of his* Nephew *and* Niece. *He stops at the door, begins to knock on it, loses his courage, tries again, loses his courage again, tries again, fails again, and then backs off and runs at the door, causing a tremendous bump against it. The* Nephew *and* Niece *are startled.* Scrooge, *poking head into room*]

59 Fred!

60 **Nephew.** Why, bless my soul! Who's that?

61 **Nephew and Niece.** [*Together*] How now? Who goes?

62 **Scrooge.** It's I. Your Uncle Scrooge.

63 **Niece.** Dear heart alive!

64 **Scrooge.** I have come to dinner. May I come in, Fred?

65 **Nephew.** *May you come in???!!!* With such pleasure for me you may, Uncle!!! What a treat!

66 **Niece.** What a treat, Uncle Scrooge! Come in, come in!

67 [*They embrace a shocked and delighted* Scrooge: Fred *calls into the other room.*]

68 **Nephew.** Come in here, everybody, and meet my Uncle Scrooge! He's come for our Christmas party!

69 [*Music in. Lighting here indicates that day has gone to night and gone to day again. It is early, early morning.* Scrooge *walks alone from the party, exhausted, to his offices, opposite side of the stage. He opens his offices. The offices are as they were at the start of the play.* Scrooge *seats himself with his door wide open so he can see into the tank, as he awaits* Cratchit, *who enters, head down, full of guilt.* Cratchit, *starts writing almost before he sits.*]

10. **farthing** (FAHR thihng) *n.* small British coin.

70 **Scrooge.** What do you mean by coming in here at this time of day, a full eighteen minutes late, Mr. Cratchit? Hallo, sir? Do you hear me?

71 **Bob.** I am very sorry, sir. I *am* behind my time.

72 **Scrooge.** You are? Yes, I certainly think you are. Step this way, sir, if you please . . .

73 **Bob.** It's only but once a year, sir . . . It shall not be repeated. I was making rather merry yesterday and into the night . . .

74 **Scrooge.** Now, I'll tell you what, Cratchit. I am not going to stand this sort of thing any longer. And therefore . . .

75 [*He stands and pokes his finger into* Bob's *chest.*]

76 I am . . . about . . . to . . . raise . . . your salary.

77 **Bob.** Oh, no, sir. I . . . [*Realizes*] what did you say, sir?

78 **Scrooge.** A Merry Christmas, Bob . . . [*He claps* Bob's *back.*] A merrier Christmas, Bob, my good fellow! than I have given you for many a year. I'll raise your salary and endeavor to assist your struggling family and we will discuss your affairs this very afternoon over a bowl of smoking bishop.[11] Bob! Make up the fires and buy another coal scuttle before you dot another i, Bob. It's too cold in this place! We need warmth and cheer, Bob Cratchit! Do you hear me? DO . . . YOU . . . HEAR . . . ME?

79 [Bob Cratchit *stands, smiles at* Scrooge: Bob Cratchit *faints. Blackout. As the main lights black out, a spotlight appears on* Scrooge: C. *Another on* Marley: *He talks directly to the audience.*]

80 **Marley.** Scrooge was better than his word. He did it all and **infinitely** more; and to Tiny Tim, who did NOT die, he was a second father. He became as good a friend, as good a master, as good a man, as the good old city knew, or any other good old city, town, or borough in the good old world. And it was always said of him that he knew how to keep Christmas well, if any man alive possessed the knowledge. [*Pauses*] May that be truly said of us, and all of us. And so, as Tiny Tim observed . . .

81 **Tiny Tim.** [*Atop* Scrooge's *shoulder*] God Bless Us, Every One . . .

82 [*Lights up on chorus, singing final Christmas Song.* Scrooge *and* Marley *and all spirits and other characters of the play join in. When the song is over, the lights fade to black.*] ❧

11. **smoking bishop** a type of mulled wine or punch that was especially popular in Victorian England at Christmas time.

infinitely (IHN fuh niht lee) *adv.* enormously; remarkably

 NOTEBOOK

Answer the questions in your notebook. Use text evidence to support your responses.

Response

1. **Personal Connections** How do you feel about the ending of the play? Explain.

Comprehension

2. **Reading Check (a)** Who are the two ghosts Scrooge encounters in Act II? **(b)** In Scene 2, what does the ghost sprinkle on people in the street? **(c)** What is the last thing the ghost shows Scrooge at the end of Scene 4?

3. **Strategy: Monitor Comprehension** At what points in the play did you pause to monitor your comprehension? In what ways did annotating details or taking notes improve your understanding?

Analysis

4. **(a)** In Scene 3, what does Scrooge learn about the Cratchit family? **(b) Analyze** Why does Scrooge care about the fate of Tiny Tim? **(c) Make Inferences** In what ways does this scene suggest that Scrooge is changing? Explain.

5. **(a)** In Scene 4, what happens to Scrooge's belongings in Christmas future? **(b) Draw Conclusions** How do Scrooge's observations of his possible future affect him? Explain, citing text evidence.

6. **(a) Analyze** Why do you think the character of Christmas Future doesn't speak? **(b) Analyze** What effect does Future's silence have on Scrooge? How might it affect an audience? Explain.

7. **Take a Position** Do you think Bob Cratchit and Scrooge's nephew do the right thing by forgiving Scrooge immediately? Explain.

EQ Notes Can people really change?

What have you learned about transformations from reading Act II of this drama? Go to your Essential Question Notes and record your observations and thoughts about *A Christmas Carol: Scrooge and Marley,* Act II.

 TEKS

5.I. Monitor comprehension and make adjustments such as re-reading, using background knowledge, asking questions, and annotating when understanding breaks down.

6.A. Describe personal connections to a variety of sources, including self-selected texts.

6.C. Use text evidence to support an appropriate response.

A CHRISTMAS CAROL: SCROOGE AND MARLEY, ACT II

Close Read

ANNOTATE

1. The model passage and annotation show how one reader analyzed part of Scene 1, paragraph 18. Find another detail in the passage to annotate. Then, write your own question and conclusion.

CLOSE-READ MODEL

[Present *is wearing a simple green robe.... Suddenly, there is a mighty roar of flame in the fireplace and now the hearth burns with a lavish, warming fire. There is an ancient scabbard girdling the* Ghost's *middle, but without sword. The sheath is gone to rust.*]

ANNOTATE: The Ghost of Christmas Present wears a rusty scabbard and there is no sword in it.

QUESTION: What idea is conveyed by these details?

CONCLUDE: The empty scabbard symbolizes the abandoning of weapons. The Ghost of Christmas Present represents peace.

MY **QUESTION:**

MY **CONCLUSION:**

2. For more practice, answer the Close-Read notes in the selection.
3. Choose a section of the drama that you found especially important. Mark important details. Then, jot down questions and write your conclusions in the open space next to the text.

Inquiry and Research

RESEARCH

NOTEBOOK

Research and Extend In Victorian England, people often played what were known as "parlor games" at parties. Conduct research to find out more about the parlor games Scrooge's nephew, wife, and guests might have played at their Christmas party. Identify and gather information from at least two relevant sources.

TEKS

8.C. Analyze how playwrights develop characters through dialogue and staging.

12.D. Identify and gather relevant information from a variety of sources.

Genre / Text Elements

Stage Directions and Character Development The written text of a play is called a **script**. The two main parts of a script are dialogue and stage directions. **Stage directions** are the playwright's instructions to the director and actors to guide them in interpreting the script and staging the performance.

TIP: If you are reading a play instead of watching a performance, you get certain information only from stage directions. Stage directions are usually printed in italics and set off by brackets or parentheses.

INFORMATION GIVEN IN STAGE DIRECTIONS	
STORY ELEMENT	**TYPES OF DETAILS**
character development, or the personalities of characters	• characters' feelings and thoughts • details about how actors should move or speak in order to portray characters accurately
setting, or time and place of the action	• scenery • sound • music • sets • lighting • costumes

NOTEBOOK

INTERACTIVITY

PRACTICE Complete the activity and answer the questions.

1. **Analyze** Use the chart to analyze how each example of stage directions helps develop the characters and scene.

EXAMPLE OF STAGE DIRECTIONS	DEVELOPMENT OF CHARACTERS
[*Lights and thunder*...Present *calls to* Scrooge.] (Scene 1, paragraph 14)	
[Scrooge *backs into...the bed; weeping.*] (Scene 4, paragraph 115)	
[*Hands paper to...money and chuckling*] (Scene 5, paragraph 34)	

2. **(a) Distinguish** Choose a different example of stage directions from Act II that you think is especially effective in developing one or more of the characters.
(b) Interpret Explain your choice, noting specific character traits that the example reveals.

A CHRISTMAS CAROL: SCROOGE AND MARLEY, ACT II

Concept Vocabulary

NOTEBOOK

Why These Words? The vocabulary words relate to Scrooge's transforming character and personality. For example, after the Spirits' visits he is an *altered* man who is *infinitely* more pleasant and willing to help other people.

parallel	strive	earnest
altered	dispelled	infinitely

PRACTICE Answer the questions.

1. How do the vocabulary words sharpen your understanding of the ways in which Scrooge changes?

2. What other words in the selection describe Scrooge's changing personality?

3. Use each vocabulary word in a sentence that shows your understanding of the word's meaning.

4. Challenge yourself to replace the vocabulary word in each sentence you wrote with a **synonym,** or word that has a similar meaning. Explain how the replacement word affects the meaning of each sentence.

WORD NETWORK

Add words that are related to transformations from the text to your Word Network.

Word Study

NOTEBOOK

Greek Prefix: *para-* The Greek prefix *para-* means "beside." In the word *parallel*, the prefix is combined with a Greek root that means "of another." So, *parallel* means "beside another." Lines that are *parallel* extend in the same direction beside one another and are always the same distance apart.

PRACTICE Complete the activity.

1. Use a dictionary to find another word that contains the Greek prefix *para-*.
2. Jot down the definition of the word you found.
3. Explain how the prefix *para-* contributes to the word's meaning.

TEKS

2.A. Use print or digital resources to determine the meaning, syllabication, pronunciation, word origin, and part of speech.

6.F. Respond using newly acquired vocabulary as appropriate.

7.A. Infer multiple themes within and across texts using text evidence.

Author's Craft

Multiple Themes The **theme** is the message or insight expressed in a literary work. Many works express more than one theme. Usually, the writer does not state themes directly. Instead, he or she builds thematic meaning through the following types of details:

- **characters:** characters' actions, statements, and emotions; the ways in which characters grow or change; what characters learn
- **conflicts:** the problems characters face and the ways in which they resolve them
- **settings:** important or dramatic places in the drama

Readers analyze the details and make connections among them to infer the themes. While readers' interpretations may vary, any valid statement of a theme must reflect all the work's important details.

TIP: A theme is not a statement about specific characters or events. It is a message or insight that applies to life in general.

NOTEBOOK

INTERACTIVITY

PRACTICE Consider both Act I and Act II of the drama as you complete the activity and answer the questions.

1. **Interpret** Consider this possible theme for the story: *Anyone can change if he or she decides to do so*. Cite at least three details from the play that support this theme. Explain your choices.

2. **Interpret** Consider this possible theme for the story: *We can't change the past, but we can learn from it*. Cite at least three details from the story that support this theme. Explain your choices.

3. **(a) Analyze** Use the chart to gather details about Scrooge's relationship with his nephew and how it changes over the course of the play. **(b) Make Inferences** What theme about compassion and forgiveness is suggested by these details?

SCROOGE AND NEPHEW	DETAILS
Act I, Scene 2	
Act II, Scene 4	
Act II, Scene 5	

4. **Draw Conclusions** What theme about happiness does the play express? Explain, citing specific details to support your thinking.

A CHRISTMAS CAROL: SCROOGE AND MARLEY, ACT II

Composition

A **friendly letter** is an informal written message addressed to a specific person or group of people.

ASSIGNMENT

Write a **friendly letter** to Scrooge in which you express your opinion about his transformation and the lessons readers can learn from his story. Share your thoughts in a personal but respectful way.

- Write the date in the top right corner of your letter, and begin with a greeting, such as "Dear Mr. Scrooge."
- In the body of your letter, discuss two key events that you think contribute the most to Scrooge's transformation.
- End by explaining your opinion about the life lessons you feel Scrooge teaches by example. Support your ideas with details from the text.
- Complete your letter with a closing, such as "Your friend." Then, sign your name.

Use New Words

Try to use one or more of the vocabulary words in your writing:

parallel, altered, strive, dispelled, earnest, infinitely

NOTEBOOK

Reflect on Your Writing

PRACTICE Think about the choices you made as you wrote. Also consider what you learned by writing. Share your experiences by responding to these questions.

1. Was it easy or difficult to write a letter to Scrooge? Explain.

2. Have your ideas about personal transformation changed after writing this letter? Why, or why not?

3. **WHY THESE WORDS?** The words you choose make a difference in your writing. Which words did you specifically choose to create a friendly tone, or attitude?

TEKS

1.D. Engage in meaningful discourse and provide and accept constructive feedback from others.

5.H. Synthesize information to create new understanding.

6.E. Interact with sources in meaningful ways such as notetaking, annotating, freewriting, or illustrating.

11.D. Compose correspondence that reflects an opinion, registers a complaint, or requests information in a business or friendly structure.

12.F. Synthesize information from a variety of sources.

Speaking and Listening

Costume plans provide descriptions and sketches or images of the clothing that actors will wear on stage during a performance.

ASSIGNMENT

With a partner, research the clothing that was worn in Victorian-era England, the time in which Dickens wrote. Then, create **costume plans** for two different characters from *A Christmas Carol: Scrooge and Marley*. Present your plans to the class.

Conduct Research Find information and images from a variety of sources that will help you develop realistic costume plans for both characters. You will need to know:

- the types of clothing the characters you chose would wear based on their social positions
- the types of clothing your characters would wear during the winter holiday season
- the types of fabrics that were popular during the time period

Create Your Plans Synthesize the information you learn through research to develop your plans. Write descriptions of each costume, giving facts about the colors and fabrics. Explain why each costume is appropriate for the characters you chose. Include drawings, photographs, illustrations, or other images of each costume.

Present and Discuss Present your plans to the class and engage in a meaningful discussion about your research and your choices. Ask for constructive feedback, considering these questions:

- In what ways are the costumes right for each character?
- Would the costumes be interesting to look at in a performance?
- What changes might make the costumes even better, and why?

After your classmates present their plans, discuss their choices, and offer constructive feedback of your own.

Informative Words

In your presentation, use concrete vocabulary, such as the words for colors, that will give your listeners an accurate picture of your costumes. Also use subject-based words that identify precise aspects of the topic. For example, Victorians used many different kinds of fabrics—linen, silks, serge—and wore types of garments that are no longer common. Use accurate terms for Victorian-era clothing.

EQ Notes Before moving on to a new selection, go to your Essential Question Notes and record any additional thoughts or observations you may have about *A Christmas Carol: Scrooge and Marley*.

A CHRISTMAS CAROL: SCROOGE AND MARLEY , ACTS I AND II

Compare Drama and Fiction

This section of Dickens's novel focuses on the Cratchit family dinner, a scene that also appears in the play you studied earlier. Pay attention to similarities and differences between the two versions of the same scene.

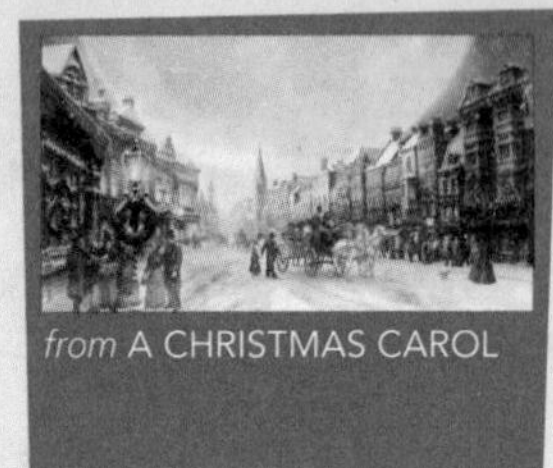

from A CHRISTMAS CAROL

About the Author

Charles Dickens (1812–1870) was one of eight children born to John Dickens and Elizabeth Barrow Dickens in a small town in southern England. When Dickens was twelve years old, his father was imprisoned for debt and young Dickens was forced to leave school and work at a boot-blacking factory. These experiences gave Dickens great sympathy for the poor and for children, concerns that many of his novels reflect. His novels include *Oliver Twist, Nicholas Nickleby, David Copperfield, A Tale of Two Cities*, and *Great Expectations.*

from A Christmas Carol

Concept Vocabulary

INTERACTIVITY

You will encounter the following words as you read the excerpt from *A Christmas Carol.* Before reading, note how familiar you are with each word. Using a scale of 1 (do not know it at all) to 6 (know it very well), indicate your knowledge of each word.

WORD	YOUR RATING
dreaded	
penitence	
grief	
rebuke	
trembling	
plaintive	

Comprehension Strategy

ANNOTATE

Make Connections

To deepen your understanding of a text, **make connections** to other texts you have read. As you read, ask yourself questions, such as *What does this remind me of?* and *How is this different from other texts with similar characters or situations?* To make connections, consider the following types of elements:

- ideas, themes, or messages in other texts
- characters in other texts
- events in other texts
- the style and language of other texts

PRACTICE As you read the novel excerpt, use the open space next to the text to note connections you make to the dramatic adaptation as well as to ideas in other texts you have read.

TEKS

5.E. Make connections to personal experiences, ideas in other texts, and society.

NOVEL EXCERPT

from

A Christmas Carol

Charles Dickens

BACKGROUND

Charles Dickens wrote *A Christmas Carol* in six weeks in 1843. The novel has since inspired many stage, screen, and radio versions. It gave the term *Scrooge* to the English language and popularized the expression "Merry (instead of *Happy*) Christmas." It also highlighted the struggle against hunger and illness faced by poor children, represented by sweet but sickly Tiny Tim. In this excerpt, the Cratchit family enjoys Christmas dinner while Scrooge and the Ghost of Christmas Present look on.

AUDIO

ANNOTATE

1 At last the dinner was all done, the cloth was cleared, the hearth swept, and the fire made up. The compound in the jug being tasted, and considered perfect, apples and oranges were put upon the table, and a shovelful of chestnuts on the fire. Then all the Cratchit family drew round the hearth, in what Bob Cratchit called a circle, meaning half a one; and at Bob Cratchit's elbow stood the family display of glass. Two tumblers, and a custard-cup without a handle.

dreaded (DREHD uhd) *v.* felt great fear or extreme reluctance

penitence (PEHN ih tuhns) *n.* sorrow for one's sins or faults

grief (greef) *n.* deep sadness

rebuke (ree BYOOK) *n.* severe or stern criticism; scolding

trembling (TREHM blihng) *v.* shaking uncontrollably

2 These held the hot stuff from the jug, however, as well as golden goblets would have done; and Bob served it out with beaming looks, while the chestnuts on the fire sputtered and cracked noisily. Then Bob proposed:

3 "A Merry Christmas to us all, my dears. God bless us!"

4 Which all the family re-echoed.

5 "God bless us every one!" said Tiny Tim, the last of all.

6 He sat very close to his father's side upon his little stool. Bob held his withered little hand in his, as if he loved the child, and wished to keep him by his side, and **dreaded** that he might be taken from him.

7 "Spirit," said Scrooge, with an interest he had never felt before, "tell me if Tiny Tim will live."

8 "I see a vacant seat," replied the Ghost, "in the poor chimney-corner, and a crutch without an owner, carefully preserved. If these shadows remain unaltered by the Future, the child will die."

9 "No, no," said Scrooge. "Oh, no, kind Spirit! Say he will be spared."

10 "If these shadows remain unaltered by the Future, none other of my race," returned the Ghost, "will find him here. What then? If he be like to die, he had better do it, and decrease the surplus population."

11 Scrooge hung his head to hear his own words quoted by the Spirit, and was overcome with **penitence** and **grief**.

12 "Man," said the Ghost, "if man you be in heart, not adamant,[1] forbear that wicked cant[2] until you have discovered What the surplus is, and Where it is. Will you decide what men shall live, what men shall die? It may be, that in the sight of Heaven, you are more worthless and less fit to live than millions like this poor man's child. Oh God! To hear the insect on the leaf pronouncing on the too much life among his hungry brothers in the dust!"

13 Scrooge bent before the Ghost's **rebuke**, and **trembling** cast his eyes upon the ground. But he raised them speedily, on hearing his own name.

14 "Mr. Scrooge!" said Bob; "I'll give you Mr. Scrooge, the Founder of the Feast!"

15 "The Founder of the Feast indeed!" cried Mrs. Cratchit, reddening. "I wish I had him here. I'd give him a piece of my mind to feast upon, and I hope he'd have a good appetite for it."

16 "My dear," said Bob, "the children! Christmas Day."

17 "It should be Christmas Day, I am sure," said she, "on which one drinks the health of such an odious, stingy, hard, unfeeling man as Mr. Scrooge. You know he is, Robert! Nobody knows it better than you do, poor fellow!"

CLOSE READ

ANNOTATE: Mark the words and phrases in paragraph 12 that relate to a person's worth or value.

QUESTION: How do these words challenge Scrooge's sense of his own importance?

CONCLUDE: Why is this an important moment in the story?

1. **adamant** (AD uh **mant**) *n.* legendary stone believed to be unbreakable.
2. **forbear that wicked cant** hold back from such morally bad, insincere talk.

^ This illustration shows Scrooge in spirit form looking on as the Cratchit family enjoys their holiday dinner. The inset image is of the author, Charles Dickens.

18 "My dear," was Bob's mild answer, "Christmas Day."

19 "I'll drink his health for your sake and the Day's," said Mrs. Cratchit, "not for his. Long life to him! A merry Christmas and a happy new year! He'll be very merry and very happy, I have no doubt!"

20 The children drank the toast after her. It was the first of their proceedings which had no heartiness. Tiny Tim drank it last of all, but he didn't care twopence[3] for it. Scrooge was the Ogre of the family. The mention of his name cast a dark shadow on the party, which was not dispelled for full five minutes.

21 After it had passed away, they were ten times merrier than before, from the mere relief of Scrooge the Baleful being done with. Bob Cratchit told them how he had a situation in his eye for Master Peter, which would bring in, if obtained, full five-and-sixpence weekly. The two young Cratchits laughed tremendously at the idea of Peter's being a man of business; and Peter himself looked thoughtfully at the fire from between his collars, as if he were deliberating what particular

3. **twopence** *n.* British sum of money equal to two pennies.

CLOSE READ

ANNOTATE: Mark words and phrases in paragraph 22 that relate to the Cratchit family's outward appearance. Mark other words and phrases that relate to their emotions and attitudes.

QUESTION: What does the contrast between these sets of words show about this family?

CONCLUDE: What is suggested by the contrast in these descriptions?

plaintive (PLAYN tihv) *adj.* sounding sad and mournful

investments he should favor when he came into the receipt of that bewildering income. Martha, who was a poor apprentice at a milliner's,[4] then told them what kind of work she had to do, and how many hours she worked at a stretch, and how she meant to lie abed tomorrow morning for a good long rest; tomorrow being a holiday she passed at home. Also how she had seen a countess and a lord some days before, and how the lord "was much about as tall as Peter" at which Peter pulled up his collars so high that you couldn't have seen his head if you had been there. All this time the chestnuts and the jug went round and round; and by-and-by they had a song, about a lost child traveling in the snow, from Tiny Tim, who had a **plaintive** little voice, and sang it very well indeed.

22 There was nothing of high mark in this. They were not a handsome family; they were not well dressed; their shoes were far from being waterproof; their clothes were scanty; and Peter might have known, and very likely did, the inside of a pawnbroker's. But, they were happy, grateful, pleased with one another, and contented with the time; and when they faded, and looked happier yet in the bright sprinklings of the Spirit's torch at parting, Scrooge had his eye upon them, and especially on Tiny Tim, until the last. ❧

4. milliner's *n.* a milliner is a person who makes hats for women.

MEDIA CONNECTION

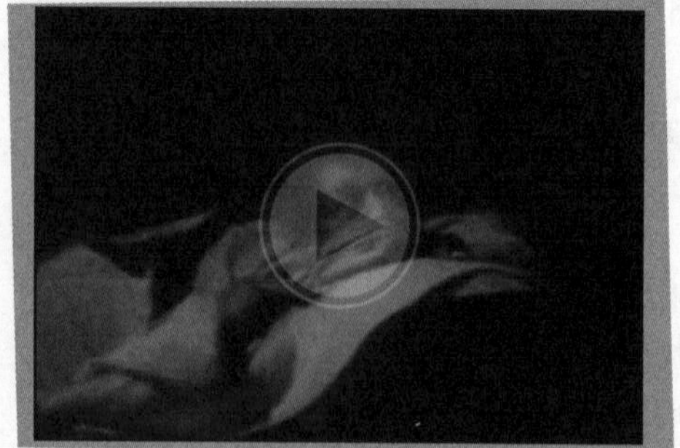

from Scrooge

VIDEO

DISCUSS IT **Does the feature-film clip reflect what you imagined the characters and setting to be like when you were reading the text? Why or why not?**

Write your response before sharing your ideas.

Answer the questions in your notebook. Use text evidence to support your response.

Response

1. **Personal Connections** If you were Bob Cratchit, would you toast Scrooge at your family dinner? Explain.

Comprehension

2. **Reading Check (a)** Where does this scene take place? **(b)** What does the ghost say about Tiny Tim's probable future? **(c)** How does Mrs. Cratchit feel about Scrooge?

3. **Strategy: Make Connections (a)** Explain one connection you made between this text and another text you have read. **(b)** Would you recommend this strategy to other readers? Why, or why not?

Analysis

4. **(a) Connect** In paragraph 1, the narrator mentions the items the family uses to hold drinks. What point does the narrator make about these items in paragraph 2? **(b) Interpret** What larger idea about the importance of wealth do these details support? Explain.

5. **Interpret** In paragraph 10, the ghost repeats words Scrooge said earlier in the story. Why do these words affect Scrooge so deeply now? What has changed for him?

6. **(a) Analyze Cause and Effect** How does the mention of Scrooge affect the family? Explain. **(b) Deduce** Given this reaction, what kinds of conversations do you think the family has had about Scrooge in the past? Explain.

7. **Contrast** In the last paragraph of the excerpt, the narrator describes the Cratchit family. Why do you think the author presents this description of the family? What point about Scrooge's life does this passage make by contrast?

EQ Notes Can people really change?

What has reading this novel excerpt taught you about people's ability to change? Go to your Essential Question Notes and record your observations and thoughts about *A Christmas Carol.*

 TEKS

5.E. Make connections to personal experiences, ideas in other texts, and society.

6.C. Use text evidence to support an appropriate response.

from A CHRISTMAS CAROL

Close Read

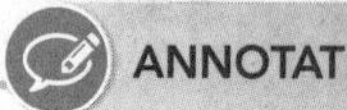
ANNOTATE

1. The model passage and annotation show how one reader analyzed paragraphs 5–6 of the novel excerpt. Find another detail in the passage to annotate. Then, write your own question and conclusion.

CLOSE-READ MODEL

"God bless us every one!" said Tiny Tim, the last of all.
He sat very close to his father's side upon his little stool. Bob held his withered little hand in his, as if he loved the child, and wished to keep him by his side, and dreaded that he might be taken from him.

ANNOTATE: These words are very powerful and show strong contrasts.

QUESTION: Why might the author have chosen to use these strong, contrasting words in a single sentence?

CONCLUDE: These words show that the character is experiencing many strong, complex feelings at the same time.

MY **QUESTION:**

MY **CONCLUSION:**

2. For more practice, answer the Close-Read notes in the selection.

3. Choose a section of the novel excerpt you found especially important. Mark important details. Then, jot down questions and write your conclusions in the open space next to the text.

Inquiry and Research

RESEARCH

NOTEBOOK

Research and Extend Often, you have to generate your own research questions. Sometimes, however, your teacher will give you research questions to explore. Practice responding to teacher-guided questions by conducting a brief, informal inquiry to find facts about the setting of this story:

What foods were commonly eaten at holiday dinners in Victorian England? Learn about the foods that were available to both the poor and the wealthy.

Cite at least three facts you discover during your research.

8.A. Demonstrate knowledge of literary genres such as realistic fiction, adventure stories, historical fiction, mysteries, humor, myths, fantasy, and science fiction.

9.E. Identify the use of literary devices, including subjective and objective point of view.

12.A. Generate student-selected and teacher-guided questions for formal and informal inquiry.

Genre / Text Elements

Narrative Point of View: Omniscient Narrator Narrative point of view is a key ingredient in all fiction. A **narrator** is the voice that tells a story. The **narrative point of view** is the perspective from which a story is told. *A Christmas Carol* uses the third-person omniscient point of view, which has these qualities:

OMNISCIENT NARRATOR	
The narrator…	is an observer and not a character in the story.
	shows how *at least two* characters feel, think, and perceive the events. (Note: If the narrator shows only the thoughts and feelings of one character, the point of view is third-person limited.)
	has the ability to reveal the inner thoughts and feelings of all the characters.
	uses third-person pronouns (*he, she, they,* etc.) to refer to all the characters.

TIP: If the narrator describes aspects of a character that any observer could see by looking, that doesn't reflect omniscience. The omniscient narrator sees through the eyes of multiple characters and shares their secrets.

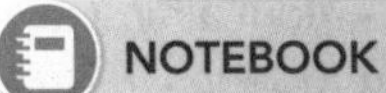
NOTEBOOK

PRACTICE Answer the questions.

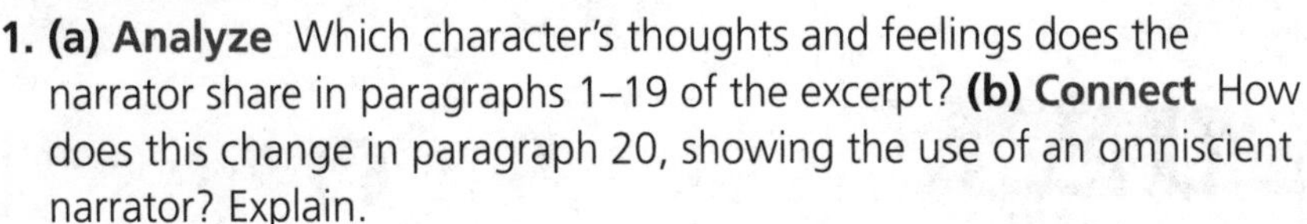
1. **(a) Analyze** Which character's thoughts and feelings does the narrator share in paragraphs 1–19 of the excerpt? **(b) Connect** How does this change in paragraph 20, showing the use of an omniscient narrator? Explain.

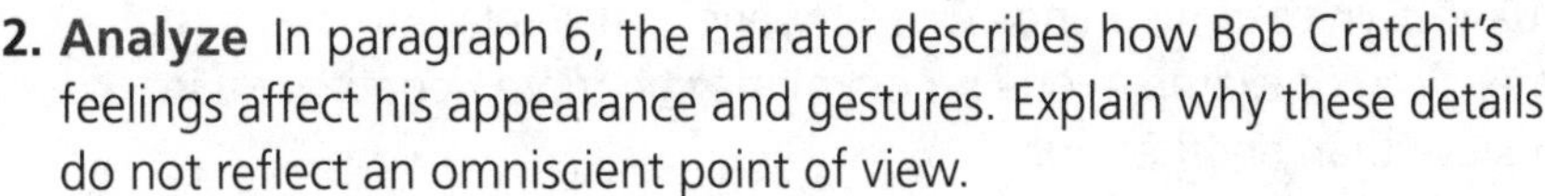
2. **Analyze** In paragraph 6, the narrator describes how Bob Cratchit's feelings affect his appearance and gestures. Explain why these details do not reflect an omniscient point of view.

3. **Interpret** Reread paragraph 22—the excerpt's ending. Could the excerpt have ended this way if the author did not use an omniscient narrator? Explain.

from A CHRISTMAS CAROL

Concept Vocabulary

NOTEBOOK

Why These Words? The vocabulary words are all related to fear and guilt. For example, a person who *dreaded* auditioning for a role in a play might *rebuke* herself later for not trying.

dreaded	penitence	grief
rebuke	trembling	plaintive

PRACTICE Answer the questions.

1. How do the vocabulary words help show the emotions Scrooge experiences and ways in which he changes?

2. Use the vocabulary words to complete the paragraph in a way that makes sense. Use each word only once.

When I was a kid, I liked TV crime shows, but my little brother __________ them. So, we'd argue about what to watch. Sometimes, he got so mad he'd start __________ a little. Later, my mom would give me a stern __________, saying how disappointed she was. I'd apologize in a __________ voice. I did feel __________ and __________ for my actions, but I still wanted to watch the shows I liked.

WORD NETWORK

Add words that are related to transformations from the text to your Word Network.

Word Study

Synonyms and Nuance: *dread* Words that have the same or similar meanings are **synonyms.** Synonyms often have subtle differences, or nuances, in their meanings. These nuances may relate to degrees of intensity. For example, one synonym may be more negative, neutral, or positive than another one.

PRACTICE Complete the activities.

The vocabulary word *dreaded* is built on the base word *dread. Dread* can be a noun that means "great fear" or a verb that means "experience great fear."

1. Use a thesaurus to find three synonyms for the word *dread*.

2. Use a dictionary to verify the definition of each synonym you find. Explain the nuances in their meanings.

3. Identify which synonyms have the most intense or negative meanings and which are more neutral.

2.A. Use print or digital resources to determine the meaning, syllabication, pronunciation, word origin, and part of speech.

6.F. Respond using newly acquired vocabulary as appropriate.

10.D.vi. Edit drafts using standard English conventions, including subordinating conjunctions to form complex sentences and correlative conjunctions such as *either/or* and *neither/nor.*

Conventions

Conjunctions Words that join other words, phrases, or clauses together are called **conjunctions.** There are three types of conjunctions:

TYPE OF CONJUNCTION	EXAMPLES	SAMPLE SENTENCES
Coordinating Conjunctions: join words or groups of words of equal importance	*and, or, but, nor, for, yet, so*	• Scrooge <u>and</u> the Ghost of Christmas Present watched the Cratchits celebrate. • Bob Cratchit wanted to toast Scrooge, <u>so</u> the rest of the family agreed.
Subordinating Conjunctions: introduce a dependent clause in a complex sentence	*after, although, because, since, unless, when, while, where*	• Bob Cratchit poured the drinks <u>while</u> chestnuts roasted on the fire. • <u>*After*</u> the Cratchits toasted Scrooge, Tiny Tim sang a song.
Correlative Conjunctions: come in pairs and join two equal grammatical terms	*both/and; either/or; neither/nor; not only/but also; whether/or*	• <u>Neither</u> Scrooge <u>nor</u> the Ghost were visible to the Cratchit family. • Scrooge felt <u>both</u> sorrow <u>and</u> remorse as the Ghost talked of Tiny Tim's bleak future.

NOTEBOOK

INTERACTIVITY

READ IT Identify the conjunctions used in these sentences about the novel excerpt. Label each conjunction as coordinating, subordinating, or correlative.

1. Mrs. Cratchit was reluctant to toast Scrooge because she thinks he is hateful and selfish.

2. The Cratchits were neither rich nor refined, but they were happy and content.

3. Unless the future is altered, Tiny Tim will suffer a very sad fate.

WRITE IT Write a paragraph about a holiday celebration. Then, edit your draft to use at least one coordinating conjunction, one subordinating conjunction, and one set of correlative conjunctions.

A CHRISTMAS CAROL: SCROOGE AND MARLEY, ACTS I AND II

from A CHRISTMAS CAROL

Compare Drama and Fiction

Multiple Choice

These questions are based on the play *A Christmas Carol: Scrooge and Marley* and the excerpt from the novel *A Christmas Carol.* Choose the best answer to each question.

1. In both the play and the novel, what does the ghost tell Scrooge about Tiny Tim's future?

A Tiny Tim will survive and regain his health.

B Unless the family's situation changes, Tiny Tim will die.

C Tiny Tim's situation will remain the same no matter what.

D Tiny Tim, who is currently well, will become sick.

2. Which statement is true of both the character of Jacob Marley in the play and the narrator in the novel?

F In the play, Marley is a character, and in the novel he is the narrator.

G Both Marley and the narrator express opinions about the characters and action.

H Neither Marley nor the narrator expresses an opinion about the characters and action.

J Marley is not an important character in the play, but he is very important in the novel excerpt.

3. Read Act II, Scene 3, paragraph 84 from the play and part of paragraph 22 from the novel excerpt. What idea is implied in the novel but stated more directly in the play?

Play

Scrooge. I am listening. [*The chorus sings full volume now, until . . . the song ends here.*] Spirit, it must be time for us to take our leave. I feel in my heart that it is . . . that I must think on that which I have seen here . . .

Novel

But, they were happy, grateful, pleased with one another, and contented with the time; and when they faded, and looked happier yet in the bright sprinklings of the Spirit's torch at parting, Scrooge had his eye upon them, and especially on Tiny Tim, until the last.

A Scrooge knows exactly what he will do to help the Cratchits.

B Scrooge feels powerless to change the Cratchits' circumstances.

C Scrooge will think deeply about the events he has just witnessed.

D Scrooge has not been affected by the events he has just seen.

TEKS

6.B. Write responses that demonstrate understanding of texts, including comparing sources within and across genres.

6.C. Use text evidence to support an appropriate response.

11.C. Compose multi-paragraph argumentative texts using genre characteristics and craft.

NOTEBOOK

Short Response

Answer the questions in your notebook. Use text evidence to support your responses.

1. Which version of the story provides more insight into Scrooge's emotions as he watches the Cratchit family? Explain your thinking.

2. **Contrast** In both the play and the novel, Tiny Tim sings a song. How is that moment in the play different from the same moment in the novel? Why do think the playwright changed it?

3. **(a) Compare and Contrast** Re-read Act 2, scene 3, paragraph 83 of the play, and paragraph 22 of the novel excerpt. How did the playwright adapt the text from the novel to suit the purposes of a play? **(b) Make a Judgment** Which version do you think is more effective? Explain your choice.

Timed Writing

A **critical review** is an essay in which you summarize and evaluate a literary or other artistic work.

ASSIGNMENT

Write a **critical review** in which you discuss how the play and the novel present the Cratchit family dinner scene. Explain whether you think the play represents the novel well in this scene.

5-MINUTE PLANNER

1. Read the assignment carefully and completely.
2. Decide what you want to say—your claim or main idea.
3. Decide which details from the texts you will use to develop and support your ideas.
4. Organize your ideas, making sure to address these points:
   - Explain how the dinner scene in the two works is similar and different.
   - Take a position about whether the scene from the play accurately reflects the novel on which it is based.

EQ Notes Before moving on to a new selection, go to your Essential Question Notes and record any additional thoughts or observations you may have about *A Christmas Carol: Scrooge and Marley* and the excerpt from the novel *A Christmas Carol.*

Write a Short Story

Short stories are brief works of fiction. They may be realistic or even based on real people and events, but they are still works of imagination.

ASSIGNMENT

Write a **short story** about a character who has a significant life experience. Shape your story to answer this question:

Does your character *truly* change?

You may write a science-fiction story, a realistic story, or another type of story you like to read. Include the elements of a short story in your writing.

ELEMENTS OF A SHORT STORY

Purpose: to tell a story that expresses an insight

Characteristics

- well-developed, interesting characters
- clearly described setting
- a deeper meaning, insight, or theme
- an effective narrative point of view
- vivid, precise word choices and descriptive details
- literary devices and craft, including dialogue
- standard English conventions

Structure

- a plot that centers on a conflict and includes a clear sequence of events

TEKS

10.A. Plan a first draft by selecting a genre appropriate for a particular topic, purpose, and audience using a range of strategies such as discussion, background reading, and personal interests.

11.A. Compose literary texts such as personal narratives, fiction, and poetry using genre characteristics and craft.

Take a Closer Look at the Assignment

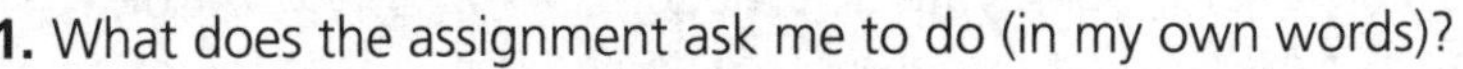

NOTEBOOK

1. What does the assignment ask me to do (in my own words)?

2. What mood, or emotional quality, do I want my story to have? What is my **purpose** for telling this story?

3. (a) Which genre interests me the most—realism, science fiction, adventure, fantasy, or another type of fiction? Why?

(b) Which type of story, or **genre**, will best help me create the mood I want and achieve my purpose?

4. What **narrative point of view** do I want to use?

- ◯ Do I want a character to tell the story?
- ◯ Do I want an outside narrator to tell the story?
- ◯ Do I want the narrator to share what everyone in the story feels and thinks, or just what one character feels and thinks?

5. Does the assignment ask me to follow a specific structure?

◯ Yes   If "yes," what structure does it require?

◯ No   If "no," how can I best structure my story?

PURPOSE

Decide your **purpose,** or reason for writing, by considering the effect you want to create. What do you want readers to feel or understand when they read your story?

GENRE

Different **genres,** create different possibilities.

- **Realistic Fiction:** true-to-life characters, settings, and events
- **Science Fiction:** futuristic settings; time travel; space travel; robots; aliens
- **Adventure:** physical challenges and danger; action-filled
- **Fantasy:** magical settings; imaginary beings; characters with special powers

NARRATIVE POINT OF VIEW

Point of view refers to the type of narrator you use.

- **First-Person:** narrator is a character in the story
- **Third-Person:** narrator is not a character; shares the thoughts and feelings of one character only
- **Third-Person Omniscient:** narrator is not a character; shares the thoughts and feelings of all the characters

Planning and Prewriting

Before you start to draft, generate first thoughts for a story you truly want to tell. For example, consider a place you've visited that might be a good story setting, or an experience you've had that suggests an interesting conflict you could turn into fiction.

Discover Your Thinking: Freewrite!

Keep your first thoughts in mind as you write quickly and freely for at least three minutes without stopping. If it helps you, fill in this sentence to start your freewrite:

What if [character] ____________, suddenly [action] ____________?

- Don't worry about spelling and grammar.
- When time is up, pause and read what you wrote.
- Mark ideas that seem strong or interesting. Repeat the process as many times as necessary to get all your ideas out. For each new round, start with the strong ideas you marked earlier.

NOTEBOOK

WRITE IT Does your character *truly* change?

TEKS

10.A. Plan a first draft by selecting a genre appropriate for a particular topic, purpose, and audience using a range of strategies such as discussion, background reading, and personal interests.

Structure Ideas: Make a Plan

 NOTEBOOK

A. Collect Your Ideas Reread your freewriting and pull out your most compelling ideas—the ones that fire up your imagination.

B. Focus on Character and Situation Write a sentence or two about the main character and his or her situation, the **setting** and circumstances of the character's life.

C. Plan a Coherent Structure Consider the **conflict** your characters face.

I. What event sparks the conflict or brings it to characters' awareness?

II. How does the conflict build or develop?

III. At what point is the conflict most intense?

IV. How does the conflict end?

CHARACTER

Consider what your main **character** is like:

- What does he or she look like?
- How does he or she think, feel, and behave?
- What does he or she want?
- What does he or she *not* want?

SETTING

Consider the **setting,** or time and place of your story's events:

- Where does the story take place?
- Does the setting have any special features?
- Will the setting affect the story's events?

CONFLICT

Every plot is driven by a **conflict**. The plot is the series of events that shows how the conflict begins, gets more intense, reaches a high point, and finally ends. Create a coherent, or unified, story by establishing a definite conflict and showing how it develops through a clear series of events.

Drafting

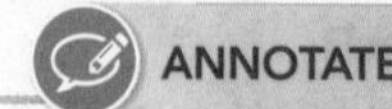

Apply your planning work to write a first draft. Work to use details that show readers how characters see the world around them as well as how they think and feel.

Read Like a Writer

Reread these two paragraphs of the Mentor Text. Mark details that show how the boy sees the world. One observation has been done for you.

MENTOR TEXT

from The Golden Windows

The boy thanked his father and kissed his mother; then he put a piece of bread in his pocket, and started off to find the house with the golden windows.

It was pleasant walking. His bare feet made marks in the white dust, and when he looked back, the footprints seemed to be following him, and making company for him. His shadow, too, kept beside him, and would dance or run with him as he pleased; so it was very cheerful.

Which details in the text grab your attention? Mark them.

The author uses sensory details to show why the boy feels walking is "pleasant" and "cheerful."

NOTEBOOK

WRITE IT Write a scene from your story. Use details to help readers understand what the character experiences.

DEPTH OF THOUGHT

Keep these ideas in mind as you draft your story.

- **Audience** Grab your reader's attention. For example, start with a dramatic event, and craft a sentence that makes readers wonder what will happen.
- **Characters** Write dialogue that gives each character a unique voice.
- **Descriptive Details** Bring the story to life by using strong details that include factual or realistic aspects of a setting, vivid examples, and powerful sensory details.

10.B.ii. Develop drafts into a focused, structured, and coherent piece of writing by developing an engaging idea reflecting depth of thought with specific facts, details, and examples; **10.D.i.** Edit drafts using standard English conventions, including complete complex sentences with subject-verb agreement and avoidance of splices, run-ons, and fragments.

Create Coherence

In a **coherent** story, the writing does not feel choppy and disjointed. Instead, events flow clearly and related ideas connect logically. Use these strategies to add to the coherence of your story.

- Don't overload one paragraph with too many actions. Instead, give separate events separate paragraphs.
- With rare exceptions (see TIP), use complete sentences that show logical sequences of ideas or actions. A **complete sentence** contains a subject and a verb and expresses a complete thought, using proper punctuation. Sentence fragments and run-ons, including comma splices, are two common errors that you should avoid.

TIP: In narrative writing, fragments can be used in dialogue or to develop style and tone. Be sure you can explain the purpose of any uncorrected fragments in your story.

TYPE OF SENTENCE ERROR	INCORRECT	CORRECT
Sentence Fragment: group of words that is missing a subject, a verb, or both, but is punctuated like a complete sentence	**Missing Subject:** *Enjoys hiking in the forest.* **Missing Verb:** *Alice never at the lake.*	**Add missing subject:** *Rosita enjoys hiking in the forest.* **Add missing verb:** *Alice never dives at the lake.*
Run-on Sentence: two or more complete sentences that are incorrectly punctuated **Comma Splice:** a type of run-on; two or more complete sentences joined by a comma without a conjunction	*Sparrows stay all winter they don't fly south.* *Sparrows stay all winter, they don't fly south.*	**Make two sentences:** *Sparrows stay all winter. They don't fly south.* **Add a conjunction and a comma:** *Sparrows stay all winter, and they don't fly south.* **Add a semicolon:** *Sparrows stay all winter; they don't fly south.*

NOTEBOOK

WRITE IT Write a paragraph of your story here. Then, edit your paragraph to correct any run-ons or unintentional fragments.

USE TRANSITIONS

Once you have corrected any fragments or run-ons, add transitions, such as *afterward* or *therefore,* that clarify relationships among ideas within a paragraph. To create coherence across paragraphs, try using transitions, such as *The next day.*

Revising

 ANNOTATE

Now that you have a first draft, revise it to be sure that the characters and other details come to life for your readers. When you revise, you "re-see" your writing, checking for the following elements:

Clarity: sharpness of your ideas

Development: vibrant, convincing characters

Organization: conflict that unfolds through a clearly sequenced plot

Style and Tone: well-written sentences of varying types, patterns, and lengths; and precise, vivid word choices

Read Like a Writer

Review the revisions made to the Mentor Text. Then, answer the questions in the white boxes.

MENTOR TEXT

from The Golden Windows

All day long the little boy had worked hard *in field and barn and shed, for his people were poor farmers, and could not pay a workman* but at sunset there came an hour that was all his own, for his father had given it to him. Then the boy would go up to the top of a hill and look across at another hill that rose some miles away. On this far hill stood a house with windows *of clear gold and diamonds. They shone and blazed so that*~~. It~~ made the boy wink to look at them: but after a while the people in the house put up shutters, as it seemed, and then it looked like any common farmhouse. The boy supposed they did this because it was suppertime; and then we would go into the house and have his supper of break and mil, and so to bed.

One day the boy's father called him and said: *"You have been a good boy, and have earned a holiday. Take this day for your own, but remember that God gave it, and try to learn some good thing."* ~~he could take the day as a holiday. He told him to remember it was a gift and to use the day wisely.~~

The additional details clarify the boy's situation.

Why did the writer add these descriptive details?

Why did the writer replace the explanation with dialogue?

TEKS
10.C. Revise drafts for clarity, development, organization, style, word choice, and sentence variety.

Take a Closer Look at Your Draft

Now, revise your draft. Use the Revision Guide for Fiction to evaluate and strengthen your short story.

REVISION GUIDE FOR FICTION

EVALUATE	TAKE ACTION
Clarity	
Does my story express an insight? Does it mean something?	If your message is unclear, simply **say** it out loud. Then, look for points where characters can express that insight or details can suggest it.
Development	
Are my characters believable and well-drawn?	**List** each character's traits. **Mark** descriptions, actions, and dialogue that reveal those traits. If there are too few, **add** details.
Do characters' actions and reactions fit their personalities?	Again, **list** each character's traits. Then, list what each character does. If any action or reaction does not reflect a character trait, **delete** or **change** it.
Organization	
Is the main conflict clear?	**Mark** the points at which the conflict begins and gets most intense. If those two points are not clear, **add** details that better show the problem.
Is the sequence of events logical?	**List** the story's events in time order. **Reorder** any that are confusing or out of place.
Style and Tone	
Does the beginning of the story engage readers?	If the beginning of the story seems flat or lackluster, **add** dialogue, an arresting detail, or a puzzling action that will grab readers' attention.
Have I used vivid sensory details to bring the characters and setting to life?	**Replace** any vague words with language that appeals to the senses of sight, hearing, taste, smell, or touch. For example, instead of saying, "The pie smelled great," say, "The pie smelled of apples, fresh butter, and cinnamon."
Have I used a variety of sentence patterns?	Review your draft, noting the types of sentences you have used. If you see a long series of short, simple sentences, combine some of them to create complex, compound, and compound-complex sentences.

Editing

Don't let errors distract readers from your story. Reread your draft and fix mistakes to create a finished narrative.

Read Like a Writer

Look at how the writer of the Mentor Text edited her draft. Then, follow the directions in the white boxes.

MENTOR TEXT

from The Golden Windows

By and by he felt hungry; and he sat down by a brown brook that ran through the alder hegde by the roadside, and ate his bread and drank the clear water. An apple tree, which nestled beside wildflowers, were heavy with fruit. Then he scattered the crumbs for the birds, as his mother had taught him to do, and went on his way.

Find and fix a spelling error.

The writer added commas before and after a nonrestrictive clause.

Find and fix an error in subject-verb agreement in a complex sentence.

Focus on Sentences

Subject-Verb Agreement in Complex Sentences A complex sentence may include an adjectival clause in the middle of the independent clause. This can lead to problems with subject-verb agreement. Make sure the subject and verb of the independent clause agree.

EXAMPLE:

Incorrect: The boy, whose parents are poor farmers, help his family.

Correct: The boy, whose parents are poor farmers, helps his family.

PRACTICE Correct the subject-verb agreement in the following sentences. Then, check your own draft for correctness.

1. The window that faces the mountains begin to shine.
2. The farmers, who are working in the field, waves at the boy.
3. The food, which cooks for several hours, are delicious.
4. The families who come for the picnic is happy.

EDITING TIPS

1. Mark any adjectival clauses.
2. Mark the subject of the independent clause.
3. If the verb in the independent clause does not agree with the subject, replace it with the correct form of the verb.

TEKS

10.D.i. Edit drafts using standard English conventions, including complete complex sentences with subject-verb agreement and avoidance of splices, run-ons, and fragments; **10.D.viii.** Edit drafts using standard English conventions, including punctuation, including commas to set off words, phrases, and clauses, and semicolons.

Focus on Spelling and Punctuation

Spelling Patterns: Use *dge* or *ge* for Ending *j* Sound In English, any word that has an ending *j* sound is spelled with *dge* or *ge*. Notice that the *e* is silent. Consider these examples:

hedge	bridge	carriage
knowledge	cabbage	damage

Check your story for words that have an ending *j* sound and make sure you have spelled them correctly.

Commas With Adjectives When you place two or more adjectives before a noun they describe, make sure to use commas correctly:

- **Use commas to separate adjectives of equal rank.** Test whether adjectives are equal by switching their order or placing the word *and* between them. If the meaning of the sentence stays the same, the adjectives are equal.
  Incorrect: Bianca asked in a civil polite way.
  Correct: Bianca asked in a civil, polite way.
- **Don't use commas to separate adjectives that must have a specific order.**
  Incorrect Order: There are large two birds in the yard.
  Correct Order: There are two large birds in the yard.
- **Don't use a comma between the last adjective in a series and the noun it modifies.**
  Incorrect: The boy walked the winding, rocky, path.
  Correct: The boy walked the winding, rocky path.

EDITING TIPS

- Read your work out loud to hear any missing or repeated words.
- Set your story aside for a while before you proofread it. This will help you notice errors more efficiently.

PRACTICE In the following sentences, fix any spelling or punctuation errors. Then, review your own draft for correctness.

1. The children live in a tiny remote villaj
2. The trees are full of sweet crisp bright, apples.
3. The boy loved the imaj of four, golden, windows.

Publishing and Presenting

Make It Multimodal

Choose an option to publish your work.

OPTION 1 Print your story and add illustrations. Share your illustrated story with your class.

OPTION 2 Record yourself giving a dramatic reading of your story. Use an app to add music or sound effects. Then, upload the reading to your school website.

Essential Question

Can people really change?

Is it truly possible to change—either over time or in an instant? If so, what can cause us to change? You will read selections that talk about changes, both big and small. Work in a small group to continue your exploration of transformation.

VIDEO

INTERACTIVITY

Peer-Group Learning Strategies

Throughout your life, in school, in your community, and in your career, you will continue to learn and work with others.

Look at these strategies and the actions you can take to practice them as you work in small groups. Add ideas of your own for each category. Use these strategies during Peer-Group Learning.

STRATEGY	MY PEER-GROUP ACTION PLAN
Prepare • Complete your assignments so that you are prepared for group work. • Take notes on your reading so that you can share ideas with others in your group.	
Participate fully • Make eye contact to signal that you are paying attention. • Use text evidence when making a point.	
Support others • Build off ideas from others in your group. • Ask others who have not yet spoken to do so.	
Clarify • Paraphrase the ideas of others to be sure that your understanding is correct. • Ask follow-up questions.	

CONTENTS

Working as a Group

1. Take a Position

In your group, discuss the following question:

> What might cause a sudden change in someone's life?

As you take turns sharing your ideas, give reasons and examples to support them. After all group members have shared, discuss the personality traits that would be necessary to make a sudden and permanent change.

2. List Your Rules

As a group, decide on the rules that you will follow as you work together. Two samples are provided. Add two more of your own. You may add or revise rules as you work through the readings and activities together.

- Everyone should participate in group discussions.
- People should not interrupt.

____

____

3. Apply the Rules

Practice working as a group. Share what you have learned about personal change. Make sure every person in the group contributes. Take notes, and be prepared to share with the class one thing that you heard from another member of your group.

4. Name Your Group

Choose a name that reflects the unit topic.

Our group's name: ____

5. Create a Communication Plan

Decide how you want to communicate with one another. For example, you might use online collaboration tools, email, or instant messaging.

Our group's plan:

____

____

1.D. Engage in meaningful discourse and provide and accept constructive feedback from others.

Making a Schedule

First, find out the due dates for the peer-group activities. Then, preview the texts and activities with your group, and make a schedule for completing the tasks.

SELECTION	ACTIVITIES	DUE DATE
Thank You, M'am		
Learning Rewires the Brain		
Trying to Name What Doesn't Change I Myself		

Build Your Vocabulary

As you work with your group to complete writing, speaking, and listening activities, you will use many kinds of vocabulary, ranging from sight words you already know, to basic terms, to academic words, to complex words for specialized ideas. The greater your vocabulary, the more clearly you will be able to express yourself, follow instructions, and comprehend others' ideas.

Use these strategies to expand your vocabulary:

Notice Routine Words: Many words in this text, such as *draft* or *tell*, appear over and over again. Build your vocabulary by learning and using other words that appear repeatedly.

Listen to Audio: Play the audio versions of the selections to hear words in context and how they are pronounced.

Use Resources: Regularly consult dictionaries and thesauri to build your word knowledge.

Keep Track: Use the Word Network chart to keep track of new words you learn or make another chart of your own. Go through your word lists periodically to remind yourself of word meanings and to see how much your vocabulary has grown.

THANK YOU, M'AM

The selection you are about to read is a realistic short story.

Reading Realistic Short Stories

A **short story** is a brief work of fiction. **Realistic short stories** are works of imagination, but feature true-to-life characters, events, and situations.

REALISTIC SHORT STORY

Author's Purpose

- to entertain and express insights

Characteristics

- settings that are realistic and may even be real places
- characters that seem like real people
- conflicts, or problems, that are like those people face in real life
- theme about life or human nature
- natural-sounding dialogue
- narrator who tells the story

Structure

- a plot, centered on a conflict; often, uses foreshadowing to generate curiosity or suspense

Take a Minute!

NOTEBOOK

CHOOSE IT Choose at least three characters and events you might find in a work of realistic fiction and three you would not. Discuss your choices with a partner.

alien being	fairy godmother	twelve-year-old chess champion
loss of a loved one	circus performer	dragons flaming a village
objects that come to life	monsters	boy who discovers a crime

TEKS

7.C. Analyze plot elements, including the use of foreshadowing and suspense, to advance the plot.

8.A. Demonstrate knowledge of literary genres such as realistic fiction, adventure stories, historical fiction, mysteries, humor, myths, fantasy, and science fiction.

Genre / Text Elements

Plot Elements A **plot** is the related sequence of events in a story. All plots center on a conflict that characters face. The conflict drives the plot, which develops in stages.

STAGES OF PLOT	
Exposition	introduces the characters, setting, and situation
Rising Action	presents the incident that starts the conflict; may also include some events that explain characters' actions
Climax	point at which the conflict becomes most intense
Falling Action	shows events that follow the climax
Resolution	point at which the conflict ends

TIP: There are two main types of conflict:

- **External Conflict:** Character struggles against an outside force, such as another person.
- **Internal Conflict:** Character struggles with his or her own feelings.

The plots of well-crafted fiction seem logical and unified to readers, even if some events are surprising. Writers create this unified quality by using **foreshadowing**, or clues that hint at later events. These clues also build the readers' interest and may create a feeling of **suspense**, or anxious curiosity about the fates of the characters.

PRACTICE Work on your own to read the passage and answer the questions.

[1] It was a spring-green day as the boy walked home, but he was lost in visions of the girl and didn't notice. [2] That morning, his father had smiled bleakly when the boy asked if he could take the girl to prom: "Sorry, son. Can't afford it." [3] Troubled by dark thoughts, the boy nearly missed the wallet, fat with cash, lying on the sidewalk. [4] It belongs to someone, he thought, and paused. [5] But a vision of the girl in a golden gown filled his mind. [6] Ignoring the guilt hammering at his heart, he picked up the wallet....

1. What conflicts does the boy in this passage face?

2. Which sentences are part of the exposition?

3. Which details foreshadow events that might come later and may cause readers to feel curiosity or suspense? Explain.

About the Author

Langston Hughes (1902–1967) published his first work just a year after his high school graduation. Though he wrote in many genres, Hughes is best known for his poetry. He was one of the main figures in the Harlem Renaissance, a creative movement among African Americans that took place during the 1920s in Harlem, an area in New York City.

Thank You, M'am

Concept Vocabulary

As you read "Thank You, M'am," you will encounter these words.

permit	release	contact

Context Clues The **context** of a word is the other words and phrases that appear close to it in a text. Clues in the context can help you determine the meanings of unfamiliar words.

Cause-and-effect clues suggest a word's meaning by showing how one thing leads to or causes another.

EXAMPLE The medicine **alleviated** Kiara's flu symptoms, so she was able to return to school.

Analysis: Since Kiara was able to return to school after taking medicine, *alleviated* must mean "helped" or "relieved."

PRACTICE As you read "Thank You, M'am," study the context to determine the meanings of unfamiliar words. Mark your observations in the open space next to the text.

Comprehension Strategy

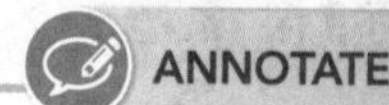

Establish a Purpose for Reading

Even when you are assigned texts to read, setting a purpose for reading can help you focus, add to your enjoyment, and learn more. Set a purpose for reading by thinking about the text and your goals—what do you want to get from your reading experience?

- **Genre:** Consider the type of text. For example, your purposes for reading a story and an essay will probably be different.
- **Background:** You may already know something about a text. For example, you might be familiar with an author's work and want to read more, or you might want to read works set in a particular place. These kinds of elements can direct your purpose for reading.

PRACTICE Before you begin to read the story, establish a purpose. Write your purpose here.

TEKS

2.B. Use context such as contrast or cause and effect to clarify the meaning of words.

5.A. Establish purpose for reading assigned and self-selected texts.

Thank You, M'am

Langston Hughes

BACKGROUND

In this story, published in 1958, Roger, the protagonist, really wants a pair of blue suede shoes. This particular fashion item became popular after Carl Perkins released his hit song "Blue Suede Shoes" in 1956. Elvis Presley also famously covered the song in the same year.

AUDIO

ANNOTATE

1 She was a large woman with a large purse that had everything in it but hammer and nails. It had a long strap, and she carried it slung across her shoulder. It was about eleven o'clock at night, dark, and she was walking alone, when a boy ran up behind her and tried to snatch her purse. The strap broke with the sudden single tug the boy gave it from behind. But the boy's weight and the weight of the purse combined caused him to lose his balance. Instead of taking off full blast as he had hoped, the boy fell on his back on the sidewalk and his legs flew up. The large woman simply turned around and kicked him right square in his blue-jeaned sitter. Then she reached down, picked the boy up by his shirt front, and shook him until his teeth rattled.

Mark context clues or indicate another strategy you used that helped you determine meaning.

permit (puhr MIHT) *v.*

MEANING:

2 After that the woman said, "Pick up my pocketbook, boy, and give it here."

3 She still held him tightly. But she bent down enough to **permit** him to stoop and pick up her purse. Then she said, "Now ain't you ashamed of yourself?"

4 Firmly gripped by his shirt front, the boy said, "Yes'm."

5 The woman said, "What did you want to do it for?"

6 The boy said, "I didn't aim to."

7 She said, "You a lie!"

8 By that time two or three people passed, stopped, turned to look, and some stood watching.

9 "If I turn you loose, will you run?" asked the woman.

10 "Yes'm," said the boy.

release (rih LEES) *v.*

MEANING:

11 "Then I won't turn you loose," said the woman. She did not **release** him.

12 "Lady, I'm sorry," whispered the boy.

13 "Um-hum! Your face is dirty. I got a great mind to wash your face for you. Ain't you got nobody home to tell you to wash your face?"

14 "No'm," said the boy.

15 "Then it will get washed this evening," said the large woman starting up the street, dragging the frightened boy behind her.

16 He looked as if he were fourteen or fifteen, frail and willow-wild, in tennis shoes and blue jeans.

17 The woman said, "You ought to be my son. I would teach you right from wrong. Least I can do right now is to wash your face. Are you hungry?"

18 "No'm," said the being-dragged boy. "I just want you to turn me loose."

19 "Was I bothering *you* when I turned that corner?" asked the woman.

20 "No'm."

contact (KON takt) *n.*

MEANING:

21 "But you put yourself in **contact** with *me*," said the woman. "If you think that that contact is not going to last awhile, you got another thought coming. When I get through with you, sir, you are going to remember Mrs. Luella Bates Washington Jones."

22 Sweat popped out on the boy's face and he began to struggle. Mrs. Jones stopped, jerked him around in front of her, put a half nelson[1] about his neck, and continued to drag him up the street. When she got to her door, she dragged the boy inside, down a hall, and into a large kitchenette-furnished room at the rear of the house. She switched on the light and left the door open. The boy could hear other roomers laughing and talking in the large house. Some of their doors were open, too, so he knew he and the woman

1. **half nelson** wrestling hold in which an arm is placed under the opponent's armpit from behind with the palm of the hand pressed against the back of the neck.

were not alone. The woman still had him by the neck in the middle of her room.

23 She said, "What is your name?"

24 "Roger," answered the boy.

25 "Then, Roger, you go to that sink and wash your face," said the woman, whereupon she turned him loose—at last. Roger looked at the door—looked at the woman—looked at the door—*and went to the sink.*

26 "Let the water run until it gets warm," she said. "Here's a clean towel."

27 "You gonna take me to jail?" asked the boy, bending over the sink.

28 "Not with that face, I would not take you nowhere," said the woman. "Here I am trying to get home to cook me a bite to eat and you snatch my pocketbook! Maybe, you ain't been to your supper either, late as it be. Have you?"

29 "There's nobody home at my house," said the boy.

30 "Then we'll eat," said the woman, "I believe you're hungry—or been hungry—to try to snatch my pocketbook."

31 "I wanted a pair of blue suede shoes," said the boy.

32 "Well, you didn't have to snatch *my* pocketbook to get some suede shoes," said Mrs. Luella Bates Washington Jones. "You could of asked me."

33 "M'am?"

34 The water dripping from his face, the boy looked at her. There was a long pause. A very long pause. After he had dried his face and not knowing what else to do dried it again, the boy turned around, wondering what next. The door was open. He could make a dash for it down the hall. He could run, run, run, *run*!

35 The woman was sitting on the day bed. After a while she said, "I were young once and I wanted things I could not get."

36 There was another long pause. The boy's mouth opened. Then he frowned, not knowing he frowned.

37 The woman said, "Um-hum! You thought I was going to say *but*, didn't you? You thought I was going to say, *but I didn't snatch people's pocketbooks*. Well, I wasn't going to say that." Pause. Silence. "I have done things, too, which I would not tell you, son—neither tell God, if He didn't already know. Everybody's got something in common. So you set down while I fix us something to eat. You might run that comb through your hair so you will look presentable."

38 In another corner of the room behind a screen was a gas plate[2] and an icebox. Mrs. Jones got up and went behind the screen. The woman did not watch the boy to see if he was going to run now, nor did she watch her purse, which she left behind her on the day

2. **gas plate** hot plate heated by gas that is used for cooking.

bed. But the boy took care to sit on the far side of the room, away from her purse, where he thought she could easily see him out of the corner of her eye if she wanted to. He did not trust the woman *not* to trust him. And he did not want to be mistrusted now.

39 "Do you need somebody to go to the store," asked the boy, "maybe to get some milk or something?"

40 "Don't believe I do," said the woman, "unless you just want sweet milk yourself. I was going to make cocoa out of this canned milk I got here."

41 "That will be fine," said the boy.

42 She heated some lima beans and ham she had in the icebox, made the cocoa, and set the table. The woman did not ask the boy anything about where he lived, or his folks, or anything else that would embarrass him. Instead, as they ate, she told him about her job in a hotel beauty-shop that stayed open late, what the work was like, and how all kinds of women came in and out, blondes, redheads, and Spanish. Then she cut him a half of her ten-cent cake.

43 "Eat some more, son," she said.

44 When they were finished eating she got up and said, "Now, here, take this ten dollars and buy yourself some blue suede shoes. And next time, do not make the mistake of latching onto *my* pocketbook *nor nobody else's*—because shoes got by devilish ways will burn your feet. I got to get my rest now. But from here on in, son, I hope you will behave yourself."

45 She led him down the hall to the front door and opened it. "Good night! Behave yourself, boy!" she said, looking out into the street.

46 The boy wanted to say something else other than "Thank you, m'am" to Mrs. Luella Bates Washington Jones, but although his lips moved, he couldn't even say that as he turned at the foot of the barren stoop and looked up at the large woman in the door. Then she shut the door. ❧

NOTEBOOK

Response

1. Personal Connections Did anything about this story surprise you? Explain.

Work on your own to answer the questions in your notebook. Use text evidence to support your responses.

Comprehension

2. Reading Check **(a)** How do Mrs. Jones and Roger meet? **(b)** What does Roger expect Mrs. Jones to do? **(c)** What does Mrs. Jones do instead?

3. Strategy: Establish a Purpose for Reading **(a)** What purpose for reading this story did you set? **(b)** In what ways did having a purpose affect your reading experience?

Analysis and Discussion

WORKING AS A GROUP

Discuss your responses to the Analysis and Discussion questions with your group.

- Note agreements and disagreements.
- Summarize insights.
- Consider changes of opinion.

If necessary, revise your original answers to reflect what you learn from your discussion.

4. Make Inferences Why does it become important to Roger that Mrs. Jones trust him? Explain, citing evidence from the story.

5. Interpret In paragraph 37, Mrs. Jones says, "Everybody's got something in common." What does she mean? Explain.

6. (a) Draw Conclusions Why is Roger unable to speak as he is leaving Mrs. Jones's apartment? **(b) Speculate** What do you think Roger wanted to say? Explain.

7. Get Ready for Close Reading Choose a passage from the text that you find especially interesting or important. You'll discuss the passage with your group during Close-Read activities.

Can people really change?

What have you learned about transformations from reading this story? Go to your Essential Question Notes and record your observations and thoughts about "Thank You, M'am."

TEKS

5.F. Make inferences and use evidence to support understanding.

6.C. Use text evidence to support an appropriate response.

6.I. Reflect on and adjust responses as new evidence is presented.

THANK YOU, M'AM

Close Read

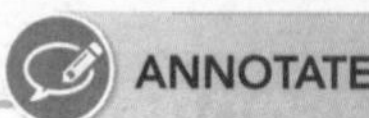

PRACTICE **Complete the following activities. Use text evidence to support your responses.**

1. **Present and Discuss** With your group, share the passages from the story that you found especially interesting. Discuss what you notice, the questions you have, and the conclusions you reach. For example, you might focus on the following passages.
   - Paragraph 37: Discuss what this passage reveals about Mrs. Jones's character, past and present.
   - Paragraph 44: Discuss why Mrs. Jones gives Roger money for the blue suede shoes.
2. **Reflect on Your Learning** What new ideas or insights did you uncover during your second reading of the text?

WORD NETWORK

Add words that are related to the concept of transformations from the text to your Word Network.

NOTEBOOK

LANGUAGE STUDY

Concept Vocabulary

Why These Words? Complete the activities. Seek support from your peers or teacher as needed.

permit	release	contact

1. The vocabulary words are related. With your group, determine what the words have in common. Write your ideas.
2. Add another word that fits the category. ______________
3. Confirm your understanding of these words by using each one in a sentence. Use context clues that hint at each word's meaning.

Word Study

Multiple-Meaning Words The vocabulary words are multiple-meaning words: they have more than one definition. Write the meaning and part of speech (noun or verb) of each word as it is used in the story. Then, use a dictionary to find two other meanings and parts of speech for each word.

TEKS

2.A. Use print or digital resources to determine the meaning, syllabication, pronunciation, word origin, and part of speech.

7.C. Analyze plot elements, including the use of foreshadowing and suspense, to advance the plot.

Genre / Text Elements

Plot Elements Every **plot** centers on one or more **conflicts**, or problems. There are two main types of conflict, external and internal.

CONFLICT TYPE	DEFINITION	EXAMPLE FROM THE STORY
External	struggle between a character and an outside force, such as another character, nature, or society	*...a boy ran up behind her and tried to snatch her purse.*
Internal	struggle caused by a character's own opposing feelings	*...the boy turned around, wondering what next.*

Foreshadowing details help to advance a plot because they suggest events that might happen later. Clues dropped early in a story carry through into later stages. These clues raise questions for readers, building curiosity and **suspense** about the fates of the characters.

PRACTICE Work with your group to complete the activity and answer the questions. Listen closely as group members share ideas. Notice academic words they use that may be new to you. Learn and use those words in your responses.

1. **(a)** What external conflict opens the story? **(b) Analyze** How does Mrs. Jones's reaction to that conflict create new conflicts? Explain

2. **Analyze** Reread the passages listed in the chart. Describe the conflict shown in each one and explain how each instance of conflict advances the story's plot.

PASSAGE	TYPE OF CONFLICT	EXPLANATION
Paragraph 22		
Paragraph 25		
Paragraph 34		

3. **(a) Analyze** Cite details in paragraph 1 that suggest Roger is small and weak. **(b) Connect** How do these details foreshadow Mrs. Jones's reaction to Roger and create suspense about his fate?

4. **(a)** In paragraphs 9–10, what question does Mrs. Jones ask, and how does Roger answer? **(b) Connect** How does this question foreshadow moments that happen later and help to advance the plot? Explain.

5. **Analyze** At what points in the story did you feel suspense about the outcome of the conflicts? What specific plot events helped to create that suspense and move the plot along?

THANK YOU, M'AM

Conventions

Prepositions and Prepositional Phrases A **preposition** relates a noun or a pronoun that follows it to another word in the sentence. In the sentence *The car is in the garage,* the preposition *in* relates the noun *car* to another word in the sentence, *garage.* A **prepositional phrase** is a group of words that has certain qualities:

- begins with a preposition and ends with either a noun or a pronoun, which is the object of the preposition. The phrase may include modifiers.
- functions as an adjective by telling which one, or as an adverb by telling *how, when*, or *where*

Note that if a prepositional phrase begins a sentence, it must be followed by a comma. In addition, the verb of a sentence must always agree with the subject of the sentence, not with the object of the preposition.

TIP There are more than 100 prepositions in English. Some of the most-common ones are *at, after, between, for, from, in, of, on, to, through, above,* and *with.*

EXAMPLES from "Thank You, M'am"

SENTENCE	EXPLANATION
Mrs. Jones got up and went *behind the screen.*	The prepositional phrase begins with the preposition *behind* and ends with the noun *screen,* which is the object of the preposition.
"Do you need somebody to go *to the store...?"*	The prepositional phrase begins with the preposition *to* and ends with the noun *store,* which is the object of the preposition.

INTERACTIVITY

NOTEBOOK

READ IT Read the story and mark at least three prepositional phrases. Identify the object of the preposition in each one.

WRITE IT Write a paragraph in which you describe someone who is important to you. Use at least two prepositional phrases. Then, edit your draft, making sure you have applied correct subject-verb agreement and included commas correctly after any prepositional phrase at the beginning of a sentence.

TEKS

10.D.iv. Edit drafts using standard English conventions, including prepositions and prepositional phrases and their influence on subject-verb agreement.

10.D.viii. Edit drafts using standard English conventions, including punctuation, including commas to set off words, phrases, and clauses, and semicolons.

Composition

A **journal entry** is a brief autobiographical record of a day's events.

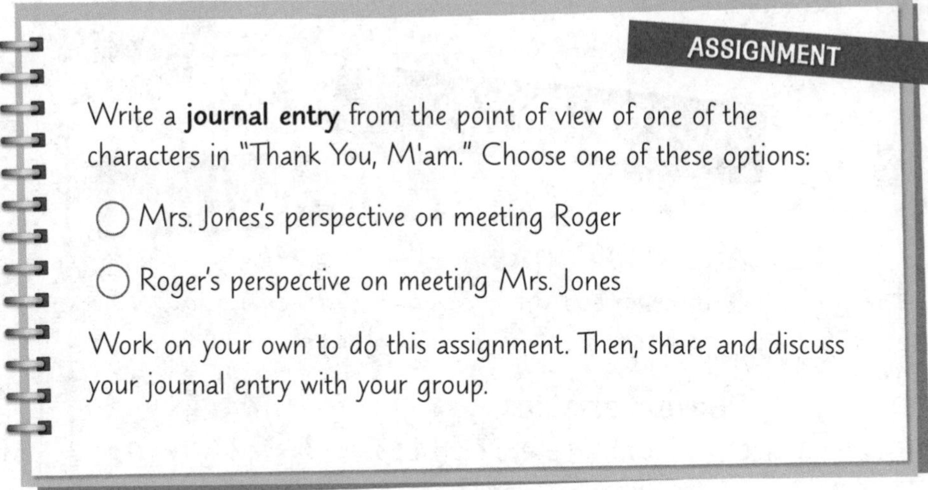

ASSIGNMENT

Write a **journal entry** from the point of view of one of the characters in "Thank You, M'am." Choose one of these options:

◯ Mrs. Jones's perspective on meeting Roger

◯ Roger's perspective on meeting Mrs. Jones

Work on your own to do this assignment. Then, share and discuss your journal entry with your group.

Plan and Draft Use the structures typical of journals in your writing:

- List the date, place, and time of the entry.
- Follow a plot structure to tell a story; you may also include reflections or explanations.

Fill in the the chart with examples, details, and facts from the story that will bring your entry to life. Then, write your draft, applying your structural choices. Use your imagination and the details you gathered from the text to create the character's voice.

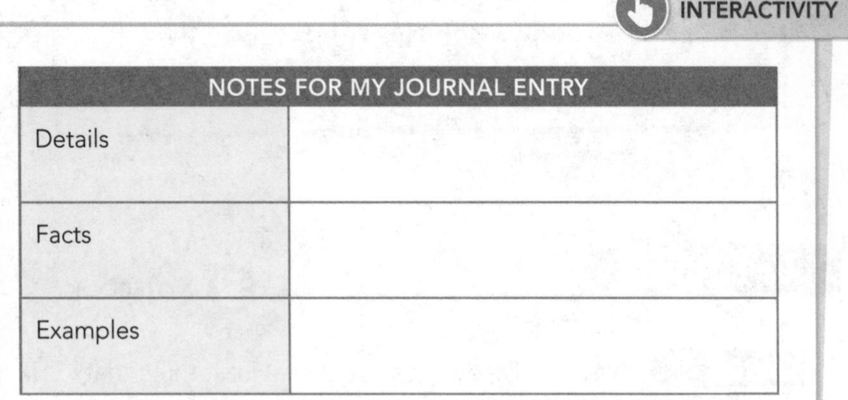

INTERACTIVITY

NOTES FOR MY JOURNAL ENTRY	
Details	
Facts	
Examples	

Revise Consider whether the entry sounds natural and true to the character. Make any changes necessary to clarify ideas and emotions.

Give and Receive Feedback Share your journal entries as a group and engage in a meaningful conversation about the choices you made. Offer and accept helpful feedback on one another's work.

EQ Notes Before moving on to a new selection, go to your Essential Question Notes and record any additional thoughts or observations you may have about "Thank You M'am."

 TEKS

1.D. Engage in meaningful discourse and provide and accept constructive feedback from others.

10.B.ii. Develop drafts into a focused, structured, and coherent piece of writing by developing an engaging idea reflecting depth of thought with specific facts, details, and examples.

11.A. Compose literary texts such as personal narratives, fiction, and poetry using genre characteristics and craft.

LEARNING REWIRES THE BRAIN

The selection you are about to read is an example of science journalism.

Reading Science Journalism

Journalism is nonfiction in which a writer (journalist) reports on current events. **Science journalism** focuses on scientific topics, issues, or discoveries.

SCIENCE JOURNALISM

Author's Purpose

- to report and explain current news about science for a general audience

Characteristics

- controlling idea, or thesis, supported with details and evidence
- scientific or technical terms
- examples and comparisons that make unfamiliar concepts clear
- often, print and graphic features that illustrate or explain concepts

Structure

- engaging first sentence or section
- logical order of ideas that creates a clear path through a complex subject

Take a Minute!

NOTEBOOK

CHOOSE IT Scan the listed topics. Identify at least three that could be the subject of science journalism. Discuss your reasons with a partner.

elections in Europe	fall fashions
landing your dream job	high-tech artificial limbs
Mars colonization	healthy holiday recipes
a cure for the common cold	how lightbulbs work

TEKS

8.D. Analyze characteristics and structural elements of informational text.

9.C. Analyze the author's use of print and graphic features to achieve specific purposes.

Genre / Text Elements

Print and Graphic Features Print and graphic features help readers grasp complex information by breaking it into sections, or categories and subcategories. These features create an order of importance, and show concepts visually. Note that both print and graphic features are types of **structural elements**. They help readers locate specific information and see how the categories and subcategories of a broader topic fit together.

TIP: Note that some print features include graphic, or visual, elements and vice versa.

STRUCTURAL ELEMENTS		
	EXAMPLES	PURPOSE
Print Features	title, heads, subheads	breaks text into chunks that show subtopics, categories, and subcategories
	bulleted lists; numbered lists	organizes data or other details into logical or numeric order
	inset boxes and features	highlights interesting aspects of the topic
Graphic Features	photos, illustrations, diagrams	provides visuals for reference; labels parts and pieces
	maps and blueprints	provides information about geography, climate, etc.
	charts, tables, graphs	organizes data into categories

NOTEBOOK

PRACTICE Work on your own to read the passage. Then, answer the questions.

The Science Behind Erosion

Have you ever heard the expression "solid as a rock"? The fact is, not even rock can resist the power of erosion.

What is erosion?

Erosion is a natural process in which Earth's surface is worn away by wind, water, and ice. This gradual process is destructive, but sometimes results in dramatic landscapes.

Natural Sculptures

Bryce Canyon National Park, Utah, is the site of dozens of spectacular rock formations known as hoodoos. These towering columns were formed when water and other natural elements eroded the softer sandstone beneath the limestone caps.

1. How do the subheads help create categories and subcategories of the broad topic?
2. What type of graphic feature might best help readers understand the "Natural Sculptures" section? Explain your thinking.

About the Author

Alison Pearce Stevens is fascinated with science and its ability to explain how the world works. She specializes in writing about science and nature topics for kids and teens. In addition to writing, Stevens teaches Environmental Curriculum at the University of Nebraska.

Learning Rewires the Brain

Concept Vocabulary

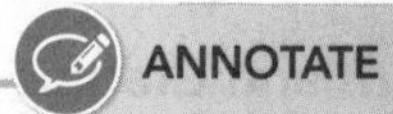

As you read "Learning Rewires the Brain," you will encounter these words.

signals	transmit	relay

Digital Resources A **digital dictionary** is a reference source you access online or through a mobile device. It provides a great deal of information about words, often including audio pronunciations.

SAMPLE DIGITAL DICTIONARY ENTRY

neuroscience *noun* [nu̇r-ō-ˈsī-ən(t)s]

Examples Word Origin Synonyms

1. scientific study of the nervous system and its effects

Analysis: This entry shows that *neuroscience* is a noun with four syllables. To hear the word pronounced, you would click the audio icon. To see it in sentences, you would click *Examples*. To learn its origins and synonyms, you would click the appropriate links.

PRACTICE As you read, use a digital dictionary to find the meanings, syllabication, pronunciations, word origins, and parts of speech of unfamiliar words. Use the open space next to the text to note information.

Comprehension Strategy

Make Connections

Deepen your understanding of a text by **making connections** as you read. You may connect with a text in several different ways:

- Consider how ideas in a text connect to your **personal experiences**, or what you already know about life.
- Notice how ideas in a text connect to **ideas in other texts** you have read, including both fiction and nonfiction.
- Analyze how ideas in a text connect to **society**, or the world around you, including your own school or community.

PRACTICE As you read, use the open space next to the text to write down connections you make to personal experiences, ideas in other texts, and society.

TEKS

2.A. Use print or digital resources to determine the meaning, syllabication, pronunciation, word origin, and part of speech.

5.E. Make connections to personal experiences, ideas in other texts, and society.

SCIENCE JOURNALISM

Learning Rewires the Brain

Alison Pearce Stevens

^ An artist's depiction of an electrical signal (yellow-orange regions) shooting down a nerve cell and then off to others in the brain. Learning strengthens the paths that these signals take, essentially "wiring" certain common paths through the brain.

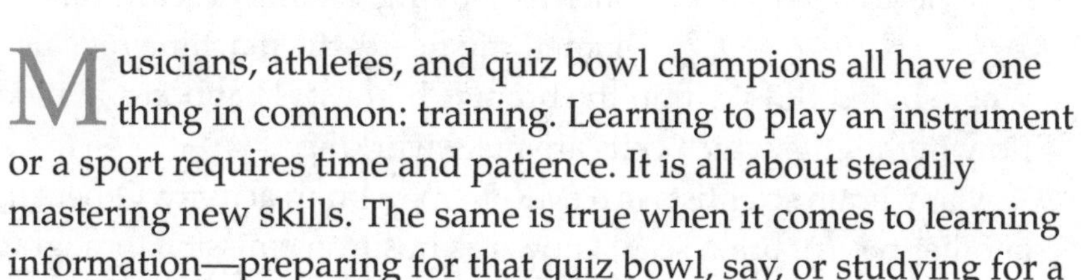

BACKGROUND

In this science article, the author reports a research finding that is truly life-changing—the discovery that as we learn, our brain cells undergo physical changes. This cause-and-effect process, much of which takes place as we sleep, helps us retain knowledge.

 AUDIO

 ANNOTATE

1 Musicians, athletes, and quiz bowl champions all have one thing in common: training. Learning to play an instrument or a sport requires time and patience. It is all about steadily mastering new skills. The same is true when it comes to learning information—preparing for that quiz bowl, say, or studying for a big test.

2 As teachers, coaches and parents everywhere like to say: Practice makes perfect.

3 Doing something over and over again doesn't just make it easier. It actually changes the brain. That may not come as a surprise. But exactly how that process happens has long been a mystery. Scientists have known that the brain continues to develop through our teenage years. But these experts used to think that those changes stopped once the brain matured.

4 No more.

5 Recent data have been showing that the brain continues to change over the course of our lives. Cells grow. They form connections with new cells. Some stop talking to others. And it's not just nerve cells that shift and change as we learn. Other brain cells also get into the act.

6 Scientists have begun unlocking these secrets of how we learn, not only in huge blocks of tissue, but even within individual cells.

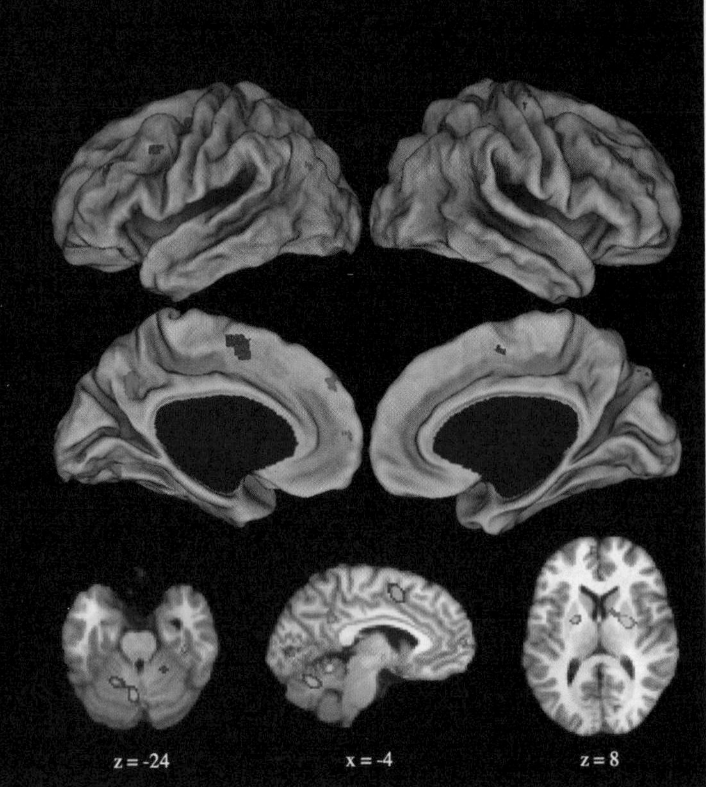

^ Blood flow reveals activity in the brain. Here, blue highlights attention-related areas that had greater blood flow when people first learned a task. Blood flow decreased in those areas as they became more familiar with the task. Red areas became more active as the task was mastered, suggesting these regions may be associated with lower externally-directed attention demands.

Rewiring

7 The brain is not one big blob of tissue. Just six to seven weeks into the development of a human embryo, the brain starts to form into different parts. Later, these areas will each take on different roles. Consider the prefrontal cortex. It's the region right behind your forehead. That's where you solve problems. Other parts of the cortex (the outer layer of the brain) help process sights and sounds. Deep in the brain, the hippocampus helps store memories. It also helps you figure out where things are located around you.

8 Scientists can see what part of the brain is active by using functional magnetic resonance imaging, or fMRI. At the heart of every fMRI device is a strong magnet. It allows the device to detect changes in blood flow. Now, when a scientist asks a volunteer to perform a particular task—such as playing a game or learning something new—the machine reveals where blood flow within the brain is highest. That boost in blood flow highlights which cells are busy working.

9 Many brain scientists use fMRI to map brain activity. Others use another type of brain scan, known as positron emission tomography, or PET. Experts have performed dozens of such studies. Each looked at how specific areas of the brain responded to specific tasks.

10 Nathan Spreng did something a little different: He decided to study the studies. Spreng is a neuroscientist at Cornell University in Ithaca, N.Y. A neuroscientist studies the brain and nervous system. Spreng wanted to know how the brain changes—how it morphs a little bit—as we learn.

11 He teamed up with two other researchers. Together, they analyzed 38 of those earlier studies. Each study had used an fMRI or PET scan to probe which regions of the brain turn on when people learn new tasks.

12 Areas that allow people to pay attention became most active as someone began a new task. But those attention areas became less active over time. Meanwhile, areas of the brain linked with daydreaming and mind-wandering became more active as people became more familiar with a task.

13 "At the beginning, you require a lot of focused attention," Spreng says. Learning to swing a bat requires a great deal of focus when you first try to hit a ball. But the more you practice, Spreng says, the less you have to think about what you're doing.

14 Extensive practice can even allow a person to perform a task while thinking about other things—or about nothing at all. A professional pianist, for example, can play a complex piece of music without thinking about which notes to play next. In fact, stopping to think about the task can actually interfere with a flawless performance. This is what musicians, athletes and others often refer to as being "in the zone."

Cells that fire together, wire together

15 Spreng's findings involve the whole brain. However, those changes actually reflect what's happening at the level of individual cells.

16 The brain is made up of billions of nerve cells, called neurons. These cells are chatty. They "talk" to each other, mostly using chemical messengers. Incoming **signals** cause a listening neuron to *fire* or send signals of its own. A cell fires when an electrical signal travels through it. The signal moves away from what is called the *cell body*, down through a long structure called an *axon*. When the signal reaches the end of the axon, it triggers the release of those chemical messengers. The chemicals then leap across a tiny gap. This triggers the next cell to fire. And on it goes.

17 As we learn something new, cells that send and receive information about the task become more and more efficient. It

Reading Environmental Print

"Learning Rewires the Brain" includes graphics that are explained with captions. Consider how the visual and text elements work together to convey meaning.

Use a dictionary or indicate another strategy you used that helped you determine meaning.

signals (SIHG nuhlz) *n.*

MEANING:

⌄ Chemical messengers—called neurotransmitters—leave the end of one nerve cell and jump across a gap to stimulate the next nerve cell.

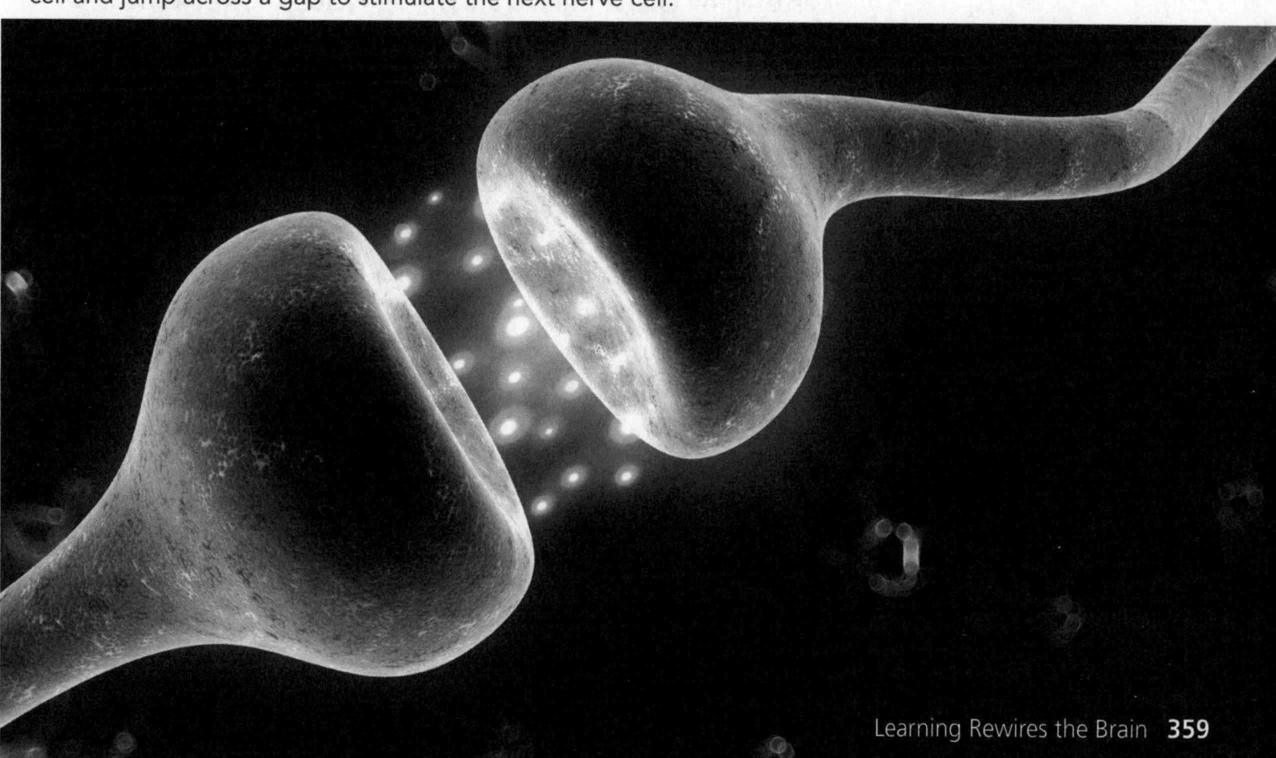

takes less effort for them to signal the next cell about what's going on. In a sense, the neurons become wired together.

18 Spreng detected that wiring. As cells in a brain area related to some task became more efficient, they used less energy to chat. This allowed more neurons in the "daydreaming" region of the brain to rev up their activity.

19 Neurons can signal to several neighbors at once. For example, one neuron might **transmit** information about the location of a baseball pitch that's flying toward you. Meanwhile, other neurons alert your muscles to get ready to swing the bat. When those neurons fire at the same time, connections between them strengthen. That improves your ability to connect with the ball.

Use a dictionary or indicate another strategy you used that helped you determine meaning.

transmit (TRANZ miht) *v.*

MEANING:

Learning while you slumber

20 The brain doesn't shut down overnight. In fact, catching some zzz's can dramatically improve learning. That's because as we sleep, our brains store memories and new information from the previous day. So a poor night's sleep can hurt our ability to remember new things. Until recently, however, researchers didn't know why.

21 A group of scientists at the University of Heidelberg in Germany provided the first clues. Specific cells in the hippocampus—that region involved in storing memories—fired when mice slept, the scientists found. But the cells didn't fire normally. Instead, electrical signals spontaneously fired near the middle of an axon, then traveled back in the direction of the cell body. In other words, the cells fired in reverse.

22 This boosted learning. It did so by making connections between cells stronger. Again, the action sort of wired together the cells. Research by Olena Bukalo and Doug Fields showed how it happens. They are neuroscientists at the National Institutes of Child Health and Human Development in Bethesda, MD.

23 Working with tissue from rat brains, the scientists electrically stimulated nerve axons. Carefully, they stimulated them just in the middle. The electrical signals then traveled in reverse. That is just what the German scientists had seen.

24 This reverse signaling made the neuron less sensitive to signals from its neighbors, the experts found. This made it harder for the cell to fire, which gave the neuron a chance to recharge, Bukalo explains. When she then applied electric stimulation near the cell body, the neuron fired. And it did so even more strongly than it had before.

25 Cells involved in learning new information are most likely to fire in reverse during sleep, Bukalo says. The next day, they will be wired more tightly to each other. Although scientists don't know for certain, it is likely that repeated cycles of reverse firing create a

strong network of neurons. The neurons **relay** information faster and more efficiently, just as Spreng found in his study. As a result, those networks reflect an improvement in understanding or physical skill.

Use a dictionary or indicate another strategy you used that helped you determine meaning.

relay (ree LAY) *v.*

MEANING:

Firing faster

26 Neurons are the best-known cells in the brain. But they are far from the only ones. Another type, called glia, actually makes up a whopping 85 percent of brain cells. For a long time, scientists thought that glia simply held neurons together. (Indeed, "glia" take their name from the Greek word for glue.) But recent research by Fields, Bukalo's colleague at the National Institutes of Child Health and Human Development, reveals that glial cells also become active during learning.

27 One type of glial cell wraps around nerve axons. (Note: Not all axons have this wrapping.) These wrapping cells create what's known as a myelin sheath. Myelin is made of protein and fatty substances. It insulates the axons. Myelin is a bit like the plastic coating that jackets the copper wires in your home. That insulation prevents electrical signals from inappropriately leaking out of one wire (or axon) and into another.

28 In axons, the myelin sheath has a second role: It actually speeds the electrical signals along. That's because glial cells force a signal to jump from one spot on the axon to the next. As it hops between glial cells, the signal moves faster. It's kind of like flying from one spot to the next, instead of taking the train.

29 Fields has found that when new skills are learned, the amount of myelin insulating an axon increases. This happens as the size of individual glial cells increases. New glial cells also may be added to bare axons. These changes improve the ability of a neuron to signal. And that leads to better learning.

30 A thicker myelin sheath helps improve all types of brainy tasks. These include reading, creating memories, playing a musical instrument and more. A thicker sheath is also linked with better decision-making.

31 Nerve cells continue to add myelin well into adulthood, as our brains continue to grow and develop. The prefrontal cortex, for example—that area where decisions are made—gains myelin well into a person's 20s. This may explain why teens don't always make the best decisions. They're not finished sheathing their nerve cells. But there is hope. And getting enough sleep certainly can help. Glial cells, like neurons, seem to change most during certain stages of sleep.

32 Exactly what causes the glial cells to change remains a mystery. Fields and his colleagues are hard at work to figure that out. It's exciting, he says, to launch into a whole new field of research.

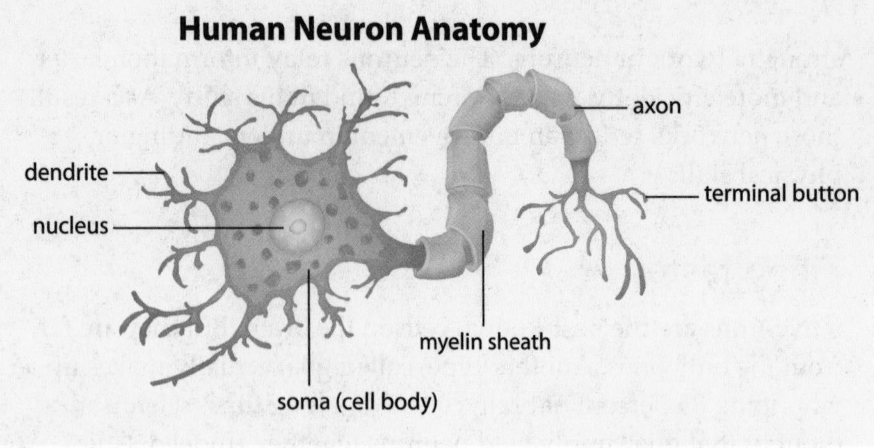

^ Artist's depiction of a nerve cell in the brain. Glial cells wrap around the axon like a blanket, forming the myelin sheath. As people learn, brain cells change in ways that increase the speed and efficiency with which signals travel down the nerve cells.

Slow and steady

33 These changes in the brain allow for faster, stronger signaling between neurons as the brain gains new skills. But the best way to speed up those signals is to introduce new information to our noggins—slowly.

34 Many students instead try to memorize lots of information the night before a test. Cramming may get them through the test. But the students won't remember the information for very long, says Hadley Bergstrom. He is a neuroscientist at the National Institutes of Alcohol Abuse and Alcoholism in Rockville, MD.

35 It's important to spread out learning over many days, his work shows. That means learning a little bit at a time. Doing so allows links between neurons to steadily strengthen. It also allows glial cells time to better insulate axons.

36 Even an "aha!" moment—when something suddenly becomes clear — doesn't come out of nowhere. Instead, it is the result of a steady accumulation of information. That's because adding new information opens up memories associated with the task. Once those memory neurons are active, they can form new connections, explains Bergstrom. They also can form stronger connections within an existing network. Over time, your level of understanding increases until you suddenly "get" it.

37 Like Fields and Bukalo, Bergstrom stresses the importance of sleep in forming the new memories needed to gain knowledge. So the next time you study for a test, start learning new information a few days ahead of time. The night before, give your brain a break and go to bed early. It will allow your brain a chance to cement that new information into its cells. And that should boost your chances of doing well.

Response

1. **Personal Connections** Cite an example of a detail or description in this article that matches your own experience with learning. Explain your choice.

Work on your own to answer the questions in your notebook. Use text evidence to support your responses.

Comprehension

2. **Reading Check (a)** What do scientists now know about the development of the brain throughout life, not just during the teen years? **(b)** What is the best way to prepare for a big test, according to the article?

3. **Strategy: Make Connections (a)** Cite one example each of a personal connection, a textual connection, and a societal connection you made while reading this article. **(b)** In what ways did making connections add to your reading experience? Explain.

Analysis and Discussion

4. **Analyze** How do our brain cells "talk" to each other, or send information?

5. **(a)** What do athletes, musicians, and other experts mean when they say they are "in the zone"? **(b) Connect** What neurological state does being "in the zone" reflect? Explain.

6. **(a) Compare and Contrast** What does research suggest about the learning abilities of those who get enough sleep and those who don't? Explain. **(b) Extend** Cite at least two ways in which information like the research explained in this article might affect people's lives. Explain your thinking, citing supporting evidence from the article.

7. **Get Ready for Close Reading** Choose a passage from the text that you find especially interesting or important. You'll discuss the passage with your group during Close-Read activities.

WORKING AS A GROUP
Discuss your responses to the Analysis and Discussion questions with your group. If you have difficulty expressing yourself, use gestures or make drawings to get your ideas across. You might also ask your group members to help you find the words you need.

EQ Notes Can people really change?

What has this science article taught you about people's ability to change? Go to your Essential Question Notes and record your observations and thoughts about "Learning Rewires the Brain."

 TEKS

5.E. Make connections to personal experiences, ideas in other texts, and society.

6.A. Describe personal connections to a variety of sources, including self-selected texts.

6.C. Use text evidence to support an appropriate response.

LEARNING REWIRES THE BRAIN

Close Read

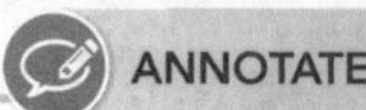

PRACTICE **Complete the following activities. Use text evidence to support your responses.**

1. **Present and Discuss** With your group, share the passages from the science article that you found especially interesting. Discuss what you notice, the questions you have, and the conclusions you reach. For example, you might focus on the following passages:
   - Paragraphs 12–14: Discuss the science behind the expression "practice makes perfect."
   - Paragraphs 17–18: Discuss the idea that neurons "chat." Consider why the author uses that comparison.
2. **Reflect on Your Learning** What new ideas or insights did you uncover during your second reading of the text?

NOTEBOOK

LANGUAGE STUDY

Concept Vocabulary

Why These Words? The vocabulary words are related.

signals	transmit	relay

1. With your group, determine what the words have in common. Write your ideas.
2. Add another word that fits the category. ____________________
3. Use each vocabulary word in a sentence. Include context clues that hint at each word's meaning.

Word Study

Latin Root: *-sign-* The vocabulary word *signal* includes the root *-sign-*. This root comes from the Latin word *signum*, a noun meaning "identifying mark." Use a print or online dictionary to determine the meanings, usage, and pronunciations of the following words that include the root *-sign-*: *signature, insignia, design.* Explain how the meaning of the Latin word *signum* is evident in the English word. Also, note when the *g* sound is pronounced and when it is silent.

WORD NETWORK

Add words that are related to transformations from the text to your Word Network.

TEKS

2.A. Use print or digital resources to determine the meaning, syllabication, pronunciation, word origin, and part of speech.

2.C. Determine the meaning and usage of grade-level academic English words derived from Greek and Latin roots such as *omni, log/logue, gen, vid/vis, phil, luc,* and *sens/sent*.

8.D.iii. Analyze characteristics and structural elements of informational text, including organizational patterns that support multiple topics, categories, and subcategories.

9.C. Analyze the author's use of print and graphic features to achieve specific purposes.

Genre / Text Elements

Organizational Patterns Many works of science journalism feature organizational patterns that break a broad topic down into subtopics, categories, and subcategories. Often, **print and graphic features** show how the text is organized. These elements also illustrate ideas, add information in compact ways, and help readers navigate the text to better understand complex topics.

TIP: An informational text may have many categories and subcategories and may use a variety of organizational patterns to clarify and order concepts, facts, examples, and other details.

EXAMPLE Organizational Pattern and Print and Graphic Features

- Broad topic, indicated by title
  - Multiple categories, indicated by heads within the text
    - Multiple subcategories, emphasized and further illustrated by print and graphic features

NOTEBOOK

INTERACTIVITY

PRACTICE Work together to complete the activity and answer the questions.

1. **Analyze** Use the chart to make an outline of the article.

Broad Topic:
Categories:
Subcategories:

2. **Analyze** Review the graphic features in each section. How does the information in each graphic feature relate to the text in the section? Using your observations, explain the role graphic features play in the organizational pattern of the article.

3. **(a) Connect** Explain why the subhead "Cells that fire together, wire together" is an effective name for the section. **(b) Distinguish** Which subhead in the article would lead you to information about why it's best to learn a little bit every day? Explain.

4. **Analyze** In what ways does the image with the caption beginning "Blood flow reveals..." clarify information presented elsewhere in the article? Explain.

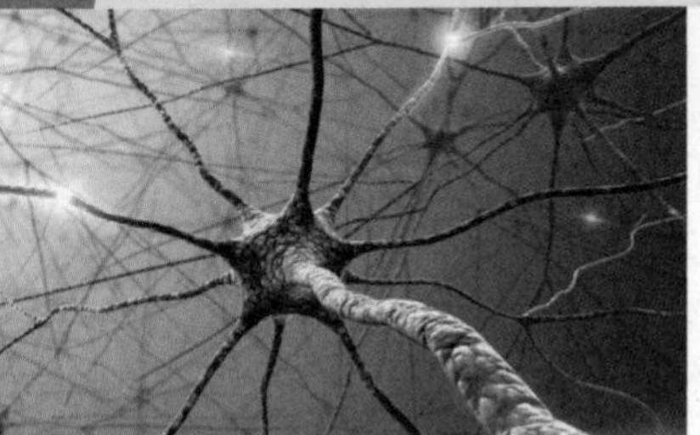

LEARNING REWIRES THE BRAIN

Author's Craft

Rhetorical Devices and Logical Fallacies Rhetorical devices are patterns of words that stress certain ideas and engage readers' interest. These devices show correct, careful reasoning. Writers may also use **logical fallacies,** language that shows faulty reasoning. Rhetorical devices strengthen informational texts; in many cases, logical fallacies weaken them.

PURPOSES OF RHETORICAL DEVICES AND LOGICAL FALLACIES		
TERM AND DEFINITION	RHETORICAL DEVICE OR FALLACY?	PURPOSE
Direct Address: use of "you" to speak directly to the reader	Rhetorical Device	engage readers; make them feel a connection to the text and author
Analogy: extended comparison between an unfamiliar concept and a familiar one	Rhetorical Device	explain unfamiliar ideas by showing connections to things readers already know
Sweeping Generalization: statement that applies a general rule too broadly	Fallacy	pull readers in with a dramatic statement; can be used unfairly to present information in a false way or create a stereotype

 NOTEBOOK

PRACTICE Work on your to answer the questions. Then, share your responses with your group.

1. **(a) Analyze** Explain how the first sentence of the article could be considered a sweeping generalization. **(b) Evaluate** What purpose does this generalization serve? **(c) Analyze** How does the rest of the passage add information that makes the sentence less of a fallacy? Explain.

2. **(a) Analyze** Explain why paragraph 2 could also be considered a sweeping generalization. **(b) Evaluate** What purpose does this generalization serve?

3. **Analyze** Explain the analogy used in paragraph 27 —what two concepts are compared? What specific purpose does the analogy serve in this article?

4. **Analyze** What rhetorical device does the author use in paragraph 37? What purpose does this device serve? Explain.

 TEKS

2.C. Determine the meaning and usage of grade-level academic English words derived from Greek and Latin roots such as *omni, log/logue, gen, vid/vis, phil, luc,* and *sens/sent.*

9.G. Explain the purpose of rhetorical devices such as direct address and rhetorical questions and logical fallacies such as loaded language and sweeping generalizations.

12.G. Differentiate between paraphrasing and plagiarism when using source materials.

12.J. Use an appropriate mode of delivery, whether written, oral, or multimodal, to present results.

Research

A **research report** is a type of nonfiction that presents information gathered from a variety of sources and conveys a clear controlling idea, or thesis.

ASSIGNMENT

Work with your group to prepare a **research report** related to text features or information from "Learning Rewires the Brain." Choose one of the following options:

◯ **Image Gallery** the art of scientific illustration

Conduct research about the types of illustrations included in the article. You might learn about the history and use of these types of images.

◯ **Word Origins** Greek origins and roots of scientific words

Conduct research about the Greek origins of three scientific terms—such as *neuron*, *axon*, and *hippocampus*—used in the article.

As you work on your report together, make sure every group member has a significant role to play in researching, planning, writing, and presenting the finished product.

Choose a Mode of Delivery After you gather information, discuss the best way to organize and present it. Mark your choice.

◯ **Written Report:** Write a polished text that includes an introduction in which you state your thesis, body paragraphs in which you present your findings, and a conclusion in which you restate your thesis.

◯ **Oral Presentation:** Write a set of detailed notes you can use to deliver your findings orally.

◯ **Multimodal Presentation:** Use slide presentation software or a set of posters to present verbal text. Enhance the information by including media elements, such as videos, music, photos, or maps.

Paraphrase, Don't Plagiarize Plagiarism is the act of using the language or ideas of another person without permission. Follow these steps to avoid plagiarism:

- Properly cite information and ideas that are not common knowledge. Use the citation style that your teacher prefers.
- **Paraphrase,** or restate the ideas of others in your own words. Note that even when you paraphrase, you must still cite the source because the ideas are not your own.
- If you want to use an author's exact words, set them in quotation marks and cite the source accurately.

EQ Notes Before moving on to a new selection, go to your Essential Question Notes and record any additional thoughts or observations you may have about "Learning Rewires the Brain."

TRYING TO NAME WHAT DOESN'T CHANGE

Poetry

Lyric poetry has a musical quality and expresses the thoughts and feelings of a single speaker. **Narrative poetry** tells a story.

I MYSELF

LYRIC POETRY

Author's Purpose

- to use focused, imaginative language and form to capture the emotions or realization of a moment

Characteristics

- themes and insights into the nature of life
- imagery, or sensory language that creates word pictures
- may have story-like elements, such as characters and dialogue
- speaker, or voice that "tells" the poem
- language that has multiple layers of meaning
- figurative language and sound devices

Structure

- divided into lines, which may be organized into stanzas

NARRATIVE POETRY

Author's Purpose

- to use focused, imaginative language to tell a story and express an insight

Characteristics

- storytelling elements, including characters, conflict, setting, and plot
- themes and insights into the nature of life
- imagery, or sensory language, that creates word pictures
- speaker, or voice that "tells" the poem
- language that has multiple layers of meaning
- figurative language and sound devices

Structure

- divided into lines which may be organized into stanzas

TEKS

7.A. Infer multiple themes within and across texts using text evidence.

8.A. Demonstrate knowledge of literary genres such as realistic fiction, adventure stories, historical fiction, mysteries, humor, myths, fantasy, and science fiction.

Genre / Text Elements

Imagery and Themes **Imagery** is language that uses details related to our senses to create word pictures. It is one of the main ways in which poets convey **themes**, or deeper meanings. A poem's title and direct statements the speaker makes also help to convey themes. Like any work of literature, a single poem may express multiple themes. Consider the example.

TIP: A theme is not just a word or phrase. It is a statement that can be applied to other literary works or to life in general.

EXAMPLE

Winter Blooms

At summer's end, sunflowers set,
their petals browned and scattered.
Husks of wildflowers rustle,
their seeds a feast for hungry jays

who cry, "Eat, eat!"
They cry, "Me! Mine!

Their feathers are the dark blue
of sky as night falls early, of shadows
on fields locked in snow,
of the cold as winter blooms.

Images of dead flowers, hungry birds, and the coming of winter create a timeline of seasonal change. Two themes the reader may infer: 1. *The cycle of the seasons is part of nature's power.* 2. *Endings and beginnings are connected.*

PRACTICE Work with a partner to read the poems and answer the questions.

Child in Rain	**I Left Her Behind**
If you see a child who scrambles wide-eyed And wondering across fields of grass, Just to watch a rainstorm passing, Applauding the raindrops with laughter, Tasting rain on her tongue like licorice tea, Please, won't you send her home to me? I have not forgotten who I am.	During the sudden storms of time's passage, I left her behind. Now she pauses with caution at every corner, Worry-eyed and wondering, The girl I was does not know me, and I no longer know her.

1. What theme about identity do both poems express? Which details help express that theme?

2. What theme about becoming an adult do both poems express? How are the themes of the two poems different? Explain.

Trying to Name What Doesn't Change

I Myself

Concept Vocabulary

As you read the poems, you will encounter these words.

explode	shrinking	distorting

Print Resources A **thesaurus** is a reference book about words. A typical thesaurus entry gives a word's part of speech, and lists synonyms and antonyms.

SAMPLE THESAURUS ENTRY

vivify *v.* synonyms: energize, enliven, animate, revive, invigorate antonyms: deaden, dull, kill

Here, synonyms *(energize, revive)* and antonyms *(deaden, dull)* indicate the meaning of the verb *vivify*, which is "give life to."

PRACTICE As you read, use a thesaurus to determine the meanings and parts of speech of unfamiliar words.

Comprehension Strategy

Create Mental Images

When you read, deepen your understanding by creating mental images, or picturing scenes in your mind. To create mental images, notice details that relate to sight, hearing, taste, touch, and smell. Allow these details to form pictures in your mind.

EXAMPLE

Notice details related to sight and smell in these lines. Use them to imagine the scene in your mind.

The widow in *the tilted house / spices her soup with cinnamon.*

PRACTICE As you read, look for details that help you create mental images and deepen your understanding. Mark the details and jot down notes in the open space next to the text.

TEKS

2.A. Use print or digital resources to determine the meaning, syllabication, pronunciation, word origin, and part of speech.

5.D. Create mental images to deepen understanding.

About the Poems

Trying to Name What Doesn't Change

BACKGROUND
"Trying to Name What Doesn't Change" was first published in Nye's 1995 collection *The Words Under the Words*. It is an example of the poet's interest in what she has called "local life, random characters met on the streets . . ." In this poem, which begins simply and gradually becomes more complex, the speaker shares different perspectives on the same subject: change.

Naomi Shihab Nye was born in St. Louis, Missouri, in 1952. Her father was a Palestinian refugee and her mother an American of German and Swiss descent. Her poetry offers a fresh perspective on ordinary people and everyday events. She lives in San Antonio, Texas.

I Myself

BACKGROUND
"I Myself," or "Yo Mismo" in the original Spanish, was translated into English in 1977. In 1985, as he accepted the Prince of Asturias Award for Literature, González spoke of himself as two people: "Here stands only the man who has contrived the words that give life to the poet." He also observed that "the way we are . . . depends on others more than we usually think." Similar ideas about human nature and identity echo in this powerful poem.

Ángel González (1925–2008) was a major 20th-century Spanish poet. He was born in Oviedo, Spain, and grew up during the Spanish Civil War and the rule of the military dictator Francisco Franco. González trained and worked as a lawyer, but eventually began writing poetry. His work earned immediate critical acclaim. González went on to publish numerous poetry collections and to win many important literary honors. For almost 20 years, he was a professor of contemporary Spanish literature at the University of New Mexico, dividing his time between the United States and Spain.

LYRIC POETRY

Trying to Name What Doesn't Change

Naomi Shihab Nye

AUDIO

ANNOTATE

Roselva says the only thing that doesn't change
is train tracks. She's sure of it.
The train changes, or the weeds that grow up spidery
by the side, but not the tracks.
I've watched one for three years, she says,
and it doesn't curve, doesn't break, doesn't grow.

Peter isn't sure. He saw an abandoned track
near Sabinas, Mexico, and says a track without a train
is a changed track. The metal wasn't shiny anymore.
The wood was split and some of the ties were gone.

Every Tuesday on Morales Street
butchers crack the necks of a hundred hens.
The widow in the tilted house
spices her soup with cinnamon.
Ask her what doesn't change.

Stars **explode**.
The rose curls up as if there is fire in the petals.
The cat who knew me is buried under the bush.

The train whistle still wails its ancient sound
but when it goes away, **shrinking** back
from the walls of the brain,
it takes something different with it every time.

Use a thesaurus or indicate another strategy you used that helped you determine meaning.

explode (ehks PLOHD) *v.*

MEANING:

shrinking (SHRINK ihng) *v.*

MEANING:

I Myself

by Ángel González
translated by Donald D. Walsh

I myself
met me face to face at a crossing.
I saw on me
a stubborn expression, and a hardness
in the eyes, like
a man who'd stop at nothing.

The road was narrow, and I said to me:
"Stand aside, make
way,
for I have to get to such and such a place."

But I was not strong, and my enemy
fell upon me with all the weight of my flesh,
and I was left defeated in the ditch.

That's the way it happened, and I never could
reach that place, and ever since
my body walks by itself, getting lost,
distorting whatever plans I make.

 AUDIO

 ANNOTATE

Use a thesaurus or indicate another strategy you used that helped you determine meaning.

distorting (dih STAWRT ihng) *v.*

MEANING:

NOTEBOOK

Work on your own to answer the questions in your notebook. Use text evidence to support your responses.

Response

1. **Personal Connections** Did you relate to one of these poems more than the other? Explain.

Comprehension

2. **Reading Check (a)** In "Trying to Name What Doesn't Change," what does Roselva say is the one thing that doesn't change? **(b)** Whom does the speaker meet in "I Myself"?

3. **Strategy: Create Mental Images (a)** Which passages in each poem were you able to picture most clearly? Why? **(b)** In what ways did this strategy deepen your understanding of the two poems?

WORKING AS A GROUP

Discuss your responses to the Analysis and Discussion questions with your group. As you listen to one another's ideas, pause to discuss unfamiliar words. These may be basic terms or ones that are more complex. Learn the words and incorporate them into your conversation.

Analysis and Discussion

4. **(a) Contrast** In "Trying to Name What Doesn't Change," what different details do Roselva and Peter notice about train tracks? **(b) Analyze** Explain how these contrasting details support the conclusions each character draws about the tracks.

5. **(a)** In lines 16-17 of "Trying to Name What Doesn't Change," what happens to the stars, the rose, and the cat? **(b) Connect** What quality do these events share?

6. **(a) Analyze** In the third stanza of "I Myself," why is the speaker defeated? **(b) Analyze Cause and Effect** What happens to the speaker as a result? **(c) Interpret** What does this poem suggest about the reasons people fail? Explain.

7. **Get Ready for Close Reading** Choose a passage from each poem that you find especially interesting or important. You'll discuss the passages with your group during Close-Read activities.

EQ Notes Can people really change?

What have you learned about transformations from reading these poems? Go to your Essential Question Notes and record your observations and thoughts about "Trying to Name What Doesn't Change" and "I Myself."

TEKS

5.D. Create mental images to deepen understanding.

6.A. Describe personal connections to a variety of sources, including self-selected texts.

6.C. Use text evidence to support an appropriate response.

TRYING TO NAME WHAT DOESN'T CHANGE • I MYSELF

Close Read

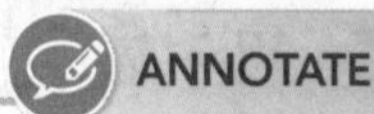
ANNOTATE

PRACTICE **Complete the following activities. Use text evidence to support your responses.**

1. **Present and Discuss** With your group, share the passages from the poems that you found especially interesting. Discuss what you notice, the questions you have, and the conclusions you reach. For example, you might focus on the following passages:
   - Lines 11–15 of "Trying to Name What Doesn't Change": Discuss the action described in this stanza and how it connects to the rest of the poem.
   - Lines 19–22 of "Trying to Name What Doesn't Change": Discuss the effect of the train whistle and what it might be taking away from the speaker.
   - Lines 1–6 of "I Myself": Discuss what the speaker's other self is like, and why he might be this way.
2. **Reflect on Your Learning** What new ideas or insights did you uncover during your second reading of the texts?

NOTEBOOK

LANGUAGE STUDY

Concept Vocabulary

Why These Words? The vocabulary words are related.

explode	shrinking	distorting

1. With your group, determine what the words have in common. Write your ideas.
2. Add another word that fits the category. ____________
3. Use each word in a sentence that describes a change.

Word Study

Latin Root: *-tort-* In "I Myself," the speaker says his body is *distorting* his plans. The word *distorting* contains the root *-tort-*, which means "twist." Using this knowledge, write a definition of *distorting*. Then, use a dictionary to find meanings for the words *retort* and *contort*. Explain how the root *-tort-* adds to the meaning of each word.

WORD NETWORK

Add words that are related to transformations from the text to your Word Network.

TEKS

2.A. Use print or digital resources to determine the meaning, syllabication, pronunciation, word origin, and part of speech.

2.C. Determine the meaning and usage of grade-level academic English words derived from Greek and Latin roots such as *omni, log/logue, gen, vid/vis, phil, luc,* and *sens/sent.*

6.F. Respond using newly acquired vocabulary as appropriate.

TIP A valid interpretation of a theme must account for all of the details in a work. If a detail doesn't fit your interpretation, re-evaluate your ideas.

Genre / Text Elements

Imagery and Theme Imagery that shares certain qualities or suggests related ideas helps to convey a poem's **theme**, or deeper message. Readers examine imagery, as well as titles and any direct statements, to infer the themes of poems.

EXAMPLES: Related Images

POEM	EXAMPLES FROM THE POEMS	SHARED QUALITIES
Trying to Name What Doesn't Change	abandoned track; track without a train	absence, emptiness, being left behind
I Myself	a stubborn expression; a hardness in the eyes	harshness, hostility

PRACTICE Work together as a group to complete the activity and answer the questions.

1. **Analyze** Use the chart to analyze the ideas suggested by the images in "Trying to Name What Doesn't Change." One item has been done for you. What similar ideas connect all of these images? Explain.

IMAGE	IDEAS SUGGESTED
weeds that grow up spidery (line 3)	*weeds* = decay and neglect; *spidery* makes the image more visual and scarier
metal wasn't shiny anymore. / The wood was split and some of the ties were gone. (lines 9–10) *tilted house* (line 13)	
Stars explode. (line 16) *The rose curls up as if there is fire in the petals.* (line 17)	

2. **(a) Analyze** What kind of change is suggested by the word *widow* (line 13)? **(b) Connect** How is this type of change reflected in other images in this poem? Explain.

3. **(a) Connect** How do the poem's details reflect its title—what idea does the speaker try to name? **(b) Make Inferences** Write a statement that expresses this idea as a theme. **(c) Make Inferences** What other theme might the poem express? Explain.

4. **Make Inferences** In "I Myself," the speaker refers to his other self as "a man who'd stop at nothing" and "my enemy." What theme do these details suggest? Explain.

7.A. Infer multiple themes within and across texts using text evidence.

TRYING TO NAME WHAT DOESN'T CHANGE • I MYSELF

Author's Craft

Poetic Structures and Purpose A **line** is a horizontal group of words. It is the most basic structure in a poem. **Stanzas** are groups of lines that are separated by space. The structures of lines and stanzas help to shape a poem's meaning and fulfill the poet's purpose for writing.

Poetic Structure: Stanzas

QUALITY	DETAILS
Stanzas are named for the number of lines they contain and may be as short as one line.	two-lines = *couplet*; three-lines = *tercet*; four-lines = *quatrain*; five-lines = *cinquain*; six-lines = *sestet*
Each stanza usually expresses a single, focused idea.	• In a lyric poem, each stanza may offer a new thought. • In a narrative poem, each stanza may show a new stage in the plot.

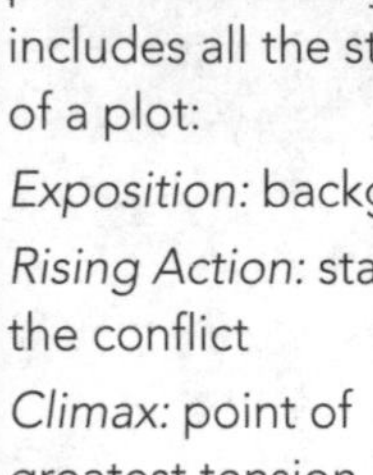

TIP: A narrative poem tells a story that includes all the stages of a plot:

Exposition: background

Rising Action: start of the conflict

Climax: point of greatest tension

Resolution: end of the conflict

NOTEBOOK

PRACTICE Work with your group to answer the questions.

1. Use the chart to complete the activity. **(a) Label** Identify each type of stanza (tercet, etc.) used in "Trying to Name What Doesn't Change." **(b) Analyze** Explain the main idea expressed in each stanza.

STANZA TYPE	IDEA EXPRESSED
Stanza 1:	One point of view:
Stanza 2:	Another point of view:
Stanza 3:	Speaker's Observations:
Stanza 4:	Speaker's Observations:
Stanza 5:	Speaker's Insight:

2. **Analyze** Explain why "I Myself" is a narrative with a complete plot that includes exposition, rising action, climax, and resolution.

3. **Generalize** Using these poems as examples, explain how the structure of a poem helps poets present their ideas clearly. Cite specific details.

TEKS

9.B. Analyze how the use of text structure contributes to the author's purpose.

TRYING TO NAME WHAT DOESN'T CHANGE

I MYSELF

Compare Lyric and Narrative Poetry

Multiple Choice

NOTEBOOK

These questions are based on "Trying to Name What Doesn't Change" and "I Myself." Choose the best answer to each question.

1. Which answer choice best describes the characters the speakers encounter in the two poems?

A In "Trying to Name...," the speaker encounters a widow. In "I Myself," the speaker encounters a stranger.

B In both poems, the speakers encounter someone they would rather not see.

C In "Trying to Name...," the speaker encounters several other characters. In "I Myself," the speaker encounters himself.

D In "Trying to Name...," the speaker encounters a butcher. In "I Myself," the speaker encounters Roselva and Peter.

2. Read stanza 4 from "Trying to Name..." and stanza 3 from "I Myself." Which statement BEST describes both stanzas?

***from* Trying to Name What Doesn't Change**

Stars explode.
The rose curls up as if there is fire in the
petals.
The cat who knew me is buried under
the bush

***from* I Myself**

But I was not strong, and my enemy
fell upon me with all the weight of my
flesh,
and I was left defeated in the ditch.

F Both stanzas give different examples of the same idea.

G Both stanzas feature two different characters' points of view.

H Both stanzas present positive aspects of change.

J Both stanzas present painful aspects of change.

3. What qualities do the two poems share?

A Both tell a complete story.

B Both organize events in chronological order.

C Both feature story elements, such as characters.

D Both attempt to name something important.

TEKS

6.B. Write responses that demonstrate understanding of texts, including comparing sources within and across genres.

7.A. Infer multiple themes within and across texts using text evidence.

NOTEBOOK

Short Response

Answer the questions in your notebook. Use text evidence to support your responses.

1. **(a) Analyze** In "Trying to Name What Doesn't Change," how are exploded stars, the curled-up rose, and the cat buried under a bush all examples of change? **(b) Analyze** What kinds of change, or lack of change, occurs in "I Myself"?

2. **(a) Contrast** In "I Myself," the speaker refers to vague locations (*such and such a place*, and *that place*). How does this differ from the references to places in "Trying to Name What Doesn't Change"? **(b) Analyze** What is the effect of this difference?

3. **Interpret** How do you think each poem answers the question of whether change is possible? Explain.

Timed Writing

A **response to literature** is a type of essay in which you analyze a literary work and explain your interpretation.

ASSIGNMENT

Write a **response to literature** in which you explain a theme each of these poems expresses and consider how they are similar and different. Then, explain which poem you think expresses a more memorable or important theme.

5-MINUTE PLANNER

1. Read the assignment carefully and completely.
2. Decide what you want to say—your main idea or claim.
3. Decide which examples you'll use from each poem.
4. Organize your ideas, making sure to address these points:
   - Explain how the themes of two poems are similar.
   - Explain how the themes are different.
   - Explain how you feel about each poem and which one you think presents a more memorable theme.

EQ Notes Before moving on to a new selection, go to your Essential Question Notes and record any additional thoughts and observations you may have about "Trying to Name What Doesn't Change" and "I Myself."

SOURCES

- Thank You, M'am
- Trying to Name What Doesn't Change
- I Myself

Deliver a Dramatic Adaptation

A **dramatic adaptation** is a play that is based on another literary work, such as a novel, work of literary nonfiction, short story, or poem. An adaptation brings a text to life and interprets it in a new way.

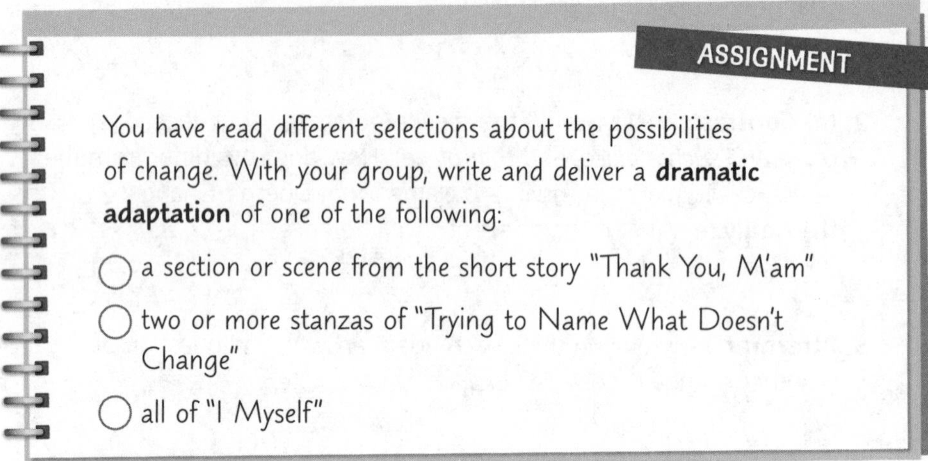

ASSIGNMENT

You have read different selections about the possibilities of change. With your group, write and deliver a **dramatic adaptation** of one of the following:

○ a section or scene from the short story "Thank You, M'am"

○ two or more stanzas of "Trying to Name What Doesn't Change"

○ all of "I Myself"

Plan With Your Group

Choose a Text Discuss the selections with your group and choose one to interpret as a play. As a group, discuss how to bring the text to life for an audience:

- What aspects of the text need to be explained by a narrator?
- How can you convey the thoughts of characters who do not speak aloud in the text?
- What language from the text do you want to use exactly? What vocabulary will you modify?

Write and Rehearse

Write the Script Follow play format and write parts for a narrator and characters. Include stage directions that tell actors how to deliver their lines.

Rehearse Practice your delivery and give one another feedback about the performance. Consider these questions:

- Is the **tone**, or emotional attitude, of each performance effective? Does it fit the character and situation?
- Does each performer use his or her voice to show a character's unique personality?
- Can improvements be made to the script, including revisions to vocabulary, that would help performers make better choices about tone and voice?

Use your rehearsal to revise the script and improve your delivery.

Deliver Your Adaptation

Present to the Class Use the following tips to make your presentation effective and engaging.

- Avoid speaking in a monotone; instead, vary the highs and lows of your voice to express emotion and convey an appropriate attitude, or tone.
- Vary the volume of your voice and also slow down or speed up to stress important vocabulary, phrases, and lines.
- Use body language and natural gestures that reinforce the meanings of your lines and add to the interest and emotional impact of the performance.

Respond to Questions After presenting, take time to discuss the presentation with your audience. Invite classmates to ask questions about choices you made in your adaptation. Listen carefully and respond thoughtfully. You might demonstrate your understanding of the questions by restating them in slightly different words before responding. For example, use these sentence starters to demonstrate your understanding before you answer:

***It seems that you're asking me about* _____________.**

***If I understand your question, you'd like me to discuss* _____________.**

Explain how you interpreted the text, which vocabulary you wanted to emphasize, and how you decided to use your voices to show your interpretation of the original text.

Listen and Evaluate

Listen Actively As other groups present their adaptations, pay close attention. Focus on the performers as you listen to the words they speak. Prepare for the discussion to follow each performance by taking notes, jotting down words and phrases that will remind you of observations you may want to share or questions you will ask.

Participate in Discussion When it's time to discuss a group's performance, express your thoughts in a respectful and helpful manner. Begin by saying what you liked or thought worked well, and then ask a question or make an observation about a less successful element. Continue to ask and respond to questions that build on the ideas other classmates share.

TEKS

1.A. Listen actively to interpret a message and ask clarifying questions that build on others' ideas.

1.D. Engage in meaningful discourse and provide and accept constructive feedback from others.

6.H. Respond orally or in writing with appropriate register, vocabulary, tone, and voice.

Essential Question

Can people really change?

As we go through life, we change physically. We also become more responsible and learn new skills. However, is there something inside all of us that does not change? In this section, you will choose a selection about change to read independently. Get the most from this section by establishing a purpose for reading. Ask yourself, "What do I hope to gain from my independent reading?" Here are just a few purposes you might consider:.

Read to Learn Think about the selections you have already studied. What questions do you still have about the unit topic?

Read to Enjoy Read the descriptions of the texts. Which one seems most interesting and appealing to you?

Read to Form a Position Consider your thoughts and feelings about the Essential Question. Are you still undecided about some aspect of the unit topic?

Reading Digital Texts

Digital texts like the ones you will read in this section are electronic versions of print texts. They have a variety of characteristics:

- can be read on various devices
- text can be resized
- may include annotation tools
- may have bookmarks, audio features, links, and other helpful elements

Independent Learning Strategies

Throughout your life, in school, in your community, and in your career, you will need to rely on yourself to learn and work on your own. Use these strategies to keep your focus as you read independently for sustained periods of time. Add ideas of your own for each category.

STRATEGY	MY ACTION PLAN
Create a schedule • Be aware of your deadlines. • Make a plan for each day's activities.	
Read with purpose • Use a variety of comprehension strategies to deepen your understanding. • Think about the text and how it adds to your knowledge.	
Take notes • Record key ideas and information. • Review your notes before sharing what you've learned.	

TEKS

4. Self-select text and read independently for a sustained period of time; **5.A.** Establish purpose for reading assigned and self-selected texts; **8.F.** Analyze characteristics of multimodal and digital texts.

AUDIO 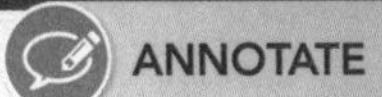 ANNOTATE  DOWNLOAD

CONTENTS

Choose one selection. Selections are available online only.

REFLECTIVE ESSAY

Little Things Are Big

Jesús Colón

Can one subway ride change a person forever?

HISTORICAL NARRATIVE

The Story of Victor d'Aveyron, the Wild Child

Eloise Montalban

Does Victor hold the key to defining what is human?

REALISTIC FICTION

A Retrieved Reformation

O. Henry

Jimmy Valentine finally proves himself in a matter of life or death.

FABLE

The Grandfather and His Little Grandson

Leo Tolstoy

SHARE YOUR INDEPENDENT LEARNING

Reflect on and evaluate the information you gained from your Independent Reading selection. Then, share what you learned with others.

Close-Read Guide

Tool Kit
Close-Read Guide and
Model Annotation

Establish your purpose for reading. Then, read the selection through at least once. Use this page to record your close-read ideas.

Selection Title: ____________________ Purpose for Reading: ____________________

Minutes Read: ____

INTERACTIVITY

Close Read the Text

Zoom in on sections you found interesting. **Annotate** what you notice. Ask yourself **questions** about the text. What can you **conclude**?

Analyze the Text

1. Think about the author's choices of literary elements, techniques, and structures. Select one and record your thoughts.

2. What characteristics of digital texts did you use as you read this selection, and in what ways? How do the characteristics of a digital text affect your reading experience? Explain.

QuickWrite

Choose a paragraph from the text that grabbed your interest. Explain the power of this passage.

Share Your Independent Learning

Essential Question

Can people really change?

When you read something independently, your understanding continues to grow as you share what you have learned with others.

 NOTEBOOK

Prepare to Share

CONNECT IT One of the most important ways to respond to a text is to notice and describe your personal reactions. Think about the text you explored independently and the ways in which it connects to your own experiences.

- What similarities and differences do you see between the text and your own life? Describe your observations.
- How do you think this text connects to the Essential Question? Describe your ideas.

Learn From Your Classmates

DISCUSS IT Share your ideas about the text you explored on your own. As you talk with others in your class, take notes about new ideas that seem important.

Reflect

EXPLAIN IT Review your notes, and mark the most important insight you gained from these writing and discussion activities. Explain how this idea adds to your understanding of transformations.

 TEKS

6.A. Describe personal connections to a variety of sources, including self-selected texts.

6.E. Interact with sources in meaningful ways such as notetaking, annotating, freewriting, or illustrating.

Short Story

ASSIGNMENT

In this unit, you have read about change and transformation from different perspectives. You also practiced writing a short story. Now, apply what you have learned.

Imagine one of the characters from this unit ten years later. What has happened to this person? Has he or she changed? Write a **short story** that explores the Essential Question:

Essential Question

Can people really change?

Review and Evaluate Your EQ Notes

INTERACTIVITY

Review your Essential Question Notes and your QuickWrite from the beginning of the unit and complete the chart. Have your ideas changed?

Yes	No
Identify at least three examples or details that made you think differently about people's ability to change.	Identify at least three examples or other details that reinforced your initial ideas about people's ability to change.
1.	1.
2.	2.
3.	3.

State your ideas now:

How might you reflect on your thinking about people's ability to change in a short story?

Share Your Perspective

The **Short Story Checklist** will help you stay on track.

PLAN Before you write, read the Checklist and make sure you understand all the items.

DRAFT As you write, pause occasionally to make sure you're meeting the Checklist requirements.

Use New Words Refer to your Word Network to vary your word choice. Also, consider using one or more of the Academic Vocabulary terms you learned at the beginning of the unit: ***omniscient, ingenious, envision, lucid, sensation.***

REVIEW AND EDIT After you have written a first draft, evaluate it against the Checklist. Make any changes needed to clarify the sequence of events or to make your characters more vivid. Then, reread your story and fix any errors you find.

EQ Notes Make sure you have pulled in details from your Essential Question Notes to support your insights about change.

SHORT STORY CHECKLIST

My short story clearly contains...

- ○ a believable, well-drawn main character and supporting characters.
- ○ a well-structured plot driven by a clearly expressed and meaningful conflict.
- ○ a consistent narrative point of view, whether first-person, third-person limited, or third-person omniscient.
- ○ dialogue that sounds natural and reveals what characters are like.
- ○ correct use of standard English conventions, including avoidance of run-ons and strictly intentional use of sentence fragments.
- ○ no punctuation or spelling errors.

10.D.i. Edit drafts using standard English conventions, including complete complex sentences with subject-verb agreement and avoidance of splices, run-ons, and fragments.

11.A. Compose literary texts such as personal narratives, fiction, and poetry, using genre characteristics and craft.

Revising and Editing

Read this draft and think about corrections the writer might make. Then, answer the questions that follow.

[1] It is a blustery spring day as the boy walks home from school. [2] Tonight is the prom, but he will not be going. [3] He leans into the wind, the wind has suddenly picked up force.

[4] Trying to change his father's decision about prom had felt like fighting a force of nature, too. [5] "Sorry, kid," his father had said, "but we just don't have the money. Another time, right?"

[6] "But Dad," the boy had protested, "There won't be another time!"

[7] His father's eyes sparked with anger. [8] His father spoke in a calm voice. [9] "I'm sorry, but sometimes things just don't work out." [10] His father turned and left and that was that.

[11] Now prom is hours away, and the boy looks around through a haze of resentment. [12] The trees, each bright with spring growth, seems to taunt him. [13] And that is the moment he sees it—a thick brown leather, wallet stuffed with cash—lying on the sidewalk. [14] The boy pauses for a moment, and then he reaches down and picks up the wallet.

1. Which revision would BEST correct the comma splice in sentence 3?

- **A** He leans into the wind and the wind has suddenly picked up force.
- **B** He leans into the wind, which has suddenly picked up force.
- **C** He leans into the wind but it has suddenly picked up force.
- **D** He leans into the wind and he has suddenly picked up force.

2. What is the best way to combine sentences 7 and 8?

- **F** His father's eyes sparked with anger, who spoke in a calm voice.
- **G** His father's eyes sparked with anger, because he spoke in a calm voice.
- **H** Although his father's eyes sparked with anger, he spoke in a calm voice.
- **J** Unless his father's eyes sparked with anger, he spoke in a calm voice.

3. What change, if any, should be made to sentence 12?

- **A** Change *each* to *one.*
- **B** Change *trees* to *tree.*
- **C** Change *seems* to *seem.*
- **D** Make no change.

4. What change, if any, should be made to correct the punctuation in sentence 13?

- **F** Delete the comma after *leather*.
- **G** Insert commas after *thick* and *wallet*.
- **H** Insert a comma after *thick* and delete the comma after *leather*.
- **J** Make no change.

Reflect on the Unit

NOTEBOOK

INTERACTIVITY

Reflect On the Unit Goals

Review your Unit Goals chart from the beginning of the unit. Then, complete the activity and answer the question.

1. In the Unit Goals chart, rate how well you meet each goal now.

2. In which goals were you most and least successful?

Reflect On the Texts

VOTE! Use this Selection Ballot to vote for three selections you would most like to see presented live, such as in a reading by the author or as a stage performance by actors. Then, discuss your choices with your group.

SELECTION BALLOT

Title	Best for live presentation (choose three)	Here's Why:
The Golden Windows		
A Christmas Carol: Scrooge and Marley		
from A Christmas Carol		
Thank You, M'am		
Learning Rewires the Brain		
Trying to Name What Doesn't Change		
I Myself		
Your Independent Reading Selection:		

Reflect On the Essential Question

Unit Scrapbook Create a class scrapbook that captures what you learned from the literature in this unit about the Essential Question: Can people really change?

- You may create a hard copy scrapbook or a digital one. Devote one page to each class member.
- Include meaningful passages from the literature you read, the writing tasks you completed, and the research you conducted. Also, include photos or other images.

TIP: Make sure your scrapbook page represents your understanding about people's ability to change. Include passages from the literary works you read, but also include your own writing and reflections.

TEKS

10.D.i. Edit drafts using standard English conventions, including complete complex sentences with subject-verb agreement and avoidance of splices, run-ons, and fragments; **10.D.iv.** Edit drafts using standard English conventions, including prepositions and prepositional phrases and their influence on subject-verb agreement; **10.D.viii.** Edit drafts using standard English conventions, including punctuation, including commas to set off words, phrases, and clauses, and semicolons.

UNIT 4

Learning From Nature

PEARSON realize™

Go ONLINE for all lessons

AUDIO

VIDEO

NOTEBOOK

ANNOTATE

INTERACTIVITY

DOWNLOAD

RESEARCH

WATCH THE VIDEO

Arctic Ice

DISCUSS IT In what way are people and animals dependent on our planet?

Write your response before sharing your ideas.

UNIT 4

UNIT INTRODUCTION

Essential Question

What is the relationship between people and nature?

MENTOR TEXT:
INFORMATIONAL TEXT–RESEARCH
Rethinking the Wild

WHOLE-CLASS LEARNING

DESCRIPTIVE ESSAY
from Silent Spring
Rachel Carson

COMPARE WITHIN GENRE

MYTH
How Grandmother Spider Stole the Sun
Michael J. Caduto and Joseph Bruchac

MYTH
How Music Came to the World
Dianne De Las Casas

PERFORMANCE TASK
WRITING PROCESS
Write a Formal Research Paper

PEER-GROUP LEARNING

POETRY COLLECTION
Turtle Watchers
Linda Hogan

Jaguar
Francisco X. Alarcón

The Sparrow
Paul Laurence Dunbar

MEDIA: PHOTO GALLERY
Urban Farming Is Growing a Greener Future
Hillary Schwei

SCIENCE FEATURE
Creature Comforts: Three Biology-Based Tips for Builders
Mary Beth Cox

MAGICAL REALISM
He—y, Come On Ou—t!
Shinichi Hoshi translated by Stanleigh Jones

PERFORMANCE TASK
SPEAKING AND LISTENING
Research and Give Instructions

INDEPENDENT LEARNING

ADVENTURE STORY
from My Side of the Mountain
Jean Craighead George

REFLECTIVE ESSAY
from An American Childhood
Annie Dillard

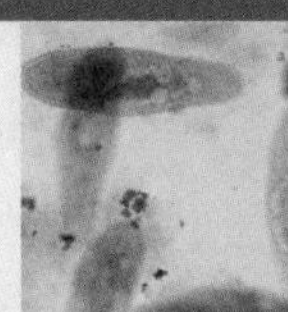

FEATURE ARTICLE
A Young Tinkerer Builds a Windmill, Electrifying a Nation
Sarah Childress

NATURE WRITING
from Of Wolves and Men
Barry Lopez

SHARE INDEPENDENT LEARNING
Share • Learn • Reflect

PERFORMANCE-BASED ASSESSMENT

Research-Based Essay

You will write a research-based essay in response to the Essential Question for the unit.

UNIT REFLECTION

Goals • Texts • Essential Question

Unit Goals

VIDEO

Throughout this unit, you will deepen your perspective about the relationship between people and nature by reading, writing, speaking, listening, and presenting. These goals will help you succeed on the Unit Performance-Based Assessment.

INTERACTIVITY

SET GOALS Rate how well you meet these goals right now. You will revisit your ratings later, when you reflect on your growth during this unit.

SCALE	1	2	3	4	5
	NOT AT ALL WELL	NOT VERY WELL	SOMEWHAT WELL	VERY WELL	EXTREMELY WELL

ESSENTIAL QUESTION	Unit Introduction	Unit Reflection
I can read selections that explore the interactions between people and nature and use what I learn as a springboard for future research.	1 2 3 4 5	1 2 3 4 5
READING	**Unit Introduction**	**Unit Reflection**
I can understand and use academic vocabulary words related to research writing.	1 2 3 4 5	1 2 3 4 5
I can recognize elements of different genres, especially descriptive essays, informational texts, and magical realism.	1 2 3 4 5	1 2 3 4 5
I can read a selection of my choice independently and make meaningful connections to other texts.	1 2 3 4 5	1 2 3 4 5
WRITING	**Unit Introduction**	**Unit Reflection**
I can write a well-documented research paper.	1 2 3 4 5	1 2 3 4 5
I can complete Timed Writing tasks with confidence.	1 2 3 4 5	1 2 3 4 5
SPEAKING AND LISTENING	**Unit Introduction**	**Unit Reflection**
I can research and give instructions.	1 2 3 4 5	1 2 3 4 5

TEKS

2.C. Determine the meaning and usage of grade-level academic English words derived from Greek and Latin roots such as *omni, log/logue, gen, vid/vis, phil, luc,* and *sens/sent.*

Academic Vocabulary: Research

Many English words have roots, or key parts, that come from ancient languages, such as Latin and Greek. Learn these roots and use the words as you respond to questions and activities in this unit.

PRACTICE Academic terms are used routinely in classrooms. Build your knowledge of these words by completing the chart.

1. **Review** each word, its root, and mentor sentences.
2. **Determine** the meaning and usage of each word using the mentor sentences and a dictionary, if needed.
3. **List** at least two related words for each word.

WORD	MENTOR SENTENCES	PREDICT MEANING	RELATED WORDS
logical GREEK ROOT: ***-log-*** "reason"; "idea"	1. The speaker's statement made no sense; it was not *logical*. 2. There must be a *logical* reason for her strange actions.		logic; illogical; logically
generate LATIN ROOT: ***-gen-*** "origin"; "race"; "family"	1. The committee wanted to *generate* enthusiasm for their project. 2. Is it possible to *generate* new life from old DNA?		
philosophy GREEK ROOTS: ***-phil- + -soph-*** "love" + "wisdom"	1. In our *philosophy* class, we study the connections between knowledge and truth. 2. The company's *philosophy* is, "the customer comes first."		
evident LATIN ROOT: ***-vid-*** "see"	1. No clues were *evident* at the crime scene; the detectives were stumped. 2. The test results were *evident*: the new drug cured the disease.		
elucidate LATIN ROOT: ***-luc-*** "bright"; "clear"	1. The mathematician attempted to *elucidate* his theory for his peers. 2. The detailed map helped *elucidate* a plan of escape.		

MENTOR TEXT | INFORMATIONAL TEXT—RESEARCH

This selection is a **research-based essay,** a type of writing in which information is supported by researched information. This is the type of writing you will develop in the Performance-Based Assessment at the end of the unit.

READ IT As you read, think about the way the writer presents information. Notice ways in which the writer weaves together elements of storytelling and informative writing.

Rethinking the Wild

AUDIO

ANNOTATE

1 There are seven billion people on the planet, and each of us has an impact on the animals and plants we share it with. It's a constant give-and-take, and people have strong opinions. Even though the correct course of action isn't always obvious, sometimes the needs of human beings have to take priority.

2 In Jon Mooallem's book *Wild Ones,* he describes the attempt of one organization to save the whooping crane from extinction. It's a story that may challenge what you thought you knew about the sometimes competing interests of people and animals.

3 The North American whooping crane—one of the few living relics of the Pleistocene era—suffered a huge drop in population in the nineteenth and twentieth centuries. In 1860 there were 1,400 whooping cranes. In 1941 there were just 15, and in 1967 the whooping crane was listed as "endangered."

4 Mooallem explains how Operation Migration planned to save the whooping crane by raising a new flock in Wisconsin. The hard part would come next: getting the birds to migrate to Florida. Here's how they did it: they led the birds there themselves. In a disguised aircraft, that looked and flew like a bird, they flew along with the flock. They avoided talking, and even wore all-white costumes, so that the cranes wouldn't get too comfortable with humans and would remain wild.

5 When the cranes reached Florida, they were put into a "release pen" with no top netting, so the birds could fly away themselves when they were ready. The complex was surrounded by houses. In fact, it was practically in the backyard of a couple named Gibbs. And that's where the second part of the story starts.

6 The Gibbses—an elderly couple who'd lived there for 50 years—loved nothing better than to sit on their back porch, sip tea, and watch the birds as they fed from the two bird feeders they'd set up in the backyard. There were all kinds of birds around—but the Gibbs' favorites were the whooping cranes that had started showing up lately.

7 As far as Operation Migration was concerned, this could destroy their project. Unless something were done about those feeders, the birds would continue to hang around the Gibbs' house. They would no longer be wary of people, and wouldn't be able to survive on their own.

8 After explaining the situation to Mrs. Gibbs, representatives from Operation Migration asked her to remove the feeders from her backyard. She refused! Her husband, it turns out, was dying of Alzheimer's and the only thing that made him happy and brought him into the present was seeing the family of whooping cranes in his own backyard.

9 The scientists were unmoved by Mrs. Gibbs' story. They were thinking of the birds that people had spent 24 hours a day trying to keep wild. They were thinking of all the time and money they had invested in this group of cranes. But in the end they had to back down. How can you ask a woman to choose between her husband and a flock of birds?

10 According to Jon Mooallem, Mrs. Gibbs did what any of us would do. As humans, we're hard-wired to put our particular set of needs above others. We also have a responsibility to be the earth's caretakers, because of the power we have over other species. And sometimes we have to be comfortable balancing our needs with theirs. ❧

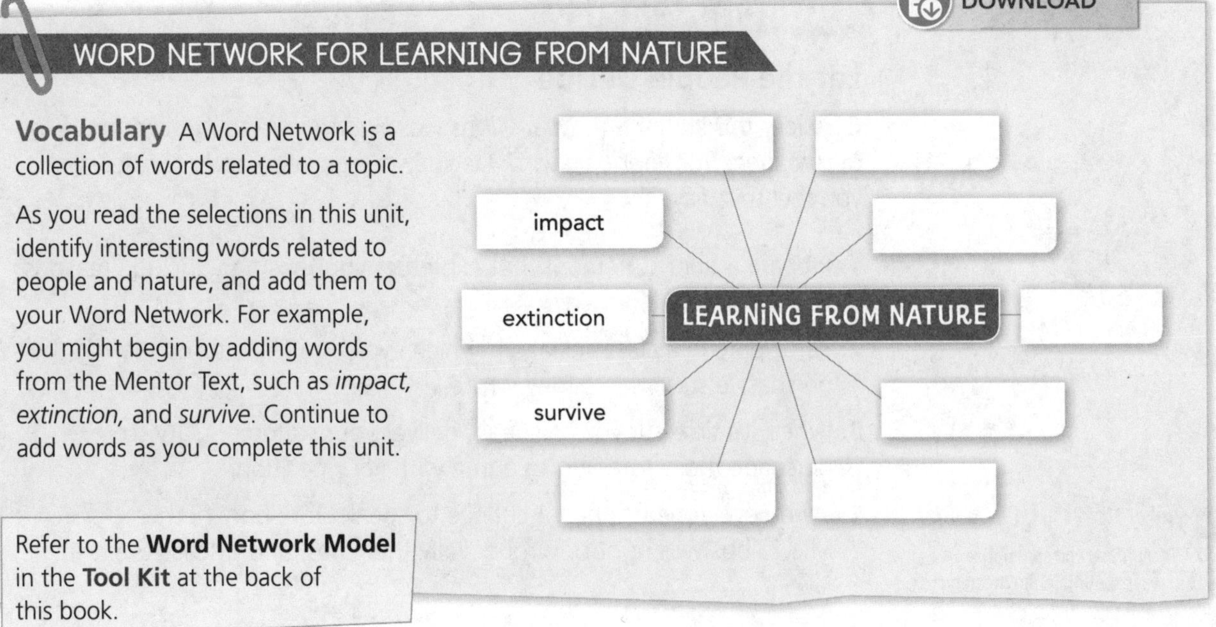

WORD NETWORK FOR LEARNING FROM NATURE

Vocabulary A Word Network is a collection of words related to a topic.

As you read the selections in this unit, identify interesting words related to people and nature, and add them to your Word Network. For example, you might begin by adding words from the Mentor Text, such as *impact, extinction,* and *survive*. Continue to add words as you complete this unit.

Refer to the **Word Network Model** in the **Tool Kit** at the back of this book.

Summary

A **summary** is a brief, complete overview of a text that maintains the meaning and logical order of ideas of the original. It should not include your personal opinions.

NOTEBOOK

WRITE IT Write a summary of "Rethinking the Wild."

Launch Activity

Let the People Decide

Consider this statement: *Mrs. Gibbs was wrong in refusing to remove the bird feeders from her backyard*. Decide your position and consider why you feel this way.

1. Prepare a brief statement that expresses your position. Include reasons you feel as you do.
2. Participate in a class activity in which everyone takes turns sharing the persuasive statements they wrote.
3. When it's time for you to speak, deliver your statement. Try to persuade those listening to agree with your position.
4. When everyone has had a chance to speak, vote on whether Mrs. Gibbs was right or wrong. Tally the votes, and discuss the results.

TEKS
6.D. Paraphrase and summarize texts in ways that maintain meaning and logical order.

QuickWrite

Consider the introductory video, the Launch Activity, your own knowledge, and the Mentor Text as you think about the Essential Question.

Essential Question

What is the relationship between people and nature?

At the end of the unit, you will respond to the Essential Question again and see how your perspective has changed.

NOTEBOOK

WRITE IT Record your first thoughts here.

EQ Notes What is the relationship between people and nature?

As you read the selections in this unit, use a chart like the one shown to record your ideas and list details from the texts that support them. Taking notes as you go will help you clarify your thinking, gather relevant information, and be ready to respond to the Essential Question.

TITLE	MY IDEAS / OBSERVATIONS	TEXT EVIDENCE / INFORMATION

Refer to the **EQ Notes Model** in the **Tool Kit** at the back of this book.

Essential Question

What is the relationship between people and nature?

Nature provides us with the necessities we need to survive—air, water, and soil in which to grow food. However, our relationship with nature goes far beyond the needs of survival. The natural world can be a mirror in which we see ourselves, a friend that gives us gifts, and even an enemy that we fight and that fights us back.

VIDEO

INTERACTIVITY

Whole-Class Learning Strategies

Throughout your life, in school, in your community, and in your career, you will continue to learn and work in large-group environments. Review these strategies and the actions you can take to practice them as you work with your whole class. Use a dictionary to check the meaning of any basic or academic vocabulary words you are unsure of. Add ideas of your own for each strategy. Get ready to use these strategies during Whole-Class Learning.

STRATEGY	MY ACTION PLAN
Listen actively • Put away personal items to avoid becoming distracted. • Try to hear the speaker's full message before planning your own response.	
Demonstrate respect • Show up on time and make sure you are prepared for class. • Avoid side conversations while in class.	
Describe Personal Connections • Recognize that literature explores human experience—the details may differ from your own life, but the emotions it expresses are universal. • Actively look for ways in which your personal experiences help you find meaning in a text. • Consider how your own experiences help you understand characters' actions and reactions.	

CONTENTS

Since the beginning of civilization, people have observed nature, tried to understand it, and told stories about it. The Whole-Class readings illustrate some of these different perspectives. After reading, you will further explore this topic by writing a formal research paper.

from SILENT SPRING

The selection you are about to read is a descriptive essay.

Reading Descriptive Essays

A **descriptive essay** is a work of nonfiction that uses words to paint a vivid picture of a subject.

DESCRIPTIVE ESSAY

Author's Purpose

- to show the importance of a subject through vivid and precise language

Characteristics

- a controlling idea, or insight
- vivid sensory details that appeal to the five senses
- imagery, or word pictures, and figurative language
- concrete details that help readers visualize abstract ideas
- a mood, or emotional quality, created by details and word choices

Structure

- a clear organization that enables readers to "see" what is being described
- usually contains an introduction, body, and conclusion, but may be structured by describing aspects of a person or thing

Take a Minute!

NOTEBOOK

LIST IT With a partner, list three subjects you think would be good for a descriptive essay. What qualities make these good subjects?

TEKS

8.D.i. Analyze characteristics and structural elements of informational text, including the controlling idea or thesis with supporting evidence.

9.F. Analyze how the author's use of language contributes to mood, voice, and tone.

Genre / Text Elements

Language and Mood Word choices are the key to strong descriptive writing. Descriptive writers often use **imagery**, or language that appeals to one or more of the five senses. The use of imagery can create **mood**, or an atmosphere that evokes feelings in readers. The mood and use of imagery lends deeper meaning to a text, helping the writer develop a strong **controlling idea,** or main point. Here is an example:

IMAGERY AND MOOD

PASSAGE	DESCRIPTION OF MOOD
The icy sharp landscape glistened in the sun, piercing the eyes of the lone onlooker. The only sound was the cracking of the ice-encrusted snow. The air hurt to breathe, as if it were an enemy and as dangerous as the knife-like shards of ice.	The landscape is described as threatening and hostile, which creates an ominous mood. It also helps develop a controlling idea about the dangers of nature.

 INTERACTIVITY

 NOTEBOOK

PRACTICE Mark language in the passage that creates imagery. Then, choose the description of the mood that best fits the passage. Finally, state a controlling idea the mood and imagery help to develop.

PASSAGE	DESCRIPTION OF MOOD
The door gently opened, and Delia stepped into the home of her past. The old wooden floor shone dully, polished by footsteps of her beloved family. The scent of lavender still hung in the air, and the grandfather clock ticked with slow confidence, the heartbeat of the home.	◯ warm and gentle ◯ carefree and uplifting ◯ exciting and electric

About the Author

Even as a child, **Rachel Carson** (1907–1964) wanted to be a writer. Once in college, she renewed her interest in nature and majored in marine biology. She later earned a master's degree in zoology. Carson had long been worried about the overuse of pesticides and wanted to raise awareness about this problem. Her book *Silent Spring* became one of the most influential environmental texts ever written.

from Silent Spring

Concept Vocabulary

You will encounter the following words as you read the essay from *Silent Spring*. Before reading, note how familiar you are with each word. Then, rank the words in order from most familiar (1) to least familiar (6).

INTERACTIVITY

WORD	YOUR RANKING
blight	
maladies	
puzzled	
stricken	
stillness	
deserted	

Comprehension Strategy

ANNOTATE

Make Connections

When you **make connections to society**, you use your background knowledge about the world, and look for relationships between ideas in the text and the larger community. For example, you might connect the author's ideas to local or national events or issues.

EXAMPLE

Here is an example of how you might make connections to society while reading the essay from *Silent Spring*.

Passage: *...no enemy action had silenced the rebirth of new life in this stricken world. The people had done it themselves.*

Connection to Society: This passage includes war-like words (enemy). It suggests a hostile relationship between society and nature.

PRACTICE As you read, make connections between ideas in the text and society. Jot down your thoughts in the page margins.

 TEKS

5.E. Make connections to personal experiences, ideas in other texts, and society.

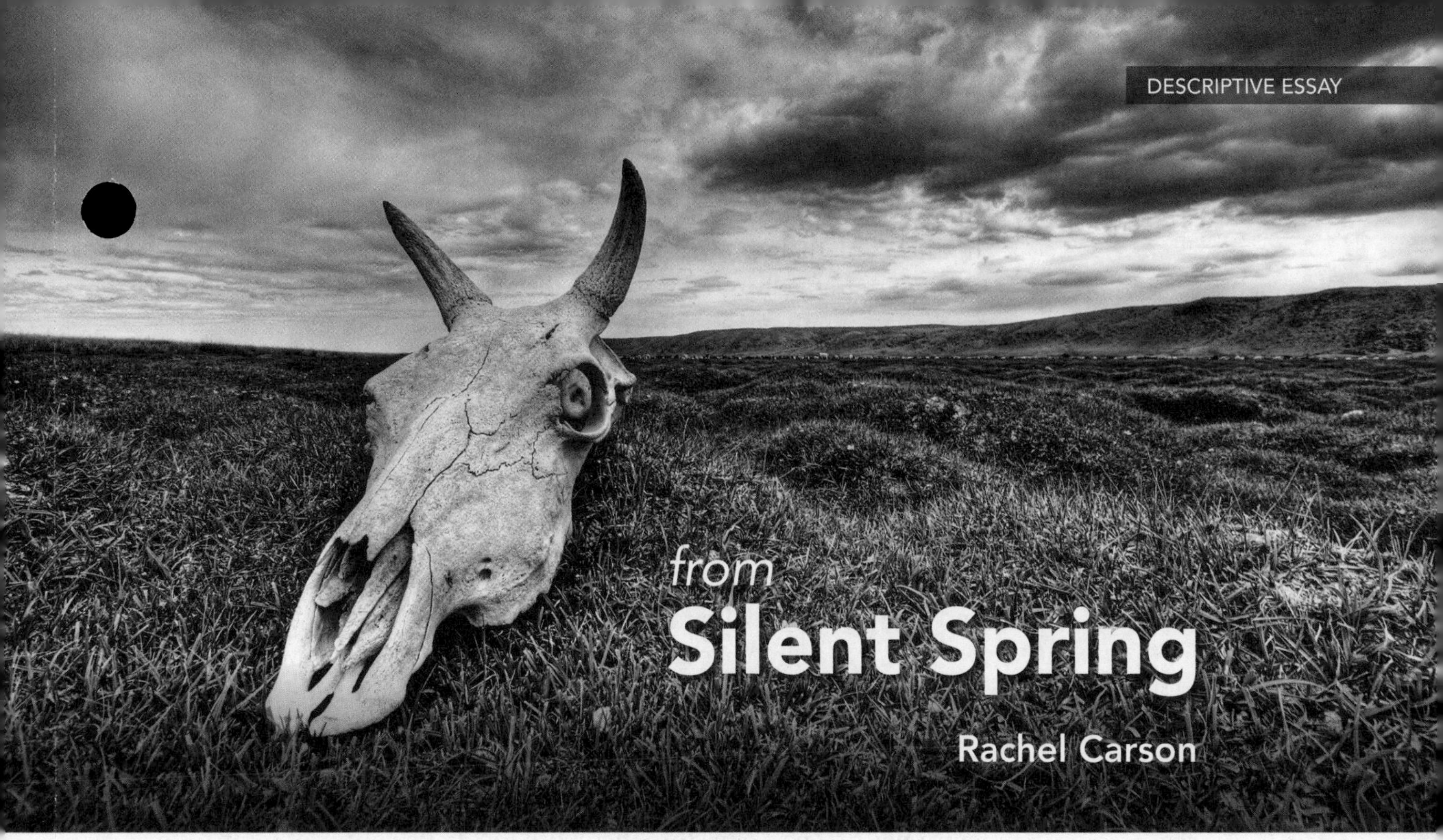

DESCRIPTIVE ESSAY

from

Silent Spring

Rachel Carson

BACKGROUND

Pesticides are chemical compounds designed to destroy crop-eating insects. Pesticides can be deadly to many species—including humans—in addition to the insects and other pests they are intended to kill. In 1962, Rachel Carson published *Silent Spring*, which revealed to the public the dangers of DDT, a pesticide in wide use at the time. The awareness raised by *Silent Spring* eventually led the United States to ban DDT entirely in 1972. This excerpt comes from the opening pages of the book.

AUDIO

ANNOTATE

1 There was once a town in the heart of America where all life seemed to live in harmony with its surroundings. The town lay in the midst of a checkerboard of prosperous farms, with fields of grain and hillsides of orchards where, in spring, white clouds of bloom drifted above the green fields. In autumn, oak and maple and birch set up a blaze of color that flamed and flickered across a backdrop of pines. Then foxes barked in the hills and deer silently crossed the fields, half hidden in the mists of the fall mornings.

2 Along the roads, laurel, viburnum and alder, great ferns and wildflowers delighted the traveler's eye through much of the year. Even in winter the roadsides were places of beauty, where countless birds came to feed on the berries and on the seed heads of the dried weeds rising above the snow. The countryside was, in fact, famous for the abundance and variety of its bird life, and when the flood of migrants was pouring through in spring and fall people traveled from great distances to observe them. Others came to fish the streams, which flowed clear and cold out of the

CLOSE READ

ANNOTATE: In paragraph 2, mark details the author uses to describe the rich environment of the town.

QUESTION: Why might the author have used such vivid, descriptive details to describe the town?

CONCLUDE: What can you conclude about the town from these details?

blight (blyt) *n.* something that spoils, prevents growth, or destroys

maladies (MAL uh deez) *n.* illnesses or diseases

puzzled (PUHZ uhld) *adj.* confused and unable to understand something

stricken (STRIHK uhn) *adj.* very badly affected by trouble or illness

stillness (STIHL nihs) *n.* absence of noise or motion

deserted (dih ZUR tihd) *adj.* abandoned; empty

hills and contained shady pools where trout lay. So it had been from the days many years ago when the first settlers raised their houses, sank their wells, and built their barns.

3 Then a strange **blight** crept over the area and everything began to change. Some evil spell had settled on the community: mysterious **maladies** swept the flocks of chickens; the cattle and sheep sickened and died. Everywhere was a shadow of death. The farmers spoke of much illness among their families. In the town the doctors had become more and more **puzzled** by new kinds of sickness appearing among their patients. There had been several sudden and unexplained deaths, not only among adults but even among children, who would be **stricken** suddenly while at play and die within a few hours.

4 There was a strange **stillness**. The birds, for example—where had they gone? Many people spoke of them, puzzled and disturbed. The feeding stations in the backyards were deserted. The few birds seen anywhere were moribund; they trembled violently and could not fly. It was a spring without voices. On the mornings that had once throbbed with the dawn chorus of robins, catbirds, doves, jays, wrens, and scores of other bird voices, there was now no sound; only silence lay over the fields and woods and marsh.

5 On the farms the hens brooded, but no chicks hatched. The farmers complained that they were unable to raise any pigs—the litters were small and the young survived only a few days. The apple trees were coming into bloom but no bees droned among the blossoms, so there was no pollination and there would be no fruit.

6 The roadsides, once so attractive, were now lined with browned and withered vegetation as though swept by fire. These, too, were silent, **deserted** by all living things. Even the streams were now lifeless. Anglers* no longer visited them, for all the fish had died.

7 In the gutters under the eaves and between the shingles of the roofs, a white granular powder still showed a few patches; some weeks before it had fallen like snow upon the roofs and the lawns, the fields and streams.

8 No witchcraft, no enemy action had silenced the rebirth of new life in this stricken world. The people had done it themselves.

9 This town does not actually exist, but it might easily have a thousand counterparts in America or elsewhere in the world. I know of no community that has experienced all the misfortunes I describe. Yet every one of these disasters has actually happened somewhere, and many real communities have already suffered a substantial number of them. A grim specter has crept upon us almost unnoticed, and this imagined tragedy may easily become a stark reality we all shall know. ❧

* **anglers** (ANG gluhrz) *n.* people who fish with a line and hook.

NOTEBOOK

Response

1. **Personal Connections** What imagery from the text affected you most, either emotionally or intellectually? Why?

Answer the questions in your notebook. Use text evidence to support your responses.

Comprehension

2. **Reading Check** **(a)** What two animals attracted visitors to the town? **(b)** What happened to the people and the animals in the town? **(c)** What fell on the roofs, lawns, fields, and streams?

3. **Strategy: Make Connections** Cite one connection you made to society as you read the essay. Explain how the connection deepened your understanding of the text.

Analysis

4. **(a) Interpret** In paragraph 1, what does the phrase "the heart of America" suggest? **(b) Speculate** Why do you think Carson uses this phrase in the first paragraph?

5. **Summarize** State the main idea of paragraph 2 in one sentence. What specific details support this main idea?

6. **Contrast** Review paragraphs 1 and 7. How do they differ? Consider the author's word choice in each paragraph.

7. **(a) Analyze** Mark all the references to people in the essay. How does the experience of the people change over time? **(b) Draw Conclusions** How does this change emphasize the author's main ideas?

8. **Make Inferences** In the book, this essay is titled "A Fable for Tomorrow." Why might Carson have chosen this title for this section of the book?

EQ Notes **What is the relationship between people and nature?**

What have you learned about the relationship between people and nature by reading this descriptive essay? Go to your Essential Question Notes and record your observations and thoughts about this essay from *Silent Spring*.

TEKS

5.E. Make connections to personal experiences, ideas in other texts, and society.

6.A. Describe personal connections to a variety of sources, including self-selected texts.

6.C. Use text evidence to support an appropriate response.

6.D. Paraphrase and summarize text in ways that maintain meaning and logical order.

from SILENT SPRING

Close Read

1. The model passage and annotation show how one reader analyzed part of paragraph 3 of the text. Find another detail in the passage to annotate. Then, write your own question and conclusion.

CLOSE-READ MODEL

Then a strange blight crept over the area and everything began to change. Some evil spell had settled on the community: mysterious maladies swept the flocks of chickens; the cattle and sheep sickened and died.

ANNOTATE: The author uses descriptive details to show the changes in the town.

QUESTION: What kind of mood do these words create?

CONCLUDE: This description creates a sense of destruction and despair.

MY **QUESTION:**

MY **CONCLUSION:**

2. For more practice, answer the Close-Read note in the selection.
3. Choose a section of the essay you found especially important. Mark important details. Then, jot down questions and write your conclusions in the open space next to the text.

Inquiry and Research

Research and Extend Practice responding to teacher-guided questions by conducting research about this question: How did different groups respond to *Silent Spring* when it was first published? Why were the reactions so varied?

Identify and gather information and evidence from at least two relevant sources. Then, synthesize the information to arrive at your own insight about the question. Write a brief **report** in which you explain your findings and insight.

TEKS

8.D.i. Analyze characteristics and structural elements of informational text, including the controlling idea or thesis with supporting evidence.

9.D. Describe how the author's use of figurative language such as metaphor and personification achieves specific purposes.

9.F. Analyze how the author's use of language contributes to mood, voice, and tone.

12.A. Generate student-selected and teacher-guided questions for formal and informal inquiry.

12.D. Identify and gather relevant information from a variety of sources.

12.F. Synthesize information from a variety of sources.

Genre / Text Elements

Language and Mood In the essay from *Silent Spring*, Rachel Carson uses language that creates a very specific **mood**, or overall feeling. To create this mood, Carson employs different kinds of descriptive details:

- **Imagery**, or words that appeal to the senses: *Then foxes barked in the hills and deer silently crossed the fields. . . .*
- **Concrete details**, or specific details that help readers visualize an abstract concept or idea: *Along the roads, laurel, viburnum and alder, great ferns and wildflowers delighted the traveler's eye. . . .*
- **Figurative language**, or non-literal language, such as metaphor and personification: *A grim specter has crept upon us. . . .*

TIP: To identify mood, visualize the scene the author describes. Is the scene bright or dark, happy or sad, safe or dangerous?

NOTEBOOK

INTERACTIVITY

PRACTICE Complete the activity and answer the questions.

1. **Analyze** Read the following passage from the first paragraph of *Silent Spring* and note Carson's use of descriptive details. Then, describe the mood the passage creates.

PASSAGE FROM *SILENT SPRING*	DESCRIPTIVE DETAILS	MOOD
There was once a town in the heart of America where all life seemed to live in harmony with its surroundings. The town lay in the midst of a checkerboard of prosperous farms, with fields of grain and hillsides of orchards where, in spring, white clouds of bloom drifted above the green fields.		

2. **(a) Describe** Reread paragraph 4. What mood has been created?
(b) Analyze Which details help to develop that mood?

3. **Compare and Contrast** Reread paragraph 9. In what way does the mood in that passage sharply differ from the mood created in paragraphs 1 and 2? Explain.

4. **(a) Analyze** What controlling idea does the author express in the essay's final paragraph?
(b) Evaluate How do the descriptive details she used and the mood she created earlier in the essay help develop that idea and give it power?

from SILENT SPRING

Concept Vocabulary

NOTEBOOK

Why These Words? The vocabulary words are related to unwelcome change—in this case, to a town's landscape. For example, after the town is *stricken* with the mysterious *blight*, there is a strange *stillness* everywhere.

blight	puzzled	stillness
maladies	stricken	deserted

PRACTICE Answer the questions.

1. How do the vocabulary words sharpen the reader's understanding of what happens to the town and its people?

2. What other words in the selection are related to this concept?

3. Correctly complete each sentence using a vocabulary word.

   (a) When she returned home from the music festival, the woman found the ________ of her apartment strange in comparison.

   (b) When the concert hall was ________, you could hear a pin drop from across the room.

   (c) After carefully following the recipe, Alfredo was _______ when the cake came out of the oven, hard as a rock.

   (d) The _______ destroyed the potatoes grown in the county.

   (e) Common ________, such as colds and flus, affect the most people during the winter.

   (f) Before the return of their lost pet, the family had been ________ with worry and fear.

WORD NETWORK

Add words that are related to people and nature from the text to your Word Network.

Word Study

NOTEBOOK

Long *i* Spelling Patterns In English, the long *i* sound can be spelled in a number of different ways. One way is with the letter sequence *igh*, as in the vocabulary word *blight*. The sound can also be spelled with the letter combinations *ig* (*sign*), *y* (*cry*), and *ie* (*tie; die*).

PRACTICE Complete the following activity.

Work with a partner to locate at least three additional words that use each of the four letter combinations discussed (*igh, ig, y,* and *ie*) to create the long *i* sound.

TEKS

6.F. Respond using newly acquired vocabulary.

9.E. Identify the use of literary devices, including subjective and objective point of view.

Author's Craft

Author's Point of View All writing expresses a point of view. In fiction and poetry, the narrator or speaker usually speaks from a first-person or third-person point of view. In nonfiction pieces like *Silent Spring*, the author him- or herself is speaking directly to you, using either an **objective point of view** or a **subjective point of view**. Here's how to distinguish between the two:

POINT OF VIEW	SAMPLE PASSAGE	LOOK FOR:
Subjective: Writers using this point of view represent primarily their own ideas, thoughts, experiences, and beliefs. Used often in narrative nonfiction, informal essays, blog posts, and some persuasion.	*Then a strange blight crept over the area and everything began to change. Some evil spell had settled on the community: mysterious maladies swept the flocks of chickens; the cattle and sheep sickened and died.* *—from* Silent Spring	• personal ideas and feelings are represented • based more on opinions than on facts
Objective: Writers using this point of view represent the ideas, thoughts, and beliefs of multiple people. Used often in formal essays, research papers, and official documents.	*Then, for some unknown reason, cows sickened and fields no longer produced crops. Farmers reported the deaths of poultry and livestock in large numbers.*	• balanced ideas • absence of bias • based more on facts than on emotions or opinions

PRACTICE

1. **Analyze** Reread the essay, and decide if it is written mostly from the objective or the subjective point of view. List evidence from the text that supports your analysis.

2. **Modify** How might you revise this subjective passage from the text to be objective: *The roadsides, once so attractive, were now lined with browned and withered vegetation as though swept by fire. These, too, were silent, deserted by all living things. Even the streams were now lifeless. Anglers no longer visited them, for all the fish had died.*

from SILENT SPRING

Composition

A **formal letter** can be used to conduct business, make a complaint or an official request, or express other serious issues.

ASSIGNMENT

In *Silent Spring*, Rachel Carson paints a harsh picture of the future. Write a **formal letter** to the author in which you answer this question: Does Carson's description inspire or discourage readers? Use an appropriate structure for a formal letter:

- Begin with a formal introduction in which you express your controlling idea, or main point.
- Develop your controlling idea in two or more body paragraphs, using transitions to make the logic of your ideas clear.
- Include details and examples that develop your controlling idea.
- Write a conclusion in which you restate your controlling idea and thank your reader.
- Include a closing expression, such as *Sincerely* or *Best Regards*, followed by your name. Make sure to capitalize the closing word or phrase and spell it correctly. For example, the word *sincerely* maintains the spelling of the base word *sincere* and simply adds the suffix *-ly*. This rule appears in similar words, such as *separately* and *merely*.

EDITING TIPS

As you review and edit your letter, make sure the salutation and closing are correctly capitalized. The first word in each element should begin with a capital letter, as should all proper names and titles, such as *Mrs.*, *Mr.*, and *Ms.*

TEKS

10.D.vii. Edit drafts, using standard English conventions, including correct capitalization.

11.D. Compose correspondence that reflects an opinion, registers a complaint, or requests information in a business or friendly structure.

12.A. Generate student-selected and teacher-guided questions for formal and informal inquiry.

12.B. Develop and revise a plan.

12.C. Refine the major research question, if necessary, guided by the answers to a secondary set of questions.

12.D. Identify and gather relevant information from a variety of sources.

12.E. Differentiate between primary and secondary sources.

12.G. Differentiate between paraphrasing and plagiarism when using source materials.

12.H.i. Examine sources for reliability, credibility, and bias.

12.H.ii. Examine sources for faulty reasoning such as hyperbole, emotional appeals, and stereotype.

12.I. Display academic citations and use source materials ethically.

NOTEBOOK

Reflect on Your Writing

PRACTICE Think about the choices you made as you wrote. Also consider what you learned by writing. Share your experiences by responding to these questions.

1. Was it easy or difficult to determine your opinion?

2. Was it easy or difficult to structure your ideas in a letter?

3. **WHY THESE WORDS?** Which words did you specifically choose to make the statement of your opinion stronger?

Research

A **research report** is an informational text in which you explain a topic using facts integrated from a variety of sources.

ASSIGNMENT

Write a **research report** about one of the following topics:

- ◯ the importance of *Silent Spring* and the impact it had
- ◯ the struggle to ban DDT and the ban's eventual victory

Develop and Revise a Research Plan

Generate Questions Think about what you already know about your topic and what you want to know. Then, use your notes to generate at least two questions that will focus a formal research inquiry. Using your questions to guide you, identify a variety of relevant materials, including both primary and secondary sources. Seek help from a peer or your teacher if you need to clarify any specialized language.

SOURCES
- Primary sources are firsthand accounts of events, such as diaries, letters, and newspaper articles.
- Secondary sources are texts written by writers who did not witness events firsthand. They include histories and biographies

Examine Sources Read your sources critically and evaluate their reliability and credibility. Make sure they are free of bias and faulty reasoning:

- Is each source reliable and credible? Who published each source? Are statements supported with balanced evidence?
- Do any sources include faulty reasoning, such as hyperbole (over-exaggeration), emotional appeals instead of logic, or stereotypes?
- Do any of them display bias, or an unfairly one-sided viewpoint?

Revise Your Plan If your sources are not reliable or credible, or if they display bias or faulty reasoning, identify a new set of sources to use. Also, decide whether you need to write different research questions, perhaps ones that are either more specific or more broad.

EQ Notes Before moving on to a new selection, go to your Essential Question Notes and record any additional thoughts or observations you may have about this essay from *Silent Spring*.

Paraphrase, Don't Plagiarize

Use Sources Ethically Follow these steps to use source materials ethically and avoid plagiarism:

- Cite information and ideas that are not common knowledge.
- **Paraphrase** by using your own words to restate the ideas of others. Make sure your paraphrases reflect the meaning and order of ideas of the original text. Note that even when you paraphrase, you must still cite the source because the ideas are not your own.
- If you want to use an author's exact words, set them in quotation marks and cite the source accurately.

HOW GRANDMOTHER SPIDER STOLE THE SUN

Fiction

The genre of fiction includes many different kinds of imagined stories. For example, a **myth** is a type of fictional story that explains the actions of divine beings, the origins of natural phenomena, or a combination of the two.

HOW MUSIC CAME TO THE WORLD

MYTH

Purpose

- to explain an aspect of the world and how it came to be
- to teach a moral lesson or value
- to share with future generations

Characteristics

- characters may be humans, animals, or gods that have magical or supernatural abilities
- settings may be imaginary or real, and centered in a particular culture
- expresses themes, or insights about life, important to the culture from which the myth comes
- includes details (plants, animals, foods, practices, etc.) that reflect the culture it comes from

Structure

- conflict-driven plot, or series of events
- often involve a series of tests or obstacles characters must overcome

TEKS

7.A. Infer multiple themes within and across texts using text evidence.

8.A. Demonstrate knowledge of literary genres such as realistic fiction, adventure stories, historical fiction, mysteries, humor, myths, fantasy, and science fiction.

Take a Minute!

NOTEBOOK

LIST IT With a partner, identify other stories (graphic novels, movies, cartoons, and so on) that are based on myths. What mythic elements do these stories have?

Genre / Text Elements

Multiple Themes A **theme** in literature is a message, or an insight, about life. For example, if crime and punishment are the topics of a text, one theme might be "crime doesn't pay." Note that a text can have multiple themes related to its topic.

In **myths,** themes about big ideas like love and hate or good and evil, are often **universal,** meaning they relate to people in all times and places. Myths also often have themes that indicate a culture's values.

Themes are generally not **explicitly,** or directly, stated. Instead, they are **implicitly** suggested. Readers must infer themes by analyzing literary details, such as characters' actions and motivations, and the ways in which conflicts are resolved.

Compare these topics and related themes.

EXAMPLES: DISTINGUISHING TOPIC FROM THEME

TOPIC	THEME
family relationships	Family helps us define ourselves.
bravery	Being brave doesn't mean being unafraid.
war and peace	People sometimes act against their best interests.

INTERACTIVITY

NOTEBOOK

PRACTICE With a partner, discuss and complete each activity.

1. Which of the items are topics and which are themes?

		TOPIC	THEME
A	Love can triumph over hate.	○	○
B	Jealousy	○	○
C	Greed can destroy lives.	○	○
D	Mysteries of the universe	○	○

2. Make up a possible theme for the topic of kindness.

HOW GRANDMOTHER SPIDER STOLE THE SUN

Compare Fiction

In this lesson, you will read and compare the myths "How Grandmother Spider Stole the Sun" and "How Music Came to the World."

HOW MUSIC CAME TO THE WORLD

How Grandmother Spider Stole the Sun • How Music Came to the World

Concept Vocabulary

INTERACTIVITY

You will encounter the following words as you read the myths. Before reading, note how familiar you are with each word. Using a scale of 1 (do not know it at all) to 5 (know it very well), indicate your knowledge of each word.

WORD	YOUR RANKING
benefit	
temperate	
passion	
cacophony	
besieged	
coaxed	

Comprehension Strategy

ANNOTATE

Adjust Fluency

When you set a purpose for reading, you decide what your focus will be. Then, you **adjust your fluency,** or the speed at which you read, to meet that goal. Consider the two purposes shown here:

- **For Analysis or Information:** Read slowly. After you finish a complex passage, pause to think about the ideas and make sure you fully understand. Mark important details, and reread if necessary.
- **For Enjoyment:** Read more quickly. You may want to linger over passages you like, but studying the text is less important.

PRACTICE As you read and analyze the myths, adjust your fluency to fit your reading purpose.

TEKS

3. Adjust fluency when reading grade-level text based on the reading purpose.

About the Myths

How Grandmother Spider Stole the Sun

BACKGROUND

"How Grandmother Spider Stole the Sun" is a Native American creation story that explains how the world became the way it is. Grandmother Spider appears in the myths of many Native American groups, such as the Hopi, Navajo, and Cherokee, as an important creator who is also a powerful teacher and helper. This story comes from the Muskogee, or Creek, people.

Michael J. Caduto (b. 1955) is an award-winning author, storyteller, educator, poet, and musician. His work emphasizes respect for the earth and the environment, as well as the scientific knowledge and cultural traditions that underline the importance of the natural world.

Joseph Bruchac (b. 1942) is a novelist, poet, and storyteller of Abenaki descent. He lives in the foothills of New York's Adirondack Mountains, where his ancestors also lived. Bruchac has written more than 70 books for children and has performed worldwide as a teller of Native American folk tales.

How Music Came to the World

BACKGROUND

The Aztecs, a native people of Central Mexico, were known for their elaborate agricultural system and the complexity of their government and military organization. At its peak, the Aztec empire had a population of 5 to 6 million people. Religion was important to Aztec culture, and the people worshipped at least 200 gods and goddess. Quetzalcoatl, the hero in this myth, is one of the most influential Aztec gods. He was revered as a great creator as well as a patron of knowledge, learning, agriculture, and the arts.

Dianne De Las Casas (1970–2017) was an award-winning author and storyteller. She was also the founder of Picture Book Month, an international initiative that celebrates print picture books during the month of November. She lived in Louisiana with her family, and frequently performed at schools, conferences, and other special events.

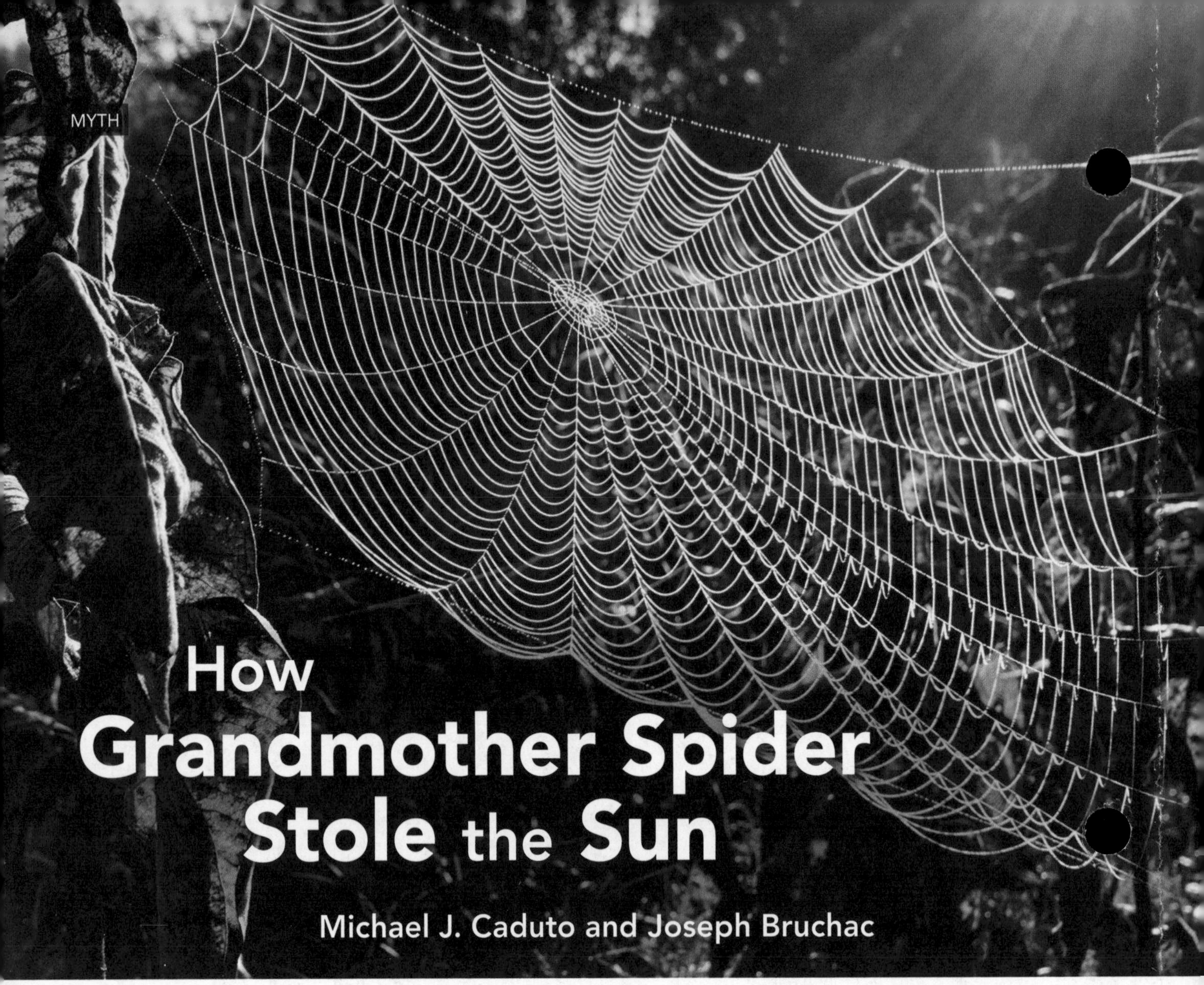

MYTH

How Grandmother Spider Stole the Sun

Michael J. Caduto and Joseph Bruchac

 AUDIO

 ANNOTATE

1 When the Earth was first made, there was no light. It was very hard for the animals and the people in the darkness. Finally the animals decided to do something about it.

2 "I have heard there is something called the Sun," said the Bear. "It is kept on the other side of the world, but the people there will not share it. Perhaps we can steal a piece of it."

3 All the animals agreed that it was a good idea. But who would be the one to steal the Sun?

4 The Fox was the first to try. He sneaked to the place where the Sun was kept. He waited until no one was looking. Then he grabbed a piece of it in his mouth and ran. But the Sun was so hot it burned his mouth and he dropped it. To this day all foxes have black mouths because that first fox burned his carrying the Sun.

5 The Possum tried next. In those days Possum had a very bushy tail. She crept up to the place where the Sun was kept, broke off a piece, and hid it in her tail. Then she began to run, bringing the Sun back to the animals and the people. But the Sun was so hot it

burned off all the hair on her tail and she lost hold of it. To this day all possums have bare tails because the Sun burned away the hair on that first possum.

6 Then Grandmother Spider tried. Instead of trying to hold the Sun herself, she wove a bag out of her webbing. She put the piece of the Sun into her bag and carried it back with her. Now the question was where to put the Sun.

7 Grandmother Spider told them, "The Sun should be up high in the sky. Then everyone will be able to see it and **benefit** from its light."

8 All the animals agreed, but none of them could reach up high enough. Even if they carried it to the top of the tallest tree, that would not be high enough for everyone on the Earth to see the Sun. Then they decided to have one of the birds carry the Sun up to the top of the sky. Everyone knew the Buzzard could fly the highest, so he was chosen.

9 Buzzard placed the Sun on top of his head, where his feathers were the thickest, for the Sun was still very hot, even inside Grandmother Spider's bag. He began to fly, up and up toward the top of the sky. As he flew the Sun grew hotter. Up and up he went, higher and higher, and the Sun grew hotter and hotter still. Now the Sun was burning through Grandmother Spider's bag, but the Buzzard still kept flying up toward the top of the sky. Up and up he went and the Sun grew hotter. Now it was burning away the feathers on top of his head, but he continued on. Now all of his feathers were gone, but he flew higher. Now it was turning the bare skin of his head all red, but he continued to fly. He flew until he reached the top of the sky, and there he placed the Sun where it would give light to everyone.

10 Because he carried the Sun up to the top of the sky, Buzzard was honored by all the birds and animals. Though his head was naked and ugly because he was burned carrying the Sun, he is still the highest flyer of all, and he can be seen circling the Sun to this day. And because Grandmother Spider brought the Sun in her bag of webbing, at times the Sun makes rays across the sky that are shaped like the rays in Grandmother Spider's web. It reminds everyone that we are all connected, like the strands of Grandmother Spider's web, and it reminds everyone of what Grandmother Spider did for all the animals and the people. ❧

CLOSE READ

ANNOTATE: Mark the repeated words in the first six sentences of paragraph 9.

QUESTION: What ideas are emphasized by the use of repetition?

CONCLUDE: Why might the author have chosen to use so much repetition in this passage? What effect does it create?

benefit (BEH nuh fiht) *v.* get good or helpful results; gain

How Music Came to the World

Dianne De Las Casas

1 Shhhh. Do you hear that? It's the sound of silence. Long ago, the world was filled with silence just like this. There was no laughter and there was no music. Tezcatlipoca, Lord of the World, walked the earth and noticed the heavy silence that blanketed the world. From the four corners of the globe, he summoned Quetzalcoatl, the feathered Lord of Spirit, who controlled the wind.

AUDIO

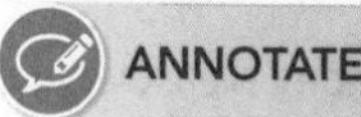
ANNOTATE

2 "Quetzalcoatl, hear my call, come as swift as the wind!"

3 Quetzalcoatl answered Tezcatlipoca's call and stood before him in feathery brilliance.

4 The lord of the world said, "Earth is sick with sad silence. The people have lost hope and laughter because there is no music to brighten the nights and days. Sun has all the music. His musicians create beautiful songs that ring through the heavens. We must bring these musicians to Earth."

5 Quetzalcoatl preened his colorful feathers, "Yes, my Lord, I will do as you ask."

6 Quetzalcoatl readied himself for the long journey to the heavens, where the Sun lived. He commanded the cold winds from the North, the warm winds from the South, the **temperate** winds from the West, and the cool winds from the East to carry him up, up, up towards the heavens.

temperate (TEHM puh riht) *adj.* not too hot or cold; mild

7 Higher and higher, the winged Lord of Spirit ascended. The Sun saw Quetzalcoatl approaching and he glowed with fury. He knew that Tezcatlipoca sent him to steal away the Sun's treasured musicians. The Sun's musicians were circling him in cheerful dance, playing their beautiful music.

8 The musician of gentle lullabies wore robes of billowy white. The musician of **passion** flaunted robes of fiery red and drummed music of love and war. The musician of dreams donned robes of fleecy blue as light as clouds. The musician of the heavens flowed in robes of bright yellow and played a golden flute, creating songs to honor kings and gods.

passion (PASH uhn) *n.* intense feeling or belief

9 The Sun harshly ordered, "Hush, my musicians. The Lord of Spirit is coming to take you to Earth, where it is lonely and sad. Stay here with me, my children, in the brightness of my kingdom."

10 The musicians quieted down just as Quetzalcoatl began climbing the stairs of the Sun's palace. He called out softly, "Oh musicians of brilliance, come with me to Earth, where the people need you."

11 The musicians cowered at the foot of the Sun as he gave them a glowering glance. The feathered lord called out once again, "The world needs your music."

CLOSE READ

ANNOTATE: Mark the sensory details in paragraph 8 related to the musicians' robes.

QUESTION: What images are evoked by the sensory details?

CONCLUDE: Why do you think the author created such vivid images to describe the musicians?

cacophony (kuh KAW fuh nee) *n.* harsh or jarring sounds; loud noise

besieged (bih SEEJD) *adj.* surrounded by armed forces with the purpose of capturing

coaxed (KOHKST) *v.* influenced or gently urged by flattery or persuasion

12 Afraid of the sun, the musicians remained silent. Down below, Tezcatlipoca was furious. "Sun won't share his music, so I'll take it from him." From the depths of Earth, he launched flashes of lightning and a **cacophony** of thunder. Together with the power of Quetzalcoatl's winds, Sun was suddenly **besieged**.

13 "It's a war! We're being attacked!" Sun cried. Quetzalcoatl offered his feathered wings to protect the frightened musicians.

14 "Come," he gently **coaxed**, "Come to Earth where it is peaceful." The musicians followed Quetzalcoatl and sailed down to Earth on the edge of the winds.

15 Suddenly, the sad silence lifted. Earth's people rejoiced as they listened to the joyous sounds of music. They laughed and again filled the world with hope. Quetzalcoatl gathered the four winds and music soared to all the corners of the world.

16 Listening to the musicians, all of Earth's creations learned to sing and create music, from the babbling brooks to the twittering birds to children playing outside. From then to now, all of Earth celebrates with the sound of music and that is how music came to the world. ❧

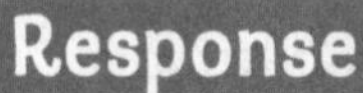

NOTEBOOK

Answer the questions in your notebook. Use text evidence to support your responses.

Response

1. **Personal Connections** What elements of these myths did you find most interesting or surprising? Explain.

Comprehension

2. **Reading Check** **(a)** Where is the Sun before Grandmother Spider steals it? **(b)** What does Grandmother Spider do differently from the others who try to steal a piece of the Sun? **(c)** What did babbling brooks and children learn to do at the end of "How Music Came to the World"?

3. **Strategy: Adjust Fluency** **(a)** What purpose did you set for reading these myths? **(b)** How did you adjust your fluency to fit that purpose? Explain.

Analysis

4. **Analyze** In "How Grandmother Spider Stole the Sun," what descriptions of the animals seem true to life? What descriptions are more imaginative? Explain.

5. **(a) Make Inferences** What do the story details suggest about Grandmother Spider? **(b) Connect** Why do you think the myth is titled as it is?

6. **Speculate** What would have happened if the sun had won the war with Quetzelcoatl in "How Music Came to the World"? Rewrite the ending of the myth with this scenario in mind, using new details about what people feel and do in the absence of music.

7. **(a) Make Inferences** In "How Music Came to the World," what can you infer about the Sun based on how the musicians act when Quetzalcoatl first arrives? **(b) Analyze** What qualities of Quetzalcoatl make him successful in his quest? Explain.

8. **Evaluate** Why do you think people still read and share myths? What qualities do these stories have that continue to give them meaning and impact? Explain, citing details from the texts.

EQ Notes What is the relationship between people and nature?

What have you learned about the relationship between people and nature from reading these myths? Go to your Essential Question Notes and record your observations and thoughts about "How Grandmother Spider Stole the Sun" and "How Music Came to the World."

TEKS

3. Adjust fluency when reading grade-level text based on the reading purpose.

5.F. Make inferences and use evidence to support understanding.

6.A. Describe personal connections to a variety of sources, including self-selected texts.

6.C. Use text evidence to support an appropriate response.

HOW GRANDMOTHER SPIDER STOLE THE SUN • HOW MUSIC CAME TO THE WORLD

Close Read

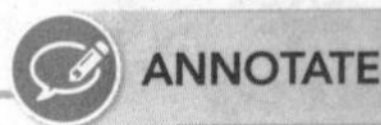

1. The model passage and annotation show how one reader analyzed part of paragraph 10 of "How Grandmother Spider Stole the Sun." Find another detail in the passage to annotate. Then, write your own question and conclusion.

CLOSE-READ MODEL

Because he carried the Sun up to the top of the sky, Buzzard was honored by all the birds and animals. Though his head was naked and ugly because he was burned carrying the Sun, he is still the highest flyer of all. . . . And because Grandmother Spider brought the Sun in her bag of webbing…

ANNOTATE: I notice that many sentences in this paragraph begin with clauses that contain *because*.

QUESTION: What is the effect of that pattern?

CONCLUDE: The author deliberately chose this pattern to emphasize the reasoning behind the myth.

MY **QUESTION:**

MY **CONCLUSION:**

2. For more practice, answer the Close-Read notes in the selection.
3. Choose a section of the myths you found especially important. Mark important details. Then, jot down questions and write your conclusions in the open space next to the texts.

 TEKS

6.C. Use text evidence to support an appropriate response.

7.A. Infer multiple themes within and across texts using text evidence.

8.A. Demonstrate knowledge of literary genres such as realistic fiction, adventure stories, historical fiction, mysteries, humor, myths, fantasy, and science fiction.

12.A. Generate student-selected and teacher-guided questions for formal and informal inquiry.

12.D. Identify and gather relevant information from a variety of sources.

12.F. Synthesize information from a variety of sources.

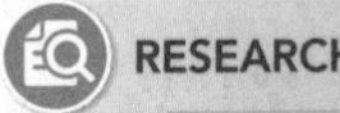

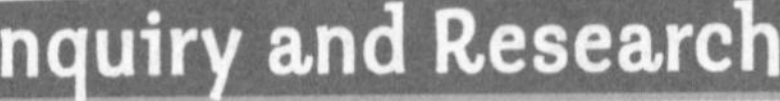

Inquiry and Research

Research and Extend Practice responding to teacher-guided questions by conducting research about this topic: What other cultures have myths about the sun? In what different ways is the sun portrayed?

Identify and gather relevant information and evidence from at least two sources. Then, synthesize the information to arrive at your own insight about the topic. Write a brief **report** in which you explain your findings and insight.

Genre / Text Elements

Multiple Themes Myths often express **themes** that comment on human nature and our relationship to the world in which we live. Themes are rarely **explicitly** stated in a text. Instead, they are **implicitly** expressed by all the details of a work. One text can express multiple themes, and different texts can express similar themes.

TIP: You can also use these strategies to infer a text's **universal themes**, or insights that are meaningful to people in all time periods, places, and cultures.

How to Infer Themes To infer the implicit thematic meaning of a text, examine details about characters and events.

- Study the text's title, and analyze its meaning or focus.
- Look for ways in which story characters grow or change.
- Analyze ways in which conflicts are resolved.

How to State Themes Once you have analyzed the clues, formulate two or three themes that apply to the text. Be sure to state themes in sentence format. Statements of themes should be worded to apply to the world, not to the text itself. See these examples:

- **Theme:** Greed leads to misery.
- **Not a theme:** In this story, Tania's greed makes her miserable.
- **Not a theme:** Misery

NOTEBOOK

INTERACTIVITY

PRACTICE Complete the activity and answer the questions.

1. **Make Inferences** Fill in the chart to identify two themes in "How Grandmother Spider Stole the Sun" and two themes in "How Music Came to the World." With a partner, discuss whether the themes you identify are explicitly or implicitly conveyed.

MYTH	TEXT EVIDENCE	POSSIBLE THEMES
How Grandmother Spider Stole the Sun		• •
How Music Came to the World		• •

2. **Interpret** Study the themes you stated in item 1. What universal theme might both myths share? What evidence in both texts supports this shared theme?

HOW GRANDMOTHER SPIDER STOLE THE SUN • HOW MUSIC CAME TO THE WORLD

Concept Vocabulary

 NOTEBOOK

Why These Words? The vocabulary words convey either gentleness or intensity. For example, the *cacophony* of thunder *besieged* Sun in "How Music Came to the World."

benefit	temperate	passion
cacophony	besieged	coaxed

PRACTICE Answer the questions and complete the activities.

1. How do the vocabulary words contribute to your understanding of the characters' conflicts in these myths?
2. Find two other words in each myth that relate to gentleness or intensity.
3. Why might someone feel *besieged* either physically or emotionally? When, on the other hand, might someone feel *coaxed*?
4. Fill in the blanks: The ______ of blaring horns and construction work disrupted her concentration, but it did not affect her ______ for her work.
5. Fill in the blanks: *Improve* is a synonym for ______; *moderate* is a synonym for ______.

WORD NETWORK

Add words that are related to people and nature from the text to your Word Network.

Word Study

 INTERACTIVITY

Anglo-Saxon Prefix: *be-* The Anglo-Saxon prefix *be-* means "on all sides" or "around." A *siege* is a long operation, usually conducted by military forces. So to *besiege* is to surround with an army for a prolonged attack.

PRACTICE **Anticipate the meanings of the *be-* words listed in the chart. Then, use a dictionary and thesaurus to confirm your definitions and find synonyms for each word.**

WORD	GUESS AT DEFINITION	DICTIONARY DEFINITION	SYNONYMS
bejewel			
bespoken			
betrothed			
befriend			

TEKS

2.A. Use print or digital resources to determine the meaning, syllabication, pronunciation, word origin, and part of speech.

6.F. Respond using newly acquired vocabulary as appropriate.

10.D.viii. Edit drafts using standard English conventions, including punctuation, including commas to set off words, phrases, and clauses, and semicolons.

Conventions

Sentence Functions and End Marks The myths you have just read contain a variety of sentence types. There are four types of sentences, which can be classified according to how they function. End marks vary according to the function of the sentence.

TYPE OF SENTENCE	FUNCTION	END MARK	EXAMPLE
Declarative	To make statements	period (.)	There should be music in this world.
Interrogative	To ask questions	question mark (?)	Why would you want to capture the Sun?
Imperative	To give commands or directions	exclamation point (!) or period (.)	Bring me the musicians at once! Put the Sun high in the sky.
Exclamatory	To call out or exclaim	exclamation point (!)	What a victory!

INTERACTIVITY

NOTEBOOK

READ IT

Fill in the chart with an example from the myths of each type of sentence. If you cannot find an example, write a sentence of your own.

TYPE OF SENTENCE	EXAMPLE
Declarative	
Interrogative	
Imperative	
Exclamatory	

WRITE IT

Using different types of sentences can make your writing more interesting to read. Write a paragraph about people and nature in which you use each type of sentence and end mark at least once.

HOW GRANDMOTHER SPIDER STOLE THE SUN

HOW MUSIC CAME TO THE WORLD

Compare Fiction

Multiple Choice

NOTEBOOK

These questions are based on the myths "How Grandmother Spider Stole the Sun" and "How Music Came to the World." Choose the best answer to each question.

1. Which statement is accurate?

A Both myths describe people's conflicts with animals.

B Both myths describe people's triumphs over nature.

C Both myths include characters that have both animal and human characteristics.

D Both myths depict people who are overpowered by nature.

2. Why might these two myths represent the sun so differently?

F Each culture believes the sun contains both good and evil.

G The myths come from different cultures with different beliefs.

H The cultures originate on different sides of the planet.

J Both myths come from cultures that were at war.

3. Read paragraph 1 from "How Grandmother Spider Stole the Sun" and paragraph 1 from "How Music Came to the World." Which does neither paragraph do?

***from* How Grandmother Spider Stole the Sun**

When the Earth was first made, there was no light. It was very hard for the animals and the people in the darkness. Finally the animals decided to do something about it.

***from* How Music Came to the World**

Shhhh. Do you hear that? It's the sound of silence. Long ago, the world was filled with silence just like this. There was no laughter and there was no music. Tezcatlipoca, Lord of the World, walked the earth and noticed the heavy silence that blanketed the world. From the four corners of the globe, he summoned Quetzalcoatl, the feathered Lord of Spirit, who controlled the wind.

A refer to a time long ago

B indicate that a hardship for people will be addressed

C indicate which character or characters will face hardship

D state morals or messages

TEKS

6.B. Write responses that demonstrate understanding of texts, including comparing sources within and across genres.

7.A. Infer multiple themes within and across texts using text evidence.

Short Response

Answer the questions in your notebook. Use text evidence to support your responses.

1. **(a) Compare and Contrast** How are the qualities of the sun similar and different in the two myths? Explain. **(b) Analyze** In what ways do the qualities of the sun in each myth contribute to the problems or conflicts the characters face?

2. **Interpret** Formulate a theme that the two myths share. Include text evidence in your response.

3. **Analyze** What qualities do the animal characters in the sun myth and the spirit characters in the music myth possess that allow them to be successful in their own stories? **(b) Draw Conclusions** What do these qualities suggest about the values of the cultures that first told these stories?

Timed Writing

A **comparison-and-contrast essay** is a piece of writing in which you discuss similarities and differences among two or more topics.

ASSIGNMENT

Write a **comparison-and-contrast essay** in which you consider what each myth suggests about what people need in life. What makes light and music so important? Do the value of these elements justify the stealing that takes place in each myth?

5-MINUTE PLANNER

1. Read the assignment carefully and completely.
2. Decide what you want to say—your controlling idea.
3. Decide what examples you'll use from the myths.
4. Organize your ideas, making sure to address these points:
   - What does each myth suggest about what people need?
   - Why are light and music so important?
   - Does the value of light and music justify their theft?

EQ Notes Before moving on to a new selection, go to your Essential Question Notes and record any additional thoughts or observations you may have about "How Grandmother Spider Stole the Sun" and "How Music Came to the World."

Write a Formal Research Paper

Research papers are reports in which a writer synthesizes research from outside sources with his or her own critical thinking and analysis to answer a research question.

ASSIGNMENT

Write a **formal research paper** in which you answer a focused research question about the following broad topic:

specific ways in which animals and people communicate

Synthesize information to create an engaging and informative text. Include the elements of research writing in your paper.

ELEMENTS OF RESEARCH WRITING

Purpose: to answer a focused research question

Characteristics

- a controlling idea, or thesis
- information gathered from a variety of sources, including primary sources and reliable secondary sources
- varied types of evidence
- citations that follow an accepted format, including a Works Cited list or bibliography
- elements of craft, including word choices that are precise and appropriate for the intended audience
- correct spelling, capitalization, and punctuation

Structure

- logical organization that includes an introduction and a conclusion
- well-chosen transitions that create coherence both within and across paragraphs

11.B. Compose informational texts, including multi-paragraph essays that convey information about a topic, using a clear controlling idea or thesis statement and genre characteristics and craft

12.A. Generate student-selected and teacher-guided questions for formal and informal inquiry.

Take a Closer Look at the Assignment

NOTEBOOK

1. What is the assignment asking me to do in my own words?

2. Is there a specific **audience** mentioned in the assignment?

◯ Yes If "yes," who is my main audience?

◯ No If "no," who do I think my audience should be?

3. Is my **purpose** for writing specified in the assignment?

◯ Yes If "yes," what is the purpose?

◯ No If "no," why am I writing this research essay (not just because it's an assignment)?

4. (a) Does the assignment ask me to use specific **types of sources**?

◯ Yes If "yes," what are they?

◯ No If "no," what types of sources do I think I need?

(b) Where will I find these sources? What details can I pull from my EQ notes?

5. Does the assignment ask me to organize my ideas in a certain way?

◯ Yes If "yes," what structure does it require?

◯ No If "no," how can I best organize my ideas?

AUDIENCE

Always keep your **audience**, or reader, in mind.

- Choose words your audience will understand.
- Explain ideas or elements that may be unfamiliar to your audience.

PURPOSE

A specific **purpose,** or reason for writing, will lead to a stronger paper.

General Purpose: *In this research paper, I'll explore communication between people and animals.*

Specific Purpose: *In this research paper, I'll explain how people benefit from communicating with animals.*

SOURCES

Use various **types of sources** to make your research paper accurate and interesting:

- **Primary Sources:** firsthand accounts of events, such as diaries, letters, or oral histories
- **Secondary Sources:** sources that discuss information originally presented in primary sources; includes articles, reference-book entries, and biographies

Prewriting and Planning

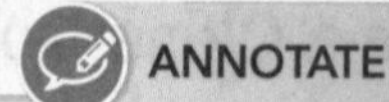

In order to choose your topic and generate a meaningful research question, you need to do some preliminary work.

SAMPLE RESEARCH QUESTIONS

- What animals have been trained to "talk," and how?
- In what ways do bees communicate?
- How do therapy dogs communicate with people?

Generate Questions to Develop a Plan

- Do a quick online search to gather background information about the broad topic. You may discuss specific topics that interest you with a partner.
- List aspects of the topic that spark your curiosity. Write them as questions. Try to use "how" and "why" questions. Write quickly and freely.
- Go back through your list of questions and mark the ones you find most exciting. Cross out the ones that don't interest you.

NOTEBOOK

WRITE IT Generate questions about your topic.

12.A. Generate student-selected and teacher-guided questions for formal and informal inquiry.
12.C. Refine the major research question, if necessary, guided by answers to a secondary set of questions.

Refine Your Research Question

NOTEBOOK

INTERACTIVITY

A. Write Your Question Pick the question you generated that you like the most. Write it here.

B. Evaluate Your Question A good question will provide a clear path for your research. A weak question will result in either too much or too little information. Use the Checklist to make sure your question is narrow enough to be interesting and answerable.

TIPS Your question will focus your research. As you conduct your research, other questions may occur to you. These new questions may lead you to modify your original question and alter the focus of your research.

Research Question Checklist

Complexity

- ◯ I can't answer the question with a simple "yes" or "no."

Clarity and Focus

- ◯ The question is precise.
- ◯ Information related to the question is plentiful but not overwhelming.
- ◯ The question will point me in a clear direction for finding information.

Significance

- ◯ The question matters to me.
- ◯ The question will matter to my readers.

C. Refine Your Question If your question doesn't meet all of the Checklist items, refine it. Write your refined question here.

STRONG RESEARCH QUESTIONS

Strong research questions have the following characteristics:

- **Level of Complexity:** The question is complex enough to warrant research, but not so complex that it becomes impossible to answer.
- **Clarity and Focus:** The question is focused enough that you're able to identify sources that will help you answer it.
- **Significance:** The question is important enough to warrant researching in the first place and is something that readers will be interested in.

Prewriting and Planning

INTERACTIVITY

Gather your research sources from the school or local library, reputable online sites, and local authorities, such as science teachers or veterinarians.

A. Identify and Gather a Variety of Sources

List sources you might use to gather information that is relevant to your research question. Plan to use at least one source from each category.

Type of Source	Title of Source
Primary Sources: texts created at the time the event actually happened • diaries or journals • original newspaper articles • eyewitness accounts • public records • ads or cartoons from the time period	
Secondary Sources: information shared by writers and researchers after the events occurred • newspaper or magazine articles • encyclopedia entries • historical writing • media (documentaries, TV programs, etc.)	
Your Own Research: information-gathering you do yourself • online surveys • in-person surveys • interviews	

TEKS

6.E. Interact with sources in meaningful ways such as notetaking, annotating, freewriting, or illustrating; **12.D.** Identify and gather relevant information from a variety of sources; **12.E.** Differentiate between primary and secondary sources; **12.H.i.** Examine sources for reliability, credibility, and bias; **12.H.ii.** Examine sources for faulty reasoning such as hyperbole, emotional appeals, and stereotype.

B. Evaluate Sources

Plan to use only those sources that are credible, reliable, unbiased, relevant, and show clear reasoning. Use these guidelines to evaluate each source on your list. After your evaluation, add or delete sources, as necessary.

Guidelines for Evaluating Sources

◯ **Credibility: Is the information believable?**

Does the author have deep knowledge of the topic?

Source Title/Explanation: ________________ ◯ Yes ◯ No

Source Title/Explanation: ________________ ◯ Yes ◯ No

Source Title/Explanation: ________________ ◯ Yes ◯ No

◯ **Reliability: Is the information accurate?**

Can you confirm the author's findings with at least one other credible source?

Source Title/Explanation: ________________ ◯ Yes ◯ No

Source Title/Explanation: ________________ ◯ Yes ◯ No

Source Title/Explanation: ________________ ◯ Yes ◯ No

◯ **Bias: Are the author's views fair?**

Does the author have unjustified negative or positive feelings about something?

Source Title/Explanation: ________________ ◯ Yes ◯ No

Source Title/Explanation: ________________ ◯ Yes ◯ No

Source Title/Explanation: ________________ ◯ Yes ◯ No

◯ **Reasoning: Is the author's logic sound?**

Some sources use rhetorical devices, such as parallelism, to emphasize key ideas. Some writers, however, use logical fallacies, or faulty reasoning. The deliberate use of fallacies generally serves one purpose: to mislead readers, making them believe things that are not true. Evaluate potential sources for their uses of such devices, including those shown here. If you find fallacies, avoid the source.

- *hyperbole*: exaggeration that distorts the facts
- *emotional appeals*: emotionally charged content unsupported by facts
- *stereotype*: unfair generalization of someone's qualities based on his or her membership in a specific group
- *sweeping generalizations:* broad general rules applied incorrectly to specific examples

CHECK ONLINE SOURCES

Some websites are reliable, but some are not.

- Consult sites from established institutions and those with expertise (.edu, .gov).
- Avoid commercial sites (.com).
- Question personal blogs and avoid anonymous sites or pages.

TAKE NOTES

Try different ways to take notes and capture information.

- Use notecards.
- Use software.
- Use digital tools, such as screenshots or bookmarks.

Choose a logical way to organize your notes.

- by source
- by topic

Be sure to record citation information for every source you consult.

REVISE YOUR PLAN

Allow enough time for your initial research. Then, review your findings and decide if you need more information. Identify your resources and leave time to gather them.

- Visit the library.
- Research online.
- Interview experts.

Drafting

Now that you've gathered the information you need, organize it and write a first draft.

Write Your Thesis

Answer your research question with one sentence; this is your thesis, or controlling idea.

Sample Thesis: Dolphins communicate in more complex and detailed ways than people realize.

My Thesis: ____

____

Make an Outline

List the points you want to make and the evidence that will support each one. Use the Outline Model as a guide.

OUTLINE MODEL

Title of Your Report

I. Introduction
   Thesis Statement
II. First main point
   A. Supporting detail #1
      1. Example
      2. Example
      3. Example
   B. Supporting detail #2
   C. Supporting detail #3
III. Second main point

WRITE IT Make an outline for your paper.

DEPTH OF THOUGHT / SYNTHESIZE INFORMATION

As you draft, show that you have synthesized research to express your own insights.

- **Audience** Explain any specialized words or concepts that you learned.
- **Development** Integrate facts, details, and examples from sources while still expressing your own point of view.
- **Citations** Mark ideas and phrases that come directly from sources so you can easily add formal citations later.

10.B.i. Develop drafts into a focused, structured, and coherent piece of writing by organizing with purposeful structure, including an introduction, transitions, coherence within and across paragraphs, and a conclusion; **12.F.** Synthesize information from a variety of sources; **12.G.** Differentiate between paraphrasing and plagiarism when using source materials; **12.I.** Display academic citations and use source materials ethically.

Create Coherence

There are different ethical ways to include information from sources. Decide how you will use specific pieces of evidence. Then, add **transitions** (words that connect ideas) to create coherence both within and across paragraphs.

Use Source Materials Ethically

Use of Source	Definition	Examples
Direct Quotation	source's exact words, set off in quotation marks	"A whale that was living close to a pod of bottlenose dolphins has learned to speak their language" ("Ocean Talk" 44).
Paraphrase	restatement of another's ideas in your own words	According to Collins, a whale living near a dolphin community has begun to use the dolphins' language ("Ocean Talk" 44).
Summary	brief statement of the main ideas and details of a text	"Ocean Talk" presents one researcher's observations about whales' remarkable ability to learn and adapt (42–47).

IN-TEXT CITATIONS: Place in-text citations in parentheses.

- Author Indicated: cite the page number
- Author Not Indicated: cite the author's last name and page number
- No Author: cite short version of the title and the page number
- No Page Number: cite short title or author only

When to Cite Information

As you use information from sources, err on the side of caution and create a citation. Otherwise, you risk **plagiarizing**, or using someone else's words and ideas as your own.

- **Citation Not Needed:** your own ideas; **common knowledge**
- **Citation Needed:** direct quote, paraphrase, or summary of someone else's idea; **specialized information**

When you finish drafting, provide full information about your sources in a Works Cited list at the end of your paper. Follow the style of the format your teacher prefers.

NOTEBOOK

WRITE IT Draft a paragraph using information from one or two sources, some of which you quote directly and some of which you paraphrase. Use well-chosen transitions, and credit the writer's ideas.

COMMON KNOWLEDGE / SPECIALIZED INFORMATION

You don't need to cite common knowledge, but you must cite specialized terms and ideas.

- **Common Knowledge:** facts most people know

EXAMPLE: Chimpanzees are mammals.

- **Specialized Information:** facts, concepts, and ideas known only by experts or those who have studied a subject in depth

EXAMPLE: Young chimps stay with their mothers for up to ten years.

Revising

Now that you have a first draft, revise it to be sure it is as clear and informative as possible. When you revise, you "re-see" your writing, checking for the following elements:

Clarity: sharpness of your ideas; clear controlling idea or thesis statement

Development: full explanations with strong supporting evidence

Organization: logical flow of ideas, connected with transitions to create coherence within and across paragraphs

Style and Tone: a variety of well-written sentence types, lengths, and patterns; precise, well-chosen words; a level of formality that suits your audience and purpose

Read Like a Writer

Review the revisions made to the Model Text. Then, answer the questions in the white boxes.

MODEL TEXT

from Sympathy in Other Species

Many researchers have reported that the great apes ~~love each other~~ *show close bonds with their offspring and adult companions.* However, according to recent research, they seem to feel sympathy for other species as well (Thompson 47).

> Why do you think the writer revised the word choice here?

Bonobos are a type of great ape that look like small chimpanzees. Researchers have observed bonobos saving birds from drowning when the birds fall into a body of water. Thompson quotes one professional observer: "They're reckless and brave," said Erin Miller, "and definitely motivated to succeed" (48).

> Why do you think the author added this information?

Koko, a gorilla famous for knowing how to communicate with humans through sign language, has been observed turning away from a scene in a movie in which a child is leaving home. *Koko was reported signing, "Mother... sad...trouble...cry" (50).*

> The author added evidence to strengthen the point.

10.C. Revise drafts for clarity, development, organization, style, word choice, and sentence variety.

Take a Closer Look at Your Draft

Now, revise your draft. Use the Revision Guide for Research Writing to evaluate and strengthen your paper.

REVISION GUIDE FOR RESEARCH WRITING

EVALUATE	TAKE ACTION
Clarity	
Is my thesis concise and clear?	If your thesis is too broad, **summarize** the main point you want to make.
Have I explained any specialized terms?	**Define** specialized terms in parentheses or within the sentence with a set-off clause.
Development	
Have I balanced researched information with my own ideas?	**Mark** researched information with one color and then your own ideas with another color. Then, **add** more sourced information or original ideas, as needed.
Do I rely too much on one source?	If most of the evidence you use is from the same source, **add** variety. • Review your source list and **integrate** relevant evidence from a different text. • Do more research, using sources you may have overlooked. Then, **replace** existing details with new evidence.
Organization	
Does every paragraph add meaningfully to my thesis?	Write your thesis in the margin beside the first sentence of each paragraph. Is the connection of that sentence to the thesis clear? If not, **revise** or **delete**.
Do all the sentences within each paragraph relate to the topic sentence?	**Delete** any sentence that is off point or **revise** it to make the relationship to the topic sentence clear.
Style and Tone	
Does my introduction engage readers?	**Add** a question, anecdote, quotation, or strong detail to interest your audience.
Is my conclusion strong and memorable?	**Add** a quotation, a call to action, an insight, or a strong statement to conclude.
Is my word choice precise?	Review your draft and mark any vague words, such as *nice, good, bad,* or *important*. **Replace** those words with precise words that make your ideas more focused and exact.

Editing

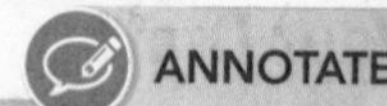

Don't let errors distract readers from your ideas and information. Reread your draft and fix mistakes to create a finished informative work.

Read Like a Writer

Look at how the writer of the Model Text edited part of a draft. Then, follow the directions in the white boxes.

MODEL TEXT

from Sympathy in Other Species

Dolphins have also been credited with saving people. For example, many stories in circulation tells about dolphins helping struggling swimmers. In one case, as a boat approached, witnesses reported that the dolphins flung themselves into the air, as if to mark the swimmer's location *("Amazing Dolphin Rescue").*

A research study led by sociologist Max Monroe and marine biologist Amelia Pantel is trying to find out whether these stories have more to them. ~~They hope they can uncover the truth by looking at these incidents in two different ways.~~ *"The tools of marine science and those of sociology are very different. We hope that the combination will show us the truth about dolphins"* (Pantel 115).

Find and fix the agreement between a subject and a verb separated by a prepositional phrase.

The author added a missing citation.

The author replaced a paraphrase with a more interesting direct quotation.

Focus on Sentences

Subject-Verb Agreement With Prepositional Phrases Subjects and verbs must agree (for example, *the gorillas swim* and *the gorilla swims*), even when you insert a prepositional phrase between the subject and verb (*the gorillas* in the water *swim* gracefully).

PRACTICE Fix the errors in subject-verb agreement in these sentences with prepositional phrases. Then, check your own draft for correctness.

1. The monkeys in the tree swings from branch to branch with ease.
2. The boy up in the branches try to swing too.
3. His sisters in the living room watches through the window.

EDITING TIPS

1. Mark the subject in each sentence and note whether it is singular or plural.
2. Read the sentence, omitting the prepositional phrase. Make sure the verb agrees with the subject in number.

TEKS

10.D.iv. Edit drafts using standard English conventions, including prepositions and prepositional phrases and their influence on subject-verb agreement; **10.E.** Publish written work for appropriate audiences. **12.I.** Display academic citations and use source materials ethically; **12.J.** Use an appropriate mode of delivery, whether written, oral, or multimodal, to present results.

Rules for Proper Citation

Works Cited List A Works Cited list is just what the name suggests—a list of all the sources you cite in your paper. There are different styles for the formatting of these lists. The rules shown here represent MLA style.

- **Capitalization of Titles:** Don't capitalize articles (*a, an, the*), prepositions, or conjunctions unless they are the first words in a title.
  Book Title: *The Incredible Complexity of Bird Song*
  Magazine Article Title: "A Conversation with My Dog"
- **Punctuation of Author Names:** Follow these models to punctuate author names correctly.
  Full-Length Book, Single Author: Bradford, Rowan. *Animal Communication*. Parker Editions, 2013.
  Full-Length Book, Multiple Authors: Bradford, Rowen, and Olivia Dasha. *Without Words: New Visions of Communication*. Parker Editions, 2018.
- **Formatting Titles:** Place the titles of shorter texts—for example, short stories, articles, poems, songs, or episodes of a show—in quotation marks. Set the titles of full-length works in italics.
  Shorter Work: Langan, Jeanette. "Whale Words." *Marine Biology Today*, 2015, pp. 9–13.
  Full-Length Work: Rain, Summer. *Speaking with Animals*. 2nd ed., CJ Press, 2011.

EDITING TIP:
Spelling The suffixes *-able* and *-ible* both mean "full of; causing." Both create adjectives when added to a verb. However, *-able* is far more common in English. Check your paper and make sure you have spelled any words that contain these suffixes correctly.

PRACTICE Refer to the rules and use the information shown here to write a correct citation.

Information: Full-Length Book	Citation
Title: Why Birds Whisper Date of Publication: 2012 Author: Marie Gonzalez Publisher: Red Wing Books	

Publishing and Presenting

Share With a Broader Audience

Share your research with your class. Choose from these options:

OPTION 1 Print your research paper and make multiple copies to share with your class or larger school community.

OPTION 2 Take turns interviewing a partner about his or her research with the class as your audience. Plan questions ahead of time and share sections of your papers during the interview.

Essential Question

What is the relationship between people and nature?

The natural world is full of amazing creatures that we interact with in countless ways, from feeling awe at their beauty to finding inspiration in their solutions to the problems of survival. In this section, you will read selections that discuss the relationship between people and nature. You will work as a group to continue your exploration of the ways in which people learn from nature.

VIDEO

INTERACTIVITY

Peer-Group Learning Strategies

Throughout your life, in school, in your community, and in your career, you will continue to learn and work with others.

Look at these strategies and the actions you can take to practice them as you work in small groups. Add ideas of your own for each category. Use these strategies during Peer-Group Learning.

STRATEGY	MY PEER-GROUP ACTION PLAN
Prepare • Complete your assignments so that you are prepared for group work. • Take notes on your reading to share with your group.	
Participate fully • Volunteer information, and use verbal and nonverbal forms of communication to get your points across. • Use text evidence when making a point.	
Support others • Build off ideas from others in your group. • Ask others who have not yet spoken to do so.	
Clarify • Paraphrase the ideas of others to check your own understanding. • Ask follow-up questions.	

CONTENTS

Working as a Group

1. Take a Position

In your group, discuss the following question:

> What is our relationship with the natural world?

As you take turns sharing your positions, be sure to provide examples that support your ideas. After all group members have shared, discuss the common characteristics of this relationship that are suggested by your responses.

2. List Your Rules

As a group, decide on the rules that you will follow as you work together. Read the two samples provided. Notice that these rules use both basic and academic words. Write two rules of your own. As you write, pay attention to the basic and academic words you use to communicate.

- Come prepared for group discussions.
- Acknowledge other people's opinions.

____

____

3. Apply the Rules

Practice working as a group. Share what you have learned about the relationship between people and nature. Make sure each person in the group contributes. Take notes and be prepared to share with the class one thing that you heard from another member of your group.

4. Name Your Group

Choose a name that reflects the unit topic.

Our group's name: ______________________________

5. Create a Communication Plan

Decide how you want to communicate with one another. For example, you might use online collaboration tools, email, or instant messaging.

Our group's plan:

____

____

TEKS

6.I. Reflect on and adjust responses as new evidence is presented.

Making a Schedule

First, find out the due dates for the peer-group activities. Then, preview the texts and activities with your group and make a schedule for completing the tasks.

SELECTION	ACTIVITIES	DUE DATE
Turtle Watchers Jaguar The Sparrow		
Urban Farming Is Growing a Greener Future		
Creature Comforts: Three Biology-Based Tips for Builders		
He—y, Come On Ou—t!		

Reflect and Adjust Your Responses

Literature can generate a wide variety of responses in different readers—and that can make your peer-group work exciting and fun. At the same time, it can be a challenge to engage in collaborative work with people who have many different opinions. Use these tips to get the most from your peer-group work:

Agree to disagree. Disagreement can be as important as agreement. It makes you focus on why you feel or think as you do and that can sharpen your reasoning.

Pause before you respond. Really reflect on what someone has said or written. Even if you agree, take a quick moment before you say something or give feedback.

Give appropriate responses. Speak up and share your thoughts, using appropriate vocabulary and a respectful tone of voice.

Other people's experiences and ways of seeing things can open your eyes to new understandings. If reflecting on evidence leads you to adjust your response, share your thinking. Your thought process may be instructive for everyone in your group.

POETRY COLLECTION

The selections you are about to read are lyric poems.

Reading Lyric Poetry

Lyric poetry is poetry that is short, with musical qualities. Lyric poems typically express feelings or emotions.

LYRIC POETRY

Author's Purpose

- to capture the emotions or insights related to a moment in time

Characteristics

- a speaker, or unnamed voice "tells" the poem
- conveys a theme, or insight about life
- imagery and figurative language that describe things in new, fresh ways
- language creates a musical effect
- may break some rules of standard English

Structure

- divided into lines, or groups of words arranged in rows
- lines are arranged in groups called stanzas
- may use rhyme scheme and meter

Take a Minute!

NOTEBOOK

LIST IT With a partner, list some songs you know that have the characteristics of lyric poems.

TEKS

7.A. Infer multiple themes within and across texts using text evidence.

8.A. Demonstrate knowledge of literary genres such as realistic fiction, adventure stories, historical fiction, mysteries, humor, myths, fantasy, and science fiction.

Genre / Text Elements

Multiple Themes The **speaker** of a poem is the voice within the poem addressing the reader. Like a character in fiction, the speaker has a specific perspective and experience—expressed in words and imagery. By analyzing what the speaker has to say you can interpret a poem's **themes**, or insights about life.

EXAMPLE POEM	SPEAKER	KEY WORDS AND IMAGERY	POSSIBLE THEMES
Twinkle, twinkle little star, How I wonder what you are. Up above the world so high, Like a diamond in the sky.	a person looking at the stars and wondering	• *twinkle* repeated twice emphasizes shining of the star • star is "little," emphasized by the distance between it and the speaker ("so high") • diamond suggests more shine, beauty, and value	• Beauty awes. • The more unknowable something is, the more valuable it is.

INTERACTIVITY

PRACTICE Complete the chart by analyzing text evidence, such as the speaker's observations, key words, and imagery. Then, state two possible themes in the form of complete sentences.

EXAMPLE POEM	SPEAKER	KEY WORDS AND IMAGERY	POSSIBLE THEMES
from "Sorrow" by Edna St. Vincent Millay Sorrow like a ceaseless rain / Beats upon my heart. / People twist and scream in pain,— / Dawn will find them still again; / This has neither wax nor wane, / Neither stop nor start.			

POETRY COLLECTION

Turtle Watchers

Jaguar

The Sparrow

Concept Vocabulary

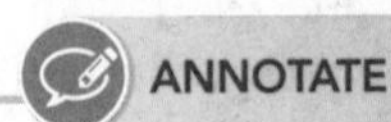

As you read the poems, you will encounter these words.

lineage	ancestors	heed

Print Resources To check the meanings of unfamiliar words, consult a print dictionary. Dictionaries provide a word's definition, pronunciation, part of speech, syllabication, and etymology, or word origin.

In the Sample Entry, notice that the pronunciation, shown in parentheses, indicates the word's syllabication.

SAMPLE DICTIONARY ENTRY

anthology (an THOL uh jee) *n., pl.* **-gies** [Gr. *anthologia*, a garland, collection of short poems < *anthologos*, gathering flowers < *anthos*, flower + *legein*, to gather] a collection of poems, stories, songs, excerpts, etc., chosen by the compiler.

PRACTICE Use a print dictionary to determine the meanings, pronunciations, and syllabications of unfamiliar words you encounter as you read.

Comprehension Strategy

Paraphrase

To **paraphrase** a text is to restate it in your own words. A paraphrase of a poem is a line-by-line or image-by-image restatement that maintains the meaning and logical order of the original text. Paraphrasing can help you clarify passages or whole poems that you find challenging. Follow these steps:

1. Read the poem, and identify any lines or sections that you don't understand.
2. Restate the challenging sections in your own words.
3. If you're still confused, seek help from peers or your teacher.

PRACTICE As you read the poems, pause to paraphrase any lines or sections that you find unclear. Write your paraphrases in the open space next to the text.

TEKS

2.A. Use print or digital resources to determine the meaning, syllabication, pronunciation, word origin, and part of speech.

6.D. Paraphrase and summarize texts in ways that maintain meaning and logical order.

About the Poems

Turtle Watchers

BACKGROUND
Some sea turtles, such as loggerhead sea turtles, travel thousands of miles to lay their eggs on the same beach where they were born. The turtles dig a small nest in the sand, where they lay their eggs, sometimes over a hundred in a single nest. When the eggs hatch, the baby turtles make the dangerous trek back to the ocean to continue the cycle.

Linda Hogan (b. 1947) is an award-winning Chickasaw novelist, essayist, poet, and environmentalist. Her writing often addresses topics such as the environment, ecofeminism, and Native American history. An activist and educator, Hogan has spoken at various global conferences and events, including the Environmental Literature Conference in Turkey in 2009. She lives in the Colorado mountains and teaches creative writing.

Jaguar

BACKGROUND
This poem comes from Alarcón's collection entitled *Animal Poems of the Iguazú,* which was inspired by the diverse creatures that inhabit the rainforest in Argentina's Iguazú National Park. In the poems, Alarcón brings the endangered rainforest to life by adopting the voices of its animal inhabitants, one of which is the jaguar.

Francisco X. Alarcón (1954–2016) grew up in California and in Guadalajara, Mexico, an upbringing that led him to call himself a "binational, bicultural, and a bilingual writer." After graduating from California State University, Alarcón earned a master's degree in Latin American literature at Stanford University. He published numerous award-winning poetry collections for both adults and children.

The Sparrow

BACKGROUND
Sparrows are one of the most common birds in the world. They are often seen in North America, but this was not always the case. In the mid-1800s, a man named Nicholas Pike decided to bring several dozen over from England and release them in New York. Since then, these small brown birds have flourished and spread across the continent.

Paul Laurence Dunbar (1872–1906) was the son of former slaves. Encouraged by his mother, he began writing poetry at an early age. Dunbar was inspired by Harriet Beecher Stowe's novel *Uncle Tom's Cabin*, and in his own work he honored people who fought for the rights of African Americans. Over the course of his life, Dunbar published more than ten volumes of poetry, four novels, and four volumes of short stories.

LYRIC POETRY

Turtle Watchers

Linda Hogan

 AUDIO

 ANNOTATE

Old mother at water's edge
used to bow down to them,
the turtles coming in from the sea,
their many eggs,
their eyes streaming water like tears,
and I'd see it all,
old mother as if in prayer,
the turtles called back to where they were born,
the hungry watchers standing at the edge of trees
hoping for food when darkness gathers.
Years later, swimming in murky waters
a sea turtle swam beside me
both of us watching as if clasped together
in the **lineage** of the same world
the sweep of the same current,
even rising for a breath of air at the same time
still watching.
My **ancestors** call them
the keepers of doors
and the shore a realm to other worlds,
both ways and
water moves the deep shift of life
back to birth and before
as if there is a path where beings truly meet,
as if I am rounding the human corners.

Use a dictionary or indicate another strategy you used that helped you determine meaning.

lineage (LIH nee ihj) *n.*

MEANING:

ancestors (AN sehs tuhrz) *n.*

MEANING:

Jaguar

Francisco X. Alarcón

AUDIO

ANNOTATE

some say
I'm now almost
extinct in this park

but the people
who say this
don't know

that by smelling
the orchids
in the trees

they're sensing
the fragrance
of my chops

that by hearing
the rumbling
of the waterfalls

they're listening
to my ancestors'
great roar

that by observing
the constellations
of the night sky

they're gazing
at the star spots
on my fur

that I am and
always will be
the wild

untamed
living spirit
of this jungle

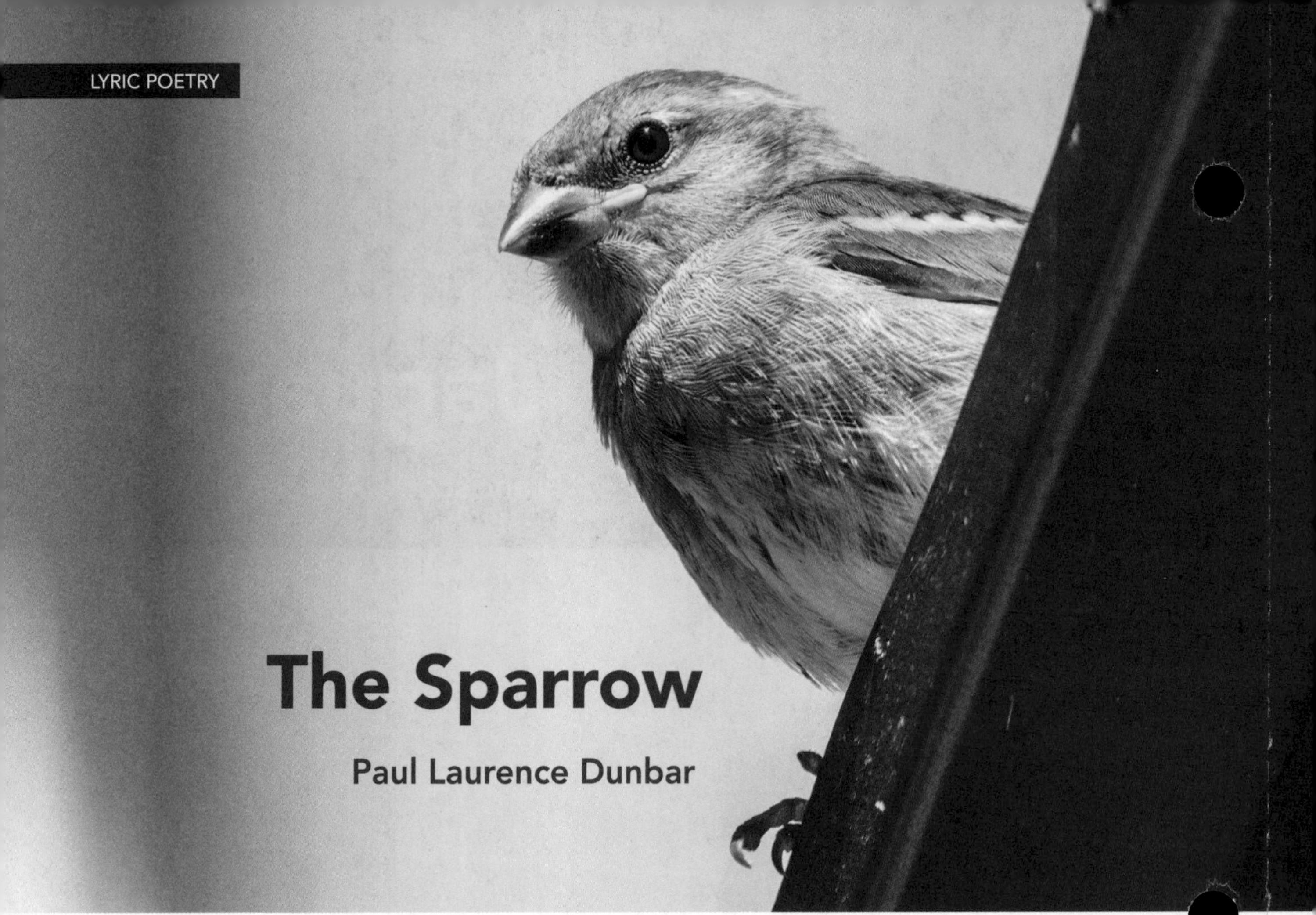

The Sparrow

Paul Laurence Dunbar

A little bird, with plumage brown,
Beside my window flutters down,
A moment chirps its little strain,
Ten taps upon my window-pane,
And chirps again, and hops along,
To call my notice to its song;
But I work on, nor **heed** its lay,*
Till, in neglect, it flies away.

So birds of peace and hope and love
Come fluttering earthward from above,
To settle on life's window-sills,
And ease our load of earthly ills;
But we, in traffic's rush and din
Too deep engaged to let them in,
With deadened heart and sense plod on,
Nor know our loss till they are gone.

* **lay** *n.* song.

Use a dictionary or indicate another strategy you used that helped you determine meaning.

heed (heed) *v.*

MEANING:

NOTEBOOK

Work on your own to answer the questions in your notebook. Use text evidence to support your responses.

Response

1. **Personal Connections** Choose one line or phrase from each poem that you found moving. Explain your choices.

Comprehension

2. **Reading Check (a)** In "Turtle Watchers," what do the turtles come in from the sea to do? **(b)** In "Jaguar," what danger is the jaguar facing? **(c)** In "The Sparrow," how does the speaker react to the bird by the window?

3. **Strategy: Paraphrase (a)** How did paraphrasing help clarify and deepen your understanding of the poems? **(b)** Would you recommend this strategy to others? Why or why not?

Analysis and Discussion

4. **(a) Analyze** In "Turtle Watchers," what understanding does the speaker gain while swimming beside the turtle? **(b) Interpret** Reread lines 18–25 of the poem. Why are turtles so meaningful to the speaker?

5. **(a) Interpret** Identify the pattern that begins in line 7 of "Jaguar." What effect does the use of patterns create? **(b) Analyze** What metaphor, or imaginative comparison, is revealed in "Jaguar"? **(c) Evaluate** Do you think this comparison is effective? Why or why not?

6. **Compare and Contrast** What similarities are there between stanza 1 and stanza 2 in "The Sparrow"? What key difference do you find?

7. **Get Ready for Close Reading** Choose a passage from the texts that you find especially interesting or important. You'll discuss the passage with your group during Close-Read activities.

WORKING AS A GROUP

Discuss your responses to the Analysis and Discussion questions with your group.

As you speak, use language that is routinely employed in academic conversations. For example, use words like *interpretation* and *consider* as you discuss the poems.

EQ Notes **What is the relationship between people and nature?**

What have you learned about the relationship between people and nature from reading these poems? Go to your Essential Question Notes and record your observations and thoughts about the Poetry Collection.

TEKS

6.A. Describe personal connections to a variety of sources, including self-selected texts.

6.C. Use text evidence to support an appropriate response.

6.D. Paraphrase and summarize texts in ways that maintain meaning and logical order.

POETRY COLLECTION

Close Read

PRACTICE **Complete the following activities. Use text evidence to support your responses. Be sure to enlist the help of peers or teachers if your group gets stuck.**

1. **Present and Discuss** With your group, share the passages from the poems that you found especially interesting. Discuss what you notice, the questions you have, and the conclusions you reach. For example, you might focus on the following passages:
   - Lines 1–13 in "Turtle Watchers": Discuss who or what the watchers are.
   - Lines 4–12 in "Jaguar": Discuss the relationship between the orchids and the jaguar.
   - Lines 9–16 in "The Sparrow": Discuss what loss the speaker describes in the final line.
2. **Reflect on Your Learning** What new ideas or insights did you uncover during your second reading of the poems?

WORD NETWORK

Add words that are related to people and nature from the text to your Word Network.

NOTEBOOK

LANGUAGE STUDY

Concept Vocabulary

Why These Words? The vocabulary words are related.

lineage	ancestors	heed

1. With your group, determine what the words have in common. Write your ideas.
2. Add another word that fits the category. ____________________
3. Use each vocabulary word in a sentence. Include context clues that hint at each word's meaning.

Word Study

Etymology The etymology, or word origin, of *ancestors* can help you understand and remember its meaning. *Ancestors* was formed from the Latin prefix *ante-*, meaning "before," and the Latin verb *cedere*, meaning "go." Thus *ancestors* literally means "those who have gone before us." Look up the word *ancestors* in a dictionary and discuss its definition with your group. How does understanding the etymology of *ancestors* deepen your understanding of the poem?

 TEKS

2.A. Use print or digital resources to determine the meaning, syllabication, pronunciation, word origin, and part of speech.

6.G. Discuss and write about the explicit or implicit meanings of text.

7.A. Infer multiple themes within and across texts using text evidence.

Genre / Text Elements

Multiple Themes A poem's **themes,** or insights about life, are usually not **explicit**, or directly stated. Instead, they are **implicit**, or left unstated. To interpret themes:

- note text evidence, such as a speaker's statements or direct observations
- note unstated ideas that are conveyed through description and imagery
- review your notes, and state an insight about life that the poem as a whole reveals

NOTEBOOK

PRACTICE Complete the activity and answer the questions.

1. **Interpret** Infer multiple themes by analyzing text evidence, both explicit and implicit, in the poems. The first item has been done as an example.

POEM	TEXT EVIDENCE	POSSIBLE THEMES
Turtle Watchers	*Explicit details:* old mother; prayer, watchers, shift of life, birth, clasped together; realm, ancestors, lineage *Implicit details:* images are mysterious and ancient; the sea seems to breathe; the speaker seems to understand the turtles	• All beings on earth share a mysterious, ancient connection. • Life is both fragile and strong.
Jaguar		
The Sparrow		

2. **Interpret** Reread "Turtle Watchers," and look at the text evidence in the chart, adding to it as necessary. What other theme can you formulate based on text evidence? Support your interpretation.

3. **(a) Compare and Contrast** Review the themes for the three poems. How are they alike and different? **(b) Interpret** What single, or universal theme, might apply to all three poems?

POETRY COLLECTION

Author's Craft

Language and Tone A poet's **diction,** or word choice, contributes to a poem's **tone**, or the author's attitude toward his or her subject. To determine tone as you read, consider the **denotations,** or definitions, of words and phrases in the text, as well as their **connotations,** or emotions they bring forth in readers.

Consider these two lines of poetry, which describe similar actions but have different tones..

TIP Try reading aloud to more readily recognize and analyze tone.

EXAMPLES	DICTION	TONE
They rolled over the swells until they slid ashore.	*rolled, swells,* and *slid* have gentle, quiet connotations	calm, peaceful
They slammed over the waves until they hit land.	*slammed* and *hit* have violent connotations	harsh, abrupt

 NOTEBOOK  INTERACTIVITY

READ IT Reread the last four lines of "The Sparrow," and mark key words in each line. Work with your group to identify connotations of the poet's word choices. Then, discuss how those words help establish the tone of the poem.

WRITE IT

1. Work with your group to revise lines 1–10 from "Turtle Watchers" by replacing the highlighted words and phrases with synonyms, or words and phrases that have similar meanings.

   Old mother at water's edge
   used to bow down to them,
   the turtles coming in from the sea,
   their many eggs,
   their eyes streaming water like tears,
   and I'd see it all,
   old mother as if in prayer,
   the turtles called back to where they were born,
   the hungry watchers standing at the edge of trees
   hoping for food when darkness gathers.

2. How do your changes to the poem's diction affect the tone?

 TEKS

9.F. Analyze how the author's use of language contributes to mood, voice, and tone.

Speaking and Listening

An **oral presentation** allows you to share your ideas directly with an audience. Various types of media may be used to illustrate ideas.

ASSIGNMENT

Work with your group to create an **oral presentation** that highlights interesting aspects of one of the poems. Choose one of these options:

- ◯ a **dramatic reading** in which you use your voice, and perhaps props, costumes, or lighting
- ◯ a **multimedia presentation** in which you use videos, images, and other digital media

Plan Your Presentation With your group, choose a poem, and decide to work on either the dramatic reading or the multimedia presentation. Discuss the poem and note elements find interesting. Be sure to look up any basic or academic vocabulary that is unclear to you. Then, assign roles for each group member, reflecting the type of presentation you have chosen. Use the graphic organizer to collect your ideas.

Poem: ________________ **Type of Presentation:** _________

What to Emphasize (aspects of the poem, such as theme or imagery)

How to Visually Emphasize (media, such as photos, illustrations, music, lighting)

How to Vocally Emphasize (ways to use speaking voices; words to choose or emphasize; tone of voice to use)

Present and Evaluate Once you have rehearsed, present your work to the class. After your presentation, invite comments and feedback from your classmates. Be prepared to answer questions. When other groups present their work, listen attentively. Evaluate their performance and provide feedback respectfully.

EQ Notes Before moving on to a new selection, go to your Essential Question Notes and record any additional thoughts or observations you may have about the Poetry Collection.

TEKS

6.E. Interact with sources in meaningful ways such as notetaking, annotating, freewriting, or illustrating.

6.H. Respond orally or in writing with appropriate register, vocabulary, tone, and voice.

About the Author

Hillary Schwei (b. 1980) studied Sustainable Food and Farming at Rutgers University and the University of Montana–Missoula and has worked on various urban gardening and farming programs, both in the United States and abroad. Schwei's belief that sustainable food production reconnects us to our environment and our communities informs her work with urban youth. She strives to educate young people about the benefits that urban, local food production can provide to the communities in which they live.

Urban Farming Is Growing a Greener Future

Concept Vocabulary

These words will be useful to you as you analyze, discuss, and write about the photographs.

rural: characteristic of the country; of or pertaining to agriculture **EXAMPLE** The family moved from a busy city to a quiet **rural** neighborhood surrounded by farms.
agricultural: related to the science and art of farming **EXAMPLE** A lot of the **agricultural** land that used to surround the town has been turned from cornfields into houses and stores.
localizing: gathering, collecting, or concentrating in a particular place **EXAMPLE** **Localizing** food production helps to provide consumers with fresher produce because the produce comes from places near where they live.

Comprehension Strategy

NOTEBOOK

Synthesize Information

When you **synthesize information,** you pull together different ideas in order to develop your own perspective. You allow your thinking about a topic to grow and change. To synthesize information from this photo gallery, notice details in both the visual elements and the text, and pull them together to deepen your understanding. Follow these steps to synthesize information:

- Identify important points in a text.
- Consider connections, similarities, and differences among those points.
- Use these sentence starters to organize your thinking and express your new understanding:

  At first I thought ________________.
  Then, I learned ________________.
  Now I think ________________.

PRACTICE As you study this photo gallery, synthesize your observations of the photographs and the captions to arrive at a new understanding. Jot your ideas in the Take Notes sections.

TEKS
5.H. Synthesize information to create new understanding.

Urban Farming Is Growing a Greener Future

Hillary Schwei

BACKGROUND

The year 2008 marked the first time that more people on Earth lived in cities than in **rural** areas. One significant consequence of this turning point is that most people no longer live in the **agricultural** areas that provide them with food.

Some city dwellers are transforming their concrete environments by establishing farms, often in the most unlikely locations. These urban farms create a new landscape that adapts the man-made structures of the city to the purposes of sustainable food production. **Localizing** food production through urban farming provides aesthetic, health, environmental, and economic benefits. Locally grown food not only supplies people with fresh, seasonal produce, but it also strengthens local economies by supporting family farmers and other local businesses. Farming in urban areas reduces the need to transport food over long distances to reach the consumer. The decrease in transportation creates environmental advantages such as lower levels of pollution and decreased fossil fuel use. This photo gallery provides a glimpse at unique and innovative urban farming projects.

AUDIO

NOTEBOOK

PHOTO 1: Urban farms are not a new idea. During both world wars, the government encouraged Americans to plant Victory Gardens where they could grow their own food. Here, in 1943, children work in a garden in New York City.

PHOTO 2: Urban farms can make use of vacant city lots that are often considered eyesores, or ugly, unpleasant sights in public places. The farms become not only a source of food and beauty, but provide a location for members of the community to gather. An area of neglected, polluted land next to a railway station in Perth, Australia, has been revived as an organic farm.

TAKE NOTES

PHOTO 3: New York City will never completely return to its long-lost agricultural origins, but in 2011, this midtown hotel began growing fruit, vegetables, and herbs on the building's roof to supply the hotel's kitchen. The hotel also keeps honeybees, which roam for miles pollinating city plants.

TAKE NOTES

PHOTO 4: Only 12 percent of Japan's land is suitable for agriculture, but in this company's headquarters in Tokyo, office workers can take time to cultivate produce. One-fifth of the nine-story building is devoted to farming.

TAKE NOTES

PHOTO 5: Urban farming, like traditional farming, is a year-round operation. The greenhouses at this farm in Chicago have to be maintained regardless of the season. Each acre of the farm produces 20,000 pounds of produce annually.

TAKE NOTES

PHOTO 6: This 30-year-old pickup truck is a mobile farm and travels around giving students in city schools a chance to experience how food grows. The farmers who own the truck made a film about their exploits and strive to support others who grow produce in creative ways.

TAKE NOTES

NOTEBOOK

Work on your own to answer the questions in your notebook. Use text evidence to support your responses.

Response

1. **Personal Connections** In what ways can farming change an individual? In what ways can it change a community?

Comprehension

2. **Reading Check (a)** What is a key consequence of more people living in cities than in rural areas? **(b)** What are the benefits of the organic farm in Perth, Australia shown in photo 2? **(c)** What is the purpose of the mobile farm shown in photo 6?

3. **Strategy: Synthesize Information (a)** Explain at least one way in which your understanding of a photograph changed when you synthesized your observations with information from a caption. **(b)** How might the strategy of synthesizing help you in other school tasks, such as writing a research paper? Explain.

Analysis and Discussion

4. **(a) Analyze** How does the author support the idea that urban farming offers various benefits? **(b) Make a Judgment** Which of those benefits do you think is most important? Explain, citing specific details from the photo gallery.

5. **Narrate** Choose one of the photographs and write a brief story about the people it depicts. Your story should reflect as many details from the image as possible.

6. **Make Inferences** What do the photos and captions suggest about the human needs that are met by urban farming? Refer to photo 4 and its caption in your answer, as well as at least one more photo and caption.

7. **Get Ready for Close Review** Choose a photo from the gallery that you find especially interesting or important. You'll discuss the photo with your group during Close-Review activities.

WORKING AS A GROUP

Discuss your responses to the Analysis and Discussion questions with your group.

- Note agreements and disagreements.
- Summarize insights.
- Consider changes of opinion.

If necessary, revise your original answers to reflect what you learn from your discussion.

What is the relationship between people and nature?

What have you learned about the relationship between people and nature from viewing this photo gallery? Go to your Essential Question Notes and record your observations and thoughts about "Urban Farming Is Growing a Greener Future."

TEKS

5.F. Make inferences and use evidence to support understanding.

5.H. Synthesize information to create new understanding.

6.C. Use text evidence to support an appropriate response.

6.I. Reflect on and adjust responses as new evidence is presented.

URBAN FARMING IS GROWING A GREENER FUTURE

Close Review

ANNOTATE

NOTEBOOK

Complete the following activities. Use text evidence to support your responses.

1. **Present and Discuss** With your group, share the photos from the gallery that you found especially interesting. Discuss what you notice, the questions you have, and the conclusions you reach. For example, you might focus on the following photos:
   - Photo 1: Discuss how urban farming may have boosted morale during the world wars.
   - Photo 4: Discuss how taking time out of one's work day to participate in farming may benefit employees.
2. **Reflect on Your Learning** What new ideas or insights did you uncover during your second reading and viewing?

NOTEBOOK

LANGUAGE STUDY

Concept Vocabulary

Use the vocabulary words in your responses to the following questions.

rural	agricultural	localizing

1. What relationship between people and nature is described in the Background section of the photo gallery?
2. Identify at least one thing that all of the photographs have in common.
3. Did the photo gallery change your views on the relationship between people and nature? Why or why not? Explain the reasons for your response.

WORD NETWORK

Add words that are related to people and nature from the text to your Word Network.

TEKS

1.B. Follow and give complex oral instructions to perform specific tasks, answer questions, or solve problems.

6.F. Respond using newly acquired vocabulary as appropriate.

Speaking and Listening

Oral instructions tell listeners how to do something in language precise enough to guide them and prevent confusion.

ASSIGNMENT

Work on your own to prepare a set of **oral instructions**. Then, take turns giving and following instructions with your group members. You may choose one of these options or pick a different, related topic.

- ◯ How can I create a garden design?
- ◯ How can I calculate the "food miles" of my favorite foods? ("Food miles" is the distance food travels from where it is grown to where it is consumed.)

Research Instructions Research the task and figure out if you'll need any materials, such as specific paper or tools.

Draft Instructions Use the chart to draft your instructions in a logical step-by-step sequence. Include precise spatial terms (*around, above, through*) and action words (*press, fold*). Also make sure to include connecting words that make the sequence of steps clear. Add rows as necessary.

INTERACTIVITY

STEPS	ORAL INSTRUCTIONS / SCRIPT
EXAMPLE: Draw a square	EXAMPLE: On an 11″ x 14″ piece of blank paper, draw a square with 1″ margins.

EQ Notes Before moving on to a new selection, go to your Essential Question Notes and record any additional thoughts or observations you may have about "Urban Farming Is Growing a Greener Future."

Give Instructions Take turns presenting your instructions. Speak clearly and observe your group. If they seem confused, find a better way to explain a step. For example, you may need to use more accurate spatial terms or exact measurements.

Follow Instructions When it is your turn to follow instructions, use these strategies:

- Listen closely for action words, as well as adverbs, such as *next* and *then*.
- Restate key points to yourself to absorb the information.
- Determine if any steps are missing or where you may be lost or confused. Ask for clarification or help if you need it. After each group member takes a turn, discuss what worked well in everyone's instructions and what could be improved.

CREATURE COMFORTS: THREE BIOLOGY-BASED TIPS FOR BUILDERS

The selection you are about to read is a science feature.

Reading Science Features

A **science feature** is a type of journalism that presents scientific information for general readers.

SCIENCE FEATURE

Author's Purpose

- to explain technical or scientific information to nonscientists

Characteristics

- controlling idea, or thesis
- supporting details and evidence, often from scientific studies, experiments, and experts
- specialized information documented by references and acknowledgements
- may contain visual elements (sidebars, charts, diagrams, images)

Structure

- engaging introduction, body paragraphs, and memorable conclusion
- background information supported by in-depth information

Take a Minute!

NOTEBOOK

LIST IT With a partner, make a list of possible subjects and titles for science features. Remember that the audience is nonscientists.

What interests you most among the topics you listed?

TEKS

8.D.ii. Analyze characteristics and structural elements of informational text, including features such as references or acknowledgements.

Genre / Text Elements

Text Features: References and Acknowledgements **References** and **acknowledgements** are characteristics of science articles. References are structures that document the writer's sources of information. Acknowledgements are passages of varying lengths in which the writer recognizes and thanks people or organizations that provided assistance. References and acknowledgements can take various forms.

EXAMPLE REFERENCES	EXAMPLE ACKNOWLEDGEMENTS
In their article "Animals' Impact," writers Wu and Smith note that having pets increases people's life expectancy (36).	I appreciate the assistance of the Wu/Smith Foundation for access to their libraries.
Research supports the idea that raising animals increases people's life expectancy (Wu and Smith, 36).	I thank Andrea Wu for helping me translate scientific language into plain English.

References and acknowledgements can help readers trust the author's process by:

- documenting specialized information.
- indicating the type and extent of research the author conducted.
- revealing the writer's process.

PRACTICE Work with a partner to mark whether each item in the chart would be better suited to a reference or an acknowledgement.

	REFERENCE	ACKNOWLEDGEMENT
1. Mentioning a grant for researching an article		
2. Thanking a physicist for explaining scientific terminology		
3. Including data about blood pressure in pet owners		
4. Quoting a newspaper article about the benefits of pet ownership		

About the Author

Mary Beth Cox is a chemist from Texas. She is a frequent contributor to Cricket Media, a global education company that publishes award-winning magazines for children on a variety of subjects.

Creature Comforts: Three Biology-Based Tips for Builders

Concept Vocabulary

As you read this science feature, you will encounter these words:

incorporate	melded	affinity

Using Resources A **thesaurus** is a resource that provides synonyms and antonyms for words and some expressions. This information can help you infer the meanings of unfamiliar words. For example, consider how the synonyms and antonyms for the adjective *pet* suggest the word's meaning, which is "favorite; preferred."

Synonyms for *pet*: beloved, cherished, dear

Antonyms for *pet*: hated, unimportant

PRACTICE As you read the article, use a thesaurus to determine the meanings of unfamiliar words. Write your notes in the margins of the text.

Comprehension Strategy

Make Predictions

When you **make predictions,** you use what you know about a text to guess at the types of ideas it might include. You then correct or confirm your predictions. Use these aspects of informational texts to make predictions:

- **Genre:** Informational texts include fact-based content. If you know the topic of a text, you can predict the kinds of facts and ideas it contains.
- **Features:** Text features—such as heads, images, and captions—can help you make predictions about the larger content.
- **Structures:** Informational texts use structures, such as cause-and-effect. Recognize those structures to make predictions. For example, if you see that an author discusses a cause, you can predict that he or she will also discuss an effect.

PRACTICE Scan the article before you read it fully. Use the characteristics of genre, text features, and structures to make predictions. Then, correct or confirm those predictions as you read more closely.

TEKS

2.A. Use print or digital resources to determine the meaning, syllabication, pronunciation, word origin, and part of speech.

5.C. Make, correct, or confirm predictions using text features, characteristics of genre, and structures.

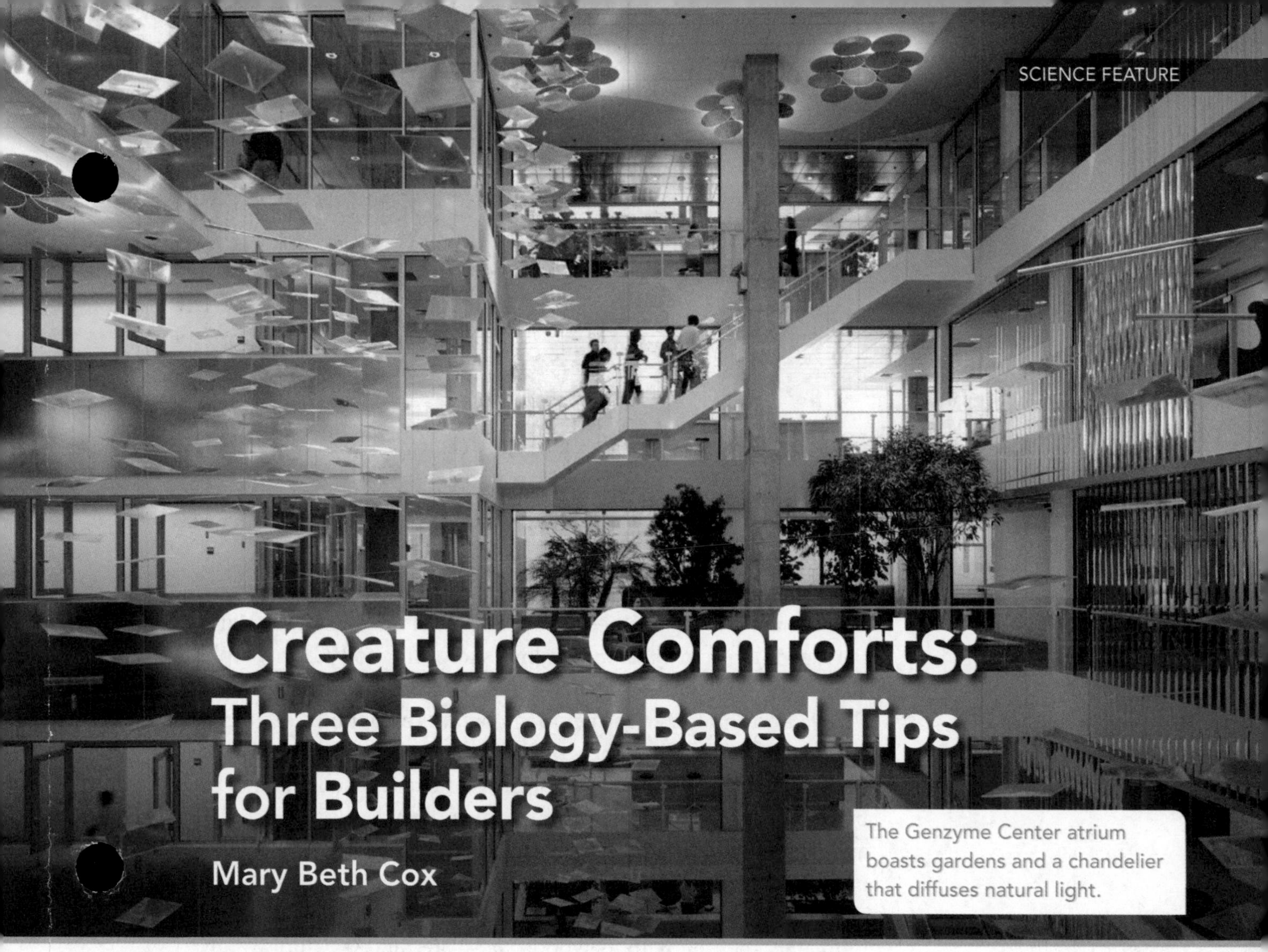

Creature Comforts: Three Biology-Based Tips for Builders

Mary Beth Cox

The Genzyme Center atrium boasts gardens and a chandelier that diffuses natural light.

BACKGROUND

Nature is full of examples of amazing solutions to the challenges of survival. From wings that are strong and light to shelters that are comfortable and cool, the creativity of nature results in designs that work incredibly well. They are also, often, beautiful. These natural solutions inspire people, who are also seeking ways to solve difficult problems. This feature explores how architects, engineers, and other designers working today look to nature for inspiration.

1 Human architects are the new kids on the block. They've been shaping their surroundings for only a few thousand years. Other life forms have done so for quite a bit longer. Life first appeared on planet Earth four *billion* years ago. Over that staggering stretch of time, creatures turned this moist rocky planet into a home. They adapted to diverse environments. They coped with fluctuating conditions. They endured tricky survival situations. So it behooves human builders to borrow what they can from the B's. Not from the hive-building insects, though they too are instructive. The B's are three biology-based ideas: biophilia, biomorphism, and biomimicry.

biophilia an appreciation for life and the living world

biomorphism using the forms, shapes, or patterns of living things

biomimicry systems based on actual living processes

Spanish architect Santiago Calatrava designed the Milwaukee Art Museum's Quadracci Pavilion.

The Company of Nature

2 Biophilia is a term coined by the esteemed biologist E. O. Wilson. *Bio* means life, and *philia* means love. According to Wilson, biophilia is an instinctive fondness humans feel for other living things (1–2). People find comfort in the company of nature. Biophilic architects build accordingly. They **incorporate** sunlight, fresh air, water, and plants into their designs. They preserve the native sense of a place by blending buildings into surroundings. They landscape appropriately for the ecosystems of their sites. They provide views of the wider outside world. Frank Lloyd Wright's Fallingwater is an example of biophilic architecture. The rough stone home is intimately **melded** with its woods and waterfall. At Fallingwater, the indoors feels like it's outside. Sometimes biophilic architects do things the other way round. They bring the great out-of-doors in. Natural light floods the atrium of Boston's Genzyme Center. A water feature splish-splashes pleasantly. Specimen trees thrive in scattered mini-gardens.

Use a digital thesaurus or indicate another strategy that helped you determine meaning.

incorporate (ihn CORP uhr ayt) *V.*

MEANING:

melded (MEL dihd) *V.*

MEANING:

Living Shapes and Patterns

3 The second B, biomorphism, is a term best defined by a quote from the naturalist Charles Darwin. Darwin famously observed that living things adopt "endless forms most beautiful and wonderful" (867). Architects who design biomorphically couldn't agree more. They are inspired by the shapes and patterns of the living world. Life forms differ from human-made forms. Humans engineer rigid structures with lots of right angles. They frequently build with inorganic materials such as metal and stone. Life tends to be more flexible. It prefers bends and curves to squared-off angles. Some creatures have inorganic bones or shells, but most are composed of organic, carbon-based materials. Biomorphic architects model their work on those wonderful forms that humans happen to enjoy. The Milwaukee Art Museum bears a

striking example. The museum's roof is outfitted with an adjustable sunscreen, or *brise soleil*. The screen looks like a pair of giant wings that grace the Wisconsin sky. A few states to the east, a Connecticut campus sports a biomorphic building. The cetacean-style[1] hockey rink is fondly known as the "Yale Whale."

Sustainable Structures

4 Biophilia and biomorphism are about **affinity** and appearance. Biomimicry is concerned with action. Biomimetic architects are interested in life's processes, mechanisms, and strategies. Their designs don't necessarily look lifelike—they *act* lifelike. Such is the case with the famed Eiffel Tower. The Parisian landmark is among the most familiar structures in the world, and yet few realize the debt it owes to biomimicry. Monsieur Eiffel's source of inspiration was his own species. His iconic tower handles off-center stresses in the same manner as the human thighbone ("Human Anatomy").

5 Biomimicry offers a wealth of ideas to architects who are interested in sustainability. It shows them how to minimize any negative impacts their structures might have on the environment. Living things have spent four billion years researching sustainable strategies. They've achieved some enviable results. They rely solely on locally available resources. They're efficient recyclers—one creature's waste is often another's raw material. Photosynthetic[2] green plants are even solar powered! Eco-sensitive biomimicry is what keeps the Eastgate Centre in Harare, Zimbabwe, cool and

Use a digital thesaurus or indicate another strategy that helped you determine meaning.

affinity (uh FIHN ih tee) *n.*

MEANING:

1. **cetacean-style** (sih TAY shun STY uhl) *adj.* modeled after a certain group of marine mammals that includes whales, dolphins, and porpoises.
2. **photosynthetic** (foh toh sihn THEH tihk) *adj.* characterized by the ability to turn water and carbon dioxide into food when exposed to light—the process by which plants make their food.

Yale University's Ingalls Rink has been nicknamed the "Yale Whale."

comfortable. The office complex is ventilated by an air-handling system that is inspired by termite mounds. The system features hollow horizontal floors, vertical vent shafts, and high-volume fans. Cool night air drawn in at the building's base pushes the day's hot air up and out. Termites use a similar strategy to control temperatures in the chambers of their mounds (except the bugs do it without the fans). The Eastgate Centre uses 90 percent less energy than comparable human-made structures (Doan).

Thoughtful Design

6 When architects borrow from the B's, they take life's lessons in new directions. Biology focuses on one goal and one goal only: Survive long enough to reproduce. It is restricted to testing random, incremental changes. It can build only on previous success. Its main advantage is eons of time.

7 Human architects get to choose their own various projects. Their work is not usually a matter of life or death (though at times it can be stressful). Architects are freer to experiment. They can build on established traditions, but they can also start from scratch. They plan with logical insight. They create with leaps of imagination. Of course, their deadlines are much tighter!

8 But the innovations of humans are not isolated from the environment shaped by other living things. All Earthlings cope with the same planetary conditions. We contend with the same ecological consequences. Humans just meet the challenges with an odd adaptation called intelligence. Intelligence improves our chances of survival. It also lets us learn from the hard-won experience of others. The value of that is impossible to overestimate. Our fellow creatures have been making themselves comfortable here for a very, very long time. ❧

French engineer Gustave Eiffel studied the way the human femur (thigh bone) supports off-center weight while designing the Paris landmark.

The termite-inspired Eastgate Centre is a renowned example of green architecture.

Acknowledgements

In writing this article, I received help from people all over the world. I wish to thank Janine Benyus and her team at the Biomimicry Institute. They see biomimicry as a way to build environments that help people live in harmony with nature rather than against it. I am also grateful to the wonderful people at The Genzyme Center in Boston, Massachusetts, and the Milwaukee Art Museum in Milwaukee, Wisconsin. The staff at both organizations spent a great deal of time with me and generously gave me tours of their facilities. They also answered my many questions with vast patience. I also wish to thank my college friend, Tenley Harper, who teaches in Harare, Zimbabwe. She alerted me to the fascinating, biomimetic design of the Eastgate Centre in that country. Finally, I would like to express my gratitude to all the visionary scientists, architects, and engineers who are including elements of the natural world in their designs. I believe their efforts will create a brighter future for everyone.

Works Cited

Benyus, Janine M. *Biomimicry: Innovation Inspired by Nature.* HarperCollins, 1997.

Brooks, Michael. "Nature Designs It Better." *The Guardian,* 5 Apr. 2000, http://www.url-website. Accessed 29 June 2017.

Darwin, Charles. *On the Origin of Species.* 1st ed., John Murray, 1859. *Project Gutenberg E-book,* http://www.url-website. Accessed 30 June 2017.

Delgado, Jacinto. Personal interview. 1 June 2017.

Doan, Abigail. "Biomimetic Architecture: Green Building in Zimbabwe Modeled After Termite Mounds." *Inhabit,* 29 Nov. 2012, http://www.url-website. Accessed 20 June 2017.

Holland, Mirabai. "What Does Your Thigh Bone Have in Common with the Eiffel Tower?" *HuffPost News: The Blog*, 3 July 2013, http://www.url-website. Accessed 25 June 2017.

"Human Anatomy and Biomimicry." *CSDT Community*, Rensselaer Polytechnic Institute, http://www.url-website. Accessed 22 June 2017.

Lee, Dora. *Biomimicry: Inventions Inspired by Nature*. Kids Can Press, 2011.

Pearce, Mick. "Biomimicry Video - 02." *Mick Pearce*, 2016, http://www.url-website. Accessed 27 June 2017.

Pearce, Mick. "Eastgate." *Mick Pearce*, 2016, http://www.url-website. Accessed 1 July 2017.

Wilson, Edward O. *Biophilia*. Harvard UP, 1984.

NOTEBOOK

Response

1. **Personal Connections** Which building did you like the most? Do you think most people would agree with you? Why or why not?

Work on your own to answer the questions in your notebook. Use text evidence to support your responses.

Comprehension

2. **Reading Check** **(a)** What are the 3 B's? **(b)** What is the "Yale Whale"? **(c)** According to the text, what is the "one goal" of biology?

3. **Strategy: Make Predictions** Cite three predictions you made about this text, one for each element—genre characteristics, text features, and structures. Which predictions were you able to confirm and which ones did you need to correct or adjust? Explain.

Analysis and Discussion

4. **(a)** What is the writer's **controlling idea,** or thesis? **(b) Analyze** How does her introduction make that idea understandable to nonscientists?

5. **Compare and Contrast** What are the three biology-based ideas, and how are they similar and different?

6. **(a) Summarize** Reread and summarize the section of the article titled "Thoughtful Design." **(b) Analyze** What purpose does this section serve?

7. **Get Ready for Close Reading** Choose a passage from the text that you find especially interesting or important. You will discuss the passage with your group during Close-Read activities.

WORKING AS A GROUP

Discuss your responses to the Analysis and Discussion questions with your group.

- Note agreements and disagreements.
- Summarize insights.
- Consider changes of opinion.

If necessary, revise your original answers to reflect what you learn from your discussion.

What is the relationship between people and nature?

What have you learned about the relationship between people and nature from reading this science feature? Go to your Essential Question Notes and record your observations and thoughts about "Creature Comforts: Three Biology-Based Tips for Builders."

 TEKS

5.C. Make, correct, or confirm predictions using text features, characteristics of genre, and structures.

6.D. Paraphrase and summarize texts in ways that maintain meaning and logical order.

6.I. Reflect on and adjust responses as new evidence is presented.

CREATURE COMFORTS: THREE BIOLOGY-BASED TIPS FOR BUILDERS

Close Read

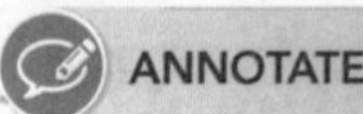

PRACTICE Complete the following activities. Use text evidence to support an appropriate response.

1. **Present and Discuss** With your group, share the passages from the science feature that you find especially interesting. Discuss what you notice, the questions you have, and the conclusions you reach. For example, you might focus on the following passages:
   - Paragraph 2: Discuss why people might "find comfort in the company of nature."
   - Paragraph 3: Discuss what the writer means by "Life tends to be more flexible."
   - Paragraph 5: Discuss why sustainability is an important issue in building design.
2. **Reflect on Your Learning** What new ideas or insights did you uncover during your second reading of the text?

WORD NETWORK

Add words that are related to people and nature from the text to your Word Network.

LANGUAGE STUDY

Concept Vocabulary

Why These Words? The vocabulary words are related.

incorporate	melded	affinity

1. With your group, discuss these words, and determine what they have in common. Write your ideas.
2. Add another word that fits the category. ______________________
3. On your own, use a thesaurus to find antonyms for each vocabulary word. Then, compare the words you found with your group.

Word Study

Latin Root: *-fin-* The word *affinity* is built from the prefix *af-*, which means "add," and the Latin root *-fin-*, which means "border" or "end." An *affinity* is a natural drawing together of two or more things across a border.

Use a dictionary to find the meanings of other words built from the root *-fin-*: *finish, infinite,* and *define*. Explain how the meaning of "end" or "border" is evident in each word.

TEKS

2.A. Use print or digital resources to determine the meaning, syllabication, pronunciation, word origin, and part of speech.

2.C. Determine the meaning and usage of grade-level academic English words derived from Greek and Latin roots such as *omni, log/logue, gen, vid/vis, phil, luc,* and *sens/sent.*

8.D.ii. Analyze characteristics and structural elements of informational text, including features such as references and acknowledgements.

Genre / Text Elements

Text Features: References and Acknowledgements A key characteristic of science features is the inclusion of references and acknowledgements. **References** cite sources used by the writer; an **acknowledgements** section recognizes the contributions other people and organizations made to the writer's work.

The author of "Creature Comforts" uses different types of references within the body of the text. At the end of the article, she compiled all the references into a Works Cited list.

EXAMPLES FROM THE TEXT	FROM THE WORKS CITED LIST
Darwin famously observed that living things adopt "endless forms most beautiful and wonderful" (867).	Darwin, Charles. *On the Origin of Species.* 1st ed., John Murray, 1859. *Project Gutenberg E-book,* http://www.url-website. Accessed 30 June 2017.
His iconic tower handles off-center stresses in the same manner as the human thighbone ("Human Anatomy").	"Human Anatomy and Biomimicry." *CSDT Community,* Rensselaer Polytechnic Institute, http://www.url-website. Accessed 22 June 2017.

PRACTICE Answer the questions to analyze the use of references and acknowledgements in this article. Work on your own, and then discuss your responses with your group.

1. **Analyze** Mark and review source references within the body of the text. Why does the writer note her references at these points?

2. **Make Inferences** Reread the acknowledgements. What does the information in the acknowledgements section suggest about the writer's research process?

3. **Make a Judgment** Scan the Works Cited list. Has the author consulted a variety of trustworthy sources? Explain why or why not.

4. **Evaluate** Does the inclusion of references and acknowledgements affect your attitude toward the information in the text? Explain.

CREATURE COMFORTS: THREE BIOLOGY-BASED TIPS FOR BUILDERS

Conventions

Verb Tenses A **verb** expresses an action or a state of being. A verb's tense indicates when an action happens or a state exists.

TIP: In English, there are six common verb tenses: present, past, future, present perfect, past perfect, and future perfect.

VERB TENSE	EXAMPLE
Present tense indicates an action that is happening now or happens regularly.	I plan a project.
Past tense indicates an action that has already happened.	You planned the last project.
Future tense indicates an action that will happen.	We will plan a project.
Present perfect tense indicates an action that happened in the past and may still be happening now.	They have planned many projects..
Past perfect tense indicates an action that ended before another action in the past.	He had planned the project before he left.
Future perfect tense indicates an action that will have ended before a specific time.	She will have planned the project by next week.

INTERACTIVITY  NOTEBOOK

READ IT Work with your group to identify examples of present, past, and future tense verbs in "Creature Comforts." Write your examples in the chart.

Present	
Past	
Future	

WRITE IT Choose a verb from the article such as *find, provide, design,* or *build.* Write two sentences using the verb in the present and past tenses. Then, edit your sentences, changing the present and past tenses to other tenses. Share your work with your group, and challenge them to identify the verb tenses you used in your second set of sentences.

 TEKS

10.D.ii. Edit drafts using standard English conventions, including consistent, appropriate use of verb tenses.

Research

In a **research report,** you present information gathered from research to support your own explanations and insights on a focused topic.

ASSIGNMENT

Work with your group to write a **research report** about some aspect of biomimicry. You may choose one of these options, or pick a different topic that you prefer.

- ◯ transportation (for example, airplanes, trains, or cars)
- ◯ athletic clothing (for example, sharkskin swimsuits)

Plan Your Work Before you begin to gather sources, make a plan to guide your work. List the tasks you will need to complete—such as research, organizing, writing, and editing, etc.—and make sure everyone has an equal and important role to play in all of them.

Gather Relevant Information Use the questions listed here to evaluate the relevance of the information you find. If any information gets a NO answer, it may not be useful for this project.

Evaluate Information for Relevance		
Does the information relate directly to the topic?	◯ No	◯ Yes
Does the information relate directly to the research question?	◯ No	◯ Yes
Does the information fill a specific gap in knowledge, such as background?	◯ No	◯ Yes
Is the information current?	◯ No	◯ Yes

Synthesize Information To synthesize information, integrate ideas, examples, and facts from a variety of sources to offer your own new insight. That insight is your thesis. Work together to synthesize information and prepare your report, including a strong thesis.

Choose a Mode of Delivery Discuss the best way to organize and present your information and ideas. Mark your choice.

- ◯ **Written Report:** Write a polished, well-structured text.
- ◯ **Oral Presentation:** Write a set of detailed notes you can use to deliver your findings orally.
- ◯ **Multimodal Presentation:** Enhance the information by including media elements, such as videos, music, photos, or diagrams. You may deliver the text and media in an oral presentation, in a slideshow, or in another digital format.

EQ Notes Before moving on to a new selection, go to your Essential Question Notes and record any additional thoughts or observations you may have about "Creature Comforts: Three Biology-Based Tips for Builders."

TEKS

12.D. Identify and gather relevant information from a variety of sources.

12.F. Synthesize information from a variety of sources.

12.J. Use an appropriate mode of delivery, whether written, oral, or multimodal, to present results.

HE—Y, COME ON OU—T!

The selection you are about to read is magical realism.

Reading Magical Realism

Magical realism is a literary genre that combines both realistic and magical, or fantastic, elements.

MAGICAL REALISM: SHORT STORY

Author's Purpose

- to tell a story that weaves together realistic and magical elements

Characteristics

- ordinary settings (the real world) with extraordinary elements, which break natural law or logic
- characters who are ordinary but who accept or expect magical events
- strange or magical events conveyed with an unsurprised tone
- dialogue
- irony, or unexpected outcomes

Structure

- plots that often center on a major, fantasy-like change or transformation

Take a Minute!

NOTEBOOK

LIST IT With a partner, think of some television shows or movies that you've seen or know about that might belong to the genre of magical realism. What makes you think so?

TEKS

7.D. Analyze how the setting influences character and plot development.

8.A. Demonstrate knowledge of literary genres such as realistic fiction, adventure stories, historical fiction, mysteries, humor, myths, fantasy, and science fiction.

Genre / Text Elements

Setting and Plot A story's **setting** is the time and place in which the events occur. The **plot** is the sequence of those events. In **magical realism,** the setting is grounded in the real world but includes fantastic, or magical, details. The plot in magical realist stories is built around the fantastic elements and characters' reactions to them.

REALISM AND MAGICAL REALISM		
ELEMENT	REALISM	MAGICAL REALISM
setting	a classroom	a classroom that fades in and out of sight
plot	initiated by a conflict between characters	initiated by a magical event
characters	react typically to the extraordinary (for example, with shock or surprise)	accept the extraordinary as normal

INTERACTIVITY

PRACTICE Mark each item as an example of either realism or magical realism.

EXAMPLE	REALISM?	MAGICAL REALISM?
1. A boy has a conversation with a talking horse.		
2. A church setting with light streaming in through stained-glass windows		
3. A legal decision gives a woman justice.		
4. A world in which time moves backwards		

About the Author

Shinichi Hoshi (1926–1997), a Japanese writer, is best known for his "short-short stories," in which he makes observations about human nature and society. Hoshi wrote more than a thousand short-short stories, as well as longer fantasy stories, detective stories, biographies, and travel articles. In addition, he was one of the first Japanese science-fiction writers. Hoshi's stories have been translated into many languages, and devoted readers enjoy their unexpected plot turns.

He—y, Come On Ou—t!

Concept Vocabulary

As you read "He—y, Come On Ou—t!" you will encounter these words.

disposal	consequences	resolved

Context Clues If these words are unfamiliar to you, try using **context clues**—or words and phrases that appear nearby in the text—to help you determine their meanings. There are various types of context clues that you may encounter as you read.

Synonyms: A **throng** gathered around the hole, so the village built a fence to keep the crowd from getting too close.

Restatement of an Idea: People traveled to the village to see the hole, and when they arrived, they were so impressed by its depth that they **gawked** at it.

Contrast of Ideas: The scientist was able to keep his **composure** despite the fact that he was scared of the deep hole.

PRACTICE As you read "He—y, Come On Ou—t!" use context clues to determine meanings of unfamiliar words. Write your definitions in the open space next to the text.

Comprehension Strategy

Make Connections to Society

When you **make connections** to society while reading, you look for relationships between ideas in a text and the larger world. For example, you might consider how characters, aspects of a setting, and the events of a story connect to real-life social issues. Then, think about the author's intentions—does the author seem to be commenting directly on society?

- Think about what a situation in a story might represent or symbolize in society.
- Consider how characters' actions and reactions reflect the attitudes people in the real world take toward the issue.

PRACTICE As you read, make connections between the story and society. Mark your observations in the open space next to the text.

2.B. Use context such as contrast or cause and effect to clarify the meaning of words.

5.E. Make connections to personal experiences, ideas in other texts, and society.

He–y, Come On Ou–t!

Shinichi Hoshi
translated by Stanleigh Jones

BACKGROUND

Each year, the world generates billions of tons of waste. Much of that waste is disposed of in landfills, where heavy metals and toxins can leak into the environment. The oceans have also been polluted with vast amounts of trash because, for many decades, it was common practice to get rid of chemicals, garbage, and even nuclear waste by dumping them directly into the ocean.

AUDIO

ANNOTATE

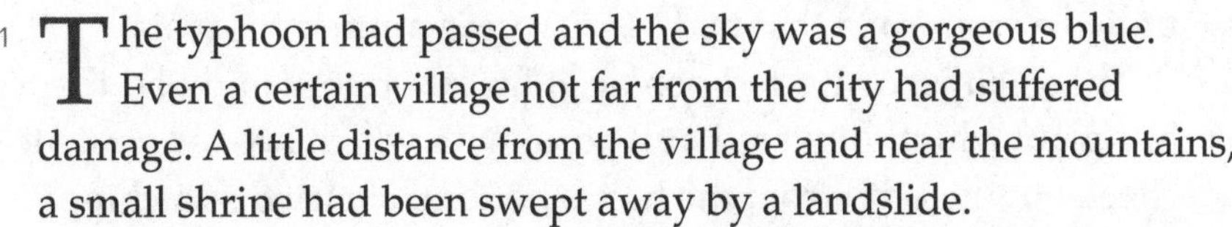

1 The typhoon had passed and the sky was a gorgeous blue. Even a certain village not far from the city had suffered damage. A little distance from the village and near the mountains, a small shrine had been swept away by a landslide.

2 "I wonder how long that shrine's been here."

3 "Well, in any case, it must have been here since an awfully long time ago."

4 "We've got to rebuild it right away."

5 While the villagers exchanged views, several more of their number came over.

6 "It sure was wrecked."

7 "I think it used to be right here."

8 "No, looks like it was a little more over there."

9 Just then one of them raised his voice. "Hey what in the world is this hole?"

10 Where they had all gathered there was a hole about a meter in diameter. They peered in, but it was so dark nothing could be seen. However, it gave one the feeling that it was so deep it went clear through to the center of the earth.

11 There was even one person who said, "I wonder if it's a fox's hole."

12 "He—y, come on ou—t!" shouted a young man into the hole. There was no echo from the bottom. Next he picked up a pebble and was about to throw it in.

13 "You might bring down a curse on us. Lay off," warned an old man, but the younger one energetically threw the pebble in. As before, however, there was no answering response from the bottom. The villagers cut down some trees, tied them with rope and made a fence which they put around the hole. Then they repaired to the village.

14 "What do you suppose we ought to do?"

15 "Shouldn't we build the shrine up just as it was over the hole?"

16 A day passed with no agreement. The news traveled fast, and a car from the newspaper company rushed over. In no time a scientist came out, and with an all-knowing expression on his face he went over to the hole. Next, a bunch of gawking curiosity seekers showed up; one could also pick out here and there men of shifty glances who appeared to be concessionaires.[1] Concerned that someone might fall into the hole, a policeman from the local substation kept a careful watch.

17 One newspaper reporter tied a weight to the end of a long cord and lowered it into the hole. A long way down it went. The cord ran out, however, and he tried to pull it out, but it would not come back up. Two or three people helped out but when they all pulled too hard, the cord parted at the edge of the hole. Another reporter, a camera in hand, who had been watching all of this, quietly untied a stout rope that had been wound around his waist.

18 The scientist contacted people at his laboratory and had them bring out a high-powered bull horn, with which he was going to check out the echo from the hole's bottom. He tried switching through various sounds, but there was no echo. The scientist was puzzled, but he could not very well give up with everyone watching him so intently. He put the bull horn right up to the hole, turned it to its highest volume, and let it sound continuously for a long time. It was a noise that would have carried several dozen kilometers above ground. But the hole just calmly swallowed up the sound.

19 In his own mind the scientist was at a loss, but with a look of apparent composure he cut off the sound and, in a manner

1. **concessionaires** (kuhn sehsh uh NAIRZ) *n.* businesspersons.

suggesting that the whole thing had a perfectly plausible explanation, said simply, "Fill it in."

20 Safer to get rid of something one didn't understand.

21 The onlookers, disappointed that this was all that was going to happen, prepared to disperse. Just then one of the concessionaires, having broken through the throng and come forward, made a proposal.

22 "Let me have that hole. I'll fill it in for you."

23 "We'd be grateful to you for filling it in," replied the mayor of the village, "but we can't very well give you the hole. We have to build a shrine there."

24 "If it's a shrine you want, I'll build you a fine one later. Shall I make it with an attached meeting hall?"

25 Before the mayor could answer, the people of the village all shouted out.

26 "Really? Well, in that case, we ought to have it closer to the village."

27 "It's just an old hole. We'll give it to you!"

28 So it was settled. And the mayor, of course, had no objection.

29 The concessionaire was true to his promise. It was small, but closer to the village he did build for them a shrine with an attached meeting hall.

30 About the time the autumn festival was held at the new shrine, the hole-filling company established by the concessionaire hung out its small shingle at a shack near the hole.

31 The concessionaire had his cohorts mount a loud campaign in the city. "We've got a fabulously deep hole! Scientists say it's at least five thousand meters deep! Perfect for the **disposal** of such things as waste from nuclear reactors."

Use context clues or indicate another strategy you used that helped you determine meaning.

disposal (dihs POH zuhl) *n.*

MEANING:

32 Government authorities granted permission. Nuclear power plants fought for contracts. The people of the village were a bit worried about this, but they consented when it was explained that there would be absolutely no above-ground contamination[2] for several thousand years and that they would share in the profits. Into the bargain, very shortly a magnificent road was built from the city to the village.

33 Trucks rolled in over the road, transporting lead boxes. Above the hole the lids were opened, and the wastes from nuclear reactors tumbled away into the hole.

34 From the Foreign Ministry and the Defense Agency boxes of unnecessary classified documents were brought for disposal. Officials who came to supervise the disposal held discussions on golf. The lesser functionaries, as they threw in the papers, chatted about pinball.

2. **contamination** (kuhn tam uh NAY shuhn) *n.* pollution by poison or another dangerous substance.

Use context clues or indicate another strategy you used that helped you determine meaning.

consequences (KON suh kwehns ihz) *n.*

MEANING:

resolved (rih ZOLVD) *v.*

MEANING:

35 The hole showed no signs of filling up. It was awfully deep, thought some; or else it might be very spacious at the bottom. Little by little the hole-filling company expanded its business.

36 Bodies of animals used in contagious disease experiments at the universities were brought out and to these were added the unclaimed corpses of vagrants. Better than dumping all of its garbage in the ocean, went the thinking in the city, and plans were made for a long pipe to carry it to the hole.

37 The hole gave peace of mind to the dwellers of the city. They concentrated solely on producing one thing after another. Everyone disliked thinking about the eventual **consequences**. People wanted only to work for production companies and sales corporations; they had no interest in becoming junk dealers. But, it was thought, these problems too would gradually be **resolved** by the hole.

38 Young girls whose betrothals[3] had been arranged discarded old diaries in the hole. There were also those who were inaugurating new love affairs and threw into the hole old photographs of themselves taken with former sweethearts. The police felt comforted as they used the hole to get rid of accumulations of expertly done counterfeit bills. Criminals breathed easier after throwing material evidence into the hole.

39 Whatever one wished to discard, the hole accepted it all. The hole cleansed the city of its filth; the sea and sky seemed to have become a bit clearer than before.

40 Aiming at the heavens, new buildings went on being constructed one after another.

41 One day, atop the high steel frame of a new building under construction, a workman was taking a break. Above his head he heard a voice shout:

42 "He—y, come on ou—t!"

43 But, in the sky to which he lifted his gaze there was nothing at all. A clear blue sky merely spread over all. He thought it must be his imagination. Then, as he resumed his former position, from the direction where the voice had come, a small pebble skimmed by him and fell on past.

44 The man, however, was gazing in idle reverie[4] at the city's skyline growing ever more beautiful, and he failed to notice. ❧

3. **betrothals** (bih TRO*TH* uhlz) *n.* promises of marriage.
4. **idle reverie** (Y duhl REHV uh ree) daydreaming.

NOTEBOOK

Work on your own to answer the questions in your notebook. Use text evidence to support your responses.

Response

1. **Personal Connections** What parts of the story surprised you most? Why?

Comprehension

2. **Reading Check (a)** Why does the old man tell the young man not to throw a pebble in the hole? **(b)** How is the hole used? **(c)** What does the workman hear at the end of the story?

3. **Strategy: Make Connections** What connections did you make between the story's events and society? In what ways did these connections affect your understanding of the text? Explain.

Analysis and Discussion

WORKING AS A GROUP
Discuss your responses to the Analysis and Discussion questions with your group.
- Note agreements and disagreements.
- Summarize insights.
- Consider changes of opinion.

If necessary, revise your original answers to reflect what you learn from your discussion.

4. **(a) Analyze** Which character do you think is most responsible for the sequence of events that leads to the story's conclusion? Why? **(b) Interpret** How does that choice shape your understanding of the conclusion?

5. **(a)** What things do people in the story throw into the hole? **(b) Draw Conclusions** What can you conclude about their society based on these details?

6. **Speculate** If the events of this story were to happen in real life, do you think people would behave similarly? Why or why not?

7. **Interpret** What comment does this story seem to be making about the idea of a "disposable society"? Explain, citing text evidence.

8. **Get Ready for Close Reading** Choose a passage from the text that you find especially interesting or important. You'll discuss the passage with your group during Close-Read activities.

TEKS

5.E. Make connections to personal experiences, ideas in other texts, and society.

6.A. Describe personal connections to a variety of sources, including self-selected texts.

6.C. Use text evidence to support an appropriate response.

6.I. Reflect on and adjust responses as new evidence is presented.

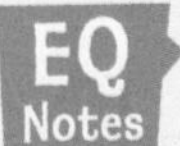

What is the relationship between people and nature?

What have you learned about the relationship between people and nature from reading this story? Go to your Essential Question Notes and record your observations and thoughts about "He—y, Come on Ou—t!"

HE—Y, COME ON OU—T!

Close Read

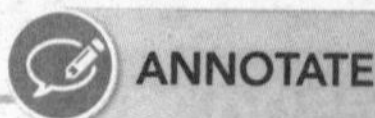
ANNOTATE

PRACTICE **Complete the following activities. Use text evidence to support your responses.**

1. **Present and Discuss** With your group, share the passages from the story that you found especially interesting. Discuss what you notice, the questions you have, and the conclusions you reach. For example, you might focus on the following passages:
   - Paragraph 1: Discuss the setting and whether it is typical of magical realism.
   - Paragraphs 18 and 19: Discuss the scientist's reactions. Explain how he might react if the story were realistic.
   - Paragraphs 41 and 42: Discuss possible explanations for what happens in these paragraphs.
2. **Reflect on Your Learning** What new ideas or insights did you uncover during your second reading of the text?

WORD NETWORK

Add words that related to people and nature from the text to your Word Network.

NOTEBOOK

LANGUAGE STUDY

Concept Vocabulary

Why These Words? The vocabulary words are related.

disposal	consequences	resolved

1. With your group, determine what the words have in common. Write your ideas.
2. Add another word that fits the category. ____________________
3. Use each vocabulary word in a sentence. Include context clues that hint at each word's meaning.

Word Study

Latin Root: *-sequ-* The Latin root *-sequ-* means "to follow." In the story, the author writes that people disliked thinking of the *consequences* of dumping things in the hole because people did not want to think of the things that might *follow* as a result of their actions.

With your group, find three more words that are built on the root *-sequ-*. Then, use the words in a short discussion.

TEKS

2.C. Determine the meaning and usage of grade-level academic English words derived from Greek and Latin roots such as *omni, log/logue, gen, vid/vis, phil, luc,* and *sens/sent.*

7.D. Analyze how the setting influences character and plot development.

8.A. Demonstrate knowledge of literary genres such as realistic fiction, adventure stories, historical fiction, mysteries, humor, myths, fantasy, and science fiction.

Genre / Text Elements

Setting and Plot In **magical-realist** stories, the limitations of real-life settings don't apply. Instead, the writer introduces impossible, magical, circumstances. The magical qualities of the setting spur characters' reactions and develop the plot. Often, the magical events and the plot that results hint at real social problems. Consider the examples of setting and other magical-realist traits from "He—y, Come on Ou—t!"

EXAMPLE: Characteristics of Magical Realism

CHARACTERISTICS	STORY EXAMPLES	NOTES
Characters are often unnamed; individuals are less important than society as a whole.	"You might bring down a curse on us. Lay off," warned an old man, but the younger one energetically threw the pebble in.	Characters are not given names.
Magical events suggest a problem or ill in society.	It was a noise that would have carried several dozen kilometers above ground. But the hole just calmly swallowed up the sound.	A large hole in the earth appeared from nowhere and is seemingly bottomless.
The magical event creates conflicts, and characters' reactions drive the plot.	Where they had all gathered there was a hole about a meter in diameter. They peered in, but it was so dark nothing could be seen.	The story's plot revolves around the discovery of a bottomless hole.

NOTEBOOK

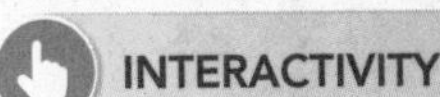
INTERACTIVITY

PRACTICE Work on your own to answer the questions and complete the activity. Then, discuss your responses with your group.

1. **(a) Analyze** What characteristics, or details, of the setting make this story an example of magical realism? Explain. **(b) Evaluate** How does this setting influence the story's plot? Cite specific details that support your response.

2. **Interpret** Use the chart to describe the significance of key events in the story. One row has been completed for you.

EVENT	INTERPRETATION/SIGNIFICANCE
loss of shrine in a landslide	The villagers have ignored the shrine for so long, they no longer know its meaning, which enables their next dangerous move.
young man yells into the hole and throws a pebble	
scientist's direction ("Fill it in.")	
concessionaire's business decisions, and government responses and actions	

HE—Y, COME ON OU—T!

Author's Craft

Irony and Theme In literature, **situational irony** occurs when something happens that is the opposite of what the reader or character expects. Such ironic moments provide clues to the text's **themes**, or insights about life.

EXAMPLES:

SITUATIONAL IRONY	THEME
expecting the adult to take charge of a chaotic situation and then discovering that a child restores order	Children can be wiser than adults.
expecting an act of kindness to have positive consequences that instead has negative ones	Kindness is not an absolute good.

NOTEBOOK

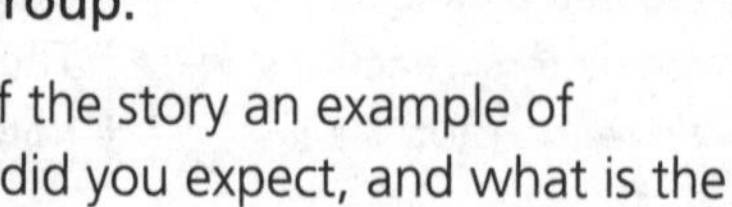

PRACTICE Answer these questions on your own. Then, discuss them with your group.

1. **(a) Analyze** How is the beginning of the story an example of situational irony? **(b) Connect** What did you expect, and what is the significance of what happens instead?

2. **(a) Draw Conclusions** What makes the ending ironic, or unexpected? **(b) Evaluate** Can the ending be both ironic and logical? Explain why or why not.

3. **(a) Interpret** What theme or themes does the story's ironic ending convey about people and how we interact with the world around us? **(b) Support** What specific details support your interpretations of the theme or themes?

TEKS

7.A. Infer multiple themes within and across texts using text evidence.

9.E. Identify the use of literary devices, including subjective and objective point of view.

Composition

An **alternate ending** is a new ending that explores a different way in which the conflicts in a work of fiction might be resolved, or come to an end.

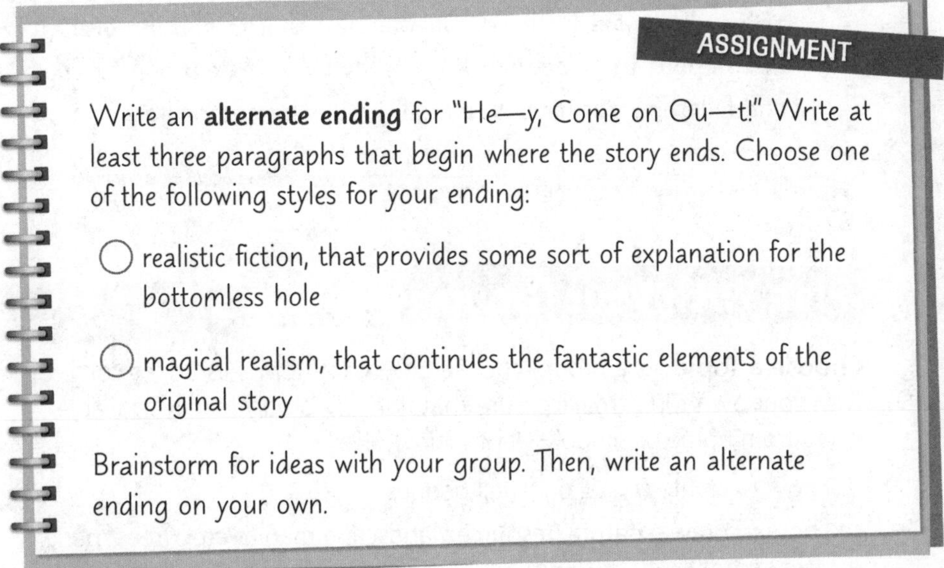

ASSIGNMENT

Write an **alternate ending** for "He—y, Come on Ou—t!" Write at least three paragraphs that begin where the story ends. Choose one of the following styles for your ending:

- ◯ realistic fiction, that provides some sort of explanation for the bottomless hole
- ◯ magical realism, that continues the fantastic elements of the original story

Brainstorm for ideas with your group. Then, write an alternate ending on your own.

Plan Your Ending With your group, discuss possibilities for what could happen next and decide which style of writing you will use. Next, brainstorm different directions alternate endings could take. Make sure your choices reflect the world of the story, including the nature of the setting and the ways characters interact. Then, on your own, choose what characters will be involved, what events will take place, and what will happen as a result.

Draft Your Ending On your own, draft at least three new paragraphs that provide a satisfying end to the story. Use strong descriptive details that help readers visualize the scene. In addition, work to create coherence in your story by using transitions—such as *later that day, meanwhile,* or *on the other side*—that help you move from the original ending to your alternative version. Continue to use transitions to link sentences and paragraphs in a clear, coherent way.

Reflect on Your Writing Share your draft with your group and ask for feedback on your form and content. Revise your draft to address that feedback.

EQ Notes Before moving on to a new selection, go to your Essential Question Notes and record any additional thoughts or observations you may have about "He—y, Come on Ou—t!"

TEKS

10.B.i. Develop drafts into a focused, structured, and coherent piece of writing by organizing with purposeful structure, including an introduction, transitions, coherence within and across paragraphs, and a conclusion.

10.B.ii. Develop drafts into a focused, structured, and coherent piece of writing by developing an engaging idea reflecting depth of thought with specific facts, details, and examples.

11.A. Compose literary texts such as personal narratives, fiction, and poetry using genre characteristics and craft.

Follow and Give Oral Instructions

ASSIGNMENT

With your group, research how to perform a specific task or activity. Then, teach the rest of your class that task, using **oral instructions** to guide them step by step. Alternate groups giving and following instructions until all groups have done both.

Plan With Your Group

Choose a Topic As a group, choose one of the topics listed, or come up with your own topic, making sure that it involves only readily available items from home or school. Mark your choice.

- ◯ how to create crystal eggshell geodes
- ◯ how to draw a natural resources/landscape map (water, trees, parks, etc.) of your city or town
- ◯ how to create a balloon greenhouse
- ◯ how to create a bottle terrarium
- ◯ how to purify water using the sun
- ◯ our own topic: ______________________________

Conduct Research Find and list at least one source—print or online—that describes the topic. Two sources are better, in case the first has any gaps. As you gather ideas, consult with group members. Ask for information to clarify any questions you might have about the research process, your project goals, or the content you find.

Write Instructions Determine the steps necessary to complete the task and write the instructions. Use specific words that make requirements clear. Consider these types of terms:

- **Action Verbs:** Start each step with a clear verb, such as *pour, stretch,* or *draw.*
- **Spatial Words:** Use terms that indicate clear spatial relationships, such as *above, over, under,* or *inside.*
- **Time-Order Terms:** Use words that clearly indicate sequence. Consider words like *before, first, next,* and *finally.*

Also, consider providing other support, such as visual aids, and make sure that you gather any materials your audience will need to complete the task.

Plan and Practice the Presentation Decide how to present these steps clearly so that the audience can easily follow them. Make sure everyone in the group has a role to play in the presentation.

Use this chart to plan your presentation. Add rows if you need them and a column for group member responsibilities, if appropriate. Then, rehearse as a group.

INSTRUCTIONS	SUPPORT MATERIALS (e.g., eggshells or visuals)
Step 1:	
Step 2:	
Step 3:	

Give Instructions

Present to the Class Once you have rehearsed, present your instructions to the class, following your group's plan. Keep these tips in mind:

- Speak slowly and clearly.
- Watch as listeners perform each step to be sure they are following along.
- Be sure that everyone who is trying to follow your instructions can see any visuals you have displayed.
- Encourage listeners to ask clarifying questions as they work.

Evaluate Once you've finished presenting, have students compare their final products. Did the instructions produce the expected results? If not, how could you revise them to be clearer?

Follow Instructions

Listen Actively Watch and listen closely as other groups give their instructions. Apply these strategies to follow instructions accurately:

- Check to be sure you have the materials that are required.
- Ask clarifying questions of the presenters as needed.
- Look at visuals to help you to understand the process steps.
- Listen closely for action verbs, spatial words, and time-order terms.

Evaluate Once you have finished following instructions, evaluate how well you completed the task. What could you have done to ensure a better result? What constructive feedback do you have for the presenters?

TEKS

1.B. Follow and give complex oral instructions to perform specific tasks, answer questions, or solve problems.

12.D. Identify and gather relevant information from a variety of sources.

Essential Question

What is the relationship between people and nature?

The natural world affects everyone and everything on the planet. In this section, you will choose one additional selection that explores the relationship between people and nature to read independently. Get the most from this section by establishing a purpose for reading. Ask yourself, "What do I hope to gain from my independent reading?" Here are just a few purposes you might consider:

Read to Learn Think about the selections you have already read. What questions do you still have about the unit topic?

Read to Enjoy Read the descriptions of the texts. Which one seems most interesting and appealing to you?

Read to Form a Position Consider your thoughts and feelings about the Essential Question. Are you still undecided about some aspect of the topic?

Reading Digital Texts

Digital texts, like the ones you will read in this section, are electronic versions of print texts. They have a variety of characteristics:

- can be read on various devices
- text can be resized
- may include annotation tools
- may have bookmarks, audio features, links, and other helpful elements

Independent Learning Strategies

Throughout your life, in school, in your community, and in your career, you will need to rely on yourself to learn and work on your own. Use these strategies to keep your focus as you read independently for sustained periods of time. Add ideas of your own for each category.

STRATEGY	MY ACTION PLAN
Create a schedule • Be aware of your deadlines. • Make a plan for each day's activities.	
Read with purpose • Use a variety of comprehension strategies to deepen your understanding. • Think about the text and how it adds to your knowledge.	
Take notes • Record key ideas and information. • Review your notes before sharing what you've learned.	

TEKS

4. Self-select text and read independently for a sustained period of time; **5.A.** Establish purpose for reading assigned and self-selected texts. **8.F.** Analyze characteristics of multimodal and digital texts.

AUDIO
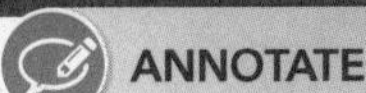
ANNOTATE

DOWNLOAD

CONTENTS

Choose one selection. Selections are available online only.

SHARE YOUR INDEPENDENT LEARNING

Reflect on and evaluate the information you gained from your Independent Reading selection. Then, share what you learned with others.

Close-Read Guide

Tool Kit
Close-Read Guide and **Model Annotation**

Establish your purpose for reading. Then, read the selection through at least once. Use this page to record your close-read ideas.

Selection Title: ____________________ Purpose for Reading: ____________________

Minutes Read: ____________________

INTERACTIVITY

Close Read the Text

Zoom in on sections you found interesting. **Annotate** what you notice. Ask yourself **questions** about the text. What can you **conclude**?

Analyze the Text

1. Think about the author's choices of literary elements, techniques, and structures. Select one and record your thoughts.

2. What characteristics of digital texts did you use as you read this selection, and in what ways? How do the characteristics of a digital text affect your reading experience? Explain.

QuickWrite

Choose a paragraph from the text that grabbed your interest. Explain the power of this passage.

Share Your Independent Learning

Essential Question

What is the relationship between people and nature?

When you read something independently, your understanding continues to grow as you share what you have learned with others.

 NOTEBOOK

Prepare to Share

CONNECT IT One of the most important ways to respond to a text is to notice and describe your personal reactions. Think about the text you explored independently and the ways in which it connects to your own experiences.

- What similarities and differences do you see between the text and your own life? Describe your observations.
- How do you think this text connects to the Essential Question? Describe your ideas.

Learn From Your Classmates

DISCUSS IT Share your ideas about the text you explored on your own. As you talk with others in your class, jot down a few ideas and take notes about new ideas that seem important.

Reflect

EXPLAIN IT Review your notes, and mark the most important insight you gained from these writing and discussion activities. Explain how this idea adds to your understanding of the relationship between people and nature.

 TEKS

6.A. Describe personal connections to a variety of sources, including self-selected texts.
6.E. Interact with sources in meaningful ways such as notetaking, annotating, freewriting, or illustrating.

Research-Based Essay

ASSIGNMENT

In this unit, you read about people's relationship to nature from different perspectives. You also practiced writing research reports and papers. Now, apply what you have learned.

Write a **research-based essay** that explores an answer to the Essential Question:

Essential Question

What is the relationship between people and nature?

Review and Evaluate Evidence

INTERACTIVITY

Review your Essential Question Notes and your QuickWrite from the beginning of the unit. Have your ideas changed?

◯ Yes	◯ No
Identify at least three pieces of evidence that caused you to think differently. **1.** **2.** **3.**	Identify at least three pieces of evidence that reinforced your initial views. **1.** **2.** **3.**

State your ideas now:

What other evidence might you need to develop a controlling idea?

Share Your Perspective

The **Research-Based Essay Checklist** will help you stay on track.

PLAN Before you write, read the Checklist and make sure you understand all the items.

DRAFT As you write, pause occasionally to make sure you're meeting the Checklist requirements.

Use New Words Refer to your Word Network to vary your word choice. Also, consider using one or more of the Academic Vocabulary terms you learned at the beginning of the unit: ***logical, generate, philosophy, evident, elucidate.***

REVIEW AND EDIT After you have written a first draft, evaluate it against the Checklist. Make any changes needed to strengthen your thesis, structure, transitions, and language. Then, reread your essay and fix any errors you find.

EQ Notes Make sure you have pulled in details from your Essential Question Notes to support your thesis.

RESEARCH-BASED ESSAY CHECKLIST

My essay clearly contains...

- ○ a clear controlling idea, or thesis, that answers a focused question about my topic.
- ○ information from varied sources, as well as my own ideas and insights.
- ○ a purposeful structure with introduction, conclusion, and clear connections among all paragraphs.
- ○ references to sources integrated into the body of the essay.
- ○ correct punctuation for references and citations.
- ○ correct use of standard English conventions, including subject-verb agreement.
- ○ no punctuation or spelling errors.

11.B. Compose informational texts, including multi-paragraph essays that convey information about a topic, using a clear controlling idea or thesis statement and genre characteristics and craft.

Revising and Editing

Read this draft and think about corrections the writer might make. Then, answer the questions that follow.

[1] People often take advantage of nature. [2] "We use animals and the Earth to satisfy desires rather than needs." [3] Consider what we do with leather. [4] Leather for shoes is arguably necessary, but for furniture it may not be. [5] Similarly, while it may be ethical to raise animals for food, it may not be if the animals live out their lives in cages.

[6] Our mistreatment of nature can hurt us as well? [7] Soze and Shue, scientists at the Northern institute for the Earth, note that pesticide is meant to "control pests," or kill other living things we find inconvenient.* [8] One ingredient in weed control, dichloropropene, has been associated with kidney and liver damage in humans and death in birds and fish. [9] Those trout in the lake behind your house swims in it.

* Soze, Daniel, and Dana Shue. *Pesticide Myths and Realities.* U of Canada P, 2016, p. 119.

1. Which revision of sentence 2 contributes to the paragraph's cohesion?

- **A** Soze explains, "We use animals and the Earth to satisfy desires rather than needs."
- **B** We take advantage of nature because "We use animals and the Earth to satisfy desires rather than needs."
- **C** Soze explains that we use animals and the Earth to satisfy desires rather than needs.
- **D** "We use animals and the Earth to satisfy desires rather than needs," meaning that we're motivated by the wrong things.

2. Which change to sentence 3 helps improve clarity?

- **F** Consider what leather does.
- **G** Consider, for example, how we use leather in day-to-day life.
- **H** Think about what we do with leather.
- **J** Leather is made from animals.

3. How should the punctuation in sentence 6 be corrected to suggest a more accurate meaning?

- **A** Replace the question mark with a semicolon.
- **B** Replace the question mark with a comma.
- **C** Replace the question mark with a period.
- **D** Replace the question mark with an exclamation point.

4. What change, if any, should be made to correct a subject-verb agreement error in sentence 9?

- **F** Change *lake* to *lakes*.
- **G** Change *it* to *them*.
- **H** Change *swims* to *swim*.
- **J** Make no change.

Reflect on the Unit

 NOTEBOOK

 INTERACTIVITY

RESEARCH

Reflect On the Unit Goals

Review your Unit Goals chart from the beginning of the unit. Then, complete the activity and answer the question.

1. In the Unit Goals chart, rate how well you meet each goal now.
2. In which goals were you most and least successful?

Reflect On the Texts

VOTE! The texts in this unit represent various genres and express different perspectives on the Essential Question. Demonstrate your knowledge of literary genres and the ways in which they help to shape an author's message by completing the chart. Then, vote for your favorite and discuss your choices with the class.

SELECTION BALLOT

Title	Genre	Genre Element that Shapes Author's Message
from Silent Spring		
How Grandmother Spider Stole the Sun How Music Came to the World		
Turtle Watchers Jaguar The Sparrow		
Urban Farming Is Growing a Greener Future		
Creature Comforts: Three Biology-Based Tips for Builders		
He—y, Come On Ou—t!		

Reflect On the Essential Question

Film Guide Using the unit texts as inspiration, think of ways in which you can continue to explore the Essential Question: **What is the relationship between people and nature?**

- Research and identify three films that explore the relationship between people and nature.
- Compile a film listing, identifying each film along with a short description of each one. Share your list with peers.

TIP: Refer to online movie guides or databases to find possible listings.

TEKS

8.A. Demonstrate knowledge of literary genres such as realistic fiction, adventure stories, historical fiction, mysteries, humor, myths, fantasy, and science fiction; **10.C.** Revise drafts for clarity, development, organization, style, word choice, and sentence variety; **10.D.iv.** Edit drafts using standard English conventions, including prepositions and prepositional phrases and their influence on subject-verb agreement.

Facing Adversity

PEARSON realize

Go ONLINE for all lessons

 AUDIO

 VIDEO

 NOTEBOOK

 ANNOTATE

 INTERACTIVITY

 DOWNLOAD

 RESEARCH

WATCH THE VIDEO

Exclusive: Bethany Hamilton

DISCUSS IT Are there any obstacles that are too difficult to overcome?

Write your response before sharing your ideas.

UNIT 5

UNIT INTRODUCTION

Essential Question

How do we overcome obstacles?

MENTOR TEXT: INFORMATIONAL TEXT
Against the Odds

WHOLE-CLASS LEARNING

COMPARE ACROSS GENRES

HISTORICAL WRITING

Black Sunday: The Storm That Gave Us the Dust Bowl
Erin Blakemore

HISTORICAL FICTION

***from* The Grapes of Wrath**
John Steinbeck

▸ MEDIA CONNECTION
Documentary: The Dust Bowl

SPORTS PROFILE

High School Teammates Carry On
Tom Rinaldi

PERFORMANCE TASK

WRITING PROCESS
Write an Informational Essay

PEER-GROUP LEARNING

COMPARE ACROSS GENRES

REALISTIC SHORT STORY

The Circuit
Francisco Jiménez

INTERVIEW

How This Son of Migrant Farm Workers Became an Astronaut
José Hernández and Octavio Blanco

ORAL HISTORY

A Work in Progress
Aimee Mullins

AUTOBIOGRAPHY

***from* The Story of My Life**
Helen Keller

▸ MEDIA CONNECTION
Interview: How Helen Keller Learned to Talk

PERFORMANCE TASK

SPEAKING AND LISTENING
Present an Informational Text

INDEPENDENT LEARNING

LYRIC POETRY

Four Skinny Trees
***from* The House on Mango Street**
Sandra Cisneros

JOURNALISM

The Girl Who Fell From the Sky
Juliane Koepcke

BIOGRAPHY

Profile: Malala Yousafzai
BBC

MEMOIR

***from* Facing the Lion: Growing Up Maasai on the African Savanna**
Joseph Lemasolai Lekuton

SHORT STORY

Rikki-tikki-tavi
Rudyard Kipling

SHARE INDEPENDENT LEARNING

Share • Learn • Reflect

PERFORMANCE-BASED ASSESSMENT

Informational Essay

You will write an informational essay in response to the Essential Question for the unit.

UNIT REFLECTION

Goals • Texts • Essential Question

Unit Goals

Throughout this unit you will deepen your perspective about facing adversity by reading, writing, speaking, listening, and presenting. These goals will help you succeed on the Unit Performance-Based Assessment.

SET GOALS Rate how well you meet these goals right now. You will revisit your ratings later, when you reflect on your growth during this unit.

SCALE	1	2	3	4	5
	NOT AT ALL WELL	NOT VERY WELL	SOMEWHAT WELL	VERY WELL	EXTREMELY WELL

ESSENTIAL QUESTION	Unit Introduction	Unit Reflection
I can read selections that reflect the experience of facing adversity and develop my own perspective.	1 2 3 4 5	1 2 3 4 5
READING	**Unit Introduction**	**Unit Reflection**
I can understand and use academic vocabulary words related to informational texts.	1 2 3 4 5	1 2 3 4 5
I can recognize elements of different genres, especially historical and realistic fiction, informational texts, and journalism.	1 2 3 4 5	1 2 3 4 5
I can read a selection of my choice independently and make meaningful connections to other texts.	1 2 3 4 5	1 2 3 4 5
WRITING	**Unit Introduction**	**Unit Reflection**
I can write a focused, well-organized informational essay.	1 2 3 4 5	1 2 3 4 5
I can complete Timed Writing tasks with confidence.	1 2 3 4 5	1 2 3 4 5
SPEAKING AND LISTENING	**Unit Introduction**	**Unit Reflection**
I can prepare and deliver an informational presentation.	1 2 3 4 5	1 2 3 4 5

TEKS
2.C. Determine the meaning and usage of grade-level academic English words derived from Greek and Latin roots such as *omni, log/logue, gen, vid/vis, phil, luc,* and *sens/sent.*

Academic Vocabulary: Informational Text

Many English words have roots, or key parts, that come from ancient languages, such as Latin and Greek. Learn these roots and use the words as you respond to questions and activities in this unit.

PRACTICE Academic terms are used routinely in classrooms. Build your knowledge of these words by completing the chart.

1. **Review** each word, its root, and the mentor sentences.
2. With a partner, read the words and mentor sentences aloud. Then, **determine** the meaning and usage of each word. Use a dictionary, if needed.
3. **List** at least two related words for each word.

WORD	MENTOR SENTENCES	PREDICT MEANING	RELATED WORDS
deviate LATIN ROOT: ***-via-*** "way"	1. Don't *deviate* from the route I gave you or you'll get lost! 2. She was making an important point, but she allowed herself to *deviate* into side issues.		viable; viaduct
persevere LATIN ROOT: ***-sever-*** "strict"; "serious"	1. Despite the difficult deadline, Diego's dedication helped him *persevere* and get his paper in on time 2. Though the soccer team was losing in the first half, they were able to *persevere* and win the game.		
determination LATIN ROOT: ***-term-*** "end"	1. Because of his *determination* to do well on the test, Robert studied for many hours. 2. Despite the heavy rain, Jenny's *determination* allowed her to complete her first marathon.		
diversity LATIN ROOT: ***-ver-*** "turn"	1. There is cultural *diversity* in the United States because people come from many different places. 2. The oceans are filled with a *diversity* of marine life.		
observation LATIN ROOT: ***-serv-*** "watch over"	1. Mastery of a skill requires more than *observation*; you have to do the activity yourself. 2. Any *observation* of the moon was impossible because it was such a cloudy night.		

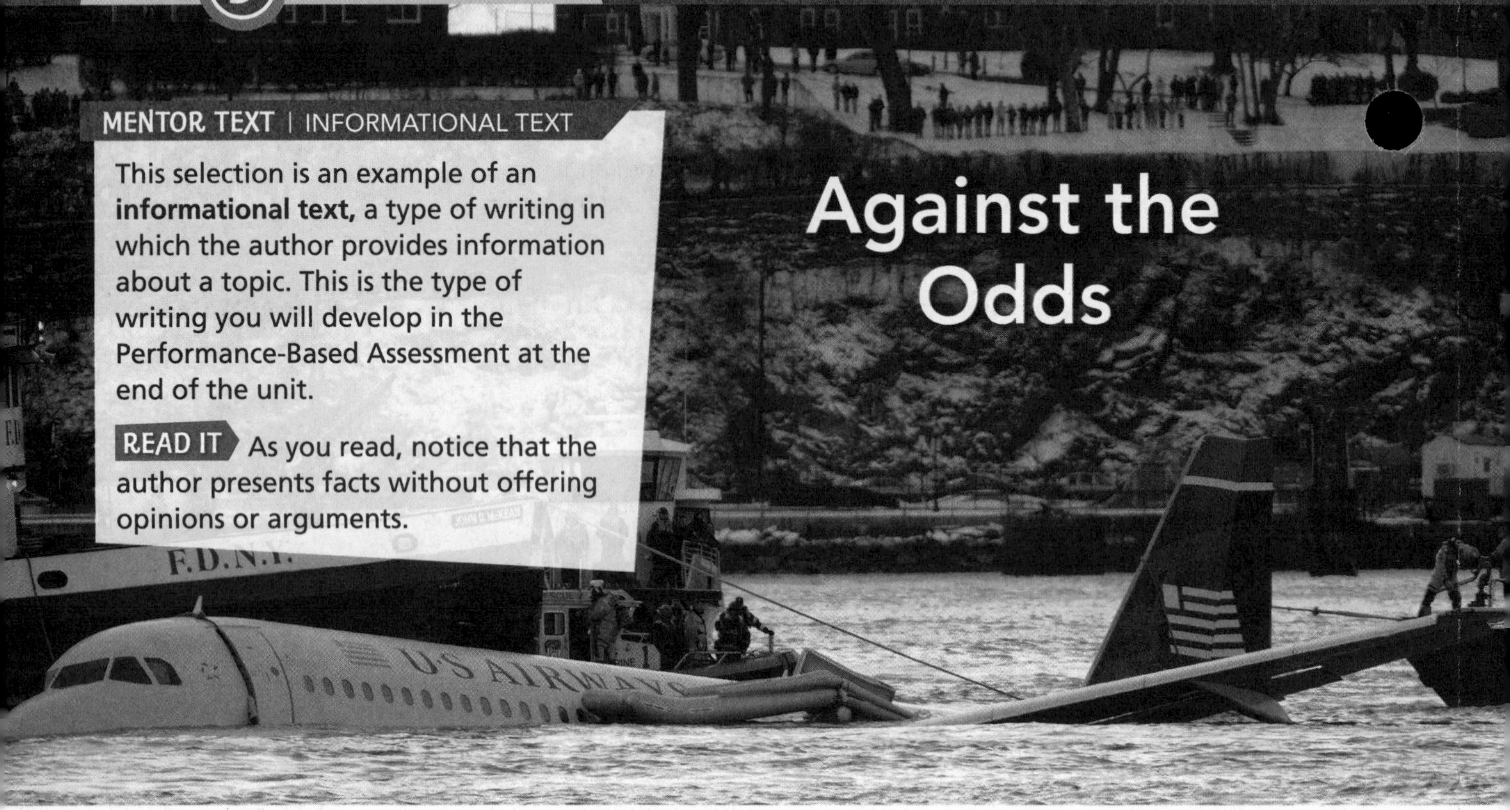

MENTOR TEXT | INFORMATIONAL TEXT

This selection is an example of an **informational text,** a type of writing in which the author provides information about a topic. This is the type of writing you will develop in the Performance-Based Assessment at the end of the unit.

READ IT As you read, notice that the author presents facts without offering opinions or arguments.

Against the Odds

AUDIO

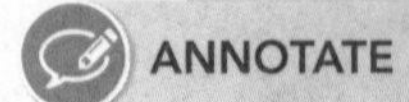
ANNOTATE

1 "If you have to ditch a commercial aircraft in the Hudson River," the news anchor joked, "this is the guy you want."

2 The "guy" was US Airways pilot Chesley "Sully" Sullenberger III, a 57-year-old former Air Force fighter pilot and a 29-year veteran of US Airways.

3 On January 15, 2009, Sullenberger was the pilot on US Airways Flight 1549 from New York's LaGuardia Airport to Charlotte, North Carolina. Flight 1549 left the tarmac at 3:25 P.M. Sullenberger thought he was in for an average flight—a routine, everyday trip.

4 The flight was unremarkable for the first 90 seconds. Then something caught the eye of copilot Jeff Skiles. At 3,000 feet, he saw a flock of Canada geese headed toward the plane. Moments later the geese struck the fuselage, wings, and engine.

5 The 150 passengers felt a powerful thud against the airplane, followed by severe vibrations from the engine. One passenger said it sounded like sneakers thumping around in a dryer. There was a loud explosion. The cabin filled up with smoke. There was a horrible smell and then an eerie quiet: both engines were disabled.

6 Sullenberger made a Mayday radio call to air traffic control and calmly explained the situation. They discussed the options: The plane could either return to LaGuardia or land at Teterboro Airport in New Jersey.

7 Sullenberger knew the situation was too dire for the plane to stay in the air long enough for either plan to be successful. He had about 30 seconds to find an alternative. The pilot decided on a

radical move: He'd ditch the plane in the Hudson River—despite the fact that passenger jets are not built to land on water.

8 "Brace for impact!" came the captain's voice over the intercom. A hush fell over the passengers. They thought they were going to die.

9 Sullenberger lowered the plane's nose in a gradual glide toward the river. The plane managed to clear the George Washington Bridge and, against the odds, land safely on the Hudson. It skidded across the water at 145 mph and finally slowed to a stop.

10 "He was thinking in nanoseconds," said a former airline pilot, speaking of Sullenberger. "He made all the right choices at all the right times. He might have been staring at the instruments, but he was feeling that airplane in his hands. He picked his landing spot and went for it."

11 Now Sullenberger's job was to get the people off the plane, which was quickly filling up with water. In this as well, he showed his tremendous capacity for calm leadership.

12 Witnesses were convinced that everyone on Flight 1549 was dead. What they couldn't see was that passengers were already exiting the plane. With water seeping into the plane, Sullenberger and Skiles walked the length of the cabin twice, calling "Is anyone there?" The water was so cold they had to walk on top of the seats. But they would not leave the plane until they were sure everyone was out.

13 "He's the man," said one of the rescued passengers. "If you want to talk to a hero, get a hold of him."

14 After all the thanking was over, Sullenberger was humble. "You're welcome," he said simply. Like most heroes, he didn't want the label. According to him, he was just doing his job.

15 But 154 men, women, and children owed their lives to a modest man who faced adversity with cool competence on one of the most remarkable days in aviation history. ❧

DOWNLOAD

WORD NETWORK FOR FACING ADVERSITY

Vocabulary A Word Network is a collection of words related to a topic.

As you read the selections in this unit, identify interesting words related to facing adversity and add them to your Word Network. For example, you might begin by adding words from the Mentor Text, such as *dire, humble,* and *competence*. Continue to add words as you complete this unit.

Refer to the **Word Network Model** in the **Tool Kit** at the back of this book.

dire

humble

FACING ADVERSITY

competence

Summary

A **summary** is a brief, complete overview of a text that maintains the meaning and logical order of ideas of the original. It should not include your personal opinions.

NOTEBOOK

WRITE IT Write a summary of "Against the Odds."

Launch Activity

Conduct a Four-Corner Debate

Consider this statement: **Chesley Sullenberger wasn't really a hero because, as he himself said, facing adversity was part of his job.**

1. Identify your position on the statement and explain your thinking.

◯ Strongly Agree ◯ Agree ◯ Disagree ◯ Strongly Disagree

2. In one corner of the room, form a group with like-minded students, and discuss what makes someone a hero, such as his or her actions and personality traits.

3. After the discussion, have a representative from each group present a brief summary of the group's position.

4. After all groups have presented their views, move into the four corners again. If you change your corner, be ready to explain why.

TEKS

6.D. Paraphrase and summarize texts in ways that maintain meaning and logical order.

6.I. Reflect on and adjust responses as new evidence is presented.

QuickWrite

Consider class discussions, presentations, the video, and the Mentor Text as you think about the Essential Question.

Essential Question

How do we overcome obstacles?

At the end of the unit, you will respond to the Essential Question again and see how your perspective has changed.

NOTEBOOK

WRITE IT Record your first thoughts here.

DOWNLOAD

EQ Notes How do we overcome obstacles?

As you read the selections in this unit, use a chart like the one shown to record your ideas and list details from the texts that support them. Taking notes as you go will help you clarify your thinking, gather relevant information, and be ready to respond to the Essential Question.

TITLE	MY IDEAS / OBSERVATIONS	TEXT EVIDENCE / INFORMATION

Refer to the **EQ Notes Model** in the **Tool Kit** at the back of this book.

Essential Question

How do we overcome obstacles?

Everyone has a bad day now and then. Most of the time we take a deep breath and keep going, but what happens when we meet an obstacle we don't think we can overcome? You will work with your whole class to explore the concept of facing adversity. The selections you are going to read present different examples of the ways in which people cope with obstacles and face adversity.

 VIDEO

 INTERACTIVITY

Whole-Class Learning Strategies

Throughout your life, in school, in your community, and in your career, you will continue to learn and work in large-group environments. Read the strategies and the actions you can take to practice them as you work with your whole class. Use a dictionary to check the meaning of any basic or academic vocabulary words you are unsure of. Then, add ideas of your own for each category. Get ready to use these strategies during Whole-Class Learning.

STRATEGY	MY ACTION PLAN
Listen actively • Put away personal items to avoid becoming distracted. • Try to hear the speaker's full message before planning your own response.	
Demonstrate respect • Show up on time and make sure you are prepared for class. • Avoid side conversations while in class.	
Describe personal connections • Recognize that literature explores human experience—the details may differ from your own life, but the emotions it expresses are universal. • Actively look for ways in which your personal experiences help you find meaning in a text. • Consider how your own experiences help you understand characters' actions and reactions.	

CONTENTS

COMPARE ACROSS GENRES

BLACK SUNDAY: THE STORM THAT GAVE US THE DUST BOWL

Historical Narratives

Historical fiction is an imaginary story that is set in a real time and place from the past. **Historical nonfiction narratives** are stories that are mostly true and include facts and the experiences of real people. You will explore the similarities and differences between these two genres.

from THE GRAPES OF WRATH

HISTORICAL NONFICTION NARRATIVE

Author's Purpose

- to explain real-life past events by providing facts and analysis

Characteristics

- a controlling idea or interpretation supported by varied evidence, including information from primary sources
- in addition to explanation, can include elements of storytelling, description, and argument

Structure

- logical progression of information
- may use a variety of organizational structures, such as chronological order or cause-and-effect

HISTORICAL FICTION

Author's Purpose

- to tell a story that combines historical and imaginary elements

Characteristics

- setting that is a real place and time
- characters who are real historical figures, or are modeled on real people from the past
- conflicts that reflect historical situations
- a theme, or insight
- dialogue that shows how people spoke in the past or in a specific place

Structure

- plot that combines real-life historical events with imaginary events

Genre/Text Elements

Theme and Controlling Idea In the literary genre of historical fiction, the author's central message or insight is the **theme.** In the genre of historical nonfiction narrative, the author's central message is the **controlling idea.** Themes and controlling ideas have similarities. For example, neither one is the topic of a work and neither can be expressed in a word or phrase. Instead, both are full thoughts that must be expressed as complete statements. They also have key differences.

SIMILARITIES AND DIFFERENCES BETWEEN GENRES	
HISTORICAL FICTION: THEME	HISTORICAL NONFICTION NARRATIVE: CONTROLLING IDEA/THESIS
general idea about life or human nature	specific statement about a topic
usually implied and not stated directly	often stated directly
developed and suggested by all the story details	developed with supporting evidence and details
one work may have multiple themes	one work has a single controlling idea with related key ideas

Why are the differences between controlling ideas and themes important? They affect how the reader approaches a text. With most informational texts, readers evaluate the strength of the controlling idea and the author's reasoning. In most literature, readers connect details to infer the theme.

NOTEBOOK

PRACTICE **Determine whether each item expresses a controlling idea or a theme, and explain your thinking.**

1. Money cannot buy love or happiness.

2. Jazz is a truly American form of music that is influenced by various musical traditions.

3. Many early women's rights activists were inspired by abolitionists.

4. One person's trash is another person's treasure.

TEKS

7.A. Infer multiple themes within and across texts using text evidence.

8.A. Demonstrate knowledge of literary genres such as realistic fiction, adventure stories, historical fiction, mysteries, humor, myths, fantasy, and science fiction.

8.D.i. Analyze characteristics and structural elements of informational text, including the controlling idea or thesis with supporting evidence.

BLACK SUNDAY: THE STORM THAT GAVE US THE DUST BOWL

Compare Nonfiction and Fiction

In this lesson, you will read a nonfiction text about the Dust Bowl and a work of historical fiction on the same subject. You will then compare how the texts portray the historical events and time period.

from THE GRAPES OF WRATH

About the Author

Erin Blakemore is a freelance journalist and author of *The Heroine's Bookshelf,* a Colorado Book Award winner. Her writing has appeared in many print and online publications, including *TIME, The Washington Post, Smithsonian Magazine, Popular Science,* and *National Geographic.*

Black Sunday: The Storm That Gave Us the Dust Bowl

Concept Vocabulary

You will encounter the following words as you read this selection. Before reading, note how familiar you are with each word. Using a scale of 1 (do not know it at all) to 5 (know it very well), indicate your knowledge of each word.

WORD	YOUR RATING
plight	
ravaged	
widespread	
unending	
demoralized	
impoverished	

Comprehension Strategy

Establish a Purpose for Reading

Setting a **purpose for reading** will help you get more meaning from a text. Answer the following questions to set a purpose for reading:

- **What is the genre?** Your purpose should reflect the type of text you are reading.
- **What is the title?** The title can help you determine what the text might be about, which will help you set your purpose.
- **What do text features tell me?** Quickly scan the text to help you set your purpose. Look for text features, such as images, subtitles, and key terms.

PRACTICE Before you read the selection, establish your purpose, and write it here.

TEKS
5.A. Establish purpose for reading assigned and self-selected texts.

HISTORICAL WRITING

Black Sunday: The Storm That Gave Us the Dust Bowl

Erin Blakemore

^ An enormous dust storm descends on the town of Springfield, Colorado, during the Dust Bowl in the 1930s.

AUDIO

ANNOTATE

BACKGROUND

Since the mid-19th century, farmers had been flocking to the Great Plains of the American Midwest, which offered large plots of land for raising crops and livestock. This migration changed the landscape of the region, replacing the native prairie grasses with plowed fields. In 1930, a severe drought hit this altered environment creating dust storms that raged for nearly a decade. This selection recounts one of the worst dust storms in the era known as the Dust Bowl.

1 It seemed like an ordinary day at first. Like any other day, folks on the Great Plains were struggling to get by. People walked to church, swept up from the dust storm that had blown through the week before, perhaps discussed the Congressional hearings that had brought the **plight** of the region, which had been **ravaged** by drought and the economic effects of the Great Depression, to the attention of the rest of the nation.

2 But Black Sunday—April 14, 1935—was no ordinary day.

3 That afternoon, a gigantic cloud swept across the Great Plains. It was 1,000 miles long and blew at speeds up to 100 miles per hour. It was made of 300,000 tons of dust whipped from the ground of northern farmlands, where poor soil conservation techniques[1] had led to **widespread** erosion made worse by the **unending** drought.

plight (plyt) *n.* serious or harmful condition or situation

ravaged (RAV ihjd) *v.* destroyed or damaged badly

widespread (WYD SPREHD) *adj.* occurring in many places

unending (uhn EHN dihng) *adj.* never stopping; constant

1. **soil conservation techniques** methods that farmers can use to stop soil from being removed by natural forces.

4 Great Plains residents were used to dust, but they had never seen anything like this. One observer compared it to "the Red Sea closing in on the Israel children[2] . . . it got so dark that you couldn't see your hand before your face, you couldn't see anybody in the room."

5 "You couldn't see the street lights," recalled Jim Williams, who watched the storm from his home in Dodge City, Kansas. "It rolled over and over and over and over and over when it came in," another witness remembered, "and it was coal black; it was coal black, and it was terrible that afternoon. It was hot and dry."

CLOSE READ

ANNOTATE: In paragraph 6, mark details that describe the reactions of humans and animals.

QUESTION: Why might the author have included these details?

CONCLUDE: What effect do these details have?

6 Humans weren't the only ones terrified by the storm. Birds fled ahead of the cloud. Confused by the dark, chickens started to go inside to roost. Cows ran in circles.

7 Once the storm subsided, a simple spring day had become the worst day in recent memory. The "black blizzard" that swept across the plains states left a trail of devastation in its wake—leveled fields, crashed cars, reports of people who had been blinded or given pneumonia by the storm. Everything was covered in dust, which choked wells and killed cattle. "Black Sunday," as the storm became known, was the death knell[3] for the poor farmers of Oklahoma and Texas. **Demoralized** and **impoverished**, thousands of so-called "Okies" cut their losses[4] and began the long migration to more favorable locations like California.

demoralized (dih MAWR uh lyzd) *adj.* discouraged; defeated

impoverished (ihm POV uhr ihsht) *adj.* extremely poor; miserable and exhausted

8 In Boise City, Oklahoma, an Associated Press reporter named Robert E. Geiger had weathered the storm with photographer Harry G. Eisenhard. "Three little words achingly familiar on a Western farmer's tongue," he wrote after the storm, "rule life in the dust bowl of the continent—if it rains." Some speculate that Geiger meant to say, "dust belt," a term he used to refer to the devastated region before and after Black Sunday.

9 Inadvertent or no, the term was picked up almost immediately. Geiger had given name to a phenomenon that would come to define the economic and social impacts of the Great Depression. But though Black Sunday and the Dust Bowl it helped name drew attention to the plight of the plains and turned soil conservation into a national priority, its effects were best summed up by a folk singer, not a reporter or politician. These are some of the lyrics to Woody Guthrie's "Dust Storm Disaster," which tells the story of the "deathlike black" cloud that enveloped America that day in 1935:

It covered up our fences, it covered up our barns,
It covered up our tractors in this wild and dusty storm.
We loaded our jalopies and piled our families in,
We rattled down that highway to never come back again.

2. **the Red Sea closing in on the Israel children** According to the Bible, the Red Sea opened up for the escaping children of Israel and then closed in on the Egyptians who were chasing them. The term "children of Israel" refers to both adults and children.
3. **death knell** *n.* sound signaling an end or failure.
4. **cut their losses** abandoned an unsuccessful occupation or activity before one suffers any more harm.

Answer the questions in your notebook. Use text evidence to support your responses.

Response

1. **Personal Connections** What passage from the text did you find most vivid or powerful? Explain.

Comprehension

2. **Reading Check** **(a)** When and where did Black Sunday occur? **(b)** What happened on that day? **(c)** How did the term "Dust Bowl" come into use?

3. **Strategy: Establish a Purpose for Reading** **(a)** How did establishing a purpose for reading help you better understand the text? **(b)** Would you recommend this strategy to others? Why or why not?

Analysis

4. **(a) Analyze Cause and Effect** What combination of factors caused the historic dust storm of Black Sunday? **(b) Support** What details from the text support your response?

5. **Analyze** Cite two examples of quotations from eyewitnesses. Explain the impact of the quotations and why you think the author chose to use them.

6. **Analyze** Note two examples of dates or numerical data the author uses. What is the effect of their inclusion? Explain.

7. **(a) Analyze** What qualities of the storm are described in paragraphs 3-5? Cite three examples of words and phrases that help convey these qualities. **(b) Draw Conclusions** What conclusion can you draw from this description about the nature of dust storms during the Dust Bowl era?

8. **(a) Interpret** Why might the author have chosen to end the article by quoting a song? Explain. **(b) Evaluate** Do you agree with the author's statement that the "effects [of Black Sunday] were best summed up by a folksinger, not a reporter or politician"? Why or why not?

EQ Notes How do we overcome obstacles?

What have you learned about facing adversity from reading this text? Go to your Essential Question Notes and record your observations and thoughts about "Black Sunday: The Storm That Gave Us the Dust Bowl."

TEKS

5.A. Establish purpose for reading assigned and self-selected texts.

6.A. Describe personal connections to a variety of sources, including self-selected texts.

6.C. Use text evidence to support an appropriate response.

6.G. Discuss and write about the explicit or implicit meanings of text.

BLACK SUNDAY: THE STORM THAT GAVE US THE DUST BOWL

Close Read

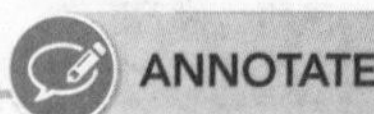

1. The model passage and annotation show how one reader analyzed part of paragraph 7 of the text. Find another detail in the passage to annotate. Then, write your own question and conclusion.

CLOSE-READ MODEL

The "black blizzard" that swept across the plains states left a trail of devastation in its wake—leveled fields, crashed cars, reports of people who had been blinded or given pneumonia by the storm. Everything was covered in dust, which choked wells and killed cattle.

ANNOTATE: The author lists a series of negative effects of the storm.

QUESTION: Why does the author list many effects rather than explain one in more depth?

CONCLUDE: The list emphasizes the scale and variety of destruction.

MY **QUESTION:**

MY **CONCLUSION:**

2. For more practice, answer the Close-Read note in the selection.
3. Choose a section of the text that you found especially important. Mark important details. Then, jot down questions and write your conclusions in the open space next to the text.

Inquiry and Research

Research and Extend Practice responding to teacher-guided research questions by conducting a brief but organized and formal inquiry into this question: *How did photography affect public understanding of the Dust Bowl?*

Consult at least two different reliable sources. Write a report of your findings in which you answer the question and discuss at least one photographer whose work is especially noteworthy.

TEKS

8.D.i. Analyze characteristics and structural elements of informational text, including the controlling idea or thesis with supporting evidence.

12.A. Generate student-selected and teacher-guided questions for formal and informal inquiry.

12.E. Differentiate between primary and secondary sources.

Genre / Text Elements

Controlling Idea and Supporting Evidence In historical writing, an author uses many types of **supporting evidence,** or information, to support his or her **controlling idea,** or interpretation. Sources can be categorized as one of two types.

TYPE OF SOURCE	EXAMPLES
Primary Source: • original account of an event or time period from a person with direct experience of it • does not include interpretations	• personal letters, diaries, blogs, and emails • journalism, interviews, and direct quotations • photographs and video or audio recordings • original art, music, or literature
Secondary Source: • analyzes, evaluates, or interprets primary sources • "one step removed" from the events or time period	• most nonfiction books, including biographies, textbooks, and reference books, such as encyclopedias • journalism written after the event or time period • reviews and criticisms • documentaries

To support a controlling idea, an author gathers evidence from both primary and secondary sources. In effective historical writing, an author structures the information in a way that combines storytelling elements with explanations and evidence.

PRACTICE Answer the questions.

1. **(a) Classify** Explain why "Black Sunday: The Storm That Gave Us the Dust Bowl" is a secondary source. **(b) Distinguish** Identify three types of primary sources the author uses as evidence.
2. **(a) Interpret** In your own words, state the controlling idea of the text. Cite two details from the text for each of the following items:
   (i) what caused the storm
   (ii) what the storm looked like and how it felt to people
   (iii) the storm's impact on the people and the land

   (b) Connect How do the details you chose support the controlling idea?

BLACK SUNDAY: THE STORM THAT GAVE US THE DUST BOWL

Concept Vocabulary

Why These Words? The vocabulary words relate to the idea of a massive, overwhelming problem. For example, the farmers were already *impoverished*, or struggling to get by economically. Then, the dust storm made their *plight* even worse.

plight	widespread	demoralized
ravaged	unending	impoverished

PRACTICE Answer the questions, and complete the activities.

1. How do the vocabulary words deepen your understanding of what life was like for people during the Dust Bowl?
2. What other words in the selection help describe the conditions during Black Sunday and the problems that arose as a result?
3. Use each vocabulary word in a sentence that demonstrates your understanding of the word's meaning.
4. Choose three of your sentences, and replace the vocabulary word with a synonym, or word with a similar meaning. How does the synonym affect the meaning of each sentence? Explain.

WORD NETWORK

Add words that are related to facing adversity from the text to your Word Network.

Word Study

Compound Words A **compound word**, such as the vocabulary word *widespread*, combines the meanings of two separate words to create a new word with a new meaning. Compound words can be open (*post office*), hyphenated (*long-term*), or closed (*sunflower*). Sometimes, spellings of compound words are modernized; for example, the word *housetop* used to be spelled *house-top*. Use a print or online dictionary to answer these questions:

1. How was the compound word *widespread* spelled differently in the past?
2. Which meaning of *spread* is used in the word *widespread*?
3. How does the word *wide* contribute to the meaning of the compound word *nationwide*?
4. Which meaning of the word *spread* is used in the compound word *bedspread*?

TEKS

2.A. Use print or digital resources to determine the meaning, syllabication, pronunciation, word origin, and part of speech.

6.F. Respond using newly acquired vocabulary as appropriate.

10.D.i. Edit drafts using standard English conventions, including complete complex sentences with subject-verb agreement and avoidance of splices, run-ons, and fragments.

Conventions

Complex Sentences A **complex sentence** consists of an independent clause and one or more dependent clauses.

- An **independent clause** has a subject and a verb and can stand alone as a sentence.
- A **dependent clause** contains a subject and a verb, but is an incomplete thought. It cannot stand alone as a sentence.

When writers add clauses, they sometimes make mistakes in subject-verb agreement. Remember that if a sentence is interrupted by a dependent clause, the main verb should still agree in person and number with the subject that comes *before* the interrupting clause; for example: The *plains*, although they were considered some of the world's best farmland, were ruined.

EXAMPLES

In each clause, the subject is underlined once and the verb is underlined twice.

COMPLEX SENTENCE	INDEPENDENT CLAUSE	DEPENDENT CLAUSE
Many farmers, after they struggle without success, abandon their land to the dust.	Many farmers abandon their land to the dust	after they struggle without success
Photographs, although they were shot with black-and-white film, capture the massive destruction.	Photographs capture the massive destruction	although they were shot with black-and-white film

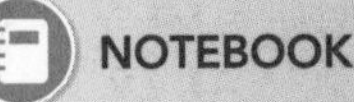

READ IT Mark the subject and verb of the independent clause in this sentence from paragraph 7 of the text:

"Black Sunday," as the storm became known, was the death knell for the poor farmers of Oklahoma and Texas.

WRITE IT **Edit these complex sentences to correct subject-verb agreement errors.**

1. Hope for a better life, although it has risks, draw many people to California.
2. A terrible drought, after farming practices damage the land, add to the disaster.
3. A disaster like the Dust Bowl, unless we change certain practices, are not unimaginable.

BLACK SUNDAY: THE STORM THAT GAVE US THE DUST BOWL

Compare Nonfiction and Fiction

You will now read an excerpt from the novel *The Grapes of Wrath,* a work of historical fiction. Then, you will compare it to the work of historical nonfiction, "Black Sunday: The Storm That Gave Us the Dust Bowl."

from THE GRAPES OF WRATH

About the Author

Few writers portray more vividly than **John Steinbeck** (1902–1968) what it was like to live through the Great Depression of the 1930s. His stories and novels capture the poverty, desperation, and social injustice experienced by many working-class Americans during this bleak period. While many of his characters suffer tragic fates, they almost always exhibit bravery and dignity in their struggles.

from The Grapes of Wrath

Concept Vocabulary

INTERACTIVITY

You will encounter the following words as you read the excerpt from *The Grapes of Wrath*. Before reading, note how familiar you are with each word. Then, rank the words in order from most familiar (1) to least familiar (6).

WORD	YOUR RANKING
ruthless	
bitterness	
toil	
sorrow	
doomed	
frantically	

Comprehension Strategy

ANNOTATE

Monitor Comprehension

As you read a text, **monitor your comprehension** to make sure you understand the ideas. If you are struggling to understand a text, use your **background knowledge,** or what you already know, to improve your grasp of new ideas and challenging passages.

- Read the Background section, and consider what you already know about the subject.
- As you read, mark new ideas and determine whether they add to, change, or contradict your background knowledge.
- If you encounter a passage and cannot figure out the meaning, clarify by drawing on your background knowledge and the ideas in the text that you do understand.

PRACTICE As you read, monitor your comprehension and make adjustments, such as using background knowledge, when needed. Jot your notes in the margins of the text.

TEKS

5.I. Monitor comprehension and make adjustments such as re-reading, using background knowledge, asking questions, and annotating when understanding breaks down.

from The Grapes of Wrath

John Steinbeck

BACKGROUND

During the Great Depression of the 1930s, a severe drought hit the American Midwest. The drought further stressed the already taxed land, producing massive dust storms that blew away topsoil and destroyed farmland. Many devastated farmers had no choice but to sell most of their belongings and seek greener pastures in western states, such as California. This is the situation faced by the Joad family in John Steinbeck's novel *The Grapes of Wrath*.

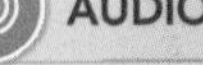

AUDIO

ANNOTATE

1 In the little houses the tenant people sifted their belongings and the belongings of their fathers and of their grandfathers. Picked over their possessions for the journey to the west. The men were **ruthless** because the past had been spoiled, but the women knew how the past would cry to them in the coming days. The men went into the barns and the sheds.

ruthless (ROOTH lihs) *adj.* having no compassion or pity

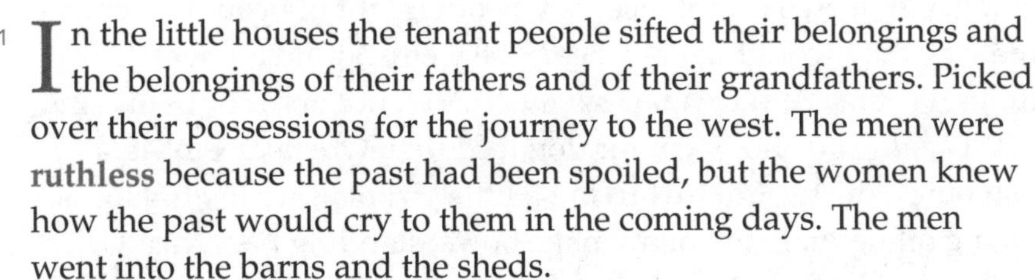

2 That plow, that harrow, remember in the war we planted mustard? Remember a fella wanted us to put in that rubber bush they call guayule?[1] Get rich, he said. Bring out those tools—get a few dollars for them. Eighteen dollars for that plow, plus freight—Sears Roebuck.[2]

1. **guayule** (gwy YOO lee) a desert shrub containing rubber, native to Mexico and Texas. During the Great Depression, it was thought that guayule could be profitably processed for rubber.
2. **Sears Roebuck** company that sold clothes, farm equipment, and other goods by mail order, which supplied much of rural America.

3 Harness, carts, seeders, little bundles of hoes. Bring 'em out. Pile 'em up. Load 'em in the wagon. Take 'em to town. Sell 'em for what you can get. Sell the team and the wagon, too. No more use for anything.

4 Fifty cents isn't enough to get for a good plow. That seeder cost thirty-eight dollars. Two dollars isn't enough. Can't haul it all back—Well, take it, and a **bitterness** with it. Take the well pump and the harness. Take halters, collars, hames, and tugs.[3] Take the little glass brow-band jewels, roses red under glass. Got those for the bay gelding.[4] 'Member how he lifted his feet when he trotted?

bitterness (BIHT uhr nihs) *n.* quality of having a sharp, unpleasant taste; condition causing pain or sorrow

5 Junk piled up in a yard.

6 Can't sell a hand plow any more. Fifty cents for the weight of the metal. Disks and tractors, that's the stuff now.

7 Well, take it—all junk—and give me five dollars. You're not buying only junk, you're buying junked lives. And more—you'll see—you're buying bitterness. Buying a plow to plow your own children under, buying the arms and spirits that might have saved you. Five dollars, not four. I can't haul 'em back—Well, take 'em for four. But I warn you, you're buying what will plow your own children under. And you won't see. You can't see. Take 'em for four. Now, what'll you give for the team and wagon? Those fine bays, matched they are, matched in color, matched the way they walk, stride to stride. In the stiff pull-straining hams[5] and buttocks, split-second timed together. And in the morning, the light on them, bay light. They look over the fence sniffing for us, and the stiff ears swivel to hear us, and the black forelocks! I've got a girl. She likes to braid the manes and forelocks, puts little red bows on them. Likes to do it. Not any more. I could tell you a funny story about that girl and that off bay. Would make you laugh. Off horse is eight, near is ten, but might of been twin colts the way they work together. See? The teeth. Sound all over. Deep lungs. Feet fair and clean. How much? Ten dollars? For both? And the wagon—I'd shoot 'em for dog feed first. Oh, take 'em! Take 'em quick, mister. You're buying a little girl plaiting the forelocks, taking off her hair ribbon to make bows, standing back, head cocked, rubbing the soft noses with her cheek. You're buying years of work, **toil** in the sun; you're buying a **sorrow** that can't talk. But watch it, mister. There's a premium goes with this pile of junk and the bay horses—so beautiful—a packet of bitterness to grow in your house and to flower, some day. We could have saved you, but you cut us down, and soon you will be cut down and there'll be none of us to save you.

toil (TOYL) *v.* work hard and with difficulty

sorrow (SOR oh) *n.* great sadness; suffering

3. **halters, collars, hames, and tugs** parts of the harnesses used to attach horses to horse-drawn plows.
4. **bay gelding** reddish-brown male horse.
5. **hams** back of a horse's knee.

8 And the tenant men came walking back, hands in their pockets, hats pulled down. Some bought a pint and drank it fast to make the impact hard and stunning. But they didn't laugh and they didn't dance. They didn't sing or pick the guitars. They walked back to the farms, hands in pockets and heads down, shoes kicking the red dust up.

9 Maybe we can start again, in the new rich land—in California, where the fruit grows. We'll start over.

10 But you can't start. Only a baby can start. You and me—why, we're all that's been. The anger of a moment, the thousand pictures, that's us. This land, this red land, is us; and the flood years and the dust years and the drought years are us. We can't start again. The bitterness we sold to the junk man—he got it all right, but we have it still. And when the owner men told us to go, that's us; and when the tractor hit the house, that's us until we're dead. To California or any place—every one a drum major leading a parade of hurts, marching with our bitterness. And some day—the armies of bitterness will all be going the same way. And they'll all walk together, and there'll be a dead terror from it.

11 The tenant men scuffed home to the farms through the red dust.

12 When everything that could be sold was sold, stoves and bedsteads, chairs and tables, little corner cupboards, tubs and tanks, still there were piles of possessions; and the women sat among them, turning them over and looking off beyond and back, pictures, square glasses, and here's a vase.

13 Now you know well what we can take and what we can't take. We'll be camping out—a few pots to cook and wash in, and mattresses and comforts, lantern and buckets, and a piece of canvas. Use that for a tent. This kerosene can. Know what that is? That's the stove. And clothes—take all the clothes. And—the rifle? Wouldn't go out naked of a rifle. When shoes and clothes and food, when even hope is gone, we'll have the rifle. When grampa came—did I tell you?—he had pepper and salt and a rifle. Nothing else. That goes. And a bottle for water. That just about fills us. Right up the sides of the trailer, and the kids can set in the trailer, and granma on a mattress. Tools, a shovel and saw and wrench and pliers. An ax, too. We had that ax forty years. Look how she's wore down. And ropes, of course. The rest? Leave it—or burn it up.

14 And the children came.

15 If Mary takes that doll, that dirty rag doll, I got to take my Indian bow. I got to. An' this roun' stick—big as me. I might need this stick. I had this stick so long—a month, or maybe a year. I got to take it. And what's it like in California?

16 The women sat among the **doomed** things, turning them over and looking past them and back. This book. My father had it. He

CLOSE READ

ANNOTATE: Mark examples of repetition of words and phrases in paragraph 10.

QUESTION: What ideas are being emphasized through repetition? Why does the narrator keep using the pronouns *us* and *we*?

CONCLUDE: What can you conclude about the narrator by the words he uses and ideas he conveys?

doomed (doomd) *adj.* destined to a bad outcome

liked a book. *Pilgrim's Progress.*[6] Used to read it. Got his name in it. And his pipe—still smells rank. And this picture—an angel. I looked at that before the fust three come—didn't seem to do much good. Think we could get this china dog in? Aunt Sadie brought it from the St. Louis Fair.[7] See? Wrote right on it. No, I guess not. Here's a letter my brother wrote the day before he died. Here's an old-time hat. These feathers—never got to use them. No, there isn't room.

CLOSE READ

ANNOTATE: Mark the punctuation in paragraphs 17 and 18.

QUESTION: What patterns are created by the questions and statements? What do the dashes indicate?

CONCLUDE: What effect do the patterns and use of dashes create?

17 How can we live without our lives? How will we know it's us without our past? No. Leave it. Burn it.

18 They sat and looked at it and burned it into their memories. How'll it be not to know what land's outside the door? How if you wake up in the night and know—and *know* the willow tree's not there? Can you live without the willow tree? Well, no, you can't. The willow tree is you. The pain on that mattress there—that dreadful pain—that's you.

19 And the children—if Sam takes his Indian bow an' his long roun' stick, I get to take two things. I choose the fluffy pilla. That's mine.

20 Suddenly they were nervous. Got to get out quick now. Can't wait. We can't wait. And they piled up the goods in the yards and set fire to them. They stood and watched them burning, and then **frantically** they loaded up the cars and drove away, drove in the dust. The dust hung in the air for a long time after the loaded cars had passed. 

frantically (FRAN tuh klee) *adv.* acting wildly with anger, worry, or pain

6. ***Pilgrim's Progress*** Christian story by John Bunyan about living virtuously.
7. **St. Louis Fair** The World's Fair of 1904, celebrating a hundred years of American ownership of lands west of the Mississippi River.

MEDIA CONNECTION

The Dust Bowl

VIDEO

DISCUSS IT **What moment, image, or detail in the documentary did you find most powerful? Why?**

Write your response before sharing your ideas.

NOTEBOOK

Answer the questions in your notebook. Use text evidence to support your responses.

Response

1. **Personal Connections** How did you relate to the characters and how they were feeling in these moments? Cite a specific passage or detail that led to your response.

Comprehension

2. **Reading Check (a)** What big change is taking place in the lives of these characters? **(b)** What are the men doing in paragraph 7? **(c)** What happens after the people burn their belongings?

3. **Strategy: Monitor Comprehension** At what points in the text did you pause to monitor your comprehension? In what ways did using your background knowledge improve your comprehension? Explain how this strategy affected your reading experience.

Analysis

4. **Make Inferences** What do Steinbeck's descriptions of the characters' selling their belongings reveal about their lives before the dust storms? Explain, citing text evidence to support your inferences.

5. **(a) Interpret** What does this excerpt suggest about the importance of memory, both to individuals and a community? **(b) Speculate** Given your answer, what do you think the future might hold for this community, even after the drought ends and the land heals? Explain, citing text evidence that supports your thinking.

6. **Interpret** What is the general attitude of the characters in the excerpt? Explain, citing specific examples to support your ideas.

7. **(a) Analyze** Why do you think some of the characters burn their belongings at the end of the excerpt? **(b) Draw Conclusions** What can you conclude about their situation based on this action?

How do we overcome obstacles?

What have you learned about facing adversity from reading this work of historical fiction? Go to your Essential Question Notes and record your observations and thoughts about the excerpt from *The Grapes of Wrath*.

 TEKS

5.F. Make inferences and use evidence to support understanding.

5.I. Monitor comprehension and make adjustments such as re-reading, using background knowledge, asking questions, and annotating when understanding breaks down.

6.A. Describe personal connections to a variety of sources, including self-selected texts.

6.C. Use text evidence to support an appropriate response.

6.G. Discuss and write about the explicit or implicit meanings of text.

from THE GRAPES OF WRATH

Close Read

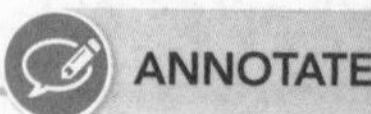

1. The model passage and annotation show how one reader analyzed part of paragraph 1 of the novel excerpt. Find another detail in the passage to annotate. Then, write your own question and conclusion.

CLOSE-READ MODEL

In the little houses the tenant people sifted their belongings and the belongings of their fathers and of their grandfathers. Picked over their possessions for the journey to the west. The men were ruthless because the past had been spoiled, but the women knew how the past would cry to them in the coming days.

ANNOTATE: This is an interesting way to describe the past.

QUESTION: Why did the author choose to say "the past would cry"?

CONCLUDE: Personifying the past gives this passage greater power.

MY **QUESTION:**

MY **CONCLUSION:**

2. For more practice, answer the Close-Read notes in the selection.
3. Choose a section of the excerpt that you found especially important. Mark important details. Then, jot down questions and write your conclusions in the open space next to the text.

Inquiry and Research

 RESEARCH

 NOTEBOOK

Research and Extend *The Grapes of Wrath* is one of the most celebrated and influential works of American historical fiction. Conduct research to learn more about the ways in which the novel has influenced or inspired films, historical writing, and other literary works.

 TEKS

7.A. Infer multiple themes within and across texts using text evidence.

7.D. Analyze how the setting influences character and plot development.

Genre / Text Elements

Multiple Themes Every successful literary work develops at least one **theme,** or central message. Themes can be expressed as general truths about people or life. Writers develop themes through careful selection of significant story details, including the following elements:

- **Setting**, or the time and place in which a story occurs; note that all aspects of the setting—the physical, cultural, and historical elements—can be important to a theme. The cultural and historical setting involves people's beliefs and practices as well as major events in the world of the story.
- **Character development,** or the ways in which characters act and react to situations

In *The Grapes of Wrath*, Steinbeck uses the setting of Oklahoma during the Great Depression to develop themes about how people respond to great hardships. The cultural setting of the novel includes the shared values and attitudes of the people living in that time and place. The historical setting includes the ongoing drought, the disappearance of usable farmland, and the resulting conditions of poverty.

PRACTICE Complete the activity and answer the questions.

1. **Connect** Complete the chart to analyze how story elements determine theme.

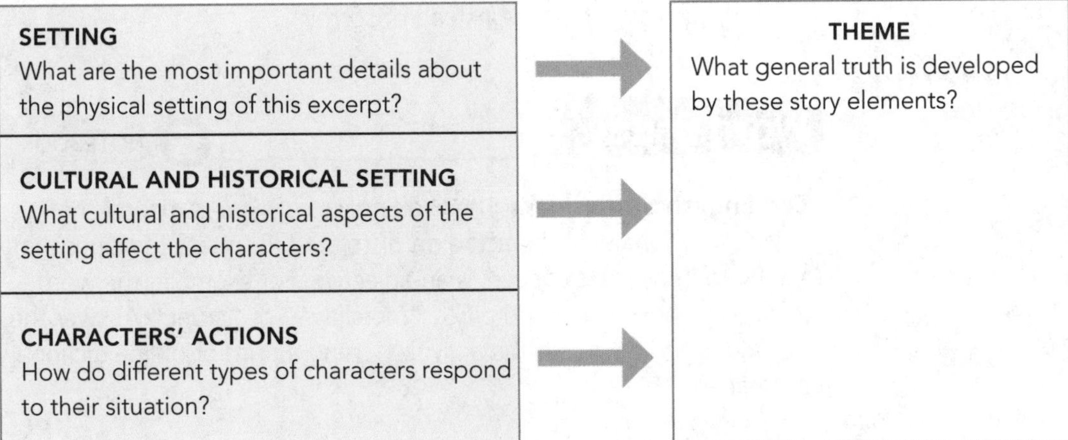

2. **Interpret** Repeated words and ideas can highlight key themes. What theme about human nature is suggested by the narrator's repetition of the noun *bitterness*?

3. **Generalize** In what other situations might these themes in this excerpt from *The Grapes of Wrath* apply? Explain your reasoning.

from THE GRAPES OF WRATH

Concept Vocabulary

NOTEBOOK

Why These Words? The vocabulary words describe extreme emotions or conditions that people experience. For example, the men feel much *bitterness* as they sell their belongings, the women feel great *sorrow* as they say good-bye to their homes, and the characters *frantically* load their cars and leave their homes behind.

ruthless	toil	doomed
bitterness	sorrow	frantically

PRACTICE Answer the questions and complete the activities.

1. How do the vocabulary words sharpen your understanding of the story's characters and setting?
2. What other words in the selection describe or relate to the difficult conditions these characters face?
3. Use each word in a sentence that demonstrates your understanding of the word's meaning.
4. Challenge yourself to write three more sentences about the characters' hopes for the future. This time, use an antonym in place of a vocabulary word, such as *happiness* instead of *sorrow*.

WORD NETWORK

Add words that are related to facing adversity from the text to your Word Network.

Word Study

NOTEBOOK

Old English Suffix: *-less* The Old English suffix *-less* means "not having" or "unable to be acted on or to act." It usually indicates that the word in which it appears is an adjective. For example, the word *ruthless* means "having no pity," "merciless," or "cruel." Answer the questions and complete the activities, using a print or online dictionary as needed.

1. Why are the men in the excerpt described as *ruthless*?
2. Using your knowledge of the suffix *-less*, write a definition for each of the following words: *clueless, heartless, purposeless.*
3. Think of two other words that have the suffix *-less*. Record a definition for each word, and write a sentence that correctly uses it.

TEKS

6.F. Respond using newly acquired vocabulary as appropriate.

9.E. Identify the use of literary devices, including subjective and objective point of view.

Author's Craft

Narrative Point of View The **narrator** is the voice that tells a story. The narrator's **point of view,** or perspective, controls the kinds of information the reader can learn. In this excerpt from *The Grapes of Wrath*, John Steinbeck uses an **omniscient third-person narrator,** which has these qualities:

- The narrator is an observer rather than a character in the story.
- The narrator can reveal the thoughts and feelings of multiple characters.

In this excerpt, the omniscient narrator shares the inner thoughts and feelings of an entire community.

NOTEBOOK

PRACTICE Answer the questions.

1. **(a)** Reread paragraph 1. What does the narrator say everyone in the community is doing? **(b) Analyze** In paragraph 2, whose voices does the reader begin to hear directly? Explain.

2. **Interpret** In what ways do the voices of the community grow and change as the narrative progresses? Cite specific details about the items people mention and the emotions they experience.

3. **Analyze** Why do you think the writer does not use quotation marks to distinguish separate speakers in this excerpt? What is the effect of that choice?

4. **Analyze** What conflict arises in paragraphs 14 and 15? Which details show this conflict?

5. **Interpret** Explain why this section of the novel could only happen with an omniscient third-person narrator. Cite specific details from the text to support your response.

BLACK SUNDAY: THE STORM THAT GAVE US THE DUST BOWL

from THE GRAPES OF WRATH

Compare Nonfiction and Fiction

Multiple Choice

NOTEBOOK

These questions are based on "Black Sunday: The Storm That Gave Us the Dust Bowl" and the excerpt from *The Grapes of Wrath.* Choose the best answer to each question.

1. Which victims of the Dust Bowl are featured in both texts?

A folk singers

B farmers

C junk traders

D newspaper reporters

2. What details about the Dust Bowl appear in the nonfiction text but *not* in the historical fiction?

F language that reveals people's thoughts and feelings

G descriptions of the dust storm and its destruction

H people fleeing to California

J information about how to recover from the storm

3. Although both texts describe the impacts of the Dust Bowl, the authors focus on different aspects to make their points. Which answer choice best states the difference in the authors' approaches?

A Blakemore focuses on the events and consequences of Black Sunday. Steinbeck focuses on how farmers and their families were impacted by Dust Bowl conditions.

B Blakemore focuses on how folk singers became popular during the Dust Bowl. Steinbeck focuses on what happened to farmers who moved to California.

C Blakemore focuses on how the term "Okie" came into use. Steinbeck focuses on how the term "Dust Bowl" came into use.

D Steinbeck focuses on the events and consequences of Black Sunday. Blakemore focuses on how Dust Bowl conditions impacted farmers and their families.

TEKS

6.B. Write responses that demonstrate understanding of texts, including comparing sources within and across genres.

NOTEBOOK

Short Response

Answer the questions in your notebook. Use text evidence to support your responses.

1. **(a) Distinguish** Cite two examples of words and phrases from each text that you feel help to paint a vivid picture of the subject.
   (b) Interpret Explain the reasons for your choices. In your view, what makes these words especially powerful?

2. **(a) Analyze** Cite three facts about the causes and effects of the Dust Bowl that Blakemore shares in her history. **(b) Make Inferences** Cite two historical facts that form the basis of Steinbeck's fiction. Explain your choices. **(c) Connect** How does the genre of each text affect the way in which the author presents historical facts? Demonstrate your knowledge by citing key aspects of the two genres shown in these texts.

3. **Synthesize** How does the information given in the nonfiction work help you better understand the work of fiction, and vice versa? Explain.

Timed Writing

A **comparison-and-contrast essay** is an informational text that analyzes the similarities and differences between two or more subjects.

EQ Notes Before moving on to a new selection, go to your Essential Question Notes and record any additional thoughts or observations you may have about "Black Sunday: The Storm That Gave Us the Dust Bowl" and the excerpt from *The Grapes of Wrath*.

ASSIGNMENT

Write a **comparison-and-contrast essay** in which you demonstrate your knowledge of literary genres. Explore the similarities and differences in how Steinbeck and Blakemore express insights about the Dust Bowl. In what ways can both genres present truths about historical events? State a clear controlling idea, or thesis, and support your ideas with evidence from both texts.

5-MINUTE PLANNER

1. Read the assignment carefully and completely.
2. Decide what you want to say—your controlling idea, or thesis.
3. Decide which examples you'll use from each text.
4. Organize your ideas, making sure to address these points:
   - Explain how the insights in each text are similar.
   - Explain how the insights in each text are different.
   - Explain how the genre of each text affects the way in which the author conveys ideas.

HIGH SCHOOL TEAMMATES CARRY ON

The selection you are about to read is a sports profile.

Reading Sports Profiles

A **sports profile** is a type of biography that tells the life story of an athlete or other person from the world of sports.

SPORTS PROFILE

Author's Purpose

- to tell a compelling story about people connected to the world of sports

Characteristics

- controlling idea that connects facts and details
- use of fiction-like techniques to bring real people alive on the page
- strong emotional appeal
- storytelling elements, such as dialogue and description
- distinct tone, or author's attitude toward the subject

Structure

- lead, or introduction that draws readers and sets the scene
- information that answers basic questions: *who, what, where, when, why,* and *how*
- often, events that are organized chronologically

Take a Minute!

NOTEBOOK

FIND IT With a partner, look up the definitions of the word *profile*. Discuss how the different meanings of the word suggest the kinds of content you would find in a written profile.

TEKS
3.D. Analyze characteristics and structural elements of informational text.

Genre / Text Elements

Direct and Indirect Characterization Like fiction writers, profile writers use **characterization,** or the art of portraying someone in words, to make their subjects come alive. Sometimes they use **direct characterization** and simply state what the person is like. Other times, they show what a person is like through **indirect characterization,** which can include the following elements:

- **anecdotes,** or brief stories that illustrate a point
- **quotations,** or a person's exact words, set in quotation marks
- **dialogue,** or conversations, which may include the writer
- **description,** or details that provide information about the person

EXAMPLES OF CHARACTERIZATION

DIRECT	
Tennis star Chris Yang is generous and talented.	
INDIRECT	
Anecdotes	Yang donated his winnings to fund college scholarships.
Quotations	"People say I'm crazy; I just work harder."
Dialogue	"How many hours do you practice?" asks a fan. "As many as it takes," says Yang with a grin.
Description	At six feet, Yang moves nimbly on the court.

INTERACTIVITY

PRACTICE Mark each item as an example of direct or indirect characterization.

	DIRECT	INDIRECT
1. "Helping kids get to college is the ultimate win," says Yang.	○	○
2. A rival player told of a time when he was ready to give up but Yang encouraged him not to quit.	○	○
3. Yang is as compassionate as he is competitive.	○	○
4. With a fluid motion, he lobs the ball over the net.	○	○

About the Author

Tom Rinaldi is an award-winning correspondent and reporter for ESPN and ABC in New York. He is well known for his critically acclaimed feature stories and reports on a wide variety of sports, including college football and golf. Prior to his career in journalism, Rinaldi was a high school English and ESL teacher in the Bronx in New York City. A native of Brooklyn, New York, Rinaldi wrote *The Red Bandana*, a best-selling biography of 9/11 hero Welles Crowther.

High School Teammates Carry On

Concept Vocabulary

You will encounter the following words as you read the sports profile. Before reading, note how familiar you are with each word. Using a scale of 1 (do not know it at all) to 5 (know it very well), indicate your knowledge of each word.

INTERACTIVITY

WORD	YOUR RANKING
foreseen	
anticipated	
glimpses	
fathom	
invested	
outcome	

Comprehension Strategy

Monitor Comprehension

When you **monitor your comprehension,** you pause to make sure you understand what you read. To clarify unfamiliar ideas or details, pause and **reread** the relevant section again. This process will help you monitor your comprehension and reread effectively:

- Pause at the end of a paragraph, and think about what you have just read.
- Then, state what you've just read in your own words.
- If you have trouble restating the information, reread the paragraph more slowly.

PRACTICE As you read, monitor your comprehension and make adjustments, such as rereading, if your understanding breaks down. Use the open space next to the text to note your observations.

5.I. Monitor comprehension and make adjustments such as re-reading, using background knowledge, asking questions, and annotating when understanding breaks down.

High School Teammates Carry On

Tom Rinaldi

BACKGROUND

The story of Dartanyon Crockett and Leroy Sutton inspired the media and public alike when ESPN aired Tom Rinaldi's "Carry On," which won the prestigious Edward R. Murrow Award for best news documentary. Their story gained even greater momentum when Lisa Fenn, the television producer who brought the story to ESPN, published a memoir about how she developed a close relationship with these young men, one in which they learned and benefitted from each other. This memoir, *Carry On: A Story of Resilience, Redemption, and an Unlikely Family,* is slated to be made into a feature film.

AUDIO

ANNOTATE

1 *"Leroy, touch your toes."*

Leroy reaches his arms out in front of him in mock effort, and says, "They're at home."

And then, the boys laugh.

2 He didn't know they were gone.

3 Staring down at the sheets of his bed, the morphine[1] starting to fade, Leroy Sutton was still numb, but he had a feeling something was wrong.

4 "It was when I tried to sit up," Leroy said, remembering that day nearly eight years ago. "I pulled the covers up, and that's when I figured everything out."

5 It was December 7, 2001, the day that shaped Leroy's body, and his life.

6 He was 11 years old at the time, walking to school with his brother along the Wheeling and Lake Erie railroad tracks near his home in East Akron, Ohio. A freight train approached, and Leroy got too close. His backpack got caught on one of the passing cars, and he was pulled beneath the wheels.

CLOSE READ

ANNOTATE: In paragraphs 7–12, mark direct quotations from Leroy Sutton.

QUESTION: Why might the author have included Leroy's exact words?

CONCLUDE: What effect do the quotations have on readers?

7 "I didn't even look down," said Leroy, now 19, recalling the first moments afterward. "I was just staring at the sun the whole time. I wasn't trying to look down because that's when I would have panicked."

8 The paramedics who arrived within minutes saved Leroy's life, but the doctors could not save his entire body. At Children's Hospital in Akron, his left leg was amputated below the knee, his right leg below the hip. He knew what had happened, but didn't understand what he'd lost until a day later, when he lifted the sheets, and looked down.

9 As the memory came back to him, his voice dropped and his head dipped.

10 "The whole time I was in the hospital, I just asked, 'Why? Why?'" he said. "Every night I could not go to sleep . . . because when I tried, I'd end up hearing the sound of a train."

11 Leroy left the hospital a month and a half later. He endured long, difficult hours of rehabilitation. He accepted that a wheelchair would be part of his life but was determined to make it a small part.

12 "I did not want to be in my chair," he said. "I had to build my arm muscles up so I could move around. . . . I move around on my arms a lot."

13 That ability to move—to lift and flip and twist his body—led him to a place few expected, and into a friendship few could have **foreseen**.

foreseen (fawr SEEN) *v.* recognized in advance; predicted

14 *"Leroy, don't forget your shoes. . . ."*
Others look down, duped. Leroy just smiles.
"You just can't see them. . . ."

---

1. **morphine** (MAWR feen) *n.* drug used to relieve severe pain.

15 In January 2008, midway through his junior year in high school, Leroy transferred to Lincoln-West High in Cleveland. By the time he was a senior, he was a familiar sight (his wheelchair flying down the hallways) with a familiar refrain (his laughter booming off the lockers). When he decided to join the wrestling team, just as he'd done at his previous school, the coaches welcomed him. They knew his story and were eager to tap his strength.

16 "I told him, 'You've been hit by a train. What else, what kid, what wrestler, what can stop you?'" said Lincoln-West coach Torrance Robinson.

17 At Leroy's first practice, his first partner was the only other wrestler on the team powerful enough to handle him. Dartanyon Crockett was Lincoln's best and strongest talent. He was 5-foot-10 with muscles bunched like walnuts, and already a winner in multiple weight classes. But when Leroy hopped off his chair and onto the wrestling mat, the competition was more than Dartanyon expected.

18 "He was a complete powerhouse," Dartanyon said, recalling their first drills together. "I never wrestled anyone as strong as him. We pushed each other to our limits, and we didn't let each other give up."

19 Hour after hour, month after month, practices connected them in ways that went beyond the gym. They went everywhere together: between classes, on team bus rides, at each other's houses—both dialed in to a wavelength[2] few others could hear. They spontaneously broke into songs only they knew. They performed imaginary superhero moves they invented. They laughed at jokes and words only they understood.

20 Yet, their simplest connection was the one everyone saw and no one **anticipated**. Not even Leroy and Dartanyon know exactly when, or how, it first happened.

anticipated (an TIHS uh payt ihd) *v.* expected

21 "One day I'm coming out of my office," said Kyro Taylor, the school's power lifting coach. "I look over to the corner of the gym where the mats were at, and right up the steps I see Dartanyon with something on his back, and the closer I get, I'm like, 'Is that Leroy?' And it was Leroy on his back. Dartanyon's carrying him."

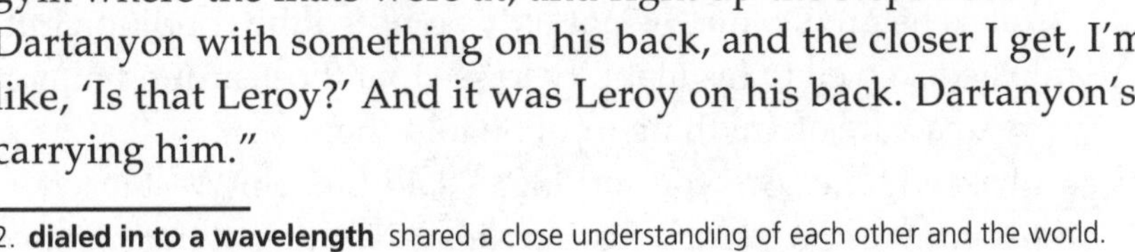

2. **dialed in to a wavelength** shared a close understanding of each other and the world.

CLOSE READ

ANNOTATE: Mark the repeated words in paragraph 23.

QUESTION: Why might the author have chosen to repeat these words?

CONCLUDE: What effect does this repetition create?

22 It was not a onetime ride.

23 Dartanyon lifted Leroy onto his back and carried him to and from every match, on and off every bus, into and out of every gym, all season long. At more than 170 pounds, Leroy was not a light load. Dartanyon never cared, and the carrying never stopped.

24 "Most of the time we wouldn't get a wheelchair lift, so I would have to carry him on the bus, take his wheelchair apart, put it on the bus, then carry him off the bus," he said. "And then, into the building and up the stairs."

25 Dartanyon lifted Leroy onto his back for the playing of every national anthem, and carried him down the bleachers before each match. Yet as inseparable as they were, a team unto themselves in a way, they also shared something greater than their sport.

26 That's because the teammate who carried Leroy on his back all season long knows about challenges himself.

27 Dartanyon Crockett knows, because he's legally blind.

28 *Dartanyon sings.*
"I can see clearly now, the rain is gone."
Leroy listens, then corrects him: "But you can't see."
"So? I can still sing."
And they pick up the song together, twice as loud.

29 Born with Leber's disease, a condition that causes acute visual loss, Dartanyon, 18, has been severely nearsighted his entire life. He can barely make out the facial features of a person sitting 5 feet away.

30 "I'm basically blind compared to someone with 20/20 vision," he said.

31 As a boy, his father watched him bump into the same table corners and fumble for the same objects over and over again, uncertain what was wrong. He received the diagnosis just after his son started elementary school.

32 "I wanted to grab him and help him, but I wasn't allowed to do that, because the world isn't like that," Arthur Harris said. "I never let him feel sorry for himself."

33 "I did feel like something was wrong with me because I was completely different from everyone," Dartanyon said. "Like I was . . . some type of freak."

34 Yet as he grew older, he not only accepted the condition but also adjusted so well to his inability to see that those around him often were unaware of anything until he told them.

35 "I asked him, 'Are you serious?'" said Lincoln-West teacher and assistant wrestling coach Justin Hons. "Nothing about him ever

gives you the hint that he has a disability. The way he carries himself, he doesn't ask for anything."

36 Still, there are signs. At times, his eyes dart back and forth as if ricocheting between objects. Boarding the city bus for the ride to school, he asks the driver to tell him when his stop is near, unwilling to trust his **glimpses** of the passing landscape. In class, often he places text just inches from his face to read. On the wrestling mat, although his moves are quick and bold, he sees little more than rough shapes lunging toward him.

glimpses (GLIHMPS ihz) *n.* brief views; glances

37 Yet his own view of his limits remains focused and clear.

38 "I'm just seeing it as a challenge God has given me and how I'm going to react to this challenge," he said. "Let it make me the person I am, or let it break me."

39 Other trials in his life could have broken him long ago.

40 After his mother died when he was 8, he moved in with his father, Harris, who struggled to take care of himself in the midst of an addiction to drugs and alcohol. There were times when Dartanyon scavenged the house for food, but found none. For most of his time in high school, he had no steady place to call home.

41 "I let him down," Harris said. "It was terrible for him."

42 Through it all, Dartanyon stayed in school, stayed on the mat, and supported his dad's effort to stay clean. Harris now has been sober, while working two full-time jobs, for more than a year.

43 That Dartanyon would pick someone else up was no surprise. He learned to carry a father before he ever carried a friend.

44 "He made a lot of mistakes in the past, and he's learned from them," Dartanyon said. "It's made our bond stronger than I could **fathom**. He's a great father."

fathom (FATH uhm) *v.* imagine; believe

45 When the words were related to Harris, he dropped his head and began to cry.

46 "Above all, I'm glad the love never left," he said. "I'm glad that stayed."

47 *Dartanyon and Leroy move down the hallway after class.*
"I am Darth Cripple," Leroy says.
"I am Blind Vader," Dartanyon replies, and they turn a corner; their laughter is all that's left behind.

48 Friends joke. They jab. They can be the least flattering of critics and the loudest of supporters. So it is with Dartanyon and Leroy. They mock each other and themselves, every chance they get, in ways others never would dare.

49 There's a sure sign of a pending joke. The pace of speech slows, and the tone becomes a notch too earnest. Leroy, in particular, has mastered the pattern. "People look up to me sometimes," he said

from his wheelchair. He waits, then says, "Well, usually, they look down to me." His laughter comes first, and easiest.

50 "They constantly make fun of each other's situation, each other's disability," Hons said. "But they do it publicly, because they're not afraid of their disabilities."

51 The one place they don't laugh is in competition. Entering gyms all season, one atop the other, each cared as much about the other's match as his own, with as much **invested** in the other's **outcome**. Every time Dartanyon wrestled, Leroy sat on the edge of the mat, serving as unofficial coach and chief encourager.

invested (in VEHST ihd) *v.* devoted one's care or interest to something

outcome (OWT kuhm) *n.* end result

52 "It's like having my brother there," Dartanyon said.

53 There was plenty to watch. Competing at 189 pounds in Ohio, one of the most wrestling-rich states in the country, Dartanyon relied more on strength than technique, preferring to overwhelm foes than to outpoint them. Nearly always the aggressor, he rarely waited for another's move, for a simple

reason. He might never see it. So he struck first, and usually, firmest.

54 He went 26–3 in his senior season, securing the league championship in his weight class.

55 "It's amazing," Robinson said. "As phenomenal as he is, and he can't see. How does that happen?"

56 As for Leroy, who's unable to generate the leverage essential in wrestling, leverage gained by using the lower body that he doesn't possess, the matches were tougher, and the wins more difficult. He expected nothing less than 100 percent from his opponents, and if he sensed any pity, he reacted with anger.

57 "Pity?!" He spits the word. "It's more than likely that I'll punch you in the face than sit here and cry."

58 Leroy would bounce on his hands and often flip his way onto the mat before matches. Then he would scream out. Then he would slap his hands down as hard as he could, making a thunderous echo, his smile dead, his arms wired. If some stared when Leroy entered the gym atop Dartanyon, even more stared as he competed.

59 Wrestling in multiple weight classes this season, Leroy won nine matches, the majority by pinning his opponents. But in every match, regardless of the outcome, he left a message. He never said it, but his coaches understood.

60 "Watching him wrestle," Robinson said, "has taught me how to stand in areas of my life that I wouldn't have wanted to."

61 *"Did you guys do the homework?" the teacher asks.*
"Dartanyon tried," says Leroy, "but he couldn't see it."
"So Leroy ran over," says Dartanyon, "and read it to me."

62 It was the final night of the school year, graduation night. The people inside the theater building of Cuyahoga Community College were there for a celebration more than a ceremony, to pay tribute to an accomplishment that meant more here than in most schools in America.

63 The majority of students at Lincoln-West High School never earn a diploma. This year, the school had a graduation rate of roughly 40 percent.

64 On that early June night, the graduates gathered on a stage, their gowns flowing and their tassels poised to swing, each ready to mark a point in a journey.

65 Leroy had dreamed of this night for a long time.

66 "My goal," he said in May, "is to actually walk across the stage."

67 No one on the stage that night understood that goal more than Dartanyon. That's why, when Leroy's name was called, Dartanyon stood, too, right beside him.

CLOSE READ

ANNOTATE: In paragraphs 56–58, mark details that show Leroy's actions and emotions.

QUESTION: Why might the author have included these details?

CONCLUDE: What do these details tell you about Leroy?

68 What would you do for a friend, one you carried on your back all year long?

69 You'd put him down, and walk beside him, which was exactly what Dartanyon did. He helped Leroy stand—upon new prosthetic legs he was fitted for just weeks earlier—then moved alongside him as Leroy crossed the stage, step for step, eye to eye.

70 When Leroy stopped, put out his hand and grasped his diploma, the audience rose and delivered a standing ovation.

71 After the photos were taken, and the music stopped, and the tears dried, the two sat in the theater, side by side.

72 "As long as I can remember," Dartanyon said, "I've been carrying him from point A to B to C. Graduation was the first time I finally got to walk beside him." He paused. "It was a privilege. It was an honor."

73 Leroy's eyes moistened, and he looked up.

74 "It meant so much to me," he said, "to know I have a friend who was there to catch me if I stumbled."

75 There was no stumble.

76 There was no pun or punch line, no joke or jab. There were just two friends, sharing one moment, and there they lingered, smiling, in silence. ❧

Answer the questions in your notebook. Use text evidence to support your responses.

Response

1. **Personal Connections** Did you find this sports profile inspiring? Explain, citing details from the text.

Comprehension

2. **Reading Check (a)** How was Leroy injured? **(b)** How has Dartanyon been physically challenged? **(c)** How did Leroy and Dartanyon meet?

3. **Strategy: Monitor Comprehension (a)** What parts of the text did you reread after pausing to monitor your comprehension? **(b)** How did making this adjustment help you better understand the text?

Analysis

4. **Analyze** Why do you think the author chose to write about Leroy and Dartanyon? What message does this profile convey? Explain, citing evidence from the text.

5. **(a) Make an Inference** What does the relationship that Dartanyon has with his father tell you about Dartanyon's personality? **(b) Evaluate** How much do the personalities of both boys seem to be a factor in their success and standing among their classmates? Explain, citing specific examples from the profile.

6. Throughout the profile, the author incorporates brief scenes and bits of dialogue that show the humor in the boy's friendship. Explain how this approach and the tone of the profile, shifts in paragraph 68.

EQ Notes How do we overcome obstacles?

What have you learned about facing adversity from reading this text? Go to your Essential Question Notes and record your observations and thoughts about "High School Teammates Carry On."

TEKS

5.F. Make inferences and use evidence to support understanding.

5.I. Monitor comprehension and make adjustments such as re-reading, using background knowledge, asking questions, and annotating when understanding breaks down.

6.A. Describe personal connections to a variety of sources, including self-selected texts.

6.C. Use text evidence to support an appropriate response.

HIGH SCHOOL TEAMMATES CARRY ON

Close Read

1. The model passage and annotation show how one reader analyzed part of paragraph 48 of the profile. Find another detail in the passage to annotate. Then, write your own question and conclusion.

CLOSE-READ MODEL

Friends joke. They jab. They can be the least flattering of critics and the loudest of supporters. So it is with Dartanyon and Leroy.

ANNOTATE: Two short, pointed sentences are followed by longer flowing ones.

QUESTION: Why does the author mix sentence lengths in this way?

CONCLUDE: The short, punchy sentences mimic the actions they describe. The mixed sentence lengths add drama to the passage.

MY **QUESTION:**

MY **CONCLUSION:**

2. For more practice, answer the Close-Read notes in the selection.
3. Choose a section of the sports profile you found especially important. Mark important details. Then, jot down questions and write your conclusions in the open space next to the text.

Inquiry and Research

Research and Extend Generate questions you could use to guide research on aspects of the profile, such as Leber's disease, the sport of wrestling, where Leroy and Dartanyon are today, or the reporter's background. Perform a quick Internet search to get answers to one of your questions.

12.A. Generate student-selected and teacher-guided questions for formal and informal inquiry.

Genre / Text Elements

Direct and Indirect Characterization In profiles, reporters reveal subjects' personalities and attitudes in two main ways.

- **Direct characterization** tells readers what a subject is like: "She is a five-time medalist in archery, arguably the best in her sport."
- **Indirect characterization** shows readers what a subject is like, as in this description: "Her hawk-like gaze never wavers as she raises her bow."

In addition to description, a reporter may share anecdotes, include quotations from other people, and weave in dialogue that suggests certain aspects of the subjects' personalities. Readers use details of indirect characterization to draw conclusions about the subjects' personalities, motivations, and behavior.

NOTEBOOK

INTERACTIVITY

PRACTICE Complete the activity and answer the questions.

1. **Analyze** Identify four examples each of direct and indirect characterization in the profile.

DIRECT CHARACTERIZATION	INDIRECT CHARACTERIZATION

2. **Evaluate** Do you think the author effectively conveys what both Leroy and Dartanyon are like? Do you get a clear sense of their characters and interactions? Explain your thinking, citing text evidence.

3. **(a) Analyze** How would this profile have been different if the author had relied solely on direct characterization? Explain. **(b) Draw Conclusions** Explain why indirect characterization is so important in this profile and in literature in general.

HIGH SCHOOL TEAMMATES CARRY ON

Concept Vocabulary

NOTEBOOK

Why These Words? The vocabulary words relate to the idea of future possibilities, or a person's expectations for the future. For example, no one could have *foreseen* that Leroy and Dartanyon would develop such a close friendship after meeting on the wrestling team.

foreseen	anticipated	glimpses
fathom	invested	outcome

PRACTICE Answer the questions.

1. How do the vocabulary words add to your understanding of how different people overcome obstacles?
2. If you are *invested* in a writing project, what are you doing?
3. How are *glimpses* different from stares?
4. Describe a situation that was different from what you *anticipated.*
5. What do you find most difficult to *fathom* about Leroy's experience?
6. When two sports teams compete, what are the possible *outcomes?*

WORD NETWORK

Add words that are related to facing adversity from the text to your Word Network.

Word Study

NOTEBOOK

Word Origins Many words and phrases in English have origins in specific occupations. For example, the vocabulary word *fathom* comes from sailing. As a noun, it is a unit of measure equal to six feet. The verb form of *fathom* has multiple meanings: It can mean "measure the depth of water" or "explore the depths of a problem; understand in a deeper way."

PRACTICE Use resources to research the word origins of these other words and phrases that derive from sailing. Explain their original meanings and their modern usage: *figurehead, footloose, above board.*

TEKS

2.A. Use print or digital resources to determine the meaning, syllabication, pronunciation, word origin, and part of speech.

6.F. Respond using newly acquired vocabulary as appropriate.

9.G. Explain the purpose of rhetorical devices such as direct address and rhetorical questions and logical fallacies such as loaded language and sweeping generalizations.

Author's Craft

Rhetorical Devices Writers often use **rhetorical devices,** which are special patterns of words that emphasize ideas and emotions. For example, **parallelism** is the deliberate repetition of grammatical structures—phrases, clauses, and sentences. Parallelism creates rhythm, giving added power and drama to a text. In this profile, the author uses parallelism to great effect.

EXAMPLES: PARALLEL STRUCTURES FROM THE TEXT

PHRASES	CLAUSES	SENTENCES
Then he would slap his hands down as hard as he could, making a thunderous echo, *his smile dead, his arms wired.*	By the time he was a senior, he was a familiar sight *(his wheelchair flying down the hallways)* with a familiar refrain *(his laughter booming off the lockers).*	*Friends joke. They jab.* They can be the least flattering of critics and the loudest of supporters.

INTERACTIVITY

PRACTICE Complete the activity.

1. **Analyze** Mark the parallel elements in each passage shown in the chart and explain the effect of the device. Then, add another example of parallelism from the text that you particularly like. Explain the reasons for your choice.

EXAMPLE OF PARALLELISM	EFFECT
"I told him, 'You've been hit by a train. What else, what kid, what wrestler, what can stop you?'" said Lincoln-West coach Torrance Robinson. (paragraph 16)	
Hour after hour, month after month, practices connected them in ways that went beyond the gym. (paragraph 19)	
They went everywhere together: between classes, on team bus rides, at each other's houses—both dialed in to a wavelength few others could hear. They spontaneously broke into songs only they knew. They performed imaginary superhero moves they invented. They laughed at jokes and words only they understood. (paragraph 19)	

HIGH SCHOOL TEAMMATES CARRY ON

Composition

A **feature film proposal** is a type of argument in which you present an idea for a film to potential producers and ask them to fund the project.

ASSIGNMENT

Work with a partner to write a **feature film proposal** for a movie based on "High School Teammates Carry On." State and defend a strong **claim,** or position, describing in detail why you think this story will make a great film. Include the following elements:

- **logline:** one or two sentences that describe the main concept of the film in a dramatic and appealing way
- **character profiles:** brief, clear descriptions of the main characters, as well as suggestions for actors who could play them
- **defense:** well-argued explanation of the reasons this story will make a strong film; include a description of a key scene with dialogue

Use Powerful Words

Remember, you are trying to convince your reader to invest money and time in a project. Use strong, convincing language that generates excitement and enthusiasm for your ideas.

Reflect on Your Writing

PRACTICE Think about the choices you made as you wrote. Also consider what you learned by writing. Share your experiences by responding to these questions.

1. How did you choose the key scene to include in your film proposal? Explain.

2. What is the most important reason people should see this film?

3. **WHY THESE WORDS?** The words you choose make a difference in your writing. Which words did you choose to appeal to emotions?

1.D. Engage in meaningful discourse and provide and accept constructive feedback from others.

6.H. Respond orally or in writing with appropriate register, vocabulary, tone, and voice.

11.C. Compose multi-paragraph argumentative texts using genre characteristics and craft.

Speaking and Listening

A **movie pitch** is a 60-second persuasive statement about why your movie should be made.

ASSIGNMENT

Working with your partner, condense your feature film proposal into a 60-second **movie pitch.** Then, present it to the class.

- Use precise vocabulary, such as *characters, actors, scene, audience,* and *drama.*
- Speak clearly, at an appropriate volume. Let your tone convey your passion for the project.
- Practice! You have one minute to persuade the class that your movie idea is worthwhile.

Evaluate Presentations

Use a presentation evaluation guide like the one shown to evaluate both your own and your classmates' movie pitches. Invite feedback on your presentation, and provide feedback after others present.

PRESENTATION EVALUATION GUIDE

Rate each statement on a scale of 1 (not demonstrated) to 5 (demonstrated).

Statement	1	2	3	4	5
The speaker communicated what the movie is about and why it should be made.	O	O	O	O	O
The speaker used precise vocabulary, such as distinguishing between *characters* and *actors*.	O	O	O	O	O
The speaker used an appropriate volume and a tone that was powerful and persuasive.	O	O	O	O	O

EQ Notes Before moving on to a new selection, go to your Essential Question Notes and record any additional thoughts or observations you may have about "High School Teammates Carry On."

Write an Informational Essay

An **informational essay** is a brief work of nonfiction in which a writer educates readers about a topic.

ASSIGNMENT

Write an **informational essay** in which you respond to the following question:

What does it mean to overcome adversity?

Support your ideas with details from your reading, background knowledge, and personal observations. Use the elements of informational essays in your writing.

ELEMENTS OF INFORMATIONAL ESSAYS

Purpose: to provide information and explanations about a topic

Characteristics

- a clear thesis statement or controlling idea
- text evidence used in a variety of different ways, including as summaries, paraphrases, and exact quotations
- elements of craft, including precise language and well-chosen transitions
- definitions of unfamiliar or technical terms
- an objective tone
- standard English conventions, including correct use of conjunctive adverbs

Structure

- an engaging introduction with a clear thesis statement
- a coherent and focused flow of ideas within and across paragraphs
- a strong conclusion

TEKS
11.B. Compose informational texts, including multi-paragraph essays that convey information about a topic, using a clear controlling idea or thesis statement and genre characteristics and craft.

Take a Closer Look at the Assignment

NOTEBOOK

1. What is the assignment asking me to do (in my own words)?

2. Is a specific **audience** mentioned in the assignment?

◯ Yes If "yes," who is my main audience?

◯ No If "no," who do I think my audience is or should be?

3. Is my **purpose** for writing specified in the assignment?

◯ Yes If "yes," what is the purpose?

◯ No If "no," why am I writing this informational essay (not just because it's an assignment)?

4. (a) Does the assignment ask me to provide specific **types of evidence**?

◯ Yes If "yes," what are they?

◯ No If "no," what types of evidence do I think I need?

(b) Where will I get the evidence? What details can I pull from my EQ Notes?

5. Does the assignment ask me to organize my ideas in a certain way?

◯ Yes If "yes," what structure does it specify?

◯ No If "no," how can I best organize my ideas?

AUDIENCE

Always keep your **audience,** or readers, in mind when you write. Define specialized terms or other information that they may not know.

PURPOSE

A specific **purpose,** or reason for writing, will lead to a stronger essay.

General Purpose: *In this essay, I will provide information about adversity.*

Specific Purpose: *In this essay, I will explain how my friend faced and overcame adversity.*

EVIDENCE

Varied **types of evidence,** or supporting details, will make your essay stronger.

- **Facts:** information that can be proved true
- **Definitions:** explanations of unfamiliar terms
- **Examples:** specific instances or brief narratives that illustrate facts or concepts
- **Direct Quotations:** people's exact words set off with quotation marks

Planning and Prewriting

Before you draft, decide what you want to say and how you want to say it. Complete the activities to get started.

Discover Your Thinking: Freewrite!

Keep your topic in mind as you write quickly and freely for at least three minutes without stopping.

- Don't worry about your spelling or grammar (you'll fix mistakes later).
- When time is up, pause and reread what you wrote. Mark ideas or details that seem strong or interesting.
- Repeat the process several times. When you begin a new round, start with the strong ideas you marked earlier.

NOTEBOOK

WRITE IT What does it mean to overcome adversity?

TEKS

10.A. Plan a first draft by selecting a genre appropriate for a particular topic, purpose, and audience using a range of strategies such as discussion, background reading, and personal interests; **10.B.i.** Develop drafts into a focused, structured, and coherent piece of writing by organizing with purposeful structure, including an introduction, transitions, coherence within and across paragraphs, and a conclusion.

Structure Ideas: Make a Plan

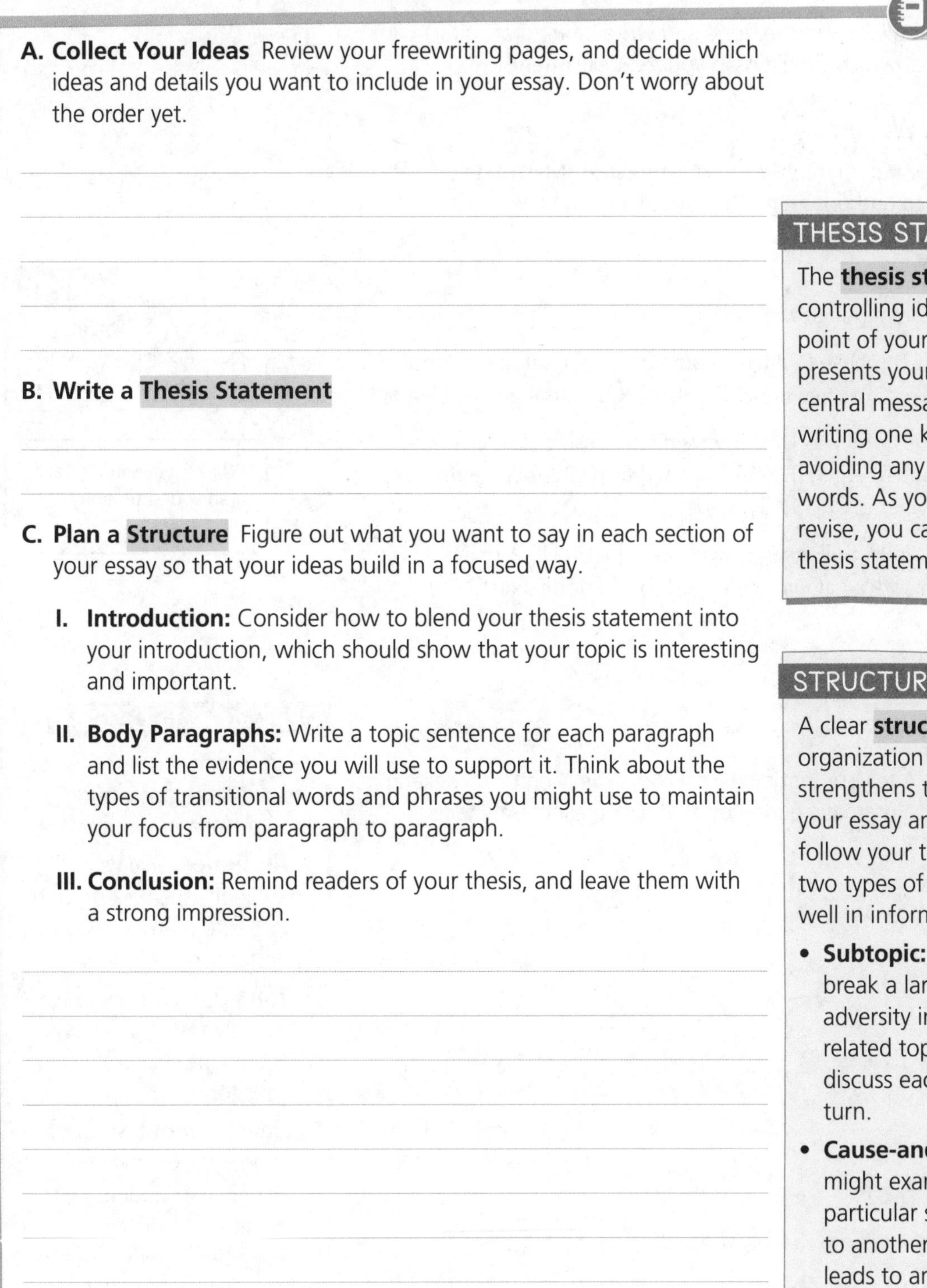

NOTEBOOK

A. Collect Your Ideas Review your freewriting pages, and decide which ideas and details you want to include in your essay. Don't worry about the order yet.

B. Write a Thesis Statement

C. Plan a Structure Figure out what you want to say in each section of your essay so that your ideas build in a focused way.

I. **Introduction:** Consider how to blend your thesis statement into your introduction, which should show that your topic is interesting and important.

II. **Body Paragraphs:** Write a topic sentence for each paragraph and list the evidence you will use to support it. Think about the types of transitional words and phrases you might use to maintain your focus from paragraph to paragraph.

III. **Conclusion:** Remind readers of your thesis, and leave them with a strong impression.

THESIS STATEMENT

The **thesis statement** is the controlling idea or main point of your essay. It presents your subject and central message. Begin by writing one key idea, avoiding any unnecessary words. As you draft and revise, you can clarify your thesis statement.

STRUCTURE

A clear **structure,** or organization of ideas, strengthens the focus of your essay and helps readers follow your thinking. These two types of structures work well in informational writing:

- **Subtopic:** You might break a large topic like adversity into smaller, related topics and then discuss each subtopic in turn.
- **Cause-and-Effect:** You might examine how a particular situation leads to another, which in turn leads to another.

Drafting

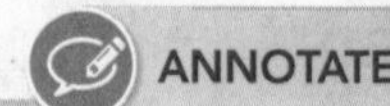

Apply the planning work you've done and write a first draft. Start with your introduction, which should grab your reader's interest.

Read Like a Writer

Reread the first few paragraphs of the Mentor Text. Mark details that make you want to find out more. One observation has been done for you.

MENTOR TEXT

from Against the Odds

"If you have to ditch a commercial aircraft in the Hudson River," the news anchor joked, "this is the guy you want."

The "guy" was US Airways pilot Chesley "Sully" Sullenberger, III, a 57-year-old former Air Force fighter pilot and a 29-year veteran of US Airways.

On January 15, 2009, Sullenberger was the pilot on US Airways Flight 1549 from New York's LaGuardia Airport to Charlotte, North Carolina.

This quotation is dramatic and also gives important facts. Readers will want to know more.

Which details in the text grab your attention? Mark them.

NOTEBOOK

WRITE IT Write your introduction. Follow the Mentor Text example, and start with a dramatic quotation that also presents key facts.

DEPTH OF THOUGHT

As you draft the rest of your essay, make your writing thoughtful and informative.

- **Audience** Give your audience the background information they need to understand your ideas.
- **Tone** Use a formal but friendly tone that shows a keen interest in your topic.
- **Development** Support your ideas with varied evidence, including facts, details, and strong examples. For instance, if you provide a quotation, back it up with facts.

10.B.ii. Develop drafts into a focused, structured, and coherent piece of writing by developing an engaging idea reflecting depth of thought with specific facts, details, and examples; **10.D.iii.** Edit drafts using standard English conventions, including conjunctive adverbs.

Create Coherence

As you draft your essay, use transitions to create coherence. A **coherent** essay "holds together" within and across paragraphs. Use **transitions** to show how ideas connect and build on one another. There are two basic types of transitions:

- **Transitional words and phrases** create smooth transitions between sentences and paragraphs, making your essay easy to follow.
- **Conjunctive adverbs** connect ideas in two independent clauses.

Sample Transitions

Relationship Between Ideas	Transitional Words / Phrases	Conjunctive Adverbs
time sequence	*before; by the time that*	*eventually; next*
contrast	*but; on the contrary*	*however; conversely*
comparison	*as; like; in the same way*	*similarly; likewise*
cause-and-effect	*because; under the circumstances*	*therefore; consequently*
add information	*also; for example*	*additionally; moreover*

TRANSITIONS AND PUNCTUATION

When you use a conjunctive adverb to connect two independent clauses, place a semicolon before the adverb and a comma after it. When you use a conjunctive adverb at the beginning of a sentence, follow it with a comma.

WRITE IT Write a paragraph of your essay here. Include specific facts, details, or examples that focus on and support your idea and convey your depth of thought. Edit to add transitions that show the connections between sentences. Then, write the first sentence of the next paragraph, including a transition.

SENTENCE VARIETY

You can add sentence variety in different ways.

- Use conjunctive adverbs to combine sentences.

EXAMPLE:
He spent decades in the military; subsequently, he became a successful pilot.

- Use a transitional word or phrase, but keep two sentences.

EXAMPLE:
He spent decades in the military. After that, he became a successful pilot.

Revising

ANNOTATE

Now that you have a first draft, revise it to be sure it conveys information as effectively as possible. When you revise, you "re-see" your writing, checking for the following elements:

Clarity: sharpness of your ideas

Development: full explanations and strong supporting facts, details, and examples

Organization: logical progression of ideas to create a focused, coherent text

Style and Tone: quality and variety of sentences and word choices; a level of formality that is appropriate for your audience and your purpose

Read Like a Writer

Review the revisions made to the Mentor Text. Then, answer the questions in the white boxes.

MENTOR TEXT

from Against the Odds

The 150 passengers felt a powerful thud against the airplane, followed by vibrations from the engine. *One passenger said it sounded like sneakers thumping around in a dryer*.

There was a loud explosion. The cabin filled up with smoke. ~~There was a loud explosion.~~ There was a horrible smell and then an eerie quiet: both engines were disabled.

Sullenberger made a Mayday radio call to air traffic control and ~~he's like all calm!~~ *calmly explained the situation.* They discussed the options: The plane could either return to LaGuardia or land at Teterboro Airport in New Jersey.

Why do you think the writer added this detail?

Why do you think the writer reorganized these sentences?

The writer changes some words to maintain an appropriately formal tone.

The writer provides relevant and accurate factual information.

 TEKS

10.C. Revise drafts for clarity, development, organization, style, word choice, and sentence variety.

Take a Closer Look at Your Draft

Now, revise your draft. Use the Revision Guide for Informational Essays to evaluate and strengthen your essay.

REVISION GUIDE FOR INFORMATIONAL ESSAYS

EVALUATE	TAKE ACTION
Clarity	
Is my thesis well integrated into the introduction?	If your thesis isn't clear, **say** your main point out loud as though you were speaking to a friend. Use that statement to help clarify the idea you want to express.
Development	
Have I provided enough information?	**List** your main ideas—the topic sentence of each paragraph. • **Add** evidence for ideas that need more support. • **Delete** details that are not relevant
Have I used a variety of evidence, including facts, details, and examples?	• **Add** facts or quotations to support your thesis. • **Add** examples to illustrate your facts.
Organization	
Have I presented ideas in a logical order to create a focused text?	Check your essay's structure to decide whether to make adjustments: • Do readers need to understand some ideas before others? If so, **reorder** to build background. • Do events feature prominently in your essay? If so, make sure the time-order sequence is clear and **reorder** if necessary.
Do my ideas connect logically?	Does each sentence have a clear connection to the ones that come before and after it? Does each paragraph? If not, **add** transitions to clarify the connections.
Style and Tone	
Does my introduction engage readers?	**Add** a question, quotation, or interesting detail to engage your audience.
Is my tone appropriate for an informational essay?	**Replace** informal language with formal language. For example: • **Substitute** academic words for slang. • **Replace** any words that seem careless or imprecise with specific details.

Editing

Don't let errors distract readers from your ideas. Reread your draft and fix mistakes to create a finished informative work.

Read Like a Writer

Look at how the writer of the Mentor Text edited her draft. Then, follow the directions in the white boxes.

MENTOR TEXT

from Against the Odds

Sullenberger knew the situation was too dire for the plane to stay in the air long enough for either plan to be successful, he had about 30 seconds to find an ~~alternateive~~ *alternative.* The pilot decided on a radical move: He'd ditch the plane in the Hudson River—despite the fact that passenger jets are not built to land on water....

Sullenberger lowered the plane's nose in a gradual glide toward the ~~river the~~ *river. The* plane managed to clear the George Washington Bridge and, against the odds, land safly on the surface of the Hudson.

Fix the comma splice.

The writer fixed a spelling error.

The writer fixed a run-on sentence.

Correct the spelling error.

Focus on Sentences

Run-Ons and Splices A **run-on sentence** happens when two or more independent clauses (complete thoughts) are connected without any punctuation or with incorrect punctuation. A **comma splice** is a run-on in which a comma incorrectly joins independent clauses. One way to fix run-ons and splices is to create complex sentences. Turn one of the independent clauses into a dependent clause by adding a subordinating conjunction. Then, connect the dependent clause to the independent clause.

Run-On: *The pilot is a hero he saved the passengers.*

Corrected as a Complex Sentence: *The pilot is a hero because he saved the passengers.*

You can also fix run-ons by separating the clauses into two sentences and adding a period or a semicolon.

PRACTICE Correct each run-on or comma splice by creating a complex sentence.

1. Some people are afraid of flying air travel is very safe.
2. It was an impressive feat, the pilot landed a huge jet on a river.
3. The pilot did not think he was a hero he was only doing his job.

EDITING TIPS

Subordinating conjunctions include the words *because, although,* and *until.* They begin subordinate, or dependent, clauses, which cannot stand alone as sentences. Instead, you must connect them to independent clauses to create complex sentences.

TEKS

10.D.i. Edit drafts using standard English conventions, including complete complex sentences with subject-verb agreement and avoidance of splices, run-ons, and fragments; **10.D.iii.** Edit drafts using standard English conventions, including conjunctive adverbs; **10.D.iv.** Edit drafts using standard English conventions, including prepositions and prepositional phrases and their influence on subject-verb agreement; **10.E.** Publish written work for appropriate audiences.

Focus on Spelling and Punctuation

Spelling: Adding Suffixes Many words in English end with a silent *e*. For example, *change, note,* and *hope* all end with the silent *e*. Follow two rules when adding suffixes to such words:

- Drop the final silent e if the suffix begins with a vowel.
- Keep the silent *e* if the suffix begins with a consonant.

EXAMPLES:

excite + -able = excitable; excite + -ment = excitement

care + -ing = caring; care + -ful = careful

Check your essay for any words that contain suffixes but are spelled with a silent *e* in their base form.

Punctuation with Conjunctive Adverbs If you use a conjunctive adverb at the beginning of a sentence, follow it with a comma. If you use a conjunctive adverb to connect two independent clauses, follow these rules for punctuation:

- Place a semicolon before the conjunctive adverb.
- Place a comma after the conjunctive adverb.

Avoid Errors: Prepositions

Prepositions (*to, for, of, in,* etc.) are small words with big impact. These words tell where, when, to whom, or how something occurs. Edit your draft, applying these rules to avoid errors:

- Don't end a sentence with a preposition.
- Don't use the preposition *of* in place of the verb *have*.

Incorrect: *I should of gone.*

Correct: *I should have gone.*

- Use *different from,* and not *different than*.

PRACTICE Fix any spelling or punctuation errors in the following sentences. Then, review your own draft for correctness.

1. People at the waterfront found it amazeing to watch the jet land on the river.
2. Staying calm makes a difference during a crisis; furthermore Captain Sullenberger had flown for US Airways for 29 years.
3. The situation looked hopless, fortunately; the pilot knew just what to do.

Publishing and Presenting

Make It Multimodal

Choose one of these options to share your work with a broader audience:

OPTION 1 Work with your class to publish your essays in an anthology. Locate or create graphic features, such as diagrams, maps, or captioned images, to add relevant information.

OPTION 2 With a classmate, create a podcast. Take turns briefly introducing each other's essays. End the podcast with a conversation in which you compare the controlling ideas of the two essays.

Essential Question

How do we overcome obstacles?

You've hit a bump in the road. Now what should you do? You will read selections that describe obstacles that people have faced and how they were able to overcome them. You will work in a group to continue your exploration of the topic of facing adversity.

VIDEO

INTERACTIVITY

Peer-Group Learning Strategies

Throughout your life, in school, in your community, and in your career, you will continue to learn and work with others.

Review these strategies and the actions you can take to practice them as you work in small groups. Add ideas of your own for each category. Use these strategies during Peer-Group Learning.

STRATEGY	MY PEER-GROUP ACTION PLAN
Prepare • Complete your assignments so that you are prepared for group work. • Take notes on your reading to share with your group.	
Participate fully • Volunteer information, and use verbal and nonverbal forms of communication to get your points across. • Use text evidence when making a point.	
Support others • Build off ideas from others in your group. • Ask others who have not yet spoken to do so.	
Clarify • Paraphrase the ideas of others to check your understanding. • Ask follow-up questions.	

CONTENTS

COMPARE ACROSS GENRES

REALISTIC SHORT STORY

The Circuit

Francisco Jiménez

Why does a cardboard box fill the narrator with dread?

INTERVIEW

How This Son of Migrant Farm Workers Became an Astronaut

José Hernández and Octavio Blanco

What can this success story teach all of us?

ORAL HISTORY

A Work in Progress

Aimee Mullins

Why be "normal," when you can be extraordinary?

AUTOBIOGRAPHY

from The Story of My Life

Helen Keller

Just one little word can make all the difference.

▸ **MEDIA CONNECTION:** How Helen Keller Learned to Talk

PERFORMANCE TASK : SPEAKING AND LISTENING

Present an Informational Text

The Peer-Group readings demonstrate how people can overcome tremendous adversity. After reading, your group will plan and present an informational text about people who faced huge obstacles, but overcame them in creative ways.

Working as a Group

1. Take a Position

In your group, discuss the following question:

> Are any challenges impossible to overcome?

As you take turns sharing your ideas, be sure to provide examples to make your response clear. After all group members have shared, discuss your responses. Were other group members' responses similar to yours? Did other group members share challenges that you had not thought of, but could understand?

2. Use Text Evidence

In this section, make sure that everyone in the group uses text evidence to support responses in both speaking and writing activities. Work to identify textual evidence in ways that reflect the demands of a question or activity:

- **Comprehension:** Identify specific, explicitly stated details.
- **Analysis:** Choose text evidence that fits the criteria for analysis.
- **Inference:** Identify clues that hint at meaning but do not directly state it.
- **Interpretation:** Draw connections among multiple details and show how they lead to deeper meanings.
- **Evaluation:** Identify textual evidence and consider it in relationship to other texts, your own values, or another measure.

3. Name Your Group

Choose a name that reflects the unit topic.

Our group's name: ____________________

4. Create a Communication Plan

Decide how you want to communicate with one another. For example, you might use online collaboration tools, email, or instant messaging.

Our group's plan:

____

____

TEKS

1.D. Engage in meaningful discourse and provide and accept constructive feedback from others.
6.C. Use text evidence to support an appropriate response.

Making a Schedule

First, find out the due dates for the Peer-Group activities. Then, preview the texts and activities with your group, and make a schedule for completing the tasks.

SELECTION	ACTIVITIES	DUE DATE
The Circuit		
How This Son of Migrant Farm Workers Became an Astronaut		
A Work in Progress		
from The Story of My Life		

Give and Accept Constructive Feedback

As you complete writing tasks and other projects with your group, make sure everyone produces the best possible work by giving and accepting constructive feedback.

- **Provide constructive feedback** by being insightful and supportive. Focus on *what works* and *what does not work,* and, most importantly, *why*. Lead off with positive comments, and always mention specific examples.
- **Accept constructive feedback** by remaining quiet and listening. Remember that comments are about your work, not about you personally. You may not agree with every point; apply the comments that are most valuable to you when you revise.

EXAMPLES: Constructive and Nonconstructive Feedback

Nonconstructive: not helpful; focuses on the person, not the writing; expresses unsupported opinions

- *I just didn't like it that much.*
- *Why didn't you make it more exciting? I was bored.*

Constructive: helpful; offers specific suggestions

- *The main character is so believable. The other characters are less vivid. You could add some description or dialogue.*
- *Descriptions of the setting are great, and very vivid. I think the story would be livelier if you mixed in some action.*

THE CIRCUIT

Fiction and Nonfiction

Realistic short stories are brief works of fiction that have characters, settings, events, and situations that seem true to life. An **interview** is a structured conversation with one person asking questions and the other answering them.

HOW THIS SON OF MIGRANT FARM WORKERS BECAME AN ASTRONAUT

REALISTIC FICTION: SHORT STORY

Author's Purpose

- to entertain readers and provide an insight about life or human nature

Characteristics

- a realistic setting that may play a key role in the story's events
- characters that seem true to life
- conflicts, or problems similar to those that people face in real life
- dialogue that reflects the way people actually speak
- a theme, or insight about life

Structure

- a plot, centered on a conflict, with events that could happen in real life

INTERVIEW

Author's Purpose

- to share the experience and knowledge of a noteworthy person

Characteristics

- an interviewer who asks questions
- a subject who answers questions
- open-ended questions that invite thoughtful responses
- interview subject has special knowledge or experience
- subject's experience often reflects a sense of place as well as historical and cultural influences

Structure

- question-and-answer format
- introduction that provides background information about the subject

TEKS

7.D. Analyze how the setting influences character and plot development.

8.A. Demonstrate knowledge of literary genres such as realistic fiction, adventure stories, historical fiction, mysteries, humor, myths, fantasy, and science fiction.

8.D. Analyze characteristics and structural elements of informational text.

Genre / Text Elements

Influence of Setting and Place No one exists in a vacuum. We all live in a place and time, traveling from home to school across fields or city blocks. Our beliefs and actions are formed by the people with whom we interact and the events that shape our lives. The same is true for characters in stories. The time, place, and historical and cultural backdrop influence how characters and plots develop.

TIP: The terms *historical context* and *cultural context* are often used interchangeably, but the first focuses on time period while the second refers to beliefs and customs.

EXAMPLES: Influence of Setting

ELEMENT OF SETTING	EXAMPLE	EFFECT ON CHARACTER AND PLOT
Historical: country, year, political events	U.S.; The Great Depression	Jacob leaves home and gets a railroad job to lift a burden from his family.
Cultural: attitudes, beliefs, customs	Mexican-American family	Luz, a 14-year-old girl, prepares for her upcoming quinceañara.
Location (for example, a specific city; a theater; a rainforest)	San Francisco; Market Street	Emily races a historic street car on foot to see if she can beat it.
Climate/Weather	Midwest prairie; tornado alert	Pat lived through a tornado two years ago and is now terrified of them.

INTERACTIVITY

PRACTICE Read the passage and complete the activity. Use different marks for items 1 and 2. Share your responses with your group.

PASSAGE	INFLUENCE OF SETTING
As a hiding place, it could be worse. At least it was dry and bug free. Hal was tired of running. He prayed that mama bear would go away and that the shed would keep him safe. A loud crack came out of nowhere. Hal ducked and grabbed a shovel. He fervently wished he were somewhere else. *Anywhere* else. It had been a lousy idea to hike in the woods alone, and he had no cell phone and no map. Hal started to make a plan.	1. What details reveal the setting? Mark them. 2. What details reveal how Hal reacts to the setting? Mark them. 3. How do details of the setting help to propel the story's plot?

THE CIRCUIT

Compare Fiction and Nonfiction

In this lesson, you will read a realistic short story, "The Circuit," and an interview, "How This Son of Migrant Farm Workers Became an Astronaut." You will then compare the realistic short story and the interview.

HOW THIS SON OF MIGRANT FARM WORKERS BECAME AN ASTRONAUT

About the Author

Francisco Jiménez (b. 1943) was born in Mexico and came to the United States with his family when he was four years old. The family settled in California and became migrant workers. Although he could not go to school before the harvest ended, Jiménez studied in the fields. His hard work paid off as he went on to become an outstanding teacher and award-winning writer.

The Circuit

Concept Vocabulary

NOTEBOOK

As you read the short story, you will encounter these words.

instinctively	enthusiastically	hesitantly

Base Words Base, or "inside" words, can help you unlock meaning.

EXAMPLE

Unfamiliar Word in Context: Louisa was *energetic*: She rarely took a break from work.

Base word: *energy*, or "great physical power"

Conclusion: Adding *-etic* makes *energy* into an adjective. *Energetic* must mean "filled with energy."

PRACTICE As you read, look for base words in any unfamiliar words. Mark your observations in the open space next to the text.

Comprehension Strategy

ANNOTATE

Make Predictions

When you **make predictions** based on the structure of a story, you use what you know about how plots work to anticipate or guess what will happen later. You then read on to confirm your predictions or to correct them. For example, every story has these structural qualities that can help you make predictions:

- Characters are introduced early in the story.
- Characters face a conflict that gets more intense until it reaches a turning point and eventually resolves.

PRACTICE Use the structures of fiction to make predictions as you read this story. Jot your predictions in the margins of the text. Then, read on to either correct or confirm the predictions you made.

TEKS

5.C. Make, correct, or confirm predictions using text features, characteristics of genre, and structures.

REALISTIC SHORT STORY

The Circuit

Francisco Jiménez

AUDIO

ANNOTATE

BACKGROUND

This selection is from *The Circuit: Stories from the Life of a Migrant Child*, a collection of autobiographical short stories by Francisco Jiménez. In this story, the narrator, Panchito, tells of his difficult early years as part of a family of migrant farm workers. To him, life consisted of constant moving and work, with school wedged in around harvesting jobs. The "circuit" in the title refers to the path migrant workers take every year to find jobs.

BUILD YOUR VOCABULARY

Concept and other higher-level words aren't the only ones that matter. As you read, actively build your understanding of sight and basic words. Listen to the audio and note words you've mastered and those you are still acquiring.

1 It was that time of year again. Ito, the strawberry sharecropper,[1] did not smile. It was natural. The peak of the strawberry season was over and the last few days the workers, most of them braceros,[2] were not picking as many boxes as they had during the months of June and July.

1. **sharecropper** (SHAIR krop uhr) *n.* one who works for a share of a crop; tenant farmer.
2. **braceros** (bruh SAIR ohs) *n.* migrant Mexican farm laborers who harvest crops.

2 As the last days of August disappeared, so did the number of braceros. Sunday, only one—the best picker—came to work. I liked him. Sometimes we talked during our half-hour lunch break. That is how I found out he was from Jalisco, the same state in Mexico my family was from. That Sunday was the last time I saw him.

3 When the sun had tired and sunk behind the mountains, Ito signaled us that it was time to go home. "*Ya esora,*"[3] he yelled in his broken Spanish. Those were the words I waited for twelve hours a day, every day, seven days a week, week after week. And the thought of not hearing them again saddened me.

4 As we drove home Papá did not say a word. With both hands on the wheel, he stared at the dirt road. My older brother, Roberto, was also silent. He leaned his head back and closed his eyes. Once in a while he cleared from his throat the dust that blew in from outside.

5 Yes, it was that time of year. When I opened the front door to the shack, I stopped. Everything we owned was neatly packed in cardboard boxes. Suddenly I felt even more the weight of hours, days, weeks, and months of work. I sat down on a box. The thought of having to move to Fresno[4] and knowing what was in store for me there brought tears to my eyes.

6 That night I could not sleep. I lay in bed thinking about how much I hated this move.

7 A little before five o'clock in the morning, Papá woke everyone up. A few minutes later, the yelling and screaming of my little brothers and sisters, for whom the move was a great adventure, broke the silence of dawn. Shortly, the barking of the dogs accompanied them.

8 While we packed the breakfast dishes, Papá went outside to start the "Carcanchita."[5] That was the name Papá gave his old black Plymouth. He bought it in a used-car lot in Santa Rosa in the Winter of 1949. Papá was very proud of his little jalopy. He had a right to be proud of it. He spent a lot of time looking at other cars before buying this one. When he finally chose the Carcanchita, he checked it thoroughly before driving it out of the car lot. He examined every inch of the car. He listened to the motor, tilting his head from side to side like a parrot, trying to detect any noises that spelled car trouble. After being satisfied with the looks and sounds of the car, Papá then insisted on knowing who the original owner was. He never did find out from the car salesman, but he bought the car anyway. Papá figured the original owner must

3. ***Ya esora*** (yah ehs AW rah) Spanish for "It's time." *(Ya es hora).*
4. **Fresno** (FREHZ noh) *n.* city in central California.
5. **"Carcanchita"** (kahr kahn CHEE tah) affectionate name for the car.

have been an important man because behind the rear seat of the car he found a blue necktie.

9 Papá parked the car out in front and left the motor running. *"Listo,"*[6] he yelled. Without saying a word Roberto and I began to carry the boxes out to the car. Roberto carried the two big boxes and I carried the two smaller ones. Papá then threw the mattress on top of the car roof and tied it with ropes to the front and rear bumpers.

10 Everything was packed except Mamá's pot. It was an old large galvanized[7] pot she had picked up at an army surplus store in Santa Maria. The pot had many dents and nicks, and the more dents and nicks it acquired the more Mamá liked it. *"Mi olla,"*[8] she used to say proudly.

11 I held the front door open as Mamá carefully carried out her pot by both handles, making sure not to spill the cooked beans. When she got to the car, Papá reached out to help her with it. Roberto opened the rear car door and Papá gently placed it on the floor behind the front seat. All of us then climbed in. Papá sighed, wiped the sweat from his forehead with his sleeve, and said wearily: *"Es todo."*[9]

12 As we drove away, I felt a lump in my throat. I turned around and looked at our little shack for the last time.

13 At sunset we drove into a labor camp near Fresno. Since Papá did not speak English, Mamá asked the camp foreman if he needed any more workers. "We don't need no more," said the foreman, scratching his head. "Check with Sullivan down the road. Can't miss him. He lives in a big white house with a fence around it."

14 When we got there, Mamá walked up to the house. She went through a white gate, past a row of rose bushes, up the stairs to the front door. She rang the doorbell. The porch light went on and a tall husky man came out. They exchanged a few words. After the man went in, Mamá clasped her hands and hurried back to the car. "We have work! Mr. Sullivan said we can stay there the whole season," she said, gasping and pointing to an old garage near the stables.

15 The garage was worn out by the years. It had no windows. The walls, eaten by termites, strained to support the roof full of holes. The dirt floor, populated by earth worms, looked like a gray road map.

---

6. ***Listo*** (LEES toh) Spanish for "Ready."
7. **galvanized** (GAL vuh nyzd) *adj.* coated with zinc to prevent rusting.
8. ***Mi olla*** (mee OH yah) Spanish for "My pot."
9. ***Es todo*** (ehs TOH thoh) Spanish for "That's everything."

16 That night, by the light of a kerosene lamp, we unpacked and cleaned our new home. Roberto swept away the loose dirt, leaving the hard ground. Papá plugged the holes in the walls with old newspapers and tin can tops. Mamá fed my little brothers and sisters. Papá and Roberto then brought in the mattress and placed it on the far corner of the garage. "Mamá, you and the little ones sleep on the mattress. Roberto, Panchito, and I will sleep outside under the trees," Papá said.

17 Early next morning Mr. Sullivan showed us where his crop was, and after breakfast, Papá, Roberto, and I headed for the vineyard to pick.

18 Around nine o'clock the temperature had risen to almost one hundred degrees. I was completely soaked in sweat and my mouth felt as if I had been chewing on a handkerchief. I walked over to the end of the row, picked up the jug of water we had brought, and began drinking. "Don't drink too much; you'll get sick," Roberto shouted. No sooner had he said that than I felt sick to my stomach. I dropped to my knees and let the jug roll off my hands. I remained motionless with my eyes glued on the hot sandy ground. All I could hear was the drone of insects. Slowly I began to recover. I poured water over my face and neck and watched the dirty water run down my arms to the ground.

Mark base words or indicate another strategy that helped you determine meaning.

instinctively (ihn STIHNGK tihv lee) *adv.*

MEANING:

19 I still felt dizzy when we took a break to eat lunch. It was past two o'clock and we sat underneath a large walnut tree that was on the side of the road. While we ate, Papá jotted down the number of boxes we had picked. Roberto drew designs on the ground with a stick. Suddenly I noticed Papá's face turn pale as he looked down the road. "Here comes the school bus," he whispered loudly in alarm. **Instinctively**, Roberto and I ran and hid in the vineyards. We did not want to get in trouble for not going to school. The neatly dressed boys about my age got off. They carried books under their arms. After they crossed the street, the bus drove away. Roberto and I came out from hiding and joined Papá. "*Tienen que tener cuidado*,"[10] he warned us.

20 After lunch we went back to work. The sun kept beating down. The buzzing insects, the wet sweat, and the hot dry dust made the afternoon seem to last forever. Finally the mountains around the valley reached out and swallowed the sun. Within an hour it was too dark to continue picking. The vines blanketed the grapes, making it difficult to see the bunches. "*Vámonos*,"[11] said Papá, signaling to us that it was time to quit work. Papá then took out a

10. ***Tienen que tener cuidado*** (tee EHN ehn kay tehn EHR kwee THAH thoh) Spanish for "You have to be careful."

11. ***Vámonos*** (VAH moh nohs) Spanish for "Let's go."

pencil and began to figure out how much we had earned our first day. He wrote down numbers, crossed some out, wrote down some more. "*Quince*,"[12] he murmured.

21 When we arrived home, we took a cold shower underneath a water hose. We then sat down to eat dinner around some wooden crates that served as a table. Mamá had cooked a special meal for us. We had rice and tortillas with "*carne con chile*,"[13] my favorite dish.

22 The next morning I could hardly move. My body ached all over. I felt little control over my arms and legs. This feeling went on every morning for days until my muscles finally got used to the work.

23 It was Monday, the first week of November. The grape season was over and I could now go to school. I woke up early that morning and lay in bed, looking at the stars and savoring the thought of not going to work and of starting sixth grade for the first time that year. Since I could not sleep, I decided to get up and join Papá and Roberto at breakfast. I sat at the table across from Roberto, but I kept my head down. I did not want to look up and face him. I knew he was sad. He was not going to school today. He was not going tomorrow, or next week, or next month. He would not go until the cotton season was over, and that was sometime in February. I rubbed my hands together and watched the dry, acid stained skin fall to the floor in little rolls.

"Finally, after struggling for English words, I managed to tell her that I wanted to enroll in the sixth grade."

24 When Papá and Roberto left for work, I felt relief. I walked to the top of a small grade next to the shack and watched the Carcanchita disappear in the distance in a cloud of dust. Two hours later, around eight o'clock, I stood by the side of the road waiting for school bus number twenty. When it arrived I climbed in. Everyone was busy either talking or yelling. I sat in an empty seat in the back.

25 When the bus stopped in front of the school, I felt very nervous. I looked out the bus window and saw boys and girls carrying books under their arms. I put my hands in my pant pockets and walked to the principal's office. When I entered I heard a woman's voice say: "May I help you?" I was startled. I had not heard

12. ***Quince*** (KEEN say) Spanish for "Fifteen."
13. ***"carne con chile"*** (KAHR nay kuhn CHIHL ay) dish of ground meat, hot peppers, beans, and tomatoes.

English for months. For a few seconds I remained speechless. I looked at the lady who waited for an answer. My first instinct was to answer her in Spanish, but I held back. Finally, after struggling for English words, I managed to tell her that I wanted to enroll in the sixth grade. After answering many questions, I was led to the classroom.

26 Mr. Lema, the sixth grade teacher, greeted me and assigned me a desk. He then introduced me to the class. I was so nervous and scared at that moment when everyone's eyes were on me that I wished I were with Papá and Roberto picking cotton. After taking

roll, Mr. Lema gave the class the assignment for the first hour. "The first thing we have to do this morning is finish reading the story we began yesterday," he said **enthusiastically**. He walked up to me, handed me an English book, and asked me to read. "We are on page 125," he said politely. When I heard this, I felt my blood rush to my head; I felt dizzy. "Would you like to read?" he asked **hesitantly**. I opened the book to page 125. My mouth was dry. My eyes began to water. I could not begin. "You can read later," Mr. Lema said understandingly.

27 For the rest of the reading period I kept getting angrier and angrier at myself. I should have read, I thought to myself.

28 During recess I went into the rest room and opened my English book to page 125. I began to read in a low voice, pretending I was in class. There were many words I did not know. I closed the book and headed back to the classroom.

29 Mr. Lema was sitting at his desk correcting papers. When I entered he looked up at me and smiled. I felt better. I walked up to him and asked if he could help me with the new words. "Gladly," he said.

30 The rest of the month I spent my lunch hours working on English with Mr. Lema, my best friend at school.

31 One Friday during lunch hour Mr. Lema asked me to take a walk with him to the music room. "Do you like music?" he asked me as we entered the building. "Yes, I like *corridos*,"[14] I answered. He then picked up a trumpet, blew on it, and handed it to me. The sound gave me goose bumps. I knew that sound. I had heard it in many corridos. "How would you like to learn how to play it?" he asked. He must have read my face because before I could answer, he added: "I'll teach you how to play it during our lunch hours."

32 That day I could hardly wait to tell Papá and Mamá the great news. As I got off the bus, my little brothers and sisters ran up to meet me. They were yelling and screaming. I thought they were happy to see me, but when I opened the door to our shack, I saw that everything we owned was neatly packed in cardboard boxes. ❧

Mark base words or indicate another strategy that helped you determine meaning.

enthusiastically (ehn thoo zee AS tihk lee) *adv.*

MEANING:

hesitantly (HEHZ uh tuhnt lee) *adv.*

MEANING:

14. ***corridos*** (koh REE thohs) *n.* ballads.

NOTEBOOK

Work on your own to answer the questions in your notebook. Use text evidence to support your responses.

Response

1. **Personal Connections** What parts of the story did you find most surprising? Explain.

Comprehension

2. **Reading Check** **(a)** What kind of work does Panchito's family do? **(b)** Why does the family move at the beginning of the story? **(c)** Why does Papá warn his sons that the school bus is coming when they are picking grapes?

3. **Strategy: Make Predictions** **(a)** Cite one prediction you made based on the story's structure. **(b)** Were you able to confirm that prediction or did you have to correct it? Explain.

WORKING AS A GROUP
Discuss your responses to the Analysis and Discussion questions with your group.
- Note agreements and disagreements.
- Summarize insights.
- Consider changes of opinion.

If necessary, revise your original answers to reflect what you learn from your discussion.

Analysis and Discussion

4. **(a) Draw Conclusions** Why does Panchito call Mr. Lema his "best friend at school"? **(b) Interpret** Based on the information in the story, how would you describe Panchito's personality?

5. **(a) Describe** What is the best thing that happens to Panchito on the last day of school? **(b) Make Inferences** What is the worst thing that happens?

6. **(a) Interpret** What theme, or insight about life, does the story convey? **(b) Evaluate** Does the story's title help to convey its theme? Why or why not?

7. **Get Ready for Close Reading** Choose a passage from the text that you find especially interesting or important. You'll discuss the passage with your group during Close-Read activities.

EQ Notes **How do we overcome obstacles?**

What has this short story taught you about how people overcome obstacles? Go to your Essential Question Notes and record your observations and thoughts about "The Circuit."

TEKS

5.C. Make, correct, or confirm predictions using text features, characteristics of genre, and structures.

6.I. Reflect on and adjust responses as new evidence is presented.

THE CIRCUIT

Close Read

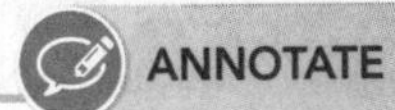

PRACTICE Complete the following activities. Use text evidence to support your responses.

1. **Present and Discuss** With your group, share the passages from the story that you found especially interesting. Discuss what you notice, the questions you have, and the conclusions you reach. For example, you might focus on the following passages:
   - Paragraphs 3–4: Discuss ways in which the author creates a specific mood through word choice.
   - Paragraph 8: Discuss the character of Papá and how the author brings him to life.
2. **Reflect on Your Learning** What new ideas or insights did you uncover during your second reading of the text?

LANGUAGE STUDY

Concept Vocabulary

Why These Words? The vocabulary words are related.

instinctively	enthusiastically	hesitantly

1. With your group, determine what the words have in common. Write your ideas.
2. Add another word that fits the category. ______________________
3. Use each word in a sentence. Include context clues that hint at each word's meaning. Share your sentences with your group.

WORD NETWORK

Add words that are related to facing adversity from the text to your Word Network.

Word Study

Spelling: *-ly* and *-ally* Endings When you add the suffix *-ly* to a base word, you create an adverb. Follow these spelling rules to add the suffix correctly:

- If the base word ends in a consonant, simply add *-ly: hesitantly.*
- If the base word ends in a silent e, keep the silent *e* and add *-ly: instinctively.*
- If the word ends in *-ic,* the suffix changes, becoming *-ally: enthusiastically.*

Correctly add the suffix *-ly* or *-ally* to the following base words: *heroic, formal, mythic, brave.* Use a dictionary to check your work.

THE CIRCUIT

Genre / Text Elements

Influence of Setting A story's setting can shape characters' personalities, attitudes, and actions. The way characters think and behave is often influenced by the world in which they live. In some stories, the setting itself fuels conflict, as characters battle elements such as snow, wind, floods, or earthquakes. As you analyze fictional stories, note details that refer to the setting, including references to:

- **time,** such as the historical period, month, seasons, or even time of day
- **place,** including both elements of nature (type of terrain, type of weather) and civilization (specific city, type of building)
- **cultural values,** including a society's beliefs, attitudes, and customs

STORY SETTING	EFFECTS ON CHARACTER / PLOT
In 1850, a family going to California breaks a wagon wheel in the Rocky Mountains. They must use natural resources to survive as night falls and the temperature drops to dangerous levels.	The setting will drive the plot of the story. Characters must race to find food and shelter before night falls.

INTERACTIVITY

PRACTICE Work with a partner to analyze how the setting affects the characters and develops the plot in "The Circuit." The first entry has been done for you. Add three more examples. Then, discuss your responses with the rest of your group.

SETTING DETAIL	EFFECT ON CHARACTERS / PLOT
It was that time of year again. Ito, the strawberry sharecropper, did not smile. . . The peak of the strawberry season was over.	The characters' livelihood depends on having crops to pick. They must now move on to where other crops are in season.

TEKS

7.D. Analyze how the setting influences character and plot development.

10.D.viii. Edit drafts using standard English conventions, including punctuation, including commas to set off words, phrases, and clauses, and semicolons.

Conventions

Commas Commas are essential tools for writers. **Commas (,)** signal a brief pause; they enable readers to absorb information in meaningful, accurate chunks.

USING COMMAS	EXAMPLES FROM "THE CIRCUIT"
Use a comma before a conjunction that joins independent clauses—groups of words that can stand on their own in sentences.	*The pot had many dents and nicks, and the more dents and nicks it acquired the more Mamá liked it.*
Use a comma after an introductory word, phrase, or clause.	**Introductory Word:** *Yes, it was that time of year.* **Introductory Phrase:** *A little before five o'clock in the morning, Papá woke everyone up.* **Introductory Clause:** *When she got to the car, Papá reached out to help her with it.*
Use commas to separate three or more words, phrases, or clauses in a series.	**Words in a Series:** *Suddenly I felt even more the weight of hours, days, weeks, and months of work.* **Phrases in a Series:** *He wrote down numbers, crossed some out, wrote down some more.*

 INTERACTIVITY  ANNOTATE

READ IT Reread these sentences from "The Circuit." Identify the function of the comma or commas in each sentence.

SENTENCE	FUNCTION
1. As the last days of August disappeared, so did the number of braceros.	
2. The buzzing insects, the wet sweat, and the hot dry dust made the afternoon seem to last forever.	
3. I sat at the table across from Roberto, but I kept my head down.	
4. After the man went in, Mamá clasped her hands and hurried back to the car.	

WRITE IT Edit the following passage to show correct use of commas. Then, discuss your edits with a partner.

The weirdest thing happened today. In the garden I paused to admire our vegetables. I saw rows of herbs stalks of corn and several tomato bushes. Guess what I saw next? Quick as a wink a beanstalk vanished under the soil! If you had been here you would have laughed. Evidently there's a gopher in our garden!

THE CIRCUIT

Compare Fiction and Nonfiction

Like the short story "The Circuit," the interview you are about to read features the son of migrant farm workers. As you read, notice similarities and differences between the two texts.

HOW THIS SON OF MIGRANT FARM WORKERS BECAME AN ASTRONAUT

About the Interviewer

Octavio Blanco is a multimedia content creator at Consumer Reports, a nonprofit organization that works to provide information and protect consumers. For 18 years, Blanco was a reporter and editor for CNN. He is an active member of the National Association of Hispanic Journalists.

How This Son of Migrant Farm Workers Became an Astronaut

Concept Vocabulary

ANNOTATE

As you read the interview, you will encounter these words.

perseverance	attain	conducive

Context Clues Using context clues, including those that relate to cause and effect, can help you figure out what some words mean.

EXAMPLE

Unfamiliar Word in Context If you practice piano every day for an hour, even when you don't feel like it, your *persistence* will pay off—you will become a better musician.

Conclusion The sentence talks about practicing repeatedly despite obstacles in order to achieve something. *Persistence* must mean "the action of repeating something to achieve a goal."

PRACTICE As you read, use cause-and-effect context clues to clarify the meanings of unfamiliar words. Mark your observations in the open space next to the text.

Comprehension Strategy

ANNOTATE

Summarize

When you **summarize,** you restate ideas in an abbreviated way while maintaining the meaning and logical order of the original text. Summarizing can help you improve your understanding of a text. You may write a summary down, but you can also simply keep it in your mind as you continue to read. Follow these steps to summarize:

- Pause after any confusing sections.
- State the key ideas and details in a shortened way.

PRACTICE As you read, summarize sections of the text that may be unclear after a first reading.

TEKS

2.B. Use context such as contrast or cause and effect to clarify the meaning of words.

6.D. Paraphrase and summarize texts in ways that maintain meaning and logical order.

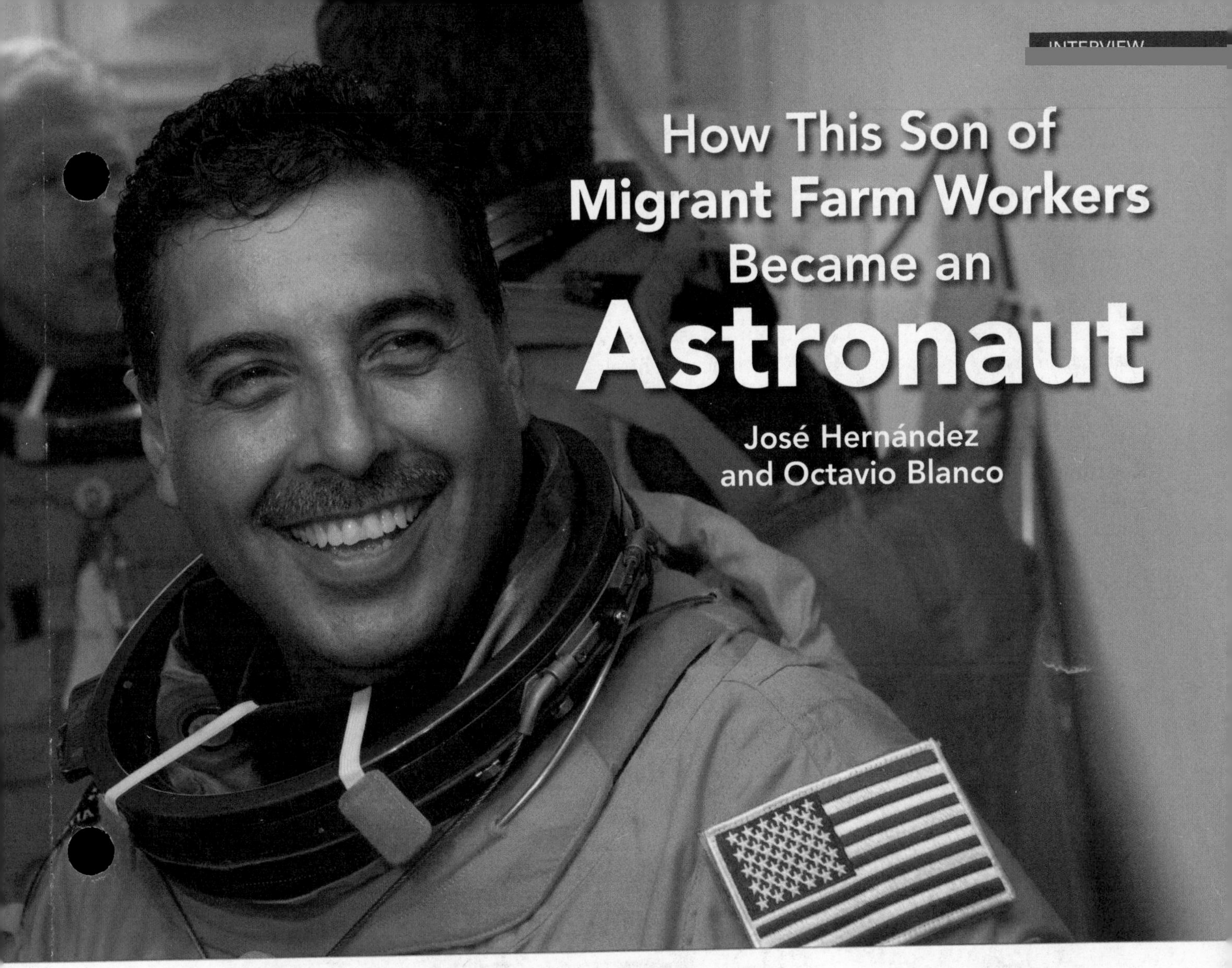

How This Son of Migrant Farm Workers Became an Astronaut

José Hernández
and Octavio Blanco

BACKGROUND

José Hernández was hard at work, hoeing a row of sugar beets in a field, when he heard the news: The first Hispanic American had been chosen to travel into space. Hernández, who was a teenager at the time, had been fascinated by science since childhood. In this interview, Hernández talks with reporter Octavio Blanco about how he went from working on "the California circuit" to working on the International Space Station.

AUDIO

ANNOTATE

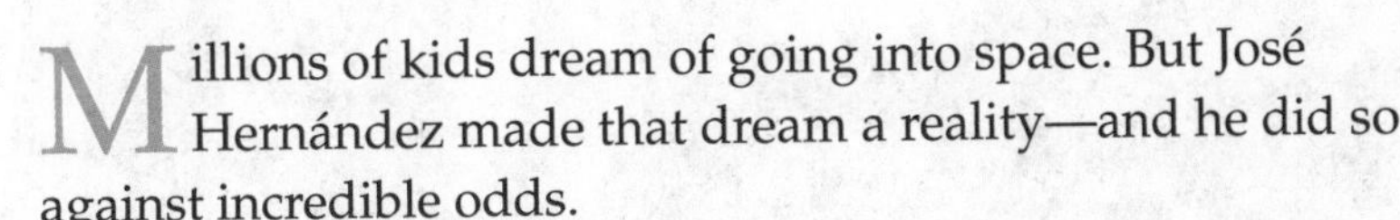

1 Millions of kids dream of going into space. But José Hernández made that dream a reality—and he did so against incredible odds.

2 As the son of Mexican migrant farm workers, his education was constantly interrupted as his family followed the changing crops. Often, they would spend December through February in Mexico.

3 Hernández and his siblings would home school themselves with assignments from their American teachers during those months. But with all of the constant interruptions, Hernández didn't become fluent in English until he was 12.

Use context clues or indicate another strategy you used that helped you determine meaning.

perseverance (puhr suh VEER uhns) *n.*

MEANING:

attain (uh TAYN) *v.*

MEANING:

Reading Environmental Print

This photograph of José Hernández shows him working on the International Space Station. Study the photograph carefully. What signs and graphics do you notice? Why do you think these signs and graphics are important in an outer space environment?

4 But through **perseverance**, Hernández managed to earn a Master's degree in electrical and computer engineering from the University of California, Santa Barbara, and **attain** his goal of becoming an astronaut. Not only has he traveled into space as the mission specialist to the International Space Station, but he now runs his own foundation, Reaching for the Stars.

5 The group aims to get youth in central California interested in STEM (science, technology, engineering and math) fields and provides first-generation[1] high school seniors with scholarships.

6 Here's Hernández's American success story:

What was life like growing up?

7 My childhood was typical of a migrant farm working family, a family that spends nine months out of the year picking fruits and vegetables from Southern California to Northern California. While others looked forward to summer vacation, I hated it. Summer vacation meant working seven days a week in the fields.

8 I had it easier than the rest of my brothers and sisters. I had three older siblings to help me with my schoolwork.

1. **first-generation** born in the United States to immigrant parents.

9 My mom would sit us down at the kitchen table and we wouldn't be allowed to leave until we finished our homework. She motivated all of us by having confidence and high expectations. It wasn't *if* we went to college, it was *when*.

10 Life was rough, but we didn't know it. It was just what we were used to.

11 But then as a teenager I was embarrassed because we lived in the barrio.[2] We lived in areas that were run down because those were the areas where we could afford to live.

12 My bi-cultural upbringing made me feel out of place—not American enough, but not Mexican enough, either.

13 My parents' love, support and high expectations helped me to find my path to success. It could have been a different story. I used to hang out with four guys in the neighborhood. I last saw one of them just a little while ago; he was out on the streets.

When did things begin to change for you?

14 I remember one day, after picking cucumbers, me and my siblings were tired, hot, sweaty, dusty and stinking.

15 My dad told us, 'You're living your future now. I'm not going to force you to go to school or to get good grades. But if you don't study, this is your future.'

16 No matter how hard we studied, however, our life moving from place to place wasn't **conducive** to a good education.

Use context clues or indicate another strategy you used that helped you determine meaning.

conducive
(kuhn DOO sihv) *adj.*
MEANING:

17 My second-grade teacher, frustrated by the constant interruptions, made a special home visit to convince my parents that this lifestyle was hurting us kids.

18 The next year, things changed. We all moved to Stockton, California, year round, visiting Mexico only during Christmas vacations.

19 This stability really helped me. I started speaking English better and was able to focus on learning.

When did your interest in space begin?

20 I began dreaming of going into space after watching the Apollo 17 moon landing when I was 10.

21 That was the last mission to the moon. I'm so glad I saw it!

22 I'd go outside and look at the moon and come back in to see them walking on the surface of it on TV.

2. **barrio** (BAHR ee oh) *n.* neighborhood in a city or town where many residents speak Spanish.

^ Hernández and crew heading to a mission on the International Space Station

23 That night I shared my dream with my dad. Instead of bursting my bubble, he gave me a recipe for success: Decide what you want to do in life. Recognize how far you are from your goal. Draw a road map from where you are to where you want to go. Get your education and make an effort.

24 "Always do more than people expect, m'hijo,"[3] he said.

Is there anything else that contributed to your success?

25 My wife played a huge part in helping me to persevere. I was rejected from NASA's[4] astronaut program eleven times. People get rejected twice, on average, before they're picked.

26 The sixth year that NASA rejected me, I crumpled up the rejection letter and threw it on the bedroom floor. I was going to quit trying, but she talked me out of it.

27 "Let NASA be the one to disqualify you, don't disqualify yourself," she told me.

3. **m'hijo** (mee EE khoh) Spanish for "my son."
4. **NASA** National Aeronautics and Space Administration, a U.S. government agency.

28 I was rejected eleven times. It wasn't until the twelfth time that I was selected. I was 41 when I became an astronaut. The average age of new astronauts is 34.

What was going through your mind in the moments before you blasted off into space?

29 In 2009, I was part of a 14-day mission to finish construction of the International Space Station.

30 Before launch, astronauts have hours aboard the shuttle for checks and reflection. I was looking at the American flag on my shoulder remembering that I was picking fruits in the field as a kid and now I'm about to blast off into space in the most complex piece of equipment we have representing America.

How have role models influenced you?

31 As a senior in high school I first heard about Franklin Chang Díaz, the first Hispanic astronaut. It was then that my childhood dream started to come into focus. Seeing someone who looked and sounded like me succeed pushed me to reach my goal.

32 He [Díaz] spoke with an accent, had brown skin and came from humble beginnings like me. I spoke broken English until I was 12 years old. Now I want to inspire the next generation through my foundation in central California. We invite companies like Google to help spark the interests of 5th graders. There's a science academy for 7th through 12th graders to help expose kids to math and tutor them. We also give scholarships to first-generation seniors. ❧

NOTEBOOK

Work on your own to answer the questions in your notebook. Use text evidence to support your responses.

Response

1. **Personal Connections** What part of Hernández's story do you find most inspiring? Why?

Comprehension

2. **Reading Check** **(a)** What does Hernández dream of becoming as a young boy? **(b)** As a child, how did Hernández initially get his education? **(c)** How did he feel about summer vacation as a child? Why?

3. **Strategy: Summarize** **(a)** How would you summarize this interview in one sentence? **(b)** What key details would you include in a longer summary? **(c)** How does summarizing help you better understand the article?

WORKING AS A GROUP

Discuss your responses to the Analysis and Discussion questions with your group.

- Note agreements and disagreements.
- Summarize insights.
- Consider changes of opinion.

If necessary, revise your original answers to reflect what you learn from your discussion.

Analysis and Discussion

4. **(a)** Why did Hernández's family move to Stockton, California? **(b) Analyze** In what ways was the move significant?

5. **Speculate** Reread Hernández's comments on being bi-cultural, applying to NASA, and learning about Franklin Chang Díaz. If you had been interviewing him, which of these topics would you want to explore in more depth? What questions would you ask?

6. **Interpret** What insight about life is conveyed by this text? Which details support your response?

7. **Get Ready for Close Reading** Choose a passage from the text that you find especially interesting or important. You'll discuss the passage with your group during Close-Read activities.

TEKS

6.A. Describe personal connections to a variety of sources, including self-selected texts.

6.C. Use text evidence to support an appropriate response.

6.D. Paraphrase and summarize texts in ways that maintain meaning and logical order.

6.G. Discuss and write about the explicit or implicit meanings of text.

EQ Notes **How do we overcome obstacles?**

What has this interview taught you about how people overcome obstacles? Go to your Essential Question Notes and record your observations and thoughts about "How This Son of Migrant Farm Workers Became an Astronaut."

HOW THIS SON OF MIGRANT FARM WORKERS BECAME AN ASTRONAUT

Close Read

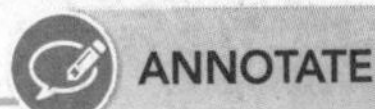

ANNOTATE

PRACTICE Complete the following activities. Use text evidence to support your responses.

1. **Present and Discuss** With your group, share the passages from the interview that you found especially interesting. Discuss what you notice, the questions you have, and the conclusions you reach. For example, you might focus on the following passages:
   - Paragraphs 7–13: Discuss what you learn about Hernández in this passage.
   - Paragraphs 23–24: Discuss the relationship that Hernández has with his father.
   - Paragraphs 25–28: Discuss the idea of perseverance and how that quality shaped Hernández's life choices.
2. **Reflect on Your Learning** What new ideas or insights did you uncover during your second reading of the text?

NOTEBOOK

LANGUAGE STUDY

Concept Vocabulary

Why These Words? Continue to develop your vocabulary by completing these activities. Enlist the help of your teacher as needed.

perseverance	attain	conducive

1. With your group, discuss what the words have in common.
2. Add another word that fits the category. ______________________
3. Use each vocabulary word in a sentence. Include context clues that hint at each word's meaning.

Word Study

Latin Root: *-duc-* In the interview, Hernández says that "moving from place to place wasn't conducive to a good education." The Latin root *-duc-* in *conducive* means "lead." Use a dictionary to analyze the following words: *producer, duchess, conductor,* and *educator*. Determine what these words have in common. Then, explain how the Latin root contributes to their meanings.

WORD NETWORK

Add words that are related to facing adversity from the text to your World Network.

TEKS

2.C. Determine the meaning and usage of grade-level academic English words derived from Greek and Latin roots such as *omni, log/logue, gen, vid/vis, phil, luc,* and / *sens/sent.*

HOW THIS SON OF MIGRANT FARM WORKERS BECAME AN ASTRONAUT

Genre / Text Elements

Influence of Setting In autobiographical writing, biographical writing, and interviews, writers often explore ways in which a setting, or environment, shapes the ideas, beliefs, and actions of a person.

As you reflect on "How This Son of Migrant Farm Workers Became an Astronaut," recall the aspects of environment that shaped Hernández's childhood. In particular, consider these factors:

- geographic locations and seasons
- the economic aspects of his family's life
- the values that his parents taught him

TIP: To determine the influence of setting, or place, notice the connections Hernández makes between his circumstances and his life choices.

INTERACTIVITY

PRACTICE Analyze each passage, and describe ways in which setting affected Hernández's early life. Share your completed chart with your group.

PASSAGE FROM THE TEXT	EFFECT ON HERNÁNDEZ
My childhood was typical of a migrant farm working family, a family that spends nine months out of the year picking fruits and vegetables from Southern California to Northern California. While others looked forward to summer vacation, I hated it. Summer vacation meant working seven days a week in the fields. (paragraph 7)	
But then as a teenager I was embarrassed because we lived in the barrio. We lived in areas that were run down because those were the areas where we could afford to live. My bi-cultural upbringing made me feel out of place—not American enough, but not Mexican enough, either. (paragraphs 11–12)	

TEKS

7.D. Analyze how the setting influences character and plot development.

8.D. Analyze characteristics and structural elements of informational text.

Author's Craft

Organizational Patterns Before they interview a person, interviewers prepare a list of questions to ask the person. The questions are organized by topic, which are then broken into categories and subcategories. This organizational pattern ensures that the interview progresses smoothly and that the questions follow logically.

For example, the interviewer may:

- present questions chronologically, so that we learn about the life of the interview subject;
- present questions according to a broad category, such as favorite musician, or favorite baseball team;
- present follow-up questions that get at subcategories, or smaller, related topics, such as favorite jazz pianist, favorite rap artist, best teacher.

TIP: Note that most transcripts of interviews also contain introductory information about the interview subject. The bulk of the interview is in **Q and A format:** Questions appear in boldface type and are followed by the answers.

NOTEBOOK

PRACTICE **Work on your own to complete the activity. Then, share your responses with your group.**

1. **Analyze** Where in the text does the interviewer provide background information about Hernández? Cite two details the background information reveals.

2. **Analyze** Review the interview questions. What basic organizational pattern does the interviewer use to arrange the questions? Within that larger pattern, what subcategories are explored?

3. **Evaluate** How effective is the organizational pattern in showing connections among different parts of Hernández's life? Provide details to support your response.

4. **Interpret** What controlling idea do the different parts of the interview help to convey?

TEKS

8.D.iii. Analyze characteristics and structural elements of informational text, including organizational patterns that support multiple topics, categories, and subcategories.

THE CIRCUIT

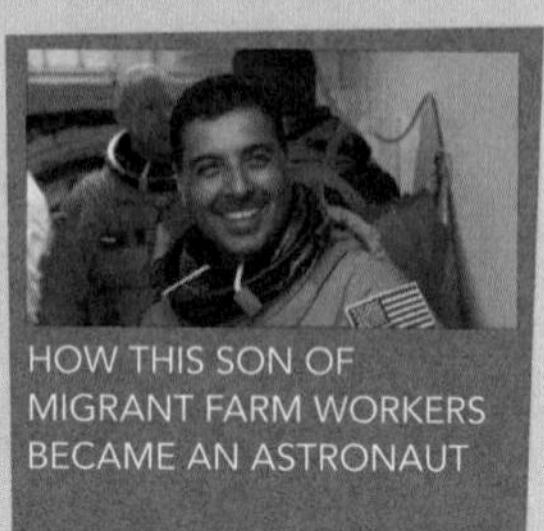
HOW THIS SON OF MIGRANT FARM WORKERS BECAME AN ASTRONAUT

Compare Fiction and Nonfiction

Multiple Choice

NOTEBOOK

These questions are based on the short story, "The Circuit," and the interview, "How This Son of Migrant Farm Workers Became an Astronaut." Choose the best answer to each question.

1. Consider the ending of "The Circuit." Which answer choice best states how Panchito's probable future compares to the life José Hernández achieved?

A Like José Hernández, Panchito will probably stop moving from farm to farm.

B Like José Hernández, Panchito will probably get an education and achieve his dreams.

C Unlike José Hernández, Panchito will probably not get an education and achieve his dreams.

D Like José Hernández, Panchito will become an astronaut.

2. Read the passages from the short story and the interview. Which answer choice best states a similarity between the challenges both Panchito and young Hernández face in these passages?

***from* "The Circuit"**

The garage was worn out by the years. It had no windows. The walls, eaten by termites, strained to support the roof full of holes. The dirt floor, populated by earth worms, looked like a gray road map. (paragraph 15)

***from* "How This Son of Migrant Farm Workers Became an Astronaut"**

But then as a teenager I was embarrassed because we lived in the barrio. We lived in areas that were run down because those were the areas where we could afford to live. (paragraph 11)

F loneliness and lack of friendship

G lack of nice clothing

H poverty and poor housing

J hunger and lack of basic necessities

3. What important insight do both the short story and the interview share?

A Not everyone has to overcome obstacles in order to be happy.

B Anyone can overcome obstacles with determination.

C Hard work is all that is needed to overcome obstacles.

D Love, stability, and education are essential to overcoming obstacles.

TEKS

6.B. Write responses that demonstrate understanding of texts, including comparing sources within and across genres.

Short Response

1. **(a)** In "The Circuit," how do Panchito and his family react when seeing the school bus during grape season? Why? **(b) Analyze** What raises Panchito's hopes when he begins attending school?
2. **(a)** In the interview, how does Hernández describe his parents' attitude about education? **(b) Connect** In your opinion, which of their actions best reflects this attitude? Support your response with text evidence.
3. **(a) Compare and Contrast** How are Panchito's and Hernández's childhoods similar and different? Consider the challenges or conflicts they face. **(b) Make Inferences** What do Panchito's and Hernández's reactions to the challenges they face reveal about the kind of people they are?

Answer the questions in your notebook. Use text evidence to support your responses.

Timed Writing

A **comparison-and-contrast essay** is a piece of writing in which you analyze the similarities and differences among two or more topics.

ASSIGNMENT

Both "The Circuit" and "How This Son of Migrant Farm Workers Became an Astronaut" explore the obstacles that children of migrant workers often face. Write a **comparison-and-contrast essay** in which you discuss similarities and differences in the insights the two texts express.

5-MINUTE PLANNER

1. Read the assignment carefully and completely.
2. Decide the most important thing you want to say—your controlling idea.
3. Decide which examples you'll use from the two texts.
4. Organize your ideas, making sure to address these points:
   - Explain how the experiences of the character in the short story and those of the subject of the interview are similar. What challenges do they both face?
   - Explain important differences between the two selections. What is the outcome of each? How do the text types differ?
   - Explain the insights expressed in both selections and how they are similar and different.

A WORK IN PROGRESS

The selection you are about to read is an oral history.

Reading Oral Histories

An **oral history** is a living person's testimony about his or her own experiences.

ORAL HISTORIES

Author's Purpose

- to capture personal experiences that are significant in some way

Characteristics

- first-person account (the speaker tells his or her own story)
- distinctive personality, or voice, of the speaker
- often transcribed, or written down, from a spoken account
- conversational, "think out loud" quality
- may not follow grammatical rules
- often, expresses deeper insights

Structure

- usually follows a time-order sequence to tell a true story
- may include an interviewer and follow a question-and-answer format

Take a Minute!

NOTEBOOK

DISCUSS IT With a partner, discuss this question: Would you rather read someone's story or hear the person tell it out loud? Explain your thinking.

TEKS

8.D. Analyze characteristics and structural elements of informational text.

9.F. Analyze how the author's use of language contributes to mood, voice, and tone.

Genre / Text Elements

Language and Voice One way in which a speaker shares an oral history effectively is by showing the audience his or her personality. An **author's voice** is the distinct personality of the speaker, or writer. Voice emerges from the the unique ways in which a writer or speaker uses language, including the following elements:

- **Diction:** writer's or speaker's choice of words and phrases
- **Syntax:** ways in which the writer or speaker organizes phrases, clauses, and sentences; for example, sentences can be short and punchy, long and flowing, or a mix of the two.
- **Tone:** writer's or speaker's attitude toward his or her subject and audience; tone can be described with words we often use to name emotions, such as *cold, warm, playful, joyous*, or *harsh*.

The language a writer chooses to discuss a subject reveals his or her personality, or voice. For example, if a writer makes a joke about an embarrassing personal experience, it suggests that he or she is playful and has a good sense of humor.

TIP: When someone refers to an author's or speaker's unique "sound," they are talking about voice.

INTERACTIVITY

PRACTICE Work on your own to read the two passages. Then, mark the set of words that best describes the voice in each one. Discuss your choices with your group.

SAMPLE PASSAGE	DESCRIPTION OF VOICE
I recently went to the TV studio to film an interview about the holiday food drive. To my surprise, there was great confusion when I arrived. Apparently, the staff expected not me, but a famous singer who shares my name! Since I cannot sing a note, we had to make the best of a deeply embarrassing situation.	◯ Serious and Formal ◯ Casual and Amused ◯ Cautious and Restrained
So, I go to the TV studio to talk about the holiday food drive, but—of course—there's a mix-up. Apparently, they think I'm "The Famous Singer"… disappointment and embarrassment all around, since my "vocals" are about as sweet as car horns in a traffic jam.	◯ Serious and Formal ◯ Casual and Amused ◯ Cautious and Restrained

About the Author

Aimee Mullins (b. 1976) is an athlete, model, and actor. At the age of one, she needed to have both of her legs amputated below the knee. Mullins learned how to walk and run with prosthetics, enabling her to participate in the 1996 Paralympic Games, where she set three world records in running and jumping events.

A Work in Progress

Concept Vocabulary

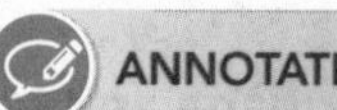
ANNOTATE

As you read "A Work in Progress," you will encounter these words.

accomplishments	extraordinary	celebrate

Context Clues The **context** of a word is the other words and phrases that appear near it in a text. Clues in the context can help you figure out the meanings of unfamiliar words.

Synonyms: His **aberrant** behavior was unexpected. It is strange for him to be impolite.

Restatement of an idea: Because of a rare bone disease, her bones are **delicate** and more likely to break.

Contrast of ideas and topics: James will not eat foods made with **artificial** ingredients; he shops only at organic food stores.

PRACTICE As you read "A Work in Progress," study the context to determine the meanings of unfamiliar words. Mark your observations in the open space next to the text.

Comprehension Strategy

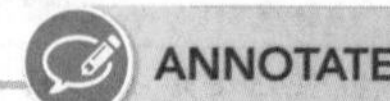
ANNOTATE

Generate Questions

To deepen your understanding and gain more information from a text, **generate questions** about it before, during, and after reading.

- **Before you read,** preview the text, including the title, text type, and any additional features, such as the background section or author bio. Write questions the text might answer.
- **As you read,** notice details that raise questions for you. Jot these questions down and read on.
- **After you read,** reflect on the questions you asked before and during reading. Then, consider whether these questions have been answered. Write any additional questions that you have.

PRACTICE Generate questions before, during, and after you read the text. Jot them down in the open space next to the text.

TEKS

2.B. Use context such as contrast or cause and effect to clarify the meaning of words.

5.B. Generate questions about text before, during, and after reading to deepen understanding and gain information.

A Work in Progress

Aimee Mullins

BACKGROUND

A prosthetic is an artificial substitute for a missing body part. Over the past few decades, prosthetic technology has advanced greatly. Modern prosthetics can often fully replace the function of a missing limb due to the invention of lighter materials and more sophisticated designs.

AUDIO

ANNOTATE

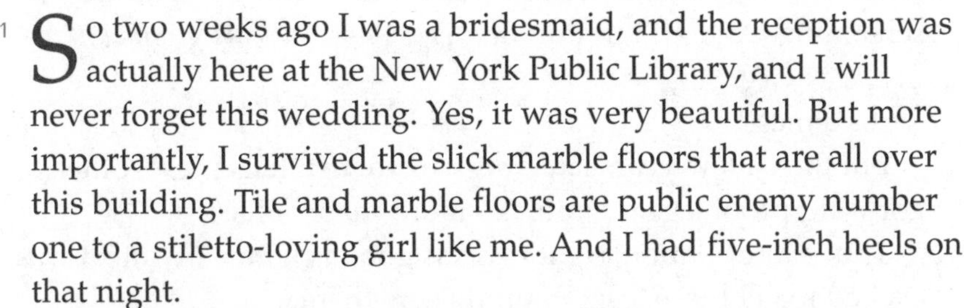

1 So two weeks ago I was a bridesmaid, and the reception was actually here at the New York Public Library, and I will never forget this wedding. Yes, it was very beautiful. But more importantly, I survived the slick marble floors that are all over this building. Tile and marble floors are public enemy number one to a stiletto-loving girl like me. And I had five-inch heels on that night.

2 Most people learn to walk in very high heels. They bend their ankle so that the ball of the foot touches the ground first; you have more stability.

3 I don't have ankles, so I hit each step on the stiletto, which makes the possibility of the banana peel wipeout very likely. But given the choice between practicality and theatricality, I say, "Go big or go home, man. Go down in flames if you're gonna go."

4 I guess I'm a bit of a daredevil. I think that the nurses at DuPont Institute would agree. I spent a lot of time there as a child. Doctors amputated[1] both of my legs below the knee when I was an infant, and then when I was five, I had a major surgery to correct the wonky direction in which my tibia was growing. So I had two metal pins to hold that—full plaster casts on both legs. I had to use a wheelchair because I couldn't wear prosthetics.

5 One of the best things about getting out of the hospital is the anticipation of the day you return to school—I had missed so much class, I just couldn't wait to get back and see all my friends. But my teacher had a different idea about that. She tried to prevent me from returning to class, because she said that in the condition I was in, I was "inappropriate," and that I would be a distraction to the other students (which of course I was, but not because of the casts and the wheelchair).

6 Clearly she needed to make my difference invisible because she wanted to control her environment and make it fit into her idea of what "normal" looked like.

7 And it would've been a lot easier for me to fit into what "normal" looked like. I know I wanted that back then. But instead I had these wooden legs with a rubber foot that the toes broke off of, and they were held on with a big bolt that rusted out because I swam in the wooden legs.

8 You're not supposed to swim in the wooden legs, because, you know, the wood rots out.

9 So there I was in second grade music class, doing the twist, and mid-twist I hear this [*makes loud cracking sound*]. And I'm on the floor, and the lower half of my left leg is in splinters across the room. The teacher faints on the piano, and the kids are screaming. And all I'm thinking is, *My parents are gonna kill me. I broke my leg!*

10 It's a mess.

11 But then a few years later, my prosthetist[2] tells me, "Aimee, we got waterproof legs for you. No more rusty bolts!"

12 This is a revelation, right? This is gonna change my life. I was so excited to get these legs . . . until I saw them.

1. **amputated** (AM pyoo tayt ihd) *v.* removed surgically.
2. **prosthetist** (PROS thuh tihst) *n.* professional who fits and designs prosthetic limbs.

13 They were made of polypropylene, which is that white plastic "milk jug" material. And when I say "white," I'm not talking about skin color; I'm talking about *the color white*. The "skin color" was the rubber foam foot painted "Caucasian," which is the nastiest shade of nuclear peach that you've ever seen in your life. It has nothing to do with any human skin tone on the planet. And these legs were so good at being waterproof that they were *buoyant*. So when I'd go off the high dive, I'd go down and come straight back up feet first. They were the bane of my existence.

14 But then we're at the Jersey Shore one summer. By the time we get there, there's three hundred yards of towels between me and the sea. And I know this is where I first honed my ability to run really fast. I was the white flash. I didn't wanna feel hundreds of pairs of eyes staring at me. And so I'd get myself into the ocean, and I was a good swimmer, but no amount of swimming technique can control buoyant legs.

15 So at some point I get caught in a rip current, and I'm migrating from my vantage point of where I could see my parents' towel. And I'm taking in water, and I'm fighting, fighting, fighting. And all I could think to do was pop off these legs and put one under each armpit, with the peach feet sticking up, and just bob, thinking, *Someone's gotta find me*.

16 And a lifeguard did. And I'm sure he will collect for therapy bills. You know? Like, they don't show that on *Baywatch*.[3]

17 But they saved my life, those legs.

18 And then when I was fourteen it was Easter Sunday, and I was gonna be wearing a dress that I had purchased with my own money—the first thing I ever bought that wasn't on sale.

19 Momentous event; you never forget it. I'd had a paper route since I was twelve, and I went to The Limited, and I bought this dress that I thought was the height of sophistication—sleeveless safari dress, belted, hits at the knee.

20 Coming downstairs into the living room, I see my father waiting to take us to church. He takes one look at me, and he says, "That doesn't look right. Go upstairs and change."

21 I was like, "What? My super-classy dress? What are you talking about? It's the best thing I own."

22 He said, "No, you can see the knee joint when you walk. It doesn't look right. It's inappropriate to go out like that. Go change."

23 And I think something snapped in me. I refused to change. And it was the first time I defied my father. I refused to hide something

3. ***Baywatch*** popular television show from the late 1990s about the lives of fictional lifeguards.

about myself that was true, and I refused to be embarrassed about something so that other people could feel more comfortable.

24 I was grounded for that defiance.

25 So after church the extended family convenes at my grandmother's house, and everybody's complimenting me on how nice I look in this dress, and I'm like, "Really? You think I look nice? Because my parents think I look inappropriate."

26 I outed them (kinda mean, really).

27 But I think the public utterance of this idea that I should somehow hide myself was so shocking to hear that it changed their mind about why they were doing it.

28 And I had always managed to get through life with somewhat of a positive attitude, but I think this was the start of me being able to accept myself. You know, okay, I'm not normal. I have strengths. I've got weaknesses. It is what it is.

29 And I had always been athletic, but it wasn't until college that I started this adventure in Track and Field. I had gone through a lifetime of being given legs that just barely got me by. And I thought, *Well, maybe I'm just having the wrong conversations with the wrong people. Maybe I need to go find people who say, "Yes, we can create* anything *for you in the space between where your leg ends and the ground."*

30 And so I started working with engineers, fashion designers, sculptors, Hollywood prosthetic makeup artists, wax museum designers to build legs for me.

31 I decided I wanted to be the fastest woman in the world on artificial legs, and I was lucky enough to arrive in track at just the right time to be the first person to get these radical sprinting legs modeled after the hind leg of a cheetah, the fastest thing that runs—woven carbon fiber.[4] I was able to set three world records with those legs. And they made no attempt at approximating humanness.

32 Then I get these incredibly lifelike silicon legs—hand-painted, capillaries, veins. And, hey, I can be as tall as I wanna be, so I get different legs for different heights. I don't have to shave. I can wear open-toed shoes in the winter. And most importantly, I can opt out of the cankles[5] I most certainly would've inherited genetically.

33 And then I get these legs made for me by the late, great Alexander McQueen, and they were hand-carved of solid ash with grapevines and magnolias all over them and a six-inch heel. And I was able to walk the runways of the world with supermodels. I was suddenly in this whirlwind of adventure and

4. **carbon fiber** (KAHR buhn FY buhr) *n.* very strong, lightweight material.
5. **cankles** (KANG kuhlz) *n.* informal term for thick ankles.

excitement. I was being invited to go around the world and speak about these adventures, and how I had legs that looked like glass, legs covered in feathers, porcelain legs, jellyfish legs—all wearable sculpture.

34 And I get this call from a guy who had seen me speak years ago, when I was at the beginning of my track career, and he says, "We loved it. We want you to come back." And it was clear to me he didn't know all these amazing things that had happened to me since my sports career.

35 So as I'm telling him, he says, "Whoa, whoa, whoa. Hold on, Aimee. The reason everybody liked you all those years ago was because you were this sweet, vulnerable, naïve girl, and if you walk onstage today, and you are this polished young woman with too many **accomplishments**, I'm afraid they won't like you."

36 For real, he said that. Wow.

37 He apparently didn't think I was vulnerable enough now. He was asking me to be *less than*, a little more downtrodden. He was asking me to disable myself for him and his audience.

38 And what was so shocking to me about that was that I realized I had moved past mere acceptance of my difference. I was having *fun* with my difference. Thank *God* I'm not normal. I get to be ***extraordinary***. And I'll decide what is a weakness and what is a strength.

Mark context clues or indicate another strategy you used that helped you determine meaning.

accomplishments (uh KOM plihsh muhnts) *n.*

MEANING:

extraordinary (ehk STRAWR duh nehr ee) *adj.*

MEANING:

39 And so I refused his request.

40 And a few days later, I'm walking in downtown Manhattan at a street fair, and I get this tug on my shirt, and I look down. It's this little girl I met a year earlier when she was at a pivotal moment in her life. She had been born with a brittle bone disease that resulted in her left leg being seven centimeters shorter than her right. She wore a brace and orthopedic[6] shoes and they got her by, but she wanted to do more.

41 And like all Internet-savvy kindergarteners, she gets on the computer and Googles "new leg," and she comes up with dozens of images of prosthetics, many of them mine. And she prints them out, goes to school, does show-and-tell on it, comes home, and makes a startling pronouncement to her parents:

42 "I wanna get rid of my bad leg," she says. "When can I get a new leg?"

43 And ultimately that was the decision her parents and doctors made for her. So here she was, six months after the amputation, and right there in the middle of the street fair she hikes up her jeans leg to show me her cool new leg. And it's pink, and it's

6. **orthopedic** (awr thuh PEE dihk) *adj.* designed to treat a muscular or skeletal problem.

tattooed with the characters of *High School Musical 3*, replete with red, sequined Mary Janes on her feet.

44 And she was proud of it. She was proud of herself. And the marvelous thing was that this six-year-old understood something that it took me twenty-something years to get, but that we both did discover—that when we can **celebrate** and truly own what it is that makes us different, we're able to find the source of our greatest creative power. ❧

Mark context clues or indicate another strategy you used that helped you determine meaning.

celebrate (SEHL uh brayt) *v.*

MEANING:

NOTEBOOK

Work on your own to answer the questions in your notebook. Use text evidence to support your responses.

Response

1. **Personal Connections** Did you find this oral history surprising? Explain, citing details from the text.

Comprehension

2. **Reading Check (a)** Why does Aimee Mullins have difficulty walking across the marble floor of the library? **(b)** What happened between Mullins and her father that caused her to be grounded? **(c)** What does Mullins do to improve the quality of her prosthetic legs?

3. **Strategy: Generate Questions (a)** Cite at least one question you asked before and during your reading of this text. **(b)** What new question can you ask now, after reading the text? **(c)** Explain how asking questions deepened your understanding of the selection.

Analysis and Discussion

4. **Make Inferences** Reread paragraphs 7–10. What does the incident in Mullins's music class suggest about her attitude toward her difference, even as a young child?

5. **Interpret** Reread paragraph 28. What does Mullins suggest is the difference between her "positive attitude" and "being able to accept myself"? Explain, citing text evidence to support your ideas.

6. Reread paragraph 29. **(a) Summarize** What realization does Mullins have in this paragraph? **(b) Analyze Cause and Effect** How does this realization influence Mullins's life and attitude? Explain, citing specific details from the text.

7. **Get Ready for Close Reading** Choose a passage from the text that you find especially interesting or important. You'll discuss the passage with your group during Close-Read activities.

WORKING AS A GROUP

Discuss your responses to the Analysis and Discussion questions with your group.

- Note agreements and disagreements.
- Summarize insights.
- Consider changes of opinion.

If necessary, revise your original answers to reflect what you learn from your discussion.

EQ Notes How do we overcome obstacles?

What have you learned about facing adversity from reading this oral history? Go to your Essential Question Notes and record your observations and thoughts about "A Work in Progress."

TEKS

5.B. Generate questions about text before, during, and after reading to deepen understanding and gain information.

6.A. Describe personal connections to a variety of sources, including self-selected texts.

6.C. Use text evidence to support an appropriate response.

6.G. Discuss and write about the explicit or implicit meanings of text.

6.I. Reflect on and adjust responses as new evidence is presented.

A WORK IN PROGRESS

Close Read

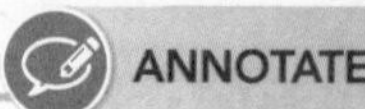
ANNOTATE

PRACTICE Complete the following activities. Use text evidence to support your responses. If necessary, ask for help from your teacher or your peers.

1. **Present and Discuss** With your group, share the passages from the text that you found especially interesting. Discuss what you notice, the questions you have, and the conclusions you reach. For example, you might focus on the following passages:
   - Paragraphs 5–6: Discuss the teacher's response to the narrator.
   - Paragraphs 15–17: Discuss the narrator's response to the rip current.
   - Paragraphs 40–44: Discuss why Mullins included the account of meeting the six-year-old girl.
2. **Reflect on Your Learning** What new ideas or insights did you uncover during your second reading of the text?

WORD NETWORK

Add words that are related to facing adversity from the text to your Word Network.

NOTEBOOK

LANGUAGE STUDY

Concept Vocabulary

Why These Words? The vocabulary words are related.

accomplishments	extraordinary	celebrate

1. With your group, determine what the words have in common. Write down your ideas.
2. Add another word that fits the category. ____________________
3. Use each vocabulary word in a sentence. Include context clues that hint at each word's meaning.

Word Study

Latin Prefix: *extra-* The Latin prefix *extra-* means "beyond the scope of" or "in addition to what is usual or expected." At the end of the selection, the author realizes that what makes her different also makes her *extraordinary*, or beyond what is ordinary or expected. With your group, identify and define two other words you know that include this prefix.

6.F. Respond using newly acquired vocabulary as appropriate.

9.F. Analyze how the author's use of language contributes to mood, voice, and tone.

Genre / Text Elements

Language and Voice Every writer has a characteristic personality, a distinctive sound or way of "speaking" on the page. That quality is **voice.** An author's voice is the result of his or her subject matter, the occasion and purpose of the writing, and his or her use of language.

LANGUAGE DEVICE	EXAMPLES FROM THE TEXT	ANALYSIS
Diction	• *So two weeks ago* • *banana-peel wipeout* • *choice between practicality and theatricality*	• starts sentences with conjunctions • mixes casual words, slang, and sophisticated words
Syntax	• *So two weeks ago… and I will never forget this wedding. Yes, it was very beautiful.* • *I broke my leg!* • *This is a revelation, right?*	• combines longer, rambling sentences with short sentences • exclamations • questions
Tone	• *banana-peel wipeout* • *I don't have ankles.*	• humor • direct statements

NOTEBOOK

PRACTICE Work on your own to answer the questions. Then, share your responses with your group.

1. **(a) Distinguish** Explain how the syntax in paragraph 15 shows that this selection was originally delivered as an informal speech. **(b) Connect** Identify another passage that has similar conversational syntax and voice. Explain your choice. **(c) Revise** Choose one of the passages and rewrite it to make it seem more like a written text. Explain your changes.

2. **Speculate** How do you think the listening audience probably reacted to paragraph 16? Why? Describe qualities in the text that develop the speaker's voice and support your thinking.

3. **Interpret** Choose three adjectives from this list that you think best describe Aimee Mullins's voice. Explain your choices.

direct	charming	conceited	humble
boastful	secretive	funny	insincere

A WORK IN PROGRESS

Conventions

Informal Grammar "A Work in Progress" is transcribed, or copied, from a speech. While speaking, Mullins chose **informal grammar,** or casual language, including the following elements:

- **Colloquial Contractions:** words such as *gonna (going to),* wanna *(want to)* and kinda *(kind of)*
- **Informal Transitions:** casual words and phrases such as *man, I'm like,* and *you know*
- **Introductory Conjunctions:** sentences that begin with *but* or *so*
- **Sentence Fragments:** deliberate use of incomplete thoughts or statements

INTERACTIVITY NOTEBOOK

READ IT Work on your own to rewrite each example of informal grammar to follow standard English grammar rules. Then, discuss with your group how these changes impact the text.

INFORMAL GRAMMAR FROM TEXT	STANDARD GRAMMAR
And all I'm thinking is, My parents are gonna kill me. (paragraph 9)	
This is a revelation, right? This is gonna change my life. (paragraph 12)	
For real, he said that. Wow. (paragraph 36)	

WRITE IT Write a paragraph that uses informal language to tell about a funny incident that happened to you or someone you know. Write as if you are speaking directly to an audience. Use colloquial contractions, sentence fragments, and other informal elements. Then, exchange paragraphs with a member of your group. Rewrite each other's paragraph in standard English. Discuss how the changes affect the voice of your paragraphs.

TEKS

1.A. Listen actively to interpret a message and ask clarifying questions that build on others' ideas.

1.D. Engage in meaningful discourse and provide and accept constructive feedback from others.

10.D.i. Edit drafts using standard English conventions, including complete complex sentences with subject-verb agreement and avoidance of splices, run-ons, and fragments.

Speaking and Listening

A **discussion** is a conversation among two or more people about a specific topic.

ASSIGNMENT

With your group, conduct a **discussion** in which you analyze one of the following quotations from the selection. Read the full quotation in the text before deciding which quotation to focus on.

- ◯ "And I had always been *athletic, ... your leg ends and the ground.'"* (paragraph 29)
- ◯ "And the marvelous thing was ... the source of our greatest creative power." (paragraph 44)

Use Questions to Guide Your Discussion As you share ideas, use the chart to take notes and add questions of your own.

DISCUSSION QUESTIONS	RESPONSES
What does the quotation mean?	
What happens that causes the author to express these ideas?	
Do you think it would help society if more people felt as this author feels? Why or why not?	

EQ Notes Before moving on to a new selection, go to your Essential Question Notes and record any additional thoughts or observations you may have about "A Work in Progress."

Listen Actively You can deepen your understanding of a discussion topic by clarifying the ideas of other speakers. Here are sentence starters that you might use to politely ask questions that build on other group members' ideas:

- I wasn't sure what you meant when you said __________________. Could you provide an example?
- I thought your idea about __________________ was interesting. Could you elaborate on it?

from THE STORY OF MY LIFE

The selection you are about to read is an autobiography.

Reading Autobiographies

An **autobiography** is the story of a person's life written by that person.

AUTOBIOGRAPHY

Author's Purpose

- to tell the author's life story in a meaningful and insightful way

Characteristics

- written in the first-person point of view
- features characters who are real people and settings that are real places
- expresses a deeper insight about the meaning of the author's life, or about life in general
- often includes storytelling techniques such as dialogue and description

Structure

- may describe the full sweep of the author's life or focus on a specific time period or incident
- usually presents events in chronological, or time, order
- may have sections or chapters

Take a Minute!

NOTEBOOK

FIND IT With a partner, use resources to research the word origins of *autobiography*. Explain how the three key word parts relate to the type of writing the word names.

TEKS

2.C. Determine the meaning and usage of grade-level academic English words derived from Greek and Latin roots such as *omni, log/logue, gen, vid/vis, phil, luc,* and *sens/sent*.

8.D. Analyze characteristics and structural elements of informational text.

9.A. Explain the author's purpose and message within a text.

Genre / Text Elements

Author's Purpose and Message There are four broad **purposes** for writing—to describe, to inform, to narrate (tell a story), and to persuade. The main purpose of autobiography is to narrate. However, by telling his or her own life story, the author of an autobiography also shares a message that may inform readers or persuade them to see a topic in a new way. Consider these examples:

- Author is a leader whose life shows how we can change society for the better.
- Author had a unique experience that changes how we think about ourselves.
- Author is a famous performer whose life shows the power of persistence.
- Author is not well-known, but his or her life story teaches lessons about how to respond to adversity.

In some autobiographies, the writer simply states his or her purpose and message. More often, you need to notice details, think about them, and draw conclusions about the message.

 NOTEBOOK  INTERACTIVITY

PRACTICE Read the passage, adapted from the autobiography *Incidents in the Life of a Slave Girl* by Harriet Jacobs. Then, answer the questions that follow.

> I was born a slave, but I did not know it till I was six years old. Those were happy years. My father loved me, and protected me from the truth. He was an intelligent and skilled carpenter, and many people hired him to manage their most difficult projects. Through an arrangement with his owner, he earned his own money. But his greatest wish was to purchase my freedom. He offered to buy me many times, but my owner never accepted.

1. What do you think is the author's purpose for writing this autobiography?

2. Which details from the passage support your answer? Explain.

About the Author

A serious illness left **Helen Keller** (1880–1968) blind and deaf before she was two years old. When Keller was nearly seven, her family hired Anne Sullivan, a teacher from the Perkins School for the Blind, to help her learn to communicate. Keller and Sullivan developed a remarkable teacher-student relationship as well as a unique friendship.

from The Story of My Life

Concept Vocabulary

As you read the autobiography, you will encounter these words.

imitate	mystery	barriers

Context Clues If these words are unfamiliar to you, try using context clues to help you determine their meanings.

EXAMPLE Restatement is one type of context clue.

Restatement: This was an **impediment** on her path, but she would not let it block her progress.

Analysis: Something that blocks progress gets in a person's way. *Impediment* must mean "obstacle."

PRACTICE As you read the excerpt from *The Story of My Life,* study the context to determine the meanings of unfamiliar words. Mark your observations in the open space next to the text.

Comprehension Strategy

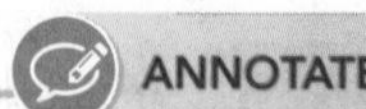

Monitor Comprehension

It can feel overwhelming to make sense of a text and all its details after you finish reading. Instead of waiting till the end, check your comprehension as you go, and **ask questions** to clarify your understanding. If you don't know an answer, **reread** to figure it out.

EXAMPLES Here are the types of questions you might ask as you read:

- *Am I clear about the problems the author faces?*
- *Do I understand why the author or other people feel the way they do?*
- *Are the reasons for events clear to me? Do I see why the author's story matters?*

PRACTICE As you read, monitor your comprehension. If you find that something is unclear, pause to ask a question and reread to find the answer. Mark your questions and answers in the open space next to the text.

TEKS

2.B. Use context such as contrast or cause and effect to clarify the meaning of words.

5.I. Monitor comprehension and make adjustments such as re-reading, using background knowledge, asking questions, and annotating when understanding breaks down.

AUTOBIOGRAPHY

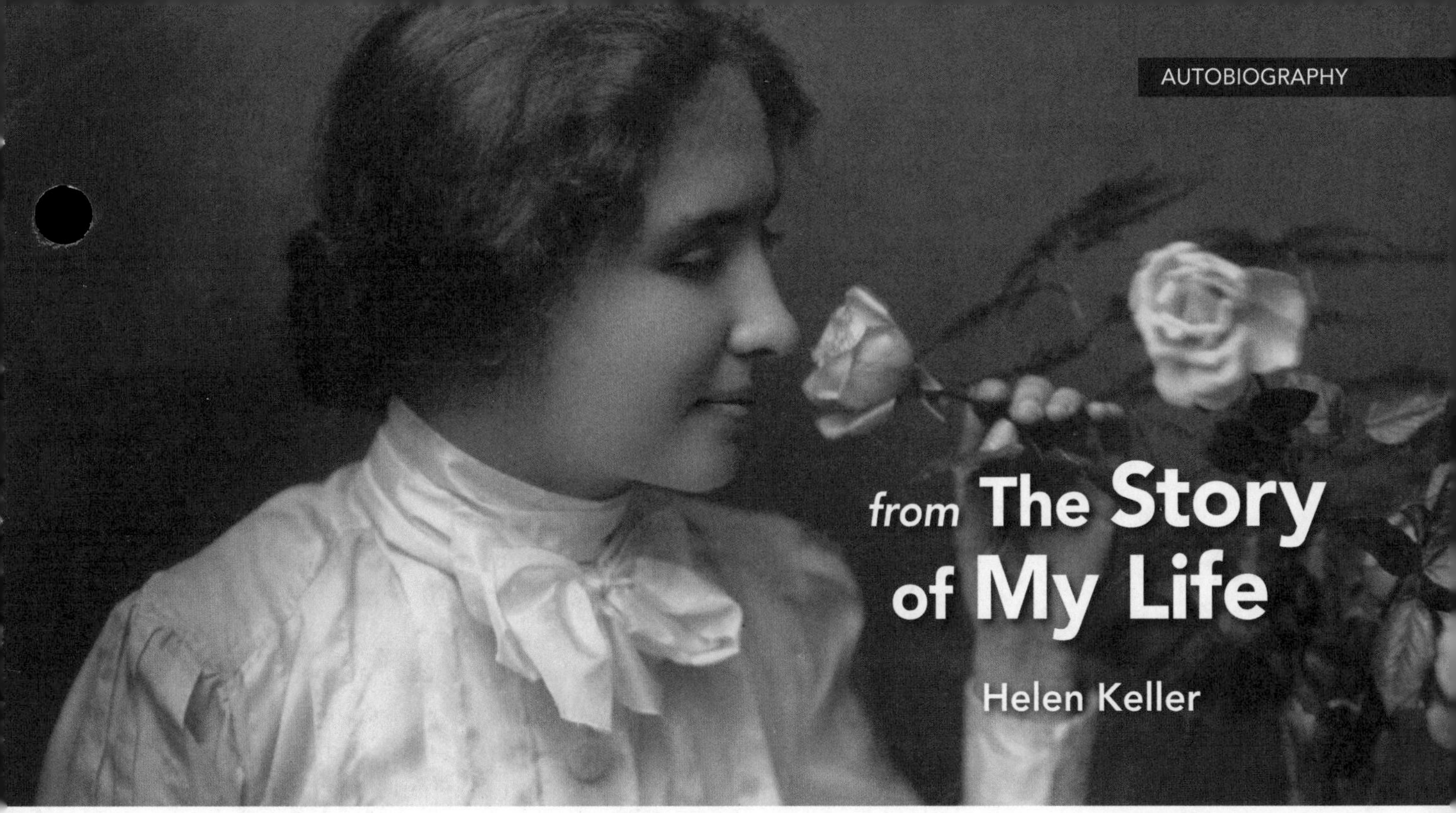

from The Story of My Life

Helen Keller

BACKGROUND

In this excerpt from her autobiography, Helen Keller describes her first experience with language at the age of six. *The Story of My Life* was published in 1903, when Keller was 23 years old.

AUDIO

ANNOTATE

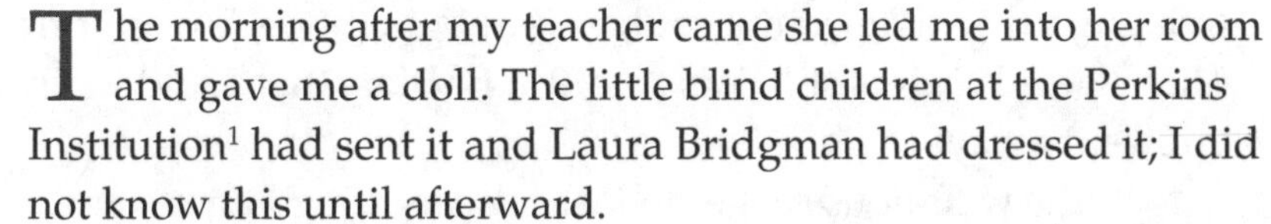

1 The morning after my teacher came she led me into her room and gave me a doll. The little blind children at the Perkins Institution[1] had sent it and Laura Bridgman had dressed it; I did not know this until afterward.

2 When I had played with it a little while, Miss Sullivan slowly spelled into my hand the word "d-o-l-l." I was at once interested in this finger play and tried to **imitate** it. When I finally succeeded in making the letters correctly I was flushed with childish pleasure and pride. Running downstairs to my mother I held up my hand and made the letters for *doll*. I did not know that I was spelling a word or even that words existed; I was simply making my fingers go in monkey-like imitation. In the days that followed I learned to spell in this uncomprehending way a great many words, among them *pin, hat, cup,* and a few verbs like *sit, stand,* and *walk*. But my teacher had been with me several weeks before I understood that everything has a name.

3 One day, while I was playing with my new doll, Miss Sullivan put my big rag doll into my lap also, spelled "d-o-l-l" and tried to make me understand that "d-o-l-l" applied to both. Earlier in the day we had had a tussle over the words "m-u-g" and "w-a-t-e-r." Miss Sullivan had tried to impress it upon me that "m-u-g" is *mug* and that "w-a-t-e-r" is *water*, but I persisted in confounding

Mark context clues or indicate another strategy you used that helped you determine meaning.

imitate (IHM uh tayt) *v.*

MEANING:

1. **Perkins Institution** The Perkins School for the Blind, founded in 1829 in Boston.

the two. In despair she had dropped the subject for the time, only to renew it at the first opportunity. I became impatient at her repeated attempts and, seizing the new doll, I dashed it upon the floor. I was keenly delighted when I felt the fragments of the broken doll at my feet. Neither sorrow nor regret followed my passionate outburst. I had not loved the doll. In the still, dark world in which I lived there was no strong sentiment or tenderness. I felt my teacher sweep the fragments to one side of the hearth, and I had a sense of satisfaction that the cause of my discomfort was removed. She brought me my hat, and I knew I was going out into the warm sunshine. This thought, if a wordless sensation may be called a thought, made me hop and skip with pleasure.

4 We walked down the path to the well-house,[2] attracted by the fragrance of the honeysuckle with which it was covered. Someone was drawing water and my teacher placed my hand under the spout. As the cool stream gushed over one hand she spelled into the other the word water, first slowly, then rapidly. I stood still, my whole attention fixed upon the motions of her fingers. Suddenly I felt a misty consciousness as of something forgotten—a thrill of returning thought; and somehow the **mystery** of language was revealed to me. I knew then that "w-a-t-e-r" meant the wonderful cool something that was flowing over my hand. That living word awakened my soul, gave it light, hope, joy, set it free! There were **barriers** still, it is true, but barriers that could in time be swept away.

Mark context clues or indicate another strategy you used that helped you determine meaning.

mystery (MIHS tuh ree) *n.*

MEANING:

barriers (BAR ee uhrz) *n.*

MEANING:

5 I left the well-house eager to learn. Everything had a name, and each name gave birth to a new thought. As we returned to the house every object which I touched seemed to quiver with life. That was because I saw everything with the strange, new sight that had come to me. On entering the door I remembered the doll I had broken. I felt my way to the hearth and picked up the pieces. I tried vainly to put them together. Then my eyes filled with tears; I realized what I had done, and for the first time I felt repentance and sorrow.

6 I learned a great many new words that day. I do not remember what they all were; I do know that *mother, father, sister, teacher* were among them—words that were to make the world blossom for me, "like Aaron's rod, with flowers."[3] It would have been difficult to find a happier child than I was as I lay in my crib at the close of that eventful day and lived over the joys it had brought me, and for the first time longed for a new day to come. ❧

MEDIA CONNECTION

How Helen Keller Learned to Talk

DISCUSS IT What does Anne Sullivan demonstrate about how Helen Keller learned to talk?

Write your response before sharing your idea.

2. **well-house** small building containing a well.
3. **"like Aaron's rod, with flowers"** in the Old Testament of the Bible, the staff of Aaron miraculously gives forth buds and flowers.

NOTEBOOK

Work on your own to answer the questions in your notebook. Use text evidence to support your responses.

Response

1. **Personal Connections** Describe a time when you, like Helen Keller, experienced a sudden moment of understanding or learned a new and exciting skill.

Comprehension

2. **Reading Check (a)** What attracts Keller and her teacher toward the well-house? **(b)** Through which sense does Keller experience the water? **(c)** Once Keller learns the word for *water,* what is she eager to do next?

3. **Strategy: Monitor Comprehension (a)** What is one question you asked to clarify your understanding as you read this text? **(b)** Were you able to find an answer by rereading? Explain. **(c)** In what ways did asking questions and rereading affect your comprehension? Explain.

Analysis and Discussion

4. **(a)** How does Keller feel when she breaks the new doll? **(b) Analyze** How do her feelings change after she understands what words are? **(c) Draw Conclusions** In what ways does language fundamentally change who Keller is? Explain.

5. **Analyze** What is the world like for Keller before she understands language? Cite specific details that show what she feels and how she understands what is happening around her.

6. **Evaluate** In your own words, what happens when Keller and Miss Sullivan are at the water spout? Why is it important?

7. **Get Ready for Close Reading** Choose a passage from the text that you find especially interesting or important. You'll discuss the passage with your group during Close-Read activities.

WORKING AS A GROUP

Discuss your responses to the Analysis and Discussion questions with your group.

- Note agreements and disagreements.
- Summarize insights.
- Consider changes of opinion.

If necessary, revise your original answers to reflect what you learn from your discussion.

EQ Notes How do we overcome obstacles?

What have you learned about overcoming adversity from reading this autobiography? Go to your Essential Question Notes and record your observations and thoughts about the excerpt from *The Story of My Life*.

TEKS

5.I. Monitor comprehension and make adjustments such as re-reading, using background knowledge, asking questions, and annotating when understanding breaks down.

6.A. Describe personal connections to a variety of sources, including self-selected texts.

6.C. Use text evidence to support an appropriate response.

from THE STORY OF MY LIFE

Close Read

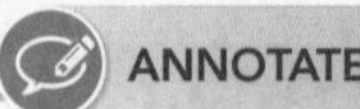
ANNOTATE

PRACTICE **Complete the following activities. Use text evidence to support your responses.**

1. **Present and Discuss** With your group, share passages from the text that you found especially important. Discuss what you notice, the questions you have, and the conclusions you reach. For example, you might focus on the following passages:
   - Paragraph 3: Discuss how Miss Sullivan tries to show Helen connections among different objects or ideas.
   - Paragraph 5: Discuss how her "strange new sight" affects Keller.

As you discuss the text, use language that is routinely employed in academic conversations. For example, use words like *message* and *concept*.

2. **Reflect on Your Learning** What new ideas or insights did you uncover during your second reading of the text?

NOTEBOOK

WORD NETWORK

Add words that are related to facing adversity from the text to your Word Network.

LANGUAGE STUDY

Concept Vocabulary

Why These Words? The vocabulary words are related.

imitate	mystery	barriers

1. With your group, determine what the words have in common. Write your ideas.

2. Add another word that fits the category. ____________________

3. Use each vocabulary word in a sentence. Include context clues that hint at each word's meaning.

Word Study

Greek Root: *-myst-* The Greek root *-myst-* means "secret." In the selection, Helen Keller describes how the mystery, or "secret," of language was revealed to her through her experience with water at the well-house. Identify another word you know with the Greek root *-myst-*, and use it in a sentence that shows your understanding of the word's meaning.

TEKS

2.C. Determine the meaning and usage of grade-level academic English words derived from Greek and Latin roots such as *omni, log/logue, gen, vid/vis, phil, luc,* and *sens/sent*.

9.A. Explain the author's purpose and message within a text.

Genre / Text Elements

Author's Purpose and Message An **author's purpose** is his or her main reason for writing. An **author's message** is the central idea or point that he or she wants to communicate. Even though an autobiography is true, the author makes choices about how to tell his or her story and which details to include. Those choices shape the message.

To understand the message of an autobiography, identify key details and think about how they connect. Consider the following types of details:

- words and phrases that show strong feelings
- descriptions of people, objects, and sensations
- related scenes that show how a situation changes or develops
- direct statements about the meaning of an experience

TIP: The four broad purposes for writing are to describe, to narrate, to inform, and to persuade. Every writer also has a specific purpose for writing a given text. For example, he or she wants to tell a certain story to convey a particular insight.

 INTERACTIVITY

 NOTEBOOK

PRACTICE **Work on your own to complete the activity and answer the questions. Then, discuss your responses with your group.**

1. **Analyze** Reread the passages listed in the chart and take notes about details in each one that seem important.

PASSAGE	NOTES
Paragraph 3	
Paragraph 4	
Paragraph 5	

2. **(a) Connect** How do details you noted in the chart relate to each other? **(b) Interpret** What larger message or insight do these details help to express? Explain.

3. **Interpret** In paragraph 4, Keller says "w-a-t-e-r" became a "living word" for her. Explain how the concept of language coming to life is central to her purpose for writing and her message.

4. **Support** Generations of readers have found meaning in Keller's life experience and message. Using details from this excerpt as examples, explain why you think this is so.

from THE STORY OF MY LIFE

Conventions

Semicolons A **semicolon (;)** is a punctuation mark that indicates a separation between ideas that is greater than that of a comma but less than that of a period.

- It is used to join two closely related independent clauses that are not already joined by a coordinating conjunction (such as *and* or *but*).
- The second clause may or may not begin with a conjunctive adverb (such as *also, however,* or *therefore*) or a transitional expression (such as *as a result* or *for instance*).

TYPE OF CONNECTION	EXAMPLES
no conjunctive adverb or transitional expression	*Then my eyes filled with tears; I realized what I had done.*
with a conjunctive adverb	*Then my eyes filled with tears; amazingly, I realized what I had done.*
with a transitional expression	*Then my eyes filled with tears; for the first time, I realized what I had done.*

Notice that the conjunctive adverb and transitional expression are preceded by a semicolon and followed by a comma.

ANNOTATE

NOTEBOOK

READ IT Mark sentences in the selection that use semicolons to connect independent clauses. Note whether each example simply connects the clauses or uses a conjunctive adverb or transitional expression.

WRITE IT Edit the passage to correct any faulty use of semicolons or punctuation. If you choose, you may add conjunctive adverbs or transitional expressions.

I was reluctant to read the text however after I did I was glad. Keller had a strong spirit Sullivan had limitless patience. Together, they released Keller's gift for language as a result she was able to contribute her wisdom to the world. Keller's life would have been dark and silent without Sullivan; my life would be poorer without both of them.

TEKS

1.C. Present a critique of a literary work, film, or dramatic production, employing eye contact, speaking rate, volume, enunciation, a variety of natural gestures, and conventions of language to communicate ideas effectively.

10.D.vi. Edit drafts using standard English conventions, including subordinating conjunctions to form complex sentences and correlative conjunctions such as *either/or* and *neither/nor*.

10.D.viii. Edit drafts using standard English conventions, including punctuation, including commas to set off words, phrases, and clauses, and semicolons.

Speaking and Listening

A **critique** is a text that presents an evaluation of a literary or artistic work. It can discuss a work's weaknesses, celebrate its strengths, or do both.

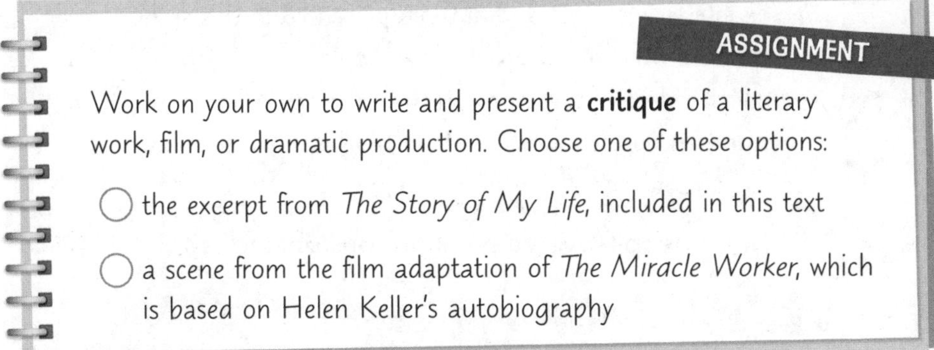

ASSIGNMENT

Work on your own to write and present a **critique** of a literary work, film, or dramatic production. Choose one of these options:

- ○ the excerpt from *The Story of My Life*, included in this text
- ○ a scene from the film adaptation of *The Miracle Worker*, which is based on Helen Keller's autobiography

Plan and Draft

Evaluate the Work Decide which work you will critique. Then, think about the qualities of the work that stand out to you. What do you most want to say about this work?

Use Conventions Effectively Grammatical structures can help you convey your ideas precisely. For example, practice using **correlative conjunctions** to show different aspects of your critique in a balanced way.

EXAMPLE: The author uses *both* description *and* dialogue to show experiences most people can't imagine.

TIP: Correlative conjunctions are pairs of joining words. They include *both/and, either/or, neither/nor,* and *not only/but also.* They always connect two elements that are grammatically the same.

Rehearse and Present

Practice Your Delivery As you speak, make sure your delivery is as strong as possible. Pay attention to each of these elements:

- **Eye Contact:** Don't stare; move your gaze from listener to listener.
- **Speaking Rate:** Vary the speed at which you speak to mirror your message. For example, slow down for emphasis and speed up for drama.
- **Volume:** Don't whisper or shout; speak loudly enough to be heard.
- **Enunciation:** Don't mumble; say each word clearly.
- **Natural Gestures:** Use gestures that are not forced and help to emphasize your ideas.
- **Language Conventions:** Use an informal tone but speak with proper grammar. When you use correlative conjunctions, place a slight emphasis on those words to ensure your meaning comes across.

Deliver and Discuss With your group, take turns delivering your critiques. Include a brief question-and-answer session after each person's turn. When you are the presenter, ask for feedback about the ideas you shared. When you are the listener, ask for more information or clarifications.

SOURCES

- The Circuit
- How This Son of Migrant Farm Workers Became an Astronaut
- A Work in Progress
- *from* The Story of My Life

Present an Informational Text

ASSIGNMENT

The interview subject and authors presented in this section faced and overcame a variety of struggles. Deepen your understanding of these people and their achievements by writing and presenting three brief **biographical profiles.** Use your texts to address this question:

How do people overcome enormous obstacles?

Plan With Your Group

Analyze the Texts With your group, analyze how each selection contributed to your understanding of the obstacles that people face and the ways they overcome them. Use the chart to organize your ideas.

SELECTION	INTERVIEW SUBJECT / AUTHOR	OBSTACLES
The Circuit		
How This Son of Migrant Farm Workers Became an Astronaut		
A Work in Progress		
from The Story of My Life		

Gather Evidence and Media Examples As a group, choose three of the authors or people portrayed in the selections on which to focus. Keep in mind that the three subjects you choose should all be real people, not fictional characters. For example, you may profile Francisco Jiménez rather than his characters. Decide how you will work to gather important information about each subject. Discuss what kind of media resources—such as online interview clips or historical photos—might be relevant to your presentation.

Organize and Draft Organize the details you have gathered and draft your profiles. Develop a coherent structure in each profile by including an introduction in which you state your main point, body paragraphs that develop your ideas, and a conclusion in which you restate the main point and leave listeners with a memorable thought. Use transitions within and across paragraphs to create a seamless flow of ideas that your listeners can easily follow. Decide whether to present your profiles in a live reading or a recorded presentation.

Rehearse and Present

Practice with Your Group As you practice delivering your part of the presentation, use this checklist to evaluate the effectiveness of your group's rehearsal. Then, use your evaluation and to guide revisions to your presentation.

CONTENT	USE OF MEDIA	PRESENTATION TECHNIQUES
◯ The presentation addresses the prompt. ◯ The presentation synthesizes information from multiple sources. ◯ The presentation provides an insightful conclusion.	◯ Visuals support the ideas and information presented. ◯ Media enhance and clarify the ideas and information presented.	◯ Speakers use an appropriately formal tone and vocabulary. ◯ Speakers use appropriate volume and pacing, and enunciate clearly. ◯ Instead of speaking in a monotone, speakers vary their registers, using the highs and lows of their voices.

Deliver the Presentation Apply the feedback you received during rehearsal to your delivery. Use your voice—including vocal register, volume, and tone—to emphasize interesting details and to express your feelings about your subject. Make sure that you speak clearly, stressing connecting words so that your listeners can follow the flow of your ideas.

Listen and Discuss

Discuss Presentations Hold a question-and-answer session after each presentation.

1. For Presenters: Listen closely to questions from your audience and respond with clear explanations.

2. For Listeners: Provide feedback about the clarity of the profiles and the use of media. Speak respectfully and offer recommendations that are genuinely helpful.

TEKS

6.H. Respond orally or in writing with appropriate register, vocabulary, tone, and voice.

10.B.i. Develop drafts into a focused, structured, and coherent piece of writing by organizing with purposeful structure, including an introduction, transitions, coherence within and across paragraphs, and a conclusion.

12.J. Use an appropriate mode of delivery, whether written, oral, or multi-modal, to present results.

Essential Question

How do we overcome obstacles?

Some people face extreme, even life-threatening obstacles. The ways in which they overcome them can inspire and teach all of us. In this section, you will choose a selection to read independently. Get the most from this section by establishing a purpose for reading. Ask yourself, "What do I hope to gain from my independent reading?" Here are just a few purposes you might consider:

Read to Learn Think about the selections you have already read. What questions do you still have about the unit topic?

Read to Enjoy Read the descriptions of the texts. Which one seems most interesting and appealing to you?

Read to Form a Position Consider your thoughts and feelings about the Essential Question. Are you still undecided about some aspect of the topic?

Reading Digital Texts

Digital texts like the ones you will read in this section are electronic versions of print texts. They have a variety of characteristics:

- can be read on various devices
- text can be resized
- may include highlighting or other annotation tools
- may have bookmarks, audio links, and other helpful features

Independent Learning Strategies

Throughout your life, in school, in your community, and in your career, you will need to rely on yourself to learn and work on your own. Use these strategies to keep your focus as you read independently for sustained periods of time. Add ideas of your own for each category.

STRATEGY	MY ACTION PLAN
Create a schedule • Be aware of your deadlines. • Make a plan for each day's activities.	
Read with purpose • Use a variety of comprehension strategies to deepen your understanding. • Think about the text and how it adds to your knowledge.	
Take notes • Record key ideas and information. • Review your notes before sharing what you've learned.	

TEKS

4. Self-select text and read independently for a sustained period of time; **5.A.** Establish purpose for reading assigned and self-selected text; **8.F.** Analyze characteristics of multimodal and digital texts.

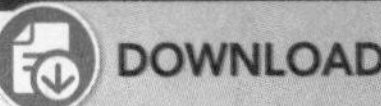

CONTENTS

Choose one selection. Selections are available online only.

LYRIC POETRY

Four Skinny Trees

from The House on Mango Street

Sandra Cisneros

A young girl finds inner strength in an unexpected place.

JOURNALISM

The Girl Who Fell From the Sky

Juliane Koepcke

Can a teenage girl survive in the rain forest all by herself?

BIOGRAPHY

Profile: Malala Yousafzai

BBC

One young woman changes the way millions of people see the world.

MEMOIR

from Facing the Lion: Growing Up Maasai on the African Savanna

Joseph Lemasolai Lekuton

Sometimes life forces a person to step way outside of "the comfort zone."

SHORT STORY

Rikki-tikki-tavi

Rudyard Kipling

Can one little mongoose protect the people and animals around him from two deadly cobras?

SHARE YOUR INDEPENDENT LEARNING

Reflect on and evaluate the information you gained from your Independent Reading selection. Then, share what you learned with others.

Close-Read Guide

Tool Kit
Close-Read Guide and **Model Annotation**

Establish your purpose for reading. Then, read the selection through at least once. Use this page to record your Close-Read ideas.

Selection Title: ____________ Purpose for Reading: ____________

Minutes Read: ____________

INTERACTIVITY

Close Read the Text

Zoom in on sections you found interesting. **Annotate** what you notice. Ask yourself **questions** about the text. What can you **conclude?**

Analyze the Text

1. Think about the author's choices of literary elements, techniques, and structures. Select one and record your thoughts.

2. What characteristics of digital texts did you use as you read this selection, and in what ways? How do the characteristics of a digital text affect your reading experience? Explain.

QuickWrite

Choose a paragraph from the text that grabbed your interest. Explain the power of this passage.

Share Your Independent Learning

Essential Question

How do we overcome obstacles?

When you read something independently, your understanding continues to grow as you share what you have learned with others.

 NOTEBOOK

Prepare to Share

CONNECT IT One of the most important ways to respond to a text is to notice and describe your personal reactions. Think about the text you explored independently and the ways in which it connects to your own experiences.

- What similarities and differences do you see between the text and your own life? Describe your observations.
- How do you think this text connects to the Essential Question? Describe your ideas.

Learn From Your Classmates

DISCUSS IT Share your ideas about the text you explored on your own. As you talk with others in your class, take notes about new ideas that seem important.

Reflect

EXPLAIN IT Review your notes, and mark the most important insight you gained from these writing and discussion activities. Explain how this idea adds to your understanding of facing adversity.

 TEKS

6.A. Describe personal connections to a variety of sources, including self-selected texts.

6.E. Interact with sources in meaningful ways such as notetaking, annotating, freewriting, or illustrating.

Informational Essay

ASSIGNMENT

In this unit, you read about adversity from different perspectives. You also practiced writing informational essays and biographical profiles. Now, apply what you have learned.

Write an **informational essay** in which you develop a thesis in response to the Essential Question.

Essential Question

How do we overcome obstacles?

Review and Evaluate Evidence

INTERACTIVITY

Review your Essential Question Notes and your QuickWrite from the beginning of the unit. Have your ideas changed?

Yes	No
Identify at least three pieces of evidence that made you think differently about the topic.	Identify at least three pieces of evidence that reinforced your initial ideas about the topic.
1.	1.
2.	2.
3.	3.

State your ideas now:

What other evidence might you need to support a thesis on the topic?

Share Your Perspective

The **Informational Essay Checklist** will help you stay on track.

PLAN Before you write, read the Checklist and make sure you understand all the items.

DRAFT As you write, pause occasionally to make sure you're meeting the Checklist requirements.

Use New Words Refer to your Word Network to vary your word choice. Also, consider using one or more of the Academic Vocabulary terms you learned at the beginning of the unit: ***deviate, persevere, determination, diversity, observation.***

REVIEW AND EDIT After you have written a first draft, evaluate it against the Checklist. Make any changes needed to strengthen your thesis, structure, transitions, and language. Then, reread your essay and fix any errors you find.

EQ Notes Make sure you have pulled in details from your Essential Question Notes to support your thesis.

INTERACTIVITY

INFORMATIONAL ESSAY CHECKLIST

My essay clearly contains . . .

- ◯ a strong thesis, or controlling idea, that shows depth of thought.
- ◯ varied types of supporting evidence, including facts, details, and examples.
- ◯ a purposeful structure that includes an engaging introduction, logical connections between body paragraphs, and an insightful conclusion.
- ◯ use of conjunctive adverbs to show logical relationships among ideas and create coherence.
- ◯ varied and precise word choices.
- ◯ correct use of standard English conventions.
- ◯ no punctuation or spelling errors.

TEKS

11.B. Compose informational texts, including multi-paragraph essays that convey information about a topic, using a clear controlling idea or thesis statement and genre characteristics and craft.

Revising and Editing

INTERACTIVITY

Read this draft and think about corrections the writer might make. Then, answer the questions that follow.

[1] Marya Sklodowska, later known as Marie Curie, spent her life overcoming adversity. [2] She was born in 1867 to a poor Polish family. [3] She could not study science in Poland, therefore; she moved to France. [4] She married Pierre Curie, she studied chemistry next. [5] Her research led to the development of X-rays. [6] Marie Curie became the first woman to win the Nobel Prize and the only person to win in two different fields, physics and chemistry.

[7] Even then, her struggles were not over. [8] Marie never gave up. [9] She coped with other scientists' envy the death of Pierre and her own illness. [10] According to her daughter and biographer, Curie said,"Life is not easy for any of us. [11] But . . . we must believe that we are gifted for something, and that this thing, at whatever cost, must be attained."

1. How should the punctuation in sentence 3 be corrected?

A Add a comma after *science*.

B Replace the comma after *Poland* with a colon, and remove the semicolon after *therefore*.

C Replace the comma after *Poland* with a semicolon, and replace the semicolon after *therefore* with a comma.

D Add a comma after *moved*.

2. Which answer choice is the best revision of sentence 4?

F After she married Pierre Curie, she studied chemistry.

G She studied chemistry, she married Pierre Curie.

H She married Pierre Curie. She studied chemistry.

J She married Pierre Curie therefore; she studied chemistry next.

3. Which answer choice combines sentences 7 and 8 using correct punctuation?

A Even then her struggles were not over; however Marie never gave up.

B Even then, her struggles were not over; however, Marie never gave up.

C Even then her struggles were not over; however; Marie never gave up.

D Even then, her struggles were not over, however, Marie never gave up.

4. Where should commas be added to correct sentence 9?

F after *coped, envy,* and *Pierre*

G after *with* and *envy*

H after *coped, death,* and *Pierre*

J after *envy* and *Pierre*

Reflect on the Unit

NOTEBOOK

INTERACTIVITY

Reflect On the Unit Goals

Review your Unit Goals chart from the beginning of the unit. Then, complete the activity and answer the question.

1. In the Unit Goals chart, rate how well you meet each goal now.
2. In which goals were you most and least successful?

Reflect On the Texts

VOTE! Use this Ballot to choose the selection that you think would make the most interesting movie or TV show. Support your choice with reasons. Then, discuss your choices.

SELECTION BALLOT

Title	Best Movie or Show [choose one]	Reasons
Black Sunday: The Storm That Gave Us the Dust Bowl		
from The Grapes of Wrath		
High School Teammates Carry On		
The Circuit		
How This Son of Migrant Farm Workers Became an Astronaut		
A Work in Progress		
from The Story of My Life		
My Independent Reading Selection:		

Reflect On the Essential Question

Talk Show As a class, conduct a talk show featuring characters and real people from this unit. Focus the discussion on the Essential Question:

How do we overcome obstacles?

- Come up with a name for your show.
- Have one person play the host and others play the "guests"—characters and real people from the unit.

TEKS

10.D.i. Edit drafts using standard English conventions, including complete complex sentences with subject-verb agreement and avoidance of splices, run-ons, and fragments; **10.D.iii.** Edit drafts using standard English conventions, including conjunctive adverbs; **10.D.viii.** Edit drafts using standard English conventions, including punctuation, including commas to set off words, phrases, and clauses, and semicolons.

RESOURCES

TOOL KIT

GLOSSARY

INDEXES

ACKNOWLEDGEMENTS

Marking the Text: Strategies and Tips for Annotation

When you close read a text, you read for comprehension and then reread to unlock layers of meaning and to analyze a writer's style and techniques. Marking a text as you read it enables you to participate more fully in the close-reading process.

Following are some strategies for text mark-ups, along with samples of how the strategies can be applied. These mark-ups are suggestions; you and your teacher may want to use other mark-up strategies.

- * Key Idea
- ! I love it!
- ? I have questions
- ◯ Unfamiliar or important word
- — Context Clues
- ▭ Highlight

SUGGESTED MARK-UP NOTES

WHAT I NOTICE	HOW TO MARK UP	QUESTIONS TO ASK
Key Ideas and Details	• Highlight key ideas or claims. • Underline supporting details or evidence.	• What does the text say? What does it leave unsaid? • What inferences do you need to make? • What details lead you to make your inferences?
Word Choice	• Circle unfamiliar words. • Put a dotted line under context clues, if any exist. • Put an exclamation point beside especially rich or poetic passages.	• What inferences about word meaning can you make? • What tone and mood are created by word choice? • What alternate word choices might the author have made?
Text Structure	• Highlight passages that show key details supporting the main idea. • Use arrows to indicate how sentences and paragraphs work together to build ideas. • Use a right-facing arrow to indicate foreshadowing. • Use a left-facing arrow to indicate flashback.	• Is the text logically structured? • What emotional impact do the structural choices create?
Author's Craft	• Circle or highlight instances of repetition, either of words, phrases, consonants, or vowel sounds. • Mark rhythmic beats in poetry using checkmarks and slashes. • Underline instances of symbolism or figurative language.	• Does the author's style enrich or detract from the reading experience? • What levels of meaning are created by the author's techniques?

Close-Reading Model

When close reading, take the time to analyze not only the author's ideas but the way that those ideas are conveyed. Consider the genre of the text, the author's word choice, the writer's unique style, and the message of the text.

Here is how one reader close read this text. You will use different mark-up tools when working digitally.

- ✱ Key Idea
- ! I love it!
- ? I have questions
- ◯ Unfamiliar or important word
- — Context Clues
- Highlight

TOOL KIT: CLOSE READING

MODEL

INFORMATIONAL TEXT

from Classifying the Stars

Cecilia H. Payne

NOTES

explanation of sunlight and starlight

What is light and where do the colors come from?

This paragraph is about Newton and the prism.

What discoveries helped us understand light?

Fraunhofer and gaps in spectrum

1 Sunlight and starlight are composed of waves of various lengths, which the eye, even aided by a telescope, is unable to separate. We must use more than a telescope. In order to sort out the component colors, the light must be dispersed by a prism, or split up by some other means. For instance, sunbeams passing through rain drops are transformed into the myriad-tinted rainbow. The familiar rainbow spanning the sky is Nature's most glorious demonstration that light is composed of many colors.

2 The very beginning of our knowledge of the nature of a star dates back to 1672, when Isaac Newton gave to the world the results of his experiments on passing sunlight through a prism. To describe the beautiful band of rainbow tints, produced when sunlight was dispersed by his three-cornered piece of glass, he took from the Latin the word *spectrum*, meaning an appearance. The rainbow is the spectrum of the Sun. . . .

3 In 1814, more than a century after Newton, the spectrum of the Sun was obtained in such purity that an amazing detail was seen and studied by the German optician, Fraunhofer. He saw that the multiple spectral tints, ranging from delicate violet to deep red, were crossed by hundreds of fine dark lines. In other words, there were narrow gaps in the spectrum where certain shades were wholly blotted out. We must remember that the word spectrum is applied not only to sunlight, but also to the light of any glowing substance when its rays are sorted out by a prism or a grating.

You can use the Close-Read Guide to help you dig deeper into the text. Here is how a reader completed a Close-Read Guide.

MODEL

Close-Read Guide

Use this page to record your close-read ideas.

Selection Title: Classifying the Stars

Close Read the Text

Revisit sections of the text you marked during your first read. Read these sections closely and **annotate** what you notice. Ask yourself **questions** about the text. What can you **conclude?** Write down your ideas.

Paragraph 3: Light is composed of waves of various lengths. Prisms let us see different colors in light. This is called the spectrum. Fraunhofer proved that there are gaps in the spectrum, where certain shades are blotted out.

More than one researcher studied this and each built off the ideas that were already discovered.

Analyze the Text

Think about the author's choices of patterns, structure, techniques, and ideas included in the text. Select one, and record your thoughts about what this choice conveys.

The author showed the development of human knowledge of the spectrum chronologically. Helped me see how ideas were built upon earlier understandings.
Used dates and "more than a century after Newton" to show time.

QuickWrite

Pick a paragraph from the text that grabbed your interest. Explain the power of this passage.

The first paragraph grabbed my attention, specifically the sentence "The familiar rainbow spanning the sky is Nature's most glorious demonstration that light is composed of many colors." The paragraph began as a straightforward scientific explanation. When I read the word "glorious," I had to stop and deeply consider what was being said. It is a word loaded with personal feelings. With that one word, the author let the reader know what was important to her.

Argument

When you think of the word *argument,* you might think of a disagreement between two people, but the word has another meaning, too. An argument is a logical way of presenting a belief, conclusion, or stance. A good argument is supported with reasoning and evidence.

Argument writing can be used for many purposes, such as changing a reader's opinion or bringing about an action or a response from a reader.

ARGUMENT

Your Purpose: to explain and defend your position

Characteristics

- a clear claim that relates to an engaging idea and shows depth of thought
- a consideration of other opinions or positions
- varied types of evidence, including specific facts, details, and examples
- language that makes a connection to your reader
- well-chosen transitions
- standard English conventions

Structure

- a well-organized structure that includes:
  - an interesting introduction
  - a logical flow of ideas from paragraph to paragraph
  - a strong conclusion

MODEL

ARGUMENT: SCORE 1

Celebrities Should Try to Be Better Role Models

A lot of Celebrities are singers or actors or actresses or athletes. Kids spend tons of time watching Celebrities on TV. They listen to their songs. They read about them. They watch them play and perform. No matter weather the Celebrities are good people or bad people. Kids still spend time watching them. The kids will try to imitate what they do. Some of them have parents or brothers and sisters who are famous also.

Celebrities don't seem to watch out what they do and how they live. Some say, "Why do I care? It's none of you're business"! Well, that's true. But it's bad on them if they do all kinds of stupid things. Because this is bad for the kids who look up to them.

Sometimes celebrity's say they wish they are not role models. *"I'm just an actor!" "I'm just a singer"!* they say. But the choice is not really up to them. If their on TV all the time, then kids' will look up to them, no matter what. It's stupid when Celebrities mess up and then nothing bad happens to them. That gives kids a bad lesson. Kids will think that you can do stupid things and be fine. That is not being a good role model.

Some Celebrities give money to charity. That's a good way to be a good role model. But sometimes it seems like Celebrities are just totally messed up. It's hard always being in the spotlight. That can drive Celebrities kind of crazy. Then they act out.

It is a good idea to support charities when you are rich and famous. You can do a lot of good. For a lot of people. Some Celebrities give out cars or houses or free scholarships. You can even give away your dresses and people can have an auction to see who will pay the most money for them. This can help for example the Humane Society. Or whatever charity or cause the celebrity wants to support.

Celebrities are fun to watch and follow, even when they mess up. I think they don't realize that when they do bad things, they give teens wrong ideas about how to live. They should try to keep that under control. So many teens look up to them and copy them, no matter what.

The claim is not clearly stated in the introduction or elsewhere.

Some of the ideas in the essay do not relate to the claim or focus on the issue.

The writer ineffectively addresses other positions.

The word choice in the essay is not effective and lends it an informal tone.

The progression of ideas is not logical or purposeful.

Errors in spelling, capitalization, punctuation, grammar, usage, and sentence boundaries are frequent. The effectiveness of the essay is affected by these errors.

The conclusion does not clearly restate the claim.

MODEL

ARGUMENT: SCORE 2

Celebrities Should Try to Be Better Role Models

Most kids spend tons of time watching celebrities on TV, listening to their songs, and reading about them. No matter how celebrities behave—whether they do good things or bad—they are role models for kids. They often do really dumb things, and that is not good considering they are role models.

Sometimes celebrity's say they wish they were not role models. "I'm just an actor!" or, "I'm just a singer!" they say. But the choice is not really up to them. If they are on TV all the time, then kids' will look up to them. No matter what. It's really bad when celebrities mess up and then nothing bad happens to them. That gives kids a false lesson because in reality there are bad things when you mess up. That's why celebrities should think more about what they are doing and what lessons they are giving to kids.

Some celebrities might say, *"Why do I care? Why should I be bothered?"* Well, they don't have to. But it's bad on them if they do all kinds of stupid things and don't think about how this affects the kids who look up to them. Plus, they get tons of money, much more even than inventors or scientists or other important people. Being a good role model should be part of what they have to do to get so much money.

When you are famous it is a good idea to support charities. Some celebrities give out cars, or houses, or free scholarships. They even sometimes give away their dresses and people have an auction to see who will pay the most money for them. This can help for example the Humane Society, or whatever charity or cause the celebrity wants to support.

Sometimes it seems like celebrities are more messed up than anyone else. That's in their personal lives. Imagine if people wanted to take pictures of you wherever you went, and you could never get away. That can drive celebrities kind of crazy, and then they act out.

Celebrities can do good things and they can do bad things. They don't realize that when they do bad things, they give teens wrong ideas about how to live. So many teens look up to them and copy them, no matter what. They should make an effort to be better role models.

The introduction does not state the claim clearly enough.

The writer ineffectively addresses other positions.

Errors in spelling, grammar, and sentence boundaries decrease the effectiveness of the essay.

The word choice in the essay contributes to an informal tone.

The writer does not make use of transitions and sentence connections.

Some of the ideas in the essay do not relate to the claim or focus on the issue.

The essay has a clear conclusion.

MODEL

ARGUMENT: SCORE 3

Celebrities Should Try to Be Better Role Models

Kids look up to the celebrities they see on TV and want to be like them. Parents may not *want* celebrities to be role models for their children, but they are anyway. Therefore, celebrities should think about what they say and do and live lives that are worth copying. Celebrities should think about how they act because they are role models.

"I'm just an actor!" or, "I'm just a singer!" celebrities sometimes say. "Their parents and teachers are the ones who should be the role models!" But it would be foolish to misjudge the impact that celebrities have on youth. Kids spend hours every day digitally hanging with their favorite stars. Children learn by imitation, so, for better or worse, celebrities are role models. That's why celebrities should start modeling good decision-making and good citizenship.

With all that they are given by society, celebrities owe a lot back to their communities and the world. Celebrities get a lot of attention, time, and money. Often they get all that for doing not very much: acting, singing, or playing a sport. It's true; some of them work very hard. But even if they work very hard, do they deserve to be in the news all the time and earn 100 or even 1000 times more than equally hard-working teachers, scientists, or nurses? I don't think so. After receiving all that, it seems only fair that celebrities take on the important job of being good role models for the young people who look up to them.

Celebrities can serve as good role models is by giving back. Quite a few use their fame and fortune to do just that. They give scholarships, or even build and run schools; they help veterans; they visit hospitals; they support important causes such as conservation, and women's rights. They donate not just money but their time and talents too. This is a great way to be a role model.

Celebrities should recognize that as role models, they have a responsibility to try to make good decisions and be honest. Celebrities should step up so they can be a force for good in people's lives and in the world.

The writer's word choice is good but could be better.

The introduction mostly states the claim.

The writer addresses other positions.

The ideas relate to the stated claim and focus on the issue.

The sentences are varied and coherent and enhance the effectiveness of the essay.

The progression of ideas is logical, but there could be better transitions and sentence connections to show how ideas are related.

The conclusion mostly follows from the claim.

MODEL

ARGUMENT: SCORE 4

Celebrities Should Try to Be Better Role Models

Like it or not, kids look up to the celebrities they see on TV and want to be like them. Parents may not *want* celebrities to be role models for their children, but the fact is that they are. With such an oversized influence on young people, celebrities have a responsibility to think about what they say and do and to live lives that are worth emulating. In short, they should make an effort to be better role models.

Sometimes celebrities say they don't want to be role models. "I'm just an actor!" or "I'm just a singer!" they protest. "Their parents and teachers are the ones who should be guiding them and showing them the right way to live!" That is all very well, but it would be foolish to underestimate the impact that celebrities have on children. Kids spend hours every day digitally hanging out with their favorite stars. Children learn by imitation, so for better or worse, celebrities act as role models.

Celebrities are given a lot of attention, time, and money. They get all that for doing very little: acting, singing, or playing a sport very well. It's true some of them work very hard. But even if they work hard, do they deserve to be in the news all the time and earn 100 or even 1,000 times more than equally hardworking teachers, scientists, or nurses? I don't think so.

With all that they are given, celebrities owe a lot to their communities and the world. One way they can serve as good role models is by giving back, and quite a few celebrities use their fame and fortune to do just that. They give scholarships or even build and run schools; they help veterans; they entertain kids who are sick; they support important causes such as conservation and women's rights. They donate not just money but their time and talents too.

Celebrities don't have to be perfect. They are people too and make mistakes. But they should recognize that as role models for youth, they have a responsibility to try to make good decisions and be honest about their struggles. Celebrities should step up so they can be a force for good in people's lives.

The writer has chosen words that contribute to the clarity of the essay.

The writer clearly states the claim in the introduction.

The writer addresses other positions.

There are no errors to distract the reader from the effectiveness of the essay.

The writer uses transitions and sentence connections to show how ideas are related.

The writer clearly restates the claim and the most powerful idea presented in the essay.

Argument Rubric

	1 (POOR)	2 (WEAK)	3 (GOOD)	4 (EXCELLENT)
Clarity and Purpose	The claim is unstated or unclear. Evidence is absent or irrelevant to the purpose. The argument is unfocused and the intended audience is not addressed.	The claim is unclear or lacks power. Evidence is weak and does not build the argument. The argument is often unfocused and not suited to its audience.	The claim is stated, but could be more powerful. The argument is mostly focused and supported by evidence. It is somewhat suited to its audience.	The claim is clear and powerful. The argument is focused and supported by ample and varied evidence. It is totally suited to the audience.
Organization	The argument has no purposeful structure. The ideas presented do not relate to one another.	The argument has a weak structure. The organization is unclear and does not help build the argument.	The structure of the argument is evident. Ideas are clearly linked with transitions.	A purposeful structure clearly builds the argument. The ideas presented are coherent and powerful.
Development of Ideas	The argument lacks specific facts, details, and examples to support the claim. Sources are not cited. Transitions are not used to link ideas. Other positions are not addressed.	The argument has few facts, details, and examples to support the claim. Sources are often unidentified. Transitions are usually absent. Other positions are ineffectively addressed.	The claim is mostly supported by facts, details, and examples. Most sources are identified. Most ideas are linked using transitions. Other positions are addressed.	Varied facts, details, and examples fully support the claim. Sources are always identified. Transitions link ideas within and among paragraphs. Other positions are addressed.
Language and Style	Word choice is vague, repetitive, or misleading. Sentences lack variety and impact.	Word choice is often vague, repetitive, or misleading. There is little sentence variety.	Word choice is often precise and to the point. Most passages contain a variety of sentence types.	Word choices are precise and purposeful. A variety of sentence types help focus and maintain the audience's attention.
Conventions	Misspellings and errors in grammar detract from the argument. Punctuation is lacking or incorrect.	The argument is weakened by occasional errors in spelling, punctuation, and grammar.	The argument contains few errors in spelling, punctuation, and grammar.	The argument is free from errors in spelling, punctuation, and grammar.

TOOL KIT: WRITING MODELS AND RUBRICS

Informational Text

Informational writing should present facts, details, data, and other kinds of evidence to communicate information about a topic. Informative writing serves several purposes: to increase readers' knowledge of a subject, to help readers better understand a procedure or process, or to provide readers with enhanced comprehension of a concept. It should also feature a clear introduction, body, and conclusion.

INFORMATIONAL TEXT

Your Purpose: to communicate information about a topic

Characteristics

- a clear thesis statement or controlling idea
- varied types of evidence
- precise language and well-chosen transitions
- definitions of unfamiliar or technical terms
- an objective tone
- standard English grammar and conventions

Structure

- an engaging introduction with a clear thesis statement
- a logical flow of ideas from paragraph to paragraph
- a strong conclusion

MODEL

INFORMATIONAL: SCORE 1

Kids, School, and Exercise: Problems and Solutions

In the past, children ran around and even did hard physical labor. Today most kid's just sit most of the time. They don't know the old Outdoor Games. Like tether ball. and th ve hard chores to do. Like milking the cows. But children should be Physically Active quite a bit every day. That doesn't happen very much any more. Not as much as it should anyway.

Even at home when kid's have a chance to run around, they choose to sit and play video games, for example. Some schools understand that it's a problem when students don't get enough exercise. Even though they have had to cut Physical Education classes. Some also had to make recess shorter.

But lots of schools are working hard to find ways to get kid's moving around again. Like they used to long ago.

Schools use volunteers to teach kid's old-fashioned games. Old-fashioned games are an awesome way to get kid's moving around like crazy people.

Some schools have before school activities. Such as games in the gym. Other schools have after school activities. Such as bike riding or outdoor games. They can't count on kid's to be active. Not even on their own or at home. So they do the activities all together. Kids enjoy doing stuff with their friends. So that works out really well.

If you don't exercise you get overweight. You can end up with high blood pressure and too much colesterol. Of course its also a problem if you eat too much junk food all the time. But not getting enough exercise is part of the problem too. That's why schools need to try to be part of the solution.

A break during class to move around helps. Good teachers know how to use exercise during classes. There are all kinds of ways to move in the classroom that don't mean you have to change your clothes. Classes don't have to be just about math and science.

Schools are doing what they can to get kids moving, doing exercise, being active. Getting enough exercise also helps kid's do better in school. Being active also helps kids get strong.

There are extensive errors in spelling, capitalization, punctuation, grammar, usage, and sentence boundaries.

Many of the ideas in the essay do not focus on the topic and are not supported by evidence. The thesis is unclear.

The word choice shows the writer's lack of awareness of the essay's purpose and tone.

The essay's sentences are not purposeful, varied, or well-controlled. The writer's sentences decrease the effectiveness of the essay.

The essay is not well organized. Its structure does not support its purpose, and ideas do not flow logically from one paragraph to the next.

The conclusion is not insightful or engaging.

MODEL

INFORMATIONAL: SCORE 2

Kids, School, and Exercise: Problems and Solutions

In the past, children ran around a lot and did chores and other physical work. Today most kid's sit by a TV or computer screen or play with their phones. But children should be active for at least 60 minutes a day. Sadly, most don't get nearly that much exercise. And that's a big problem.

Some schools understand that it's a problem when students don't get enough exercise. Even though they have had to cut Physical Education classes due to budget cuts. Some also had to make recess shorter because there isn't enough time in the schedule. But they are working hard to find creative ways that don't cost too much or take up too much time to get kid's moving. Because there's only so much money in the budget, and only so much time in the day, and preparing to take tests takes lots of time.

Schools can use parent volunteers to teach kid's old-fashioned games such as kick-the-can, hopscotch, foursquare, tetherball, or jump rope. Kid's nowadays often don't know these games! Old-fashioned games are a great way to get kid's moving. Some schools have before school activities, such as games in the gym. Other schools have after school activities, such as bike riding or outdoor games. They can't count on kid's to be active on their own or at home.

A break during class can help students concentrate when they go back to work. There are all kinds of ways to move in the classroom. And you don't have to change your clothes or anything. Wiggling, stretching, and playing a short active game are all good ideas. Good teachers know how to squeeze in time during academic classes like math and language arts.

Not getting enough exercise is linked to many problems. For example, unhealthy wait, and high blood pressure and colesterol. When students don't' get enough exercise, they end up overweight.

Physical activity also helps kid's do better in school. Kids who exercise have better attendance rates. They have increased attention span. They act out less. They have less stress and learn more. Being active also helps muscles and bones. It increases strength and stamina.

Schools today are doing what they can to find a solution by being creative and making time for physical activity before, during, and after school. They understand that it is a problem when kid's don't get enough exercise.

Not all the ideas in the essay focus on the topic or are supported by evidence. The thesis is not completely clear.

The writer uses some transitions and sentence connections.

Some ideas are well developed. Some examples and details are well chosen and specific and add substance to the essay.

Ideas do not always flow logically from one paragraph to the next.

There are errors in spelling, punctuation, grammar, usage, and sentence boundaries that decrease the effectiveness of the essay.

The essay's organizing structure does not effectively support its purpose.

The conclusion lacks focus and insight.

MODEL

INFORMATIONAL: SCORE 3

Kids, School, and Exercise: Problems and Solutions

A 2008 report said school-age children should be physically active for at least 60 minutes a day. Sadly, most children don't get nearly that much exercise. Lots of schools have cut Physical Education classes because of money and time pressures. And there's less recess than there used to be. Even at home when kids have a chance to run around, many choose screen time instead. No wonder so many of us are turning into chubby couch potatoes!

Not getting exercise is linked to many problems, for example unhealthy weight, and high blood pressure and cholesterol. Studies show physical activity also helps students do better in school: it means better attendance rates, increased attention span, fewer behavioral problems, less stress, and more learning. Being active helps develop strong muscles and bones. It increases strength and stamina.

Many schools around the country get that there are problems when students are inactive. They are working hard to find creative solutions that don't cost too much or take up precious time in the school schedule.

Some schools are using parent volunteers to teach kids active games such as kick-the-can, hopscotch, foursquare, tetherball, or jump rope. These games are more likely to get kids moving than just sitting gossiping with your friends or staring at your phone. Some schools have before school activities such as run-around games in the gym. Other schools have after school activities such as bike riding or outdoor games. They can't count on kids to be active on their own.

There are all kinds of fun and healthy ways to move in the classroom, without changing clothes. An active break during class can help students concentrate when they go back to work. Creative teachers know how to squeeze in active time even during academic classes. Wiggling, stretching, and playing a short active game are all good ideas.

Schools today understand that it is a problem when kids don't get enough exercise. They are doing what they can to find a solution by being creative and making time for physical activity before, during, and after school.

The essay is fairly thoughtful and engaging.

Almost all the ideas focus on the topic, and the thesis is clear.

The ideas in the essay are well developed, with well-chosen evidence.

The writer uses transitions and connections between sentences and paragraphs, such as *"Not getting exercise is linked..."* *"Many schools ..."* *"Some schools..."* *"Other schools..."*

Ideas in the essay are mostly well developed and flow logically.

Words are chosen carefully and contribute to the clarity of the essay.

MODEL

INFORMATIONAL: SCORE 4

Kids, School, and Exercise: Problems and Solutions

In 2008, the U.S. Department of Health and Human Services published a report stating that all school-age children need to be physically active for at least 60 minutes a day. Sadly, most children don't get nearly the recommended amount of exercise. Due to budget cuts and time pressure, many schools have cut Physical Education classes. Even recess is being squeezed to make room for more tests and test preparation.

> The writer explains the problem and its causes in the thesis and provides evidence.

Lack of exercise can lead to many problems, such as unhealthy weight, high blood pressure, and high cholesterol. Physical activity helps develop strong muscles and bones, and it increases strength and stamina. Studies show physical activity leads to better attendance rates, increased attention span, fewer behavioral problems, less stress, and more learning. When kids don't get enough physical activity, a lot is at stake!

> The writer clearly lays out the effects of the problem.

Many schools around the country are stepping up to find innovative solutions—even when they don't have time or money to spare. Some have started before-school activities such as active games in the gym. Others have after-school activities such as bike riding or outdoor games. Just a few extra minutes a day can make a big difference!

> The writer turns to the solution. The essay's organizing structure supports its purpose.

Some schools try to make the most of recess by using parent volunteers to teach kids active games such as kick-the-can, hopscotch, foursquare, tetherball, or jump rope. Volunteers can also organize races or tournaments—anything to get the kids going! At the end of recess, everyone should be a little bit out of breath.

> The writer includes specific examples and well-chosen details.

Creative educators squeeze in active time even during academic classes. It could be a quick "brain break" to stretch in the middle of class, imaginary jump rope, or a game of rock-paper-scissors with legs instead of fingers. There are all kinds of imaginative ways to move in the classroom, without moving furniture or changing clothes. And research shows that an active break during class can help students focus when they go back to work.

> The progression of ideas is logical.

> Details and examples add substance to the essay.

Schools today understand the problems that can arise when kids don't have enough physical activity in their lives. They are meeting the challenge by finding opportunities for exercise before, during, and after school. After all, if students do well on tests but end up unhealthy and unhappy, what is the point?

> The conclusion is insightful and engaging.

Informational Text Rubric

	1 (POOR)	2 (WEAK)	3 (GOOD)	4 (EXCELLENT)
Clarity and Purpose	The thesis is unstated or unclear. Evidence is absent or irrelevant to the purpose. Ideas are unfocused.	The thesis is unclear. Ideas are often unfocused and not supported by evidence.	The thesis is clear. Most of the ideas are focused and supported by evidence.	The thesis is completely clear. The ideas are focused and are supported by ample and varied evidence.
Organization	The topic is not clearly stated, and ideas do not follow a logical progression. The conclusion does not follow from the rest of the essay.	The introduction sets forth the topic. Ideas often do not progress logically, and the conclusion does not completely follow from the rest of the essay.	The introduction is somewhat engaging and compelling. Ideas progress somewhat logically. The conclusion does not completely follow from the rest of the essay.	The introduction is engaging and sets forth the topic in a compelling way. Ideas progress logically. The conclusion is insightful and follows from the rest of the essay.
Development of Ideas	The topic is not developed with reliable or relevant evidence. Sources are not cited. Transitions are not used to link ideas.	The topic is supported with few facts, details, and examples. Sources are often unidentified. Transitions are usually absent.	The topic is supported by facts, details, and examples. Most sources are identified. Transitions are often used to link ideas.	Varied facts, details, and examples fully support the topic. Sources are always identified. Transitions consistently link ideas.
Language and Style	Word choice is vague or repetitive. Sentences lack variety and impact. Technical words are not defined. The tone is not objective.	Word choice is often vague or repetitive. There is little sentence variety. Most technical words are not defined. The tone is often not objective.	Word choice is often precise and varied. Most passages contain a variety of sentence types. Most technical words are defined. The tone is usually objective.	Word choice is precise and varied. Sentences types are varied throughout. Technical words are defined. The tone is consistently objective.
Conventions	The essay contains numerous misspellings and errors in standard English conventions. Punctuation is lacking or incorrect.	The essay contains some misspellings and errors in standard English conventions. Punctuation is sometimes lacking or incorrect.	The essay contains few misspellings and errors in standard English conventions. Punctuation is usually correct.	The essay is free from errors in spelling, punctuation, and standard English conventions.

Narrative Text

Narrative writing conveys an experience, either real or imaginary, and uses time order to provide structure. Usually its purpose is to entertain, but it can also instruct, persuade, or inform. Whenever writers tell a story, they are using narrative writing. Most types of narrative writing share certain elements, such as characters, setting, a sequence of events, and, often, a theme.

NARRATIVE TEXT

Your Purpose: To tell a fiction or nonfiction story that expresses an insight

Characteristics

- a clear sequence of events
- details that show time and place
- well-developed, interesting characters (fiction) or real people (nonfiction)
- a conflict, or problem, and a resolution (fiction) or clear main idea (nonfiction)
- description and dialogue
- a clear narrative point of view
  - first-person (fiction or nonfiction)
  - third-person (fiction or nonfiction)
  - third-person omniscient (usually fiction)
- word choices and sensory details that paint a picture for readers
- standard English conventions

Structure

- a well-organized structure that includes
  - an engaging beginning
  - a chronological organization of events
  - a strong ending that expresses an insight

MODEL

NARRATIVE: SCORE 1

Mind Scissors

There's a bike race. Right away people start losing. But me and Thad were winning. Thad is the kid who always wins is who is also popular. I don't like Thad. I pumped pumping hard at my pedals, I knew the end was coming. I looked ahead and all I could see was Thad, and the woods.

I pedaled harder and then I was up to Thad. That was swinging at me, I swerved, I kept looking at him, I was worried!

That's stick had untied my shoelace and it was wrapped around my pedal! But I didn't know it yet.

We were out of the woods. I still wanted to win, I pedaled even faster. than my pedals stopped!

I saw with my mind the shoelace was caught in my pedal. No worries, I have the superpower of mind scissors. That's when my mind looked down and I used my mind scissors. I used the mind scissors to cut the shoelace my right foot was free.

That's how I became a superhero. I save people with my mind scissors now.

The story's beginning is not clear or engaging. The conflict is not well established.

The narrative does not include sensory language or precise words to convey experiences and develop characters.

Events do not progress logically. The ideas seem disconnected, and the sentences do not include transitions.

The narrative contains mistakes in standard English conventions of usage and mechanics.

The resolution does not connect to the narrative.

MODEL

NARRATIVE: SCORE 2

Mind-Scissors

When I was a baby I wound up with a tiny pair of scissors in my head. What the doctors couldn't have predicted is the uncanny ability they would give me. This past summer that was when I discovered what I could do with my mind-scissors.

Every summer there's a bike race. The kid who always wins is Thad who is popular.

The race starts. Right away racers start losing. After a long time pumping hard at my pedals, I knew the end was coming. I looked ahead and all I could see was Thad, and the woods.

I pedaled harder than ever. I was up to Thad. I turned my head to look at him. He was swinging a stick at me, I swerved, I kept looking at him, boy was I worried.

We were now out of the woods. Still hopeful I could win, I pedaled even faster. Suddenly, my pedals stopped!

Oh no! Thad's stick had untied my shoelace and it was wrapped around my pedal!

I was going to crash my bike. That's when my mind looked down. That's when I knew I could use my mind-scissors. I used the mind scissors to cut the shoelace my right foot was free.

That's how I won the race.

The story's beginning introduces the main character.

Events in the narrative progress somewhat logically, but the conflict is not completely clear. The writer uses some transition words.

The writer uses some description in the narrative.

The narrative demonstrates some accuracy in standard English conventions of usage and mechanics.

The words vary between vague and precise. The writer uses some sensory language.

The resolution is weak and adds very little to the narrative.

MODEL

NARRATIVE: SCORE 3

Mind-Scissors

When I was a baby I wound up with a tiny pair of scissors in my head. Lots of people live with pieces of metal in their heads. We just have to be careful. What the doctors couldn't have predicted is the uncanny ability they would give me.

Every summer there's a bike race that ends at the lake. The kid who always wins is Thad Thomas the Third, who is popular. This past summer that was about to change. It's also when I discovered what I could do with my mind-scissors.

The race starts. Right away racers start falling behind. After what seemed an eternity pumping hard at my pedals, I knew the end had to be in sight. I looked ahead and all I could see was Thad, and the opening to the woods—the last leg of the race.

I felt like steam was coming off my legs. I could see Thad's helmet. I turned my head to flash him a look. Only, Thad was the one who was gloating! And then I saw it—he was holding a stick he had pulled off a low-hanging branch.

He jabbed it toward me. I swerved out of the way. I kept pedaling, shifting my eyes to the right, to see what he was going to do.

But I waited too long. Then Thad made a slashing motion. Then he tossed the stick aside, yelled, "Yes!" and zoomed forward.

What happened? I felt nothing. We were now out of the woods and into the clearing before the finish line. Still hopeful I could win, I pedaled even faster. Suddenly, there was a jerk. My pedals had stopped!

I looked down. Oh no! My shoelace was wrapped around my pedal! Thad's stick had untied it!

I looked for a place to crash. That's when my head started tingling. I looked down at the shoelace. I concentrated really hard. I could see the scissors in my mind, floating just beside the pedal. Snip! The shoelace broke and my foot was free.

Thad was too busy listening to his fans cheer him on as I rode past him. Thanks to the mind-scissors, I won.

The story's beginning is engaging and clearly introduces the main character and situation.

Events in the narrative progress logically, and the conflict is clear. The writer uses transition words frequently.

The writer uses precise words and some sensory language to convey the experiences in the narrative and to describe the characters and scenes.

The writer uses some description and dialogue to add interest to the narrative and develop experiences and events.

The narrative demonstrates accuracy in standard English conventions of usage and mechanics.

The resolution follows from the rest of the narrative.

MODEL

NARRATIVE: SCORE 4

Mind-Scissors

As long as I wear my bike helmet, they say I'll be okay. Lots of people live with pieces of metal in their heads. We just have to be careful. When I was a baby I wound up with a tiny pair of scissors in mine. What the doctors couldn't have predicted is the uncanny ability they would give me.

Every summer there's a bike race that ends at the lake. The kid who always wins is Thad Thomas the Third, who is popular, but if you ask me, it's because he knows how to sweet-talk everyone. This past summer that was about to change. It's also when I discovered what I could do with my mind-scissors.

The race starts. Right away, racers start falling behind. After what seemed an eternity pumping hard at my pedals, I knew the end had to be in sight. I looked ahead and all I could see was Thad and the opening to the woods—the last leg of the race.

I put my stamina to the test—pedaling harder than ever, I felt like steam was coming off my legs. Thad's red helmet came into view. As I could sense I was going to overtake him any second, I turned my head to flash him a look. Only, to my befuddlement, Thad was the one who was gloating! And then I saw it—he was holding a stick he had pulled off a low-hanging branch.

He jabbed it toward me. I swerved out of the way. Was he trying to poke me with it? I kept pedaling, shifting my eyes to the right, to see what he was going to do.

But I waited too long. Thad made a slashing motion. Then he tossed the stick aside, yelled, "Yes!" and zoomed forward.

What happened? I felt nothing. We were now out of the woods and into the clearing before the finish line. Still hopeful I could win, I pedaled even faster. Suddenly, there was a jerk. My pedals had stopped!

I looked down. Oh no! My shoelace was wrapped around my pedal! Thad's stick had untied the shoelace!

I coasted as I looked for a place to crash. That's when my head started tingling. I got this funny notion to try something. I looked down. I had the tangled shoelace in my sights. I concentrated really hard. I could see the scissors in my mind, floating just beside the pedal. Snip! The shoelace broke and my right foot was free.

Thad was busy motioning his fans to cheer him on as I made my greatest effort to pedal back up to speed. Guess who made it to the finish line first?

The story's beginning is engaging and introduces the main character and situation in a way that appeals to a reader.

The writer uses techniques such as dialogue and description to add interest to the narrative and to develop the characters and events.

Events in the narrative progress in logical order and are linked by clear transitions. The conflict is well established.

The writer uses vivid description and sensory language to convey the experiences in the narrative and to help the reader imagine the characters and scenes.

The writer uses standard English conventions of usage and mechanics.

The resolution follows from the events in the narrative.

Narrative Rubric

	1 (POOR)	2 (WEAK)	3 (GOOD)	4 (EXCELLENT)
Clarity and Purpose	The beginning does not introduce characters or a situation. The conflict is unclear.	The beginning does not clearly introduce the situation or characters. The conflict is not well established.	The beginning introduces the characters and the situation. The conflict is established, but is not entirely developed.	An engaging beginning introduces the characters and situation in an appealing way. The conflict is well established and developed.
Organization	Events are jumbled and hard to follow and do not progress in chronological order.	Events are sometimes difficult to follow. They often do not progress in chronological order.	Most events are easy to follow and appear to progress in chronological order.	Events are easy to follow and clearly progress in chronological order.
Development of Ideas	Events do not progress logically and ideas seem disconnected. Sentences are not linked using transitions. The ending does not connect to the narrative or present an insight.	Events progress somewhat logically. Ideas are sometimes connected using transitions. The ending adds little to the narrative and provides a weak insight.	Most events progress logically. Ideas are often linked using transitions. The ending mostly follows from the narrative and provides an insight.	Events progress logically and are linked using clear transitions. The ending effectively follows from the narrative and provides and interesting insight.
Language and Style	Dialogue and description are absent. The narrative does not include sensory language or precise words to convey experiences and develop characters. The point of view is inconsistent.	The narrative includes some dialogue and description. Some precise words and sensory language are included. The point of view is not always consistent.	Dialogue and description are use to develop the story. Most words are precise and sensory language is included. The point of view is consistent.	Dialogue and description are used to add interest and develop the story. Word choice and sensory language are effectively used. The point of view is consistent.
Conventions	The narrative contains numerous misspellings and errors in standard English conventions. Punctuation is lacking or incorrect.	The narrative contains some misspellings and errors in standard English conventions. Punctuation is sometimes lacking or incorrect.	The narrative contains few misspellings and errors in standard English conventions. Punctuation is usually correct.	The narrative is free of errors in spelling, punctuation, and standard English conventions.

Conducting Research

You can conduct research to gain more knowledge about a topic. Sources such as articles, books, interviews, or the Internet have the facts and explanations that you need. Not all of the information that you find, however, will be useful—or reliable. Strong research skills will help you find accurate information about your topic.

Narrowing or Broadening a Topic

The first step in any research is finding your topic. Choose a topic that is narrow enough to cover completely. If you can name your topic in just one or two words, it is probably too broad. Topics such as mythology, hip hop music, or Italy are too broad to cover in a single report. Narrow a broad topic into smaller subcategories.

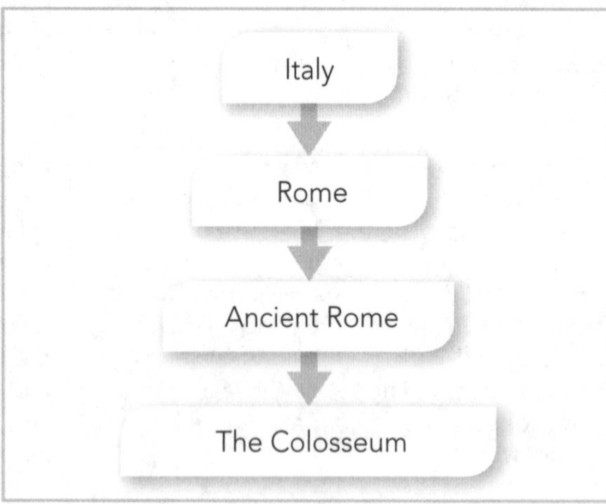

When you begin to research, pay attention to the amount of information available. If there is way too much information on your topic, you may need to narrow your topic further.

You might also need to broaden a topic if there is not enough information for your purpose. A topic is too narrow when it can be thoroughly presented in less space than the required size of your assignment. It might also be too narrow if you can find little or no information in library and media sources. Broaden your topic by including other related ideas.

Generating Research Questions

Use research questions to focus your research. Specific questions can help you avoid wasting time. For example, instead of simply hunting for information about Peter Pan, you might ask, "What inspired J. M. Barrie to write the story of Peter Pan?" or "How have different artists depicted Peter Pan?"

A research question may lead you to find your topic sentence. The question can also help you focus your research plan. Write your question down and keep it in mind while you hunt for facts. Your question can prevent you from gathering unnecessary information. As you learn more about your topic, you may need to refine your original question.

Consulting Print and Digital Sources

An effective research project combines information from multiple sources. It is important not to rely too heavily on a single source. The creativity and originality of your research depends on how you synthesize, or combine, ideas from many places. Plan to include a variety of these resources:

- **Primary and Secondary Sources:** Use both primary sources (firsthand or original accounts, such as interview transcripts and newspaper articles) and secondary sources (accounts that are not created at the time of an event, such as encyclopedia entries).
- **Print and Digital Resources:** The Internet allows fast access to data, but print resources are often edited more carefully. Plan to include both print and digital resources in order to guarantee that your work is accurate.
- **Media Resources:** You can find valuable information in media resources such as documentaries, television programs, podcasts, and museum exhibitions.
- **Original Research:** Depending on your topic, you may wish to conduct original research to include among your sources. For example, you might interview experts or eyewitnesses or conduct a survey of people in your community.

Using Online Encyclopedias

Online encyclopedias are often written by anonymous contributors who are not required to fact-check information. These sites can be very useful as a launching point for research, but should not be considered accurate. Look for footnotes, endnotes, or hyperlinks that support facts with reliable sources that have been carefully checked by editors.

Evaluating Sources It is important to evaluate the credibility and accuracy of any information you find. Ask yourself questions such as these to evaluate sources:

- **Reliability and Credibility:** Is the author well known? What are the author's credentials? Does the source include references to other reliable sources? Does the author's tone win your confidence? Why or why not?
- **Bias:** Does the author have any obvious biases? What is the author's purpose for writing? Who is the target audience?
- **Currency:** When was the work created? Has it been revised? Is there more current information available?

Using Search Terms

Finding information on the Internet is easy, but it can be a challenge to find facts that are useful and trustworthy. If you type a word or phrase into a search engine, you will probably get hundreds—or thousands—of results. However, those results are not guaranteed to be relevant or accurate.

These strategies can help you find information from the Internet:

- Create a list of topic keywords before you begin using a search engine. Use a thesaurus to expand your list.
- Enter six to eight keywords.
- Choose unique nouns. Most search engines ignore articles and prepositions. Verbs may lead to sources that are not useful. Use modifiers, such as adjectives, when necessary to specify a category. For example, you might enter "ancient Rome" instead of "Rome."
- Use quotation marks to focus a search. Place a phrase in quotation marks to find pages that include exactly that phrase. Add several phrases in quotation marks to narrow your results.
- Spell carefully. Many search engines correct spelling automatically, but they cannot catch every spelling error.
- Scan search results before you click them. The first result isn't always the most useful. Read the text and notice the domain before you make a choice.
- Consult more than one search engine.

Evaluating Internet Domains

Not everything you read on the Internet is true, so you have to evaluate sources carefully. The last three letters of an Internet URL identify the site's domain, which can help you evaluate the information on the site.

- **.gov**—Government sites are sponsored by a branch of the United States federal government and are considered reliable.
- **.edu**—Information from an educational research center or department is likely to be carefully checked, but may include student pages that are not edited or monitored.
- **.org**—Organizations are often nonprofit groups and usually maintain a high level of credibility but may still reflect strong biases.
- **.com and .net**—Commercial sites exist to make a profit. Information might be biased to show a product or service in a good light.

Taking Notes

Use different strategies to take notes:

- Use index cards to create notecards and source cards. On each source card, record information about each source you use—author, title, publisher, date of publication, and relevant page numbers. On each notecard, record information to use in your writing. Use quotation marks when you copy exact words, and indicate the page number(s) on which the information appears.
- Photocopy articles and copyright pages. Then, highlight relevant information. Remember to include the Web addresses of printouts from online sources.
- Print articles from the Internet or copy them directly into a "notes" folder.

You will use these notes to help you write original text.

Source Card

Papp, Joseph
and Kirkland, Elizabeth

Shakespeare Alive!

New York: Bantam Books, 1988

Notecard

Education
Papp, p.5

Only the upper classes could read.

Most of the common people in Shakespeare's time could not read.

Quote Accurately Responsible research begins with the first note you take. Be sure to quote and paraphrase your sources accurately so you can identify these sources later. In your notes, circle all quotations and paraphrases to distinguish them from your own comments. When photocopying from a source, include the copyright information. Include the Web addresses of printouts from online sources.

Reviewing Research Findings

You will need to review your findings to be sure that you have collected enough accurate and appropriate information.

Considering Audience and Purpose

Always keep your audience in mind as you gather information. Different audiences may have very different needs. For example, if you are writing a report for your class about a topic you have studied together, you will not need to provide background information in your writing. However, if you are writing about the topic for a national student magazine, you cannot assume that all of your readers have the same information. You will need to provide background facts from reliable sources to help inform those readers about your subject. When thinking about your research and your audience, ask yourself:

- Who am I writing for?
- Have I collected enough information to explain my topic to this audience?
- Do I need to conduct more research to explain my topic clearly?
- Are there details in my research that I can leave out because they are already familiar to my audience?

Your purpose for writing will also affect your research review. If you are researching to satisfy your own curiosity, you can stop researching when you feel you understand the answer completely. If you are writing a research report that will be graded, you need to think about your assignment. When thinking about whether or not you have enough information, ask yourself:

- What is my purpose for writing?
- Will the information I've gathered be enough to achieve my purpose?
- If I need more information, where might I find it?

Synthesizing Sources

Effective research writing is more than just a list of facts and details. Good research synthesizes—gathers, orders, and interprets—those elements. These strategies will help you synthesize effectively:

- Review your notes. Look for connections and patterns among the details you have collected.
- Organize notes or notecards to help you plan how you will combine details.
- Pay close attention to details that emphasize the same main idea.
- Also look for details that challenge one another. For many topics, there is no single correct opinion. You might decide to conduct additional research to help you decide which side of the issue has more support.

Types of Evidence

When reviewing your research, also think about the kinds of evidence you have collected. The strongest writing combines a variety of evidence. This chart describes three of the most common types of evidence.

TYPE OF EVIDENCE	DESCRIPTION	EXAMPLE
Statistical evidence includes facts and other numerical data used to support a claim or explain a topic.	Statistical evidence are facts about a topic, such as historical dates, descriptions about size and number, and poll results.	Jane Goodall began to study chimpanzees when she was 26 years old.
Testimonial evidence includes any ideas or opinions presented by others. Testimonies might come from experts or people with special knowledge about a topic.	Firsthand testimonies present ideas from eyewitnesses to events or subjects being discussed.	Goodall's view of chimps has changed: "When I first started at Gombe, I thought the chimps were nicer than we are. But time has revealed that they are not. They can be just as awful."
	Secondary testimonies include commentaries on events by people who were not directly involved.	Science writer David Quammen points out that Goodall "set a new standard, a very high standard, for behavioral study of apes in the wild."
Anecdotal evidence presents one person's view of the world, often by describing specific events or incidents.	An anecdote is a story about something that happened. Personal stories can be part of effective research, but they should not be the only kind of evidence presented. Anecdotes are particularly useful for proving that broad generalizations are not accurate.	It is not fair to say that it is impossible for dogs to use tools. One researcher reports the story of a dog that learned to use a large bone as a back scratcher.

Incorporating Research Into Writing

Avoiding Plagiarism

Whether you are presenting a formal research paper or an opinion paper on a current event, you must be careful to give credit for any ideas or opinions that are not your own. Presenting someone else's ideas, research, or opinion as your own—even if you have phrased it in different words—is plagiarism, the equivalent of academic stealing, or fraud.

Do not use the ideas or research of others in place of your own. Read from several sources to draw your own conclusions and form your own opinions. Incorporate the ideas and research of others to support your points. Credit the source of the following types of support:

- Statistics
- Direct quotations
- Indirectly quoted statements of opinions
- Conclusions presented by an expert
- Facts available in only one or two sources

When you are drafting and revising, circle any words or ideas that are not your own. Follow the instructions on pages R30 and R31 to correctly cite those passages.

Reviewing for Plagiarism Take time to review your writing for accidental plagiarism. Read what you have written and take note of any ideas that do not have your personal writing voice. Compare those passages with your resource materials. You might have copied them without remembering the exact source. Add a correct citation to give credit to the original author. If you cannot find the questionable phrase in your notes, think about revising your word choices. You want to be sure that your final writing reflects your own thinking and not someone else's work.

Quoting and Paraphrasing

When including ideas from research in your writing, you will decide to quote directly or paraphrase.

Direct Quotation Use the author's exact words when they are interesting or persuasive. You might decide to include direct quotations in these situations:

- to share a strong statement
- to reference a historically significant passage
- to show that an expert agrees with your position
- to present an argument to which you will respond

Include complete quotations, without deleting or changing words. If you need to leave out words for space or clarity, use ellipsis points to show where you removed words. Enclose direct quotations in quotation marks.

Paraphrase A paraphrase restates an author's ideas in your own words. Be careful to paraphrase accurately. Beware of making sweeping generalizations in a paraphrase that were not made by the original author. You may use some words from the original source, but a good paraphrase does more than simply rearrange an author's phrases, or replace a few words with synonyms.

Original Text	"Some teens doing homework while listening to music and juggling tweets and texts may actually work better that way, according to an intriguing new study performed by two high-school seniors." *Sumathi Reddy, "Teen Researchers Defend Media Multitasking"*
Patchwork Plagiarism phrases from the original are rearranged, but they too closely follow the original text.	An intriguing new study conducted by two high-school seniors suggests that teens work better when they are listening to music and juggling texts and tweets.
Good Paraphrase	Two high-school students studied homework habits. They concluded that some people do better work while multitasking, such as studying and listening to music or checking text messages at the same time.

Maintaining the Flow of Ideas

Effective research writing is much more than just a list of facts. Maintain the flow of ideas by connecting research information to your own ideas. Instead of simply stating a piece of evidence, use transitions to connect information you found from outside resources with your own thinking. The transitions shown here can be used to introduce, compare, contrast, and clarify.

Choosing an effective organizational strategy for your writing will help you create a logical flow of ideas. Once you have chosen a clear organization, add research in appropriate places to provide evidence and support.

Useful Transitions

When providing examples:

for example | for instance | to illustrate | in [name of resource], [author]

When comparing and contrasting ideas or information:

in the same way | similarly | however | on the other hand

When clarifying ideas or opinions:

in other words | that is | to explain | to put it another way

ORGANIZATIONAL STRUCTURE	USES
Chronological order presents information in the sequence in which it happens.	historical topics; science experiments; analysis of narratives
Part-to-whole order examines how several categories affect a larger subject.	analysis of social issues; historical topics
Order of importance presents information in order of increasing or decreasing importance.	persuasive arguments; supporting a bold or challenging thesis
Comparison-and-contrast organization presents similarities and differences.	addressing two or more subjects

Formats for Citing Sources

When you cite a source, you acknowledge where you found your information and you give your readers the details necessary for locating the source themselves. Within the body of a paper, you provide a short citation, a footnote number linked to a footnote, or an endnote number linked to an endnote reference. These brief references show the page numbers on which you found the information. Prepare a reference list at the end of a research report to provide full bibliographic information on your sources. These are two common types of reference lists:

- A bibliography provides a listing of all the resources you consulted during your research.
- A works-cited list indicates the works you have referenced in your writing.

The chart on the next page shows the Modern Language Association format for crediting sources. This is the most common format for papers written in the content areas in middle school and high school. Unless instructed otherwise by your teacher, use this format for crediting sources.

Focus on Citations When you revise your writing, check that you cite the sources for quotations, factual information, and ideas that are not your own. Most word-processing programs have features that allow you to create footnotes and endnotes.

Identifying Missing Citations These strategies can help you find facts and details that should be cited in your writing:

- Look for facts that are not general knowledge. If a fact was unique to one source, it needs a citation.
- Read your report aloud. Listen for words and phrases that do not sound like your writing style. You might have picked them up from a source. If so, use your notes to find the source, place the words in quotation marks, and give credit.
- Review your notes. Look for ideas that you used in your writing but did not cite.

MLA (8th Edition) Style for Listing Sources

Book with one author	Pyles, Thomas. *The Origins and Development of the English Language.* 2nd ed., Harcourt Brace Jovanovich, 1971. [Indicate the edition or version number when relevant.]
Book with two authors	Pyles, Thomas, and John Algeo. *The Origins and Development of the English Language.* 5th ed., Cengage Learning, 2004.
Book with three or more authors	Donald, Robert B., et al. *Writing Clear Essays.* Prentice Hall, 1983.
Book with an editor	Truth, Sojourner. *Narrative of Sojourner Truth.* Edited by Margaret Washington, Vintage Books, 1993.
Introduction to a work in a published edition	Washington, Margaret. Introduction. *Narrative of Sojourner Truth,* by Sojourner Truth, edited by Washington, Vintage Books, 1993, pp. v–xi.
Single work in an anthology	Hawthorne, Nathaniel. "Young Goodman Brown." *Literature: An Introduction to Reading and Writing,* edited by Edgar V. Roberts and Henry E. Jacobs, 5th ed., Prentice Hall, 1998, pp. 376–385. [Indicate pages for the entire selection.]
Signed article from an encyclopedia	Askeland, Donald R. "Welding." *World Book Encyclopedia,* vol. 21, World Book, 1991, p. 58.
Signed article in a weekly magazine	Wallace, Charles. "A Vodacious Deal." *Time,* 14 Feb. 2000, p. 63.
Signed article in a monthly magazine	Gustaitis, Joseph. "The Sticky History of Chewing Gum." *American History,* Oct. 1998, pp. 30–38.
Newspaper article	Thurow, Roger. "South Africans Who Fought for Sanctions Now Scrap for Investors." *Wall Street Journal,* 11 Feb. 2000, pp. A1+. [For a multipage article that does not appear on consecutive pages, write only the first page number on which it appears, followed by the plus sign.]
Unsigned editorial or story	"Selective Silence." Editorial. *Wall Street Journal,* 11 Feb. 2000, p. A14. [If the editorial or story is signed, begin with the author's name.]
Signed pamphlet or brochure	[Treat the pamphlet as though it were a book.]
Work from a library subscription service	Ertman, Earl L. "Nefertiti's Eyes." *Archaeology,* Mar.–Apr. 2008, pp. 28–32. *Kids Search,* EBSCO, New York Public Library. Accessed 7 Jan. 2017. [Indicating the date you accessed the information is optional but recommended.]
Filmstrips, slide programs, videocassettes, DVDs, and other audiovisual media	*The Diary of Anne Frank.* 1959. Directed by George Stevens, performances by Millie Perkins, Shelley Winters, Joseph Schildkraut, Lou Jacobi, and Richard Beymer, Twentieth Century Fox, 2004. [Indicating the original release date after the title is optional but recommended.]
CD-ROM (with multiple publishers)	Simms, James, editor. *Romeo and Juliet.* By William Shakespeare, Attica Cybernetics / BBC Education / Harper, 1995.
Radio or television program transcript	"Washington's Crossing of the Delaware." *Weekend Edition Sunday,* National Public Radio, 23 Dec. 2013. Transcript.
Web page	"Fun Facts About Gum." ICGA, 2005–2017, www.gumassociation.org/index.cfm/facts-figures/fun-facts-about-gum. Accessed 19 Feb. 2017. [Indicating the date you accessed the information is optional but recommended.]
Personal interview	Smith, Jane. Personal interview, 10 Feb. 2017.

All examples follow the style given in the MLA Handbook, 8th edition, published in 2016.

TOOL KIT: RESEARCH PROCESS AND MODELS

MODEL

EQ Notes

Unit Title: Discovery

Perfomance-Based Assessment Prompt:
Do all discoveries benefit humanity?

My initial thoughts:
Yes - all knowledge moves us forward.

As you read multiple texts about a topic, your thinking may change. Create EQ Notes like these to record your thoughts, to track details you might use in later writing or discussion, and to make further connections.

Here is a sample to show how one reader's ideas deepened as she read two texts.

TITLE	MY IDEAS/OBSERVATIONS	TEXT EVIDENCE/INFORMATION
Classifying the Stars	Newton shared his discoveries and then other scientists built on his discoveries.	Paragraph 2: "Isaac Newton gave to the world the results of his experiments on passing sunlight through a prism." Paragraph 3: "In 1814 . . . the German optician, Fraunhofer . . . saw that the multiple spectral tints . . . were crossed by hundreds of fine dark lines."

How does this text change or add to my thinking? This confirms what I think.

Date: Sept. 20

TITLE	MY IDEAS/OBSERVATIONS	TEXT EVIDENCE/INFORMATION
Cell Phone Mania	Cell phones have made some forms of communication easier, but people don't talk to each other as much as they did in the past.	Paragraph 7: "Over 80% of young adults state that texting is their primary method of communicating with friends. This contrasts with older adults who state that they prefer a phone call."

How does this text change or add to my thinking?

Date: Sept. 25

Maybe there are some downsides to discoveries. I still think that knowledge moves us forward, but sometimes there are negative effects.

MODEL

Word Network

A word network is a collection of words related to a topic. As you read the selections in a unit, identify interesting theme-related words and build your vocabulary by adding them to your Word Network.

Use your Word Network as a resource for your discussions and writings. Here is an example:

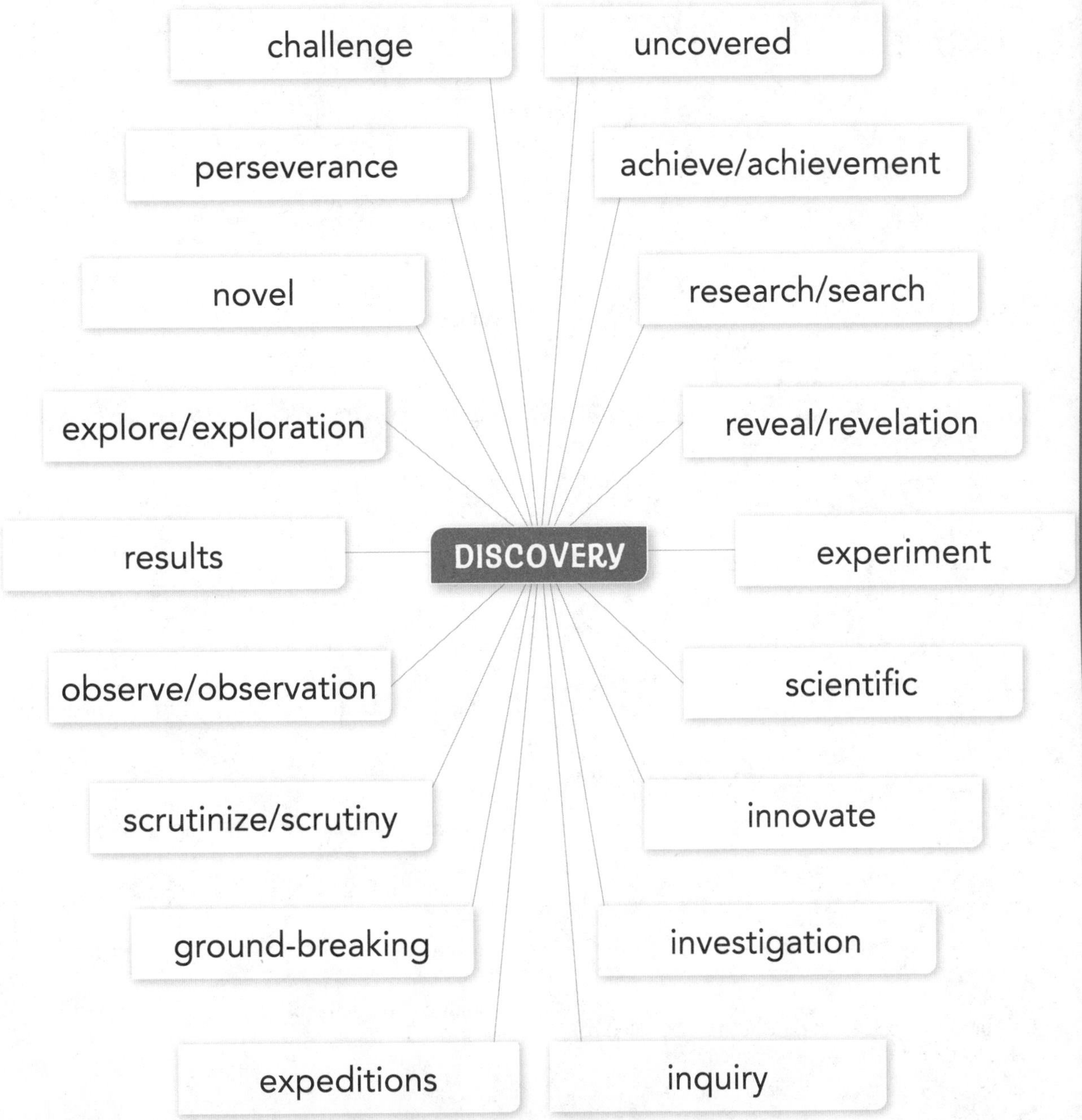

DISCOVERY

- challenge
- uncovered
- perseverance
- achieve/achievement
- novel
- research/search
- explore/exploration
- reveal/revelation
- results
- experiment
- observe/observation
- scientific
- scrutinize/scrutiny
- innovate
- ground-breaking
- investigation
- expeditions
- inquiry

Academic vocabulary appears in **blue type**.

Pronunciation Key

Symbol	Sample Words	Symbol	Sample Words
a	*at, catapult, Alabama*	oo	*boot, soup, crucial*
ah	*heart, charms, argue*	ow	*now, stout, flounder*
ai	*care, various, hair*	oy	*boy, toil, oyster*
aw	*law, maraud, caution*	s	*say, nice, press*
awr	*pour, organism, forewarn*	sh	*she, abolition, motion*
ay	*ape, sails, implication*	u	*full, put, book*
ee	*even, teeth, really*	uh	*ago, focus, contemplation*
eh	*ten, repel, elephant*	ur	*bird, urgent, perforation*
ehr	*merry, verify, terribly*	y	*by, delight, identify*
ih	*it, pin, hymn*	yoo	*music, confuse, few*
o	*shot, hopscotch, condo*	zh	*pleasure, treasure, vision*
oh	*own, parole, rowboat*		

A

accomplishments (uh KOM plihsh muhnts) *n.* goals reached; achievements; tasks done skillfully

actors' delivery (AK tuhrz) (dih LIH vuh ree) *n.* the ways in which actors speak their lines

affinity (uh FIHN ih tee) *n.* a liking or sympathy with something; a similarity of characteristics suggesting a relationship

agricultural (ag ruh KUHL chuhr uhl) *adj.* related to the science and art of farming

altered (AWL tuhrd) *adj.* changed

ancestors (AN sehs tuhrz) *n.* people from whom one is descended; forefathers

anticipated (an TIHS uh payt ihd) *v.* expected

aptitude (AP tuh tood) *n.* natural ability or talent

assumption (uh SUHMP shuhn) *n.* fact or statement taken for granted

atmosphere (AT muhs fihr) *n.* the gas surrounding the earth; the air

attain (uh TAYN) *v.* reach or achieve

awe (aw) *n.* reverential respect mixed with fear or wonder

B

background music (BAK grownd) (MYOO zihk) *n.* music that is not the focus of the performance

barriers (BAR ee uhrz) *n.* obstructions; things that block passage

benefit (BEHN uh fiht) *v.* get good or helpful results; gain

besieged (bih SEEJD) *adj.* surrounded for the purpose of capturing

bitterness (BIHT uhr nihs) *n.* a feeling caused by pain, sorrow, or regret

blight (blyt) *n.* something that spoils, prevents growth, or destroys

C

cacophony (kuh KOF uh nee) *n.* harsh or jarring sounds; loud noise

canals (kuh NALZ) *n.* artificial waterways for transportation or irrigation

catapulted (KA tuh puhl tihd) *v.* launched forward with machine-like force

celebrate (SEHL uh brayt) *v.* mark a happy occasion by engaging in a pleasurable activity

certainty (SUR tuhn tee) *n.* sure fact; freedom from doubt

charitable (CHAIR ih tuh buhl) *adj.* kind and forgiving; lenient

coaxed (kohkst) *v.* influenced or gently urged by flattery or persuasion

composition (kom puh ZIHSH uhn) *n.* arrangement of elements in a work of visual art

conducive (kuhn DOO sihv) *adj.* tending to promote or assist

consequence (KON suh kwehns) *n.* result; outcome; effect

consequences (KON suh kwehns ihz) *n.* results of an action or actions

contact (KON takt) *n.* connection; communication

contradict (kon truh DIHKT) *v.* dispute or disagree with

covetous (KUHV uh tuhs) *adj.* greedy and jealous

D

demoralized (dih MAWR uh lyzd) *adj.* discouraged; defeated

deserted (dih ZUR tihd) *adj.* abandoned; empty

determination (dih tuhr muh NAY shuhn) *n.* conclusion; firm decision

devastated (DEH vuh stay tihd) *v.* destroyed; completely upset

deviate (DEE vee ayt) *v.* depart from an established plan

dialogue (DY uh log) *n.* conversation; words spoken by characters in a story, drama, etc.

dire (dyr) *adj.* extremely serious or urgent

discordant (dihs KAWRD uhnt) *adj.* lacking harmony

discredit (dihs KREHD iht) *v.* disbelieve; cast doubt on *n.* loss of trust or faith; disbelief

dispelled (dihs PEHLD) *v.* driven away; scattered

disposal (dihs POH zuhl) *n.* act of getting rid of somehting

dissent (dih SEHNT) *v.* disagree; *n.* disagreement

distorting (dih STAWRT ihng) *v.* pulling or twisting out of meaning or shape

diversity (dy VUR suh tee) *n.* variety; differences within a group

doomed (doomd) *adj.* destined to a bad outcome

dreaded (DREHD ihd) *v.* felt great fear or extreme reluctance

E

earnest (UR nihst) *adj.* serious and heartfelt; not joking

elucidate (ih LOO suh dayt) *v.* make clear especially by explanation, demonstration, or analysis

enthusiastically (ehn thoo zee AS tihk lee) *adv.* with eager interest

envision (ehn VIH zhuhn) *v.* picture to oneself

evident (EH vih duhnt) *adj.* clear to the vision or understanding

explode (ehk SPLOHD) *v.* burst or shatter violently

extinct (ehk STIHNGKT) *adj.* no longer in existence

extraordinary (ehk STRAWR duh nehr ee) *adj.* better than ordinary; exceptional

F

fathom (FATH uhm) *v.* understand; come to comprehend

fluently (FLOO uhnt lee) *adv.* easily and smoothly

flung (fluhng) *v.* threw with force

forlorn (fawr LAWRN) *adj.* abandoned or deserted

foreseen (fawr SEEN) *v.* recognized in advance; predicted

frantically (FRAN tuh klee) *adv.* acting wildly with anger, worry, or pain

frivolity (frih VOL uh tee) *n.* the state of being frivolous; lacking weight or importance

frustrated (FRUHS trayt ihd) *adj.* feeling anger and annoyance

G

generate (JEHN uhr ayt) *v.* bring into existence; cause

glimpses (GLIHMPS ihz) *n.* brief views; glances

grief (greef) *n.* deep sadness

H

heed (heed) *v.* pay close attention to

hesitantly (HEHZ uh tuhnt lee) *adv.* in an unsure or cautious way

I

imitate (IHM uh tayt) *v.* act the same as; copy

immense (ih MEHNS) *adj.* very large

impairments (ihm PAIR muhnts) *n.* injury; damage; weakness

impossible (ihm POS uh buhl) *adj.* disagreeable; unreasonable

impoverished (ihm POV uhr ihsht) *adj.* extremely poor; miserable and exhausted

impractical (ihm PRAK tih kuhl) *adj.* not practical; unwise

incorporate (ihn KAWR puh rayt) *v.* include as part of the whole

indignity (ihn DIHG nuh tee) *n.* feeling that one has been disrespected

infinitely (IHN fuh niht lee) *adv.* enormously; remarkably

ingenious (ihn JEEN yuhs) *adj.* marked by originality, resourcefulness, and cleverness

instinctively (ihn STIHNGK tihv lee) *adv.* done automatically, without thinking

interview subject (IHN tuhr vyoo) (*SUHB* jehkt) *n.* the person being interviewed

invested (ihn VEHST ihd) *v.* devoted one's care or interest to something

J

justify (JUHS tuh fy) *v.* give sufficient reason for an action

L

lamented (luh MEHNT ihd) *v.* expressed regret

lecture (LEHK chuhr) *v.* talk in a critical way that seems unfair

light/shadow (lyt) / (SHAD oh) *n.* elements that define and enhance parts of an image

lineage (LIH nee ihj) *n.* ancestry or pedigree

linguists (LIHN gwihsts) *n.* people who study how language works

localizing (LOH kuh lyz ihng) *v.* gathering, collecting, or concentrating in a particular place

logical (LOJ ih kuhl) *adj.* supported by reason or evidence

looming (LOO mihng) *adj.* appearing large or threatening

lucid (LOO sihd) *adj.* clearly understandable; having full use of one's faculties

lurched (lurcht) *v.* staggered; moved unsteadily

M

maladies (MAL uh deez) *n.* illnesses or diseases

malcontent (MAL kuhn tehnt) *n.* person who is always unhappy

melded (MEHL dihd) *v.* blended; combined

miser (MY zuhr) *n.* greedy person who keeps and refuses to spend money, even at the expense of his or her own comfort

morose (muh ROHS) *adj.* gloomy; ill-tempered

mosaic (moh ZAY ihk) *adj.* made of many small pieces of colored glass or stone

mutation (myoo TAY shuhn) *n.* change in form, nature, or qualities

mystery (MIHS tuh ree) *n.* quality of being unexplained or kept secret

N

notable (NOH tuh buhl) *adj.* important; remarkable

O

observation (ob zuhr VAY shuhn) *n.* act of watching or noticing; something observed

omniscient (om NIH shuhnt) *adj.* all-knowing

outcome (OWT kuhm) *n.* end result

P

parallel (PAR uh lehl) *adj.* having the same direction or nature; similar

passion (PASH uhn) *n.* intense feeling or belief

penitence (PEHN ih tuhns) *n.* sorrow for one's sins or faults

permit (puhr MIHT) *v.* allow

perseverance (pur suh VIHR uhns) *n.* continued, patient effort

persevere (puhr suh VIHR) *v.* continue despite difficulty

perspective (puhr SPEHK tihv) *n.* particular way of looking at something; point of view

perspective (puhr SPEHK tihv) *n.* technique used to create the illusion of a three-dimensional world on a two-dimensional surface, such as a piece of paper

philanthropist (fih LAN thruh pihst) *n.* wealthy person who donates to charities

philosophy (fih LOS uh fee) *n.* pursuit of wisdom; system of beliefs and attitudes

plaintive (PLAYN tihv) *adj.* sounding sad and mournful

plight (plyt) *n.* serious or harmful condition or situation

pronouncing (pruh NOWN sihng) *v.* speaking words correctly

proportion (pruh PAWR shuhn) *n.* size of objects in relation to each other or to background

puzzled (PUHZ uhld) *adj.* confused and unable to understand something

R

ravaged (RAV ihjd) *v.* destroyed or damaged badly

rebuke (rih BYOOK) *n.* severe or stern criticism; scolding

recording (rih KAWR dihng) *v.* storing sounds in a form, such as a digital file, so that they can be heard again in the future

relay (ree LAY) *v.* pass along, communicate

release (rih LEES) *n.* act of letting go; *v.* let go; set free

reproach (rih PROHCH) *n.* criticism or disapproval

resilience (rih ZIHL yuhns) *n.* ability to recover quickly

resolute (REHZ uh loot) *adj.* determined

resolved (rih ZOLVD) *v.* offered a solution for; solved

rural (RUR uhl) *adj.* characteristic of the country; of or pertaining to agriculture

ruthless (ROOTH lihs) *adj.* having no compassion or pity

S

sensation (sehn SAY shuhn) *n.* state of excited interest; an indefinite bodily feeling

set (seht) *n.* where the interview takes place

severe (suh VEER) *adj.* (of something bad or undesirable) very great; intense

shrinking (SHRIHNK ihng) *v.* moving back or away

signals (SIHG nuhlz) *n.* gestures, actions, or sounds used to convey information or instructions

sorrow (SOR oh) *n.* great sadness; suffering

sound effects (sownd) (uh FEHKTS) *n.* sounds produced artificially for a radio production

squabbling (SKWOB lihng) *v.* fighting noisily over small matters

squandered (SKWON duhrd) *v.* spent extravagantly or foolishly

stillness (STIHL nihs) *n.* absence of noise or motion

stricken (STRIHK uhn) *adj.* very badly affected by trouble or illness

strive (stryv) *v.* make a great effort; try very hard

struggling (STRUHG lihng) *v.* trying to do with difficulty

submerged (suhb MURJD) *adj.* completely covered with a liquid

supervision (soo pur VIH zhun) *n.* act of watching over someone

T

temperate (TEHM puh riht) *adj.* not too hot or cold; mild

term (turm) *n.* word or expression that has a specific meaning

threatening (THREHT uhn ihng) *adj.* dangerous

toil (toyl) *v.* work hard and with difficulty

tone (tohn) *n.* the emotional quality of the conversation between the interviewer and the subject

transmit (tranz MIHT) *v.* cause something to pass from one thing to another

trembling (TREHM blihng) *v.* shaking uncontrollably

U

unending (uhn EHN dihng) *adj.* never stopping

V

vast (vast) *adj.* immense

W

wanderlust (WON duhr luhst) *n.* a strong desire to travel aimlessly

widespread (WYD SPREHD) *adj.* occurring in many places

El vocabulario académico está en **letra azul**.

A

accomplishments / logros *s.* objetivos alcanzados; hazañas; tareas realizadas hábilmente

actors' delivery / elocución de los actores *s.* manera en que los actores dicen sus diálogos

affinity / afinidad *n.* gusto o simpatía por algo; similitud de características que sugiere relación entre dos cosas

agricultural / agrícola *adj.* relativo a la ciencia o al arte del cultivo y la labranza de la tierra

altered / alteró *v.* cambió

ancestors / ancestros *s.* personas de las cuales alguien desciende; antepasados

anticipated / previó *v.* vio con anticipación, esperó

aptitude / aptitud *s.* habilidad natural o talento

assumption / supuesto *s.* dato o enunciado que se da por hecho

atmosphere / atmósfera *s.* el gas que envuelve la Tierra; el aire

attain / alcanzar *v.* conseguir o lograr

awe / sobrecogimiento *s.* respeto reverencial mezclado con temor o asombro

B

background music / música de fondo *s.* música que no es el centro de lo que ocurre en escena

barriers / barreras *s.* obstáculos; cosas que bloquean el paso

benefit / beneficiar *v.* obtener resultados positivos o útiles; ser favorecido por

besieged / sitiado *adj.* rodeado para su captura

bitterness / amargura *s.* sentimiento causado por el dolor, la tristeza o el arrepentimiento

blight / plaga *s.* algo que se echa a perder, impide el crecimiento o destruye

C

cacophony / cacofonía *s.* sonidos desagradables o discordantes; ruido de alto volumen

canals / canales *s.* cauces de agua artificial para el transporte o el riego

catapulted / catapultó *v.* lanzó con la fuerza de una máquina

celebrate / celebrar *v.* ensalzar una ocasión especial realizando una actividad placentera

certainty / certeza *s.* conocimiento de que algo es cierto; libre de toda duda

charitable / comprensivo *adj.* benévolo y flexible; indulgente

coaxed / persuadió *v.* indujo a alguien a hacer algo, convenció por medio de adulaciones

composition / composición *s.* disposición de elementos en una obra de artes visuales

conducive / propicio *adj.* que promueve o favorece algo

consequence / consecuencia *s.* resultado; efecto

consequences / consecuencias *s.* resultados de una acción o acciones

contact / contacto *s.* conexión; comunicación

contradict / contradecir *v.* discutir o estar en desacuerdo con alguien o algo

covetous / codicioso *adj.* envidioso, avaricioso

D

demoralized / desmoralizado *adj.* desalentado; derrotado

deserted / abandonado *adj.* que está desatendido; vacío

determination / determinación *s.* conclusión; decisión firme

devastated / devastó *v.* destruyó; apenó profundamente

dialogue / diálogo *s.* conversación; palabras dichas por los personajes en un cuento, drama, etc.

dire / aciago *adj.* funesto, sumamente grave o urgente

discordant / discordante *adj.* sin armonía

discredit / desacreditar *v.* no creer; dudar de

discredit / descrédito *s.* pérdida o falta de fe; desprestigio

dispelled / disipó *v.* desvaneció; esparció

disposal / desecho *s.* acción de deshacerse de algo

dissent / disentir *v.* estar en desacuerdo

dissent / disentimiento *s.* desacuerdo

distorting / distorsionando *v.* torciendo formas o sentidos hasta deformarlos

diversity / diversidad *s.* variedad; diferencias dentro de un grupo

doomed / condenado *adj.* destinado a un final desgraciado

dreaded / se aterró *v.* sintió gran temor o renuencia extrema

E

earnest / serio *adj.* que no bromea

elucidate / esclarecer *adj.* dejar en claro, especialmente por medio de la explicación, la demostración o el análisis

enthusiastically / con estusiasmo *adv.* con interés y ganas

envision / visualizar *v.* imaginar

evident /evidente *adj.* *claro* para la visión o el entendimiento

explode / explotar *v.* estallar o hacerse añicos violentamente

extinct / extinto *adj.* que ya no existe

extraordinary / extraordinario *adj.* mejor que lo ordinario; excepcional

F

fathom / desentrañar *v.* entender; llegar a comprender algo

fluently / fluidamente *adv.* fácilmente, con soltura

flung / lanzó *v.* arrojó con fuerza

forlorn / abandonado *adj.* dejado atrás o desierto

foreseen / previsto *v.* reconocido con anticipación; predicho

frantically / frenéticamente *adv.* actuando atacadamente, con enojo, preocupación o dolor

frivolity / frivolidad *s.* cualidad de frívolo; carente de peso o importancia

frustrated / frustrado *adj.* enojado y molesto

G

generate / generar *v.* crear, causar la existencia de algo; provocar

glimpses / vistazos *s.* miradas breves; ojeadas

grief / pesar *s.* gran pena o tristeza

H

heed / prestar atención *v.* mantener plena concentración en algo o alguien

hesitantly / con vacilación *adv.* de manera reacia

I

imitate / imitar *v.* actuar igual a como lo hace alguien; copiar

immense / inmenso *adj.* enorme

impairments / deficiencias *s.* lesiones; daños; debilidades

impossible / imposible *adj.* incapaz de existir u ocurrir

impoverished / empobrecido *adj.* reducido a la pobreza extrema

impractical / impráctico *adj.* poco práctico; insensato

incorporate / incorporar *v.* incluir como parte de un todo

indignity / indignidad *s.* cualidad de no sentirse digno o respetado

infinitely / infinitamente *adv.* de manera enorme o muy notable

ingenious / ingenioso *adj.* caracterizado por su originalidad, maña y astucia

instinctively / instintivamente *adv.* hecho de manera automática, sin pensar

interview subject / entrevistado *s.* persona a la que se entrevista

invested / invirtió *v.* dedicó su cuidado o interés a algo

J

justify / justificar *v.* dar razones suficientes para un acto

L

lamented / lamentó *v.* expresó arrepentimiento

lecture / sermonear *v.* hablar de un modo crítico que se considera injusto

light/shadow / luz y sombra *s.* elementos que definen y mejoran partes de una imagen

lineage / linaje *s.* ascendencia o genealogía

linguists / lingüistas *s.* personas que estudian el modo en que funciona el lenguaje

localizing / localizando *v.* juntando, reuniendo o concentrando en un lugar particular

logical / lógico *adj.* fundado en la razón o en la evidencia

looming / amenazante *adj.* que parece peligroso

lucid / lúcido *adj.* claro y comprensible; en pleno uso de sus facultades

lurched / se tambaleó *v.* dio tumbos, se movió a tropezones

M

maladies / enfermedades *s.* dolencias

malcontent / insatisfecho *s.* persona que está siempre descontenta

melded / mezcló *v.* unió, combinó

miser / avaro *s.* persona tacaña que se niega a gastar dinero, aun cuando sacrifique su propia comodidad

morose / taciturno *adj.* malhumorado; melancólico

mosaic / mosaico *s.* obra hecha con muchas piezas pequeñas de vidrio o piedras de colores

mutation / mutación *s.* cambio de forma, naturaleza o atributos

mystery / misterio *s.* cualidad de ser inexplicable o un secreto

N

notable / notable *adj.* extraordinario; destacado

O

observation / observación *s.* acción de contemplar; algo que se observa

omniscient / omnisciente *adj.* que todo lo sabe

outcome / resultado *s.* consecuencia final de algo

P

parallel / paralelo *adj.* que va en la misma dirección o tiene la misma naturaleza; similar

passion / pasión *s.* sentimiento o creencia intensos

penitence / penitencia *s.* pesar por los propios pecados o defectos

permit / permitir *v.* dar permiso, autorizar

perseverance / perseverancia *s.* esfuerzo constante y paciente

persevere / perseverar *v.* seguir pese a las dificultades

perspective / perspectiva *s. manera particular de* ver *las cosas; punto de vista*

perspective / perspective *s.* técnica usada para crear la ilusión de un mundo tridimensional en una superficie bidimensional, como un pedazo de papel

philanthropist / filántropo *s.* persona rica que hace donativos a causas benéficas

philosophy / filosofía *s.* búsqueda de sabiduría; sistema de creencias y actitudes

plaintive / lastimero *adj.* que suena triste y quejumbroso

plight / aprieto *s.* situación o condición grave o perjudicial

pronouncing / pronunciando *v.* diciendo palabras correctamente

proportion / proporción *s.* tamaño de los objetos en relación con otros objetos o con el fondo

puzzled / perplejo *adj.* confundido y sin poder entender algo

R

ravaged / asoló *v.* destruyó o dañó gravemente

rebuke / reprimenda *s.* crítica severa; regaño

recording / grabando *v.* registrando sonido, por ejemplo, en formato digital, para que pueda volver a oírse en el futuro

relay / comunicar *v.* hacer llegar información

release / liberación *s.* acción de dejar ir

release / liberar *v.* soltar; dejar libre

reproach / reproche *s.* desaprobación; crítica

resilience / resiliencia *s.* capacidad de recuperarse rápidamente

resolute / resuelto *adj.* firme y con un propósito claro

resolved / resolvería *v.* ofrecería una solución

rural / rural *adj.* relativo al campo; perteneciente a la agricultura

ruthless / despiadado *adj.* sin compasión o piedad

S

sensation / sensación *s.* interés fuerte; impresión corporal indefinida

set / set *s.* donde tiene lugar una entrevista

severe / severo *adj.* (de algo malo o indeseable) muy fuerte o intenso

shrinking / replegándose *v.* retrocediendo o alejándose

signals / señales *s.* gestos, actos o sonidos que se usan para transmitir información o instrucciones

sorrow / pena *s.* tristeza profunda; sufrimiento

sound effects / efectos de sonido *s.* sonidos producidos artificialmente para acompañar a un guión radiofónico

squabbling / reñir *v.* pelearse en voz muy alta sobre asuntos de poca importancia

squandered / despilfarró *v.* malgastó, derrochó

stillness / quietud *s.* ausencia de ruido o movimiento

stricken / afligido *adj.* muy afectado por problemas o por una enfermedad

strive / esforzarse *v.* hacer un gran esfuerzo; luchar

struggling / luchando *v.* intentando salir adelante con dificultad

submerged / sumergido *adj.* cubierto completamente por un líquido

supervision / supervisión *s.* acción de vigilar a alguien

T

temperate / templado *adj.* ni frío ni caliente; moderado

term / término *s.* palabra o expresión que tiene un significado específico

threatening / amenazador *adj.* peligroso

toil / esforzarse *v.* trabajar arduamente

tone / tono *s.* cualidad emocional de la conversación entre el entrevistador y el entrevistado

transmit / transmitir *v.* trasladar, transferir; hacer llegar de una cosa a otra

trembling / estremeciéndose *v.* temblando descontroladamente

U

unending / infinito *adj.* sin fin

V

vast / vasto *adj.* inmenso

W

wanderlust / espíritu viajero *s.* fuerte deseo de viajar sin rumbo

widespread / generalizado *adj.* que ocurre en muchos lugares

ANALOGY An ***analogy*** makes a comparison between two or more things that are similar in some ways but otherwise unalike.

ANECDOTE An ***anecdote*** is a brief nonfiction story about an interesting, amusing, or strange event. Writers tell anecdotes to entertain or to make a point.

ARGUMENT In an ***argument***, the writer states and supports a claim, or opinion, based on factual evidence and logical reasoning. Most arguments are composed of an ***introduction***, in which a claim is stated; the ***body***, in which the claim is supported by evidence; and the ***conclusion***, in which the claim is summarized or restated.

AUDIENCE The ***audience*** of a literary work is the person or people that a writer or speaker is addressing. The writer or speaker must consider the interests, knowledge, and education of his or her intended audience, which will help shape the work.

AUTHOR'S POINT OF VIEW The attitude toward a topic an author reveals in a piece of nonfiction writing shows the ***author's point of view***.

AUTHOR'S PURPOSE An ***author's purpose*** is his or her main reason for writing. For example, an author may want to entertain, inform, or persuade the reader. Sometimes an author is trying to teach a moral lesson or reflect on an experience. An author may have more than one purpose for writing.

AUTOBIOGRAPHY An ***autobiography*** is the story of the writer's own life, told by the writer. Autobiographical writing may tell about the person's whole life or only a part of it.

Because autobiographies are about real people and events, they are a form of nonfiction. Most autobiographies are written in the ***first-person point of view***.

BIOGRAPHY A ***biography*** is a form of nonfiction in which a writer tells the life story of another person. Most biographies are written about famous or admirable people. Although biographies are nonfiction, the most effective ones share the qualities of good narrative writing.

BLOG A ***blog post*** is a piece of online writing added to an online journal, called a ***blog***. Writers of blogs provide information or express thoughts on various subjects.

BOOK FEATURES ***Book features*** can include acknowledgements, a foreword, a preface, an introduction, and references to help the audience gain background information. In an ***acknowledgements*** section, the author of a book expresses gratitude to all those who have helped him or her in researching, writing, and editing the book. A ***foreword*** is an introductory note that is written by a person other than the author. A ***preface*** is the author's own statement about the book. It usually includes reasons why he or she wrote the book, the type of research used, and any other background information that may help readers understand the book. An ***introduction*** appears either in the front of the book or at the beginning of the text. It focuses on the content of the book, rather than its origins and background. ***References*** for a book usually appear in the back of the book before the index, if there is one. They provide all the necessary documentation for the work.

CHARACTER A ***character*** is a person or an animal that takes part in the action of a literary work. The main, or ***major,*** character is the most important character in a story, poem, or play. A ***minor*** character is one who takes part in the action but is not the focus of attention. Character qualities include the characteristics, attitudes and values that a character possesses—such as dependability, intelligence, selfishness, or stubbornness. These qualities influence the resolution of the conflict in the story.

Characters are sometimes classified as flat or round. A ***flat character*** is one-sided and often stereotypical. A ***round character,*** on the other hand, is fully developed and exhibits many traits—often both faults and virtues. Characters can also be classified as dynamic or static. A ***dynamic character*** is one who changes or grows during the course of the work. A ***static character*** is one who does not change.

CHARACTER TRAITS ***Character traits*** are the individual qualities that make each character unique.

CHARACTERIZATION ***Characterization*** is the act of creating and developing a character. Authors use two major methods of characterization—***direct*** and ***indirect.*** When using direct characterization, a writer states the ***characters' traits,*** or characteristics.

When describing a character indirectly, a writer depends on the reader to draw conclusions about the character's traits. Sometimes the writer tells what other participants in the story say and think about the character.

CITATION A ***citation*** gives credit in the body of a research paper to an author whose ideas are either quoted directly or paraphrased. It usually gives the author's last name, the year of publication, and a page number or range in parentheses after the words or ideas that are borrowed. To complete the citation, the entire bibliographic entry is included in the References at the end of the research paper. ***Footnotes*** are numbered notes that are placed at the foot or bottom of a page. They cite sources and references or comment on a particular part of the text on the page. ***Endnotes*** are numbered notes that are placed at the end of the article or book and provide the source of the information quoted within it.

CLAIM A ***claim*** is a statement of the author's position on an issue. In an argument, an author supports his or her claim with data, examples, or other types of evidence.

CLIMAX The ***climax,*** also called the turning point, is the high point in the action of the plot. It is the moment of greatest tension, when the outcome of the plot hangs in the balance. See ***Plot.***

COLLABORATIVE DISCUSSION The exploration of a topic in a group setting in which all individuals participate is called a ***collaborative discussion.***

COMEDY A ***comedy*** is a literary work, especially a play, which is light, often humorous or satirical, and ends happily. Comedies frequently depict ordinary characters faced with temporary difficulties and conflicts. Types of comedy include ***romantic comedy,*** which involves problems between lovers, and the ***comedy of manners,*** which satirically challenges social customs of a society.

CONFLICT A ***conflict*** is a struggle between opposing forces. Conflict is one of the most important elements of stories, novels, and plays because it causes the action. There are two kinds of conflict: external and internal. An ***external conflict*** is one in which a character struggles against some outside force, such as another person. Another kind of external conflict may occur between a character and some force in nature.

An ***internal conflict*** takes place within the mind of a character. The character struggles to make a decision, take an action, or overcome a feeling.

CONNOTATIONS The ***connotation*** of a word is the set of ideas associated with it in addition to its explicit meaning. The connotation of a word can be personal, based on individual experiences. More often, cultural connotations—those recognizable by most people in a group—determine a writer's word choices.

CONTROLLING IDEA The ***controlling idea*** is a statement of the main idea or purpose of an informational text or research paper. See ***Thesis***.

COUNTERCLAIM An opposing view to the main claim of an argument is called a ***counterclaim***. Another name for counterclaim is ***counterargument.***

CONSTRUCTIVE CRITCISM Respectful disagreements and critiques, meant to improve an outcome, are referred to as ***constructive criticism***.

CULTURAL CONTEXT The ***cultural context*** of a literary work is the economic, social, and historical environment of the characters. This includes the attitudes and customs of that culture and historical period.

DENOTATION The ***denotation*** of a word is its dictionary meaning, independent of other associations, that the word may have. The denotation of the word ***lake,*** for example, is "an inland body of water." "Vacation spot" and "place where the fishing is good" are connotations of the word ***lake.***

DESCRIPTION A ***description*** is a portrait, in words, of a person, place, or object. Descriptive writing uses images that appeal to the five senses—sight, hearing, touch, taste, and smell.

DIALECT ***Dialect*** is the form of a language spoken by people in a particular region or group. Dialects differ in pronunciation, grammar, and word choice. The English language is divided into many dialects. British English differs from American English.

DIALOGUE A ***dialogue*** is a conversation between characters. In poems, novels, and short stories, dialogue is usually set off by quotation marks to indicate a speaker's exact words.

In a play, dialogue follows the names of the characters, and no quotation marks are used.

DICTION ***Diction*** is a writer's word choice and the way the writer puts those words together. Diction is part of a writer's style and may be described as formal or informal, plain or fancy, ordinary or technical, sophisticated or down-to-earth, old-fashioned or modern.

DIGITAL TEXT ***Digital text*** is the electronic version of a written text. Digital text is accessed on the Internet or on a computer or other electronic device.

DIRECT QUOTATIONS Quotations that show a person's exact words in quotation marks are ***direct quotations. Personal interviews*** are a research method often used by authors as a source of direct quotations.

DRAMA A ***drama*** is a story written to be performed by actors. Although a drama is meant to be performed, one can also read the script, or written version, and imagine the action. The ***script*** of a drama is made up of dialogue and stage directions. The ***dialogue*** is the words spoken by the actors. The ***stage directions,*** usually printed in italics, tell how the actors should look, move, and speak. They also describe the setting, sound effects, and lighting.

Dramas are often divided into parts called ***acts.*** The acts are often divided into smaller parts called ***scenes.***

EDITORIAL An ***editorial*** is a type of argument that typically appears in a newspaper and takes a position on a specific topic.

ESSAY An ***essay*** is a short nonfiction work about a particular subject. Most essays have a single major focus and a clear introduction, body, and conclusion.

There are many types of essays. An ***informal essay*** uses casual, conversational language. A ***historical essay*** gives facts, explanations, and insights about historical events. An ***expository essay*** explains an idea by breaking it down. A ***narrative essay*** tells a story about a real-life experience. An ***informational essay*** explains a process. A ***persuasive essay*** offers an opinion and supports it. A ***humorous essay*** uses humor to achieve the author's purpose. A ***descriptive essay*** creates an engaging picture of a subject, by using vivid, sensory details. A ***how-to essay*** is a step-by-step explanation of how to make or do something. An ***explanatory essay*** is a short piece of nonfiction in which the author explains, defines, or interprets ideas, events, or processes. A ***reflective essay*** is a brief prose work in which an author presents his or her thoughts or feelings—or reflections—about an experience or an idea.

An ***objective point of view*** is based on fact. It does not relate opinions, feelings, or emotions. A ***subjective point of view,*** on the other hand, may include personal opinions, emotions, and feelings. A persuasive essay is an example of subjective point of view, or ***bias.*** The persuasive essay writer attempts to get the reader to agree with his or her opinion.

EVIDENCE ***Evidence*** is all the information that is used to support an argument. Various types of evidence include facts, examples, statistics, quotations, expert testimony, observations, or personal experiences.

EXAMPLE An ***example*** is a fact, idea or event that supports an idea or insight.

EXPOSITION In the plot of a story or a drama, the ***exposition,*** or introduction, is the part of the work that introduces the characters, setting, and basic situation.

EXPOSITORY WRITING ***Expository writing*** is writing that explains or informs.

FANTASY A ***fantasy*** is highly imaginative writing that contains elements not found in real life. Examples of fantasy include stories that involve supernatural elements, stories that resemble fairy tales, stories that deal with imaginary places and creatures, and science-fiction stories.

FICTION ***Fiction*** is prose writing that tells about imaginary characters and events. Short stories and novels are works of fiction. Some writers base their fiction on actual events and people, adding invented characters, dialogue, settings, and plots. Other writers rely on imagination alone.

There are many types of fiction. An ***adventure story*** describes an event that happens outside a character's ordinary life. It is often characterized by danger and much action, with a plot that moves quickly. A ***fantasy*** is highly imaginative writing that contains elements not found in real life. Examples of fantasy include stories that involve supernatural elements, stories that resemble fairy tales, stories that deal with imaginary places and creatures, and science-fiction stories. A ***mystery*** usually involves a mysterious death or other crime that must be solved. Each suspect must have a reasonable motive and opportunity to commit the crime. The main character must work as a detective who solves the mystery from the facts that are presented in the story. A ***myth*** is an tale meant to explain the actions of gods (and the human heroes who interact with them) or the causes of natural phenomena. ***Science fiction*** combines elements of fiction and fantasy with scientific fact. Many science-fiction stories are set in the future. ***Historical fiction*** is set in the past during a particular historical time period, but with fictional characters or a combination of historical and fictional characters.

FIGURATIVE LANGUAGE ***Figurative language*** is writing or speech that is not meant to be taken literally. The many types of figurative language are known as ***figures of speech.*** Common figures of speech include metaphor, personification, and simile. Writers use figurative language to state ideas in vivid and imaginative ways.

FLASHBACK A ***flashback*** is a scene within a narrative that interrupts the sequence of events to relate events that happened in the past. Writers use flashbacks to show what motivates a character or to reveal something about a character's past. A flashback is part of a ***nonlinear plot*** since it interrupts the normal chronological order of events to go back into the past. In a ***linear plot***, all the events are told in chronological order.

FORESHADOWING ***Foreshadowing*** is the use of clues hinting at events that are going to happen later in the plot of a narrative. This technique helps create suspense, which keeps the reader wondering what will happen next.

FRAME STORY A ***frame story*** is a story that brackets—or frames—another story or group of stories. This framing device creates a story-within-a-story narrative structure.

FREE VERSE ***Free verse*** is poetry not written with a ***formal structure***, or in a regular, rhythmical pattern, or meter. The poet is free to write lines of any length or with any number of stresses, or beats. Free verse is therefore less constraining than ***metrical verse,*** in which every line must have a certain length and a certain number of stresses.

GENRE A ***genre*** is a division or type of literature. Literature is commonly divided into three major genres: poetry, prose, and drama. Each major genre is, in turn, divided into lesser genres, as follows:

1. ***Poetry:*** lyric poetry, concrete poetry, dramatic poetry, narrative poetry, epic poetry
2. ***Prose:*** fiction (novels and short stories) and nonfiction (biography, autobiography, letters, essays, and reports)

3. ***Drama:*** serious drama and tragedy, comic drama, melodrama, and farce

GRAPHIC FEATURE A ***graphic feature*** is a visual aid that helps the reader better understand information in a text. Graphic features can include images, graphs, charts, type treatments, icons, and other visual elements that organize, emphasize, or augment certain aspects of a text. Authors use these features to achieve a certain purpose.

HISTORICAL CONTEXT The ***historical context*** of a literary work includes the actual political and social events and trends of the time. When a work takes place in the past, knowledge about that historical time period can help the reader understand its setting, background, culture, and message, as well as the attitudes and actions of its characters. A reader must also take into account the historical context in which the writer was creating the work, which may be different from the time period of the work's setting.

HUMOR ***Humor*** is writing intended to evoke laughter. While most humorists try to entertain, humor can also be used to convey a serious theme.

HYPERBOLE ***Hyperbole*** is a form of figurative language that uses exaggeration for effect.

IDIOM An ***idiom*** is an expression that has a meaning particular to a language or region.

IMAGERY ***Imagery*** is a technique of writing with images.

IMAGES ***Images*** are words or phrases that appeal to one or more of the five senses. Writers use images to describe how their subjects look, sound, feel, taste, and smell. Poets often paint images, or word pictures, that appeal to the senses. These pictures help you to experience the poem fully.

INFERENCES An ***inference*** is a guess based on clues. Very often in literature, authors leave some details unstated; it is up to readers to "fill in the blanks" and infer details about characters, events, and setting.

IRONY ***Irony*** is a contradiction between what happens and what is expected. There are three main types of irony. ***Situational irony*** occurs when something happens that directly contradicts the expectations of the characters or the audience. ***Verbal irony*** is created when words are used to suggest the opposite of their meaning. In ***dramatic irony,*** the audience is aware of something that the character or speaker is not aware of. The result is suspense or humor.

JOURNAL A ***journal*** is a daily or periodic account of events and the writer's thoughts and feelings about those events. Personal journals are not normally written for publication, but sometimes they do get published later with permission from the author or the author's family.

LETTERS A ***letter*** is a written communication from one person to another. In personal letters, the writer shares information and his or her thoughts and feelings with one other person or group. Although letters are not normally written for publication, they sometimes do get published later with the permission of the author or the author's family.

LOGICAL FALLACY A ***logical fallacy*** is an argument that may appear to be logical but is actually based on a faulty assumption. There are many types of logical fallacies. ***Loaded language*** is a specific choice of words designed to persuade an audience by appealing to emotions or stereotypes. A ***sweeping generalization*** applies a general rule to a specific instance without sufficient evidence. A ***bandwagon appeal*** argues that if something is popular and everybody else is doing it, so should you. ***Circular reasoning*** asserts its conclusion as one of the premises of the argument, thus expecting the listener to accept the conclusion when it has not been proven.

MAIN IDEA The ***main idea*** is the ***central idea*** or most important point in a text.

MEDIA Stories and information are shared using different forms of ***media***. Books and magazines are a type of media. Film, video, and digital are other forms of media. A ***multimedia presentation*** is created from a combination of words, images, sounds, and video.

MEDIA ACCOUNTS ***Media accounts*** are reports, explanations, opinions, or descriptions written for television, radio, newspapers, and magazines. While some media accounts report only facts, others include the writer's thoughts and reflections.

METAPHOR A ***metaphor*** is a figure of speech in which something is described as though it were something else. A metaphor, like a simile, works by pointing out a similarity between two unlike things. An ***extended metaphor*** is a metaphor that is sustained and developed over several lines or an entire poem.

METER The ***meter*** of a poem is its rhythmical pattern. In poetry with a regular meter, this pattern is based on the number and arrangement of strong and weak beats, or stresses, in each line.

MONOLOGUE A ***monologue*** is a dramatic speech presented by a single character in a play. The character speaks from the first-person point of view and relates his or her thoughts and feelings.

MOOD The ***mood*** is the feeling created in a reader by a piece of writing. Writers create mood by using imagery, word choice and descriptive details.

MOTIVE A ***motive*** is a reason that explains or partially explains a character's thoughts, feelings, actions, or speech. Writers try to make their characters' motives, or motivations, as clear as possible. If the motives of a main character are not clear, then the character will not be believable.

Characters are often motivated by needs, such as food and shelter. They are also motivated by feelings, such as fear, love, and pride. Motives may be obvious or hidden.

MULTIMODAL TEXT A ***multimodal text*** uses two or more modes of communication to convey meaning—for example, images, spoken language, sound effects, and music in addition to written language. Examples of multimodal texts include picture books that have both images and text and web pages with oral language, sound effects, images, animations, and written language.

NARRATION ***Narration*** is writing that tells a story. The act of telling a story is also called narration. Any story told in fiction, nonfiction, poetry, or even drama is called a narrative.

Writers of narratives employ many techniques to bring their stories to life. For example, most narratives contain a plot, setting, characters, and theme. The readers' experience can be enhanced by varied **narrative pacing**, in which the writer speeds up or slows down the plot events to create effects such as suspense.

NARRATIVE A ***narrative*** is a story. Novels and short stories are types of fictional narratives. Biographies and autobiographies are nonfiction narratives.

NARRATOR A ***narrator*** is a speaker or a character who tells a story. The narrator's perspective is the way he or she sees things. A ***third-person narrator*** is one who stands outside the action and speaks about it. A ***first-person narrator*** is one who tells a story and participates in its action.

NONFICTION ***Nonfiction*** is prose writing that presents and explains ideas or that tells about real people, places, objects, or events. Autobiographies, biographies, essays, reports, letters, memos, and newspaper articles are all types of nonfiction.

NOVEL A ***novel*** is a long work of fiction. Novels contain such elements as characters, plot, conflict, and setting. The writer of novels, or novelist, develops these elements. In addition to its main plot, a novel may contain one or more subplots, or independent, related stories. A novel may also have several themes. See ***Fiction*** and ***Short Story.***

ONOMATOPOEIA ***Onomatopoeia*** is the use of words that imitate sounds. ***Crash, buzz, screech, hiss, neigh, jingle,*** and ***cluck*** are examples of onomatopoeia. ***Chickadee, towhee,*** and ***whippoorwill*** are onomatopoeic names of birds.

ORGANIZATION The structure of a text or media presentation is referred to as its **organization**. Common organizational structures are cause-and-effect, comparison-and contrast, order of importance, and chronological order. Writers choose organizational structures that best suit their topic and purpose.

OXYMORON An ***oxymoron*** (pl. ***oxymora***) is a figure of speech that links two opposite or contradictory words in order to point out an idea or situation that seems contradictory or inconsistent but on closer inspection turns out to be somehow true.

PARAPHRASE When you ***paraphrase***, you restate a text using your own words.

PERSONIFICATION ***Personification*** is a type of figurative language in which a nonhuman subject is given human characteristics.

PERSUASION ***Persuasion*** is used in writing or speech that attempts to convince the reader or listener to adopt a particular opinion or course of action. Newspaper editorials and letters to the editor use persuasion. So do advertisements and campaign speeches given by political candidates.

Writers use a combination of persuasive techniques to argue their point of view. ***Appeals to authority*** use the statements of experts. ***Appeals to emotion*** use words that convey strong feelings. ***Appeals to reason*** use logical arguments backed by facts.

PLAYWRIGHT A ***playwright*** is a person who writes plays. William Shakespeare is regarded as the greatest playwright in English literature.

PLOT ***Plot*** is the sequence of events in which each event results from a previous one and causes the next. In most novels, dramas, short stories, and narrative poems, the plot involves both characters and a central conflict. The plot usually begins with an ***exposition*** that introduces the setting, the characters, and the basic situation. This is followed by the ***inciting incident,*** which introduces the central conflict. The conflict then increases during the ***development*** until it reaches a high point of interest or suspense, the ***climax.*** The climax is followed by the ***falling action,*** or end, of the central conflict. Any events that occur during the ***falling action*** make up the ***resolution*** or ***denouement.*** A ***subplot*** is a secondary story line that complicates or adds depth to the main plot in a narrative. For example, a novel or play may have one or more subplots, or minor stories, in addition to the central conflict.

Some plots do not have all of these parts. Some stories begin with the inciting incident and end with the resolution. See ***Conflict.***

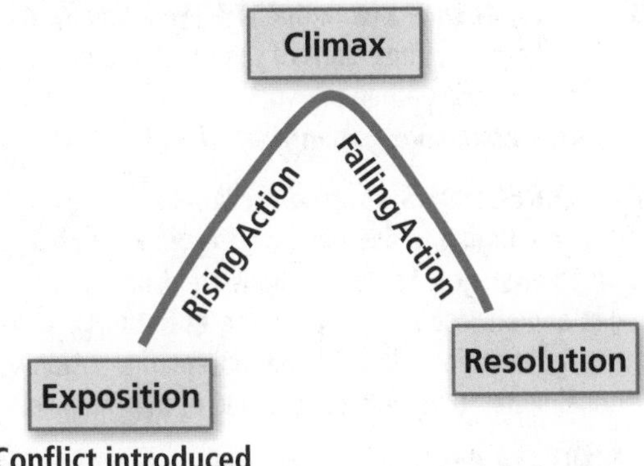

POETRY ***Poetry*** is one of the three classic types of literature, the others being prose and drama. Most poems make use of highly concise, musical, and emotionally charged language. Many also make use of imagery, figurative language, and special devices of sound such as rhyme. Poems often make use of graphical elements in language such as punctuation and capitalization. Some poems may have no punctuation at all. Types of poetry include ***lyric poetry, narrative poetry, epic poetry***, and ***humorous poetry.***

A ***lyric poem*** is a highly musical verse that expresses the observations and feelings of a single speaker. It creates a single, unified impression. A ***narrative poem*** is a story told in verse. Narrative poems often have all the elements of short stories, including characters, conflict, and plot. An ***epic poem*** is a long narrative poem about a larger-than-life hero engaged in a dangerous journey, or quest, that is important to the history of a nation or culture. ***Humorous poems*** are written to make the reader laugh. They are usually brief and often contain word play, puns, interesting rhyme, and alliteration.

POINT OF VIEW ***Point of view*** is the perspective, or vantage point, from which a story is told. It is either a narrator outside the story or a character in the story. ***First-person point of view*** is told by a character who uses the first-person pronoun "I."

The two kinds of ***third-person point of view,*** limited and omniscient, are called "third person" because the narrator uses third-person pronouns such as *he* and *she* to refer to the characters. There is no "I" telling the story.

In stories told from the ***omniscient third-person point of view,*** the narrator knows and tells about what each character feels and thinks.

In stories told from the ***limited third-person point of view,*** the narrator relates the inner thoughts and feelings of only one character, and everything is viewed from this character's perspective.

PRESENTATION A presentation is the act of showing or demonstrating something to an audience. ***Oral presentations***, spoken aloud to a live audience, may include other ***visual presentation*** forms, such as charts, diagrams, illustrations, and photos. Video clips and slide shows often are key parts of ***digital presentations***, which are created partly or entirely on a computer.

PROSE ***Prose*** is the ordinary form of written language. Most writing that is not poetry, drama, or song is considered prose. Prose is one of the major genres of literature and occurs in fiction and nonfiction.

QUOTATION ***Quotations*** are groups of words that are taken from a text, a speech, or an interview and are used or repeated by someone other than the original author or speaker. Quotations must be attributed to the original writer or speaker.

READ CLOSELY To ***read closely*** involves careful analysis of a text, its ideas, and the ways in which the author chooses to express those ideas.

REPETITION ***Repetition*** is the use, more than once, of any element of language—a sound, word, phrase, clause, or sentence. Repetition is used in both prose and poetry.

RESEARCH PAPER A ***research paper*** provides detailed information on a topic or thesis. Effective research papers are built on information from a variety of credible sources, which are credited.

RESOLUTION The ***resolution*** is the outcome of the conflict in a plot.

RETELLING A ***retelling*** of a story can be either written or oral and should include a clear sequence of events and narrative techniques such as dialogue and description.

RHETORICAL DEVICES ***Rhetorical devices*** are special patterns of words and ideas that create emphasis and stir emotion, especially in speeches or other oral presentations. Some of the most common rhetorical devices include ***rhetorical questions,*** or questions asked in order to make a point or create a dramatic affect rather than to get an answer. ***Direct address*** is a rhetorical device wherein a speaker or writer directs a message directly to an individual or a group of people. An ***analogy*** is a comparison that points out the similarities between two things, often explaining something unfamiliar by likening it to something familiar. Analogies are usually extended comparisons. ***Juxtaposition*** as a rhetorical device places two or more ideas or characters side by side for the purpose of comparing and contrasting them.

RHYME ***Rhyme*** is the repetition of sounds at the ends of words. Poets use rhyme to lend a songlike quality to their verses and to emphasize certain words and ideas. Many traditional poems contain ***end rhymes,*** or rhyming words at the ends of lines.

Another common device is the use of ***internal rhymes,*** or rhyming words within lines. Internal rhyme also emphasizes the flowing nature of a poem.

RHYTHM ***Rhythm*** is the pattern of stressed and unstressed syllables in spoken or written language.

SCAN To ***scan*** is to run your eyes over the text to find answers to questions, to clarify, or to find supporting details.

SCENE A ***scene*** is a section of uninterrupted action in the act of a drama.

SCRIPT A ***script*** is the written version of a play or film. It includes ***dialogue*** and ***stage directions***.

SENSORY LANGUAGE ***Sensory language*** is writing or speech that appeals to one or more of the five senses.

SETTING The ***setting*** of a literary work is the time and place of the action. The setting includes all the details of a place and time—the year, the time of day, even the weather. The place may be a specific country, state, region, community, neighborhood, building, institution, or home. Details such as dialects, clothing, customs, and modes of transportation are often used to establish setting. In most stories, the setting serves as a backdrop—a context in which the characters interact. Setting can also help to create a feeling, or atmosphere.

SHORT STORY A ***short story*** is a brief work of fiction. Like a novel, a short story presents a sequence of events, or plot. The plot usually deals with a central conflict faced by a main character, or protagonist. The events in a short story usually communicate a message about life or human nature. This message, or central idea, is the story's theme.

SIMILE A ***simile*** is a figure of speech that uses ***like*** or ***as*** to make a direct comparison between two unlike ideas. Everyday speech often contains similes, such as "pale as a ghost," "good as gold," "spread like wildfire," and "clever as a fox."

SKIM To ***skim*** is to look over the text quickly, to get a sense of important ideas before reading.

SOUND DEVICES ***Sound devices*** are techniques used by writers to give musical effects to their writing. Some of these include ***onomatopoeia, alliteration, rhyme, meter,*** and ***repetition.***

SPEAKER The ***speaker*** is the imaginary voice a poet uses when writing a poem. The speaker is the character who tells the poem. This character, or voice, often is not identified by name. There can be important differences between the poet and the poem's speaker.

SPEECH A ***speech*** is a work that is delivered orally to an audience. There are many kinds of speeches suiting almost every kind of public gathering. Types of speeches include ***dramatic, persuasive,*** and ***informative.***

STAGE DIRECTIONS ***Stage directions*** are notes included in a drama to describe how the work is to be performed or staged. Stage directions are usually printed in italics and enclosed within parentheses or brackets. Some stage directions describe the movements, costumes, emotional states, and ways of speaking of the characters.

STAGING ***Staging*** includes the setting, lighting, costumes, special effects, and music that go into a stage performance of a drama.

SUMMARY A ***summary*** is a short, clear description of the main ideas of something, such as a text, a film, or a presentation. Effective summaries are objective—free from bias or evaluation.

SUSPENSE ***Suspense*** is the growing curiosity, tension, or anxiety the reader feels about the outcome of events in a literary work. Suspense builds until the ***climax***, the high point of tension in the plot, when the conflict reaches a peak. The tension of suspense is part of what keeps the reader engaged in a story and anxious to find out what will happen next.

SYMBOL A ***symbol*** is anything that stands for or represents something else. Symbols are common in everyday life. A dove with an olive branch in its beak is a symbol of peace. A blindfolded woman holding a balanced scale is a symbol of justice. A crown is a symbol of a king's status and authority.

SYMBOLISM ***Symbolism*** is the use of symbols. Symbolism plays an important role in many different types of literature. It can highlight certain elements the author wishes to emphasize and also add levels of meaning.

TEXT FEATURE A ***text feature***, which can also be called a ***print feature***, is a design element that helps to show or augment the organization of a text. Text features can include headings, subheadings, captions, and sidebars.

TEXT STRUCTURE ***Text structure*** is the way in which information in a text is organized or put together. An author chooses a particular text structure according to his or her purpose. An ***advantage and disadvantage*** structure addresses the positive and negative aspects of a topic and then gives an opinion. ***Cause-and-effect*** text structure examines the relationship between events. It provides reasons or an explanation for why something has happened. ***Chronological order*** text relates events in the order in which they happened. ***Classification*** text structure creates categories and then provides examples of things that fit into each category. In ***comparison and contrast*** text structure, an author presents the similarities and differences between two subjects. A comparison and contrast text can be organized using **point-by-point organization** in which one aspect of both subjects is discussed, then another aspect, and so on. **Block method organization** presents all the details of one subject, and then all the details about the next subject.

THEME A ***theme*** is a central message in a literary work that can usually be expressed in a general statement about human beings or about life. The theme of a work is not a summary of its plot.

Although a theme may be stated directly in the text, it is more often presented indirectly. When the theme is stated indirectly, or implied, the reader must figure out what the theme is by looking at what the work reveals about people or life. A single text may have multiple themes. The various sub-themes are usually closely related to the central theme.

THESIS The ***thesis*** of a text is the main idea or purpose of an essay or research paper. See ***Controlling Idea.***

TONE The ***tone*** of a literary work is the writer's attitude toward his or her audience and subject. The tone can often be described by a single adjective, such as ***formal*** or ***informal, serious*** or ***playful, bitter*** or ***ironic.*** Factors that contribute to the tone are word choice, sentence structure, line length, rhyme, rhythm, and repetition.

UNIVERSAL THEME A ***universal theme*** is a message about life that is expressed regularly in many different cultures and time periods. Folk tales, epics, and romances often address universal themes like the importance of courage, the power of love, or the danger of greed.

VOICE ***Voice*** is the author's individual writing style or manner of expression that make his or her writing distinctive or unique. *Voice* can also refer to the speech and thought patterns of the narrator of a work of fiction.

WEIGHTED WORDS Words that have strong emotional associations beyond their basic meanings are ***weighted words.***

WORD CHOICE A writer's ***word choice*** is the way the writer puts those words together. Diction is part of a writer's style and may be described as formal or informal, plain or fancy, ordinary or technical, sophisticated or down-to-earth, old-fashioned or modern.

ANALOGY / ANALOGÍA Una ***analogía*** establece una comparación entre dos o varias cosas que comparten similitudes, pero son distintas en todo lo demás.

ANECDOTE / ANÉCDOTA Una ***anécdota*** es un relato corto de no ficción sobre un acontecimiento extraño, interesante o divertido. Los escritores cuentan anécdotas para entretener o explicar algo importante.

ARGUMENT / ARGUMENTO En un ***argumento*** los escritores exponen y defienden una afirmación o una opinión, para lo cual se basan en hechos probados o razonamientos lógicos. Casi todos los argumentos tienen una ***introducción***, en la que se expone una afirmación; un ***desarrollo***, en el que se respalda la afirmación con evidencia; y una ***conclusión***, en la que se resume o replantea la afirmación.

AUDIENCE / PÚBLICO El ***público*** de una obra literaria es la persona o el conjunto de personas a quienes se dirige un escritor u orador. Tomar en cuenta los intereses, los conocimientos y la educación del público destinatario ayuda al escritor u orador a dar forma a la obra.

AUTHOR'S POINT OF VIEW / PUNTO DE VISTA DEL AUTOR La postura hacia el tema que revela el autor de un texto de no ficción muestra el ***punto de vista del autor***.

AUTHOR'S PURPOSE / PROPÓSITO DEL AUTOR El ***propósito del autor*** es la razón principal por la que este autor o autora escribe. Por ejemplo, un autor puede buscar entretener, informar o persuadir al lector. En ocasiones un autor intenta enseñarnos una lección moral o reflexionar sobre una experiencia. Un autor puede tener más de un propósito por los que escribir.

AUTOBIOGRAPHY / AUTOBIOGRAFÍA Una ***autobiografía*** es la historia de la vida del propio autor. Los textos autobiográficos pueden hablar de la vida completa del autor o solo de una parte.

Como las autobiografías tratan sobre gente y acontecimientos reales, son consideradas como no ficción. La mayoría de las autobiografías están escritas en narrador en primera persona.

BIOGRAPHY / BIOGRAFÍA Una ***biografía*** es un tipo de texto de no ficción donde el escritor explica la historia de la vida de otra persona. La mayoría de las biografías son sobre gente famosa y admirable. Aunque las biografías están consideradas libros de no ficción, las de mayor calidad suelen compartir cualidades con los buenos textos narrativos.

BLOG / BLOG Una ***entrada de blog*** es un texto en línea que se aporta a un diario en línea llamado ***blog***. Los autores de blogs ofrecen información o expresan su opinión sobre distintos temas.

BOOK FEATURES / SECCIONES ESPECIALES Las ***secciones especiales*** de los libros son partes tales como los agradecimientos, el prólogo, el prefacio, la introducción y las referencias, que ayudan al público a obtener información general. En la sección de ***agradecimientos***, el autor expresa su gratitud a todos aquellos que lo ayudaron a investigar, escribir y editar el libro. El ***prólogo*** es una nota preliminar que escribe alguien que no es el autor. El ***prefacio*** es lo que dice el autor acerca de su propio libro. Allí suele mencionar los motivos por los que lo escribió, el tipo de investigación que usó y demás información general que pueda ayudar a los lectores a entender la obra. La ***introducción*** aparece en las primeras páginas del libro o al comienzo del texto principal. Trata del contenido del libro, en lugar de sus orígenes o su contexto. Las ***referencias*** suelen estar al final del libro, antes del índice, cuando lo hay. Proporcionan toda la documentación necesaria para la obra.

CHARACTER / PERSONAJE Un ***personaje*** es una persona o un animal que participa en la acción de una obra literaria. El personaje ***principal*** o protagonista es el más importante de una historia, poema u obra teatral. El personaje ***secundario*** participa también en la acción pero no es el centro de atención. Las cualidades de un personaje son sus características, actitudes y valores; por ejemplo, confiabilidad, inteligencia, egoísmo o terquedad. Estas cualidades influyen en la resolución del conflicto de la historia.

A menudo se clasifican los personajes como planos o redondos.

Un ***personaje plano*** es unilateral y a menudo estereotipado.

Un ***personaje redondo***, por el contrario, está desarrollado completamente y presenta muchos rasgos (a menudo tanto defectos como virtudes). También se pueden clasificar a los personajes como dinámicos o estáticos. Un ***personaje dinámico*** es aquel que cambia o evoluciona a lo largo de la obra. Un ***personaje estático*** es aquel que no cambia.

CHARACTER TRAITS / RASGOS DEL PERSONAJE Los ***rasgos del personaje*** son las características particulares que hacen que cada personaje sea único.

CHARACTERIZATION / CARACTERIZACIÓN La ***caracterización*** es la acción de crear y desarrollar un personaje. Los autores utilizan dos métodos principales de caracterización: ***directa*** e ***indirecta.*** Cuando se utiliza la caracterización directa, el escritor describe los ***rasgos del personaje*** o sus características.

En cambio, cuando se describe a un personaje indirectamente, el escritor depende del lector para que pueda extraer conclusiones sobre los rasgos del personaje. A veces el escritor cuenta lo que otros personajes que participan en la historia dicen o piensan sobre el personaje en cuestión.

CITATION / CITA Las ***citas*** reconocen, en el cuerpo de un trabajo de investigación, a un autor cuyas ideas se tomaron textualmente o se parafrasearon. Por lo general, la cita incluye el nombre del autor, el año de publicación de su obra, y un número o un rango de páginas entre paréntesis, después de las palabras o ideas que se tomaron de allí. Para completar la cita, la nota bibliográfica íntegra se incorpora en las Referencias, al final del trabajo de investigación. Las ***notas al pie*** son notas numeradas que se ubican en el pie de página, es decir, abajo de todo el texto. En ellas se mencionan fuentes y referencias, o se comenta una parte determinada del texto de la página. Las ***notas al final*** son notas numeradas que se ubican al final del artículo o libro, y que proporcionan la fuente de la información mencionada en él.

CLAIM / AFIRMACIÓN Una ***afirmación*** es donde el autor expone su posición sobre una cuestión determinada. Se usa como punto principal para demostrar un argumento. En su argumento, el autor defiende su afirmación con datos, ejemplos u otros tipos de evidencia.

CLIMAX / CLÍMAX El ***clímax,*** también llamado momento culminante, es el punto más elevado de la acción de una trama. Es el momento de mayor tensión, es decir, cuando el desenlace de la trama pende de un hilo.

Ver ***Trama.***

COLLABORATIVE DISCUSSION / DISCUSIÓN COLABORATIVA Se conoce como ***discusión colaborativa*** a la exploración de un tema en grupo, con la participación de todos los miembros del grupo.

COMEDY / COMEDIA Una ***comedia*** es una obra literaria, especialmente una obra de teatro, que es ligera, a menudo cómica o satírica y tiene un final feliz. Las comedias describen a personajes normales que se enfrentan a dificultades y conflictos temporales. Algunos tipos de comedia incluyen la ***comedia romántica***, que contiene problemas entre amantes, y la ***comedia de costumbres,*** que cuestiona satíricamente las costumbres sociales de un sector de la sociedad.

CONFLICT / CONFLICTO Un ***conflicto*** es una lucha entre fuerzas opuestas. El conflicto es uno de los elementos más importantes de los cuentos, novelas y obras de teatro porque provoca la acción. Hay dos tipos de conflictos: externos e internos.

Un ***conflicto externo*** se da cuando un personaje lucha contra una fuerza ajena a él, como por ejemplo otra persona. Otro tipo de conflicto externo puedo ocurrir entre un personaje y una fuerza de la naturaleza.

Un ***conflicto interno*** tiene lugar en la mente de un personaje. El personaje lucha por tomar una decisión, llevar a cabo una acción o frenar un sentimiento.

CONNOTATIONS / CONNOTACIONES La ***connotación*** de una palabra es el conjunto de ideas que se asocian con esta, más allá de su significado explícito. La connotación de una palabra puede ser personal, basada en una experiencia individual. Con frecuencia son las connotaciones culturales, aquellas que son reconocibles por la mayoría de las personas de un grupo, las que determinan la elección de palabras de un autor.

CONTROLLING IDEA / IDEA CONTROL La ***idea control*** es la exposición de la idea principal o el propósito de un texto informativo o un trabajo de investigación.

Ver ***Tesis***.

COUNTERCLAIM / CONTRAARGUMENTO Se llama ***contraargumento*** a una opinión contraria a la afirmación principal de un argumento.

CONSTRUCTIVE CRITICISM / CRÍTICA CONSTRUCTIVA Se conoce como ***crítica constructiva*** a las diferencias de opinión que se exponen de manera respetuosa y que tienen como fin mejorar un resultado.

CULTURAL CONTEXT / CONTEXTO CULTURAL El ***contexto cultural*** de una obra literaria es el entorno económico, social e histórico de los personajes. Este incluye los comportamientos y costumbres de dicho período cultural e histórico.

DENOTATION / DENOTACIÓN La ***denotación*** de una palabra es su significado del diccionario, independientemente de otras asociaciones que se le puedan otorgar. La denotación de la palabra ***lago*** sería "una masa de agua que se acumula en un terreno". "Un lugar de vacaciones" o "un lugar adonde se puede ir de pesca" son connotaciones de la palabra ***lago.***

DESCRIPTION / DESCRIPCIÓN Una ***descripción*** es un retrato en palabras de una persona, lugar u objeto. Los textos descriptivos utilizan imágenes que se relacionan con los cinco sentidos: vista, oído, tacto, gusto y olfato.

DIALECT / DIALECTO Un ***dialecto*** es la variedad de una lengua que habla un grupo o las personas de una región particular. Los dialectos se diferencian en la pronunciación, gramática y elección de las palabras utilizadas. La lengua inglesa está dividida en muchos dialectos. Por ejemplo, el inglés británico es distinto del inglés estadounidense.

DIALOGUE / DIÁLOGO Un ***diálogo*** es una conversación entre personajes. En los poemas, novelas y cuentos en inglés, los diálogos se indican normalmente entre comillas para señalar que estas son las palabras exactas que dice un personaje.

En una obra de teatro, los diálogos se colocan después de los nombres de los personajes y no se utilizan comillas.

DICTION / DICCIÓN La ***dicción*** es tanto la elección de las palabras que hace un escritor como la manera de combinarlas. La dicción forma parte del estilo de un escritor y puede ser descrita como formal o informal, sencilla o elegante, corriente o técnica, sofisticada o popular, anticuada o moderna.

DIGITAL TEXT / TEXTO DIGITAL Un ***texto digital*** es la versión electrónica de un texto escrito. Se accede a los textos digitales por Internet, con una computadora o con otro aparato electrónico.

DIRECT QUOTATIONS / CITAS DIRECTAS Las ***citas directas*** presentan las palabras exactas que dijo alguien y se ponen entre comillas. Las ***entrevistas personales*** son uno de los métodos de investigación que utilizan los autores como fuente de citas directas.

DRAMA / DRAMA Un ***drama*** es una historia escrita para ser representada por actores. Aunque está destinada a ser representada, también se puede, únicamente, leer su texto e imaginar la acción. El ***texto dramático***, o guión, está compuesto de diálogos y acotaciones. Los ***diálogos*** son palabras que dicen los personajes. Las ***acotaciones*** aparecen normalmente en cursiva e indican cómo deben verse, moverse o hablar los personajes. También describen el decorado, los efectos de sonido y la iluminación.

Los dramas suelen estar divididos en distintas partes denominadas ***actos.*** Los actos aparecen a menudo divididos en partes más pequeñas denominadas ***escenas.***

EDITORIAL / EDITORIAL Un ***editorial*** es un tipo de argumento que suele aparecer en los periódicos y que adopta una postura en un asunto determinado.

ESSAY / ENSAYO Un ***ensayo*** es un texto de no ficción corto sobre un tema particular. La mayoría de los ensayos se concentran en un único aspecto fundamental y tienen una introducción clara, un desarrollo y una conclusión.

Hay muchos tipos de ensayos. Un ***ensayo informal*** emplea lenguaje coloquial y conversacional. Un ***ensayo histórico*** nos presenta hechos, explicaciones y conocimientos sobre acontecimientos históricos. Un ***ensayo expositivo*** expone una idea desglosándola. Un ***ensayo narrativo*** cuenta una historia sobre una experiencia real. Un ***ensayo informativo*** explica un proceso. Un ***ensayo argumentativo*** ofrece una opinión y la argumenta. Un ***ensayo humorístico*** utiliza el humor para lograr el propósito del autor. Un ***ensayo descriptivo*** crea un retrato cautivador del sujeto, usando detalles vívidos y sensoriales. Un ***ensayo instructivo*** explica paso por paso cómo crear o hacer algo. Un ***ensayo explicativo*** es una obra de no-ficción corta en la que el autor aclara, define e interpreta ideas, acontecimientos o procesos. Un ***ensayo reflexivo*** es una obra de prosa corta en la que el autor presenta sus pensamientos y sentimientos, es decir, sus reflexiones, sobre una experiencia o idea.

Punto de vista objetivo es aquel que se apoya en los hechos. No hace mención de opiniones, sentimientos ni emociones. El ***punto de vista subjetivo,*** en cambio, puede incorporar opiniones personales, emociones y sentimientos. El ensayo persuasivo es un ejemplo de punto de vista subjetivo, también llamado ***sesgo.*** El autor de un ensayo persuasivo procura conseguir que el lector concuerde con su opinión.

EVIDENCE / EVIDENCIA La ***evidencia*** es toda la información que se usa para defender un argumento. Hay diversos tipos de evidencia, como los datos, los ejemplos, las estadísticas, las citas, los testimonios de especialistas, las observaciones y las experiencias personales.

EXAMPLE / EJEMPLO Un ***ejemplo*** es un dato, idea o suceso que respalda un concepto o una visión de las cosas.

EXPOSITION / PLANTEAMIENTO En el argumento de una historia o drama, el ***planteamiento*** o introducción es la parte de la obra que presenta a los personajes, escenarios y situación básica.

EXPOSITORY WRITING / TEXTO EXPOSITIVO Un ***texto expositivo*** es un texto que explica e informa.

FANTASY / LITERATURA FANTÁSTICA La ***literatura fantástica*** son textos con elementos muy imaginativos que no pueden encontrarse en la vida real. Algunos ejemplos de literatura fantástica incluyen historias que contienen elementos supernaturales, historias que recuerdan a los cuentos de hadas, historias que tratan de lugares y criaturas imaginarias e historias de ciencia ficción.

FICTION / FICCIÓN La ***ficción*** son obras en prosa que hablan de sucesos y personajes imaginarios. Los cuentos y las novelas son obras de ficción. Algunos escritores se inspiran para sus obras de ficción en sucesos y personas reales, a los que añaden también personajes, diálogos, escenarios y tramas inventados. Otros escritores se sirven únicamente de la imaginación.

Existen muchos tipos de ficción. Las ***historias de aventuras*** describen sucesos fuera de lo común que ocurren en la vida de un personaje. Suelen caracterizarse por situaciones de peligro y mucha acción, y por una trama que avanza con rapidez. La ***literatura fantástica*** incluye textos muy imaginativos que contienen elementos que no pueden hallarse en la vida real. Las historias con elementos sobrenaturales, las que recuerdan a los cuentos de hadas, las que tratan de lugares y criaturas imaginarios, y las de ciencia ficción son ejemplos de literatura fantástica.

Las ***historias de misterio*** generalmente tratan de una muerte misteriosa u otro crimen que hay que resolver. Cada sospechoso tiene que tener un móvil y una oportunidad razonable para haber cometido el crimen. El personaje principal debe trabajar como detective que resuelve el misterio a partir de los hechos que se le presentan en la historia. Los ***mitos*** son relatos que intentan explicar los actos de los dioses (y de los héroes humanos que interactúan con ellos) o las causas de fenómenos naturales. La ***ciencia ficción*** combina elementos de la ficción y la literatura fantástica con datos científicos. Muchas historias de ciencia ficción están situadas en el futuro. La ***ficción histórica*** se sitúa en el pasado, durante un período histórico particular, pero se desarrolla con personajes ficticios o con una combinación de personajes históricos y ficticios.

FIGURATIVE LANGUAGE / LENGUAJE FIGURADO El ***lenguaje figurado*** es un texto o diálogo que no se debe interpretar literalmente. A los numerosos tipos de lenguaje figurado se los llama ***figuras retóricas.*** Algunas de las más comunes son las metáforas, las personificaciones y los símiles. Los escritores utilizan el lenguaje figurado para expresar ideas de una manera imaginativa y vívida.

FLASHBACK / FLASHBACK Un ***flashback*** es una escena de un relato que interrumpe la secuencia de acontecimientos para narrar sucesos ocurridos en el pasado. Los escritores usan los *flashbacks* para mostrar lo que motiva a un personaje o para revelar algo de su historia personal. Los *flashbacks* son parte de una ***trama no lineal***, puesto que interrumpen el orden cronológico normal de los acontecimientos para volver al pasado. En una ***trama lineal,*** todos los acontecimientos se cuentan en orden cronológico.

FORESHADOWING / PRESAGIO El ***presagio*** es el uso de indicios de sucesos que van a ocurrir más adelante en la trama de un relato. Esta técnica ayuda a crear suspenso, que hace que el lector no deje de preguntarse cómo seguirá la historia.

FRAME STORY / NARRACIÓN ENMARCADA Una ***narración enmarcada*** es una historia que pone entre paréntesis o enmarca otra historia o grupo de historias. Este recurso literario crea la estructura narrativa de una historia dentro de otra historia.

FREE VERSE / VERSO LIBRE El ***verso libre*** es poesía que no tiene una ***estructura formal***; es decir, que no sigue un patrón rítmico ni métrico normal. El poeta es libre de escribir versos de la extensión que prefiera y con un número libre de acentos. Por consiguiente, el verso libre es menos restrictivo que el ***verso métrico***, en el que cada verso debe ser de determinada extensión y contener un número concreto de acentos.

GENRE / GÉNERO Un ***género*** es una clase o tipo de literatura. La literatura se divide normalmente en tres géneros principales: poesía, prosa y drama. Cada uno de estos géneros está, a su vez, dividido en otros géneros menores:

1. ***Poesía:*** poesía lírica, poesía concreta, poesía dramática, poesía narrativa, poesía épica
2. ***Prosa:*** ficción (novelas y cuentos cortos) y no ficción (biografías, autobiografías, cartas, ensayos y reportajes)
3. ***Drama:*** drama serio y tragedia, comedia, melodrama y farsa

GRAPHIC FEATURE / ELEMENTO GRÁFICO Un ***elemento gráfico*** es un recurso visual que ayuda al lector a entender mejor la información contenida en un texto. Los elementos gráficos pueden ser imágenes, diagramas, gráficos, tratamientos tipográficos, íconos y otros recursos visuales que organizan, enfatizan o hacen foco en ciertos aspectos de un texto. El autor usa esos elementos para lograr un objetivo determinado.

HISTORICAL CONTEXT / CONTEXTO HISTÓRICO El ***contexto histórico*** de una obra literaria lo constituyen los verdaderos acontecimientos y tendencias político-sociales de la época. Cuando una obra tiene lugar en el pasado, el conocimiento previo sobre ese período histórico puede ayudar al lector a comprender la ambientación, trasfondo, cultura y mensaje, así como las actitudes y acciones de sus personajes. Un lector también debe tener en cuenta el contexto histórico en el que el escritor creó su obra, ya que puede ser distinto del contexto real en el que se desarrolla la obra.

HUMOR / HUMOR El ***humor*** es una forma de escribir que incita a la risa. Si bien es cierto que la mayoría de los humoristas tratan de entretener, también se puede utilizar el humor para transmitir un tema serio.

HYPERBOLE / HIPÉRBOLE La ***hipérbole*** es un tipo de figura retórica que utiliza la exageración para provocar un efecto en el lector.

IDIOM / MODISMOS Los ***modismos*** son expresiones idiomáticas que tienen un significado particular en una lengua o región.

IMAGERY / IMAGINERÍA La ***imaginería*** es la técnica de escribir con imágenes.

IMAGES / IMÁGENES La ***imágenes*** son palabras o frases que se relacionan con uno o varios de los cinco sentidos. Los escritores utilizan imágenes para describir qué apariencia tienen, cómo suenan, sienten, saben y huelen las personas u objetos descritos. Los poetas suelen dibujar imágenes o hacer una descripción visual que se vincula con los sentidos. Estas descripciones visuales nos ayudan a experimentar el poema en su totalidad.

INFERENCES / INFERENCIAS Una ***inferencia*** es una suposición que se basa en pistas. Es frecuente en la literatura que los autores no lo expliquen todo; les corresponde a los lectores "llenar los espacios en blanco" e inferir detalles sobre los personajes, sucesos y ambiente.

IRONY / IRONÍA Una ***ironía*** es una contradicción entre lo que ocurre realmente y lo que se espera que pase. Hay tres tipos principales de ironía. La ***ironía situacional*** se da cuando ocurre algo que se contradice directamente con aquello que los personajes o el público espera. La ***ironía verbal*** se crea cuando se usan las palabras para insinuar algo opuesto a su significado literal. En la ***ironía dramática,*** el público conoce algo que el personaje o la persona que habla no sabe. El resultado es el suspenso o el humor.

JOURNAL / DIARIO Un ***diario*** es un relato periódico o diario de acontecimientos y reflexiones u opiniones que el escritor tiene sobre esos acontecimientos. Los diarios personales no se escriben normalmente para ser publicados, pero en ocasiones se publican más tarde con el permiso del autor o de la familia del autor.

LETTERS / CARTAS Una ***carta*** es una comunicación escrita de una persona a otra. En las cartas personales, los escritores comparten información, así como sus opiniones y sentimientos, con otra persona o grupo. Aunque las cartas no se escriben normalmente para ser publicadas, a veces se publican más tarde con el permiso del autor o de la familia del autor.

LOGICAL FALLACY / FALACIA LÓGICA Una ***falacia lógica*** es un argumento que puede parecer lógico pero que, en realidad, se apoya en un supuesto incorrecto. Hay muchos tipos de falacias lógicas. El ***vocabulario emotivo*** es una elección de palabras diseñada para persuadir al público apelando a emociones y a estereotipos. La ***generalización indiscriminada*** consiste en aplicar una regla general a una instancia específica sin suficiente evidencia. La ***apelación a la tendencia*** sostiene que, si algo es popular y todos lo hacen, uno también debería. El ***razonamiento circular*** afirma su conclusión entre las premisas del argumento, y así pretende que el interlocutor acepte una conclusión sin que se la haya demostrado.

MAIN IDEA / IDEA PRINCIPAL La ***idea principal*** es la ***idea central*** o lo más importante de un texto.

MEDIA / MEDIOS Los relatos y la información se transmiten usando distintos ***medios***. Los libros y las revistas son un tipo de medios. El cine, el video y el formato digital son otras formas de medios. Las ***presentaciones multimedios*** son las que combinan palabras, imágenes, sonidos y video.

MEDIA ACCOUNTS / REPORTAJES PERIODÍSTICOS Los ***reportajes periodísticos*** son relatos, explicaciones, opiniones o descripciones escritas para televisión, radio, periódicos o revistas. Si bien algunos reportajes periodísticos solo relatan hechos, otros incluyen también las opiniones y reflexiones del autor.

METAPHOR / METÁFORA Una ***metáfora*** es una figura retórica que se utiliza para identificar una cosa con algo distinto. Una metáfora, al igual que un símil, se obtiene analizando las similitudes que comparten dos cosas distintas. Una ***metáfora ampliada*** es una metáfora que se sostiene y desarrolla a lo largo de varios versos o de un poema entero.

METER / MÉTRICA La ***métrica*** de un poema es su estructura rítmica. En la poesía con métrica regular, esa estructura consiste en la cantidad y disposición de pulsos fuertes y débiles, o acentos, en cada verso.

MONOLOGUE / MONÓLOGO Un ***monólogo*** en una obra de teatro es un discurso dramático por parte de un personaje. El personaje habla desde el punto de vista de primera persona y comparte sus pensamientos y sentimientos.

MOOD / ATMÓSFERA La ***atmósfera*** es la sensación que un texto produce en el lector. Los escritores crean la atmósfera mediante el uso de imaginería, su elección de palabras y los detalles descriptivos.

MOTIVE / MOTIVACIÓN Una ***motivación*** es una razón que explica total o parcialmente las opiniones, sentimientos, acciones o diálogos de los personajes. El escritor intenta exponer las motivaciones o motivos de sus personajes de la manera más clara posible. Si las motivaciones de un personaje principal no están claras, el personaje no será creíble.

Las motivaciones que mueven con frecuencia a los personajes son necesidades tales como encontrar comida o un refugio. Además les pueden motivar también sentimientos como el miedo, el amor y el orgullo. Las motivaciones pueden ser claras u ocultas.

MULTIMODAL TEXT / TEXTO MULTIMODAL ***Texto multimodal*** es el que utiliza dos o más modos de comunicación para transmitir sentido: por ejemplo, imágenes, lenguaje oral, efectos sonoros y música, además de lenguaje escrito. Los libros ilustrados, que tienen tanto imágenes como texto, y las páginas web que contienen lenguaje oral, efectos sonoros, imágenes, animaciones y lenguaje escrito son ejemplos de texto multimodal.

NARRATION / NARRACIÓN Una ***narración*** es un texto que cuenta una historia. También se denomina narración a la acción de contar una historia. Una historia contada en ficción, no ficción, poesía o incluso en drama es conocida como narración.

Los escritores emplean distintas técnicas para darles vida a sus historias. Por ejemplo, las narraciones suelen tener una trama, un escenario, varios personajes y un tema. La experiencia de los lectores se enriquece con el uso de distintos ***ritmos narrativos***, mediante los que el escritor acelera o desacelera los sucesos de la narración para crear una variedad de efectos como el suspenso.

NARRATIVE / TEXTO NARRATIVO Un ***texto narrativo*** es una historia. Las novelas y los cuentos son tipos de textos narrativos de ficción. Las biografías y las autobiografías son textos narrativos de no ficción.

NARRATOR / NARRADOR Un ***narrador*** es la persona o personaje que cuenta una historia. El punto de vista del narrador es la manera en la que él o ella ve las cosas. Un ***narrador en tercera persona*** es aquel que solo habla de la acción sin implicarse en ella. Un ***narrador en primera persona*** es aquel que cuenta una historia y además participa en su acción.

NONFICTION / NO FICCIÓN Un texto de ***no ficción*** es un texto en prosa que presenta y explica ideas, o que trata de personas, lugares, objetos o acontecimientos de la vida real. Las autobiografías, biografías, ensayos, reportajes, cartas, memorandos y artículos periodísticos son todos diferentes tipos de no ficción.

NOVEL / NOVELA Una ***novela*** es una obra larga de ficción. Las novelas contienen elementos tales como los personajes, la trama, el conflicto y los escenarios. Los escritores de novelas, o novelistas, desarrollan estos elementos. Aparte de su trama principal, una novela puede contener una o varias subtramas, o narraciones independientes o relacionadas con la trama principal. Una novela puede contener también diversos temas.

Ver ***Ficción*** y ***Cuento.***

ONOMATOPOEIA / ONOMATOPEYA Una ***onomatopeya*** es el uso de las palabras que imitan sonidos. ***Cataplam, zzzzzz, zas, din don, glu glu glu, achís*** y ***crag*** son ejemplos de onomatopeyas. El ***cuco,*** la ***urraca*** y el ***pitirre*** son nombres onomatopéyicos de aves.

ORGANIZATION / ORGANIZACIÓN La estructura de un texto o de una presentación audiovisual es lo que se conoce como su ***organización***. Algunas estructuras organizativas comunes son: causa y efecto, comparación y contraste, orden de importancia y orden cronológico. Los escritores eligen la organización que mejor se adapte al tema y propósito de su texto.

OXYMORON / OXÍMORON Un ***oxímoron*** es una figura retórica que vincula dos palabras contrarias u opuestas con el fin de indicar que una idea o situación, que parece contradictoria o incoherente a simple vista, encierra algo de verdad cuando la analizamos detenidamente.

PARAPHRASE / PARÁFRASIS Una ***paráfrasis*** ocurre cuando explicamos un texto con nuestras propias palabras.

PERSONIFICATION / PERSONIFICACIÓN La ***personificación*** es una figura retórica con la que se atribuyen características humanas a un animal o una cosa.

PERSUASION / PERSUASIÓN La ***persuasión*** se utiliza cuando escribimos o hablamos para convencer a nuestro lector o interlocutor de que debe adoptar una opinión concreta o tomar un rumbo determinado en sus decisiones. Los editoriales periodísticos y las cartas al editor emplean la persuasión. Asimismo, la publicidad y los discursos electorales que los políticos pronuncian en campaña también la utilizan.

Los escritores emplean distintas técnicas persuasivas para defender sus opiniones. Las ***apelaciones a la autoridad*** usan lo que han dicho diversos expertos. Las ***apelaciones a las emociones*** usan palabras que transmiten sentimientos profundos. Las ***apelaciones a la razón*** utilizan argumentos lógicos fundamentados con datos.

PLAYWRIGHT / DRAMATURGO Un ***dramaturgo*** es una persona que escribe obras de teatro. Muchos consideran a William Shakespeare el mejor dramaturgo de la literatura inglesa.

PLOT / TRAMA Una ***trama*** es la secuencia de acontecimientos en la cual cada acontecimiento es el resultado de otro acontecimiento anterior y la causa de uno nuevo que lo sigue. En la mayoría de novelas, dramas, cuentos y poemas narrativos, la trama contiene personajes y un conflicto central. La trama suele comenzar con un ***planteamiento*** o introducción que presenta el escenario, los personajes y la situación básica. A esto le sigue el ***suceso desencadenante***, que presenta el conflicto central. El conflico va aumentando durante el ***desarrollo*** hasta que alcanza el punto más elevado de interés o suspenso, el ***clímax.*** El clímax va seguido de una ***acción descendente*** del conflicto central. Todos los acontecimientos que ocurren durante la acción descendente forman el ***desenlace***. La ***subtrama*** es una línea narrativa secundaria que complica o profundiza la trama principal de un relato. Por ejemplo, una novela u obra de teatro puede tener una o más subtramas, o historias secundarias, además del conflicto central.

Algunas tramas no tienen todas estas partes. Algunas historias comienzan con el suceso desencadenante y acaban con un desenlace.

Ver ***Conflicto.***

POETRY / POESÍA La ***poesía*** es uno de los tres géneros clásicos de la literatura junto con la prosa y el drama. La mayoría de los poemas utilizan lenguaje muy conciso, musical y cargado de emoción. Muchos también emplean imágenes, lenguaje figurado y recursos sonoros especiales como la rima. En la poesía también suele hacerse uso de elementos gráficos del lenguaje, como la puntuación y las mayúsculas. Algunos poemas pueden omitir toda puntuación. Algunos tipos de poesía son: la ***poesía lírica,*** la ***poesía narrativa,*** la ***poesía épica*** y la ***poesía humorística.***

Un ***poema lírico*** es una obra en verso muy musical que expresa las observaciones y los sentimientos de un solo yo poético, lo que da como resultado una impresión unificada. Un ***poema narrativo*** es una historia contada en verso. Los poemas narrativos suelen tener todos los elementos de los cuentos, como personajes, conflicto y trama. Un ***poema épico*** es un poema narrativo extenso sobre un héroe extraordinario que se embarca en una peligrosa travesía o misión importante para la historia de una nación o una cultura. Los ***poemas humorísticos*** se escriben para hacer reír al lector. Suelen ser cortos y a menudo contienen juegos de palabras, rimas interesantes y aliteración.

POINT OF VIEW / PUNTO DE VISTA El ***punto de vista*** es la perspectiva, o el punto de observación, desde la que se cuenta una historia. Puede tratarse de un narrador situado fuera de la historia o un personaje dentro de ella. El ***punto de vista en primera persona*** corresponde a un personaje que utiliza el pronombre "yo" o la conjugación de los verbos en primera persona de singular. Los dos tipos de ***punto de vista en tercera persona***, limitado y omnisciente, son conocidos como "tercera persona" porque el narrador utiliza los pronombres de tercera persona como "él" y "ella" y la conjugación de los verbos en tercera persona para referirse a los personajes. Por el contrario, no se utiliza el pronombre "yo".

En las historias contadas desde el ***punto de vista en tercera persona omnisciente***, el narrador sabe y cuenta todo lo que sienten y piensan los personajes.

En las historia contadas desde el ***punto de vista en tercera persona limitado***, el narrador relata los pensamientos y sentimientos de solo un personaje, y se cuenta todo desde la perspectiva de ese personaje.

PRESENTATION / PRESENTACIÓN Una ***presentación*** es el acto de mostrar o enseñar algo a un público. Las ***presentaciones orales***, que se comunican a un público en vivo, pueden incluir ***presentaciones visuales*** como tablas, diagramas, ilustraciones y fotografías. Los videoclips y las diapositivas suelen ser parte de las ***presentaciones digitales***, que se crean parcial o totalmente en computadora.

PROSE / PROSA La ***prosa*** es la forma más corriente del lenguaje escrito. La mayoría de los textos escritos que no se consideran poesía, drama o canción son textos en prosa. La prosa es uno de los géneros más importantes de la literatura y puede ser de ficción o de no ficción.

QUOTATION / CITA Las ***citas*** son grupos de palabras que se toman de un texto, de un discurso o de una entrevista y que son usadas o repetidas por alguien distinto al autor original. Siempre se debe atribuir una cita al autor original.

READ CLOSELY / LEER CON ATENCIÓN ***Leer con atención*** conlleva un análisis cuidadoso del texto, sus ideas y la manera en la que el autor expresa esas ideas.

REPETITION / REPETICIÓN La ***repetición*** se da cuando se utiliza más de una vez cualquier elemento del lenguaje (un sonido, una palabra, una expresión, un sintagma o una oración). La repetición se emplea tanto en prosa como en poesía.

RESEARCH PAPER / DOCUMENTO DE INVESTIGACIÓN Un ***documento de investigación*** brinda información detallada acerca de un tema o una tesis. Los documentos de investigación eficaces se elaboran a partir de información tomada de diversas fuentes creíbles, que se citan en el documento.

RESOLUTION / DESENLACE El ***desenlace*** es la resolución del conflicto en una trama.

RETELLING / VOLVER A CONTAR Las historias se pueden ***volver a contar*** de manera escrita u oral. Al volverse a contar una historia, se debe seguir una secuencia clara de los sucesos y utilizar técnicas narrativas como el diálogo y la descripción.

RHETORICAL DEVICES / FIGURAS RETÓRICAS Las ***figuras retóricas*** son formas especiales de organizar palabras e ideas para producir énfasis y provocar emoción, especialmente en discursos y otras presentaciones orales. Algunas de las figuras retóricas más frecuentes son las ***preguntas retóricas,*** que se formulan para insistir en una idea o para producir un efecto dramático más que para obtener una respuesta. La ***apelación directa*** es una figura retórica en la que el orador o escritor apunta un mensaje directamente a una persona o a un grupo de personas. La ***analogía*** es una comparación que destaca las semejanzas entre dos cosas, a menudo para explicar algo con lo que el público está poco familiarizado equiparándolo a algo más conocido. Muchas veces, las analogías son comparaciones ampliadas. La ***yuxtaposición*** es una figura retórica que coloca dos o más ideas o personajes uno al lado del otro para compararlos y contrastarlos.

RHYME / RIMA La ***rima*** es la repetición de los sonidos finales de las palabras. Los poetas emplean la rima para revestir de musicalidad sus versos y resaltar ciertas palabras e ideas. Muchos poemas tradicionales contienen ***rimas finales*** o palabras rimadas al final de los versos.

Otro recurso muy común es el uso de ***rimas internas*** o palabras que riman entre ellas en un mismo verso. La rima interna también resalta la fluidez propia de un poema.

RHYTHM / RITMO El ***ritmo*** es el patrón de sílabas acentuadas y no acentuadas en el lenguaje hablado o escrito.

SCAN / OJEAR ***Ojear*** es mirar por encima un texto para buscar la respuesta a una pregunta, clarificar algo o buscar detalles de apoyo.

SCENE / ESCENA Una ***escena*** es una sección de acción ininterrumpida dentro de uno de los actos de un drama.

SCRIPT / GUIÓN Un ***guión*** es la versión escrita de una obra de teatro o de una película. Los guiones se componen de ***diálogos*** y ***acotaciones***.

SENSORY LANGUAGE / LENGUAJE SENSORIAL El ***lenguaje sensorial*** es texto o diálogo que tiene relación con uno o varios de los cinco sentidos.

SETTING / ESCENARIO El ***escenario*** de una obra literaria es el tiempo y lugar en los que ocurre la acción. El escenario incluye todos los detalles sobre el tiempo y el lugar: el año, el momento del día o incluso el tiempo atmosférico. El lugar puede ser un país concreto, un estado, una región, una comunidad, un barrio, un edificio, una institución o el propio hogar. Los detalles como los dialectos, ropa, costumbres y medios de trasporte se emplean con frecuencia para componer el escenario. En la mayoría de historias, los escenarios sirven de telón de fondo, es decir, de contexto en el que los personajes interactúan. El escenario también puede contribuir a crear una determinada sensación o un ambiente.

SHORT STORY / CUENTO Un ***cuento*** es una obra corta de ficción. Al igual que una novela, los cuentos presentan una secuencia de acontecimientos o trama. La trama suele contener un conflico central al que se enfrenta un personaje principal o protagonista. Los acontecimientos en un cuento normalmente comunican un mensaje sobre la vida o la naturaleza humana. Este mensaje o idea central es el tema del cuento.

SIMILE / SÍMIL Un ***símil*** es una figura retórica que utiliza ***como*** o ***igual que*** para establecer una comparación entre dos ideas distintas. Las conversaciones que mantenemos a diario también contienen símiles como, por ejemplo, "pálido como un muerto", "se propaga igual que un incendio" y "listo como un zorro".

SKIM / ECHAR UN VISTAZO ***Echar un vistazo*** a un texto es mirarlo rápidamente para tener una idea de lo más importante antes de comenzar a leerlo.

SOUND DEVICES / RECURSOS SONOROS Los ***recursos sonoros*** o fónicos son técnicas utilizadas por los escritores para dotar de musicalidad a sus textos. Entre ellos se incluyen la ***onomatopeya,*** la ***aliteración,*** la ***rima***, la ***métrica*** y la ***repetición.***

SPEAKER / YO POÉTICO El ***yo poético*** es la voz imaginaria que emplea un poeta cuando escribe un poema. El yo poético es el personaje que cuenta el poema. Este personaje o voz no suele identificarse con un nombre. Pueden existir notables diferencias entre el poeta y el yo poético.

SPEECH / DISCURSO Un ***discurso*** es una creación que se pronuncia de manera oral ante un público. Hay muchas clases de discursos que se ajustan a diversos tipos de reuniones y actos públicos. Algunos tipos de discursos son el ***dramático,*** el ***persuasivo*** y el ***informativo.***

STAGE DIRECTIONS / ACOTACIONES Las ***acotaciones*** son las notas de un texto dramático en las que se describe como se debe interpretar o escenificar la obra. Las acotaciones suelen aparecer en cursiva y encerradas entre paréntesis o corchetes. Algunas acotaciones describen los movimientos, el vestuario, los estados de ánimo y el modo en el que deben hablar los personajes.

STAGING / ESCENOGRAFÍA La ***escenografía*** incluye la ambientación, iluminación, vestuario, efectos especiales y música que debe aparecer en el escenario donde se representa un drama.

SUMMARY / RESUMEN Un ***resumen*** es una descripción corta y clara de las ideas principales de algo como un texto, una película o una presentación. Los resúmenes eficaces son objetivos; es decir, son imparciales y no ofrecen valoraciones.

SUSPENSE / SUSPENSO El ***suspenso*** es la curiosidad, tensión o ansiedad en aumento que siente el lector por el devenir de la trama en una obra literaria. El suspenso se acrecienta hasta llegar al *clímax*, el punto máximo de tensión en la trama, cuando el conflicto alcanza su pico. La tensión del suspenso es parte de lo que mantiene al lector interesado en una historia y deseoso de descubrir cómo seguirá.

SYMBOL / SÍMBOLO Un ***símbolo*** es algo que representa una cosa diferente. Los símbolos son muy comunes en nuestra vida diaria. Una paloma con una rama de olivo en el pico es un símbolo de la paz. Una mujer con los ojos vendados sujetando una balanza es un símbolo de la justicia. Una corona es un símbolo del poder y la autoridad de un rey.

SYMBOLISM / SIMBOLISMO El ***simbolismo*** es el uso de los símbolos. El simbolismo juega un papel importante en muchos tipos de literatura. Puede ayudar a destacar algunos elementos que el autor quiere subrayar y añadir otros niveles de significado.

TEXT FEATURE / ELEMENTO TEXTUAL Un ***elemento textual*** es un elemento de diseño que ayuda a mostrar o incrementar la organización de un texto. Los títulos, subtítulos, pies de ilustración y apartados son ejemplos de elementos textuales.

TEXT STRUCTURE / ESTRUCTURA TEXTUAL La ***estructura textual*** es el modo en que está organizada la información en un texto. El autor elige una estructura textual determinada en función de su propósito. La estructura de ***ventajas y desventajas*** aborda los aspectos positivos y negativos de un tema, y luego da una opinión. La estructura de ***causa y efecto*** examina la relación entre distintos sucesos. Proporciona razones o una explicación de algo que ocurrió. El texto estructurado en ***orden cronológico*** narra una serie de sucesos en el orden en que ocurrieron. La estructura de ***clasificación*** crea categorías y luego da ejemplos de cosas que corresponden a cada una de ellas. En un texto estructurado como ***comparación y contraste***, el autor presenta las semejanzas y diferencias entre dos asuntos. Los textos de comparación y contraste pueden adoptar una **organización punto por punto,** en la que se analiza un aspecto de ambos asuntos, luego otro, y así sucesivamente. En la **organización en bloque,** en cambio, se presentan todos los detalles sobre uno de los asuntos, seguidos de todos los detalles sobre el otro.

THEME / TEMA El ***tema*** es el mensaje central de una obra literaria. Se puede entender como una generalización sobre los seres humanos o la vida. El tema de una obra no es el resumen de su trama.

Aunque el tema puede exponerse directamente en el texto, se suele presentar indirectamente. Cuando se expone el tema indirecta o implícitamente, el lector lo podrá deducir al observar lo que se muestra en la obra sobre la vida y las personas. Un texto puede tener muchos temas. Los diversos subtemas suelen estar estrechamente relacionados con el tema central.

THESIS / TESIS La ***tesis*** de un texto es la idea principal o el propósito de un ensayo o trabajo de investigación.

Ver ***Idea control.***

TONE / TONO El ***tono*** de una obra literaria es la actitud del escritor hacia sus lectores o hacia aquello sobre lo que escribe. El tono se puede describir con un único adjetivo como, por ejemplo, ***formal*** o ***informal, serio*** o ***jocoso, amargo*** o ***irónico.*** Los factores que contribuyen a crear el tono son la elección de las palabras, la estructura de la oración, la longitud de un verso, la rima, el ritmo y la repetición.

UNIVERSAL THEME / TEMA UNIVERSAL Un ***tema universal*** es un mensaje sobre la vida que se expresa habitualmente en muchas culturas y períodos históricos diferentes. Los cuentos populares, las epopeyas y los romances suelen abordar temas universales como la importancia de la valentía, el poder del amor o el peligro de la avaricia.

VOICE / VOZ La ***voz*** es el estilo personal del autor, la forma de expresarse que distingue su escritura de la de los demás. *Voz* puede referirse también a la organización del habla y el pensamiento del narrador de una obra de ficción.

WEIGHTED WORDS / PALABRAS EMOCIONALMENTE CARGADAS Las palabras que producen fuertes asociaciones emocionales que van más allá de sus significados básicos son ***palabras emocionalmente cargadas.***

WORD CHOICE / ELECCIÓN DE PALABRAS La ***elección de palabras*** es la forma que tiene un escritor de escoger su lenguaje. La dicción es parte del estilo de un escritor y se describe como formal o informal, llana o elaborada, común o técnica, sofisticada o popular, anticuada o moderna.

PARTS OF SPEECH

Every English word, depending on its meaning and its use in a sentence, can be identified as one of the eight parts of speech. These are nouns, pronouns, verbs, adjectives, adverbs, prepositions, conjunctions, and interjections. Understanding the parts of speech will help you learn the rules of English grammar and usage.

Nouns A **noun** names a person, place, or thing. A **common noun** names any one of a class of persons, places, or things. A **proper noun** names a specific person, place, or thing.

Common Noun	Proper Noun
writer, country, novel	Charles Dickens, Great Britain, *Hard Times*

Pronouns A **pronoun** is a word that stands for one or more nouns. The word to which a pronoun refers (whose place it takes) is the **antecedent** of the pronoun.

A **personal pronoun** refers to the person speaking (first person); the person spoken to (second person); or the person, place, or thing spoken about (third person).

	Singular	Plural
First Person	I, me, my, mine	we, us, our, ours
Second Person	you, your, yours	you, your, yours
Third Person	he, him, his, she, her, hers, it, its	they, them, their, theirs

A **reflexive pronoun** reflects the action of a verb back on its subject. It indicates that the person or thing performing the action also is receiving the action.

I keep *myself* fit by taking a walk every day.

An **intensive pronoun** adds emphasis to a noun or pronoun.

It took the work of the president *himself* to pass the law.

A **demonstrative** pronoun points out a specific person(s), place(s), or thing(s).

this, that, these, those

A **relative pronoun** begins a subordinate clause and connects it to another idea in the sentence.

that, which, who, whom, whose

An **interrogative pronoun** begins a question.

what, which, who, whom, whose

An **indefinite pronoun** refers to a person, place, or thing that may or may not be specifically named.

all, another, any, anybody, both, each, everyone, few, most, much, none, no one, several, somebody

Verbs A **verb** expresses action or the existence of a state or condition.

An **action verb** tells what action someone or something is performing.

gather, read, work, jump, imagine, analyze, conclude

A **linking verb** connects the subject with another word that identifies or describes the subject. The most common linking verb is *be*.

appear, be, become, feel, look, remain, seem, smell, sound, stay, taste

A **helping verb,** or **auxiliary verb,** is added to a main verb to make a verb phrase.

be, can, could, do, have, may, might, must, shall, should, will, would

Adjectives An **adjective** modifies a noun or pronoun by describing it or giving it a more specific meaning. An adjective answers the questions:

What kind?	*purple* hat, *happy* face, *loud* sound
Which one?	*this* bowl
How many?	*three* cars
How much?	*enough* food

The articles *the, a,* and *an* are adjectives.

A **proper adjective** is an adjective derived from a proper noun.

French, Shakespearean

Adverbs An **adverb** modifies a verb, an adjective, or another adverb by telling *where, when, how,* or *to what extent*.

will answer *soon, extremely* sad, calls *more* often

Prepositions A **preposition** relates a noun or pronoun that appears with it to another word in the sentence.

Dad made a meal *for* us. We talked *till* dusk. Bo missed school *because of* his illness.

Conjunctions A **conjunction** connects words or groups of words.

A **coordinating conjunction** joins words or groups of words of equal rank.

bread *and* cheese, brief *but* powerful, milk *or* water

Correlative conjunctions are used in pairs to connect words or groups of words of equal importance.

both Luis *and* Rosa, *neither* you *nor* I, *either* Jon *or* his sister

Subordinating conjunctions indicate the connection between two ideas by placing one below the other in rank or importance. A subordinating conjunction introduces a subordinate, or dependent, clause (in a complex or compound-complex sentence).

We will miss her *if* she leaves. Hank shrieked *when* he slipped on the ice.

Conjunctive adverbs do not subordinate a clause. Rather, they connect independent clauses of equal importance. They show the relationship between the two clauses and provide a smooth transition between the two ideas.

I love skiing; *however*, my sister hates the snow and cold weather. [*However* shows a contrast relationship between the two clauses.]

Skiing can be dangerous; *therefore*, I always wear a helmet. [*Therefore* shows a cause-and-effect relationship between the two clauses.]

Interjections An **interjection** expresses feeling or emotion. It is not related to other words in the sentence.

ah, hey, oh, ouch, well, wow, ugh, yippee

PHRASES AND CLAUSES

Phrases A **phrase** is a group of words that does not have both a subject and a verb and that functions as one part of speech. A phrase expresses an idea but cannot stand alone.

Prepositional Phrases A **prepositional phrase** is a group of words that begins with a preposition and ends with a noun or pronoun that is the **object of the preposition.**

before dawn   as a result of the rain

An **adjective phrase** is a prepositional phrase that modifies a noun or pronoun.

Eliza appreciates the beauty **of a well-crafted poem.**

An **adverb phrase** is a prepositional phrase that modifies a verb, an adjective, or an adverb.

She reads Spenser's sonnets **with great pleasure.**

Appositive Phrases An **appositive** is a noun or pronoun placed next to another noun or pronoun to add information about it. An **appositive phrase** consists of an appositive and its modifiers.

Mr. Roth, **my music teacher**, is sick.

Verbal Phrases A **verbal** is a verb form that functions as a different part of speech (not as a verb) in a sentence. **Participles, gerunds,** and **infinitives** are verbals.

A **verbal phrase** includes a verbal and any modifiers or complements it may have. Verbal phrases may function as nouns, as adjectives, or as adverbs.

A **participle** is a verb form that can act as an adjective. Present participles end in *-ing;* past participles of regular verbs end in *-ed*.

A **participial phrase** consists of a participle and its modifiers or complements. The entire phrase acts as an adjective.

Jenna's backpack, **loaded with equipment,** was heavy.

Barking incessantly, the dogs chased the squirrels out of sight.

A **gerund** is a verb form that ends in *-ing* and is used as a noun.

A **gerund phrase** consists of a gerund with any modifiers or complements, all acting together as a noun.

Taking photographs of wildlife is her main hobby. [acts as subject]

We always enjoy **listening to live music.** [acts as object]

An **infinitive** is a verb form, usually preceded by *to,* that can act as a noun, an adjective, or an adverb.

An **infinitive phrase** consists of an infinitive and its modifiers or complements, and sometimes its subject, all acting together as a single part of speech.

She tries **to get out into the wilderness often.** [acts as a noun; direct object of *tries*]

The Tigers are the team **to beat.** [acts as an adjective; describes *team*]

I drove twenty miles **to witness the event.** [acts as an adverb; tells why I drove]

Clauses A **clause** is a group of words with its own subject and verb.

Independent Clauses An **independent clause** can stand by itself as a complete sentence.

George Orwell wrote with extraordinary insight.

Subordinate Clauses A **subordinate clause** cannot stand by itself as a complete sentence. Subordinate clauses always appear connected in some way with one or more independent clauses.

George Orwell, **who wrote with extraordinary insight,** produced many politically relevant works.

An **adjective clause** is a subordinate clause that acts as an adjective. It modifies a noun or a pronoun by telling *what kind* or *which one.* Also called relative clauses, adjective clauses usually begin with a **relative pronoun:** *who, which, that, whom, or whose*.

"The Lamb" is the poem **that I memorized for class.**

An **adverb clause** is a subordinate clause that, like an adverb, modifies a verb, an adjective, or an adverb. An adverb clause tells *where, when, in what way, to what extent, under what condition,* or *why.*

The students will read another poetry collection **if their schedule allows.**

When I recited the poem, Mr. Lopez was impressed.

A **noun clause** is a subordinate clause that acts as a noun.

William Blake survived on **whatever he made as an engraver.**

SENTENCE STRUCTURE

Subject and Predicate A **sentence** is a group of words that expresses a complete thought. A sentence has two main parts: a *subject* and a *predicate*.

The **subject** tells *whom* or *what* the sentence is about. The **predicate** tells what the subject of the sentence does or is.

A subject or a predicate can consist of a single word or of many words. All the words in the subject make up the **complete subject.** All the words in the predicate make up the **complete predicate.**

Complete Subject **Complete Predicate**

Both of those girls | have already read *Macbeth*.

The **simple subject** is the essential noun, pronoun, or group of words acting as a noun that cannot be left out of the complete subject. The **simple predicate** is the essential verb or verb phrase that cannot be left out of the complete predicate.

Both of those girls | **have** already **read** *Macbeth*.
[Simple subject: *Both;* simple predicate: *have read*]

A **compound subject** is two or more subjects that have the same verb and are joined by a conjunction.

Neither the horse nor the driver looked tired.

A **compound predicate** is two or more verbs that have the same subject and are joined by a conjunction.

She **sneezed and coughed** throughout the trip.

Complements A **complement** is a word or word group that completes the meaning of the subject or verb in a sentence. There are four kinds: *direct objects, indirect objects, object complements,* and *subject complements.*

A **direct object** is a noun, a pronoun, or a group of words acting as a noun that receives the action of a transitive verb.

She drove **Zach** to the launch site.

We watched **how the rocket lifted off.**

An **indirect object** is a noun or pronoun that appears with a direct object and names the person or thing to which or for which something is done.

He sold the **family** a mirror. [The direct object is *mirror.*]

An **object complement** is an adjective or noun that appears with a direct object and describes or renames it.

The decision made her **unhappy**.
[The direct object is *her*.]

Many consider Shakespeare the greatest **playwright.** [The direct object is *Shakespeare*.]

A **subject complement** follows a linking verb and tells something about the subject. There are two kinds: *predicate nominatives* and *predicate adjectives.*

A **predicate nominative** is a noun or pronoun that follows a linking verb and identifies or renames the subject.

"A Modest Proposal" is a **pamphlet.**

A **predicate adjective** is an adjective that follows a linking verb and describes the subject of the sentence.

"A Modest Proposal" is **satirical.**

Classifying Sentences by Structure

Sentences can be classified according to the kind and number of clauses they contain. The four basic sentence structures are *simple, compound, complex,* and *compound-complex.*

A **simple sentence** consists of one independent clause.

Terrence enjoys modern British literature.

A **compound sentence** consists of two or more independent clauses. The clauses are joined by a conjunction or by a semicolon.

Terrence enjoys modern British literature, but his brother prefers the classics.

A **complex sentence** consists of one independent clause and one or more subordinate clauses.

Terrence, who reads voraciously, enjoys modern British literature.

A **compound-complex sentence** consists of two or more independent clauses and one or more subordinate clauses.

Terrence, who reads voraciously, enjoys modern British literature, but his brother prefers the classics.

Classifying Sentences by Function

Sentences can be classified according to their function or purpose. The four types are *declarative, interrogative, imperative,* and *exclamatory.*

A **declarative sentence** states an idea and ends with a period.

An **interrogative sentence** asks a question and ends with a question mark.

An **imperative sentence** gives an order or a direction and ends with either a period or an exclamation mark.

An **exclamatory sentence** conveys a strong emotion and ends with an exclamation mark.

Errors in Sentence Structure

A **fragment** is a group of words that does not express a complete thought. It lacks a subject, a predicate, or both.

A **run-on** sentence is made of two or more independent clauses run together as a single sentence.

A **comma splice** is a type of run-on sentence. It contains two independent clauses joined only by a comma. Independent clauses should be joined either by a semicolon or by a comma plus a coordinating conjunction. Independent clauses may also stand alone as sentences.

AGREEMENT

Subject and Verb Agreement

A singular subject must have a singular verb. A plural subject must have a plural verb.

Dr. Boone uses a telescope to view the night sky.

The **students use** a telescope to view the night sky.

A verb always agrees with its subject, not its object.

Incorrect: The best part of the show were the jugglers.

Correct: The best part of the show was the jugglers.

A phrase or clause that comes between a subject and verb does not affect subject-verb agreement.

His **theory** about black holes **lacks** support. [prepositional phrase in simple sentence]

The library **books,** which are on the table, **are** due tomorrow. [subordinate clause in complex sentence]

Two subjects joined by *and* usually take a plural verb.

The **dog** and the **cat are** healthy.

Two singular subjects joined by *or* or *nor* take a singular verb.

The **dog** or the **cat is** hiding.

Two plural subjects joined by *or* or *nor* take a plural verb.

The **dogs** or the **cats are** coming home with us.

When a singular and a plural subject are joined by *or* or *nor,* the verb agrees with the closer subject.

Either the **dogs** or the **cat is** behind the door.

Either the **cat** or the **dogs are** behind the door.

Pronoun and Antecedent Agreement

Pronouns must agree with their antecedents in number and gender. Use singular pronouns with singular antecedents and plural pronouns with plural antecedents.

Doris Lessing uses **her** writing to challenge ideas about women's roles.

Writers often use **their** skills to promote social change.

Use a singular pronoun when the antecedent is a singular indefinite pronoun such as *anybody, each, either, everybody, neither, no one, one, or someone.*

Judge **each** of the articles on **its** merits.

Use a plural pronoun when the antecedent is a plural indefinite pronoun such as *both, few, many,* or *several.*

Both of the articles have **their** flaws.

The indefinite pronouns *all, any, more, most, none,* and *some* can be singular or plural depending on the number of the word to which they refer.

Most of the *books* are in **their** proper places.

Most of the *book* has been torn from **its** binding.

USING VERBS

Principal Parts of Regular and Irregular Verbs

A verb has four principal parts:

Present	Present Participle	Past	Past Participle
learn	learning	learned	learned
discuss	discussing	discussed	discussed
stand	standing	stood	stood
begin	beginning	began	begun

Regular verbs such as *learn* and *discuss* form the past and past participle by adding *-ed* to the present form. **Irregular verbs** such as *stand* and *begin* form the past and past participle in other ways. If you are in doubt about the principal parts of an irregular verb, check a dictionary.

Verb Tense

The different tenses of verbs indicate the time in which an action or condition occurs.

The **present tense** expresses an action that happens regularly or states a current condition or general truth.

Tourists **flock** to the site yearly.

Daily exercise **is** good for your heallth.

The **past tense** expresses a completed action or a condition that is no longer true.

The squirrel **dropped** the nut and **ran** up the tree.

I **was** very tired last night by 9:00.

The **future tense** indicates an action that will happen in the future or a condition that will be true.

The Glazers **will visit** us tomorrow.

They **will be** glad to arrive from their long journey.

The **present perfect tense** expresses an action that happened at an indefinite time in the past or an action that began in the past and continues into the present.

Someone **has cleaned** the trash from the park.

The puppy **has been** under the bed all day.

The **past perfect tense** shows an action that was completed before another action in the past.

Gerard **had revised** his essay before he turned it in.

The **future perfect tense** indicates an action that will have been completed before another action takes place.

Mimi **will have painted** the kitchen by the time we finish the shutters.

Unnecessary Shift in Verb Tense

A shift in verb tense is a change in verb tense—for example, from past tense to present tense, or from present to past. Shifting from one tense to another unnecessarily can cause confusion. Use a single verb tense unless there is a good reason to shift.

The cat **is** hungry, so Margot **fed** her. [confusing shift from present tense to past tense]

The cat **was** hungry, so Margot **fed** her. [consistent use of past tense]

Verb Voice

The **voice** of a verb shows whether the subject of a sentence is performing the action or receiving the action.

Active voice shows that the subject of the verb is performing the action.

Josephine Baker **bought** her chateau in southern France in 1947.

Passive voice shows that the subject of the verb is receiving the action. It is often used when the person or thing doing the action is unknown or unimportant.

The chateau **was built** in the fifteenth century.

Unnecessary Shift in Verb Voice

Do not shift needlessly from active voice to passive voice in your use of verbs.

Elena and I **searched** the trail for evidence, but no clues **were found**. [shift from active voice to passive voice]

Elena and I **searched** the trail for evidence, but we **found** no clues. [consistent use of active voice]

USING MODIFIERS

Degrees of Comparison

Adjectives and adverbs take different forms to show the three degrees of comparison: the *positive*, the *comparative*, and the *superlative*.

Positive	Comparative	Superlative
fast	faster	fastest
crafty	craftier	craftiest
abruptly	more abruptly	most abruptly
badly	worse	worst

Using Comparative and Superlative Adjectives and Adverbs

Use comparative adjectives and adverbs to compare two things. Use superlative adjectives and adverbs to compare three or more things.

This season's weather was **drier** than last year's.

This season has been one of the **driest** on record.

Jake practices **more often** than Jamal.

Of everyone in the band, Jake practices **most often.**

USING PRONOUNS

Pronoun Case

The **case** of a pronoun is the form it takes to show its function in a sentence. There are three pronoun cases: *nominative, objective,* and *possessive*.

Nominative	Objective	Possessive
I, you, he, she, it, we, you, they	me, you, him, her, it, us, you, them	my, mine, your, yours, his, her, hers, its, our, ours, their, theirs

Use the **nominative case** when a pronoun functions as a *subject* or as a *predicate nominative.*

They are going to the movies. [subject]

The biggest movie fan is **she.** [predicate nominative]

Use the **objective case** for a pronoun acting as a *direct object*, an *indirect object,* or the *object of a preposition.*

The ending of the play surprised **me**. [direct object]

Mary gave **us** two tickets to the play. [indirect object]

The audience cheered for **him.** [object of preposition]

Use the **possessive case** to show ownership.

The red suitcase is **hers.**

COMMONLY CONFUSED WORDS

Diction The words you choose contribute to the overall effectiveness of your writing. **Diction** refers to word choice and to the clearness and correctness of those words. You can improve one aspect of your diction by choosing carefully between commonly confused words, such as the sets of words listed below.

accept, except

Accept is a verb that means "to receive" or "to agree to." *Except* is a preposition that means "other than" or "leaving out."

Please **accept** my offer to buy you lunch this weekend.

He is busy every day **except** the weekends.

affect, effect

Affect is usually a verb meaning "to influence" or "to bring about a change in." *Effect* is usually a noun meaning "result."

The distractions outside **affect** Steven's ability to concentrate.

The teacher's remedies had a positive **effect** on Steven's ability to concentrate.

among, between

Among is usually used with three or more items, and it emphasizes collective relationships or indicates distribution. *Between* is generally used with only two items, but it can be used with more than two if the emphasis is on individual (one-to-one) relationships within the group.

I had to choose a snack **among** the various vegetables.

He handed out the booklets **among** the conference participants.

Our school is **between** a park and an old barn.

The tournament included matches **between** France, Spain, Mexico, and the United States.

amount, number

Amount refers to overall quantity and is mainly used with mass nouns (those that can't be counted). *Number* refers to individual items that can be counted.

The **amount** of attention that great writers have paid to Shakespeare is remarkable.

A **number** of important English writers have been fascinated by the legend of King Arthur.

assure, ensure, insure

Assure means "to convince [someone of something]; to guarantee." *Ensure* means "to make certain [that something happens]." *Insure* means "to arrange for payment in case of loss."

The attorney **assured** us we'd win the case.

The rules **ensure** that no one gets treated unfairly.

Many professional musicians **insure** their valuable instruments.

bad, badly

Use the adjective *bad* before a noun or after linking verbs such as *feel, look,* and *seem*. Use *badly* whenever an adverb is required.

The situation may seem **bad**, but it will improve over time.

Though our team played **badly** today, we will focus on practicing for the next match.

beside, besides

Beside means "at the side of" or "close to." *Besides* means "in addition to."

The stapler sits **beside** the pencil sharpener in our classroom.

Besides being very clean, the classroom is very organized.

can, may

The helping verb *can* generally refers to the ability to do something. The helping verb *may* generally refers to permission to do something.

I **can** run one mile in six minutes.

May we have a race during recess?

complement, compliment

The verb *complement* means "to enhance"; the verb *compliment* means "to praise."

Online exercises **complement** the textbook lessons.

Ms. Lewis **complimented** our team on our excellent debate.

compose, comprise

Compose means "to make up; constitute." *Comprise* means "to include or contain." The whole comprises its parts or is composed of its parts, and the parts compose the whole.

The assignment **comprises** three different tasks.

The assignment is **composed** of three different tasks.

Three different tasks **compose** the assignment.

different from, different than

Different from is generally preferred over *different than,* but *different than* can be used before a clause. Use *different from* before a noun or pronoun.

Your point of view is so **different from** mine.

His idea was so **different from** [or **different than**] what we had expected.

farther, further

Use *farther* to refer to distance. Use *further* to mean "to a greater degree or extent" or "additional."

Chiang has traveled **farther** than anybody else in the class.

If I want **further** details about his travels, I can read his blog.

fewer, less

Use *fewer* for things that can be counted. Use *less* for amounts or quantities that cannot be counted. *Fewer* must be followed by a plural noun.

Fewer students drive to school since the weather improved.

There is **less** noise outside in the mornings.

good, well

Use the adjective *good* before a noun or after a linking verb. Use *well* whenever an adverb is required, such as when modifying a verb.

I feel **good** after sleeping for eight hours.

I did **well** on my test, and my soccer team played **well** in that afternoon's game. It was a **good** day!

its, it's

The word *its* with no apostrophe is a possessive pronoun. The word *it's* is a contraction of "it is."

Angelica will try to fix the computer and **its** keyboard.

It's a difficult job, but she can do it.

lay, lie

Lay is a transitive verb meaning "to set or put something down." Its principal parts are *lay, laying, laid, laid. Lie* is an intransitive verb meaning "to recline" or "to exist in a certain place." Its principal parts are *lie, lying, lay, lain.*

Please **lay** that box down and help me with the sofa.

When we are done moving, I am going to **lie** down.

My hometown **lies** sixty miles north of here.

like, as

Like is a preposition that usually means "similar to" and precedes a noun or pronoun. The conjunction *as* means "in the way that" and usually precedes a clause.

Like the other students, I was prepared for a quiz.

As I said yesterday, we expect to finish before noon.

Use **such as,** not **like,** before a series of examples.

Foods **such as** apples, nuts, and pretzels make good snacks.

of, have

Do not use *of* in place of *have* after auxiliary verbs such as *would, could, should, might,* or *must.* The contraction of *have* is formed by adding *-ve* after these verbs.

I **would have** stayed after school today, but I had to help cook at home.

Mom **must've** called while I was still in the gym.

principal, principle

Principal can be an adjective meaning "main; most important." It can also be a noun meaning "chief officer of a school." *Principle* is a noun meaning "moral rule" or "fundamental truth."

His strange behavior was the **principal** reason for our concern.

Democratic **principles** form the basis of our country's laws.

raise, rise

Raise is a transitive verb that usually takes a direct object. *Rise* is intransitive and never takes a direct object.

Iliana and Josef **raise** the flag every morning.

They **rise** from their seats and volunteer immediately whenever help is needed.

than, then

The conjunction *than* is used to connect the two parts of a comparison. The adverb *then* usually refers to time.

My backpack is heavier **than** hers.

I will finish my homework and **then** meet my friends at the park.

that, which, who

Use the relative pronoun *that* to refer to things or people. Use *which* only for things and *who* only for people.

That introduces a restrictive phrase or clause, that is, one that is essential to the meaning of the sentence. *Which* introduces a nonrestrictive phrase or clause—one that adds information but could be deleted from the sentence—and is preceded by a comma.

Ben ran to the park **that** just reopened.

The park, **which** just reopened, has many attractions.

The man **who** built the park loves to see people smiling.

their, there, they're *Their* is a possessive pronoun. *There* is an adverb that shows location. *They're* is the contraction of "they are."

They're meeting **their** friends over **there.**

to, too, two *To* is a preposition that can mean "in the direction toward." *To* is also the first part of an infinitive. *Too* means "also" or "excessively." *Two* is the number after one.

The **two** friends were careful not **to** wave **to** each other **too** quickly.

who, whom

In formal writing, use *who* only as a subject in clauses and sentences. Use *whom* only as the object of a verb or of a preposition.

Who paid for the tickets?

I wonder **who** was able to get them.

Whom should I pay for the tickets?

I can't recall to **whom** I gave the money for the tickets.

your, you're

Your is a possessive pronoun expressing ownership. *You're* is the contraction of "you are."

Have you finished writing **your** informative essay? **You're** supposed to turn it in tomorrow. If **you're** late, **your** grade will be affected.

EDITING FOR ENGLISH LANGUAGE CONVENTIONS

Capitalization

First Words

Capitalize the first word of a sentence.

Stories about knights and their deeds interest me.

Capitalize the first word of direct speech.

Sharon asked, "**D**o you like stories about knights?"

Capitalize the first word of a quotation that is a complete sentence.

Einstein said, "**A**nyone who has never made a mistake has never tried anything new."

Proper Nouns and Proper Adjectives

Capitalize all proper nouns, including geographical names, historical events and periods, and names of organizations.

Thames **R**iver	**J**ohn **K**eats	the **R**enaissance
United **N**ations	**W**orld **W**ar II	**S**ierra **N**evada

Capitalize all proper adjectives.

Shakespearean play	**B**ritish invasion
American citizen	**L**atin **A**merican literature

Abbreviations

An **abbreviation** is the shortened form of a word or a phrase.

Capitalize the first letter of many common abbreviations.

Dr.	**M**r.	**M**s.	**D**ept.
Inc.	**A**ve.	**B**lvd.	**S**t.

Capitalize the first letter of the traditional abbreviations for states and both letters of the postal abbreviation.

Calif. **CA** (California) **F**la. **FL** (Florida)

An **acronym** is a type of abbreviation that is created from the first letters or from parts of a compound term. An acronym is read or spoken as a single word.

Capitalize all the letters in most acronyms.

NASA (National Aeronautics and Space Administration)

NATO (North Atlantic Treaty Organization)

SAT (Scholastic Aptitude Test)

UNESCO (United Nations Educational, Scientific, and Cultural Organization)

Some acronyms have become words and are not capitalized, such as *radar* (radio detection and ranging), and *scuba* (self-contained underwater breathing apparatus).

Initialisms are another type of abbreviation made from the first letters of a compound term. However, they are spoken letter by letter, not as one word.

Capitalize all the letters in most initialisms.

DVD (Digital Video Disk)

FBI (Federal Bureau of Investigation)

FDA (Food and Drug Administration)

UN (United Nations)

URL (Uniform Resource Locator)

Academic Course Names

Capitalize course names only if they are language courses, are followed by a number, or are preceded by a proper noun or adjective.

Spanish **H**onors **C**hemistry **H**istory 101
geology **a**lgebra **s**ocial **s**tudies

Titles

Capitalize personal titles when followed by the person's name.

Senator Pérez **K**ing George
At the time, George was **k**ing.

Capitalize titles showing family relationships when they are followed by a specific person's name, unless they are preceded by a possessive noun or pronoun.

Uncle Oscar Mangan's **s**ister his **a**unt Tessa

Capitalize the first word and all other key words in the titles of books, stories, songs, and other works of art.

Frankenstein "**S**hooting an **E**lephant"

Punctuation

End Marks

Use a **period** to end a declarative sentence or an imperative sentence.

We are studying the structure of sonnets.
Read the biography of Mary Shelley.

Use periods with initials and abbreviations.

D. H. Lawrence Mrs. Browning
Mt. Everest Maple St.

Use a **question mark** to end an interrogative sentence.

What is Macbeth's fatal flaw?

Use an **exclamation mark** after an exclamatory sentence or a forceful imperative sentence.

That's a beautiful painting! Let me go now!

Commas

Use a **comma** before a coordinating conjunction to separate two independent clauses in a compound sentence.

The game was very close, but we were victorious.

Use a comma in a complex sentence if the subordinate clause precedes the independent clause.

If it rains, we will cancel the game.

Do not use a comma if the subordinate clause follows the independent clause.

We will cancel the game if it rains.

Use commas to separate three or more words, phrases, or clauses in a series.

William Blake was a writer, artist, and printer.

Use commas to separate coordinate adjectives.

It was a witty, amusing novel.

Use a comma after an introductory word, phrase, or interjection. Use a comma in direct address, after the noun that names the person(s) being addressed.

Well, I haven't decided yet.
Carmen, have you made up your mind?

Use a comma after a transition word or phrase at the beginning of a sentence.

Last week, I studied for my math exam. This week, I will study for my science exam and finish my research project.

Use commas to set off nonrestrictive phrases and clauses in the middle of a sentence.

Old English, of course, requires translation.
Middle English, which was spoken from about 1100 to 1500, eventually became Modern English.

Use commas with places and dates.

Coventry, England September 1, 1939

Semicolons

Use a **semicolon** to join closely related independent clauses that are not already joined by a conjunction.

Tanya likes to write poetry; Heather prefers prose.

Use semicolons to avoid confusion when items in a series contain commas.

They traveled to London, England; Madrid, Spain; and Rome, Italy.

Colons

Use a **colon** before a list of items following an independent clause.

Notable Victorian poets include the following: Tennyson, Arnold, Housman, and Hopkins.

Use a colon to introduce information that summarizes or explains the independent clause before it.

She just wanted to do one thing: rest.
Malcolm loves volunteering: He reads to sick children every Saturday afternoon.

Quotation Marks

Use **quotation marks** to enclose a direct quotation.

"Short stories," Ms. Hildebrand said, "should have rich, well-developed characters."

An **indirect quotation** does not require quotation marks.

Ms. Hildebrand said that short stories should have well-developed characters.

Use quotation marks around the titles of short written works, episodes in a series, songs, and works mentioned as parts of collections.

"The Lagoon" "Boswell Meets Johnson"

Italics

Italicize the titles of long written works, movies, television and radio shows, lengthy works of music, paintings, and sculptures.

Howards End *60 Minutes* *Guernica*

For handwritten material, you can use underlining instead of italics.

The Princess Bride Mona Lisa

Dashes

Use **dashes** to indicate an abrupt change of thought, an interrupting idea, or a summary statement.

I read the entire first act of *Macbeth*—you won't believe what happens next.

The director—what's her name again?—attended the movie premiere.

Hyphens

Use a **hyphen** with certain numbers, after certain prefixes, with two or more words used as one word, and with a compound modifier that comes before a noun.

seventy-two
pre-Columbian
president-elect
five-year contract

Parentheses

Use **parentheses** to set off asides and explanations when the material is not essential or when it consists of one or more sentences. When the sentence in parentheses interrupts the larger sentence, it does not have a capital letter or a period.

He listened intently (it was too dark to see who was speaking) to try to identify the voices.

When a sentence in parentheses falls between two other complete sentences, it should start with a capital letter and end with a period.

The quarterback threw three touchdown passes. (We knew he could do it.) Our team won the game by two points.

Apostrophes

Add an **apostrophe** and an *s* to show the possessive case of most singular nouns and of plural nouns that do not end in *-s* or *-es*.

Blake's poems the mice's whiskers

Names ending in *s* form their possessives in the same way, except for classical and biblical names, which add only an apostrophe to form the possessive.

Dickens's Hercules'

Add an apostrophe to show the possessive case of plural nouns ending in *-s* and *-es*.

the girls' songs the Ortizes' car

Use an apostrophe in a contraction to indicate the position of the missing letter or letters.

She's never read a Coleridge poem she didn't like.

Brackets

Use **brackets** to enclose clarifying information inserted within a quotation.

Columbus's journal entry from October 21, 1492, begins as follows: "At 10 o'clock, we arrived at a cape of the island [San Salvador], and anchored, the other vessels in company."

Ellipses

Use three ellipsis points, also known as an **ellipsis,** to indicate where you have omitted words from quoted material.

Wollestonecraft wrote, "The education of women has of late been more attended to than formerly; yet they are still . . . ridiculed or pitied. . . ."

In the example above, the four dots at the end of the sentence are the three ellipsis points plus the period from the original sentence.

Use an ellipsis to indicate a pause or interruption in speech.

"When he told me the news," said the coach, "I was . . . I was shocked . . . completely shocked."

Spelling

Spelling Rules

Learning the rules of English spelling will help you make **generalizations** about how to spell words.

Word Parts

The three word parts that can combine to form a word are roots, prefixes, and suffixes. Many of these word parts come from the Greek, Latin, and Anglo-Saxon languages.

The **root** carries a word's basic meaning.

Root and Origin	Meaning	Examples
-log- [Gr.]	word, discourse	*logic, monologue*
-pel- [L.]	force, drive	*expel, compel*

A **prefix** is one or more syllables added to the beginning of a word that alter the meaning of the root.

Prefix and Origin	Meaning	Example
anti- [Gr.]	against	*antipathy*
inter- [L.]	between	*international*
mis- [A.S.]	wrong	*misplace*

A **suffix** is a letter or group of letters added to the end of a word that changes the word's meaning or part of speech.

Suffix and Origin	Meaning and Example	Part of Speech
-ful [A.S.]	full of: *scornful*	adjective
-ity [L.]	state of being: *adversity*	noun
-ize (-ise) [Gr.]	to make: *idolize*	verb
-ly [A.S.]	in a manner: *calmly*	adverb

Rules for Adding Suffixes to Words

When adding a suffix to a word ending in *y* preceded by a consonant, change *y* to *i* unless the suffix begins with *i*.

ply + -able = pliable   happy + -ness = happiness
defy + -ing = defying   cry + -ing = crying

For a word ending in *e*, drop the *e* when adding a suffix beginning with a vowel.

drive + -ing = driving   move + -able = movable
SOME EXCEPTIONS: traceable, seeing, dyeing

For words ending with a consonant + vowel + consonant in a stressed syllable, double the final consonant when adding a suffix that begins with a vowel.

mud + -y = muddy   submit + -ed = submitted
SOME EXCEPTIONS: mixing, fixed

Rules for Adding Prefixes to Words

When a prefix is added to a word, the spelling of the word remains the same.

un- + certain = uncertain   mis- + spell = misspell

When a prefix is added to a proper noun, add a hyphen before the noun.

pro- + Europe = pro-Europe
post- + Victorian = post-Victorian

Orthographic Patterns

Certain letter combinations in English make certain sounds. For instance, *ph* sounds like *f*, *eigh* usually makes a long *a* sound, and the *k* before an *n* is often silent.

pharmacy   n**eigh**bor   **k**nowledge

Understanding **orthographic patterns** such as these can help you improve your spelling.

Forming Plurals

The plural form of most nouns is formed by adding *-s* to the singular.

computers   gadgets   Washingtons

For words ending in *s, ss, x, z, sh,* or *ch,* add *-es*.

circus**es**   tax**es**   wish**es**   bench**es**

For words ending in *y* or *o* preceded by a vowel, add *-s*.

key**s**   patio**s**

For words ending in *y* preceded by a consonant, change the *y* to an *i* and add *-es*.

cit**ies**   enem**ies**   troph**ies**

For most words ending in *o* preceded by a consonant, add *-es*.

echo**es**   tomato**es**

Some words form the plural in irregular ways.

women   oxen   children   teeth   deer

Foreign Words Used in English

Some words used in English are actually foreign words that have been adopted. Learning to spell these words requires memorization. When in doubt, check a dictionary.

sushi   enchilada   au pair   fiancé
laissez faire   croissant   al fresco   piñata

Text Analysis

Composition

INDEX OF SKILLS

Comprehension Skills

Conventions

INDEX OF SKILLS

Inquiry and Research

Response Skills

Speaking and Listening

Vocabulary

INDEX OF SKILLS

Assessment

INDEX OF SKILLS

The following authors and titles appear in the print and online versions of *myPerspectives*.

The following Independent Learning titles appear only in the online version of myPerspectives.

The following selections appear in Grade 7 of *myPerspectives*. Some selections appear online only.

Abner Stein "Two Kinds" from *The Joy Luck Club* by Amy Tan. Used with permission of Abner Stein.

AOL's Makers Makers Profile: *Ellen Ochoa, Director, Johnson Space Center* ©AOL's Makers.

Arte Publico Press "Abuelita Magic" by Pat Mora is reprinted with permission from the publisher of *My Own True Name* (©1984 Arte Público Press - University of Houston).

BBC News Online "Profile: Malala Yousafzai" from BBC, December 10, 2014; http://www.bbc.com/news/world-asia-23241937. Used with permission.

BBC Worldwide Americas, Inc. "Maya Angelou: Learning to love my mother" ©BBC Worldwide Learning.

Best Part Productions *Cyber-Seniors Documentary* - Official Trailer ©Best Part Productions.

Bloomsbury Publishing Plc From *The House on Mango Street.* Copyright ©1984 by Sandra Cisneros. Published by Vintage Books, a division of Penguin Random House, and in hardcover by Alfred A. Knopf in 1994. By permission of Bloomsbury Publishing Plc.

C.S. Lewis Company "Science-Fiction Cradlesong" from *Poems* by C. S. Lewis. Copyright ©1964 by the Executors of the Estate of C.S. Lewis and renewed 1992 by C.S. Lewis Pte Ltd. Reprinted by permission of C.S. Lewis Company.

Coffee House Press Linda Hogan, "Turtle Watchers" from *Dark. Sweet.: New & Selected Poems.* Copyright ©2008 by Linda Hogan. Reprinted with the permission of The Permissions Company, Inc., on behalf of Coffee House Press, www.coffeehousepress.org.

Cricket Media "The Case of the Disappearing Words: Save the World's Endangered Languages" by Alice Andre-Clark/ Cricket Media; "Creature Comforts: Three Biology-Based Tips for Builders" by Mary Beth Cox/Cricket Media.

Curtis Brown, Ltd. (UK) "Chapter 9," from *The Grapes of Wrath* by John Steinbeck, copyright 1939, renewed ©1967 by John Steinbeck. Used by permission of Curtis Brown, Ltd.

Curtis Brown, Ltd. "First Men on the Moon" ©2001 by J. Patrick Lewis, renewed. Reprinted by permission of Curtis Brown, Ltd.

de Las Casas, Dianne *How Music Came to the World: An Aztec Myth* Retold by Dianne de Las Casas ©2008 The Story Connection.

Don Congdon Associates, Inc. "Dark They Were and Golden-Eyed" originally published in *Thrilling Wonder Stories*, as "The Naming of Names." Copyright 1949 by Ray Bradbury; copyright renewed 1976 by Ray Bradbury.

Elaine Markson Literary Agency "Family" from *Begin Again:* Collected Poems by Grace Paley. Used with permission of Elaine Markson Literary Agency.

ESPN Magazine, LLC "High School Teammates Carry On" ©ESPN. Reprinted courtesy of *ESPN The Magazine.*

Farrar, Straus and Giroux "Family" from *Begin Again: Collected Poems* by Grace Paley. Copyright ©2000 by Grace Paley. Reprinted by permission Farrar, Straus and Giroux, LLC; "One Friday Morning" and "Thank You, M'am" from *Short Stories* by Langston Hughes. Copyright ©1996 by Ramona Bass and Arnold Rampersad. Reprinted by permission of Hill and Wang, a division of Farrar, Straus and Giroux, LLC. CAUTION: Users are warned that this work is protected under copyright laws and downloading is strictly prohibited. The right to reproduce or transfer the work via any medium must be secured with Farrar, Straus and Giroux, LLC.

Fulcrum Publishing, Inc. "How Grandmother Spider Stole the Sun" from *Keepers of the Earth* by Michael Caduto and Joseph Bruchac. Reprinted by permission of Fulcrum Publishing.

Hachette Book Group USA "A Work in Progress" from *The Moth* edited by Catherine Burns. Copyright ©2013 by The Moth. Copyright ©2013 by Aimee Mullins. Reprinted by permission of Hachette Books.

Harold Ober Associates Reprinted by permission of Harold Ober Associates Incorporated. Copyright ©1994 by The Estate Of Langston Hughes; "One Friday Morning" and "Thank You, M'am" from *Short Stories* by Langston Hughes. Copyright ©1996 by Ramona Bass and Arnold Rampersad. Reprinted by permission of Harold Ober Associates.

HarperCollins Publishers From *An American Childhood* by Annie Dillard. Copyright ©1987 by Annie Dillard. Used with permission of HarperCollins Publishers.

Houghton Mifflin Harcourt Publishing Co. "Science-Fiction Cradlesong" from *Poems* by C. S. Lewis. Copyright ©1964 by the Executors of the Estate of C.S. Lewis and renewed 1992 by C.S. Lewis Pte Ltd. Reprinted by permission of Houghton Mifflin Harcourt Publishing Company. All rights reserved; "A Fable for Tomorrow" from *Silent Spring* by Rachel Carson. Copyright ©1962 by Rachel L. Carson, renewed 1990 by Roger Christie. Reprinted by permission of Houghton Mifflin Harcourt Publishing Company. All rights reserved.

International Publishers Adapted from "Little Things are Big" from *A Puerto Rican in New York and Other Sketches* by Jesús Colón. Colon. Copyright ©1982. Used with permission of International Publishers.

Jemison, Mae Carol Mae Jemison "Starship" courtesy of Dr. Mae Jemison.

Johnson, Sophie "'Gotcha Day' Isn't a Cause for Celebration" by Sophie Johnson, from Huffington Post, November 3, 2014. Used with permission of the author.

Jones, Stanleigh "He-y, Come On Ou-t!" from *The Best Japanese Science Fiction Stories* by Shinichi Hoshi, translated by Stanleigh Jones. Reprinted by permission of the translator.

Lee & Low Books "Jaguar" from *Animal Poems of the Iguazu.* Text ©2008 by Francisco X. Alarcón. Permission arranged with Lee & Low Books, Inc. New York, NY 10016. All rights not specifically granted herein are reserved. Levine Greenberg Literary Agency "A Work in Progress" from The Moth by Aimee Mullins. Copyright © Aimee Mullins.

Ludlow Music, Inc. "Dust Storm Disaster" a/k/a "The Great Dust Storm" Words and Music by Woody Guthrie WGP/ TRO-© Copyright 1960 (Renewed) 1963 (Renewed) Woody Guthrie Publications, Inc. & Ludlow Music, Inc., New York, NY administered by Ludlow Music, Inc. International Copyright Secured. Made in U.S.A. All Rights Reserved Including Public Performance For Profit. Used by Permission.

Malala Fund "Malala Yousafzai United Nations Speech" Used with permission of Malala Fund.

McCormick, John "Bridging the Generational Divide between

ACKNOWLEDGEMENTS AND CREDITS

a Football Father and a Soccer Son" by John McCormick, originally appeared in Huffington Post, September 30, 2014. Used with permission of the author.

Mental Floss, Inc "Black Sunday: The Storm That Gave Us the Dust Bowl," used with permission from Mental Floss.

Minna Murra, Inc. "The Last Dog" by Katherine Paterson. Copyright ©1999 by Minna Murra, Inc. Used by permission of PearlCo Literary Agency, LLC.

Moth "A Work in Progress" from *The Moth* by Aimee Mullins. Copyright © Aimee Mullins.

National Geographic Books Excerpt from *Facing the Lion: Growing Up Maasai on the African Savanna* published by National Geographic Society, 2003. Copyright ©2003 by Joseph Lemasolai Lekuton with Herman Viola.

National Public Radio ©2011 National Public Radio, Inc. News report titled "Tutors Teach Seniors New High-Tech Tricks" by Jennifer Ludden was originally published on NPR.org on December 27, 2011, and is used with the permission of NPR. Any unauthorized duplication is strictly prohibited.

New York Public Library "To James" © Schomburg Center for Research in Black Culture, The New York Public Library.

Nye, Naomi Shihab "Trying to Name What Doesn't Change", by permission of the author, Naomi Shihab Nye, 2017.

OneWorld Publications From *Packing for Mars: The Curious Science of Life in the Void* by Mary Roach. Copyright ©2010 by Mary Roach. Used by permission of OneWorld Publications.

PARS International Corporation "Mars Can Wait. Oceans Can't." From CNN.com, August 17, 2012 ©2012 Turner Broadcast Systems, Inc. All rights reserved. Used by permission and protected by the Copyright Laws of the United States. The printing, copying, redistribution, or retransmission of this Content without express written permission is prohibited;

New York Times "Danger! This Mission to Mars Could Bore You to Death!" from The New York Times, July 21, 2013 ©2013 The New York Times. All rights reserved. Used by permission and protected by the copyright laws of the United States. The printing, copying, redistribution, or retransmission of this content without express written permission is prohibited.

Penguin Books, Ltd. (UK) "Chapter 9," from *The Grapes of Wrath* by John Steinbeck, copyright 1939, renewed ©1967 by John Steinbeck. Used by permission of Penguin Books, Ltd.

Penguin Publishing Group "Two Kinds" from *The Joy Luck Club* by Amy Tan, copyright ©1989 by Amy Tan. Used by permission of G. P. Putnam's Sons, an imprint of Penguin Publishing Group, a division of Penguin Random House LLC.; "The Old, Old Tree" from *My Side of the Mountain* by Jean Craighead George. Copyright ©1959, 1988 by Jean Craighead George. Used with permission of Penguin Random House; "Chapter 9," from The Grapes of Wrath by John Steinbeck, copyright 1939, renewed ©1967 by John Steinbeck. Used by permission of Viking Books, an imprint of Penguin Publishing Group, a division of Penguin Random House LLC.

Pollinger Limited Extract from *Silent Spring* by Rachel Carson reprinted by permission of Pollinger Limited (www.pollingerltd.com) on behalf of the Estate of Rachel Carson.

Princeton University Press Republished with permission of Princeton University Press from "I, Myself," from *Harsh World and Other Poems* by Ángel González; permission conveyed through Copyright Clearance Center, Inc.

Public Domain "A Retrieved Reformation" by O.Henry, originally appeared in *Cosmopolitan Magazine,* April 1903; "The Sparrow" from *The Complete Poems of Paul Laurence Dunbar* by Paul Laurence Dunbar; "Rikki-tikki-tavi" from *The Jungle Book* (1894) by Rudyard Kipling; *The Story of My Life.* Parts I & II by Helen Keller (1880-1968); Part III from the letters and reports of Anne Mansfield Sullivan (ca.1867-1936); Edited by John Albert Macy. New York: Doubleday, Page & Company, 1905; *The Golden Windows: A Book of Fables for Young and Old* by Laura E. Richards, 1903.

Purch "Future Space Exploration Could See Humans on Mars, Alien Planets" from Purch. Used with permission.

Random House, Inc. "Mother to Son," from *The Collected Poems of Langston Hughes* by Langston Hughes, edited by Arnold Rampersad with David Roessel, Associate Editor, copyright ©1994 by the Estate of Langston Hughes. Used by permission of Alfred A. Knopf, an imprint of the Knopf Doubleday Publishing Group, a division of Penguin Random House LLC. All rights reserved. Any third party use of this material, outside of this publication, is prohibited. Interested parties must apply directly to Penguin Random House LLC for permission; "Chapter 3," and "Chapter 4" from *Mom & Me & Mom* by Maya Angelou, copyright ©2013 by Maya Angelou. Used by permission of Random House, an imprint and division of Penguin Random House LLC. All rights reserved. Any third party use of this material, outside of this publication, is prohibited. Interested parties must apply directly to Penguin Random House LLC for permission;

Scholastic, Inc. "An Hour With Abuelo" from *An Island Like You* by Judith Ortiz Cofer. Copyright ©1995 by Judith Ortiz Cofer. Reprinted by permission of Orchard Books, an imprint of Scholastic Inc.

Simon & Schuster Inc. "The Grandfather and His Little Grandson" Reprinted with the permission of Little Simon, an imprint of Simon & Schuster Children's Publishing Division from *Twenty-Two Russian Tales for Young Children* by Leo Tolstoy. Selected, Translated, and with an afterword by Miriam Morton. translated, copyright 1969 Miriam Morton; copyright renewed ©1998 Miriam Morton.

Society for Science & the Public "Learning Rewires the Brain" by Alison Pearce Stevens, September 2, 2014. Reprinted with Permission of *Science News for Students.*

Sterling Lord Literistic, Inc. Excerpt from *Of Wolves and Men.* Reprinted by permission of SLL/Sterling Lord Literistic, Inc. Copyright by Barry Holstun Lopez.

Susan Bergholz Literary Services "Four Skinny Trees" from *The House on Mango Street.* Copyright ©1984 by Sandra Cisneros. Published by Vintage Books, a division of Penguin Random House, and in hardcover by Alfred A. Knopf in 1994. By permission of Susan Bergholz Literary Services, New York, NY and Lamy, NM. All rights reserved.

Time-Life Syndication "Neil deGrasse Tyson on the Future of U.S. Space Exploration After *Curiosity* ©2012 Time Inc. All rights reserved. Reprinted/Translated from TIME and published with permission of Time Inc. Reproduction in any manner in any language in whole or in part without written permission is prohibited. TIME and the TIME logo are registered.

Title Town Publishing "The Girl Who Fell From the Sky"

from *When I Fell from the Sky* by Juliane Koepcke. Courtesy of TitleTown Publishing LLC.

Turner Broadcasting System, Inc. "How This Son of Migrant Farm Workers Became an Astronaut" from CNNMoney.com, March 14, 2016 ©2016 Turner Broadcast Systems. All rights reserved. Used by permission and protected by the Copyright Laws of the United States. The printing, copying, redistribution, or retransmission of this content without express written permission is prohibited.

University of Georgia Press "Lineage"from *This Is My Century: New and Collected Poems* by Margaret Walker. Copyright ©1989. Used with permission of University of Georgia Press.

University of New Mexico Press (Rights) From *The Circuit* by Francisco Jiménez. Copyright ©1997 University of New Mexico Press, 1997.

Virago Press "Chapter 3," and "Chapter 4" from *Mom & Me & Mom* by Maya Angelou, copyright ©2013 by Maya Angelou. Used by permission of Virago Press.

W. W. Norton & Co. "Water Names" from *Hunger* by Lan Samantha Chang. Copyright ©1998 by Lan Samantha Chang. Used by permission of W.W. Norton & Company, Inc.; From *Packing for Mars: The Curious Science of Life in the Void* by Mary Roach. Copyright ©2010 by Mary Roach. Used by permission of W.W. Norton & Company, Inc.

Wall Street Journal Republished with permission of Dow Jones, Inc., from "A Young Tinkerer Builds a Windmill, Electrifying a Nation" by Sarah Childress, *The Wall Street Journal* December 12, 2007; permission conveyed through Copyright Clearance Center, Inc.

WGBH Stock Sales Mae Jemison "Starship" ©WGBH.

William Morris Endeavor *A Christmas Carol: Scrooge and Marley* Copyright ©1979 by Fountain Pen, LLC All rights reserved. CAUTION: Professionals and amateurs are hereby warned that *A Christmas Carol: Scrooge and Marley* is subject to a royalty. It is fully protected under the copyright laws of the United States of America and of all countries covered by the International Copyright Union (including the Dominion of Canada and the rest of the British Commonwealth), the Berne Convention, the Pan-American Copyright Convention and the Universal Copyright Convention as wells as all countries with which the United States has reciprocal copyright relations. All rights, including professional/amateur stage rights, motion picture, recitation, lecturing, public reading, radio broadcasting, television, video or sound recording, all other forms of mechanical or electronic reproduction, such as CD-ROM, CD-I, information storage and retrieval systems and photocopying, and the rights of translation into foreign languages, are strictly reserved. Particular emphasis is laid upon the matter of readings, permission for which must be secured from the Author's agent in writing. Inquiries concerning rights should be addressed to: William Morris Endeavor Entertainment, LLC, 11 Madison Avenue, New York, New York 10010, Attn: Emily Dooley.

Wylie Agency "Water Names" from *Hunger* by Lan Samantha Chang. Copyright ©1998 by Lan Samantha Chang. Used by permission of the Wylie Agency.

Photo locators denoted as follows: Top (T), Center (C), Bottom (B), Left (L), Right (R), Background (Bkgd)

Cover: Pearson; iii C: Romolo Tavani/Shutterstock; iii CL: Ollyy/Shutterstock; iii CR: Stephan Kaps/EyeEm/Getty Images; iii TC: Sergey Novikov/Shutterstock; iii TR: Mehau Kulyk/Science Photo Library/Getty Images; viii: Sergey Novikov/ Shutterstock; x: Mehau Kulyk/Science Photo Library/Getty Images; xii: Ollyy/ Shutterstock; xiv: Romolo Tavani/Shutterstock; xvi: Stephan Kaps/EyeEm/ Getty Images; 002 Bkgrd: Sergey Novikov/Shutterstock; 002 BL: National Geographic Creative; 003 BC: © Mica Hendricks; 003 BCR: Dean Conger/ Corbis; 003 BR: Ronnie Kaufman/Larry/Blend Images/AGE Fotostock; 003 C: Everett Collection Historical/Alamy Stock Photo; 003 CC: BBC Worldwide Learning; 003 CL: Lucky Team Studio/Shutterstock; 003 CR: Dan Dalton/ Caiaimage/Getty Images; 003 T: Keith Bell/123RF; 003 TC: Paul Maguire/ Alamy Stock Photo; 003 TCR: © Alyson Aliano; 003 TL: Weimin Liu/Flickr RF/ Getty Images; 003 TR: Everett Collection Inc/Alamy Stock Photo; 006: Keith Bell/123RF; 011 B: Lucky Team Studio/Shutterstock; 011 T: Weimin Liu/Flickr RF/Getty Images; 012: Weimin Liu/Flickr RF/Getty Images; 014: J.J.Guillen/ EPA/Newscom; 015: Weimin Liu/Flickr RF/Getty Images; 018: Curt Teich Postcard Archives/Lake County Museum/Getty Images; 025: Dmitrimaruta/123RF; 028: Weimin Liu/Flickr RF/Getty Images; 030: Weimin Liu/Flickr RF/Getty Images; 032: Weimin Liu/Flickr RF/Getty Images; 034: Lucky Team Studio/Shutterstock; 037: Lucky Team Studio/Shutterstock; 038: Photographs by Yuri Marder; 040: Photographs by Yuri Marder; 041: Photographs by Yuri Marder; 042: Photographs by Yuri Marder; 044: Lucky Team Studio/Shutterstock; 046: Lucky Team Studio/Shutterstock; 048: Lucky Team Studio/Shutterstock; 054: Keith Bell/123RF; 056: Keith Bell/123RF; 058: Keith Bell/123RF; 061 BCR: © Mica Hendricks; 061 CR: BBC Worldwide Learning; 061 TCR: Everett Collection Historical/Alamy Stock Photo; 061 TR: Paul Maguire/Alamy Stock Photo; 064: Paul Maguire/Alamy Stock Photo; 066: John Poole/NPR; 067: Paul Maguire/Alamy Stock Photo; 068: Best Part Productions; 070: Paul Maguire/Alamy Stock Photo; 072: Paul Maguire/Alamy Stock Photo; 074 TL: Everett Collection Historical/Alamy Stock Photo; 074 TR: BBC Worldwide Learning; 076 CL: Ken Charnock/Getty Images; 076 TL: Everett Collection Historical/Alamy Stock Photo; 076 TR: BBC Worldwide Learning; 077: Everett Collection Historical/Alamy Stock Photo; 080: Sam Shere/The LIFE Picture Collection/Getty Images; 083: Everett Collection Historical/Alamy Stock Photo; 084: Everett Collection Historical/Alamy Stock Photo; 086 CL: BBC Worldwide Learning; 086 TL: Everett Collection Historical/Alamy Stock Photo; 086 TR: BBC Worldwide Learning; 087: BBC Worldwide Learning; 089: BBC Worldwide Learning; 090 B: BBC Worldwide Learning; 090 T: Everett Collection Historical/Alamy Stock Photo; 092: © Mica Hendricks; 093: © Mica Hendricks; 094 BL: © Mica Hendricks; 094 CL: © Mica Hendricks; 094 R: © Mica Hendricks; 094 TL: © Mica Hendricks; 095 B: © Mica Hendricks; 095 T: © Mica Hendricks; 096 BR: © Mica Hendricks; 096 TL: © Mica Hendricks; 098: © Mica Hendricks; 103 BR: Schomburg Center for Research in Black Culture; 103 CR: Everett Collection Inc/Alamy Stock Photo; 103 TR: Pat Mora; 104: Aditya Gujaran/EyeEm/Getty Images; 105: Cardinal/ Corbis; 117 BCR: Dean Conger/Corbis; 117 BR: Ronnie Kaufman/Larry/Blend Images/AGE Fotostock; 117 CR: Dan Dalton/Caiaimage/Getty Images; 117 TCR: © Alyson Aliano; 117 TR: Everett Collection Inc/Alamy Stock Photo; IL1 C: Everett Collection/Alamy Stock Photo; IL1 T: Everett Collection Inc/Alamy Stock Photo; IL12: Ronnie Kaufman/Larry/Blend Images/AGE Fotostock; IL14: Courtesy Everett Collection/AGE Fotostock; IL2 C: Nancy Kaszerman/ZUMA/ Corbis; IL2 T: © Rue des Archives/Mary Evans; IL3 C: © Alyson Aliano; IL3 T: © Alyson Aliano; IL5: Dan Dalton/Caiaimage/Getty Images; IL8 C: Eddie Ledesma/Contra Costa Times/ZUMAPRESS/Newscom; IL8 T: Dean Conger/ Corbis; 124 Bkgrd: Mehau Kulyk/Science Photo Library/Getty Images; 124 BL: Johnson Space Center/NASA; 125 B: Armando Arorizo/ZUMA Press/Newscom; 125 BCR: NASA/ZUMA Press/Newscom; 125 BR: Makers Profile: *Ellen Ochoa, Director, Johnson Space Center* ©AOL's Makers.; 125 C: NASA; 125 CL: Patrick Koslo/Stockbyte/Getty Images; 125 CR: Michael Lewis/Corbis; 125 T: Everett Historical/Shutterstock; 125 TC: Susan Dykstra/Design Pics/ Perspectives/Getty Images; 125 TL: Martin Lovatt/iStock/Getty Images; 128: Everett Historical/Shutterstock; 133 B: Patrick Koslo/Stockbyte/Getty Images; 133 T: Martin Lovatt/iStock/Getty Images; 134 TL: Martin Lovatt/iStock/Getty Images; 134 TR: Patrick Koslo/Stockbyte/Getty Images; 136 CL: Everett Collection Inc/Alamy Stock Photo; 136 TL: Martin Lovatt/iStock/Getty Images; 136 TR: Patrick Koslo/Stockbyte/Getty Images; 137: Martin Lovatt/iStock/ Getty Images; 141: Lonia/Shutterstock; 145: Altanaka/Shutterstock; 152: Martin Lovatt/iStock/Getty Images; 154: Martin Lovatt/iStock/Getty Images; 156 CL: ©Michael McDonough; 156 TL: Martin Lovatt/iStock/Getty Images; 156 TR: Patrick Koslo/Stockbyte/Getty Images; 157: Patrick Koslo/Stockbyte/ Getty Images; 159: Patrick Koslo/Stockbyte/Getty Images; 160 B: Patrick Koslo/Stockbyte/Getty Images; 160 T: Martin Lovatt/iStock/Getty Images; 166: Everett Historical/Shutterstock; 168: Everett Historical/Shutterstock; 170: Everett Historical/Shutterstock; 173 BCR: WaterFrame/Alamy Stock Photo; 173 BR: Armando Arorizo/ZUMA Press/Newscom; 173 TR: Susan Dykstra/Design Pics/Perspectives/Getty Images; 176: Susan Dykstra/Design Pics/Perspectives/ Getty Images; 178: Susan Dykstra/Design Pics/Perspectives/Getty Images; 179 CR: J. Patrick Lewis; 179 TR: AF Archive/Alamy Stock Photo; 180: Susan Dykstra/Design Pics/Perspectives/Getty Images; 182: NASA; 184: Susan Dykstra/Design Pics/Perspectives/Getty Images; 186: Susan Dykstra/Design Pics/Perspectives/Getty Images; 190: Byron Purvis/AdMedia/Newscom; 208 TL: WaterFrame/Alamy Stock Photo; 208 TR: Fer Gregory/Shutterstock; 210 CL: Agencja Fotograficzna Caro/Alamy Stock Photo; 210 TL: WaterFrame/ Alamy Stock Photo; 210 TR: Fer Gregory/Shutterstock; 211: WaterFrame/ Alamy Stock Photo; 215: WaterFrame/Alamy Stock Photo; 216: WaterFrame/ Alamy Stock Photo; 218 CL: © Jen Siska; 218 TL: WaterFrame/Alamy Stock Photo; 218 TR: Fer Gregory/Shutterstock; 219: Fer Gregory/Shutterstock; 220: Armando Arorizo/ZUMA Press/Newscom; 223: Fer Gregory/Shutterstock; 224: Fer Gregory/Shutterstock; 226 TCL: Fer Gregory/Shutterstock; 226 TL: WaterFrame/Alamy Stock Photo; 231 BCR: NASA/ZUMA Press/Newscom; 231 BR: AOL's Makers; 231 TCR: Michael Lewis/Corbis; 231 TR: NG Images/Alamy Stock Photo; DELETE: Agencja Fotograficzna Caro/Alamy Stock Photo; IL1 C: Wenn Ltd/Alamy Stock Photo; IL1 T: NG Images/Alamy Stock Photo; IL10 C: NASA; IL10 T: AOL's Makers; IL3 C: Leah Shaffer; IL3 T: Michael Lewis/Corbis; IL7: NASA/ZUMA Press/Newscom; 238 Bkgrd: Ollyy/Shutterstock; 238 BL: Jamesdeanny/Shutterstock; 239 B: Matthias Clamer/Getty Images; 239 BCR: Vladimir Salman/123RF; 239 BR: Dave Lawrence/Flickr Flash/Getty Images; 239 CR: AF Archive/Alamy Stock Photo; 239 T: akg-images/Newscom; 239 TC: ktsdesign/Shutterstock; 239 TCR: Chad McDermott/Fotolia; 239 TL: C.M.Pennington-Richards/Everett Collection; 242: konradlew/Getty Images; 244: Olivier Le Queinec/Shutterstock; 249 CR: Entertainment Pictures/Alamy Stock Photo; 249 TR: C.M.Pennington-Richards/Everett Collection; 250 TL: C.M.Pennington-Richards/Everett Collection; 250 TR: C.M.Pennington-Richards/Everett Collection; 252 TL: C.M.Pennington-Richards/Everett Collection; 252 TR: C.M.Pennington-Richards/Everett Collection; 253: C.M.Pennington-Richards/ Everett Collection; 261: C.M.Pennington-Richards/Everett Collection; 264: Hulton Archive/Getty Images; 271: C.M.Pennington-Richards/Everett Collection; 278: C.M.Pennington-Richards/Everett Collection; 280: C.M.Pennington-Richards/Everett Collection; 282 TL: C.M.Pennington-Richards/Everett Collection; 282 TR: C.M.Pennington-Richards/Everett Collection; 283: C.M.Pennington-Richards/ Everett Collection; 289: C.M.Pennington-Richards/Everett Collection; 294: John Springer Collection/Corbis; 302: Hulton Archive/Moviepix/Getty Images; 305: John Springer Collection/Corbis; 310: C.M.Pennington-Richards/Everett Collection; 312: C.M.Pennington-Richards/Everett Collection; 314:

C.M.Pennington-Richards/Everett Collection; 316 TL: C.M.Pennington-Richards/Everett Collection; 316 TR: Entertainment Pictures/Alamy Stock Photo; 317: Entertainment Pictures/Alamy Stock Photo; 319: *A Christmas Carol* by Charles Dickens (gouache on paper), Nicolle, Pat (Patrick) (1907-95)/Private Collection/Look and Learn/Bridgeman Images; 320: Twickenham Film Studios/Paramount Pictures; 322: Entertainment Pictures/Alamy Stock Photo; 324: Entertainment Pictures/Alamy Stock Photo; 326 TCL: Entertainment Pictures/Alamy Stock Photo; 326 TL: C.M.Pennington-Richards/Everett Collection; 332: konradlew/Getty Images; 334: konradlew/Getty Images; 336: konradlew/Getty Images; 339 BCR: incamerastock/Alamy Stock Photo; 339 BR: Matthias Clamer/Getty Images; 339 TCR: ktsdesign/Shutterstock; 339 TR: akg-images/Newscom; 342: akg-images/Newscom; 344: Fred Stein Archive/Archive Photos/Getty Images; 345: akg-images/Newscom; 350: akg-images/Newscom; 352: akg-images/Newscom; 354: ktsdesign/Shutterstock; 357: ktsdesign/Shutterstock; 358: Courtesy of Gary R. Turner; 359: Sebastian Kaulitzki/Shutterstock; 362: BlueRingMedia/Shutterstock; 364: ktsdesign/Shutterstock; 366: ktsdesign/Shutterstock; 368 TL: incamerastock/Alamy Stock Photo; 368 TR: Matthias Clamer/Getty Images; 370 TL: incamerastock/Alamy Stock Photo; 370 TR: Matthias Clamer/Getty Images; 371 CR: Sofia Moro/Cover/Getty Images; 371 TR: Handout/KRT/Newscom; 372: incamerastock/Alamy Stock Photo; 373: Matthias Clamer/Getty Images; 375 TCR: incamerastock/Alamy Stock Photo; 375 TR: Matthias Clamer/Getty Images; 377 TCR: incamerastock/Alamy Stock Photo; 377 TR: Matthias Clamer/Getty Images; 378 TCL: Matthias Clamer/Getty Images; 378 TL: incamerastock/Alamy Stock Photo; 381 BCR: Vladimir Salman/123RF; 381 BR: Dave Lawrence/Flickr Flash/Getty Images; 381 TCR: AF Archive/Alamy Stock Photo; 381 TR: Chad McDermott/Fotolia; IL1: Chad McDermott/Fotolia; IL15 C: RIA Novosti/Alamy Stock Photo; IL15 T: Dave Lawrence/Flickr Flash/Getty Images; IL4: AF Archive/Alamy Stock Photo; IL7 C: Culture Club/Hulton Archive/Getty Images; IL7 T: Vladimir Salman/123RF; 390 Bkgrd: Romolo Tavani/Shutterstock; 390 BL: Arctic Bear Productions; 391 B: Loree Johnson/Shutterstock; 391 BC: Courtesy of the Genzyme Center; 391 BCR: Lucas Oleniuk/ZUMApress/Newscom; 391 BR: Carlos Violda/Shutterstock; 391 C: C.P. Cushing/ClassicStock/Corbis; 391 CL: Budimir Jevtic/Shutterstock; 391 T: Christina N. Elbers/AP Images; 391 TC: Idreamphoto/Shutterstock; 391 TCR: Artem Povarov/123RF; 391 TL: Christopher Meder/Shutterstock; 391 TR: Happetr/Shutterstock; 394: Christina N. Elbers/AP Images; 399 C: Budimir Jevtic/Shutterstock; 399 T: Christopher Meder/Shutterstock; 400: Christopher Meder/Shutterstock; 402: Alfred Eisenstaedt/The Life Picture Collection/Getty Images; 403: Christopher Meder/Shutterstock; 406: Christopher Meder/Shutterstock; 408: Christopher Meder/Shutterstock; 410: Christopher Meder/Shutterstock; 412: Budimir Jevtic/Shutterstock; 414: Budimir Jevtic/Shutterstock; 415: Eric Jenks/Awasos Entertainment; 416: Budimir Jevtic/Shutterstock; 422: Budimir Jevtic/Shutterstock; 424: Budimir Jevtic/Shutterstock; 426: Budimir Jevtic/Shutterstock; 436: Christina N. Elbers/AP Images; 438: Christina N. Elbers/AP Images; 441 BCR: Courtesy of the Genzyme Center; 441 BR: Loree Johnson/Shutterstock; 441 TCR: C.P. Cushing/ClassicStock/Corbis; 441 TR: Idreamphoto/Shutterstock; 444: Idreamphoto/Shutterstock; 446: Idreamphoto/Shutterstock; 447 B: Anthony Barboza/Archive Photos/Getty Images; 447 T: Chris Felver/Archive Photos/Getty Images; 448: Idreamphoto/Shutterstock; 449: Staffan Widstrand/Nature Picture Library/Getty Images; 450: Erik Karits/Shutterstock; 452: Idreamphoto/Shutterstock; 454: Idreamphoto/Shutterstock; 456: hillary schwei; 457: C.P. Cushing/ClassicStock/Corbis; 458 B: Anthony Behar/Sipa/AP Images; 458 T: Chris Martin Bahr/REX/Newscom; 459 B: Scott Olson/Getty Images; 459 T: Tomohiro Ohsumi/Bloomberg/Getty Images; 460: New York Daily News Archive/Getty Images; 462: C.P. Cushing/ClassicStock/Corbis; 464: Courtesy of the Genzyme Center; 467: Courtesy of the Genzyme Center; 468 TL: Sue Stokes/Shutterstock; 468 TR: ifong/Shutterstock; 469 BL: f11photo/Shutterstock; 469 BR: Miles Away Photography/Shutterstock; 470: WDG Photo/Shutterstock; 471 L: edella/Shutterstock; 471 R: Tom Cockrem/Getty Images; 474: Courtesy of the Genzyme Center; 476: Courtesy of the Genzyme Center; 478: Loree Johnson/Shutterstock; 480: Koichi Saito/AFLO/Nippon News/Corbis; 481: Loree Johnson/Shutterstock; 486: Loree Johnson/Shutterstock; 488: Loree Johnson/Shutterstock; 493 BR: Carlos Violda/Shutterstock; 493 CR: Lucas Oleniuk/ZUMApress/Newscom; 493 TCR: Artem Povarov/123RF; 493 TR: Happetr/Shutterstock; IL1: Happetr/Shutterstock; IL12 C: Galen Rowell/Corbis; IL12 T: Carlos Violda/Shutterstock; IL5 B: Richard Howard/The LIFE Images Collection/Getty Images; IL5 T: Artem Povarov/123RF; IL8: Lucas Oleniuk/ZUMApress/Newscom; 500 Bkgrd: Stephan Kaps/EyeEm/Getty Images; 500 BL: ABC News - Permissions Dept.; 501 BC: AKG-images; 501 BCR: Images of Africa Photobank/Alamy Stock Photo; 501 BL: Kolman Rosenberg; 501; BR: Oleg Senkov/Shutterstock; 501 C: Lynn Johnson/National Geographic Creative/Corbis; 501 CC: Jim Grossmann/NASA; 501 CL: Everett Collection Inc/Alamy Stock Photo; 501 CR: European Pressphoto Agency b.v./Alamy Stock Photo; 501 T: Justin Lane/EPA/Corbis; 501 TC: Library of Congress; 501 TCR: Johan Swanepoel/Shutterstock; 501 TL: Science History Images/Alamy Stock Photo; 501 TR: Triff/Shutterstock; 504: Justin Lane/EPA/Corbis; 509 BR: Kolman Rosenberg; 509 CR: Everett Collection Inc/Alamy Stock Photo; 509 TR: Science History Images/Alamy Stock Photo; 510 TL: Science History Images/Alamy Stock Photo; 510 TR: Everett Collection Inc/Alamy Stock Photo; 512 CL: Erin Blakemore/Juli Dimos; 512 TL: Science History Images/Alamy Stock Photo; 512 TR: Everett Collection Inc/Alamy Stock Photo; 513: Science History Images/Alamy Stock Photo; 516: Science History Images/Alamy Stock Photo; 518: Science History Images/Alamy Stock Photo; 520 CL: Heritage Image Partnership Ltd/Alamy Stock Photo; 520 TL: Science History Images/Alamy Stock Photo; 520 TR: Everett Collection Inc/Alamy Stock Photo; 521: Everett Collection Inc/Alamy Stock Photo; 524: CriticalPast; 526: Everett Collection Inc/Alamy Stock Photo; 528: Everett Collection Inc/Alamy Stock Photo; 530 TCL: Everett Collection Inc/Alamy Stock Photo; 530 TL: Science History Images/Alamy Stock Photo; 532: Kolman Rosenberg; 534: Scott Clarke/ESPN Images; 535: Kolman Rosenberg; 537: Kolman Rosenberg; 540: Kolman Rosenberg; 542: Kolman Rosenberg; 544: Kolman Rosenberg; 546: Kolman Rosenberg; 548: Kolman Rosenberg; 554: Justin Lane/EPA/Corbis; 556: Justin Lane/EPA/Corbis; 558: Justin Lane/EPA/Corbis; 561 BR: AKG-images; 561 CR: Lynn Johnson/National Geographic Creative/Corbis; 561 TCR: Jim Grossmann/NASA; 561 TR: Library of Congress; 564 TL: Library of Congress; 564 TR: Jim Grossmann/NASA; 566 CL: Francisco Jimenez; 566 TL: Library of Congress; 566 TR: Jim Grossmann/NASA; 567: Library of Congress; 572: Michael Rougier/The LIFE Picture Collection/Getty Images; 575: Library of Congress; 576: Library of Congress; 578 CL: Octavio Blanco; 578 TL: Library of Congress; 578 TR: Jim Grossmann/NASA; 579: Jim Grossmann/NASA; 580: NASA; 582: JSC/NASA; 585: Jim Grossmann/NASA; 586: Jim Grossmann/NASA; 590: Lynn Johnson/National Geographic Creative/Corbis; 592: Adam Hunger/Reuters/Corbis; 593: Lynn Johnson/National Geographic Creative/Corbis; 598 TCL: Jim Grossmann/NASA; 598 TL: Library of Congress; 602: Lynn Johnson/National Geographic Creative/Corbis; 604: AKG-images; 606: Time Life Pictures/The LIFE Picture Collection/Getty Images; 607: AKG-images; 608: ITN Source/Fox Movietone; 610: AKG-images; 612: AKG-images; 617 BCR: Images of Africa Photobank/Alamy Stock Photo; 617 BR: European Pressphoto Agency b.v./Alamy Stock Photo; 617 CR: Oleg Senkov/Shutterstock; 617 TCR: Triff/Shutterstock; 617 TR : Johan Swanepoel/Shutterstock; IL1 C: David Livingston/Getty Images; IL1 T: Triff/Shutterstock; IL12 C: Margaret Thomas/The Washington Post/Getty Images; IL12 T: Images of Africa Photobank/Alamy Stock Photo; IL17 C: Ullstein bild/Getty Images; IL17 T: Oleg Senkov/Shutterstock; IL21: Evgeniya Uvarova/Shutterstock; IL24: Heiko Kiera/Shutterstock; IL26: Lovely Bird/Shutterstock; IL29: Paolo Koch/Science Source; IL3 C: Franziska Krug/German Select/Getty Images; IL3 T: Johan Swanepoel/Shutterstock; IL8: European Pressphoto Agency b.v./Alamy Stock Photo